The Thirty-sev
North Carolina T

ALSO BY MICHAEL C. HARDY
AND FROM MCFARLAND

*The Battle of Hanover Court House: Turning Point of
the Peninsula Campaign, May 27, 1862* (2006)

THE THIRTY-SEVENTH NORTH CAROLINA TROOPS

Tar Heels in the Army of Northern Virginia

Michael C. Hardy

McFarland & Company, Inc., Publishers

Jefferson, North Carolina, and London

Dedicated to the memory of the men of
the Thirty-seventh North Carolina Troops,
to their families, and to their descendants,

and to my uncle, Jeffery Allen Hardy, who, in November 1982,
ignited my obsession with 19th century America.

The present work is a reprint of the illustrated case edition of
The Thirty-seventh North Carolina Troops: Tar Heels
in the Army of Northern Virginia, *first published in 2003*
by McFarland.

LIBRARY OF CONGRESS CATALOGUING-IN-PUBLICATION DATA

Hardy, Michael C.
The thirty-seventh North Carolina troops :
Tar Heels in the Army of Northern Virginia / Michael C. Hardy.
p.   cm.
Includes bibliographical references and index.

ISBN 978-0-7864-4580-6
softcover : 50# alkaline paper ∞

1. Confederate States of America. Army. North Carolina Infantry Regiment, 37th.
2. North Carolina — History — Civil War, 1861–1865 — Regimental histories.
3. United States — History — Civil War, 1861–1865 — Regimental histories.
4. North Carolina — History — Civil War, 1861–1865 — Personal narratives.
5. United States — History — Civil War, 1861–1865 — Personal narratives, Confederate.
6. Confederate States of America. Army. North Carolina Infantry Regiment, 37th — Registers.
I. Title.
E573.537th.H37   2009   973.7'456 — dc21   2003002512

British Library cataloguing data are available

On the cover: Confederate Veterans' parade, Blowing Rock, Watauga County,
North Carolina; map of Appomattox, Virginia, and vicinity, April 1865

Manufactured in the United States of America

McFarland & Company, Inc., Publishers
Box 611, Jefferson, North Carolina 28640
www.mcfarlandpub.com

Table of Contents

Table of Contents

Preface

The circumstances surrounding the American Civil War can be seen as a complex mosaic. From a distance, the picture sometimes appears simple, but closer examination reveals a multitude of minute pieces that contribute to the whole. Many segments of that mosaic remain unseen. The annals of the men who served in the Thirty-seventh Regiment of North Carolina Troops are a part of that mosaic and contribute to a greater comprehension of the larger image.

This narrative of the Thirty-seventh is told largely in the troops' own words: war-time letters, diaries, official reports, newspaper articles, and credible postwar reminiscences. An attempt has been made, as much as possible, to let the soldiers speak for themselves. While there are obvious costs to this method in terms of simplicity and precision, the benefits of hearing their tone and phraseology outweigh those costs.

There have been other studies of regiments from North Carolina during the war, but this is the first modern analysis of a component of the Branch-Lane brigade. The Thirty-seventh's exploits were just as important as those of her sister regiments from the state. The sacrifice made by her members was greater than that of any other Tar Heel regiment and, in perspective, that makes their story well worth telling.

There are two subjects addressed in this book: did the Appalachian soldiers of North Carolina view and experience war differently from their "flatland" counterparts; and the age-old question, why did these men fight?

This book would not have been possible without the help of the hundreds of descendants who so freely gave of their families' pasts. It seemed that I almost daily received a letter, email, or phone call from a person that had a letter or two, a photograph, or some postwar account or anecdote that has been handed down through the past hundred and forty years. This story would not be so rich without these personal touches.

There is a vast amount of material related to the Thirty-seventh North Carolina

Troops in public institutions. I am especially grateful to the librarians and historians at the University of North Carolina, Chapel Hill; the University of North Carolina, Charlotte; Duke University; Auburn University; the Virginia Military Institute; the North Carolina State Archives; the Gaston County History Museum; and the public libraries in West Jefferson, Sparta, North Wilkesboro, Taylorsville, Boone, Monroe, Charlotte, and Gastonia.

   And finally, I would publicly like to thank my readers: Eddie Foeller, Kyle Rains, Daphne Baird, and, most importantly, Elizabeth Hardy.

1

"A free and independent people"
August–September 1861

strange! But still would have been called 'boys by other commanders'. Reference in fiction.

The volunteers who would constitute the Thirty-seventh Regiment of North Carolina Troops were not the boys of '61; they were the men of '61. During the months of May and June of 1861, an initial surge of volunteerism swept through the state, carrying with it ardent young men who rushed to the excitement and adventure of war. One major battle, Manassas, and several smaller engagements, such as Ball's Bluff and Bethel Church, had already been fought and won by the Confederacy. But by August of 1861, many people within North Carolina, and the Confederacy as a whole, certainly realized that this would not be a six-month war. In fact, as the men of the future Thirty-seventh collected around training camps near High Point to sign on for their first, year-long term, the war was already into its seventh month, and the tide of victory was beginning to shift away from the South. Volunteering had begun to abate across the state by the time the Thirty-seventh formed, and these men volunteered out of a sense of duty rather than adventure. Who were these men who must have had some understanding of the seriousness of the strife that they entered?

Most North Carolinians had an ingrained awareness of freedom. Almost a century earlier, on May 20, 1775, the residents of Mecklenburg County, who would furnish two companies to the future Thirty-seventh, adopted the Mecklenburg Declaration of Independence. This celebrated document, which pre-dated the American Declaration of Independence by a year, confirmed that the inhabitants of Mecklenburg County were "a free and independent people" and possessed the right "to be a sovereign and self governing association, under the control of no power, other than that of our God and the general government of the Congress." The Founders of North Carolina had been inspired by the ideas of John Locke, who believed that a people had the right to revolt against a corrupt government. The Mecklenburg Declaration

Pay in Reference to their the revolutionary action.

went on to state that "the crown of Great Britain never can be considered as holding rights, privileges, or authorities" and that "whosoever directly or indirectly abets, or in any way, form, or manner countenance the uncharted and dangerous invasion of our rights, as claimed by Great Britain, is an enemy to this country … and to the inherent and unalienable rights of man." The debate over these "unalienable rights" would occupy much of the time of the new government of the United States, coming to a head in the 1850s with such acts as the Nebraska Bill, the Compromise of 1850, the Wilmont Proviso, the Homestead Bill, and the Morrill Tariff. Much of the discussion regarded slavery: with each new Congressional bill that sought to limit the expansion of slavery into the new territories and states came a new round of talks over disunion and the constitutionality of disunion. Many of North Carolina's political leaders, grounded in the Revolutionary concepts of independence and self-determination, thought that it was unconstitutional for Congress to limit the expansion of slavery. Some were divided on the issue of a state having the right to abandon the Union. Others thought that the North retained aggressive views towards the South. This is not to say that the state would go to war over the right of an individual to possess slaves. On the contrary, North Carolina would go to war over the right of a state to decide for itself if it wanted to be a slave state or not.[1]

For the majority of the men who volunteered with the Thirty-seventh, personal freedom and choice were far more relevant than abstract concepts such as states' rights or emancipation. Like their ancestors during the Revolutionary War, they saw armed conflict as a means of obtaining or keeping their personal independence. Their grandfathers had fought in the Revolution; some had probably even been a part of the Overmountain Men, who had come from beyond the Blue Ridge and defeated the British under Major Patrick Ferguson at the Battle of Kings Mountain. Others had grown up on anecdotes of Bunker Hill and the Minute Men: Walter W. Lenoir's grandfather was General Lenoir, and John B. Petty was a collateral descendant of George Washington. Many of the ancestors of the men in the future Thirty-seventh had moved into the westward counties of North Carolina after receiving land grants as payment for their services in the Continental Army. Some of their fathers had picked up their muskets when the British invaded America during the War of 1812; others had been involved in the Cherokee Removals of the 1830s.

The men who would make up the Thirty-seventh came from two intensely different geographical and cultural regions. Forty percent of the men would hail from the southern section of the piedmont portion of the state: Gaston, Mecklenburg, and Union counties. Sixty percent would hail from the Blue Ridge and its foothills: Alexander, Alleghery, Ashe, Watauga, and Wilkes counties.

Created in 1846, Gaston County was a fast-growing community in the 1840s and 1850s, with several industries, including the Mountain Island Manufacturing Company, which made red bricks; the Mountain Island Mill, which had 150 looms and 3,000 spindles; and another mill located at Woodlawn with 600 spindles and machinery from England. Added to this were the High Shoals Iron Works, the Mountain Island Cotton Factory, ore mines, and gold mines. In 1860, the county seat, Dallas, had "four churches, two hotels, a carriage factory, and numerous stores and shops" along with two practicing physicians. Overall, the county boasted fourteen flour and grist mills, seventeen churches, three textile mills, an iron manufactory, three gold mines, two of which also produced ore, and two horse racing tracks. The Wilmington, Charlotte, and Rutherford Railroad Company was making inroads into the county by 1861.[2]

Mecklenburg County, established in 1762, with its county seat of Charlotte, founded in 1766, had been named in honor of Princess Charlotte of Mecklenburg, wife of England's King George III. Regardless of its royal pedigree, the area had been nicknamed the "Hornet's Nest" by Lord Cornwallis, who thought that "the people were more hostile to England than any in America." Despite its rowdy reputation, Mecklenburg, like Gaston County, was a growing industrial center. The county possessed many mines, and a branch of the United States Mint operated in the "Queen City." The largest industry was woolen mills, followed by flour and wheat mills, tanneries, cotton mills, saw mills, and carriage makers. The population in 1860, including slaves, was 17,374.[3]

Union County, originally populated by a Native American tribe known as the Waxhaws, was created from portions of Anson and Mecklenburg counties in 1842. The area had been settled since the early 1700s by Presbyterian Scots-Irish and Germans. While Mecklenburg County, to the west, had prospered with an "industrial revolution" in the 1850s and 1860s, Union County was still predominantly a planter and tenant farmer–based society, with a small number of artisans. The county, one of the largest cotton-producing counties in North Carolina, also produced an abundant amount of tobacco.[4]

Gaston, Mecklenburg, and Union counties, while still having large plantations and small tenant farms, were also counties with growing numbers of the middle class, which included skilled workers, factory employees, and merchants.

Ashe County (founded 1799), Allegheny County (founded 1858–59), and Watauga County (founded 1849), were all beyond the Blue Ridge, and all shared a common "geographical situation, socio-economic makeup, political sentiments, and citizenry, individually and collectively." Just as in the other counties, in the westernmost counties the population fell into socio-economic categories that saw slave owners occupying the upper level of society. However, in the western counties they were usually merchants and not members of the planter class. In Watauga County, slave owners represented only two percent of the population. The middle class—the widespread majority of the mountain population who owned their own property, grew food to live on, and raised hogs and other livestock to sell for money—was the most copious class. The lower class, "poor tenants of small farms, or parts of farms or still ruder mountaineers, dwelling in squalid log huts, and living by fishing … illicit distilling, roguery of all sorts and other invisible means of support" made up the last class. Many considered the towns of these counties to be "rude," but these town/villages included hotels, jails, and courthouses, often made of brick, not the quaint log cabins of writers' colorful prose. However, these counties did lack good methods of transportation. While there were carriage routes and turnpikes, railroads into the area were still only hotly debated "self-improvement" topics during elections.[5]

The last two counties that would contribute men to the Thirty-seventh were located in the foothills of the Blue Ridge: Wilkes County (founded 1778) and Alexander County (founded 1846). These counties contained elements of both the piedmont to their east, and the mountain citizenry to their west. The planter class was very evident, as were the rural classes. The rural lifestyle was certainly not unique to the southern mountains: it existed in countless other regions of America throughout the nineteenth century. Wilkes and Alexander County shared many common characteristics. The area had originally been settled by Moravians from the piedmont. Wilkes County would become one of the strongest pro–Union counties within the state as the war progressed, with many of its Unionists laying claim to Alexander County as well. Ironically, many of the most prominent Unionists in these counties were also possessors of the area's largest slave capital.[6]

Despite their differences, all these counties would experience the tension within North Carolina which was beginning to reach its peak in 1859. On January 1, the new governor, John W. Ellis, would reflect the state's unfaltering pro–Southern views during his inaugural address: "We are not prepared for the acknowledgment that we cannot enjoy all our constitutional rights in the Union. Should the day unfortunately come, but little doubt need be entertained that our people will act as best comports with their interest and honor and with sacred memories of the past, to whatever the result may lead." Many of the state's newspapers would take up the cry of disunion. The Charlotte *Bulletin* would support "an abandonment of party lines and a complete union in the South for the protection of its rights and institutions." The North Carolina *Standard* believed that the election of a "Black Republican" in 1860 "will and ought to sound the knell of this Union." Thomas Ruffin added that if a Republican was elected president, he "was in favor of N.C. assuming her Sovereignty and proclaiming resistance to Federal authority under such a rule."[7]

John Brown's October 1859 raid on the United States Arsenal in Harpers Ferry, Virginia, "the work of a wretched lunatic and fanatic; and a handful of desperadoes" would compel the state further toward disunion. People across North Carolina, and the South, became unsettled. The Wilmington *Journal* observed "that the abolitionists of the North stop not with stealing and political robbery — they resort to actual violence on our own soil." The *Raleigh Register* would add: "These disclosures are 'startling' indeed, and show a settled determination on the part of the abolitionist to leave no means untried to deprive the South of its slave property." Zebulon Baird Vance, representing most of the mountain counties in the United States House, wrote in February 1860: "what restraint is there upon the furious and bloodthirsty fanaticism which led John Brown, bristling with arms, into a sleeping southern city?" One historian has asserted that "it was not so much the raid itself which created alarm for the safety of Southern institutions, but rather the widespread sympathy for Brown which soon became manifest in the North." Prominent individuals within the state began to request that the governor place the state in a position of military readiness.

"We can only keep these ... [radical abolitionists] back by showing them we are prepared to defend ourselves when attacked by their lawless bands," wrote one North Carolina citizen. Editor William W. Holden would espouse his views in his newspaper: "If about one thousand of the prominent abolitionists could be hanged by the neck until they were dead, the country would be benefited, and all good men everywhere would be more assured of a continuance of concord between the States." Anxiety and animosity gripped citizens across the state.[8]

Some people within the state began calling for an economic separation from the North. The Asheville *News*, in 1857, contended that "the only way to stop the infernal whining of Northern Abolitionists is to cut of[f] the supplies on which they grow fat. Let us trade at home and drink at home, travel for business and pleasure in the South; learn to supply each other's wants and to rely on ourselves." Again, in 1859, the Asheville *News* chronicled the opinion of many people in the western portion of the state, when it declared that "a large majority of them are in favor of a perpetual non-intercourse with the north. If they had their choice they would never again buy a dollar's worth of goods in any Northern state."[9]

The 1860 presidential elections, and the events that followed, compelled the state even further toward separation from the Union. There were three men on the 1860 presidential ballot: John Bell, John C. Breckinridge, and Stephen A. Douglas. Abraham Lincoln did not appear on the North Carolina ticket. The real contest in North Carolina was between John Bell and John C. Breckinridge. Breckinridge's platform "fairly and squarely recognized the rights of the South and the equality of the States." Breckinridge, if elected, promised to stand by and defend the rights of the Southern people. Bell stood for reason and restraint. The race was close, and in the end, Breckinridge carried the state with 48,539 votes to Bell's 44,990. Douglas came in a distant third with 2,701 votes.[10]

As the days waned prior to the fall elections, many people began to recognize the inevitability of a Republican triumph. There were some within the state who had been saying, since the Presidential election of 1856, that the selection of a Republican would lead to the dissolution of the United States. "It is not simply a slab-sided, rail-splitting Illinois politician that we look at," the Wilmington *Journal* would write about Lincoln, "it is the system he represents...." Some citizens of the state had vehement feelings regarding the topic. Thomas L. Clingman stated in August that if Lincoln was elected he thought the Union ought to be dissolved. Others were a little more guarded concerning leaving the Union. In Wilkesboro, four days before North Carolina's day at the ballot boxes, nearly five thousand people gathered to hear Zebulon Vance and others speak and assert the need to eschew rash action in response to the success of Lincoln. A few days later, on October 27, 4,000–5,000 people, men and women, gathered at the courthouse in Jefferson for a "Union" rally. The platform was decked in crimson cloth, and the Salisbury Brass Band, which had performed at the Wilkesboro gathering, were dressed in blue. A large arched sign proudly proclaimed: "We march to the music of the Union." Orating that day were Zebulon Vance, former congressman Nathaniel Boyden, and James M. Leach. The speaking lasted into the evening hours, and during a speech by Nathaniel Boyden he specifically addressed the ladies in the crowd, reportedly 500 strong, and requested them to "vote with their menfolk on the issue of whether the Union should be dissolved if Lincoln was elected." Both the men and the women in the crowd responded with a "hearty 'No, Never.'" In comparison, no voice was heard when asked if they would support secession.[11]

When North Carolina's sister state, South Carolina, received the telegram announcing Abraham Lincoln's election, she began to make preparations to abandon the Union. On December 17, 1860, a convention met in Columbia, "determined to resume the exercise of her rights as a sovereign State."

A few days later, South Carolina voted to leave the Union, followed, over the course of the next couple of weeks, by other states from the deep South. North Carolina still would not cast her lot with these states. While she believed that a state had the constitutional right to leave the Union, she was not yet willing to take that step. On January 29, 1861, the North Carolina General Assembly adopted a bill which asked the people to vote on the proposition to call a convention and elect 120 delegates to discuss disunion. The measure was not adopted. Concurrently, another meeting was held at the courthouse in Jefferson in Ashe County. This time, a resolution was adopted by both political parties asserting their loyalty to the United States, and pledging that "as immovably attached to the institutions of the South, as [much as we] deeply deplore the election of Lincoln and Hamlin, and have as much abhorrence of the personal liberty laws of the North as any people on this continent ... we can see no safety for our institutions and no remedy for our ills in a dissolution of the Union." The people of Ashe would meet again for a third pro-union meeting on March 13, resolutions passing that supported the propositions of the Washington Peace Conference and "reiterating the communities' strong opposition to secession."[12]

The controversy of whether North Carolina would remain in the Union or join her sister states was resolved in April 1861. On April 12, based upon information that secret reinforcements were on their way to re-supply and strengthen the garrison at Fort Sumter in Charleston Harbor, the South Carolinians opened fire upon the fort, causing it to capitulate a day later. President Lincoln, on April 15, took the next step toward forcing North Carolina out of the Union. On this date he issued a call for 75,000 men to put down the Southern "insurrection," including two regiments from North Carolina. Governor Ellis of the Old North State replied to Lincoln's demands:

> Your dispatch is received, and if genuine, which its extraordinary character leads me to doubt, I have to say in reply, that I regard the levy of troops made by the administration for the purpose of subjugating the states of the South, as in violation of the Constitution, and a gross usurpation of power. I can be no party to this wicked violation of the laws of the country and to this war upon the liberties of a free people. You can get no troops from North Carolina.

The governor circulated a proclamation for a special session of the state's legislature to assemble on May 1. Prewar militia companies began mustering across the state, and the forts along the coast were quickly seized. The scheduled convention met on May 20 in Raleigh. Weldon N. Edwards was voted chairman, and soon thereafter the ordnance of secession was passed amidst the cheers of people and the peals of cannons in the streets.[13]

All across the state, men began to enlist in companies, often led by important men in local communities. These companies gave themselves grandiose names, such as the "Enfield Blues," the "Halifax Light Infantry," the "Washington Grays," the "Hornets' Nest Rifles," or the "Southern Stars." The companies often congregated near Raleigh at one of the training camps, where they formed groups of ten companies and received a numerical or regimental designation. Afterwards, they elected their field officers and were sworn into state, and later Confederate, service. Finally, each regiment would be assigned to either a location on the coast or be transferred to the seat of the eastern war in Virginia.

Some 2,021 men would eventually serve under the banner of the Thirty-seventh Regiment. They would come from a diversity of backgrounds, occupations, talents, and ages. One thing is certain: as the war progressed, they would become one of the best fighting forces in Robert E. Lee's Army of Northern Virginia. They would have their moments of victory, their trials under fire, and their seasons of defeat. They came from many different places: thirty-seven North Carolina counties, twelve other states (Alabama, Maryland, South Carolina, Georgia, Virginia, Indiana, Tennessee, Kentucky, Mississippi, New York, Pennsylvania, and Texas), and three foreign countries (Germany, England, and Ireland). They would put aside their differences of culture and upbringing, and, through the process of war, would be forged into a cohesive fighting force.[14]

And they were men. The overall average age of a member of the regiment was 30.4 years. The oldest member, at the age of 65, was Alexander County resident, Private Edward Turner. He served five months in what would become Company G before being discharged "by reason of general debility from age and disease." Fellow Company G member Private James Campbell was 56 when he enlisted. He probably was discharged in November when his company was mustered into State service. Private William Garner (of Company F) was 55 when he enlisted, as was Captain Jonathan Horton of Watauga County's "Watauga Marksmen." Garner lasted only until December 1, 1861, while Horton served until July 15, 1862. On the other end of the age bracket, the youngest enlistees appear to have been Demarcus Hodges and Levi Potter. They were both from Watauga County and both of the tender age of 15. Both Hodges and Potter were rejected for service. Hodges reenlisted a year later, was wounded, and deserted. Potter apparently later served in Company D of the Fifty-eighth North Carolina Troops. There were many 16-year-olds who enlisted. Some of them were rejected: William S. Gragg, Company B; Andrew J. Hunter, Company C; and Edmund P. Harrington and B. A. Manus, Company D. Several other 16-year-olds actually served, most notably Dallas M. Rigler, a Mecklenburg County native who would rise to the rank of Third Lieutenant of Company I. He was wounded at least three times before being captured at Petersburg, Virginia. Despite their overall maturity, the men

Captain Jonathan Horton, Company B (courtesy of Overmountain Press).

of the Thirty-seventh were also largely unmarried. A search of Watauga County's 1860 census rolls reveals twice as many unmarried men as married men in the future Companies B and E.[15]

Their occupations were as varied as their ages. The vast majority of the rank and file were farmers, as was the case in most of the Confederate regiments. But there was a smattering of other occupations within the future Thirty-seventh's ranks. They could boast of two lawyers, seven teachers, three clergymen, two coach makers, two millwrights, twenty-three carpenters, two doctors, eight students, six merchants, four mechanics, two wheelwrights, three miners, two masons, and at least one each of harness makers, blacksmiths, printers, cabinetmakers, saddlers, shoemakers, tinners, paper makers, moulders, clerks, artists, and cotton spinners. Added to this were at least 852 farmers, who owned farms of varying sizes, to produce a colorful mixture. Company I would be the most diverse: they had at least 13 different professions among their members, and not all of their professions were listed on the company descriptive rolls.[16]

Many of the men had undoubtedly served in North Carolina's prewar militia. The militia system of the state dated back to the Charter of 1663, granted to the eight Lords Proprietor by Charles II. The militia was "compromised of all freemen in the colony between the ages of seventeen and sixty." The system was reorganized in 1714, after the Tuscarora War of 1711–1712. This Militia Act of 1715 arranged for weapons, regular muster dates, and a method of fines to promote compliance with the state requirements. The state militia continued to be strengthened throughout the French and Indian War (1754–1763) and the American Revolution (1775–1783). The Militia Law of 1836–37 authorized, among other things, that the companies would meet twice a year for drill, with the regiments meeting once a year, the brigades once every two years, and the divisions once every three years. These drills, or dress parades, were usually a highlight of a community's event calendar. While some of the northwestern counties lacked the resources of Mecklenburg or Buncombe counties, this description probably held true throughout the state:

> Many people regard military parade as the most desirable of events and the prime objective of human existence, military titles as the only honors and badges of merit and importance worth having.... As such matters occupy most of their thoughts ... changes in these matters were to these people the most absorbing considerations of their entire lives where the accomplishments of their supreme bliss was in a dress parade, keeping step, and a liberal display of gaudy colored clothes, brass buttons and flaunting banners accompanied by loud and curt shouts of command....[17]

The laws of the State of North Carolina in 1855 declared that: "All free white men and white apprentices, citizens of this State ... who are or shall be of the age of eighteen and under the age of forty-five, shall as soon as practicable, be severally and respectively enrolled in the militia of this State." The laws went further to state that a citizen enrolled in the militia should "provide himself with a good musket, smooth bored gun or good rifle, shot pouch, and powder horn...."[18]

Some who would join the ranks of the Thirty-seventh obtained their military experience in other regiments. Walter W. Lenoir came from Company H of the Fifty-eighth North Carolina Troops; Collet A. Greer earlier served in the Twenty-second North Carolina Troops; Willis Whitaker had previously been with Company A of the First Regiment of Texas Infantry, Hood's brigade. These varied backgrounds would add to the diversity of the Thirty-seventh. At least one other soldier had served in a previous conflict: Daniel C. Robinson had served in Company A of the Third United States Dragoons during the war with Mexico in the 1840s.[19]

The men averaged five feet, eight-and-one-third inches in height. The shortest soldier seems to have been Amos Estes of Watauga County (Company B). He was five feet, one-and-a-quarter inches tall. The tallest soldier appears to have been Jackson M. Gibbs of Mecklenburg County (Company C), at an impressive six feet, seven inches tall. There were at least 90 soldiers who stood six feet or taller, with at least 18 of that number in Company C (not all records contain height information). Clearly, these men defy the stereotype that all nineteenth-century people were short. Conflicting with another common stereotype, there was at least one free black man in the ranks of the Thirty-seventh. His name was Franklin Cossens, of Watauga County. He volunteered on September 14, 1861, and would later be killed in action. There was also at least one Native American, Larkin Oxentine, also of Watauga County. He too volunteered on September 14, 1861, and would serve until being captured on March 25, 1865, south of Petersburg.[20]

Suprisingly, a large portion of the men in the companies could read and write. Only 22 percent of the Alexander County company could not write. Ashe County had the largest number of illiterate men, at 45 percent. The Union County men boasted of the lowest number, at 9 percent. Twelve percent of the Wilkes County men could not read in 1861, while the Gaston County company had only a 19 percent illiteracy rate. One of the Watauga companies had a 29 percent rate of illiteracy. Granted, "literate" men may have only been capable of writing their names, but they were certainly not reduced to "making a mark" on their enlistment papers. Several members of the future regiment had attended some of the best colleges in the United States. Charles C. Lee had graduated from the United States Military Academy at West Point, New York. William G. Morris attended St. James University in Maryland, James Hickerson the Jefferson Medical College in Philadelphia, and Jackson L. Bost had graduated from the University of Pennsylvania Medical School.[21]

On May 10, 1861, the North Carolina General Assembly authorized the governor to accept up to 50,000 12-month volunteers. In most cases, prominent men of a township or county advertised that they were forming a company. In Mecklenburg,

Union, and Gaston counties, a person might run an advertisement in a local paper, such as the Charlotte *Home-Democrat*. In the mountain counties, where there was no local newspaper, news of the formation of a company was undoubtedly passed by word of mouth. The roles of community and kinship were crucial in this process. Jonathan Horton and William Y. Farthing, both from Watauga County, raised companies that would later be incorporated into the Thirty-seventh. Horton was from the Boone Township and Farthing was from the Beaver Dams Township. Horton's company was essentially composed of men from the Boone and Blue Ridge townships, and the men in Farthing's company hailed primarily from the Beaver Dams, Valle Crucis, and Cove Creek townships.[22]

Family bonds were also an extremely important part of the community recruiting process. Many times, whole kinship groups would enlist together. There were many sets of brothers in the future regiment: Dulin, Jacob, and Brown Starnes from Union County; Cunningham, James, John, Joseph, and Silas Orr from Mecklenburg County. Watauga County's two companies bequeathed thirty-one sets of brothers to the future regiment. There were even some father-son enlistees: James Brewer and his two sons, Phillip M. and David E. Brewer; William Y. Farthing and his son John S. Farthing; Redmond Price and his sons Calvin and John Price, all of Company E. Many times, the kinship ties extended to cousins, in-laws, and other distant relations. An example would be the Austins of Union and Alexander counties. Brothers James K. P. and Jonathan Austin enlisted, as did their uncle, Milton S. Austin, and their fourth cousin, Joseph H. Austin. They all served in the "North Carolina Defenders" from Union County. The Austins of Alexander County were just as closely related: John L. Austin and David Austin were brothers; their uncle was Merrit Austin; and John L. Austin, of Union County, was Merrit Austin's first cousin.[23]

The story of John Tally furnishes a good illustration of the complexity and importance of kinship ties. Tally was born in 1816 in Chatham County. By 1850, "John Tally was an illiterate, 30-year-old laborer who had no property of any value, making him undeniably a member of the poor-white class at that time." Just ten years later, Tally had risen in social standing to a carpenter with a net worth of $200. This rise in social status is directly attributable to his wife's kinship group. When he married Susan Montgomery in 1837, moving to her family's home county of Mecklenburg, he became part of her extended family, permitting his social mobility. One of the ways that Tally demonstrated his loyalty to the community where he resided was by enlisting. At the age of 45, with three children at home, he was certainly under no legal obligation to do so. He enlisted with several others from his kinship group.[24]

Ashe County was one of the first counties to assemble a company that would be incorporated into the Thirty-seventh, the "Ashe Beauregard Riflemen," named for the recent hero of Manassas. On August 27, 1861, men primarily from the Old Fields, Southeastern, and Jefferson townships gathered at the muster grounds in Jefferson, and 94 men enlisted to serve for twelve months. They elected John Hartzog, a prominent member of the community, as their captain. He was 43 years old at the time. James J. Goodman, 25 years old, was elected First Lieutenant. Second Lieutenant

Private Calvin P. Goodman, Company A, who enlisted in the Ashe Beauregard Riflemen on August 27, 1862 (courtesy of Barbara H. Pendry).

was Richard G. Goodman, at the young age of 19. Filling the role of Third Lieutenant was William A. Stuart, 26 years old. All these men listed their occupations as farmer. Hartzog, the Goodmans, and Stuart were all Ashe County natives.[25]

The "Watauga Marksmen" were the next company to form. Jonathan Horton and 93 other men and boys congregated on September 14, 1861, in Boone. Watauga County had one of the smallest populations of any North Carolina county but contributed over 850 men to the Confederate cause. Fifty-five-year-old Horton was elected Captain. He would be the oldest company commander in the soon-to-be-formed Thirty-seventh. Jordan Cook was elected First Lieutenant. He was 26 years old. At the post of Second Lieutenant was 34-year-old Calvin Carlton. At the age of 27, Andrew J. Critcher executed the role of Third Lieutenant. All these men, like the ones from their parent county of Ashe, listed their vocation as farmer.[26]

A day later, in another Appalachian county, the "Allegheny Tigers" formed. Seventy-five of the Tigers met on September 15 and elected John Ross, a 43-year-old son of neighboring Ashe County, as Captain. James M. Grimsley, age 50, filled the role of First Lieutenant. Elected to Second Lieutenant was William Halsey, age 23 and also an Ashe County son. John Williams, a Guilford County native, was elected Third Lieutenant, at the age of 36. Farming was again the most prevalent occupation.[27]

The day after that, "Mecklenburg's Wide Awakes" met in Mecklenburg County and held their elections. James M. Potts, at the age of 21, was elected Captain. Thomas A. Wilson, 34 years old, became First Lieutenant. Filling the office of Second Lieutenant was 21-year-old James J. Johnston. And, in the role of the Third Lieutenant was William B. Osborne, 33. All these men were born in Mecklenburg County and all registered their trade as farmer.[28]

On the same day, one county east of Mecklenburg, 116 men met in Monroe, the county seat of Union County, and formed the "North Carolina Defenders." The Defenders elected 27-year-old John B. Ashcraft Captain. The company skipped the First Lieutenant position and elected two Second Lieutenants. The first was Vachel T. Chears, 24. The second was Jackson L. Bost, 28. Picked to fill the role of Third Lieutenant was 21-year-old William A. Gaddy. Ashcraft, born in Union County, was a teacher. Chears, also from Union County, and Gaddy, born in Anson County, were farmers, while Bost, a Cabarrus County native, was a medical doctor.[29]

The "Watauga Minute Men" were the next group to enlist. They met on September 18, 1861, in Sugar Grove, in western Watauga County, North Carolina. A 49-year-old farmer, William Y. Farthing, was elected Captain of the Minute Men. His brother-in-law, 40-year-old Paul Farthing, was given the position of First Lieutenant. Second Lieutenant was 25-year-old William F. Shull. Isaac Wilson, 28, was also elected to the post of Second Lieutenant. Wilson and Shull were Watauga County natives; William Farthing had been born in Orange County; Paul Farthing was a native of Wake County. All of the men were farmers.[30]

A week later, on September 24, 1861, 111 men gathered in Wilkesboro, the county seat of Wilkes County, and formed the "Western Carolina Stars." Their first Captain was 27-year-old William M. Barber, a lawyer. The position of First Lieutenant went to James Hickerson, 27 years old. Daniel L. Clary, a 25-year-old student, and William W. Beard (at the age of 17 the youngest officer in the soon-to-be-formed Thirty-seventh), also a student, were both elected to the position of Second Lieutenant. Samuel N. Shepard, one of the many Wilkes County farmers, was also elected to the office of Second Lieutenant. Barber and Beard were from Rowan County, Clary was a Wilkes County native, and Shepherd was born in Indiana.[31]

Two more weeks passed before the meeting of the next unit to muster in. On October 6, 1861, the "Gaston Blues" gathered and formed a company. They elected Gaston County native William R. Rankin as Captain. He was 38 years old. Another Gaston County native, George W. Hanks, 30, was appointed First Lieutenant. William G. Morris, also born in Gaston County and 36 years old, filled the position of Second Lieutenant. The last member of the command structure for the Gaston Blues was Third Lieutenant Henry C. Fite, 38. All these men were farmers, along with many of the 93 men who also enlisted that day in Gaston County.[32]

Alexander County's sons provided the next company. On October 9, 1861, a group of 104 men met at Taylorsville and formed the "Alexander Soldiers." The Soldiers elected John G. Bryan, a 53-year-old Rowan County native, Captain. Clergymen James Reed and Robert L. Steele, both Burke County natives, were elected First Lieutenants. Reed was 41 years old, and Steele was 53. There appears to be no Second Lieutenant in the roster. At the Third Lieutenant post was Burke County son Joel H. Brown, a 26-year-old farmer. All of these men abided in Alexander County at the time of their enlistment and elections.[33]

The last group to be formed for the Thirty-seventh were the "Mecklenburg Rifles." They met on October 22, 1861, in Charlotte and elected local merchant John K. Harrison, age 46, Captain. First Lieutenant of the Rifles was Robert M. Oates, also

Flag of the Gaston Blues.

Lieutenant Joseph B. Todd, Company B (courtesy of Overmountain Press).

a merchant and 32 years old. Moses N. Hart, a 39-year-old farmer, was elected Second Lieutenant. And to fill the role of Third Lieutenant was William M. Smith. Smith was also a farmer and was 25 years old.[34]

Enlistment day was generally a period of enormous excitement. Some volunteer company commanders hosted a lavish dinner, the best that the local folks could supply. Other companies received flags from their respective communities. These flags, "emblems of freedom," would "serve both as a reminder of the community's determination to resist tyranny and of the transparent relationship between public and private duty in the disunion crisis." The Gaston Blues received one such flag, made from the dresses of local ladies, as did the Watauga Minute Men. Joseph B. Todd, who initially served with Company D of the First North Carolina Cavalry (Ninth North Carolina State Troops), then with Company B of the Thirty-seventh, and later as Colonel of the postwar Watauga County Home Guard, was forced to stand in the doorway of the Watauga County courthouse and wave his sword, preventing the over-joyous members of the militia from riding their horses into and through the building.[35]

The new companies elected their officers, an antiquated practice within the militia system of the United States. This did not necessarily mean that the "best qualified" man became captain or his lieutenants; only the most popular man, or the one who had the most relationships in the new company, was likely to be chosen. There was one captain within each company, and he was the most important man within that company. He drilled the men, passed on rules and regulations, made sure they received their clothing or food, heard the more serious complaints, and administered judgment and punishments, if necessary. Each company usually had three lieutenants who assisted the captain with all the duties of the company. The first lieutenant was in charge of one half of the company, and the second lieutenant was in charge of the other half. If the captain was away on official business, on leave, captured, or sick, then the first lieutenant assumed the captain's responsibilities.

The new captain also appointed his noncommissioned officers. There were usually five sergeants and eight corporals in each company. The first or orderly sergeant was the hardest working man in the company. He was the person who had immediate supervision of the company, getting his orders from the captain and seeing that those orders were carried out. He kept the roster, called the roll three times a day, made out the morning reports, and assisted the company clerk in making out all of the required forms. The other sergeants "have a more general supervision of the men" and served as file closers for the company, meaning that they were responsible for keeping the company in a straight line. The sergeants had permission to "shoot men down when they attempt to run away" and to "see that the men fill their canteens with water, and not whiskey...." They served as the sergeants of the guard, policing the camps, and were in charge of the fatigue parties. Corporals were "usually selected from the most intelligent privates ... who are noted for their military appearance and attention to duty." Corporals usually had small groups of men that they were in charge of, and oversaw small details of police and fatigue duty in camp. There was usually a company quartermaster sergeant. His duties included receiving fuel and forage for the company, taking charge of company property, and receiving and helping the first sergeant distribute clothing and camp equipage.[36]

After receiving gifts and exchanging mementos, the men marched away from their home counties. Noah Collins, from Union County, reminisced after the war: "[I] left home on the 15th day of October 1861, met the Company at Meadow Branch Church, where we remained till ... the morning of the 16th, when after the farewell compliments and extentions and hearty grasping and shaking of the trembling hands of relatives, friends and neighbors; which was a very heartrending scene, especially to the more tender hearted of the assembly, we started on our march...." As the new volunteers transferred from their home counties to centrally located camps of instruction that had been established by the state, many were taken with both excitement and despondency. Many of the volunteers had never been far from the areas where they had been born and raised. The pressure upon the community was also considerable. Many of the young, healthy farmers, the backbone of rural America in the nineteenth century, marched away, leaving a strain upon the local economy. Men were leaving their fathers and mothers, their wives and sweethearts, and their children. When William M. Kissiah of the Mecklenburg Rifles marched away from his home in Mecklenburg County, he left his wife, Mary Jane Shoemake, with child. Also there was a psychological shock to the people left behind in the communities. Before the onset of the war, so many men had never been away at the same time.[37]

It is hard to say why these men fought. An undated article in the *Western Democrat* avowed, "It is the People's War. Every Soldier on our side fights with the alacrity of one avenging a personal insult and injury." Some, of course, volunteered because of the adventure; others, out of a sense of duty or patriotism, or possibly pressure from family or friends. An Ashe County church resolution, written in October 1861, probably summed up the attitudes for most:

> Where as our Country is involved in a revolutionary war, the North against the South of the unjust savage caractor [character] the North having denied the South her constitutional guarantees, not withstanding peaceful overtures, was made by the South and called on the North again and again to settle the difficulties by Equitable negotiations to prevent the resort to the sacrifice of human life, all was proudly denied and nothing was left the South but stern resistance on object submission to unconstitutional power, and so on.[38]

Daniel C. Robinson's wife passed on words of encouragement and advice to her husband when he enlisted in the Mecklenburg Rifles: "at least don't do one thing— don't get shot in the back."[39]

2

"We have a fine Drill master"
October 1861–January 1862

The creation of the Thirty-seventh occurred at a time when the momentum of the war had begun to shift from the Confederates, who had won several early engagements, to the Federals, who would dominate from November 1861 through May of 1862, with victories at Mill Springs, Kentucky; Forts Henry and Donelson in Tennessee; and Pea Ridge in Arkansas.[1] These Confederate reverses were brought closer to home with the loss of Hatteras, North Carolina, on August 28–29, 1861. Confederate enlistment had also begun to decline as many realized the severity of a protracted war.

By late October, many of the independent companies that would constitute the Thirty-seventh had arrived at Camp Fisher, near High Point. For Noah Collins and the Defenders, the excursion had been "four days' toilsome journey in cold rainy weather...." To be in such a place, much further from home than many had ever been, was very exciting for many. James M. Tugman, of Captain Horton's Company, wrote home on the tenth of November about the things he had encountered and seen: "I saw twelve cannons ... a rifled one that weight 50.00 pounds...." Another private, A. L. Sterns, would write home a month later: "I got my likeness taken yesterday I have not got that dress yet but as son as I a chance to sedit to you I will send it...."[2]

Camp Fisher, the new home for the future members of the Thirty-seventh, was named for Colonel Charles E. Fisher, a North Carolinian killed during the first battle of Manassas. The camp was located one half mile from High Point, and where the Fayetteville and Western Plank Road intersected with the North Carolina Railroad. There were between 400 and 600 men stationed at the camp of instruction when the independent companies began arriving from the western portions of the state.

By October 31, eight of the companies had arrived at the camp and had started

Lieutenant Colonel William Groves Morris, field and staff (courtesy of C. D. Wilson).

to undergo drill. William Groves Morris, who entered the service as a Second Lieutenant of the Gaston Blues and would later rise to Lieutenant Colonel and command the regiment, started to write to his wife and children on a regular basis on the thirty-first: "There has been One Company Landed Every Day since we came heare. Though we are formed into a Redgement Next week ... we commenced Drilling yesterday. we have a fine Drill master by the name of Barnhardt A Methodist Preacher who was in the battle at Bull Run & was wounded."[3]

Instruction in company drill was one of the most important aspects of a soldier's life, and the volunteers at Camp Fisher drilled five hours a day.[4] Tactics had not changed drastically since the time of Napoleon, and what the men were taught in their company drill was intended to prepare them for the engagements that they must meet. Marching by the flanks; deploying from a column into a battle line; forming a line of battle on a certain company; firing by company, by file, by ranks, at will; listening for orders: all of these things were the basis for fighting a modern war with less than modern tactics.

These tactics, the "movement of troops in the presence of the enemy,"[5] used by Confederate and Union generals had largely been developed during the Napoleonic Wars. During the Napoleonic time period, armies would line up facing each other, march toward the opposing side, and open fire with smoothbore muskets. The first side to break under the fire of the opposing force would flee the field. Several things made these tactics obsolete during the American conflict. Most Union troops, and, as the war progressed, Confederate troops, were armed with a newly popular military invention called the rifled musket, which fired a conical bullet that gave the soldiers an accurately firing weapon, and one with a greater killing range than smoothbore muskets. Another, and even greater, advance was the addition of breastworks or field works, fortifications constructed in the field by one side or the other, usually by excavating a ditch and cutting down trees. The most elaborate breastworks had head logs, trees placed vertically on top of the breastworks, with openings or slots for muskets beneath, to protect the entire soldier. These two improvements, weapons that fired with great accuracy and field fortifications that protected the defending troops, would defeat the tactics of a previous generation. But most soldiers would spend more time in camp than on a battlefield.

Camp life was an abrupt adjustment for the men. Personal freedom had always been something these men took for granted and highly prized. Now that freedom was suppressed by the highly regulated duties of a soldier's life. There were squad and company drills, guard mounting, dress parades every evening, and "cleanly and provisional duties" to attend to. Also, there was an intermixing of classes that the men had to deal with. Before the war, the privileged and less privileged had been separated by the rural nature of Southern life. Members of the gentry were now forced to tent with common tenant farmers. The companies had been given tents for sleeping quarters, but soldiers still wore their clothes from home and carried their hunting rifles and shotguns. When the individual companies offered their services to the state, they were accepted, provided that they could arm themselves. While the men expected to receive uniforms from the state, they were oftentimes slow in arriving. Private Tugman wrote home again commenting on the lack of attire: "I want you to make me a pair of pants and a shirt [.] if we could get our uniforms this winter I would not need them." Another solider, Doctor John B. Alexander of Charlotte, a private in Company C, wrote to his wife that many of the boys were "extremely home sick." But, a few days later, in a letter dated November 18, he would write that most of the men in Company C "have concluded to take it easy and saw very little." Doctor Alexander probably wrote for many a young man that was home sick. In a third letter, dated November 26, he confessed to his wife that his "bed is not as soft as yours[,] neither is J. L. Jetton as warm to sleep with as you." Sergeant John L. Jetton, also of Company C, probably shared Doctor Alexander's sentiments.[6]

Their Methodist preacher had not proven to be an effective drillmaster. He had been "found to be a bad Case" and was discharged. A new drillmaster, James Parsons, who had also been wounded at the battle of Manassas, was assigned to drill the companies. One of the most common drill manuals of the time for North Carolina soldiers was Brigadier General William J. Hardee's *Rifle and Light Infantry Tactics.* Hardee was an officer in the United States Army prior to resigning and joining the Confederacy. He had written his tactics manual while in the service of the United States. He later revised his drill manual, and that revision was published throughout the South and adopted by Confederate regiments. Officers in command of companies in North Carolina were issued a volume of Hardee's manual, creating a demand that soon exceeded the supply of available copies.[7]

The companies had been assigned to their tents and spent their days in drill and learning new duties. One company officer wrote home: "I haft to Drill all day and studdy at Night. an officer has No time to play that wants to Discharge his Duty." Company officers received two tents for the Captain and Lieutenants. The enlisted men were often confined to larger numbers in small dwellings. The life of a soldier in the future regiment probably followed the schedule of a neighboring camp of instruction, Camp Magnum: "Reveille at Daybreak, Breakfast call at 6½ A.M., Sick Call at 7 A.M., Guard-Mounting at 730 A.M., Squad Drill from 8 to 9 A.M., Company Drill from 10 to 12 m., Orderly call 12 m., Dinner Call at 12½ p.m., Battalion Drill from 3 to 430 p.m., Dress Parade at 530 p.m., Tattoo at 8 p.m., Taps at 830 p.m." In addition to adjusting to a new schedule, the men also had to adapt to different eating habits. Their diets consisted of flour, bacon, sweet potatoes, and cabbage.[8]

Religion, particularly Christianity, was one of the most important aspects of a soldier's life. From his spiritual beliefs a soldier could draw strength during the many trials that he would face. And many concerned individuals sought to keep a soldier strong in his faith. When a company marched out to war, many times the pastor of a local church would pray with and over the men. The concern for the soldiers' spiritual well-being continued from the home front to the encampments. Lieutenant Morris wrote home, reporting at least six preachers in camp, with sermons every night, and sometimes three sermons going on simultaneously. Thousands of Bibles and tracts were printed and distributed throughout the war. Many of these four-page tracts, under such titles as "The Act of Faith," "All-sufficiency of Christ," "Private Devotion," "Motives to Early Piety," and "Self-Dedication to God," were distributed by W. J. W. Crowder of the American Bible Society. The distribution of such large quantities of religious materials led to huge revivals that later swept through the Confederate armies.[9]

On November 12, the companies then in camp received their first issue of uniforms. "We have received over coats and dress pants of the finest kind," one private wrote. Another private echoed the same thoughts: "I drawed a fine overcoat worth fifteen dollars and a dress coat worth ten dollars and a fine pair of pants and haversack...." The soldiers were issued six-button gray sack coats, with sewn-down black epaulettes, as specified by the 1861 North Carolina uniform regulations from the adjutant general. Company K's letter book, in which issued items were documented, shows that each man in the company received one great coat, one sack coat, two pairs of pants, two pairs of drawers, one pair of shoes, one blanket, one knapsack, one haversack, one cap box, one belt, one cartridge box with strap, one gun sling, one gun, thirty cartridges, forty percussion caps, one canteen with strap, one bayonet with scabbard, and one pair of socks. The next day, November 13, there were more requisitions, and more needed supplies were received: one desk, two spilt bottom chairs, one fair bank seal, four tents for hospital with a fly, one wall tent for the assistant surgeon, one field officer's tent, four wall tents, two flies for tents, and two field officer tents with flies.[10]

In February 1861, the North Carolina Legislature had passed a bill outlining the way a company would be accepted by the state, and how those companies would be arranged together to form a regiment. After forming the company, the captain of the company would "tender the[ir] services ... to the Governor." After the governor accepted the company, they were equipped and armed at the expense of the state. When six or more companies had all presented themselves to the governor, then the companies met and elected "by a ballot a colonel, lieutenant colonel, and major, under the direction of the captains...." The captains then presented the election results to the governor, who "commission[ed] the same."[11]

Elections for field officers were held on November 20, 1861. Charles Cochrane Lee was elected Colonel; William Morris Barber, Lieutenant Colonel; and John G. Bryan, Major. Adjutant was William T. Nicholson. Assistant Quartermaster was Robert M. Oates. Assistant Commissary of Substance was Herbert D. Stowe. Filling the role of surgeon was James Hickerson, with James Wright Tracy, as Assistant Surgeon. The Chaplain was Alfred L. Stough, a Baptist minister who lived in the Monroe area. The colonel was the commander of the regiment, responsible for leading the regiment on the battlefield and at regimental drills. Other duties of the colonel included appointing staff (adjutants, quartermasters) and instructing both officers and men in their duties. The lieutenant colonel was the next in command and responsible for the right half of the regiment, while the major was third in command and responsible for the left half of the regiment. The adjutant of a regiment was responsible for communicating the

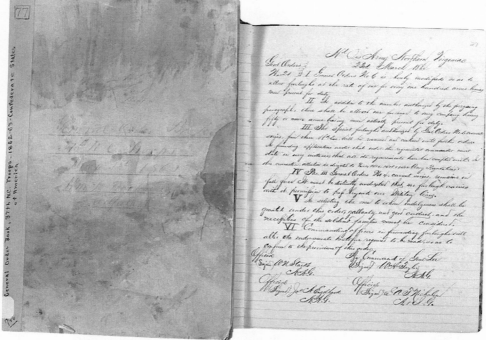

Top: **Lieutenant Herbert D. Stowe, Assistant Commissary of Substance** (courtesy of the North Carolina Division of Archives and History). *Bottom:* **General Order Books of the Thirty-seventh** (courtesy of Rare Book, Manuscript, and Special Collections Library, Duke University).

orders of the commanding officer of the regiment to the companies. He also kept up with the numerous amounts of paperwork generated by the regiment, and copied general and special orders from brigade or division headquarters into the regimental order book. An assistant quartermaster would receive and take note of stores received, and then issue those stores to the soldiers. The assistant commissary of substance made out the provision returns, drew rations for the regiment, and superintended their distribution and cooking.

Charles Cochrane Lee was the first colonel of the newly formed Thirty-seventh North Carolina Troops. Lee was born on February 2, 1834, to Stephen and Carolina Lee in Charleston, South Carolina. His father, a West Point graduate, moved the family to Asheville, North Carolina, in 1846 and opened a boys' school. Charles was appointed from North Carolina to the United States Military Academy at West Point in 1852. He graduated in 1856, fourth in his class, was assigned to the ordnance branch, and stationed at the Waterlivet Arsenal in New York. Lee resigned his commission in 1859 and took a professorship at the newly formed North Carolina Military Institute in Charlotte. He taught mineralogy, geology, chemistry, infantry tactics, and served as commandant of cadets. In January 1861, Governor John W. Ellis designated Lee to arrange the purchase of military munitions that the state of North Carolina had agreed to buy in preparation for the expected conflict. Lee traveled to Richmond, Wilmington (Delaware), Baltimore, Philadelphia, New York, New Haven, Springfield, and Hartford. He succeeded in purchasing what the state needed. In March of 1861, Lee served in his native Charleston, South Carolina, under General Pierre G. T. Beauregard in the ordnance department, and might well have witnessed the bombardment and capitulation of Fort Sumter.

May of 1861 found Lee serving under his old dean of the North Carolina Military Institute, Daniel H. Hill, who had been elected to command the First Regiment of North Carolina Volunteers. Lee was elected to the role of lieutenant colonel. This regiment was known throughout the war as the "Bethel Regiment," due to the part they played during the first land action during the war, the Battle of Big Bethel Church, Virginia. After Hill had been promoted, Lee was elected to fill his role as colonel of the First. The First was mustered out of service on November 12, and on November 20 Lee was elected colonel of the Thirty-seventh. An admirer of Lee's said he was "a splendid officer—cool and courageous and [who] has the entire confidence of his regiment."[12]

The independent companies were now each assigned a unit letter.

Company A . . . . Ashe Beauregard Riflemen
Company B . . . . Watauga Marksmen
Company C . . . . Mecklenburg's Wide Awakes
Company D . . . . North Carolina Defenders
Company E . . . . Watauga Minute Men
Company F . . . . Western Carolina Stars

Company G . . . . Alexander Soldiers

Company H . . . . Gaston Blues

Company I . . . . Mecklenburg Rifles

Company K . . . . Allegheny Tigers

These companies would bear this system of lettering throughout the war. Letter J was skipped because of its resemblance to the letter I. These ten companies were given the regimental designation of the Thirty-seventh Regiment of North Carolina Troops. A textbook regiment was to have 1,000 men and officers. On the date of their muster, the Thirty-seventh numbered 939 rank and file. Each company had a set of officers (Captain, First, Second, and Third Lieutenant), and was given a position in the regiment. From left to right, the companies' positions were D, B, E, C, K, I, H, G, A, F. The two flanking companies, D and F, were the sharpshooting companies of the regiment.[13]

The company was the backbone of the regiment; it might even be said to be the backbone of the army. Besides its Captain and Lieutenants, a company had a First or Orderly Sergeant, four other sergeants, and at least five corporals. In addition, there was an adjutant or company clerk for each company, along with a commissary and sometimes a quartermaster sergeant. While the companies were to number 100 men, they seldom did after the first days of the war, as the ranks were depleted by death and desertion, and were not always replenished.

With two of the company captains (Barber and Bryan) and two of the lieutenants (Oates and Hickerson) being elected or appointed to the field and staff, elections were held again in their companies to replace the vacant slots. Their composition now was as follows:

Company A	John Hartzog, Captain; James J. Goodman, First Lieutenant; Richard G. Goodman, Second Lieutenant; William A. Stuart, Third Lieutenant.
Company B	Jonathan Horton, Captain; Jordan Cook, First Lieutenant; Thomas D. Cook, Second Lieutenant; Andrew J. Critcher, Third Lieutenant.
Company C	James M. Potts, Captain; Thomas A. Wilson, First Lieutenant; James S. Johnston, Second Lieutenant; William B. Osborne, Third Lieutenant.
Company D	John B. Ashcraft, Captain; Jackson L. Bost and Vachel T. Chears, Second Lieutenants; William A. Gaddy, Third Lieutenant.
Company E	William Y. Farthing, Captain; Paul Farthing, First Lieutenant; William F. Shull, Second Lieutenant; Isaac Wilson, Third Lieutenant.
Company F	Charles N. Hickerson, Captain; Samuel N. Shepherd, First Lieutenant; Daniel L. Clary and William W. Beard, Second Lieutenants.
Company G	James Reed, Captain; Robert L. Steele, First Lieutenant; Daniel Austin, Second Lieutenant; Joel H. Brown, Third Lieutenant.

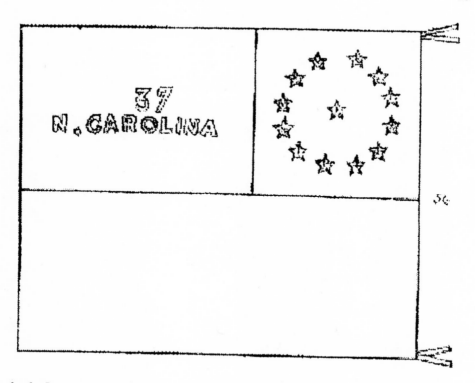

Sketch of a flag presumed to have been carried by the Thirty-seventh (courtesy of Howard M. Madaus).

Company H	William R. Rankin, Captain; George W. Hanks, First Lieutenant; William G. Morris, Second Lieutenant; Henry C. Fite, Third Lieutenant.
Company I	John K. Harrison, Captain; Moses N. Hart, Second Lieutenant; Julius G. Price, Third Lieutenant (the position of First Lieutenant was vacant until elections in 1862).
Company K	John Ross, Captain; Lowrey Grimsley, First Lieutenant; William Halsey, Second Lieutenant; John Williams, Third Lieutenant.

It was also around this time that the new regiment received its state battle flag. While most regiments received a standard North Carolina issue flag, manufactured at first in Richmond and later in Raleigh, it appears that the Thirty-seventh received an unusual variation of that flag. The flag measured 36 inches by 42 inches in length. It contained two bars, a white one on the top and a red one on the bottom. There was a blue canton, with thirteen white stars, and the letter "37" and "N. Carolina" in gold lace on one side only in the white bar. The flag had two or three sets of ties.[14]

Even as the new regiment received its new flag, disease had already begun to take its toll. Many of the men had spent their entire lives on farms and had never been exposed to many childhood ailments, such as mumps and the measles. Lieutenant

Morris reported two cases of the measles in his letter home, dated November 12, 1861. Private Silas Green (Company B) wrote home on December 29: "there is right smart sickness in our regiment mostly with Measles and sum mups...." Private Tugman, in an undated letter sometime after the ninth of December, echoed Green's sentiments when he stated that "there is a heap of sickness in camp ... a great many have died ... only one of our company [B] that died Will Triplett and too of Capt. hartzog and three of Capt. Farthing has died...." One of the first deaths belonged to the first company, Company A. Benjamin Owens died of disease on November 14, 1861, six days before

Private Mecager Tugman, Company B, with his wife Nancy Greer (courtesy of the Watauga County Historical Society).

the regiment was officially mustered into state service. Jesse D. Pierce of Company D died next, sometime in November 1861, of disease, at home. James W. Tant, of Company G, succumbed next on November 25, 1861, of disease. These three were followed by James W. Triplett of Company B on December 9; Henry A. Pilkinton and Samuel Teaster of Company E, and Robert Foster of Company H, on December 12; Riles Johnson of Company E on December 14; Logan Armstrong of Company H on December 18; James Bruce of Company I on December 25; and R. A. Craig of Company H on December 28. Most of the sick soldiers were taken to Barbee Hotel/Hospital in High Point where they succumbed to their ailments.[15]

With the loss from disease also came the loss through rejections. Most of those turned away were rejected on the basis of unfitness for duty. And one had to be really unfit not to qualify for the Confederate service. Most medical examinations consisted of a doctor thumping a person on the chest and pronouncing him sound. Age could also be a factor in fitness. Many of those discharged were deemed either too old or too young to serve. Company B lost Amos Estes, William S. Gragg, William Hayes, Demarcus Hodges, William Hodges, Levi Potter, and Mecager Tugman. Company

C lost Andrew Hunter. From Company D, Wilson P. Gaddy, Edmond Harrington, Jesse C. Hasty, William T. Hendrix, B. A. Manus, William T. Marsh, Jesse H. Pierce, Thomas H. Steele, Richard Syms, and Hampton Usry were all discharged. Company E lost William H. Calloway, Bartlett Y. Hilliard, and Hodges Moody. Rejected from Company G were James Campbell, William F. Dison, and Malee McAlpin. John M. Armstrong and Marcus Smith were rejected from Company H, along with Robert M. Wyatt of Company K.[16]

On November 20, 1861, the same day the companies were mustered and officers elected, the regiment reported its first three cases of desertion. William P. Miller of Company A, David J. Smith of Company H, and William A. Richardson of Company K all deserted from the regiment and never returned. The men had probably signed on when the companies were mustered in the counties, and had not returned to their companies when they left for High Point. These would be the first of many absences without leave and desertions within the regiment throughout the course of the war. Soldiers who absented themselves from the regiment without permission but returned to the regiment were oftentimes reported as absent without leave, while soldiers who never returned were classified as deserters.

After the formation of the regiment and the election of the officers, the men were sworn into state service. The Thirty-seventh received praise from many different sources. Lieutenant Morris wrote home: "Coln Lee & his Regmt has the prase for being able & willing to Fight." Consequently, the men were not given winter quarters so that they might be ready to "be sint Where ever the Most Danger is apprehended."[17]

On December 31, 1861, the regiment turned in its Form 51, showing the equipment received in the prior year. They had received 157 caps—most men probably still wore their civilian or slouch hats from home, 621 private's coats, 630 pairs of trousers, 76 shirts, 126 pairs of drawers, 64 pairs of gloves, 770 overcoats, 166 knapsacks, 826 knapsack straps, 34 wall tents, 111 wall tent flies, and two iron pots, along with other items such as chairs and a desk. Obviously, most still wore their shirts and drawers from home.[18] Some men may not have worn drawers at all, if they were not accustomed to doing so in civilian life. Officers did not receive clothing from the depots. They were responsible for the purchase of their own clothing and often had tailors or family at home custom make their uniforms.

The two iron pots were quickly replaced with tin mess pans and camp kettles. Cast iron pots and skillets were too heavy to be transported in regimental wagons. Mess pans were usually six inches high by 12 inches in diameter at the top, and held approximately six quarts. The camp kettles varied in size, sometimes being made of copper, but often of tin or sheet iron.[19]

The Thirty-seventh departed from Camp Fisher near High Point on December 27, 1861, and moved, by rail, to Camp Mangum. "None of us," wrote Doctor Alexander to his wife on January 1, 1862, "knew how to appreciate good living while we were at High Point. There we fared sumptuously every day." Camp Mangum was located near the state capital of Raleigh. Alexander continued his thoughts of their new location: "At High Point we had many of the conveniences of home, here we have none; many of our men have had next to nothing to eat since Monday morning." The Thirty-seventh's camp was located on a hill, with deep hollows on either side. Besides not having received food, the camp's water was in "limited supply," the regiment's cooking utensils had not yet arrived, and there was no straw, nor planks for the floors of the tents, with the ground being "very damp." The Doctor continued: "A good number of the boys are carrying oak leaves to make beds of...." Besides the living conditions which Alexander found disagreeable, he also wrote of the wood they used, with the pines being the primary source of heat. The soldiers themselves had to "cut and carry" the wood, and he thought that "so we will be as black & dirty as the negroes...."[20]

While at Camp Magnum, Camp Fisher, and other various camps, the men had a constant stream of visitors from their home counties. Private Tugman's father, mother, brother, and sister had all visited him some time after the ninth of December. There were many other visitors to camp at various times. In addition to family, local dignitaries, preachers, and even ladies' organizations often called upon the soldiers, bringing encouragement and gifts from the nearby communities. But some soldiers did not want their wives to visit camp. "I never want to see you here ... if you value your modesty I beg you not to come ... I think the place for a soldier's wife, during his absence is at home," Doctor Alexander would write to his wife Annie in Mecklenburg County.[21]

Sickness continued to plague the Thirty-seventh. Morris wrote to his wife:

> We have about 30 Men on the Sick Roll at this Time. We sent Five to the hospital to Day. One very bad Case of Pneumonia by the name of Damson. the most of the cases are Yellow Janders following the measles. W R D Abernathy has Measles. I just Started him to the hospital. he is not Much Sick. I think as he is Going to the hospital where he can be taken care of will soon be well.[22]

Every morning, after reveille and roll call, there was sick call. The soldiers who were sick, or thought they were sick, were escorted to the surgeon's quarters by their company first sergeants. The surgeon either pronounced them well, or prescribed medicine, or bed rest, or sent them to the hospital or home on furlough to recover. The regiment continued to suffer deaths due to sickness and disease. William McGuire of Company A succumbed in January, along with John Cox and John H. Dameron of Company H. Dameron died on January 12, while Cox passed away on January 14. If Lieutenant Morris's figures are true for the rest of the regiment, then as many as one-third of the Thirty-seventh were out sick at this time.

On January 7, the men were prepared to be mustered and paid. An officer wrote: "The Whole Brigade Made out there pay Roll yesterday. Tomorrow was the day appointed by the paymaster to Come & pay us all off."[23] "I have got to be an officer" one soldier wrote, "third corporal I get thirteen dollars a month."[24] Their pay was not much, and this was probably the first time they had been paid since they were mustered into state service on November 20, 1861, excluding the $50 bounties, of which $10 had been paid upon enlistment and the remaining $40 in December. A pay scale for the time period looked like this:

Private . . . . $11.00 per month
Corporal . . . . $13.00 per month
Sergeant . . . . $17.00 per month
First Sergeant . . . . $20.00 per month
Second Lieutenant . . . . $80.00 per month
First Lieutenant . . . . $90.00 per month
Captain . . . . $130.00 per month
Major . . . . $150.00 per month
Lieutenant Colonel . . . . $170.00 per month
Colonel . . . . $195.00 per month[25]

The regiment was scheduled to go through the ritual of mustering for pay once every two months, when they got paid, which, except for the summer of 1862, was fairly regularly. The company officers would labor over the mustering sheets for days, producing two copies containing the names of every enlisted man in their company. When the officer designated as the paymaster arrived, the companies were formed, inspected, and as each name was read, the soldier would move his musket from the position of support arms to shoulder arms. When the name of the next soldier was called, the first soldier would move his musket to the position of order arms. This was continued throughout the company. The soldier then approached the table where the paymaster was, either signed his name or, if illiterate, made his mark, and received his pay. If the soldier owed any money to the company laundress, or for the destruction of military property, such as musket cartridges, then the amount was deducted prior to the soldier's receiving his pay. Officers were not required to go through this ritual. The paymaster would go to the officers' quarters and pay them privately.

Camp Magnum, located near Raleigh and later renamed Camp Bethel in April 1862, was another recruit and drilling camp in North Carolina. Many other regiments had been sworn into service and drilled at Camp Magnum, including the First/ Eleventh North Carolina Troops, also known as the Bethel Regiment. The Thirty-seventh spent just sixteen days at Camp Magnum, and the weather played havoc the whole time. Lieutenant Morris reported sleet. Doctor Alexander authored another letter to his wife on January 7: "Since last Saturday night we have been surrounded with ice[,] our tents have been covered ½ an inch thick with for the last three days…." In Lt. Morris' letter home, also dated January 7, the regiment had just received marching orders and was told to be ready to march the next morning. Colonel Lee was working on acquiring transportation for the men to their next assignment and their first test under fire, New Bern.[26]

3

"Our Men are allmost Crazy to Meet the Enemy"
January–April 1862

Orders came on January 9, 1862, for the regiment to "strike tents," and within an hour they had started to convey their baggage to the railroad, in a "very hard [rain] all the time," one soldier wrote. "[w]e Got as wet as watter could make us but I Dont Know as it has hurt Me." By January 12, the Thirty-seventh had arrived at their new camp, which one soldier called "a lovely place," on the fairgrounds near New Bern, about 50 yards from the Neuse River. New Bern, the old colonial capital of the state, was the second oldest town in North Carolina and was located at the confluence of the Neuse and Trent rivers, 35 miles from the Atlantic Ocean. When the Thirty-seventh arrived, it was placed under the command of the newly appointed Brigadier General Lawrence O'Bryan Branch. Lawrence O. Branch came from a distinguished background. His grandfather, John Branch, was a notable North Carolinian who had served the county of Halifax, the state of North Carolina, as Lieutenant Colonel under General Nathaniel Green, in the North Carolina Constitutional Convention, and in the state legislature. Lawrence's uncle, also named John, was a three-time governor of North Carolina, a state representative in the General Assembly, a United States Senator, Secretary of the Navy during President Andrew Jackson's term, and a one-term governor of the then–newly formed state of Florida.[1]

Lawrence Branch was born on November 28, 1820, in Enfield, North Carolina. He spent his early years growing up in Tennessee and Washington, D.C. Some of his first education was received in Washington, D.C., where he was tutored by Salmon P. Chase. Branch then attended school at the Bingham Military School (N.C.), the University of North Carolina, and, in 1838, succeeded in graduating from Princeton with honors. He studied law in Tennessee and gained entrance to the bar in Tallahassee,

Florida, where his brother, as well as his uncle (the governor of the new state), lived. In 1841 he served as an aide-de-camp to General Leigh Reid during one of the numerous campaigns against the Seminole Indians.

In 1846 Branch entered the political scene for the first time. He was a candidate for the General Assembly of Florida, representing Leon County. He lost. The year 1848 found Branch living permanently in Raleigh, North Carolina, and the next year he received his law license from his home state. Between 1850 and 1855 he held a variety of jobs and posts: North Carolina Literary Board; director for the North Carolina Institution for the Deaf and Dumb; director for the State Bank; Democratic presidential elector; and director and president of the Raleigh and Gaston Railroad Company. In 1855 Branch was elected to his first term in the House of Representatives in the

Brigadier General Lawrence O'Bryan Branch.

United States Congress. He had defeated noted orator James B. Shepard for the seat.

Congressman Branch "was a partisan Democrat who advocated states' rights and who looked after the interest of his state and section," but he was not an extremist. "His statesmanship, his loyalty to democratic ideals, his desire for peace, and his fight for the rights of minorities" brought him to the forefront of antebellum politics. During his consecutive terms in the House, he witnessed much of the nation's political crisis leading up to the separation of the states. He watched the debate on the punishment of Representative Brooks, who had caned Senator Sumner; he denounced the Republicans and the Homestead Act; he sided for the Nebraska Bill; he felt that a surplus of the budget "was a bad thing, for Congress wrongfully collected more money from the people than it needed to run the government." In December 1857 he was appointed to the Committee of Territories, an appointment he had coveted since his election to Congress. May 1858 found Branch an appointee to the committee on Foreign Relations, replacing fellow North Carolinian Thomas L. Clingman, who had been appointed to the United States Senate. Branch's dedication to state politics was so sincere that some sought even higher aspirations for him, with one newspaper "Propos[ing] his name for Senator." The *Greensborough Patriot* thought he should be a candidate for governor. Branch did not pursue either path, and was reelected for another term in Congress, his most important.[2]

In early December 1860, Branch was offered the post of Secretary of the Treasury, which he declined, not wanting to vacate his seat in Congress. With so many of the Southern congressmen having left by early February 1861, Branch became the premier spokesman for the South. William A. Eaton, who had left the Congress and returned home to Alabama, wrote to Branch and said that Branch "occupied a high place in Congress among those who had left." What were Branch's views on the impending crisis? In January 1861 he wrote to Dr. William Lewis: "I am satisfied that the North will make no concession and consent to no compromise. They intend to carry on their agitation against the slaveholding states as precisely as they have heretofore...." Branch was staunchly dedicated to his position, and expressed some reluctance to "throw down the pillars of the Union, but the honor and security of North Carolina are dearer to me than life itself."[3]

Branch returned to Raleigh on March 6, never again to orate from the floor of the house. In April he joined the "Raleigh Rifles" as a private, but had only attended one drill when the governor appointed him a colonel and gave him the position of quartermaster and paymaster of the North Carolina Troops. This position made him responsible for the task of supplying munitions, clothing, and other material to all the North Carolina forces, some of which had already left the state for Virginia. By September, Branch had resigned this position and been awarded another: to confer with President Davis "about the coast defenses of North Carolina...." Branch returned from his meeting with the president, and a few days later was commissioned colonel of the Thirty-third North Carolina Troops.[4]

After six weeks, Branch was commissioned a brigadier general, to serve in the a post vacated by fellow North Carolinian Daniel H. Hill. Some North Carolinians were against his promotion. William W. Holden, editor of the Raleigh *Standard*, disapproved of Branch's appointment because Branch had no military education and had been advanced over others who were older and did have experience and education. Holden thought that the appointment put "at hazard the vital interest of North Carolina."[5] Despite some dissenting voices, Branch was assigned to one of the three departments on North Carolina's coast, his command focusing on the defenses of the New Bern area. Brigadier General Branch would eventually be given six regiments of regular troops, an infantry battalion, several unattached militia companies, and eight batteries of artillery.

When the Thirty-seventh arrived on the outskirts of New Bern, the members were sworn into Confederate service and placed under Branch's command. Colonel Lee had some reluctance about serving under Branch. In a letter written to old friend and fellow colonel of the Twenty-eighth North Carolina Troops, James H. Lane, Lee scoffed at Branch's lack of military knowledge and his being "more fond of his own position than the best interest of the service."[6]

At least one soldier had a problem with the oath that the soldiers took upon being placed into the service of the Confederate Army. Private Collins (Company D) thought that the oath was entrapment, and "gave them the dodge in that manner." Collins was called out by his first sergeant, George W. Davis, and later by Captain Ashcraft, who instructed Collins that he "had better be there and that very soon, if

I knew what was best for myself." Private Collins slipped off when it came time for the rolls to be called, and "did not reappear till the tumult of confusion was over and quiet restored." Just what the "tumult of confusion" was he did not record, nor any punishment he might have received for not being present to answer for his name during the roll call. How many of the other men might have felt as Private Collins did regarding the Confederate oath is not known.[7]

As the soldiers of the Thirty-seventh pitched their tents, they traded their shotguns, squirrel rifles, and hog rifles for flintlocks that had been sent down from Richmond, Virginia. An officer wrote home: "we have Recd flint Lock Muskets but Lee says he will not Leed his Men in to battle without Number One arms." Colonel Lee himself traveled to Fayetteville to inquire about the new arms, and one soldier wrote hopefully of Lee's excursion, "I suppose he will bring us some excellent arms...." General Richard C. Gatlin, commander of the Department of North Carolina, wrote to Branch that the "600 flint and steel" muskets would "be replaced in a day or two by percussion from Fayetteville Arsenal." These new weapons from Fayetteville were probably little better than those they already had. The Raleigh Depot Record of Issue reported that the Thirty-seventh was armed with altered muskets and 1842 percussion muskets.[8]

The altered muskets were also .69 caliber and smoothbore, and they were probably some of the 37,000 stands of antiquated muskets, some dating back to the War of 1812, that had been captured with the arsenal. These weapons had started out as "flint and steel," but had been converted to percussion as soon as workmen could be found. The 1842 percussion muskets were also smoothbore and had a limited range of 150 yards.[9] The muskets fired a buck-and-ball cartridge: one .64 caliber round ball, with three .30 caliber "buck" on top of that. This load was placed on top of 110 grains of powder. The balls and the powder were wrapped together in paper, forming cartridges. Prior to a battle, each soldier was issued 40 to 60 rounds of cartridges. During a battle, a soldier dropped the butt of the musket to the ground on his left side, and inclined the barrel toward the right, holding the musket in his left hand. With his right hand, he retrieved a cartridge from his cartridge box, and, with his teeth, tore off the end containing the powder, exposing the powder. He then dumped the entire cartridge into the muzzle of the musket, and drew his rammer from beneath the barrel, ramming the cartridge down into the breach of the musket. After withdrawing his rammer, he either held it in his left hand, stuck it into the ground, or replaced it in its tube beneath the muzzle. The soldier then raised his piece with his right hand, and, balancing it over his cap pouch, produced a small, copper percussion cap, and placed it on the cone or nipple of the weapon. His musket was now ready to be fired. Once that was accomplished, he had to go back through the steps all over again, the musket becoming harder and harder to load each time due to the fouling created by the black powder. A good soldier of the time period could fire about three rounds a minute.

Many members of the Thirty-seventh were also issued blocks of lead, ladles, dies, and bullet molds to manufacture their own rounds in the field prior to the battle.[10]

How long the soldiers of the regiment made their own bullets in the field is not known, but the process was a rare one for Civil War soldiers. Most received their cartridges ready-made from factories, such as the ones in Richmond, Virginia, or Selma, Alabama.

In addition to adapting to the new weapons, the men had to adjust to new diets. It seems that the diets of the men had made some improvements since moving closer to the coastal area. Lieutenant Morris wrote home on the eighteenth of January: "but One thing is Certain we Get fresh bacon & fish & oysters in a bundance ... [but] My Throat is a Little sore at this Time but I think the Oysters will Cure it." Private Jordan S. Councill, of Company B, also described his fare in a letter to his mother: "[we have] pork en sugar en pees en molases an soap...." Another soldier, Private William F. Carrigan (Company C) would write his thoughts of the military fare in late February: "I had got too fatt I have to quit eating so much fat meat...." Another soldier wrote of "a gang of oald nigars hear a roun the gard line seling sweat bread and pyes and they dont look like they was fit to eat nothing eats good like it does at home."[11]

Camp Tadpole would be the Thirty-seventh's next destination. The men broke bivouac and left the fairgrounds on January 19, and moved by rail to their new camp, three miles east of New Bern. One private described the area around Camp Tadpole as "a boggy, low level, black sandy, wet, and very muddy, long strawed piney region, abounding in gallberry bushes and cypress." Private Green (Company B) wrote on February 18: "But the worst rain and mud you ever did see...." The men of the Thirty-seventh spent their time at Camp Tadpole working on the fortifications around New Bern, namely Fort Thompson. Fort Thompson was located about six miles below New Bern and was an earthen fort located on the Neuse River, containing 13 pieces of artillery. General Branch reported that he had 500 men at a time working on the fortifications around New Bern. When not engaged in this endeavor, the soldiers were digging wells, building chimneys for their tents, flooring the guard tent, and dealing with an overabundance of rain and black mud, which Private Collins said was "about a half a leg deep all the time." Doctor Alexander would echo Private Collins's sentiments regarding their new camp when he wrote that the encampment was in a "very low, wet, boggy place, [with] grass 1½ feet high ... scarcely any other timber than the long leaf pine and sweet gum." He would once again be complaining of the water, saying that it was "hard to get" and had to be carried three-quarters of a mile: "and it taste very strong of turpentine , [with] some of it look[ing] like milk...."[12]

By contrast, Lieutenant Morris was quite impressed with his camp. On February 8 he wrote to his "Deare Companion":

> We have made a comciderable improvement in Our Camp by putting woodin Chimneys To Our Tents. we have our tents floored. the first Night after I Got My Tent floored & chimney built & Bed fixed up & a Good fire I thought To Myself that If You & the Children Could be there I would feel like I was at home. Coln Lee had a stove in his Tent but after Seeing Our Chimneys he throwed his Stove away & put a Chimney in his Tent.[13]

February 8 was possibly the first time a brigade drill was held, adding another element to their already taxing schedules. Brigade drill involved two or more regiments, and getting these new regiments to move in synchronization posed a major obstacle. Most of the regiments under Branch's command had yet to master the company and battalion drills. Orders such as "to break to the front, to the right, into column" or "to the left, forward into line" would cause mass confusion. One officer would write, either out of awe or amazement, "To see 3 Thousand Men armed & Equiped In Line of battle is a Considerable Scene."[14]

The soldiers of the Thirty-seventh were quickly approaching their first encounter with the yankees. Several times the Federal gunboats had approached the land, close enough for an alarm to be raised, but every time they had been on some other mission, such as sounding out the bay. On one occasion it was rumored that the entire Thirty-seventh had been captured and taken prisoner. Colonel Lee's reply to this was "that if the 37th R G was ever taken prisoner they would have to be killed first." Company and regimental drill still progressed, as did the constant strains of sickness and deaths. The soldiers' diets were still improving greatly. One officer authored a letter to his wife stating, "we get plenty to eat but have to pay for it. 20 cts a lb for pickled pork, 4 Dollars pr hundred for Flower, butter is Selling at 60 cts a Pound.... Chickens Sells at 50 cts a peace & Eggs Not at all." Another officer noted that he had even gained 18 pounds since he enlisted. Since the food could be costly, the men were also concerned about pay. Lieutenant Morris wrote home: "Our quarter master went to Raleigh Last week for our Money but did Not bring it from the fact that he could Not Get it Onley in One hundred Dollar bills & that Sort of Money would Not be of any use in Camp." A furlough home, the one thing that most soldiers sought more than anything else, had been halted by order of General Branch on February 10, in anticipation of an upcoming battle.[15]

By February 20, the regiment had left Camp Tadpole and arrived at Camp Lee, their new home for the next month. Camp Lee was about one mile southwest of Camp Tadpole, near the Trent River, and in sight of New Bern. The camp was described by one mountain soldier of the Thirty-seventh as "a pore contry ... it is a white sandy lan and just as full of grean briars as it can be...." By contrast, an officer in the Thirty-seventh from the piedmont portion of the state said Camp Lee was on "the Edge of an old field Rather a high Sandy Ridge a very Nice place for a camp." To many, and justly so, the water was so bad as to warrant a complaint in their letters home. Private Jordan S. Councill wrote: "the water is bad an we have to tote it...." Private Bennett Smith, of Watauga County, wrote: "The water is bad hear I had rather drink out of them mud holes thare on Brushy Fork...." As the men pitched their tents in their new camp, they began to work on new chimneys. "[We] have our chimneys up better than Ever. I have My Chimney Lined with Brick...." Lieutenant Morris wrote home to his spouse.[16]

Private William F. Carrigan, of Company C, wrote to his mother and father back in Mecklenburg County not long after arriving at Camp Lee. He wrote that he had "nothing worth writing" about, but gave them all of the details of his recent sickness: "I have had colds and incessant coughing.... I had Diarhea for about 2 weeks & these boiles on the back of my neck for the last week has been right hard on me but I'll keep in fine spirits.... I have the good will of my tentmates & all of my company & the Physicians of the Regt...." On the same day, Carrigan would write to his daughter, Margaret, who was staying with his parents. "I want you to be a fine girl and be obedient to your Grandfather and Grandmother," he wrote. "I have bought you a dress & is sending it to you with your uncle.... I want you to strive to Read & learn to write well as much as you can...." Clearly, even as the members of the Thirty-seventh faced the impending battle, their thoughts were focused on the ones at home for whom they were fighting.[17]

The men continued to toil on the fortifications around New Bern, with their primary concern being the land approaches. General Branch had been given a task all too common for the Confederacy: He was required to defend a piece of land that required more troops than he had available. So, like a wise commander, he sought to shorten his line of works. Men were detailed from regiments in the area to provide the work force to construct these lines, and were provided a "number of worn and broken shovels and axes, without picks or grubbing-hoe." The Fort Thompson line of works, which Branch deemed the best for his small force, stretched from Fort Thompson on the Neuse River, one and a quarter miles to the west, passing over the railroad, with its right resting on a swamp. Branch would write in an official report: "The line of small breastworks from the rail road to the swamp was partially finished for about half the distance." The woods in front of these works had been cleared for about 350 yards, providing a clear field of fire for the defending Confederates.[18]

The regiments that Branch had at his disposal were as follows:

Seventh North Carolina State Troops, Colonel Reuben P. Campbell
Twenty-sixth North Carolina Troops, Colonel Zebulon B. Vance
Twenty-seventh North Carolina State Troops, Major John A. Gilmer
Thirty-third North Carolina Troops, Colonel Clark M. Avery
Thirty-fifth North Carolina Troops, Colonel James Sinclair
Thirty-seventh North Carolina Troops, Colonel Charles C. Lee
Brem's Battery, Tenth North Carolina State Troops (First North Carolina Artillery)
Latham's Battery, Fortieth North Carolina Troops (Second North Carolina Artillery)
Whitehurst's Company (garrisoning Fort Thompson)
Nineteenth North Carolina Troops (Second North Carolina Cavalry) Companies E & F[19]

The preparations conducted by these troops were in response to a Federal threat to North Carolina's coastline. On January 7, 1862, fifteen thousand Federal troops under the command of General Burnside had embarked from the Chesapeake Bay and sailed south. Their orders were to seize and occupy Roanoke Island, New Bern, Beaufort, and Fort Macon. After the eventual seizing of New Bern, the Federal forces were ordered to "endeavor to seize the railroad as far west as Goldsborogh," cutting off supplies from Wilmington.[20] Another objective of the mission was to try and return the eastern portions of the state to the Union. Many people were claiming that these areas were ready to "secede" from North Carolina and go back into the Union.

As Burnside pursued his capture of the eastern coast of the Old North State, camp life continued for the everyday, common soldier of the Thirty-seventh. Of shared concern was the recent loss of the North Carolina Outer Banks and of Roanoke Island. "We have Rather unfavorable News in Regard to Ronoke Island," wrote one officer. "[I]t is Sirtainlet Taken by the Enemy.... Since the Ronoke affair ... Our men are allmost Crazy to Meet the Enemy."[21] While they may have been eager for war, much of their time was spent in amusing themselves until the need for their services should arise.

"There is awl sorts of amusements going on hear," wrote Bennett Smith to his wife Jane. "[F]idling dancing plaing bast bool pen jumping rasling and a heap of other things & some of the wickeds men you evry saw and the uglyes that you evr heard tel of...." He continued with: "I caint find out how it come I was fetch here." Letter writing occupied many a soldiers' mind. One wrote so often that he assumed that his wife "will be tired of reading; but it affords me more pleasure to write to you than to do anything else." But mail service was somewhat unreliable. Doctor Alexander wrote to his spouse twice a week, but complained that "Our mail agent is not always what he should be, frequently drunk." Many members of the Thirty-seventh were discouraged that the yankees had not come sooner. They were there to give battle to yankees and not to "Fight the Muskeetoes...." Some would cast an air of indifference: "whether they come or not I do not know (or Care)," wrote one member of the regiment.[22]

There was a dearth of reading material in the camps. "We hardly ever see a newspaper here, therefore we know nothing," one soldier of the Thirty-seventh wrote. Chaplain Stough complained that there were "few or no books" and asked people to send religious papers, which were "more highly prized than many might suppose."[23]

Many of the men used this time as an opportunity to strengthen their spiritual lives. A strong revival had already started to take place among the soldiers of the Thirty-seventh. Private Smith penned another letter home: "They hav preaching here every fiew dayes he is able preacher I go evry time to meeting[.]" Chaplain Stough wrote to the *Biblical Recorder*, a publication printed by the Southern Baptists within the state, on February 24. He found the "religious interest in the 37th regiment" very strong and "attentive." Stough asked for more "religious reading matter" and praised the work being made to circulate "Bibles among" the soldiers. "The enterprise is glorious in its orgins," he wrote, and thought that "the interest of our country, the happiness of our families, the preservation of pure religion, requires alike our exertions in supplying the destitute with the Gospel of the Son of God." He would close his letter with, "Pray for us. Pray for our unfortunate nation, that we may have a speedy and honorable peace." Lieutenant Morris, in a letter to his wife on February

Chaplain Alfred L. Stough (courtesy of the North Carolina Division of Archives and History).

26, reported that "The Camp Life is in Some respects better that I Expected." Morris attributed the better camp life to his Colonel, Charles C. Lee. Morris thought that Lee was "an Exception" and a "Devoted Christian." Morris painted this picture of a Sunday service:

We had a fine Sermon Last Sabbeth from a preacher Living in Sight of our Camp. at the Close of his Sermon he told us that there would be Servis at 3 o.clock P M at which time Coln Lee would Make Some remarks…. Coln Lee appeared, Read a chapter from the bible had prayer & preached I Believe the Best Sermon I ever heard. he told us While we was Contending for Our Wrights and Lebertyes that we Should be Careful that While We was Engaged in a ware against the yankees Who desire to bring us under SugJection & in to bondage that we be Not Slaves to a worse foe than Man. that foe he represented to be Sin. he contended that we was Engaged in a Just war but Not Lay Down our arms that God had given us to defend our selves against the foe that would hold us in Chains through Eternity. he caled on us to Come out from under the bondage of Sin that we Might be free people indeed. he told us that we could Not Expect Sucksess in our Struggle for freedom as a Nation if we Stooped So Low as to become Slaves to Sin. I hope & trust that God will Every Keep us on Guard Against the Enemy both Speritual & temporal.[24]

    While the religious services encouraged men to think of their heavenly homes, many were far more homesick for their homes in the western part of the state. The sentimental tone of the letters home conveys the constant thoughts many men had of being with their loved ones. Bennett Smith wrote: "Jiney I don't bleve ther is a half a hour but what I think of you & that Boy and you don't know how bad I want to be with you I hope they day is coming when we will pas a heap of happy hours together." Lieutenant Morris finished one of his letters with: "Tell the Children To not Neglect to Say there Prayers Every Night & God will smile on them & hope it will Not [be] Long Now till I Can come home to see you."[25] The spiritual support the men received must have been comforting in their homesickness and in their first taste of combat.

    By early March, as the soldiers prepared to defend New Bern, most of the town's citizens had fled the city for safer havens. Colonel Lee had even been witness to some of the town's men donning women's apparel to escape the coming battle and occupation. The Colonel wrote with disgust that "Such persons seem hardly worth fighting for, but then we must remember it is a part of the Old North State and we do not wish the enemy to take a foot more of this soil if we can prevent it."[26]

While the *Monitor* and the *Virginia* (sometimes referred to as the *Merrimac*) were fighting their famous battle to a draw some 80 miles away, General Burnside was loading his boats with ordnance and supplies for the upcoming campaign, proposing to possibly go as far as Raleigh. Colonel Lee could not see the importance of holding the area around New Bern. His thoughts were "that if we were to leave the place the enemy would never come here at all...." Occupation, if it did occur, would be for "a month or two [then] they would be so badly fleeced that they would be most happy to withdraw their forces and retire to their homes[,] for the shopkeepers here can beat the yankees 2 to 1 at that trade." A later historian had a different view. "The denial of the waterway and the railhead of New Bern was paramount ... in ... [the] scheme for cutting the flow of supplies to [the Confederacy]."[27]

At 7:00 A.M. on March 12, the Union assault on New Bern got underway. Spring had just begun to show its colors. At 4 P.M. that afternoon, General Branch was informed of the enemy's arrival in the Neuse River, "and at dark I learned that twelve vessels had anchored below the mouth of Otter Creek." The Federal forces commenced to land on shore near Slocum's Creek, thirteen miles from New Bern, and their brass bands played until midnight. Branch dispatched the Thirty-fifth and two other regiments to contest the Federal landing. Colonel Lee had been in command of the left wing of the Confederate field forces, consisting of the Twenty-seventh and Thirty-seventh Regiments, while Lieutenant Colonel Barber was given command of the Thirty-seventh. Lee was ordered to "guard the remainder of the shore, support the river batteries, and re-enforce Colonel Campbell in case he should be hard pressed." Colonel Campbell had been given command of the right wing. Work continued on the fortifications and breastworks. One soldier wrote home that day that 500 men were still laboring even as the Federals began the campaign.[28]

At 3 o'clock on the morning of the thirteenth, the Thirty-seventh took up position in the breastworks. Private Collins, out of curiosity, went over to the banks of the Neuse and observed the Federal gunboats and transporters. Collins saw:

> ...the distant fleet, which presented a scene very much like that of a very large city, at a great distance, and behold there were three gunboats detached and steaming up the river towards Fort Thompson.... These three gunboats in their war-like maneuvers, aligned themselves as skirmishers at proper intervals or distances from each other, acrosswise of the river, with their broadsides up the river ... when after remaining in that condition for some forty minutes, as if daring of and waiting for Fort Thompson to cast the first shot; a flash like that of lighting was seen to emerge or proceed from the broadside of one of the nearest to the southeastern bank of the river ... a very large cannon shot came howling up the river, like a terrible thunder bolt, the very noise of which seemed like lascerating or tearing us to pieces, which caused us to fall to the ground to dodge it, just as it fell in the river about 500 yards above us ... at which disturbance of the peace and quietude which never before reigned....[29]

The event seemed to only draw a little attention for the rest of the regiment. Lieutenant Colonel Barber, in his official record, only stated that "During the day shells were thrown frequently from the enemy's gunboats at our position without any damage to us." Barber went on in his official record to say that "toward evening some of the men built fires (which were immediately extinguished), when our lines were shelled for about one and a half hours, without injury to anyone."[30]

The night of March 13 was a wretched one for Branch's regiments, as well as for the Union division that had landed on Slocum's Creek, a low and wooded shore six miles below Otter Creek. Heavy thunderstorms, mud, and cold weather, along with nothing to eat and only one blanket apiece, made life miserable for the Confederates. Artillery fire from the Federal gun boats forced the withdrawal of the three Confederate regiments sent out under Colonel Campbell back to the main line. The positions of the regiments on that line were from Fort Thompson on the left: the Twenty-seventh, Thirty-seventh, Seventh, Thirty-fifth, a militia company commanded by Colonel H. J. B. Clark, and the Twenty-sixth, with the Thirty-third occupying a position to the right and rear of the main line in reserve. The force numbered less than 4,000 men. While none of Branch's force had ever been under fire, the weakest part of the line was the Clark's Militia. This force had only been mobilized two weeks prior and was armed with a variety of shotguns and squirrel rifles. In contrast, the Federal forces were coming fresh from their recent victories at Hatteras and Roanoke Islands. The Federal forces consisted of "13 regiments of infantry, 8 pieces of artillery,"[31] in addition to their gunboats.

March 14 started very early for the men of the Thirty-seventh. The rain had stopped sometime before daybreak, but had been replaced by a visibility-limiting fog.[32] Privates Dugger and Lawrance (Company E) were ordered back to camp to cook rations for their company. Private Dugger related his tales for the newspaper years after the war:

> On the return [to the company] we had about a half dozen camp kettles full of peas. The kettles were strung on a pole, with George [Lawrance] at one end and I at the other. We had to go through a pine grove, and while going through there, we heard our first bomb shells, and we did not know what they were, and there we stood looking and wondering what on earth they could be as they went whizzing through the air. Presently one cut the top out of a pine, and then we found out what they were and forthwith proceeded to hug the earth without getting our arms around it. As soon as the sound of the shell died away we gathered our pole and started to the Fort. When we got there we had peas all over us, so that we could hardly be told from the peas.[33]

Several hours before the battle began, the Confederates were ordered "to discharge, or fire off our wet guns and recharge them again...." About 7:30, or daylight, the waterlogged yankees appeared in the early spring foliage in front of the Thirty-seventh, "in full force ... partially concealed by the woods, and immediately opened a heavy fire of artillery and musketry...." Private Smith stated it in simpler, mountain terms: "the yankees Commenced bum shelling us...." The Thirty-seventh fired a few volleys, then the men were ordered by Colonel Lee to fire at will, each man firing when he was loaded and had a target. Facing the Thirty-seventh were the

Twenty-fourth and Twenty-fifth Massachusetts Infantry. After an unsuccessful attempt to flank the left of the Confederate line and storm Fort Thompson, the Federal soldiers settled for trading volleys with the Tar Heels. Private Collins left a graphic description: "shell after shell was exchanged with grape and canister, which lascerated or tore the pine forest astonioshingly ... all became a continual roar ... with [t]he grape and cannister opened lane after lane through the Union lines." Many of the Federals' shots passed over the heads of the men in the Thirty-seventh, but a few did come close. Several men of Company H reported holes in their clothing. Lieutenant William A. Stuart, of Company A, was shot in the elbow, and Private Benjamin H. Brookshire, of Company G, in the leg. Lieutenant Colonel Barber was moving up and down the line, encouraging the men in his regiment. The Federals charged the works three times and were repulsed. Private Smith wrote to his brother, a few weeks after the fight, about his first time in battle:

> ...you wanted to [know] if I was skerd or not I felt agitated rite Smart when they opened fire on us ... them big cannons roard so loud they threw shels at us from the river & when they would burst they would make as big a nois as when they fired the canons I could here the canon bauls pas by me the[y] would make thing fairly shake and the bullets would whirle over my hed they hit the pines at my back went like a thousand Sapsucors was a pecing the trees I was looking over the breastworks at the yankees ... about 100 yards from us And our men fired canons at them ... the way they pore felows fell was asite & run into the woods....[34]

Doctor Alexander, who had replaced the furloughing Hickerson as surgeon for the regiment, echoed Private Smith's thoughts: "No man knows what a battle is until he is in one."[35]

As the yankees probed the Confederate defenses, they found and exploited the weak point in the line: the position held by the militia. The untrained militiamen were soon overwhelmed and fled in disorder. This opened a hole in the center of the Confederate lines. General Branch rushed reinforcements into the breach, calling upon Colonel Lee to send half of the Thirty-seventh to bolster the right side of his faltering line. Barber chose the left wing, Companies D, B, E, C, and K, to assist. After traversing more than 400 yards, "through the thickest of the iron and leaden hail storm" and "with their muskets on the right shoulder," the left wing of the Thirty-seventh arrived too late to turn back the Union soldiers surging into the ever-widening gap. Some members of that left wing "fell in behind the fortifications just to the right of Latham's Battery" and continued to fight. The "small arms balls passed so thickly that they resembled a sward of bees passing," Private Collins wrote, and Private Smith thought that the "bawls fel thick" in their new location. Casualties mounted quickly as the Union soldiers strove to gain the rear of the Confederate line. Company E's First Sergeant, Albert P. Wilson, was shot in the left hand; Sergeant James C. Jones of Company K was hit in the thigh, and fellow Company K member Private John Richardson was struck and killed. After a few moments, the right side of the line was ordered to retreat. Concerning the retreat, Collins wrote of

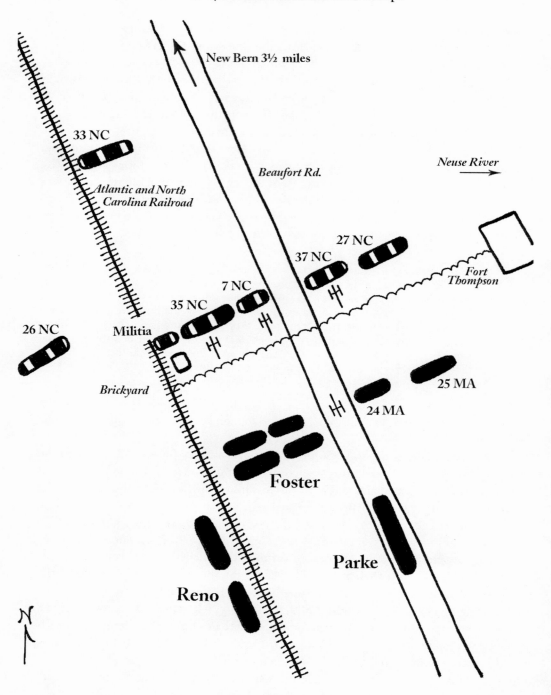

New Bern 3½ miles

Neuse River

33 NC

Beaufort Rd.

Atlantic and North
Carolina Railroad

27 NC

37 NC

Fort
Thompson

7 NC

35 NC

26 NC

Militia

25 MA

Brickyard

24 MA

Foster

Parke

N

Reno

Battle of New Bern, North Carolina, March 14, 1862.

"crossing the mud bogs, when in consequence of the shells, grape, cannister, and small arms balls passing by so thickly all the time that it did not look like anything could escape with life...." The right wing's retreat passed through the camp of the Thirty-third, where they could hear the "Union balls passing through the tents...." Other members of the Thirty-seventh passed through the recently vacated camp of the Twenty-sixth. "We found Col. Vance's liquor," wrote one member of the Thirty-seventh, "and stopped to drink it. As we went through town, we heard the Yankee cavalry was charging us and I undertook to jump a canal, which did not look to be wider than a ditch, and to be sure, I did not get over, and before I could get out, I had to loose my accouterments and swim to the bank. You can imagine how I felt when I fell plump into the water."[36]

Things were not going so well on the left side of the line either. Colonel Lee rode to the center to ascertain what the action on the other side was. After a moment, he rode back and ordered the half of the Thirty-seventh still in place and the entire Twenty-seventh to retreat. Private Andrew J. Stuart and Lieutenant William A. Stuart, brothers in Company A, were both wounded while trying to carry William Jones, also of Company A, off the field. According to the newspaper, Private Stuart shot and killed one yankee after receiving a flesh wound in both legs. Private William Sifford of Company G was wounded, and Private George M. Bradely of Company F and Musician Thomas P. Kixer of Company I were captured in the retreat. Some members of the left wing boarded on a "steam car" (train) and took it back to the bridge. Finding that the regiment's baggage (tents, spare uniforms, knapsacks) that had been stored in an old house could not be saved for want of wagons, Barber ordered it burned, to prevent its capture.[37]

At the word to fall back, Lieutenant Colonel Barber "proceeded with [his] remaining five companies toward the railroad bridges, and at that point where the Beaufort road crosses the railroad [he] found the five companies, which had been sent to the right, drawn up in a line of battle and awaiting the arrival of the remaining five companies." Barber then sought General Branch for further instructions. Branch ordered Barber to cross the bridge and reform on the other side in New Bern. After finding that a space of only 15 feet was available, Barber moved the reunited Thirty-seventh to the depot and formed a line of battle. Soon after, Colonel Robinson, General Branch's acting assistant adjutant-general, ordered the Thirty-seventh to move on toward Kinston. New Bern was in flames as the wounded were loaded into a train and the remaining soldiers marched out of town. One soldier wrote: "the flames of the city[,] bridge[,] and Rebel quarters still towering and expanding, presented an awful scene, which happily were extinguished in time to save most of the city...."[38]

The tired and worn members of the Thirty-seventh arrived about one hour before dark at the Tuscarora Depot, some eight miles from New Bern. Trains soon arrived and transported them to Kinston, where, according to Private Collins, the citizens of the town put the soldiers up in their own houses for the evening. Many of the wounded were transferred to the Female College or the Fair Grounds in Raleigh.

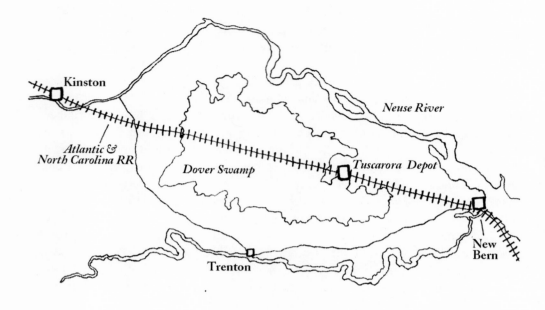

New Bern and vicinity, 1861–1865

Of the engagement, Lieutenant Colonel Barber wrote: "The men under my command behaved with great coolness and deliberation during the entire day, retreated in good order, and brought with them all their guns and ammunition." They arrived in Kinston with nothing but what they had on their backs. Private Smith wrote that "we lost awl our close and bed close…." Lieutenant Morris wrote: "I have Nothing Except that is on my back. that is My Brown soote. I Did Not have on My uniform." Doctor Alexander would provide his wife a better description of items lost during the retreat, stating that he had lost his "Haversack, Bowie Knife, Canteen, one Linen Shirt, two Collars, one flanel undershirt, one pair of pants, all [of his] bedding, nearly all of my tobacco, [and] one volume of Bryan." But the doctor was happy to say that he had saved his valise.[39]

Causalities had been extremely light, with one killed, six wounded, and two captured. It is not possible to know how many the Thirty-seventh took into the fight. Many had been on furlough, so a conservative estimate might be between three and four hundred men. At least three of the companies were under the commands of lieutenants.

The rest of March and April brought about a reorganization of the Thirty-seventh. One of the biggest topics that occupied the soldiers was the soon-to-be-implemented Conscription Act. The concept of conscription was contradictory to the ideas of many Southerners. They believed in the right of the individual to determine his own course of action rather than to be compelled to serve. But, while conscription was not a concept embraced by most Southern citizens and lawmakers, the Confederate Army needed soldiers that only a draft could provide. On April 16, 1862, the

Conscription Act passed the Confederate Congress. This Act stipulated that the President was empowered to order into military service "all white males between eighteen and thirty-five except those legally exempt." Furthermore, "men already in service were to be continued for three years or the duration" of the war.[40] The companies were allowed to reorganize and elect new officers, and those below the age of eighteen and over the age of thirty-five who were in military units to be reorganized were required to continue in their regiments for ninety days except where their space could be filled sooner by other soldiers. So the men of the Thirty-seventh had two options: not re-enlist and let the "draft" put them in another regiment, or, reenlist with the regiment in which they had already been serving. Almost all chose the latter option. Those who did reenlist were given a $100 bounty and a furlough home. Even before the Conscription Act went into effect, the furlough allowance was already being given to many men of the Thirty-seventh, who realized that reenlistment was by far their better choice. As early as February, men were reenlisting and getting the promised furloughs. Although the chance for time away from the army was certainly a morale booster, this furlough caused major problems during the battle of New Bern. Branch should have had 8,000–10,000 men to fight the battle. Instead, he had less than 4,000.

Reenlistment talk dated as far back as January and February. Lieutenant Morris wrote home on February 23: "Coln Lee formed the Regmt in a Line of battle & Gave us a Speech on the Subject of the war & caled on us to Volunteer During the war. he Requested all those that were willing to Go During the war to advance 15 Steps to the front. there was about 500 walked out. the 3 Mecklinburg Companys nearly all Stept out." In the end, only one man, Company C's William F. Carrigan, did not reenlist. He later served with the Fourth Regiment, North Carolina Senior Reserves. Doctor Alexander would write to his wife on April 27, giving some insight into the reasons why he had chosen to reenlist for the war. He said he had to join "willingly or unwillingly.... I would rather go in of my own accord than to be forced in." There were many other soldiers who felt the same as the doctor.[41]

In April there were new officer elections, since one of the provisions of the reenlistment act was that the men could reelect their officers. This, coupled with previous officer resignation, established a new leadership for the Thirty-seventh. The first officer to resign and leave was Third Lieutenant Isaac Wilson of Company E. The reason for his resignation is not clear. Wilson was later killed by Union bushwhackers as he plowed his cornfield. Company A's Richard G. Goodman, a Second Lieutenant, and Second Lieutenant Thomas D. Cook of Company B were the next to leave. Both of these men resigned on January 6, 1861. Goodman later served as a private in the First North Carolina Cavalry, while Cook seems to have disappeared from military life. William B. Osborne submitted his resignation from the position of Third Lieutenant of Company C on January 20, 1862. His reasoning was a "disease of the kidneys." He was discharged on February 4, 1862, and may have later served as a private in Company K of the Fifty-sixth North Carolina Troops. Company F's First Lieutenant, Samuel N. Shepherd, submitted his resignation on February 3, his reason

Lieutenant Thomas D. Cook, Company B (courtesy of Terry Van Dyke).

being: "severe hemorrhage of the lungs which my medical advisors say will be fatal if I remain in the service...." His resignation was accepted on February 10, 1862. Second Lieutenant James S. Johnson, of Company C, was next. He presented his resignation on February 10 due to being "predisposed to consumption, which is hereditary in my family" and his "gradually declining" health. His resignation was accepted on February 14, 1862. On February 25, 1862, the officer corps of the Thirty-seventh lost its first member to the largest killer in the war, disease. Thomas A. Wilson, First Lieutenant of Company C, died at home.[42]

During the first four months of service, the Thirty-seventh lost seven of its company grade officers, but only commissioned officers were able to tender their resignations. Common enlisted men (privates) and non-commissioned officers (corporals and sergeants) could not resign. They had to be declared "unfit" for duty and discharged by a doctor or regimental surgeon. Another rash of resignations from officers followed on April 14 and 15, just before the second election for the soon-to-be-reorganized Thirty-seventh. An officer was not allowed to run for election if he was not willing to serve for three years or the war. Company A lost First Lieutenant James J. Goodman; Company C, Second Lieutenant John L. Jetton; Company H, First Lieutenant George W. Hanks; Company I, Second Lieutenant Julius G. Price; and Company K, Third Lieutenant John Williams. These men probably foresaw their defeat in the upcoming election and chose to resign instead of being defeated. Elections for field and company grade officers were held on April 16. Major William R. Rankin was defeated, along with Captain John K. Harrison (Company I), First Lieutenants Paul Farthing (Company E) and Lowery Grimsley (Company K), and Second Lieutenant David J. Green (Company B). Rankin, former Captain of Company H, had only been promoted a month before, on the resignation of Major John G. Bryant, due to Bryant's "asthma." Rankin would later serve as a private in Company B of the Twenty-eighth North Carolina Troops; Farthing would serve as a first sergeant of Company A of the Eleventh Battalion North Carolina Home Guard;

Crowell was a private in Company H, Eleventh North Carolina Troops; and Grimsley was a second lieutenant in Company I of the Sixty-first North Carolina Troops.

Of the new company and field grade officers, 12 had been elected or promoted from the ranks. The Thirty-seventh's command structure now was as follows:

Charles C. Lee, Colonel

William M. Barber, Lieutenant Colonel

Charles N. Hickerson, Major

Company A: Captain John Hartzog; First Lieutenant Isham C. Hartzog; Second Lieutenant William H. Goodman; Third Lieutenant William A. Stuart

Company B: Captain Jonathan Horton; First Lieutenant Jordan Cook; Second Lieutenant Andrew J. Critcher; Third Lieutenant Calvin Carlton

Company C: Captain James M. Potts; First Lieutenant Owen N.

Major William Rufus Rankin, field and staff (courtesy of David R. Rankin, Jr.).

Brown; Second Lieutenant Joseph R. Gillespie; Third Lieutenant Thomas J. Kerns

Company D: Captain John B. Ashcraft; Second Lieutenants Jackson L. Bost and Vachel T. Chears; Third Lieutenant William A. Gaddy

Company E: Captain William Y. Farthing; First Lieutenant William F. Shull; Third Lieutenants Harvey Bingham and Johiel S. Eggers

Company F: Captain Daniel L. Clary; First Lieutenant William W. Beard; Second Lieutenant George R. Gilbreath; Third Lieutenant John K. Smith

Company G: Captain James Reed; First Lieutenant Robert L. Steele; Second Lieutenant Daniel L. Hudson; Third Lieutenant Joel H. Brown

Company H: Captain William G. Morris; First Lieutenant John H. Roberts; Second Lieutenant William W. Glenn; Third Lieutenant Henry C. Fite

Company I: Captain Moses N. Hart; First Lieutenant Thomas K. Samonds; Second Lieutenant James G. McCoy; Third Lieutenant William M. Stitt

Company K: Captain John Ross; First Lieutenant William Halsey; Second Lieutenant John J. Owen; Third Lieutenant Melvin C. Williams

The reorganization of the regiment was brought about by a promise by the government. If the men chose to reenlist for three years or the war, then they were given a furlough home and were able to elect new officers. In some instances, incompetent officers were replaced. In other cases, officers who were highly effective in drill and maintaining discipline were not reelected.

In February 1862, a North Carolina ordinance provided for strengthening each company's members up to 125 men. The Thirty-seventh, through death, desertion, discharges, and resignations, was down to approximately 853 men (this does not count men who were sick or out on furlough). Eight of the companies sent out recruiters back to their respective counties. Through their efforts, the regiment added 107 new recruits, bringing their strength up to 960. Company A added five, Company B twelve, Company C four, Company D twenty-three, Company E twenty, Company G thirty-

Lieutenant Harvey M. Bingham, Company E (courtesy of Overmountain Press).

one, Company H four, and Company I eight. Companies F and K did not recruit any new soldiers. For many, this was the last opportunity to "volunteer" before the grace period ran out and they were conscripted into the service. Colonel Lee would help with the recruiting, running an advertisement in the *Raleigh Register*, trying to increase the size of the regiment to 1250.[43]

After reorganization, the regiment was resupplied. While at Camp Relief, Private Collins wrote about losing most of their "blankets and most of our clothes in our precipitate or hasty retreat from Newbern...." Among their issued supplies were the new North Carolina shell jackets. These were devoid of colored shoulder trim and had a stand up collar instead of a falling collar. The Regiment's men still received items from home and homemade items from the government. Lacking supplies to equip his troops, the North Carolina governor appealed to the people to send what they could spare to be issued to the troops. Apparently these appeals were met, as Company I passed a resolution on March 17 expressing their "gratitude to the good citizens of Mecklenburg, for their prompt aid in this, our time of need." Company C would likewise pass a resolution, thanking the "patriotic and liberal citizens of Gaston county for their prompt and efficient aid in this our day of need." Several Mecklenburg County ladies received thanks in the local newspaper for their contributions of items such as blankets, quilts, socks, clothing, and even a pillow case.[44]

The Thirty-seventh's stay in the eastern part of the state brought a return to the normal routine of a soldier's life. William Morris, now Captain of Company G, wrote of the new Christian association of the Thirty-seventh: "C C Lee is [the] President.

It includes all Denominations. We have over 500 members…. We Meet Every Night a candle light for prayer…. Lee … is among the Most Devoted Christians I ever was acquainted." Doctor Alexander thought that the organization would do "much good in our Reg." Private Daniel W. Chamber (Company D) penned a letter to the *Biblical Recorder* on April 10, also describing the new association:

> Seven weeks ago, our beloved Chaplain [A. L. Stough,] with the aid of our esteemed Col. [Charles C. Lee,] and others formed a religious association, for the promotion of morality and piety among the soldiers. All the members of this association embrace some seven or eight denominations…. For the past two nights, it has rained stopping the assembling of ourselves together. Notwithstanding, all are engaged in our nightly devotions, in our tents…. The number of seekers for salvation reminds us of the day of pentecost…. Seldom do we hear the name of our Redeemer taken in vain. Since the good work has begun, five have found relief in our Savior's blood…. Our Chaplain and Colonel are, with many good brethren, ministering spirits throughout the our camp. Give us your influence and much good will be done in the cause of saving sinners.[45]

Private Smith wrote about another, more earthly aspect of camp life: "I expect you would like to no how we manage a bout cooking there is fifteen of us messes together & that number a lowes us a cook…. I don't cook any I fetch water sometimes & make a fire & the rest cooks As to washing I hav not don none yet but I will hav to wash this week…." In another letter a few weeks later, Smith wrote: "we hav hired Alfred Green to cook a month We stil git flour & meal Beacon & sugar it don eat like vituals at home did it is not cooked good you have no idy the nasnes we eat, we eat like it was clean & well cooked There is no grumbling…." He concluded his letter home with, "There is a heap of fun maid in camps of the yong men in Watauga there is some of the bigist lafs about them I hav seen some letters that the gals has sent to the boys the way they giv it to the boys back there is a site it is lafable to read them[.]" The common aspects of a soldier's life were still present: guard duty, drill, dress parade. And there were rules against everything. A person could not pass outside of the picket lines without a pass, nor could a person use profane language. Smith wrote on March 30: "it is a gainst the ruils for the soldiers to use any profain langueg…." But some soldiers still lacked a note of seriousness: "This from Silas Green" wrote a member of Company E, "tell the girls not to be uneasy ha ha ha[.]"[46]

"Our officers now bear down on us with a heavy hand," Doctor Alexander concluded in a letter dated March 29. "[W]e now … drill five hours in the day with all our accoutriments on, knapsack, haversack, canteen, cap box, cartrige box; Branch thinks we ought to become use to carrying everything."[47] A fully loaded solider commonly carried 40 pounds of gear and ammunition, sometimes more.

The Thirty-seventh spent the next six weeks in the general vicinity of Kinston. They moved to Camp Relief, which was eight miles from Kinston, on March 24, but returned to the town by April 1. On April 3, Lieutenant Colonel Barber presided over a court martial of two soldiers in the regiment (probably the regiment's first court martial). Privates Eli Patterson and John Higginson, both of Company I, were tried for violations of the 44th and 99th Articles of War. The 44th was absent without leave during a dress parade and the 99th was not carrying out their penalty regarding the former. The findings of the court were "guilty" and they were ordered to "walk for 3 hours around Gd tents with arms reversed, to walk for 1 hour before Sentinel, to perform 2 hours labor digging Stumps, [and] be confined to Gd tent for 3 days on bread and water[.]"[48] Patterson would die of wounds received during a later engagement, and Higginson was eventually captured and went over to the Union.

But Patterson and Higginson would not be the only two brought up on charges in the weeks following the battle at New Bern. Second Lieutenant John J. Owens (Company K) was dropped for "cowardice at the battle of New Bern." He would reenlist in Company K as a private. James M. Potts, Captain of Company C, was another. Potts, who would later resign due to "general debility and a predisposition of [the] breast," had already been ill for some time prior to the battle. Against the advice of Doctor Alexander and Assistant Surgeon Tracy, Potts had taken the field the day the Thirty-seventh had moved into the breastworks south of New Bern. But he was unable to keep up, and was a half mile behind the company when they reached the battle line. When he finally reached the works, he "lay about the breastworks on the ground all day ... until sundown, when the cannonading ceased...." The Captain then gained the permission of Lieutenant Colonel Barber to go to the rear to camp "to get out of the rain." On the following morning, determined to be with his men, he once again started to the battlefield, against the recommendations of the doctors. "He was walking very feebly," related Doctor Alexander, "and of course he had to go very slow; a great part of the road was half leg deep in mud." By the time Captain Potts got within a half mile of the battlefield, the battle was over and the Thirty-seventh was in retreat. Captain Potts was able to catch a loose horse and make his escape with the other troops. Potts was placed under arrest by Colonel Lee, which Doctor Alexander considered "a most unjust charge." Colonel Lee offered to drop the charges if Potts would resign, which Potts at the time refused to do. Because of Potts's medical condition, he was probably not able to command the company effectively, and Lee needed good officers.[49]

Colonel Lee would have been well-acquainted with the articles of war and the formalities of the courts-martial. Military law was one of the subjects he would have spent a semester studying during his years at West Point, and the chance of his sitting on the bench of a few courts-martials during his years in the United States Army is conceivable. According to Article of War Number 66, "Every officer commanding a regiment or corps may appoint, for his own regiment or corps, courts-martial, to consist of three commissioned officers for the trial and punishment of offenses not capital, and decide upon their sentences...." But there was a limit to the power of these regimental courts. Article of War Number 67 continued: "No ... Regimental courts-martial shall have the power to try capital cases or commissioned officers...." Colonel Lee would have been the convening authority. Any commissioned line or staff officer was eligible to be appointed to the court, except chaplains and surgeons. Colonel Lee would have been responsible for appointing a judge advocate and for reviewing the cases after they were completed. He had the power to mitigate "all or a portion of any sentence handed down" by the court. Any soldier who felt that he had been wronged by his company officer could appeal to the commanding officer of the regiment. If the soldier still felt aggrieved, he could appeal to a general courts-martial.[50]

The judge advocate was the law officer of the court. He was both the "prosecutor for the government and guardian of the rights of the prisoner." The judge advocate was the individual responsible for securing the witnesses for both prosecution and defense. He was also "required to establish that charges and specifications were properly drawn" up, and to "furnish a copy of the charges and specifications to the prisoner." After the officers selected to act as the judge and jury had been summoned, the trial would commence. It was the responsibility of the judge advocate to swear in all the members of the court, after which the president of the court, the highest ranking officer present, would swear in the judge advocate. The judge advocate would then ask the prisoner if he had "any objections … to any member of the court sitting in judgement against him." If he raised any objection, the court retired to deliberate the "validity of the prisoner's request." If the court agreed to the request, then those officer(s) would be dismissed, and other officers would be summoned.[51]

After the court had been seated, sworn in, and any challenges completed, the judge advocate would read the charges to the prisoner and the court. The soldier would be addressed by his proper rank and name: "You have heard the charge preferred against you; how say you, are you guilty or not guilty?" The soldier would then plead guilty, not guilty, or refuse to answer. He could also plead guilty to a specification and not a charge. Once the soldier had entered his plea, the judge advocate would call the first witness, who would be sworn in, and his name, rank, and unit would be recorded. His examination was conducted in the presence of the whole court and the defendant. Most of the testimony was "given in response to questions delivered by the judge advocate." If the accused soldier wished to question a witness, he had to submit his questions in writing to the judge advocate. Likewise, the members of the court had to submit their questions. After all the prosecution's witnesses had testified, the prosecution closed and the prisoner was ready to begin his defense. Any witnesses for the defense were called and questioned. After the defense rested, the soldier on trial was allowed to address the court. Once all the evidence was heard by the members of the court, the trial closed, the judge advocate performed a "summation of the whole case," and the members of the court met for deliberation. After their deliberation, a vote was taken on the innocence or guilt of the soldier. Both the taking of votes for innocence or guilt and the sentence, if the soldier were found guilty, were determined by a simple majority. The findings were then reviewed by the reviewing authority, and he issued orders for either punishment or acquittal.[52] Regimental courts-martials would take place time and time again throughout the war.

After the Battle of New Bern and the regiment's return to camp, the men prepared for a series of camp inspections by generals Branch and Holmes. Special orders were issued to the Thirty-seventh. Special orders were usually sent directly to the individual or regiments and were on a need-to-know basis. General orders were sent to the whole, or large segments of, the army. Special Order No. 2, dated April 2, stated: "The Regiment will be formed in line of battle at 2 PM for Review by Gen Branch. Men will wear their best clothes, knapsacks, c. All will attend...." The next day, Special Order No. 3, dated April 3, 1862, read in part:

> I. Captains will have everything put in good order by 12 N, so to be ready for the inspection by Genl Holmes. Streets must be swept and made clean of *all trash*. Tents must be arranged in *exact lines*. *All* clothing and blankets must be rolled in knapsacks: *Nothing* of the kind must be seated in the tents. Tents, of Officers as well as Privates must be in good order, for the reputation of the Regiment will be affected thereby. Men will wear their *best* and *cleanest* clothes, with coats buttoned and muskets in good order. Officers must wear Swords. The entire morning will be devoted to putting everything in perfect order. *The Camp of the 37th must be the Model Camp of the Brigade. "Let every man do his duty."*[53]

Not everyone was impressed with the review. Private Green (Company E) wrote in a letter home dated April 11, "We was reviewed by gen Holmes he is a sour looking old fellow...."[54]

Private Bennett Smith wrote from camp on April 6: "When we got to Camp Releif the Col oferd 2 blankets to the Company that would volenteer the most noing that we was awl without blankets." On April 16, the Thirty-seventh was officially "reorganized to serve for three years or the duration of the war...."[55] Nothing in their prewar lives could have possibly prepared the men of the Thirty-seventh for the experiences they would undergo in the next three years.

Second Lieutenant Bost (Company D) would provide a glimpse of everyday life in the waning days of April 1862:

> We are still near Kinston drilling more or less every day and a part of the brigade all the time on picket guard ... last Sunday we [Company D] took a trip down in 16 miles of Newbern to tear up the Rail Road and bring back iron on the cars.... Our infantry pickets go only about ten miles below here while the cavalry go some twenty miles.... We are all getting along pretty well, some sickness, none seriously at present. We are rather scarce of tents yet.... Tell Patsy I would like to get back home now on a thirty day furlough and talk and laugh and eat some of her cooking for a varity—like in time past.[56]

For most of the men of the Thirty-seventh, their lives would never again be like they were "in time past."

4

"Coln Lees men stood ... as firm as rocks"

May–June 1862

General Branch's brigade was officially created on March 17, 1862, and entitled the Second North Carolina Brigade. The Second North Carolina Brigade was at first composed of the Eighteenth, Twenty-fifth, Twenty-eighth, Thirty-third, and Thirty-seventh Regiments of North Carolina Troops. However, the stay of the Twenty-fifth was of short duration. They were soon transferred to Ransom's brigade and replaced by the Seventh Regiment. This would be the composition of the brigade until the waning days of the war.

The first days of May would bring a lifelong transformation to the men of the Thirty-seventh and the other members of the brigade. They were ordered to withdraw from their native state of North Carolina and join the Confederate Army of the Potomac, under General Joseph E. Johnston, in Virginia. Johnston was facing General George McClellan's Army of 105,000 men on the peninsula east of Richmond at Fort Monroe, as well as General Irving McDowell's 40,000-man army around Fredericksburg. General Johnston sought to concentrate a massive force of soldiers near the Confederate capital in order to entice General McClellan's army away from its supply base at Fort Monroe, thus making it vulnerable to attack and defeat.[1]

On May 5, General Branch ordered his brigade to prepare for its move. In a letter written on May 13, General Lee, advisor to President Davis, would provide details to General Holmes, commanding in North Carolina, as to why Branch's brigade was transferred: "Such is the pressure in Virginia that it is imperatively necessary to concentrate our forces to enable us successfully to meet the heavy columns of the enemy."[2] The Confederacy, after the early victories, was now in dire straits: Federal soldiers were within sight of the Confederate capital; the coast of North Carolina

53

belonged to General Burnside's army; Kentucky was lost; Tennessee was largely controlled by the Federals, as was New Orleans and Virginia west of the Alleghenies. Branch was ordered to take his Tar Heel brigade, move by rail, and report to General Richard S. Ewell at Gordonsville, Virginia. Gordonsville was a base of operation for the Confederate forces and the place where the Virginia Central Railroad and the Orange and Alexander Railroad converged. It was also a strategic point between the Shenandoah Valley and Fredericksburg.

The Thirty-seventh's trip to the Eastern seat of conflict was not without mishap. After being issued three days' rations, consisting of "hard dry crackers, a little musty meat," the regiments of Branch's brigade boarded a train in Kinston that transferred them to Goldsboro. From Goldsboro they made their way north via the Weldon Railroad. This line was a vital support to the Army in Virginia, bringing supplies to the men from points further to the south, such as the port of Wilmington. The Thirty-seventh boarded the trains on May 1 and began the journey northward. Traveling by train (or steam car) was a novel experience for many, for most had never even seen a train prior to the war. Oftentimes the men would ride on the tops of the cars, or take their muskets and knock holes in the sides of the cars for ventilation. This train ride was more than just a curiosity; it proved to be quite dangerous. As the train neared the Virginia–North Carolina border, the engine and cars ran off the tracks, because of the "neglect of spiking the railing when the road was under repair." Some of the cars just turned over on their right sides; other cars, including the engine, were completely demolished. Several soldiers were injured, including privates Clarence M. Carter of Company A; Fielden Asher and George Norris of Company B; and William A. Helms of Company D. The men had to wait until the next morning for another train to come by, pick them up, and continue on to Gordonsville, taking many of their injured to a hospital in Petersburg. In another instance during the same journey, one member of the Thirty-seventh was killed: Private Hugh F. Icehower of Company I. Icehower "was a drinking he had un cuppled the cars 3 times and them a running he was on top of the train and would climb down between them and pull the cupling pin out and the 4th time he fell between them and the wheels cut him in 3 pieces.... He was a well looking yong man[.]"[3]

As the trains rambled along, many members of the Thirty-seventh experienced sights and sounds they had never been exposed to before. Private Smith of Watauga County wrote to his wife, "[Richmond] is a big place ... I saw the Stutute of Washington he was siting on a horse Jest looked like man drest in milatery close ... the nigurs was drest finer than the white people in Watauga...." As they went through Richmond, "the ladies," wrote Chaplain Stough, "cheered us by waving white handkerchiefs from every cottage, This with Southern flags waving at other places, with many bouquets thrown to our boys as we passed by...."[4] The regiment arrived in Richmond at eleven o'clock on Sunday night and remained until Tuesday when the men boarded the train for Gordonsville.

The Thirty-seventh went into camp on the outskirts of Gordonsville, near the railroad, on May 4. Captain Morris complained that he had "Not Slept in a tent More than 3 nights" since leaving North Carolina. Chaplain Stough complained about "leaving our baggage in Richmond" and having to do without their blankets. But the regiment's spirits remained high. "Our religious interest is getting stronger," continued Stough, and "not an oath have I heard for many days. Drinking liquor is not tolerated in the camp, and but few want it." Apparently, the reason for the loss of baggage was the seizing of "a huge number of ... mules" by General Theophilus H. Holmes, who then gave them to General Robert Ransom, an act that infuriated General Branch.[5]

It was about this time that two companies of the regiment were able to trade their .69 caliber smoothbore Springfields for British-made .577 caliber Enfield Tower Rifled Muskets, a more formidable weapon with a greater killing range. The rifled Enfields used a conical bullet called a minié ball. The bullet had a hollow cavity in its base, and rings around the outside. When the weapon was fired, the explosion forced the base of the bullet to expand and the groves to grab the rifling of the gun, thus creating a spin which gave the minié greater accuracy and trajectory. These modern rifles had been purchased and brought over through the blockade from England.

In their new location, the regiments of the brigade were to serve as an obstacle between the Federal forces on the Peninsula and McDowell's forces near Fredericksburg. The entire brigade, which should have been able to muster 5,000 men, could only count 2,735 men and 199 officers present for duty. Some of the soldiers were still away on furlough, some were sick, and others had deserted or were absent without leave. The remaining men would spend the next two weeks in the general vicinity guarding supplies and performing picket duty at Gordonsville and Rapidan Station.[6]

"This is a very wet day," Doctor Alexander wrote to his wife on May 14 from "Camp Rapidan." "We have no tents in camp except for the officers." May 16 would bring the first period of active campaigning for the members of the Thirty-seventh. They, along with the rest of Branch's brigade, had been ordered into Western Virginia, through Fisher's Gap and into the Laurel Valley, to join Ewell and Jackson and drive the yankee forces north. The men were ordered to carry five days' worth of cooked rations and no excess baggage. The rain was coming down in torrents as the men marched out on the night of the sixteenth. After marching twelve mud-laden miles, the brigade received orders from Ewell to halt. At noon on May 17 the regiment was once again ordered to proceed. After covering thirteen miles, again in a driving rain, Branch ordered the brigade to halt, but following a brief rest they resumed their march, covering three more miles before Branch received orders to return to Gordonsville. The men spent the night "at the foot of the Blue Ridge in a Large Clover field and had plenty of wheat straw to ly on." John Tally (Company I) thought that the area was "a very Rough Country for soldiers ... [and that] our alowance is small...." The night of the eighteenth brought more orders from Ewell. Branch was to stay where he was. General Branch wrote his wife that evening: "This foolish ordering and counter-ordering results from rivalry between Gens. Jackson and Ewell. It is very unfortunate...." Doctor Alexander wrote on May 19: "I never was so completely worn out in my life as when we halted Saturday night, we had march ... with all we had on our backs ... you know that I was always opposed to walking."[7] May 19 would bring more orders, this time from General Johnston. Branch would immediately proceed to Hanover Court House. The members of the Thirty-seventh, tired, footsore, and wet, reversed their course and returned to Gordonsville. They arrived at Gordonsville around 9 A.M. on May 21, and after resting three hours, the men loaded their baggage upon the flat cars and took to the rails once again. By evening they had pitched their tents in the mud around Hanover Court House and retired to bed without waiting for supper.

The area surrounding Hanover Court House was steeped in history. It possessed one of the oldest courthouses in Virginia. The tavern, built in 1723, was the former home of Patrick Henry, the famous statesman, patriot, orator, and first governor of Virginia. The area held a strategic vantage point for both the Union and Confederate armies. For the Confederates, a force at this location kept McDowell, with an army of 40,000 men near Fredericksburg, from joining McClellan's army east of Richmond. For the Union forces, this position was vital for the protection of the Union army's right flank and the arrival of overland reinforcements from Washington. McClellan wanted McDowell and his army to join him north of Richmond and to be instrumental in the siege and capture of the Confederate capital. After the withdrawal from Ashland of three Confederate brigades under Joseph R. Anderson, Branch's brigade now formed the extreme left of Johnston's army. McClellan deemed it necessary to remove this threat and assigned the operation to Fitz John Porter and his V Corps.

The Thirty-seventh would shift camps several times during the next few days. After spending the night of the twenty-second near the Court House, the regiment moved about 500 yards to a grove of trees. Private Collins wrote that this new area was a "wet and muddy state of ... camp." Doctor Alexander, using the bottom of a tin frying pan as a writing desk, was still troubled by their "scanity rations, we get flower enough, but not much meat. [We had] cow pea today for dinner, which I can assure you was a great treat. If our negroes complain of their eating any more they ought to starve." On May 25 Branch sent orders to Colonel Lee to prepare the regiment to change locations once again. This time, however, all the sick and what remained of the excess baggage were ordered to Richmond, in confident expectation of a confrontation. By noon of the twenty-sixth, the regiments of the brigade had formed and were moving south from Hanover Court House. The precipitation kept falling, once again creating deplorable conditions. After a march of four and a half miles, the Thirty-seventh turned southwest on the Ashcake Road, a route that led to the town of Ashland. Their camp for the night was around the old Slash Church, organized in 1701.[8]

Branch's brigade would spend another night in the most wretched of situations. The rain continued to fall in torrents, turning the roads to quagmires "[between] ½ leg to knee deep all the way," related one officer in the Thirty-seventh. The men were traveling light and had no tentage, only their knapsacks or blanket rolls. Around

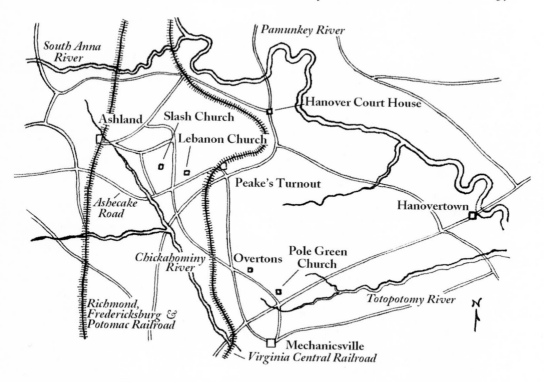

Hanover Court House, Virginia, and vicinity, 1861–1865.

midnight, two companies of the Thirty-seventh, companies D and E, were sent by General Branch to picket the Pamunkey River. Another company, B, was detailed to guard the two wagons that General Branch had brought along: an ammunition wagon and an ambulance. Companies D and E would find themselves between the proverbial rock and hard place. During the early morning hours of May 27, the Twenty-fifth New York Infantry would come up in their rear, cutting them and the Twenty-eighth North Carolina off from the rest of the brigade. Colonel Lane and his Twenty-eighth fought a detailed engagement, driving off the Twenty-fifth New York, but both he and the two companies of the Thirty-seventh, who did not participate in the fight much, were between two Federal forces: segments of Porter's V Corps to the north, and Stoneman's cavalry to the south. Captain Ashcraft (Company D) led 44 of his men and 15 of Company E's men on an elusive route and evaded the Federal soldiers. Captain Ashcraft did not return to camp until the morning of the thirty-first, having been forced to build rafts out of fence rails to cross the river and elude the enemy. Wagons were sent out to pick up the men, many "too much fatigued to come further without resting." The other men from these two companies, 78 of them, were mostly captured, with one killed, Andrew J. Hasty, Company D, and one wounded, Elijah J. Parker, also of Company D.[9]

Around 11:30 AM, cavalry pickets informed Colonel Lee that Federal soldiers had been spotted, probably a small "marauding party which might be captured by prompt action," advancing up the road a half mile from camp. Colonel Lee sent out companies F and I of the Thirty-seventh, under Lieutenant Colonel Barber, to ascertain the danger, while also sending word back to General Branch, whose headquarters were several hundred yards away. The two companies proceeded through the woods in front of the church, changing direction to the left in an attempt to catch the Federals in the flank. It is not known if the cavalry videttes had spotted the Twenty-fifth New York, which had moved toward the Twenty-eighth and the Thirty-seventh's pickets, or the Twenty-second Massachusetts Infantry, who were just beginning to deploy along the road and move toward the Thirty-seventh's camp. Colonel Lee also ordered Company A of the Thirty-seventh to the intersection of the roads to reinforce his pickets. The Federals soon moved a section of battery into position and began to throw shells into the two companies of the Thirty-seventh, which had formed up near the railroad station. Colonel Lee, realizing that his present force was not adequate, deployed the rest of his regiment and the Twelfth North Carolina Troops. He positioned the Twelfth on his right, and arrayed the Thirty-seventh across the road, sending out Company A on the left in skirmish order to protect that flank. Lieutenant Colonel Barber assumed command of the seven companies of the Thirty-seventh present, while Colonel Lee commanded this demi-brigade. Captain Latham moved a section (two guns) of his battery to support Colonel Lee and his two regiments. The Federal forces soon brought up another regiment into the fray, the Second Maine Volunteers. The Second Maine deployed to the right of the road, toward the railroad tracks, and commenced to tear up the tracks and cut the telegraph wires. So far, this had only been an artillery engagement. The Federal artillery soon caused the Confederate section to retire, but the Confederates quickly brought up a fresh section. Company F of the Thirty-seventh, one of the two companies armed with the .577-caliber Enfield rifle-muskets (the others were still armed with .69-caliber smoothbores), began to fire on the Federal battery, "killing a lieut. and 2 men and 2 horses and wounding seven [other] men." The Federals soon retired back to the New Bridge Road.[10]

General Branch presently arrived on the field and took charge of the situation. He ordered Colonel Lee, now commanding both the Thirty-seventh and the Eighteenth regiments, to assault the right and center of the Federal line, while the Twelfth and Thirty-third worked their way to the left side of the Federal line. At noon the regiments stepped off. The Twelfth and Thirty-third moved through an area described by a federal officer as being a "swampy piece of ground." These Confederates had a rough go of it, being hampered by the terrain and the Federal skirmishers. The Eighteenth fared little better. William H. McLaurin, adjutant of the Eighteenth, wrote about the action in the regiment's history: "The Eighteenth Regiment made a splendid attack on Porter's front line and drove it back to the Mechanicsville road, where the ditch bank and wicker fence afforded fine defense. From this cover Porter's volleys did great damage, and the Eighteenth was compelled to move by the right flank to a wood some 200 yards to the right to get some protection."[11]

The Thirty-seventh on the right was having a hard time also. Captain Morris described the area the Thirty-seventh was moving through as "a Dence forest in which the under growth was so thick that a man could not be seen more than 30 steps." The Thirty-seventh was moving toward the flank of the Second Maine. The Twenty-fifth New York, which had been engaged earlier in the morning with the Twenty-eighth North Carolina Troops, was ordered to relieve the Second Maine. As the transition was taking place, Colonel Charles W. Roberts, of the Second Maine, "ascertained that the enemy were rapidly advancing on my right through the woods. Informing the general commanding of the fact, he ordered me to meet them. I immediately did so, and had just time to get outside of a hedge fence on this side of the woods when through the fence muzzle met muzzle, the fight waxing warm."[12]

Private Calvin C. Miller, Company B, captured at Hanover Court House on May 27, 1862 (courtesy of the North Carolina Division of Archives and History).

Captain Morris would share Colonel Roberts's opinions of the actions:

> The 37th Rushed forward with Enthusiasm until it encountered the yankeys who were concealed behind logs, trees and in the cut of the road way which bordered by a fence ... heare the enemy had every advantage of position while his force was vastley superior, but Coln Lees men stood like victorious officers & men stood as firm as rocks within 15 or 20 paces of the Yankee line. Volley after volley of grape from their cannon & Minié Balls from there Infantry Mowed Down our men. Still the 37th moved forward Driving the enemy before it....[13]

Captain Moses N. Hart, of Company I, placed his own thoughts on paper, and mailed them to the *Weekly Catawba Journal*:

> [There was a] strip of woodland separating us—we passed through it and marched up to within thirty yards of the enemy before we discovered them. We then opened on them, which was returned with great vigor, and I suppose, the conflict while it lasted, was as fierce as any during the war. Our regiment lost a good many men... I went into the fight with 60 men and came out with 36.... When we met the enemy we thought there was 1500, but I don't suppose there were much less than 15,000.[14]

Under the intensity of the action, the men of the Thirty-seventh rapidly began falling by the scores. Benjamin Coldrion (Company A) went down with a minié ball through the right eye and brain, dying a few days later. Robert C. Gentry's (Company A) wounds were also mortal: he was struck in the chest, head, side, and arm. James L. Cardwell (Company F) suffered a round through his lungs and right thigh. Thomas

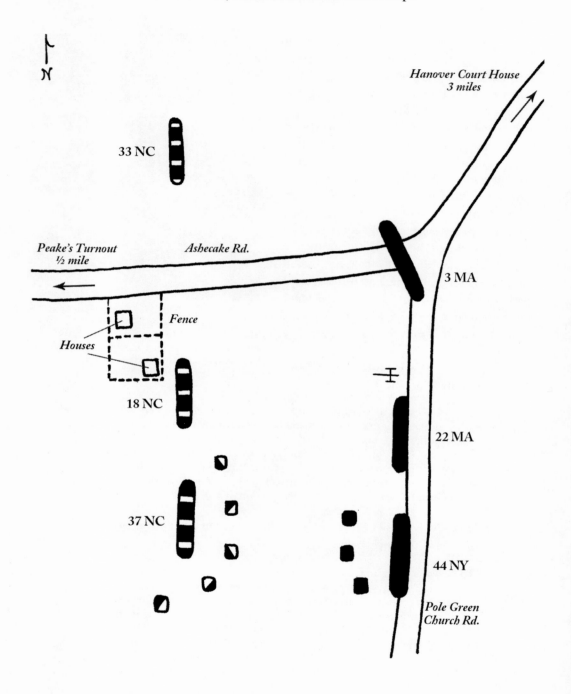

Battle of Hanover Court House, morning of May 27, 1862.

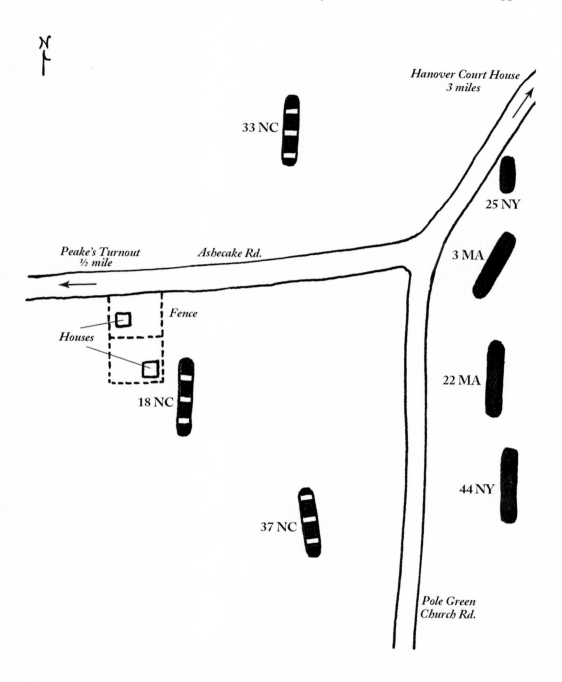

Battle of Hanover Court House, afternoon of May 27, 1862.

Mash rolled to the ground with a wound in the gluteal region and his second verte-bra. Martin V. Mullus's (Company A) wounds were also fatal: he was struck in the rectum, testicles, and left side. Henry F. Echard (Company G) had a minié ball "carry away all of the teeth and the greater part of the alveolar process of the inferior max-ilary."[15] His wound would earn him a discharge from the army. Both Colonel Lee and Major Hickerson were knocked from their horses by the explosion of a shell. Lieutenant Colonel Barber was wounded in the neck and had his horse shot and killed from underneath him. John Eldrich (Company A); Welsey Anderson, Larkin Barlow, Richard M. Hinchey (Company F); Jehua N. Austin, Brinsley Branes, Moses G. Fox, William Fox, Sr., James W. Robnett (Company G); John R. Armstrong, Oliver Brown, George McGinnas, James A. Stowe, Andrew Summey, Pickney W. Watson (Company H); Abraham Clontz, Jeptha Spears, Elm B. Wolf (Company I); and Jeptha K. Bingham, Abram Evans, Felix Long, and William Miller (Company K) were all killed. Probably the worst misfortune of the day was the fate of the Robnett brothers of Alexander County (Company G). Joel B., John C., and William P. were all killed in the fighting in the woods.

The action lasted an hour. The Thirty-seventh would drop to the ground, load their muskets and rifled-muskets, rise, and fire, and drop to the ground again to reload. The Twenty-fifth New York was forced off the field, along with the gunners of Battery C, Massachusetts Light Artillery. The Second Maine had expended almost all of their ammunition in the contest when they were reinforced by the Fourteenth New York. The fresh Federal regiment was more than the Thirty-seventh could han-dle, and the Tar Heels began to retire, "Stubbornly Contesting the ground"[16] that they had fought so hard to achieve. The seven companies of the Thirty-seventh engaged here would sustain 25 killed, 60 wounded, and 91 captured (including 29 of the wounded). Add to this the 76 captured, one wounded, and one killed from Companies B, D, and E, for a total of 26 killed, 61 wounded, and 167 captured — about one of every three men the Thirty-seventh had engaged that day. The cap-tured soldiers were taken to the Confederate prison at Fort Columbus, New York Harbor.

After receiving reports from his cavalry of large columns of Federal forces mov-ing in his direction, General Branch ordered a withdrawal. The Seventh North Car-olina covered the retreat of the other regiments. Branch had wisely kept a reserve this time, learning from a mistake made at New Bern. As the Seventh prevented the Federal forces from pursuing, the Thirty-seventh "marched to the rear without haste or confusion and went up the Ashland road." The Thirty-seventh's dead were buried on the field by the Federals, while the wounded not left upon the field were taken to Ashland, where they were loaded upon the railroad cars and taken to Richmond. Once there, they were placed in one of the many hospitals in the city, or in a private home. Noah Collins, who was sick at the time of the battle, related his journey:

> When the battle had progressed till they began to bring the wounded back and lay them in the Church House yard ... [we were soon] sent back to Ashland ... at which place we arrived just before dark.... The next morning we resumed our journey

again, by rail, to Richmond.... When we arrived in Richmond ... we were very cordially received and kindly entertained by the ladies of Richmond.... On the night of the 28th we were conducted to a very large house on Broad Street, which was set appart for a hospital, where we remained that night and received another supper....[17]

The Thirty-seventh traveled all night after having fought all day, but, due to the dismal conditions of the road, only covered eight miles. It was not until May 30 that they were issued rations, many men going two or three days with nothing to eat. The survivors began to write home again, this time with a notable solemnity in their letters. Captain Morris would write: "Tell Luly and all the Children that I thought of you all while I was in the engagement & prayed that I mite be saved from the enemy. I believe my prayers were heard because I was more exposed to the fier than any of my men...." Private Daniel W. Chambers (Company D) would write on the thirty-first: "we have had a battle with the enemy ... our regiment was very much cut up...."[18]

Not everyone was pleased with the outcome of the battle nor the way in which Branch had handled the regiments under his command. Using the pseudonym "Hanover," two officers in the brigade submitted a letter to the Richmond *Examiner* in which they accused the general of leaving three regiments to battle a vastly superior Federal force, and that Branch was not on the field until after the battle. General Branch made some inquiries, and found that Adjutant William T. Nicholson of the Thirty-seventh was one of the men who had submitted the letter. Branch sent for Nicholson, and another officer of the Thirty-third, and

> ...received them in that open, easy manner of which he was the master, and entertained them with such courtesy as put them entirely at ease. Handing each his communication he asked "Is that your signature for the purpose therein expressed," with the deliberation of a clerk in chancery probating a paper.
> They recognized that a condition, not a theory, confronted them, sweated the great sweat of confusion and acknowledged their deeds.[19]

General Branch then handed Captain Nicholson a letter and asked him to read it aloud. The letter was from General Lee, praising General Branch for his "discharge of duties ... and ... the gallant manner in which your troops opposed a very superior force of the enemy.... [Your troops have] my hearty approval of their conduct...." The two officers returned to their commands, and the congratulatory letter was read to the entire brigade that evening during dress parade. A few days later, this letter appeared in the Richmond *Examiner*:

> *To the Editor of the Richmond Examiner:*
> In your paper of May 31st appeared an article on the battle of Hanover, by "Hanover." The Author afterwards found some of the facts had been unintentionally misstated, and that certain expressions had been used which might, if unexplained, be constructed to reflect upon the personal bravery or generalship of General L. O'B. Branch; therefore "Hanover," requested you, on June 1st, to insert an article explanatory of this first article, and was told by your clerk that the article would appear if

possible. Will you, sir, please publish said article, if possible, and if not please pub-lish enough to assure the public that "Hanover" is now satisfied that General Branch was on the field before a gun had been fired, and that he ordered all of his forces into position, and did not keep a battery or four regiments idle at his side while the enemy was mowing down the Eighteenth and Thirty-seventh, as was at first stated.[20]

On June 9, General Branch sought to protect his reputation with a letter of his own, published in newspapers throughout the state of North Carolina. In this open letter he publicly revealed the identity of "Hanover," and called for a court of inquiry "to spread upon the records of the War Department other evidence of those facts than my own report...." Both Colonel Lee and Adjutant Nicholson were to be called to testify, and the "doors of the court will be wide open to critics...." General Branch concluded his letter with:

> Having been forced to the mortifying extremity of bringing my individual *action* to the attention of my peers and associates in arms, now that the thoughts of all are engrossed by the great transactions in which we are participating.
> I shall rest my reputation upon their verdict. Whilst I shall not attempt to fore-stall the judgment of the public, I ask no suspension of it. The North Carolina pub-lic will form its opinion on such materials as it thinks fit, or when it thinks fit — on no material at all. Those who are too cowardly to take the field themselves, and too mean to do justice to those who are in the field, will continue to slander me as they have done heretofore. If there is not honor and justice enough left in the State to protect me, whilst absent in the discharges of duties to the county, from such base and fool attacks, I will remain without defense until time and circumstances permit me to return.[21]

On May 29, Colonel Lee would pen his official report, a practice that all regi-mental, brigade, division, and corps commanders were required to do. These reports were forwarded to the commander of the Army, and in this case, General Lee and one of the General's staff members would draft another official report that was for-warded to the Secretary of War. Colonel Lee closed his report with, "but the battle of Lebanon Church [Hanover Court House] will be remembered by North Car-olinians as one of the bloodiest in which her sons have ever been engaged." Unfor-tunately for the brave North Carolinians, this battle would pale in comparison with things to come.[22]

5

"Waiting for the Yankees—
to come over and see us"
June–July 1862

The day before Branch's modest command battled elements of Fitz John Porter's V Corps, Branch's brigade was transferred to a new division in the Army of the Potomac and placed under the recently appointed division commander, Ambrose P. Hill. The Thirty-seventh would serve under Hill's command for the remainder of the war and would become part of Hill's famed "Light Division."

Ambrose Powell Hill, called Powell Hill by family and historians alike to separate him from fellow Confederate General Daniel H. Hill, was born in Culpeper, Virginia, on November 9, 1825. His family traced their lineage back to England, coming to Virginia in the 1630s. Since establishing roots in the Old Dominion, the Hills had produced Revolutionary War heroes, legislators, and plantation owners. Powell's father, Thomas Hill, was a well-regarded farmer, merchant, and politician. Thomas's wife and Powell's mother, Fannie Russell Baptist Hill, "was a small, frail, bespectacled introvert...."[1] The Hills had seven children, Powell being the last son.

Powell's childhood was similar to that of many other planters' children of the time: fishing, hunting, horseback riding, and reading of the campaigns of Napoleon Bonaparte in France. He attended schools under the Reverend Andrew Broadus and later, at the Black Hills, a private boarding academy. In April 1842 Hill was accepted at West Point Military Academy. Hill's classmates, acquaintances, and friends were some of the future players in the upcoming conflict: Birkett D. Fry, Dabney H. Maury, Thomas J. Jackson, Darius N. Crouch, John G. Foster, David R. Jones, Samuel B. Maxey, Cadmus M. Wilcox, Henry Heth, Ambrose E. Burnside, Julian McAllister, Truman Seymour, Samuel D. Sturgis, George Stoneman, Jesse L. Reno, and George E. Pickett. Hill's roommate was George B. McClellan, who later married one of Hill's former sweethearts.

Hill graduated from West Point in 1847, was promoted to second lieutenant, and assigned to the First Regiment, United States Artillery. His assignment led him to Mexico. While in Mexico, Hill was assigned to a horse artillery company of Capt. Francis Taylor, a supply train commander and acting adjutant of Maj. Samuel P. Heintzelman's battalion. After the end of that conflict, and after surviving a bout of yellow fever, Hill was transferred to many posts: Fort McHenry, Maryland (1848–49); Fort Clinch, Florida (1849–50); Key West, Florida (1850–51); Camp Ricketts, Texas (1851–52); Fort Barrancas, Florida (1852–53); Fort Capron, Florida (1853–55); and with the Coast Survey of the U.S. Navy, Washington, D.C. (1855–61). On July 18, 1860, Hill married Kitty Morgan McClung, a Kentuckian he had met at a party in Washington. Kitty's brother was future Confederate General John Hunt

Lieutenant General Ambrose Powell Hill (courtesy of the Library of Congress).

Morgan. In February 1861 Hill tendered his resignation from the U.S. Army. He had been offered a post that would not require him to bear arms against the South, but had declined. Hill had written in a letter in 1847: "There is one regiment on which I would stake my life, and that is the one from dear old Virginia." Powell Hill had owned no slaves, and after the war, his widow, Kitty, whom he always referred to as "Dolly," would write that Hill "never approved of the institution of slavery, but thought the Government should not take the slaves from their masters without paying something for them."[2]

Hill was soon commissioned Colonel of the Thirteenth Virginia Infantry. A year later, on February 26, 1862, Hill was appointed a brigadier general and assigned a brigade of Virginians, General James Longstreet's former command. Soon thereafter, on May 26, 1862, he was appointed a major general and given a division to command. Hill's command consisted of James J. Archer's brigade of Tennessee and Alabama troops, William Dorsey Pender's North Carolina brigade, Maxcy Gregg's South Carolina brigade, Charles W. Fields's brigade of Virginians, Joseph R. Anderson's Georgia brigade, and Branch's brigade of North Carolinians.[3]

The first of June found the Thirty-seventh hungry, without tents and clean clothes, and hundreds of miles from the state the men thought they had enlisted to fight in and for. Many thought that after the current crisis was defused, they would be returned to North Carolina. This was a feeling that they kept during the entire war, even though many never returned to the state from whence they came.

"Annie we have had a hard road to travel ever since we came to V[irginia]," Doctor Alexander would write on June 2. "Sometimes I get so tired that I can scarcly drag my-seilf along." For the better part of the next month, the men would change camps several times and perform picket duty often. The

Private John V. Miller, Company A, and his wife (courtesy of the Ashe County Historical Society).

Thirty-seventh would remain at a camp on the Chickahominy River until June 13, then take up the march and set up a new camp near the Brook Run Creek. Private John V. Miller (Company A) would write his brother on June 17: "we expect to hav a batle here very day we think … that we can whip them … it is very worm here.…" After seven days at Brook Run Creek, the Thirty-seventh once again took to the roads and moved to a camp near Brook Church. Their stay there in their shelter tents would be six days long. John Tally (Company I) would take the opportunity to pen a few lines home, from a "noll" on June 22, describing life for the soldiers around Richmond. He would write that "There is Little Skirmishing evy day [but] not mutch damage done … we are Laying a few miles of Richmond waiting for the Yankees—to come over and see us.…" Some complained of their plight. Private Lawson Potts, of Company C, wrote that he "would rather be one of his Pa's dogs trotting through the yard than to lead the life" that the soldiers of the Thirty-seventh currently had to live.[4]

On June 3, Doctor Alexander was ordered by Colonel Lee to visit Charlottesville, Gordonsville, and Petersburg, Virginia, and Wilson and Goldsboro, North Carolina, to "gather up all of our men who have been in the Hospital, and are fit for duty." Some men would "prolong their illnesses to keep from returning to the front lines, and some doctors would neglect to release men that were well enough to return to the regiment. Alexander thought that Lynchburg was the "most uncouth, hideously ugly city" that he ever had seen. Alexander would reach Goldsboro on June 10, and on June 12 would return to the camp of the Thirty-seventh near Richmond. He did not record how many men he sent back to the camp.[5]

The regiment suffered greatly from sickness and disease at this time. One soldier of the Thirty-seventh reported that on June 15 the regiment could only muster 450 men. Company C alone had 25 men in the hospital. Also, near the middle of

June, Colonel Lee stopped the prewar practice of electing company level officers, and began to appoint them. Doctor Alexander wrote home to his wife that he thought the practice "a good idea in our company." By June 20, the doctor estimated that the regiment had lost 50 men to sickness and disease.[6]

It was during this time that the new commander of the army around Richmond, Robert E. Lee, formulated his plans. Lee, a West Point graduate and a military advisor to President Davis, had been placed in command after General Joseph E. Johnson had been seriously wounded during the battle of Seven Pines on May 31. Lee believed that the opportunity for the Confederates to win the war rested much more on Northern morale and their willingness to continue to fight than on Southern victories. Lee would write to President Davis: "It is plain to my understanding that everything that will tend to repress the war feeling in the Federal States will insure to our benefit." As Lee took field command, there were several fundamental principles that he believed had already been established after the first thirteen months of war. He understood that the Confederacy faced overwhelming general disadvantages. The Northern resources, their finances, and their skilled workers and craftsmen, were almost unlimited. The North also possessed more manpower than the South could ever hope to draw upon. The South would lack the outside intervention that had made the American Revolution possible. The South's only hope was that the North would grow weary of the war and tired of having her sons killed and buried in Southern soil. It was with these thoughts that Lee took to the field in late June. His goal was to push back and, if possible, destroy the Federal army poised on Richmond's doorstep. He also sought to show the North how costly this war would be.[7]

Richmond, the capital of the Confederate States, was the object that the Federal army under General McClellan sought. This Federal army was just a few miles to the east, within viewing distance of the church spires of the city. But Richmond was more than the Confederate capital. The city had key railroad connections, connections that provided men and supplies from other parts of the Confederacy. The city itself also provided most of the munitions of war to Lee's army. The factories in the County of Henrico alone "excelled half of the eleven states of the Confederacy" combined.[8] In addition to the city's physical importance, its fall would have greatly diminished the morale of the entire Confederacy. Thus, General McClellan landed his army on the Peninsula and moved toward Richmond, causing the Confederates to fall back closer and closer to their capital. It was McClellan's army positioned on the very outskirts of Richmond that forced General Lee to adopt a policy of offensive war.

On June 24 orders came for the Thirty-seventh to "draw two days rations ... to be issued and cooked and put into Haversacks.... Knapsacks will be left behind in camp ... the men taking but one blanket."[9] The morning of June 26 brought orders for the men to break camps and prepare to move out. The Thirty-seventh, along with the rest of Branch's brigade, was to be ready to cross the river at 3 A.M. and march in an eastern direction toward Mechanicsville. At least that was the scheme. Branch was to act as a liaison between Stonewall Jackson's command arriving from the valley and the rest of the Confederate army. As Jackson approached, he would

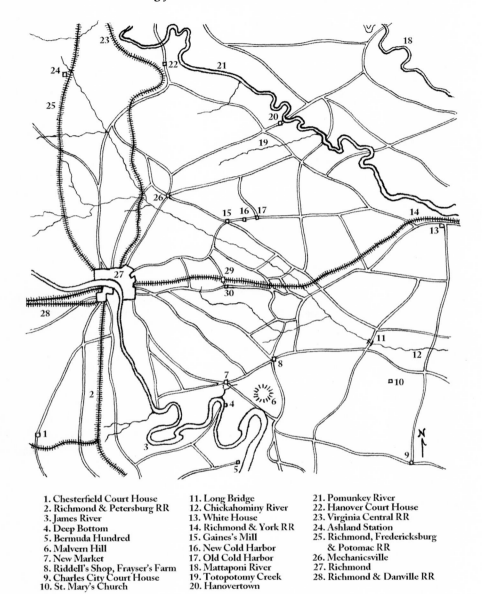

1. Chesterfield Court House	11. Long Bridge	21. Pomunkey River
2. Richmond & Petersburg RR	12. Chickahominy River	22. Hanover Court House
3. James River	13. White House	23. Virginia Central RR
4. Deep Bottom	14. Richmond & York RR	24. Ashland Station
5. Bermuda Hundred	15. Gaines's Mill	25. Richmond, Fredericksburg
6. Malvern Hill	16. New Cold Harbor	& Potomac RR
7. New Market	17. Old Cold Harbor	26. Mechanicsville
8. Riddell's Shop, Frayser's Farm	18. Mattaponi River	27. Richmond
9. Charles City Court House	19. Totopotomy Creek	28. Richmond & Danville RR
10. St. Mary's Church	20. Hanovertown	

Overview of action around Richmond, Virginia, June through July 1862.

send word to Branch. Branch would begin his drive on the Federals, while sending word to A. P. Hill to commence his attack. Hill would make a demonstration on the Federal front as Jackson drove into their rear, cutting the Federal Army off from its base of supplies. At 4 A.M., the Thirty-seventh moved out of the encampment near Brook Church to a position at Half Sink. There, in an open field, they waited for Jackson. By 8 A.M., he had not materialized, and Hill sent orders to Branch to continue to wait. The Thirty-seventh moved back away from the river to a spot in the woods about half a mile from their starting point, near their former camp at Brook Church. Finally, just after 10 A.M., Jackson sent word to Branch that he was at the Virginia Central rail line near Slash Church. The patient Branch launched his attack within ten minutes of Jackson's note. Jackson would not arrive on the field until late that evening, some twelve hours late and after the outcome of the battle had already been determined.

The Federals put up ineffectual resistance as the brigade crossed the bridge over the Chickahominy River, commencing the start of the Seven Days campaign. Three companies of the Seventh were thrown out in front, acting as skirmishers, followed by the rest of the brigade. The progress was slow, with the Federals making at least two stands, one of which was at Atlee's Station. The Thirty-seventh was somewhere near the rear of the column. In his letter home, Captain Morris wrote of the spoils of war the men encountered: "they [Federals] burned Every thing they could but they left any amount of Camp Equippage & persuing them we could pick us any thing you want, Napsacks, Haversacks, Guns & all kinds of Clothing Scatterd for Miles wide in the Direction they went."[10]

About a half hour before dark, they arrived on the field at Mechanicsville amid a storm of shot and shell. General Hill had not been as patient as he had cautioned General Branch to be, and had begun the battle without waiting for General Jackson to arrive. The Thirty-seventh was assigned to protect a battery then dueling with the Federals. Its position was "in a very thick piney old field...." The artillery contest lasted until 10 P.M. that evening, and the men of the Thirty-seventh spent the night around the artillery, sleeping on their arms, the second such night they had spent in a row. The next morning, before dawn, the Federal artillery opened upon the Confederate lines with a tremendous barrage. Branch wisely ordered the regiments to lie down, providing smaller targets for the deadly Federal missiles. The Thirty-seventh was ordered to prepare to charge around 10 A.M. Branch's orders were "as soon as you see any movement on the right or left, or hear heavy musket firing, advance also and storm the [Beaver Dam] Creek." When they reached the Federal lines they discovered that the Federals had withdrawn during the night. "Here the Yankee dead had not been moved," described Private John B. Alexander, "and the swarms of horse flies that arose from the dead carcasses rendered it necessary for each man to hold one hand over his mouth and nose." Casualties for the day had been light among the Thirty-seventh. Private John R. Norris of Company B and First Sergeant John L. Crouch of Company G were the only wounded. Crouch would later die of his wounds.[11]

After discovering the Federals gone, A. P. Hill put his tired brigades on the road the yankees had taken, attempting to catch the Union army. That army had entrenched on high ground behind Boatswains Creek, a thirty-foot deep, wooded ravine that some also called a swamp. The area in front of the creek, from whence the Confederates had to move to attack, was a large, open, rolling field. Gregg's brigade, also of A. P. Hill's Division, was the first to stumble into the Federal lines, around noon. Hill waited until the rest of the brigades were up to commence an attack.

The Thirty-seventh came upon the field around 1 P.M., and the men could see "nothing but a huge or very large and dense or thick cloud of white smoke...." Private Collins wrote: "the artillery [was] firing away about as thickly as the sound of about one hundred wood choppers' axes...." Things were in a state of confusion. Private Alexander chronicled after the war:

> A rare site I witnessed. Some man, I never knew who he was, was riding back and forth in front of our firing line, talking to the men, telling them to aim low, don't shoot too high; he was bare-headed.... A large spotted hound appeared at the same time, running, barking as heavy limbs were cut off by shells, licking the blood from the dead and wounded.[12]

Branch's position was between two roads, not far from Gaines's Mill. The one on the left was the road that led back to New Cold Harbor. The road on his right ran directly toward the Union line of battle.

Around 3:30 P.M. Hill ordered his men to attack in force. Gregg's brigade hit and pierced the Federal line held by Sykes's Regular Infantry brigade, only to be driven back. Branch was called upon to send his brigade to support Gregg's brigade. Branch first deployed two of his regiments, the Seventh and the Twenty-eighth. Finding his position in great peril, he deployed the remaining three regiments, the Eighteenth, Thirty-third, and the Thirty-seventh. Once the Thirty-seventh's troops entered the thick brush lining the creek, all semblance of order was lost. The Thirty-seventh went from a column to a battle line on their left flank. Once arrayed, the men opened fire upon the troops in front of them, which were unfortunately not Federals, but their sister unit, the Thirty-third. One private recalled:

> ...[W]hen discovering all was not right, we fell back a few yard, reloaded, rallied and fired again.... When becoming better satisfied that all was not right, we fell back about two hundred yards to a branch, reloaded and rallied a second time, when a majority fired a third time.... Major Cowan of the 33rd North Carolina Regiment came down with out-stretched arms, screaming at the top of his voice "Cease firing, cease firing gentlemen, cease firing" for we were ... killing our own men[.]

It took Major Cowan and Colonel Lee several minutes to gain control of the men. Lee stormed about, "looking more like a maniac or mad-man at the time, than the Honorable Colonel of the regiment...."[13]

The Thirty-seventh fell back once more, across the branch, and reformed next to its field hospital. For the fourth time the men charged into the melee. One soldier likened the action to a "prairie fire of a hot stormy day...." Things at the front were not much better this time. The Thirty-seventh ran into a wall of their own troops, and were forced to lie down and seek any shelter they could find. A few would occasionally rise up and fire at the Federals, even though in some places the Confederate ranks were seven men deep at the base of the ravine. Colonel Lee, in utter disgust, stood, turned his back to the enemy, placing both hands upon his sword, the point resting upon his left foot, and defied the yankee "missiles of death." Major Hickerson

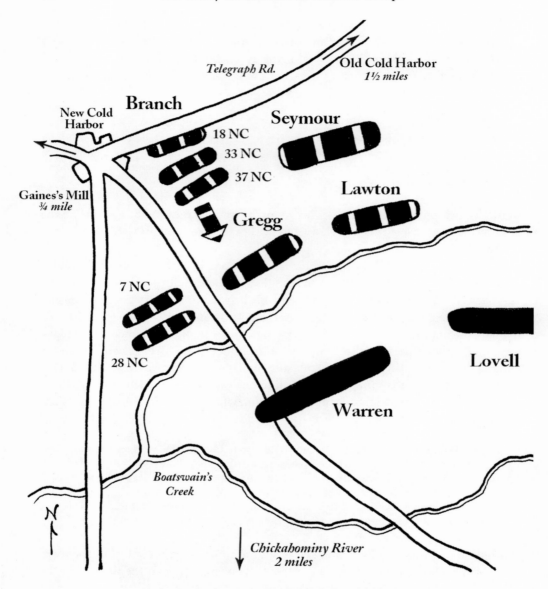

Battle of Gaines's Mill, Virginia, June 27, 1862.

approached Colonel Lee and, while attempting to pull him to safety, said, "Colonel, such as this will never do, it will never do to become so enraged at your misfortune." Doctor Alexander would have his canteen shot off and have three minié balls pierce his hat. Casualties soon began to mount. Company B seems to have been the worst hit: Lieutenant Jordan Cook would lose an eye; John M. Brown was struck in both legs, Charles Davis in the arm, and Thomas Dula in the thigh. Joseph W. Green was struck in the leg, Tarlton Hendrix in the side and arm, and Wyatt Hayes in the foot. Lindsey M. Bishop, Vinson Greer, Thomas Hodges, and Calvin Triplett were all killed. In all, the Thirty-seventh suffered eleven killed, forty-four wounded, and one captured. Eleven of the wounded would later die of their wounds.[14]

Soon the Thirty-seventh fell back once more across the creek to reform. And for the fifth time that day, around 7 P.M., they once more charged valiantly ahead to confront the foe, and finally became "engaged in a very severe and bloody contest...."[15] Around 9 P.M. the Federals were finally driven from the field. The Thirty-seventh, exhausted, bivouacked on the field that night, their third night under arms.

Morning would find them looking over a landscape transformed into a ghastly terrain, and faced with the grim task of burying the dead. While the Thirty-seventh would not move out of the area for a day, the assignment of burial detail was not one highly sought after. Private Collins would write of the duty as an "odious of hateful and offensive task...." Large trenches were dug and the dead were unceremoniously placed within, to be covered with a little dirt. "I was all over the battle field," wrote Captain Morris, "the Enemy in Every fight Carryed back there dead, some ½ a Mile. There was 800 found in one pile." Another soldier described his travels over the field of battle at Gaines's Mill: "the pools of blood being so very thickly scattered about that a person could scarcely set his feet clear of them...."[16] The Tar Heels would spend this night near the battlefield, in rain-drenched woods, and receive two days of rations that they proceeded to cook and eat.

Sunday morning, June 29, the Thirty-seventh would start once again on the trail of the retreating Federals, who, due to few roads and poor reconnaissance, occupied only one road, the Quaker Road. Recrossing the Chickahominy at New Bridge and following the Darbytown Road to the Long Bridge Road, the Thirty-seventh would continue to march until 11:00 P.M. that night, a hard day of soldiering by any account, and once more they would spend the night in a pouring rain.

The next day started out the same: up early and on the road in a sweltering heat. The Thirty-seventh moved down the Long Bridge Road toward Glendale and Frayser's Farm. In the early afternoon the command was given to halt, and the men found comfort in the shade of the woods adjacent to the road. Longstreet's division, which had been in front since leaving the field at Gaines's Mill, was deployed, with A. P. Hill's division held in reserve. Soon Longstreet sent word back to Hill to send up a brigade to reinforce the Confederate right. Branch's brigade was chosen and came upon the field, and "with spring steps pressed forward."[17]

The area the Federal forces had chosen for defense was once again fronted by a swamp, which gave the Federals the advantage of a slightly elevated position. The ground the Confederate troops had to pass over was "greatly cut up by ravines and covered with heavy timber and tangled undergrowth." By a strange chance, the Confederate forces outnumbered their Union counterparts on June 30. The Confederate Army was divided up into four contingents, each with its role to play in the upcoming battle. If each of the four parts executed its orders, then the Federal army would be trapped and destroyed.[18]

Branch's brigade soon arrived and was posted on the right of the line, next to Kemper's brigade. With no guide and uncertain of their purpose, the brigade's troops

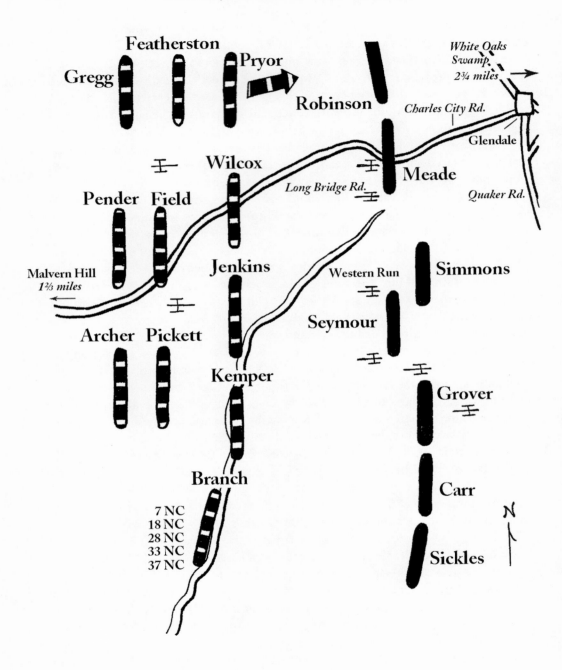

Battle of Frayser's Farm, Virginia, June 30, 1862.

deployed in some woods at the rear of the Whitlock house. The Federal artillery soon found their range, and shells began to drop among the North Carolinians. Longstreet ordered his division forward at around 5 o'clock in the afternoon, leaving Branch still without a guide. Hill soon sent word to Branch to also advance and offer protection to Longstreet's right flank. By this time, the Federal division commanded by Hooker extended across Branch's front and right flank.

Branch's attack on the Federal line was met by the Federals of Grover's brigade of Hooker's division. The Federal troops were ready, and had posted their artillery on high ground, in the rear of the Federal infantry. As the Thirty-seventh advanced, they were met by rifle and grape shot from the Federal line, forcing them to seek shelter in a ravine. Soon the Tar Heels started their advance once more across an open field toward the Federal battery that was plaguing them and that had driven back some of Kemper's brigade. Colonel Lee was encouraging his men with "On, my brave boys!" when he was killed by a blast from a cannon. The Thirty-seventh advanced and drove the gunners from their guns. A Federal soldier who was in front of the Thirty-seventh would write: "The Johnnies climbed the hill with a rush, causing the line to waver for a moment, then it closed up and gave them a murderous fire." Newton Greer of Company B was shot in the face, John L. Austin of Company D in the right leg. John M. Beard and John Wiley of Company C were killed. In all, five were killed, twenty wounded, and three were captured. Soon the Thirty-seventh was ordered to move forward again and take a second battery, which they did, finally stopping that night around 10 P.M. Captain Morris wrote of a great number of Federal prisoners captured, and "as we marched them out they seemed to bee almost as many as we had men. I cannot tell you the number."[19]

When told of Colonel Lee's death, "his men wept as if they had lost a father." A private in the Thirty-seventh said Lee was "as gallant an officer as ever trod the battle field of Virginia; he was as brave as a lion and gentle as a lamb and thought it not inconsistent with his profession as a soldier, to acknowledge Jesus Christ as the Captain of his Salvation." Captain Morris told his wife in a letter home that Lee was "Brave & so Much Loved…." Lieutenant Colonel Barber would write of Lee in his official report: "He was a brave, experienced officer, and a pure man. His loss will be severely felt." General Branch would also write highly of Lee: "A thoroughly educated soldier and an exemplary gentleman, whose life had been devoted to the profession of arms, the service in him lost one of its most promising soldiers." Colonel Lee's body was returned to North Carolina, where the newspapers continued to sing his praise. The *North Carolina Standard* declared "that he met his fate like a hero." The *Western Democrat*'s headline read: "A Brave Man Fallen." The *North Carolina Whig* would sing the highest praise with: "Thus has died upon the altar of our country one of nature's noblemen, none who knew him but to love him, a gentleman, a scholar and a true soldier fallen. May his memory ever remain fresh in our hearts, his monument a nations gratitude. Peace to his ashes."[20] Colonel Lee's remains were returned to Charlotte, where he was laid to rest in the Elmwood Cemetery. In honor to his memory, all of the stores in Charlotte were closed on the day of his funeral.

Gravestone of Colonel Charles Cochrane Lee, Elmwood Cemetery, Charlotte, North Carolina.

The Thirty-seventh would spend another night on the battlefield where they had fought so hard and bled so profusely, without gaining a clear victory, near the intersection of the Darbytown and Long Bridge roads. The Federals still held various locations along their front, but withdrew during the night to a new defensive position: Malvern Hill. The Thirty-seventh remained in camp until being relieved by General Magruder's division. They were called upon to be in the reserve of the fighting while the battle raged over Malvern Hill, marching at the double quick to the Confederate left. But the regiment would only suffer a few casualties by long range artillery fire: George M. Rushing, of Company D, was killed, and John H. Patterson and Duncan C. Shaw of Company I were wounded. Patterson lost his fore and middle fingers of his left hand, while Shaw was wounded in the right hand. The brigade returned to its camp of the previous night at dusk. The next day, July 2, brought more showers. The Thirty-seventh would spend the following week on picket duty around Malvern Hill.

General Lee's first offensive campaign had failed to achieve its main objective, the destruction of General McClellan's Army, but the Confederate Army under Lee had achieved some major successes. The enemy had been driven twenty-five miles to the south and east, away from the doorsteps and spires of Richmond. The Federal army had been forced to go on the defensive, and the South had received a major morale boost with its costly victories.

The men of the Thirty-seventh ended their first month and a half of service in the Army of Northern Virginia with a tremendous number of men killed, wounded and captured. Since its transfer to Virginia, the regiment had lost 42 killed, 140 wounded (of which another 33 would die), and 169 captured. Battlefield medical treatment was still rudimentary at this time, but was improving. Prior to the war, a person wanting to become a doctor either attended a medical university (of which there were few in the United States); apprenticed to a practicing physician for about

$100 a year, or attended a proprietary school that offered lectures on medical treatment. Degrees from the latter were not difficult to obtain. But even with degrees and education, the common physician's experience was relegated to "occasional cases of trauma, lancing boils and pulling teeth."[21] Surgery was considered by most to be anything but practical.

According to directives issued after the battle of Williamsburg, each brigade was authorized to have its own hospital provisions, "consisting of ambulance wagons, transportation wagons and carts, tents, stretchers, bedding, bandages, lints, medicines, [and] instruments...." Each brigade had a senior surgeon, who oversaw the regimental surgeons. Each of the regiments ordinarily had one surgeon and one assistant surgeon. Usually, between 20 and 30 men per regiment were authorized to serve as stretcher or litter bearers, under the direction of the assistant surgeon. Sometimes this detail was assisted by the regimental band, trading their instruments for stretchers. These men, on occasion armed with a pistol but usually unarmed, and sometimes wearing some sort of marking, were responsible for removing men too seriously wounded to walk from the field. During a battle, such as the one at Gaines's Mill, Branch's brigade hospital was set up in the rear, near the action, in a secure place. Men, when wounded or sick, would make their way to this field hospital for treatment or transfer. Those whose wounds were serious enough to prevent their walking were borne off the field on stretchers. Amputations were performed "with the least possible delay"[22] at these brigade or division field hospitals. The projectiles used by the rifled muskets of the Federal armies were conical in shape and made of soft lead. The muskets produced a low velocity when fired, causing the minié balls to flatten upon impact, often producing wounds that were large and ragged. Amputations were often the only "cure" for a soldier wounded in the arm or leg, especially if the bone had been destroyed. While the loss of a limb might be devastating to a soldier, without amputation, gangrene or other infection would almost inevitably set in and take his life, making amputation a harsh treatment but definitely the lesser of two evils. The limbs were usually removed without the use of any anesthesia, as ether, the most widely used chemical to produce unconsciousness, was highly volatile and therefore a hazard near combat situations. Supply difficulties also created a severe shortage of necessary drugs, such as painkillers. Frequently the surgeons, for whom germs were a far-fetched theory, would go from patient to patient without cleaning their instruments or the operating table between surgeries. Thus, even amputation was not a lifesaver for many men, but a prolonging of death that came later but with no less finality. These field hospitals often produced ghastly scenes, with piles of amputated arms and legs, hordes of flies, and the continual groans of the wounded, some beyond any hope. As soon as the wounded men were able, they were loaded into wagons or ambulances, of which there were never enough on hand, and transferred to hospitals that had been established in Richmond and Petersburg. While the ride might transport them to better conditions, the ambulances and wagons, overloaded, uncomfortable, and frequently traveling on poor roads, would have been misery for the wounded men, many of whom died long before reaching a hospital.

Wounded soldiers were often transported by rail when the theater of conflict was too far distant from a permanent hospital to allow a journey by ambulance.

Private Noah Collins left a vivid description of the travels of a sick or wounded soldier after the battle of Hanover Court House:

> When the battle had progressed till they began to bring the wounded back and lay them in the Church House yard.... [Soon we were] sent back to Ashland ... at which place we arrived just before dark that evening, and being entertained in a citizen's dwelling that night, we fared tollerably well. When next morning, being the 28th [May], we resumed our journey again, by rail, to Richmond.... When we arrived in Richmond on the morning of the 28th ... we were cordially received and kindly entertained by the ladies of Richmond.... On the night of the 28th we were conducted to a very large house on Broad Street, which was set apart for a hospital, where we remained that night and received another supper.... The next day ... we were removed from that house and conducted to a large house on Third Street.... [The] next day being the 30th, we were removed from that house. That wounded might be put in it, in consequence of the Battle of Seven pines having commenced ... from which the wounded were fastly filling up the city; and conducted to the Saint Charles Hotel.... Early on the morning of the 1st day of June 1862, we received orders to go to Richmond and Petersburg depot, from which by rail, we went to the North Carolina Hospital at Petersburg....[23]

In April 1862 there were 20 Confederate and state hospitals in Richmond. The most famous of these hospitals was Chimborazo, with the capacity to treat over eight thousand patients. Of almost equal size was Winder, with a capacity for 5,000 patients. North Carolina also maintained six hospitals in Richmond and two in Petersburg. These hospitals usually had their own soup kitchens, bakeries, icehouses, laundries, and bathhouses. The North Carolina hospital in Petersburg was located on Perry Street, "within a few yards of the Southern Rail Road...." The building was three stories tall, with each floor being divided up into wards, with functioning windows for ventilation, gas lighting, and hot and cold water. The hospital had one Surgeon-in-Chief, two or three Assistant Surgeons, an Apothecary, a Secretary and Clerk, a Steward and Treasurer, one Matron and two or three assistants, and a number of nurses, servants, cooks, and washers. Many times, local ladies would donate their time to the hospitals, caring for soldiers and baking food in their homes. Besides the General Hospitals in Richmond, the state of North Carolina established hospitals across the state.[24] Soldiers who were sick, but could survive relocation, were transported to their home state for convalescent care.

Many of the slightly wounded were not included on the official casualty reports of the regiments; nor were the men who simply fell out of ranks due to sheer exhaustion recorded. After the end of the battles that came to be called the Seven Days, Captain Morris recorded in a letter to his wife that he was in command of the regiment as senior officer present, and that the regiment only contained 100 men. Doctor Alexander would write on July 6 that Company C could only muster 15 men, that Company H could only muster two men, and that the regiment as a whole was only fielding 170 men.[25] At the end of the battles of Seven Days, the aggregate present of the Thirty-seventh was 593 men. If Morris and Alexander's figures are correct, then there were approximately 493 men who were either sick or slightly wounded and would later return to the ranks. One interesting case of a wounded solider was recorded by Alexander, who had been promoted from the ranks to assistant surgeon of the Thirty-seventh:

> One peculiar case of gun shot wound I will mention: A soldier by the name of Rankin, Company H ... [was] shot in the base of the skull of the medulla oblongata, [which] did not prevent him from walking about, was examined by a half dozen surgeons who were unable to trace or locate the bullet, when Dr. Campbell, of the Seventh Regiment called me as the youngest surgeon to try my hand. In a jest I placed my hand upon his forehead and told him to open his mouth; at once I saw a swelling in the roof of his mouth: it was hard and smooth. I made a slit with a scalpel, and showed a minnie ball to the astonished surgeons. How the ball got there without killing him has always been a mystery.

The surgeons of the regiment would have plenty of opportunities to ponder this and the many other horrors of war: the Thirty-seventh would be in the thick of the fight for the next three years.[26]

6

"I Doo not knew where Jackson will stop"
July–September 1862

The outset of July 1862 would find the Thirty-seventh well beneath regimental half-strength. Many men had been killed, wounded, and permanently disabled, or were in Northern prisons. Disease also ran rampant. The months of July and August 1862 witnessed more disease-related deaths in the Thirty-seventh than at any other point during the war. At least 76 members of the regiment succumbed to a host of sicknesses during this period of time, but one disease in general, *febris typhoides*, or typhoid fever, produced the most casualties. Typhoid fever was mainly caused by impure drinking water, water that was oftentimes located too near the regimental sinks (latrines). Symptoms of typhoid fever include high fever and chills, headaches, joint pain, and constipation followed then by diarrhea, which leads to dehydration and death. In the 19th century, typhoid was treated by isolating the victims in well-ventilated rooms or tents, administering saline purgatives followed by stimulants, and cold cloths and sponge baths.[1]

The regiment would also lose one of its first prisoners of war to disease. Most of the men who had been captured during the battle of Hanover Court House, Virginia, on May 27, 1862, had been sent to either the Fort Columbus Prison in New York Harbor, or Fort Delaware, on Pea Patch Island in the Delaware River. Private David Eldridge of Company A was one of the first to succumb: he died on July 9, 1862, in the hospital at Fort Columbus, of "pneumonia & diarrhoea following measles." Diarrhea was a symptom of many other diseases, rather than a disease itself. The majority of the cases of diarrhea not related to other diseases were caused by poor food preparation. The food itself was sometimes spoiled, or inadequate sanitation was used in washing and cooking. There were many different treatments for diarrhea, and most doctors realized that a proper diet and rest were more important than medication to treat "a disorder of the bowels." A military handbook of the time called for a diet of "Panada [sic]," toast-water, beef-tea, chicken, beef or veal broth, water gruel, rice-gruel, milk porridge, wine whey, or calves' feet broth. Soon after the death of Eldridge, passed Private William Cox, Sr., who died on August 5, 1862, after being exchanged from a Northern prison. His son, Private William Cox, Jr., had died in Richmond of disease almost a month before, on July 16, 1862. Both the senior and junior Cox were from Ashe County and members of Company A.[2]

On July 7 the Thirty-seventh moved out from the vicinity of Malvern Hill and went into camp on the Charles City Court House Turnpike, 13 miles east of Richmond. General Lee recognized that he had lost initiative after the battle at Malvern Hill and was forced to withdraw closer to Richmond to be able to thwart any new offensives by General McClellan up the James River, or from its southern banks. Lee established a 30-mile semi-circle around the capital, protecting all of the important approaches. "We expect to have a battle here every day," wrote Pvt. John V. Miller (Company A) to his brother back in Ashe County. "[We've] got brest works and forts all around Richmond...." Captain Morris would write home on the twenty-first of July: "Since we have our tent & Nothing to Doo but to Cook & Eat I am Nearly Cleare of My Caughf & feel better than I have since I came to Virginia[.]" Barzilla C. Green (Company B) also wrote home to his uncle back in Watauga County: "the health of the regiment is not so very good at this time there is a great deal of sickness among the soldiers[.]" The low, swampy area on the east side of Richmond was not good for the health of the Tar Heels. Doctor Alexander would concur with Private Green, adding that he had seen "100 men at one time with their shirts off looking for lice...."[3]

On July 27 the regiments in A. P. Hill's division received marching orders: their destination, "Stonewall" Jackson's command. A. P. Hill and James Longstreet had been involved in a disagreement that had almost led to a duel. General Lee had intervened, and Hill's division was soon transferred from their temporary position under Longstreet to Jackson's command. Jackson's troops had moved to the area around Gordonsville on July 13, blocking General John Pope's 47,000-man Federal Army, called the Army of Virginia, that threatened Richmond from the north, Lee's flank and rear, and the important supply lines from the valley.

By mid-afternoon on July 27, the Thirty-seventh's troops were on the cars of the Virginia Central Railroad, headed to Jackson's relief and their new command for the next year. With the transfer of A. P. Hill's division and a brigade of Louisianans to Jackson's command, Jackson's orders changed. He was no longer to watch the Federals under Pope; he was now ordered to go on the offensive against Pope. The Thirty-seventh arrived and went into camp on the same day, five miles southeast of Gordonsville. The Thirty-seventh's time around camp was spent in regimental and brigade level drill. Their ranks once more began to fill out with the return of men formerly wounded or forced to drop out of the ranks because of fatigue or sickness.

Private Luther D. Penley, Company B, who died at Brook Church, Virginia, July 20, 1862 (courtesy of the North Carolina Division of Archives and History).

"[We] are getting ready for another terrible conflict," Doctor Alexander wrote on August 6 from a camp near Gordonsville. He, like many others in the regiment, thought that they would soon "be camped on Yankee soil." Alexander would go on with his thoughts on what he felt would win the war:

> I am inclined to think now that peace will not be made untill we win it from them in their own country. They will first have to feel our power at home before they will acknowledge our independence; and the sooner we can march our armies into the north and beard the lion in his own den, the sooner will we be blessed with peace.[4]

Alexander would confirm his devotion for the Southern cause in a more solemn tone a few weeks later when he wrote to his wife about the death of her brother: "It is hard my dear Annie for us to sacrifice our Brothers, but without great sacrifices we *cannot* achieve our liberty. And Annie, we cannot lay down our lives in a more noble cause; life without liberty would be a burden to us."[5]

Marching orders came again on August 7. By 5:15 A.M. on August 8, the Thirty-seventh was on the road waiting to move out, Branch's brigade probably taking position as the second brigade in A. P. Hill's line. By 4:00 P.M., on a day when the temperature soared to 96 degrees, Hill's Division had moved about a mile. They went into camp for the evening. The commissaries were soon busy issuing rations, and the soldiers were busy cooking them during the night. "We were often without cooking utensils to prepare our rations," wrote Walter W. Lenoir, a Caldwell County resident, a former lieutenant in Company H, Fifty-eighth North Carolina Troops, and the newly appointed captain of Company A,

> And the men would make their flour into dough, on oil cloths, and bake it into cakes at the bivouac fires on pieces of staves, around sticks, etc. The beef and bacon they would roast on sticks, but generally preferred to eat the bacon raw. I learned to eat fat bacon raw, and to like it. The beef roasted on sticks and the hard and dry army crackers which I generally used for bread, were so delicious to my taste after the fierce appetite gained by hard marching that I never enjoyed eating so much.[6]

Captain Morris was soon busy writing to his wife. "I have onley 21 men for Duty with Me. The rest are sick & Broke Down ... they [yankees] are sayd to be throwing up Breast works. I Suppose they are rather afraid to be so far from there Gun boats without Breastworks."[7] Considering Captain Lenoir's comments on the soldiers' appetite for raw bacon, it is not surprising that so many of Captain Morris's men were out sick.

General Jackson, in an effort to relieve some of the pressure on Richmond, devised a plan to destroy a portion of the Federal army concentrating near Culpeper Court House, annihilating it before the Federals could bring up reinforcements. The problem with Jackson's plan was that Pope already had his army concentrated in the area.

At 1:00 A.M. on August 9, Federal cavalry probed into the Confederate lines. Branch formed his Tar Heels regiments, and soon the regiments would move out on a march that lasted twelve hours. Captain Lenoir wrote that the "weather was generally hot and dry.... Sometimes the dust was very oppressive.... The march [was] very trying and it was only by constant effort that I had prevented a number of the men from falling out of the ranks." The temperature that day would reach 98 degrees. Their route would take them over the Rapidan and the Robertson rivers. Several hours later, as Hill's brigades approached Cedar Run, they could clearly hear the sounds of the battle raging ahead. The Thirty-seventh (and the rest of Branch's brigade) was deployed to the left of the Culpeper Road in the woods. The Seventh started out on the left of the brigade, followed by the Eighteenth, Thirty-third, Twenty-eighth, and the Thirty-seventh on the right, next to the road. The men dropped their knapsacks before going into the fight. Captain Lenoir recorded his thoughts of going into battle for the first time:

> As we went into ... battle ... I had very serious and uncomfortable thought of death, being conscious that I was in its immediate presence and greatly exposed to it, and reflecting how unprepared I was to meet.... Plenty of other thoughts besides those of danger, such as indulging curiosity, a disposition to chat about the battle to officers standing or passing near, an occasional sense of ludicrous, etc. Although most men become very serious on the approach of a battle and during its progress, yet the absence of cowardly fear, and the coolness amounting in appearance almost to indifference with which they fight among the showering balls and dreadful sounds and sights to the battlefield, are on the whole one of the most marvelous things in human nature.... I think most men who are engaged in battle think very seriously of the danger they are in, and find the thought anything but comfortable.[8]

Soon the Tar Heels began to encounter retreating soldiers, almost panic-stricken, from the Twenty-seventh Virginia of the Stonewall Brigade, with Federals close upon them. Doctor Alexander later told his wife that the Virginia troops had "run like turkeys." Branch sought to inspire courage among his troops, and launched into a rousing speech. Stonewall Jackson himself soon came galloping along the line, and ordered Branch to "Push Forward, General, push forward." Branch's regiments went forward at the double-quick, shouting "Stonewall Jackson! Stonewall Jackson!" "The brigade, my company included," wrote Captain Lenoir, "pressed steadily on through

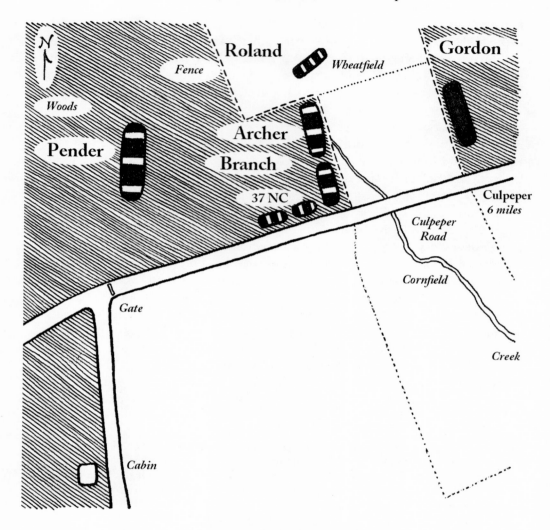

Battle of Cedar Mountain, August 9, 1862.

woods, chasing the yankees who turned and fled as soon as they appeared in view and raised the shout [with] which they are accustomed to go into battle." The yankees they encountered were of Crawford's brigade, Williams's division: the Fifth Connecticut, Tenth Maine, Twenty-eighth New York, and the Forty-sixth Pennsylvania. The Federals had become disorganized while in the woods. The Tar Heels advanced 300 to 400 yards, drove the yankees back to the edge of the field, and took a position behind a fence. The Seventh had now shifted positions to the right of the line, beyond the Thirty-seventh. "[T]he Union troops were within about sixty yards of our company," wrote Private Noah Collins, "which was immediately on the ... turnpike, at which place I gave the Union troops seven well directed rounds, taking rest on a lane fence every time." Captain Lenoir would echo his fellow soldier's words:

Lieutenant Octavius A. Wiggins, Company E (courtesy of the North Carolina Division of Archives and History).

"I was busy in my own position encouraging the men around me of my own company and others whom I knew and helping them to load."[9]

The Thirty-seventh was soon refused to the right, or at right angles to the rest of the brigade. They fronted the Culpeper Road, protecting Branch's flank. Not long after the Thirty-seventh took position, half of the First Pennsylvania Cavalry came charging down the road, but was repulsed by volleys from the brigade. Lieutenant Octavius A. Wiggins, of Company E, chronicled after the war: "The Thirty-seventh, with the whole brigade, reserved its fire until the column came in point blank range, when it poured a withering volley into it, sending it back in 'confusion worse confounded.' This cavalry charge was never forgot by the regiment; it always expressed the desire to receive a similar one." As soon as the Federal cavalry retreated, Branch, along with the brigades of Archer, Pender, and Ronald, launched an attack of his own across the wheatfield. The Thirty-seventh had moved about one hundred yards when Branch ordered a halt along a stream. The men soon began to cheer wildly as Jackson appeared and rode along the front of the brigade. Soon the regiments were moving again, this time at a right wheel, across the road and into the cornfield on the other side. "We were so worn out by the march and the fight," chronicled Captain Lenoir, "that though much exhausted myself I had to assist two of my men in the last charge through the corn field by letting them lean for a while on my shoulder. I was ill able to help them as I was very much exhausted myself."[10]

Private Noah Collins was unable to keep up with his company as they charged across the road and into the cornfield. After a short period of rest, he and a member of the Twenty-eighth started forward to find their respective commands:

> [We soon] saw a dark figure coming up between the rows of corn toward us, as we thought rather slyly, it being so very dark that we could not distinguish a Union soldier from a rebel ... we let it approach within about fifteen paces of us, closely watching of it, with regards to combative signs, with our rifles at a charge and ready, when the other cried out, who come there? Have you got arms? When I added ... if you have any side arms about you, you had better not raise a hand, for if you do you are a dead man that very instant; to which the wounded man replied, falling down at the same time; No my God, I have no arms, neither do I want any ... we left ... and went on in quest or search of our command....[11]

Darkness had now descended on the field of battle. The Thirty-seventh had helped push the remnants of the Federal forces out of the cornfield. Orders were given to halt and to go into bivouac for the night. The men simply fell out from where they had been standing and went to sleep immediately, their fatigue being great. Casualties had been light: three killed (Privates William Bryant of Company B, James F. Perry of Company D, and Corporal John A. Gibbs of Company C) and thirteen wounded. But this number does not include the vast numbers that had fallen out due to extreme heat or fatigue. A Northern journalist, who was permitted to enter the Confederate lines on August 11 with a burial party, left a vivid description of the battlefield of Cedar Mountain:

> The road and fields were strewn with knapsacks, haversacks, jackets, canteens, cartridge-boxes, shoes, bayonets, knives, buttons, belts, blankets, girths, and sabres.... Some of the treetops ... were scarred, split, and barked.... The ground looked, for limited areas, as if there had been a rain of kindling-wood; and there were furrows in the clay, like those made by some great mole which had ploughed into the bowels of the earth.[12]

August 10 greeted the Thirty-seventh with the rattle of musketry in their front, along the skirmish line. By noon, the regiment had pulled out of line and was helping with the removal of the wounded and the burying of the dead. The men would spend part of the day resting in the shade of the woods where they had fought the previous day. Late afternoon brought a small relief from the heat by the way of rain. The Thirty-seventh received orders to withdraw around midnight, which they did, re-crossing the Rapidan River and reaching their old campground around Gordonsville, named Camp Third. General Jackson had met and defeated a portion of the Federal army, but was unable to follow up on his victory. The Federal forces that he now confronted outnumbered him two to one.

Even as the battle raged on the slopes of Cedar Mountain, General Lee was putting things in motion to break the virtual strategic stalemate in which he was engaged. On August 9 Lee ordered Longstreet's command and the two divisions of Evans and D. R. Jones to Gordonsville. A few days later he would order Hood's brigade and Stuart's cavalry to the same place.

The Thirty-seventh would remain at Camp Third for six days, resting from their hard fight and preparing for the next contest, which would come soon enough. On August 16 they started on the campaign trail once more, stopping that evening on the Orange and Culpeper Court House Turnpike. Their goal had been "to cut off a portion of General Pope's Army, by getting between them and his main army; but they proved too smart for us, and slipped out by the right...."[13] General Pope had caught word of General Lee's plans after capturing a saddlebag full of orders from a member of J.E.B. Stuart's staff. The Thirty-seventh would remain at this camp for three days. During this time they would stand witness to the execution of three deserters, two of whom were in Taliaferro's brigade. This was a sad but necessary measure to maintain discipline.

On August 19 Brazilla C. Green (Company B) would take the time to pen a letter. This letter is a good example of the quick notes jotted to loved ones back home. In his letter to his uncle and aunt back in Watauga County, he wrote:

I this morning take the present time [to] write you a few lines which will inform you that I am in common health.... I have nothing much to write that will interest you more than BC and Brother silas has got back from the North and I was glad to see them come for we all thought Silas was killed[.] uncle is as fat as a grisley bear but silas look sorty slim and the rest of our co has got back but the capt and lieut Eggers and George Townsend[.] the capt and lieut was sent ... to Ohio and Townsend died after they got to New York[.] as in regard to war news they keep fighting a little almost every day.... I want you to have a fat goose killed and cooked for by ... dinner for we eat everything we can git hear duck sells at $1 a pound and chickens about the size of a robbin at 75 cents[.] I want you to write to me as soon as you have the chance[.] I must bring my short letter to a close....[14]

Around 2:00 A.M., on August 20, Jackson woke up his divisions, and the Thirty-seventh was on the road to the Somerville Ford by 4 A.M. Since daylight savings time had not yet been instituted, this was almost sunrise. By that evening they gained the Rapidan River and beyond, camping near the town of Stevensburg. By mid-morning the next day, Jackson's Corps had reached the Rappahannock River and Beverly's Ford. The Federal army was entrenched on the high ground on the northern bank of the river. The Thirty-seventh would spend the rest of the twenty-first and twenty-second strung out along the Rappahannock Valley. Around 6:00 P.M. on August 24, Longstreet's men began to replace Jackson's. General Lee had decided to move farther to the south, cross the Bull Run Mountains and emerge far in Pope's rear to cut the Federals' supply lines on the Orange and Alexandria Railroad. The Thirty-seventh went into camp not far from the river, and the men were issued three days' rations. They were instructed to leave behind their knapsacks and were issued sixty rounds of ammunition, twenty more than they normally carried.

The columns of Jackson's three divisions started the march around 4:00 A.M. As usual with Jackson's men, they did not know of their final destination. Jackson's plan was to march past the Union right flank, turn north, and get behind Pope's rear. Jackson set as his target Bristoe Station. That first day the men would cross the Rappahannock, with pants and shoes still on, at Hinson's Mill and finally stop around 11 P.M. near the small town of Salem, covering some 26 miles. The march would begin again at 4:00 A.M. the next morning. When the Thirty-seventh reached Salem, they quickly learned of Jackson's intent. Instead of turning to the left towards the Shenandoah Valley, Maryland, or points further north, they turned to the right, Pope's rear. That evening they would stop near Gainesville after covering fifty-four miles in thirty-six hours. Ewell's division was left at Bristoe Station, and the other two divisions under Jackson continued on toward Manassas Junction. On August 27, shortly after sunrise, Branch's brigade marched into the Federal storehouses of Manassas. After being held in reserve as Hill's division put to flight Taylor's New Jersey Brigade, the Tar Heels returned to the Federal depot. Jackson issued orders that the men could have as much food as they could carry. A Virginian in Hill's division spoke well for all of the Confederates around Manassas when he wrote:

It was more than funny to see the ragged, rough, dirty fellows, who had been living on roasted corn and green apples for days, now drinking Rhine wine, eating lobster

Private Emberry Walters, Company D, wounded in the head August 24, 1862 (courtesy of Carol Bullins).

salad, potted tongue, cream biscuit, pound cake, canned fruits, and the like; and filling his pockets and haversacks with ground coffee, tooth-brushes, condensed milk, [and] silk handkerchiefs.[15]

Assistant Surgeon John B. Alexander would also leave a description after the war of what he called the "wonderful capture" on the 27th: "The depot was an immense building, filled with unlimited supplies of flour, crackers, bacon, mollasses, sugar, coffee, whiskey, clothing, harness for wagons and artillery, fixed ammunition for small arms and for cannon. We tarried here all day, got out whatever we needed that we could carry of rations; swapped our old harness for new, replenished our cartridge boxes and filled our caissons with shells and shrapnel...."[16]

Soon the depot was in flames. "This was a great sight," continued Alexander, " the grease run probably twenty yards blazing on the ground. The thousands of shell exploding sounded like a battle in earnest."[17] About 1 A.M., Branch moved his brigade out, following the rest of Hill's division, across the Bull Run at Blackburn's Ford toward Centerville. The Thirty-seventh

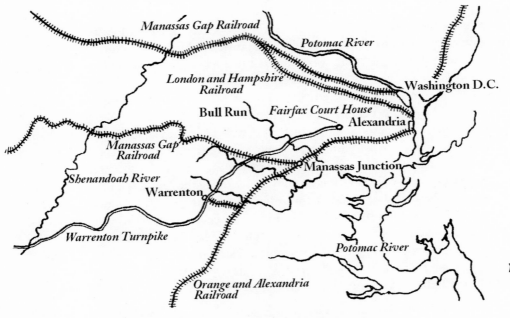

Manassas and vicinity, August through September 1862.

would halt around daybreak, with orders to cook rations and rest. Near midday they resumed their march back to Jackson's main force, near Grovetown.

Thursday, August 28, would dawn cloudy and warm, and find the Thirty-seventh in some woods alongside the road to Sudley Springs. They were now near the field of the first battle of Manassas and would soon participate in the second battle along the Bull Run. From here they would listen to the clatter of musketry and the roar of the cannons. Near dusk, Archer's and Branch's brigades were moved into a supporting position behind Ewell's and Taliaferro's divisions, but neither would see any action and were only exposed to sporadic artillery fire. After the engagement at Grovetown petered out, Jackson withdrew all three divisions back to "a long flat-topped ridge a mile north of the Warrenton-Centerville Road."[18] An uncompleted railroad that ran 500 yards below the ridge was used as breastworks. Hill placed, from right to left, the brigades of Gregg, Thomas, and Field. Behind them was his second line of brigades: Archer, Pender, and Branch. Orders were given to fight rigorously on the defensive.

The night had been a long and restless one. Branch was soon shifted to the far left of the Confederate line, now in support of Gregg. Soon Gregg was heavily engaged with the Federals of the First Brigade, Third Division, under Brig. Gen. A. Schimmelfenning. General Branch ordered the Thirty-seventh to bolster Gregg's line. The regiment rushed forward, across the Grovetown-Sudley Road, but soon found its own right flank exposed to enemy fire. "In a few minutes two thirds of my company had been struck," Captain Lenoir would write. "It required my utmost efforts to keep others from giving way. I more than once seized men by the shoulders who began to give back, and then forced them back into the ranks." In Lenoir's Company A, James M. Baker was wounded in both thighs, Abraham Baker in the groin, George H. Bryant in the shoulder, Isaac Ham in the leg, and Joel Huffman in the left thigh. William J. Davis, Elijah Owens, and Zachariah Owens were also wounded. William H. Weaver was killed. Lenoir would write of Weaver's death:

> ...the ball had passed through the head of William Weaver, a brave soldier ... who fell dead at my feet and seemed to look me in the face with an expression that I cannot forget, a gentle smile on his lips and a look from the eyes that seemed to ask for aid. The blood gushing from his forehead and from the back of his head gave too plain evidence that the look was unconscious.[19]

Captain Lenoir would return to the site of Weaver's death and dig the piece of lead that had killed him out of a tree.

The fire was so great that individual companies of the Thirty-seventh soon started to give way. General Branch, upon seeing that the Thirty-seventh needed support, rode back and called upon the Seventh and the Eighteenth to support the Thirty-seventh. The regiment retired about fifty yards, re-formed near the lower slopes of the Stony Ridge, and went after the yankees again. After being reinforced, the three regiments, along with fresh men from Early's brigade, moved forward and "swept the enemy back in almost the twinkling of an eye, regaining the ground lost

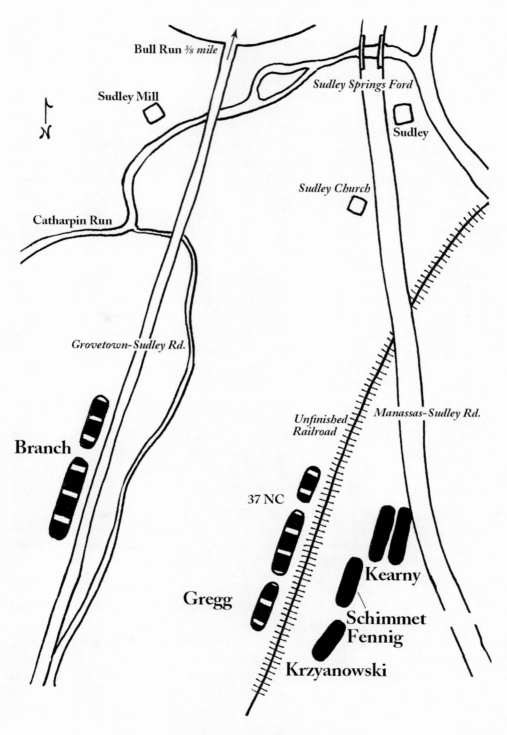

Battle of Manassas, Virginia, August 29, 1862.

by General Gregg and re-establishing our line at that point." The Federal troops re-formed and came after the Tar Heels once more. A Thirty-seventh company officer wrote: "we were soon assailed by them again quite fiercely, and afterwards a second time in the same position. There was no more falling back by my men who continued to fight with coolness...." Another officer would chronicle after the war: "several well directed volleys hurled them back." General Branch could be seen moving up and down his battle lines, encouraging the men and lending help where help was needed.[20]

The action here had been extremely fierce. Captain Lenoir would write: "At the railroad cut at the spot where my company fought I counted where 20 balls struck a white oak not much larger than a man's body, and nearly all within six feet of the ground. Not a bush had been missed. Most of the trees had been struck many times." The casualties continued to mount. Robert M. McGinnas of Company H was struck in the abdomen and arm. Company I's Sergeant Adam F. Yadle was hit in the thigh, mouth, and testicles. George W. Cable of Watauga County's Company E had his hearing destroyed by a shell. In all, the Thirty-seventh would have 11 killed and 62 wounded in that afternoon's fight (eight of those wounded would later die of their wounds). They had suffered more killed and wounded than any other regiment in Branch's brigade. Most of the brigade's wounded probably filtered back to a hospital near the Sudley Church. "We had a hard day's work at our field hospital," wrote Assistant Surgeon Alexander. "We had nothing to eat for two days, except some hard apples, which we baked."[21]

Ammunition was now almost completely exhausted, with many of the men having none left at all. The entire brigade could only account for 24 rounds total. Luckily, the Federals were also spent. Branch's brigade was withdrawn that night from the front lines and ordered to replenish the cartridge boxes from the divisional ammunition trains. General Branch, on learning that some of the Federals who had assailed his line during the day had been a part of Burnside's IX Corps, remarked: "Burnside whipped us at New Bern but we have whipped him this evening."[22]

The next day,

Private George Washington Cable, Company E, and Elizabeth Cook Cable (courtesy of North Carolina Division of Archives and History).

Saturday, August 30, would begin arid and hot, and the Thirty-seventh was held in reserve for most of the day. Around 6 P.M. they were called upon to assail the disorganized Federal troops. Longstreet had arrived during the evening before, attacked the exposed Federal flank, and had thrown the yankees into a half retreat, half rout. Hill saw an opportunity and ordered his entire Light Division to advance. Branch's brigade initiated the movement. They advanced through woods until about 10:00 P.M., capturing Federal soldiers and a large Federal hospital filled with wounded, but meeting little resistance. Darkness that evening brought rain. General Hill would write in his official report: "The battle being thus gloriously won, my men slept among the dead and the dying enemy." General Lee would pen his praise to Richmond that evening:

> This army achieved today on the plains of Manassas a signal victory over the combined forces of Genls McClellan and Pope. On the 28th and 29th each wing under Genls Longstreet and Jackson repulsed with valour attacks made on them separately. We mourn the loss of our gallant dead in every conflict yet our gratitude to Almighty God for His mercies rises higher and Higher each day, to Him and the valour of our troops a nation's gratitude is due.[23]

The armies awoke to a steady shower the next morning, a shower that translated into difficult marches for the Thirty-seventh. Another flanking march was in store for the day. Jackson was going to try to get between the retreating army of Pope and the Federal capital of Washington. The maneuver started around noon, wandered through a "single track country road ... through a post-oak forest over quicksand subsoil"[24] and ended 10 miles later near the Pleasant Valley Baptist Church on the Little River Turnpike. The advance resumed at daybreak on September 1, on what looked to be the beginning of a clear and warm day. After covering three miles in half a day, Hill ran into the Federals at Ox Hill, near Fairfax Courthouse. The time was 2:30 P.M. About 4:30 the brigades of Branch and Field were ordered into the fray. General Jackson, as he was probing the Union forces in front of his position, discovered Federal troops advancing on his right flank. The two Confederate brigades deployed their men, threw out skirmishers, and advanced into some thick woods south of the Little River Turnpike.

After moving into the woods, they crossed into a field bordered by a fence near the Reid farmhouse. They promptly encountered Stevens's division of Reno's corps, and were subjected to a testing Federal fire. A few moments after the battle began, the dark clouds that had been building overhead began to produce torrents of rain that badly fouled the muzzle-loading muskets and rifles of the men. The Federals attempted to flank the Confederates, but the movement was countered by the Eighteenth. The Federals then advanced directly across the field, but paid with heavy casualties. One officer of the Thirty-seventh said that this was "the hottest fire to which my company [had] been exposed." Another officer thought that the Federals were using explosive balls. Captain Morris wrote, "I was Struck Several times with spent Balls and Shells but not hurt." The Thirty-seventh was now running low on ammunition, and the little ammunition they had was damaged by the damp weather. Branch sent this message back to A. P. Hill, and Hill ordered Branch "to hold his position at the point of the bayonet." The command would hold their position until dark as the rain slowed to a drizzle and the temperature dropped. The Thirty-seventh went into the fight with fewer than 150 men. During the course of action, they suffered a loss of two killed and sixteen wounded (three of whom would die of their wounds), and one captured. Those killed were Sergeant William L. Sample of Company C and Private Alfred Rhyne of Company H. The captured man was Private William A. Walker of Company A (he was also wounded). Among the wounded was Captain Lenoir:

> In the twilight, toward the close of the battle, I had thrown myself on the ground siting with my body raised so as to rest on my elbow, and my legs stretched on the ground, across the fire, instead of towards the rear as they should have been, I had just been talking to Capt. Morris who was sitting by me in a similar attitude, and having turned my face from him to observe and speak to my men, when I felt an awful pain in my leg, and said, in my ordinary voice, Captain Morris, my leg is broken. A musket ball had passed through my right leg, a little nearer the foot than the knee, from side to side, about the middle of the leg....[25]

Captain Lenoir was soon wounded again, in the same leg; this time, the ball struck the shin bone and also took off his big toe. Captain Lenoir's gripping account accurately describes what soldiers wounded on the battlefield experienced:

> ...I determined to try to crawl to the rear in search of some of the infirmary corps to bear me off the field, as I was utterly disabled, and feared that an artery might have been severed which would require prompt surgical aid. I managed to drag myself about ten steps when I stopped from exhaustion, finding myself in an open place caused by a little road, and a little more elevated than the fence at which we had been fighting, where though probably more elevated than the fence to the fire.... While lying there I had sand thrown on my cheek twice by musket balls which struck the ground by my head ... I wondered afterwards at the degree of calmness and resignation to my fate which I felt in this very alarming situation. I feared the wounds I had already received would prove fatal, and that I would be struck again and killed. But I felt that I was in the hands of a good and merciful God and that he would do with me what was right.... It occurred to me that I ought to be thankful that I had lost a leg instead of an arm ... and from that I commenced thinking of the things of which I would be deprived by the loss of my leg. First I thought of my favorite sport of trout fishing, which I would have to give up. Then I thought of skating, swimming, and partridge hunting. My other favorite sports which it also occurred to me that I could never enjoy again.... It had rained hard during the night, and I was chilled and thoroughly wet when I was found a little after dark by one of my men. As none of the infirmary corps seemed to be near I was borne off by four men on my blanket stretched between two fence rails.... On that night, Sept 1st, I was carried about a quarter of a mile to a house were I was laid upon a narrow porch already so crowded with wounded men that there was only room for me at the entry, where my wounded leg was struck occasionally during the night to my great torture by the feet of persons passing in and out. On the next morning I was carried on stretchers about three quarters of a mile, and deposited on the ground in an old field where

some wounded men had been brought together, here I lay without receiving any surgical aid till about ten o'clock on the morning of the 3rd, when to my great relief I found several surgeons were in attendance and ready to proceed with the amputation of my leg. I was placed under the influence of chloroform, and my leg soon taken off by Dr. Shaeffner, surgeon of the 33rd NC, and the stump dressed. I waked up just as the dressing was complete without retaining the slightest consciousness of any part of the operation.[26]

Captain Lenoir was then loaded into "the bed of a rough and heavy army road wagon without springs," and started on the road toward Middleburg, Virginia. He would spend the night in the wagon, and part of the next day, with "every little jolt of the wagon causing a pang which felt as if my stump was thrust into liquid fire...." Lenoir was able on the second morning of his trip "to secure a Rockway with springs" to complete his journey. Most of the common soldiers were not that lucky. After reaching Middleburg, the captain secured the services of a local lady, who found him a room with the Reverend Richey. Captain Lenoir was soon found by his brother, who acquired a carriage and they started off toward home. Through the entire ordeal Captain Lenoir would never lose his faith:

Admist the cares and fatigues of the campaign I continued to read daily in the testament and to try to pray, and was making some effort, I own with shame that it was but a feeble one, to seek the favor of God. After being wounded and while I was suffering so much, the world seemed farther from me than it ever seemed before. I was reading the gospel of St. John at the time, and when I attempted to read out as I sometimes did to Tom Norrwood and Liet. Goodman who was in the same room, severely wounded in the neck and shoulder, I could not read many lines without tears and a trembling voice. The words seemed full of new meaning. Rude wit and coarse and vulgar ideas and conversation were not only without any relish but very distasteful.[27]

While Lenoir was still lying on the field, praying for assistance, the Thirty-seventh was pulled back under the cover of darkness. The Federal troops were gone by daylight. In a letter to his wife, General Branch described the condition of the men: "Fighting all day and marching night.... The little sleep we have had has been generally on the battle field surrounded by the dead and wounded[.] Some of the soundest sleep I have ever had has been on the naked ground without cover and with rain pouring down in torrents. The only rations we have had for a week are fresh beef without salt or bread...."[28] September 2 would dawn without a cloud in the sky. General Lee was resolved to strike Pope and finish his Federal army. The remaining men of the Thirty-seventh were up early, ready to finish the job. But the Federals had pulled out during the night and had taken a strong defensive position behind Difficult Creek. The day was spent in skirmishing, with some much deserved rest, considering the distance they had covered and the battles the Tar Heels had fought.

"I drop you a Line ... to Let you Know that I am Stout and Hearty," Captain Morris wrote on the morning of September 2. "I Can say to you that we have been in Several Engagements Since we left Gordonsville & have been Suckessful in Every fight...." He would conclude, "May God have Mercy on us all, Guide & protect us all through all Dangers."[29] The Thirty-seventh would move out September 3, heading toward Loundon County and Leesburg for some rest and refitting. The Confederate Army's position in Leesburg would threaten Maryland and the Union garrisons in the Shenandoah Valley. Orders were issued for the regiments under Jackson's command to move along the Ox Road, passing the Frying Pan Church and crossing the Alexandria, Loudoun, and Hampshire Railroad at Herndon Station. They were then ordered onto the Leesburg Pike near Dranesville, and on to Leesburg. The evening of the third they camped along the road on the north side of Dranesville. The next morning, under a bright sun but with a little frost, the Tar Heels would move out once again. Both General Lee and General Jackson issued orders against straggling or falling out of ranks. Lee's orders stated that men dropping out of ranks were to be rounded up and returned to their commands. Jackson's orders said that men leaving the ranks without excuse were to be shot. Nevertheless, there was straggling, due mostly to the exhausted state of the men. They had been on the move, constantly, for four months and had fought numerous battles and skirmishes.

Around noon, General Hill was placed under arrest by General Jackson. The causes of the incident are debatable, but the outcome was that General Branch was placed in command of the Light Division, and Colonel Lane of the Twenty-eighth was placed in command of Branch's brigade. Later that day the men passed through Leesburg, Virginia, and encamped that evening around 10:00 P.M., only a mile from Conrad's Ferry on the Potomac River. Jackson ordered the men to prepare two days' worth of rations. Word was sent back to Jackson that the men had nothing to prepare. General Lee would take time to issue a general order preparing his soldiers for their foray into Maryland. The main thrust of the General's order, read to all of the men as soon as possible, was to limit their transportation and wagons to "a mere sufficienct [for] cooking utensils and the absolute necessaries of a regiment." Friday, September 5, would be another cloudless and increasingly warm day. Orders came for the Thirty-seventh, along with the rest of the men from Jackson's corps, to cross into Maryland. The Tar Heels crossed the Potomac using White's Ford. Fording a river was a delicate task, usually requiring the men to take off their shoes, and sometimes their pants and drawers. But the cool water was probably a relief on the warm day. Orders came to General Branch, still in command of Hill's division, to be prepared to place the Light Division in a line of battle one mile east of the road to prevent the Federal artillery from slowing the progress of the supply trains.[30]

On September 6, one week after the battle at Manassas, the Light Division would march into Frederick, Maryland, the second largest city in Maryland, for a few days of rest, slightly better food (they were now able to roast their corn instead of eating it raw), and a chance to bathe. The long column of Confederate soldiers, consisting of four divisions, marched from Buckeystown to Monocacy Junction. The Light Division, along with Ewell's division, took up a position to the right of the junction to guard the road and the bridge. "This morning," Captain Morris would write on September 7, "finds Me well & hearty & in Fredrick City in Meriland. this is a fine

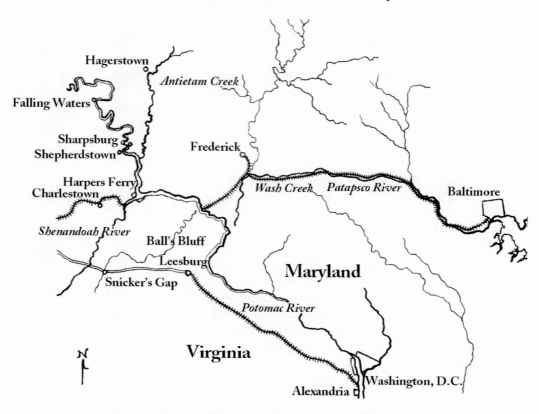

Western Virginia and Maryland, August and September 1862.

country. Pleanty of Everything…. We find More & better friends heare than in Va."
He would end this letter with, "I Doo not knew where Jackson will stop."[31] General
Lee, in an effort to continue his string of successes and to provide forage for his hun-
gry army, took the Confederate forces to Maryland, a slave state still within the
Union. He also desired to draw the beaten Federal Army out of its entrenchments
around Washington and to a battlefield of Lee's choosing, and to impress Maryland-
ers with his army's good behavior, hoping to draw more recruits for the Army of
Northern Virginia.

The period of rest would come to a close late on September 9. Orders came for
the men to cook three days' rations and to be ready to move at dawn. Their destination: the Federal garrison at Harpers Ferry, located along the Confederates' new
lines of communication and support. The Confederate army was to be split, with General Jackson taking a large force to eliminate the Federal threat, and Generals
Longstreet and D. H. Hill guarding against the main Federal army coming from the
entrenchments around Washington, D.C. The orders went on further to say that all
soldiers who were sick or unable to walk were ordered to Winchester. The Confederate soldiers would begin their march at dawn on Wednesday, September 10. Weather
conditions were so adverse that orders went out to commanders that the rate of march

should be limited to three miles per hour, with a ten minute rest every hour. Those who could not keep up were placed in wagons and ambulances. Later that afternoon, Hill was returned to the command of the Light Division, and Branch returned to the command of his brigade. The division would travel westward from Frederick on the National Turnpike, crossing the Catoctin mountain range at Hagan's Gap, through Middletown, before stopping just south of South Mountain near the junction of the Old Sharpsburg Road around three or four P.M.[32]

Reveille would once again come early for the members of the Thirty-seventh — on the eleventh of September. The Tar Heels moved toward the Federal garrison at Martinsburg, attempting to capture the stores located there. This day would not be bright and sunny as the days before had been. Gray skies that hung heavy with dampness greeted the soldiers with each step they took. A mile west of Boonsboro, the Thirty-seventh left the National Turnpike and turned left on a macadam road that led to Williamsport. A light rain greeted the men as they approached Light's Ford, directly across from Williamsport. They crossed the ford and continued to move down the road toward Martinsburg. As the rain increased and darkness fell, the exhausted men dropped to the ground for some much-needed sleep; many of them had covered an average of twenty-three miles that day.[33] Friday, September 12, was a pleasant, warm day. The rain of the night before had settled much of the dust that the Confederates had encountered during the previous days. By midmorning, the "Light Division" had covered the five miles between their encampment of the previous night and Martinsburg. In their haste to escape, the Federals had not destroyed all of the military stores located about the town, and the famished Confederates captured many badly needed supplies. After plundering the Federal munitions in town, Hill's division advanced three miles toward Harpers Ferry and set up camp on the banks of the Opequon Creek.

Saturday, September 13, dawned warm and sunny. The Thirty-seventh arrived west of the town around noon, and took up a position on School House Ridge, west of the main Union line on Bolivar Heights. On the night of the fourteenth, Hill ordered Branch and Gregg to move their brigades along the river and around the Federal left, which was weakly defended and without artillery support. Part of the Seventh was thrown out in front as skirmishers, where they dislodged some of the "enemy's sharpshooters from a high position overlooking the railroad."[34] From there they scaled the heights and worked through the ravines, sometimes having to pull themselves up by roots and bushes. They were in position by 3 A.M. The men of the Thirty-seventh spent the rest of the night sleeping on their arms, in readiness for a battle in the morning.

The battle on the morning of September 15 was short — one hour of artillery fire that began at 6:10, catching the Federals in a three-way crossfire and convincing them of the futility of trying to hold their position. At 7:15 the Federal fire slackened and the Confederates prepared to charge. Their advance was met by the white flags of the surrendering Federal troops. The Thirty-seventh suffered no casualties during the short fight. Captain Morris chronicled to the folks at home the events: "we went to harpers Ferry & captured Twelve Thousand yankeys and all of there arms & stores. they surrendered without Much fighting. We had a fine time at harpers fery. Got Plenty Shugar & Coffee, in fact all most any thing we could wish, clothing, etc." Since Hill's brigades had done most of the heavy work (including an assault by Pender's brigade), Jackson placed Hill's Light Division in charge of paroling prisoners and securing captured Federal munitions. Two other divisions that had been under Jackson's command (Walker and McClaws), and had been instrumental in the capture of the Federal garrison, left during the night to reinforce Lee at Sharpsburg. One captured Federal remarked: "we were most civily treated by the rebels, whom we found to be ... men like ourselves; only the rebels were not nearly as profane as our men — in fact, they used no profane language at all. They shamed us." The Thirty-seventh used this opportunity to re-clothe themselves. This was probably the first chance the men had to re-supply themselves since they had left North Carolina four months earlier (excluding the store capture at Manassas Junction). They traded their ragged and threadbare uniforms for Federal uniforms. After they had finished, the quartermaster could only report 305 pairs of shoes, ninety pairs of socks, and fourteen blankets among the tons of other secured equipment. The Light Division's new attire caused some confusion and concern when they arrived on the battlefield at Sharpsburg. The uniforms may even have offered tactical advantages, but most men probably were only concerned with owning clean, warm clothes. Captain Morris wrote a week later: "I have Clothes plenty to Doo Me all winter as we all Got what we wanted at Harpers Ferry."[35]

The Thirty-seventh spent all of September 16 in Harpers Ferry, paroling prisoners and securing captured stores. General Lee believed that the Federals might attempt to recapture the post, and kept A. P. Hill and his division there to prevent the retaking of the town.

At 6:30 on the morning of September 17, A. P. Hill received orders from Lee. Hill was to move out as soon as possible and reinforce Lee's army, then battle McClellan and the Army of the Potomac on the defensive heights of Antietam Creek. The Tar Heels were on the road by 7 that morning and soon took up a rapid gait through the hot, humid, dusty day. The sounds of the booming cannon could be heard all day long as they made their way through the countryside. Around two in the afternoon the men began fording the Potomac River at Boteler's Ford, south of Sharpsburg.

The forced march of 17 miles in the humid September air had taken its toll on the dust-covered and exhausted men of the Thirty-seventh. The regiment, under the command of Captain Morris, could only field 50 men. Around 4:00 P.M., the brigade deployed along the Harpers Ferry road, crossed over a rail fence, and moved along a small cornfield to a recently plowed field. In this field were the men of the Eighth Connecticut Volunteers, who had just charged over a clover-laden field and engaged Archer's brigade. Colonel Edward Harland of the Eighth would write on September

Opposite: Branch's brigade's approach, September 17, 1862.

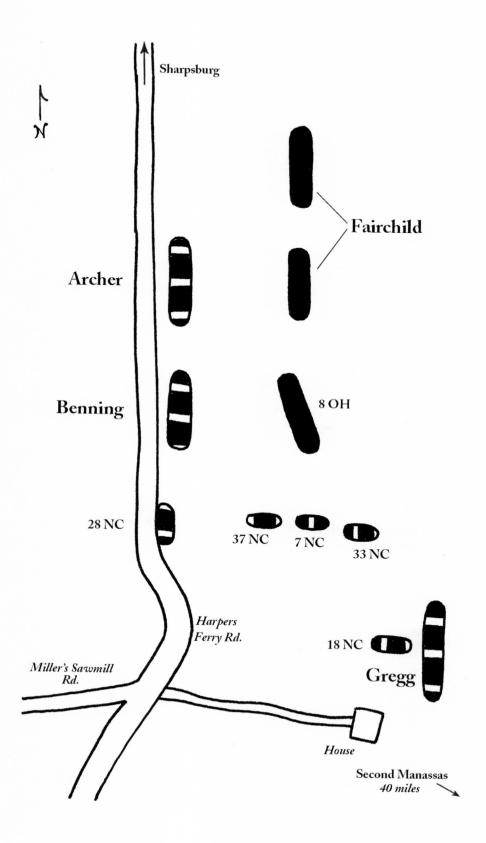

22: "I turned ... and saw some infantry belonging to the enemy advancing upon our left flank ... [knowing] that if that were not checked it would be impossible to hold this part of the field...." The fire being delivered by the brigades was sharp. "[W]e ... lost over 50 percent of our regiment," wrote Major J. Edward Ward of the Eighth Connecticut. "The fire from artillery and musketry was very severe, the regiment receiving fire in front and on both flanks."[36] The Eighth was forced to retire.

The Thirty-seventh now turned its attention upon the Twenty-third Ohio Volunteers. The Twenty-third, led by a future president, Rutherford B. Hayes, had taken a position behind a stone fence. As the other members of the Light Division assaulted the position from the front, Branch swung his brigade through the clover field and struck the Ohioians on their left flank. Colonel Hayes was struck and carried from the field. An officer in the Twenty-third wrote: "a heavy enfilading fire was open upon our whole line, when I received orders ... to change front perpendicularly to the rear...." Soon thereafter, the Ohioians were forced out of their position and across a deep ravine in their rear to the top of another hill. Captain Morris related these simple details to his wife: "We whipped them badly with little loss...." The setting of the sun (6:16 P.M.) caused a cease of the hostilities for the day, even though Burnside's IX Corps and Hill's Light Division were separated only by a ravine. Casualties had been light for the two hours that the Thirty-seventh had been in the field: only four men had been wounded.[37]

One of the greatest casualties that day would not occur in the ranks of the Thirty-seventh, but it would have a profound impact on the regiment. After helping to drive the Federal forces back toward the bridge spanning the Antietam Creek, General Gregg and General Archer rode over to confer with General Branch. After their attention had been called to a certain portion of the field, General Branch was in the act of raising his field glasses to his eyes when an enemy sharpshooter fired into the group, hitting Branch in the right cheek, killing him instantly. General Branch was lamented by many. Octavius Wiggins would write after the war that the Thirty-seventh "was called upon to morn the loss of its brigade commander ... who was then so rapidly rising in military prominence and was so dearly beloved by his troops." General Hill would speak highly of Branch when he wrote: "He was my senior brigadier, and one to whom I could have instructed the command of the Division with all confidence." Colonel James H. Lane of the Twenty-eighth, and senior colonel in the brigade, was called upon to take command of the brigade that evening.[38]

Branch's body was borne off the field, supposedly by Wiley, "his faithful Negro servant," and returned to Raleigh. The general's remains reached the capital city on Thursday afternoon, September 27, and were laid in state in the rotunda of the capital until Friday morning, when his body was borne to the City Cemetery. Bells were tolled at 9 A.M., stores closed, and a military escort, commanded by General J. G. Martin, proceeded to the cemetery. The procession was declared by some to be "the largest concourse of people ever seen in Raleigh since the visit of Mr. Clay to it in 1844." The funeral service was conducted by the Reverend Doctor Mason of the Episcopal Church and "concluded by the usual firing of three volleys by the military at the grave." Not long after the general's death, members of his brigade drew up a petition "for the purpose of erecting a monument ... in memory of our late commander.... And in doing so, we desire to express our high appreciation of one who has nobly earned it by his self sacrificing spirit as a patriot, his gallantry & faithfulness as an officer, and his bearing & character as a man...."[39]

After their fallen brigade commander's body was taken from the field, the Thirty-seventh would stay in their position along the stone wall all night and the next day, and would not be subjected to any more than a few rounds of artillery fire and occasional snipers, but would be subjected to a torrent of rain. On the morning of the nineteenth, around 1:00 A.M., the Thirty-seventh, which had formed part of the rear guard, was withdrawn from its lines. By mid-morning, they had recrossed the Potomac River to camp five miles south of Shepherdstown. General Lee's plan was to move his army west to Martinsburg, then east to Williamsport, crossing the army back over into Maryland on the twentieth or twenty-first, turning the flank and gaining the rear of McClellan's forces. The next morning brought the Thirty-seventh's return to battle. The regiment, even with the return of stragglers, could not number more than 150 men. McClellan had launched a portion of Porter's V Corps in pursuit of the Confederates and their rearguard. Jackson ordered Hill to counter this movement. Hill sent his entire division back and denied the Federals use of the Boteler's Ford.

Hill formed his brigades into two lines. The first line was composed of the brigades of Pender, Gregg, and Thomas. The second line was made up of Branch (Lane), Archer, and Brockenbrough (Field). They were positioned in a corn field, 1,000 yards from the Potomac River and across the Trough Road. The ground in front of them was open, spotted with wheat stacks. Upon Hill's command, the brigades launched forward toward the Federals "in the face of a withering artillery fire," according to one officer. Pender was soon outflanked, and Lane (in command of the brigade), rushed to his assistance. The two brigades pushed forward to the top of a hill and, in the words of Lane, "raised a yell, and poured a deadly fire into the enemy, who fled precipitately and in great confusion to the river." The Thirty-seventh then advanced at the double-quick to the river's edge and, "whipping them badly, [we] drove them across the River capturing 300 prisoners, killing a great many of them." Assistant Surgeon Alexander would add after the war: "As the enemy were driven back to the water's edge they threw down their arms and cried for quarters.... [Captain] Morris ordered his men to cease firing, repeating the order three times, but they refused to obey the order until all who had crossed the river were put hors-de-combat." The regiment suffered four more wounded: Corporal William W. Torrence, Company C; Captain Daniel L. Clary, who would die of his wounds, Company F; and Privates James G. Blanchard and William J. Hunsucker of Company I. Alexander would leave his embellished view of the battle some sixty years later when he wrote: "the 37th N.C. Regiment in command of the rear guard was ordered by Gen. A. P. Hill to about face and charge the enemy as they essayed to cross the river; one color-bearer after another was shot down, the flag staff cut away, [when] Morris seized the bunting and waving it aloft rushed into the thick of the fight; he was surprised by a slap on the shoulder by Gen. Hill, who asked what troops are these, he replied a part of Lane's Brigade, the quick rejoinder was 'brave men — brave men.'"[40]

The fighting at the river crossing would last until mid-morning, when the brigades slowly made their way back to the main army. The Thirty-seventh went into camp near Martinsburg for a few days, but Lane was soon ordered to have the brigade once again prepare three days' rations and to report to General Jackson for special duty. Soon the Thirty-seventh was on its way to the North Mountain depot, near Hedgesville. Their mission: destroy the tracks of the Baltimore and Ohio railroad, which they did with "thoroughness." Finally, the regiments returned to Camp Branch for some much needed recuperation. They spent this time occasionally doing picket duty at Snicker's Gap.

The Maryland Campaign had taken its toll on the Thirty-seventh. Arriving at Gordonsville in mid–August, they numbered approximately 450 men, under the command of Lieutenant Colonel Barber. Now, toward the end of September, they numbered less than 150, under the command of Captain Morris. In that span of a few weeks, they had lost 16 killed, 72 wounded (12 of whom would later die of those wounds), and five captured. Added to this were many men, like Private Collins, who were too sick to continue with the army. The regiment had suffered greatly, but had also gained great laurels. A. P. Hill issued this proclamation four days after the Shepherdstown battle:

> Soldiers of the Light Division: You have done well and I am pleased with you. You have fought in every battle from Mechanicsville to Shepherdstown, and no man can yet say that the Light Division was ever broken. You held the left at Manassas against overwhelming numbers and saved the army. You saved the day at Sharpsburg and Shepherdstown. You were selected to face a storm of round shot, shell, and grape such as I have never before seen. I am proud to say that your services are appreciated by our general, and that you have a reputation in this army which it should be the object of every officer and private to sustain.[41]

This was a reputation that the Thirty-seventh had helped to make, many times with the highest sacrifice a man could give: his life. Since that first fight at Mechanicsville, the division as a whole had suffered 9,000 killed and wounded.

7

"I believe I hav roat a bout awl I can think of that is worth riting"

September 1862–April 1863

On September 24 the Thirty-seventh received a much-needed recruitment boost: conscripts. Conscription was despised by people all over the South. It forced men between the ages of eighteen and thirty-five (and after September 1862, eighteen and forty-five) into the army. Many men took to hiding out in the mountains to avoid joining the army. Under the conscription system, each state was to establish two conscription camps or camps of instruction. A place and time was announced by the local recruiting officer, and local men between the appropriate ages were expected to present themselves. Sometimes a lottery was used, in which a soldier drew a colored slip of paper or a certain colored marble. The men thus selected or required to enlist were shipped to one of the camps of instruction. Upon arriving at the camp, the new "recruit" was examined by a surgeon, given a small pox vaccination, and drilled in the rudimentary evolutions of rifle tactics. From there, the new soldier was sent to the front, at first to a regiment of his choice, but later, as the war progressed, to whatever regiment needed men. Thomas Deboard was one of those new recruits. He was conscripted into the Thirty-seventh on August 15, 1862, the same day that his brother, Elijah DeBoard (Company A), died of disease.[1]

Brazilla C. Green (Company B) wrote home to his aunt and uncle: "I left the hospital at Richmond on Sunday last and came to this place [Gordonsville] and found the 37th reg. conscripts and some of the Watauga boys with them…." The conscripts and men returning to the regiment moved to Winchester shortly after Private Green wrote his letter. On September 23 Captain Morris wrote to his wife on the progress of the new members: "Our conscripts are at winchester some 20 Miles from us & will be heare tomorrow." On September 24 he wrote: "Our conscripts have Just landed." And on September 28: "Our conscripts are with us. some of them have Measels." The Thirty-seventh would receive a total of 346 new conscripts from around the state. Sadly, 75 of them (or twenty-two percent) would succumb to death by disease in a year's time. Captain Morris mentioned the new soldiers one more time in a letter dated October 4: "the conscripts are in fine Sperrits Generally but they have not Seen the Elephant yet. I Don't Know how they will Stand the Shells and Shot."[2]

Conscription increased the number of enlisted men, but the command of the Thirty-seventh was a shambles. No replacement for Colonel Lee had yet been elected or promoted. Lieutenant Colonel Barber had been absent, probably sick, since Second Manassas; Major Ashcraft had been afflicted "with attacks of fever ... chronic dysentery and a renal affection...."[3] Captain Morris had been in command for over a month. Company officers present were limited:

Field and Staff
Colonel . . . . vacant
Lieutenant Colonel . . William M. Barber — absent sick/wounded
Major . . . . John B. Ashcraft — absent sick

Company A
Captain . . . . Walter W. Lenoir — permanently disabled due to wound
First Lieutenant . . . . . . William H. Goodman — permanently disabled due to wound
Second Lieutenant . . . William A. Stuart — prisoner of war at Fort Columbus, New York
Third Lieutenant . . . . Thomas L. Norwood — temporarily disabled due to wound

Company B
Captain . . . . Jordan Cook — permanently disabled due to wound
First Lieutenant . . . . . Andrew J. Critcher — temporarily disabled due to wound
Second Lieutenant . . . Calvin Carlton — permanently disabled due to wound
Third Lieutenant . . . . Joseph B. Todd

Company C
Captain . . . . Owen N. Brown
First Lieutenant . . . . . Thomas J. Kerns
Second Lieutenant . . . Lawson A. Potts — temporarily disabled due to wounds
Second Lieutenant . . . George H. Beatty — killed in action at Second Manassas
Third Lieutenant . . . . none

Company D
Captain . . . . Jackson L. Bost — prisoner of war at Johnson's Island, Ohio
First Lieutenant . . . . . Vachel T. Cheers — resigned on August 28, 1862
First Lieutenant . . . . . Daniel L. Walters — promoted September 1862
Second Lieutenant . . . Henry C. Grady — absent on parole
Third Lieutenant . . . . vacant

Company E
Captain . . . . William Y. Farthing — prisoner of war at Johnson's Island, Ohio
First Lieutenant . . . . . . William F. Shull — permanently disabled due to wounds
Second Lieutenant . . . . vacant
Third Lieutenant . . . . . Harvey Bingham — temporarily disabled due to wounds
Third Lieutenant . . . . . . Johiel S. Eggers — prisoner of war at Johnson's Island, Ohio

Company F
Captain . . . . Daniel L. Clary — permanently disabled due to wounds
First Lieutenant . . . . . . William W. Beard — permanently disabled due to wounds
Second Lieutenant . . . . John B. Petty
Third Lieutenant . . . . . vacant

Company G
Captain . . . . Robert L. Steele — prisoner of war at Johnson's Island, Ohio
First Lieutenant . . . . . . Joel H. Brown — permanently disabled due to wounds
Second Lieutenant . . . . Daniel L. Hudson
Third Lieutenant . . . . . James B. Pool — temporarily disabled due to wounds

Company H
Captain . . . . William G. Morris — in command of regiment
First Lieutenant . . . . . . John H. Roberts — absent due to illness
Second Lieutenant . . . . vacant
Third Lieutenant . . . . . Henry C. Fite

Company I
Captain . . . . John I. Elms — Absent(?)
First Lieutenant . . . . . . William M. Stitt
Second Lieutenant . . . . William D. Elms
Third Lieutenant . . . . . John J. Wilson — permanently disabled due to wounds

Company K
Captain . . . . John Ross (probably absent)
First Lieutenant . . . . . . William Halsey — prisoner of war at Fort Warren, Boston, Massachusetts
Second Lieutenant . . . . Thomas J. Armstrong
Second Lieutenant . . . . William M. Fetter — temporarily disabled due to wounds
Third Lieutenant . . . . . vacant

At the end of September, the Thirty-seventh's command looked like this:

Commanding . . . . Captain William G. Morris
Company A . . . . First Sergeant Elijah A. Carter
Company B . . . . Third Lieutenant Joseph B. Todd
Company C . . . . Captain Owen N. Brown

Company D . . . . either Sergeant George W. Baucom or Sergeant Malachi Staton
Company E . . . . probably First Sergeant Lawson A. Farmer
Company F . . . . Second Lieutenant John B. Petty
Company G . . . . probably Sergeant Francis M. Cochrane
Company H . . . . Third Lieutenant Henry C. Fite
Company I . . . . First Lieutenant William M. Stitt
Company K . . . . Second Lieutenant Thomas J. Armstrong

Fortunately, October was a quiet time for the regiment, stationed near Bunker's Hill, not far from Winchester, Virginia. Besides the mundane routine of camp life, there was picket duty and the occasional foray into the countryside to destroy railroad tracks. On October 5 the army was placed on rations of "one and one forth pound ... of beef." This created some complaining among the men, but sometimes they did not even get the reduced rations. Private Andrew Jackson Teague of Alexander County, one of the new conscripts, would write home: "we had nothing but 1⅛ of a pound of flour and had nit thing [nothing] to bake it on nor salt to put in it but we bake it. Some bake on bords you may think it was a no acount but it eat mighty well for we very hungrey...." But the veterans of the unit had a different outlook on things. Captain Morris wrote: "we Guet very Good fruit here. this is a rich contry...." Another member of the regiment, Sergeant Tally of Company I, would paint his loved ones at home this picture from "Camp Uncertainty": "Albert is well and doing firstrate he is baking pies this morning, he had to pay 60 cents a Dozen for appels, and they are quire onry at that. Vegetables are very scearse here. the army has done consumed evrything that can be got to Eat."[4]

Camp life settled into a routine that the men had not experienced for the last four months. Sergeant Tally would continue his letter home: "we have been longer in camp [here] now than we have been since July." On October 8 James M. Gentry and Paul Hartzog were appointed special commissioners for the Thirty-seventh. They were given "the authority to enlist men for the 37th Regt. NCT...." The orders further stated that they were to "give public notice ... and to enlist and swear in all men who may wish to join said Regiment and afterward to bring them to the Regiment." Even with the recent arrival of conscripts, the ranks were painfully thin. Hartzog would only be partially successful in his quest. In a letter dated October 30, 1862, he was credited with bringing in six new recruits to the understrength regiment.[5]

Promotions came some time around the tenth of October. William M. Barber was promoted to colonel, John B. Ashcraft was promoted to lieutenant colonel, and William G. Morris was promoted to major. Doctor Alexander thought that Morris was "altogether worthy of the position. He has been in *every* fight (15) that the Reg. has been in and has acted the part of a hero and a Patriot. He deserves the highest praise for his gallantry." Morris himself wrote: "I am Major of the 37th Regt. I Could Not Well Deny. I will be compelled to have a horse."[6]

The Thirty-seventh's new colonel, who had been in command of the regiment

Above: Colonel William M. Barber (courtesy of Betsy Barber Hawkins). *Right:* Lieutenant Colonel John Benjamin Ashcraft, field and staff (courtesy of North Carolina Division of Archives and History).

since the death of Charles C. Lee at Frayser's Farm on June 30, was 28-year-old William Morgan Barber. Barber had been born in Rowan County, North Carolina. His ancestry traced back to St. Mary's County, Maryland, and one of his ancestors had been an early lieutenant governor of that colony. Barber was first educated under the tutelage of Peter S. Ney, sometimes thought to be Marshal Michael Ney, one of Napoleon's field marshals. Ney was reportedly very fond of Barber and called him his "Military Boy." After studying under Ney, Barber went to St. James College in Hagerstown, Maryland. Following his graduation from St. James, Barber studied law under Anderson Mitchell and was admitted to the North Carolina bar in 1859. Barber soon relocated to Wilkesboro and was reported to have been one of the best lawyers in Western North Carolina. He married Miss Ada Alexander of Mecklenburg County, and served on the vestry of St. Paul's Episcopal Church, along with future Confederate General James B. Gordon. When the war came, he was elected captain of the "Western Carolina Stars" and then elected Lieutenant Colonel when the Thirty-seventh was created in November 1861.

A good example of the process of promotion in the Confederate Army was the case of Henry C. Fite of Company H. After Morris was promoted from captain of Company H to major of the Thirty-seventh, the captain's position in that company was open. Colonel Barber, under the advice of Major Morris, nominated Third Lieutenant Fite for the position of captain of Company H. Barber wrote a letter to the

Secretary of War, asking that Fite be promoted. But before the letter reached the Secretary of War's office, it went through a series of "approvals." First the letter went to Colonel Lane, temporarily in command of Branch's brigade, for his endorsement. After Lane, the letter went to General A. P. Hill, in command of the Light Division, for his endorsement. From there the letter progressed to General Jackson, then to General Lee, who both signed it, and finally it was forwarded to the Secretary of War. The letter (and promotion) at any time could have been refused and returned to Colonel Barber, for a reason as simple as being worded incorrectly. Then the process would have had to be initiated again. Luckily, this did not happen. The Secretary of War's office returned the promotion on November 6, 1862, with the following note: "I am directed by the Sec. of War to say the promotion is approved and the same is hereby confirmed."[7]

In late October and early November, the officers of the brigade passed around a petition among themselves asking that Colonel Lane be promoted to brigadier general and given official command of Branch's brigade. On October 27 General Lee agreed with the officers' requests and forwarded the letter to the war department with the following note: "I consider it just and proper that the Colonel of Branch's brigade, who has been recommended for promotion, be assigned to the command."[8] On November 6 the promotion became official, and Branch's brigade became known as Lane's brigade.

James Henry Lane was born at Matthews Court House, Virginia, on July 28, 1833. Lane's great grandfather was one of the founders of Matthews County, and was active in the military and political affairs of colonial Virginia. Lane's grandfather, William Lane, also a military man, served as a private in the Revolutionary War, and as a sergeant in the War of 1812. James H. Lane's father, Walter G. Lane, was a justice of the peace, a colonel of the militia, and served one term in the Virginia Legislature. Lane was first educated in a small, one-room schoolhouse in his local community. From there he was privately tutored until his entrance to the Virginia Military Institute in Lexington, Virginia, the "West Point of the South." One of his professors at VMI was now his corps commander, Thomas Jonathan Jackson. At the end of his sophomore year, Lane was ranked fourth out of twenty-one students. In his last year he ranked second. Lane graduated on June 4, 1854, and after graduation he became a private school teacher on the plantation of Robert Douthat, near Charles City Court House, Virginia. In 1856 Lane entered the University of Virginia and pursued scientific courses. In 1857 he was an assistant professor of mathematics at his alma mater, the Virginia Military Institute; and in 1858 he became the principal of the Upperville Academy, a boy's school in Upperville, Virginia. After several other brief teaching jobs, and work at a factory owned by his brother in Richmond, Lane decided that his true calling in life was to be a teacher. In 1859 he was named Chair of the Departments of Mathematics and Military Tactics at the State Seminary in Tallahassee, Florida. From there, in 1860 he would become Professor of Natural Philosophy and Instructor in Military Tactics at the North Carolina Military Institute in Charlotte, North Carolina. Lane received this appointment based on a recommendation from Thomas Jackson to his brother-in-law, Daniel Harvey Hill, who was superintendent of the Institute.

Soon Lane was in Raleigh, as drill master and adjutant of the camp of instruction there. On May 11 he was elected major of the First North Carolina Volunteers, a regiment in which D. H. Hill served as colonel, and Charles C. Lee, the first colonel of the Thirty-seventh, served as lieutenant colonel. Lane moved with the regiment to Virginia, where he was involved in the battle of Bethel Church, the first important land victory for the Confederate forces. On September 2 he was promoted to lieutenant colonel of the First North Carolina Volunteers. A Richmond newspaper published this about Lane regarding his promotion:

Brigadier General James H. Lane (courtesy of the Library of Congress).

> He is deservedly the most popular man, perhaps, in the regiment, and is every way worthy the honor conferred by his promotion. He possesses the necessary qualifications to make an officer the idol of his men, viz.: theory and practice of military science, firmness in discipline, with the affable manners and sociality of a gentleman.[9]

On September 21, 1861, Lane was unanimously elected colonel of the Twenty-eighth North Carolina Troops. When he departed the First North Carolina, the men presented him with a sword, bridle and saddle, and two pieces of silver plate. The men of his new command would include in their letter to Lane: "It would afford us great pleasure and satisfaction to have for our leader an officer so well and so favorably known for bravery, courtesy and professional attainment as Lieutenant-Colonel Lane...."[10]

By early October, Lane was with the Twenty-eighth. In February of 1862 Lane and his regiment were ordered to the New Bern area and placed under the command of General Branch. From there he was involved in all the same actions as the Thirty-seventh.

Despite the changes in command, most of November was spent in the indifference

Captain William Young Farthing, Company E (courtesy of Cliff Farthing).

that was associated with camp life. On November 12 Captain William Y. Farthing (Company E) tendered his resignation. Farthing wrote:

> In 1861 I brought into service my Co. and enlisted it for twelve months. Last April I re-enlisted "for the war" and induced most of my company to follow me. I am fifty years old and have two sons; one of my sons is now a member of my Co. and the other is about to enter the army being subject to the Conscription law. I own no slaves, therefore my wife and daughters are left without any male assistance on the plantation.

Just returned as a prisoner of war from Johnson's Island, Ohio, Captain Farthing was paroled on November 10 and submitted his resignation letter on November 12. On November 28 his resignation was accepted, but it is unclear if Farthing knew of it. He died the same day in a hospital in Winchester, Virginia, of "pleuritis." Farthing was not the only member of Company E to meet a tragic death that November. Private Michael Goodwin, a fifty-six-year-old soldier from Alexander County, died in a hospital in Rockingham County, Virginia, of unknown causes. He had enlisted in Iredell County on August 15, 1862, as a substitute for his son.[11]

However, for most members of the Thirty-seventh, their experiences that month were far more mundane and typical of camp life. Major Morris provided a glimpse of that life for an officer:

> Camp Lee Neare Winchester Nov 19th 1862.... Tomorrow I will bee 38 years old. I expect to have a fat Goose for Dinner. Tomorrow I wish you & the Children Could take dinner with Me.... We Live on Beef, Bread & coffee. it is Good Enough for Me though Some of the Men complain. I Mess with Lieut Coln Ashcraft, Chaplain Stough & Sergeant Theadore Stowe. We have a free boy hired at $12 pr Month to cook & wash for us.... I Doo Not Know how Long we will Stay here.[12]

The newly appointed Major did not have long to wonder how long they would stay near Winchester. After receiving decent food, but little in the way of clothing and shoes, the Thirty-seventh and the rest of the Light Division were called upon by General Lee once more. The Thirty-seventh was now in the newly created Second Corps of the Army of Northern Virginia (but still under the command of General Jackson). At 2:30 on the morning of November 22, the Thirty-seventh broke camp and started south. The weather was bitterly cold. A lady in Winchester spoke of the Light Division as they passed through the town: "They were very destitute, many without shoes, all without overcoats or gloves, although the weather was freezing. Their poor hands looked so red and cold holding their muskets in the bitter wind." They traveled down the Valley Turnpike, turning east at New Market, crossing the Massanutten Mountains, and fording the Shenandoah River. Sleet fell on the men as they crossed the Blue Ridge at Thornton's Gap. On November 26 the Thirty-seventh rested near Madison Court House. Here, due to the lack of shoes, many men made moccasins out of leather hides. After twelve days and 175 miles, the Thirty-seventh set up camp at Yerby's farm, five miles south of Fredericksburg. Lieutenant Finely P. Shull (Company B) would recall a few days later: "[several] have bin sent to the Hospital on this march from fatigue of marching...."[13] The weather conditions probably played as large a role as the march.

At this time the Thirty-seventh received its new regimental colors. In the early days of the war, regiments often carried state or homemade flags, most fashioned after the Confederate First National. During the battle of Manassas, the Confederate and Union officers had a difficult time distinguishing friend from foe on the smoke-filled battlefield. Soon after this, at a gathering at the headquarters of the Army of the Potomac (later renamed the Army of Northern Virginia), Generals Gustavus Smith, Joseph Johnston, and P. G. T. Beauregard, and Congressman William P. Miles, created a battle flag for the army. The Richmond Depot started manufacturing the flag, and all regiments in the eastern army were ordered to adopt the flag and send their state flags back to their respective state capitals. The Thirty-seventh would receive a third-bunting flag, which was 48 inches square, with a 5-inch-wide blue Saint Andrew's Cross with 3½ inch stars. The flag was inscribed with battle honors, painted with white paint. It read, on the reverse, "Manassas Junction, Sharpsburg, Harpers Ferry, Mechanicsville, and Shephedtown[*sic*]," and on the obverse, "New Berne, Hanover, Manassas, Ox Hill, Cold Harbor, Craziers [*sic*] Farm, Cedar Run, and Malvern Hill."

A snowfall of four inches greeted the Thirty-seventh on the morning of December 5. Many of the men, in addition to lacking shoes, did not have tents either. On the morning of December 11 the temperature was twenty-four degrees. That evening the Thirty-seventh received orders to cook two days' rations. At 6:30 A.M. on the twelfth, the Light Division moved into lines once held by Hood's division, which had been moved to a new defensive position down the line. Hill's new position was a wooded, mile-and-a-half-long ridge, with the Richmond, Fredericksburg, and Potomac Railroad in front of the entire line. The area in front of the lines, the Confederate's field of fire, was exposed and somewhat flat — an ideal place to defend. At eight A.M., Lane's brigade was placed on the front line, along the railroad, at a position

Obverse of the Thirty-seventh's battle flag (courtesy of the Museum of the Confederacy).

somewhat advanced of the rest of the division. To Lane's right was a hole in the line (approximately six hundred yards) that stretched to the position held by Archer's brigade. Many thought this gap in the line did not need defenders, for it was an impassable low area of underbrush, woods, and swamp. Just for good measure, Hill placed Gregg's South Carolina Brigade in the rear of the gap. Lane placed his men from left to right: the Seventh, Eighteenth, Thirty-third, Twenty-eighth, and the Thirty-seventh, whose right flank opened into the six-hundred-yard void. Sporadic artillery fire would annoy the men until late in the afternoon.

Lieutenant Edward A. T. Nicholson, who transferred to Company E on December 1, 1862 (courtesy of the North Carolina Division of Archives and History).

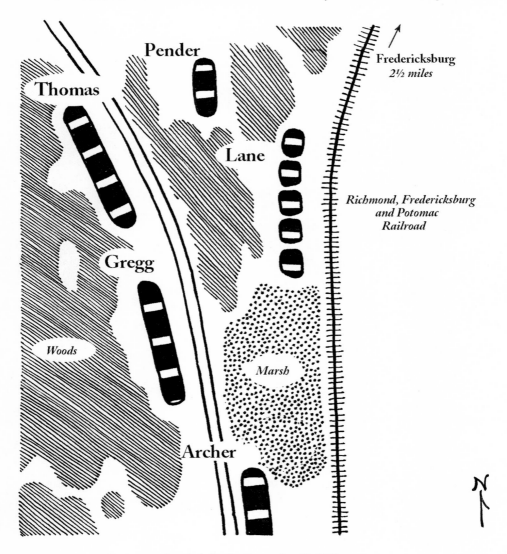

Lane's brigade, December 12, 1862.

The morning of the thirteenth began with a thick fog, which began to dissipate around 10 A.M., and the Federals began to bombard the Confederate positions, trying to learn the whereabouts of the masked Confederate artillery emplacements. Several members of the regiment were struck during this intense fire. Sampson Collins and William T. Griffin of Company D were both struck, as were two members of Company E: John C. Lusk had his head "bruised by a shell," and James W. Munday was "bruised badly" by a shell that hit his thigh. As the Federals began to mount their charge across the field, Colonel Barber saw the Thirty-seventh's precarious situation. He sent a courier back to General Lane requesting instructions on what to do if the Federals should move into the gap on his exposed right flank. Lane's only reply was

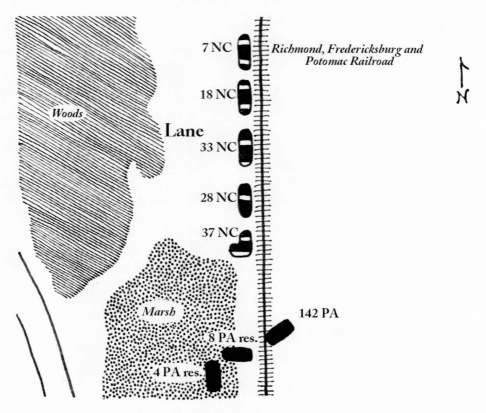

The Thirty-seventh refuses their right flank, Fredericksburg, Virginia, December 13, 1862.

to hold at all costs. Soon Barber's fears were realized as Federal troops came pouring over the railroad embankment and into the gap. Thinking quickly, Barber refused his right three companies (probably companies G, A, and F). His line now formed a backwards L-shape. The One-hundred-and-forty-second Pennsylvania and the Eighth Pennsylvania Reserves soon found their way into the aperture. Barber ordered his right companies to open fire, sending volleys of lead crashing into the Federal forces. Both Federal regimental commanders were wounded, and the One hundred and forty-second was driven back behind the railroad embankment. The Thirty-seventh's three refused companies had stifled two Federal regiments for a time, but had taken serious casualties of their own. Company A's Second Lieutenant, William A. Stuart, went down with wounds in an arm and in both legs. Company G's First Lieutenant, James B. Pool, was struck in the head. John Parsons of Company F had a "finger shot off," and his fellow member of Company F, Archibald Bell, was killed.

As things on the right of the regiment slowed into a lead-slinging contest, the rest of the line erupted into fire as portions of Gibbon's division came into a range of 150 yards. Colonel Barber was soon struck by a projectile in the neck and taken to the rear. The wound incapacitated him for several days. Command of the regiment devolved once again upon Major Morris. Morris was soon struck in the ear and "as bloodey as a Hog." He wrote, "I Doo Not Like to Beare old Abes Mark but am thankful to God it is no worse[.]"[14] He had another ball pass through his canteen and strike his haversack, lodging in a piece of hardtack. Other men began to fall from the ranks, killed instantly or wounded, falling to the ground and writhing in pain. James M. Farthing of Company E was killed by a minié ball to the skull. Third Lieutenant John W. Pettus of Company C was struck in the head also, but he lived. Samuel J. Stewart of Company C was struck in the right arm. Company D's James C. Nance would lose his life to a wound in his thigh. Alexander L. Bullison went down with wounds in his back, right knee, and right arm, and would also succumb to his wounds. The recently promoted Captain Henry C. Fite, of Company H, was struck in the breast and left arm and was taken to the rear. Private Rowland A. Laney of Company D was wounded in the shoulder. Private Robert B. Smith (Company G) was in the process of loading his musket, the butt of the weapon on the

Private Rowland A. Laney, Company D (courtesy of Mike Laney).

ground, when a round struck him in the temple just behind his left eye, coming out just under his right ear. He was able to walk a mile to the rear and find the hospital. The Thirty-seventh would suffer 19 killed and 82 wounded in the battle of Fredericksburg, once again more than any other regiment in the brigade. Seven of the wounded would later die of their wounds.

After sustaining repeated attacks along their front and flank, the Thirty-seventh's men began to run out of ammunition. They scavenged the bodies of the dead and wounded nearby their position for more rounds. The Federals advanced once more, and the Thirty-seventh "had to use the bayonet & buts of [their] guns." Peter Smith was killed by a butt stroke from one of the yankees of Colonel Root's brigade of Gibbon's division. The Federals overwhelmed the thin lines of the Thirty-seventh, forcing them and the Twenty-eighth to the rear. Lieutenant John W. Pettus of the Thirty-seventh's Company C was captured by the Federals, and in the words of one officer, dragged by "the Yankee wretchers ... some distance to the rear after he had been wounded in the head and leg." Other members of the Thirty-seventh were also

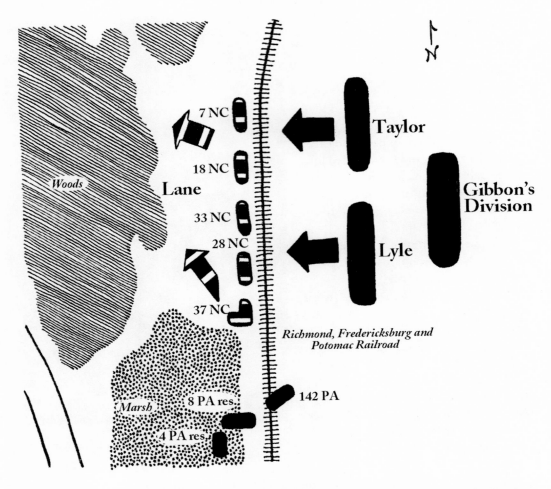

The Thirty-seventh and the rest of Lane's brigade is flanked, Fredericksburg, Virginia, December 13, 1862.

captured, some of them wounded and others just overwhelmed. William S. McGee of Company G went down with a wound in his head and face before being captured. Lowery Dula of the same company was suffering with wounds in the right side and left hand when he was taken prisoner. In all, five wounded men were captured and twenty unwounded men were taken by the Federals. The rest of Lane's line retreated a short distance into the woods, where they re-formed and engaged the Federals once more. The Thirty-seventh and the Twenty-eighth retreated back beyond the front line in search of a source to replenish their exhausted supplies of ammunition. Private Collins called the battle "flagitious [*sic*] or grossly wicked...." Major Morris called the fight "the hardest fight that I have ever been in." Colonel Barber wrote in his official report: "My whole regiment behaved very gallently throughout the whole engagement and the conduct of the men is highly creditable...."[15]

About dark, after being resupplied with ammunition, the Thirty-seventh returned to the line held by the rest of the brigade. Part of Lane's brigade, with the help of Thomas' Georgia Brigade, had driven the Federals back away from the railroad that the Tar Heels had fought behind and had sealed off the breach in the lines. The Thirty-seventh spent the night along these tracks, waiting for Stonewall Jackson to launch a night attack against the Federal lines. Jackson's attack was called off, and the men spent the time reinforcing their improvised breastworks. Around 10 A.M. the next morning, the Thirty-seventh moved to the rear to rest. Their rest was short lived. By 1 P.M. the Thirty-seventh, along with the rest of Jackson's Second Corps, was on its way to Port Royal to counter a possible threat from Burnside's Army. The threat proved to be a rumor, and the men made camp around Moss Neck.

Colonel Barber started home on December 27 on a furlough, granted due to his wounds received on December 13, leaving Major Morris in command of the regiment. During this time the regiment was occupied with picket duty and watching over the Federals, who were just on the other side of the river. Being so near the Federal lines often gave the men chances to converse with the yankees. Major Morris recorded one of these conversations to his wife in a letter home, dated December 28, 1862:

> I cannot say but one thing is Sertain, the Northern Soldiers are out of hart of Ever whipping us & the athorityes at the North are Mitely pusselled how to Manage the affair. there Generals have all been whiped badly. The Enemy pickets on the River Called over to our Pickets yesterday to Know if we had a Soory Corporal in our armey that we would Swap for General Burnside. They said if they could Not Guet a corporal for him they would swap him for a Poore horse. I think Burnside has Got pay for his trip to NewBern.[16]

Major Morris was again on picket duty in January, and wrote again to his wife about conversations with the Federals:

> We was on Picket Duty a fiew Days ago. the Enemy on one Bank of the river & we on the other about 200 yds wide. they are very Friendley & want to talk a Great Deal. they curse the war & Say there time will bee out Next May & will Go Home Peace or No peace & if the Abolitionist want the Negroes Set free they will have to Doo there own fighting.[17]

Private Brazilla C. Green echoed his Major's thoughts when he wrote home about his encounter with the Federal pickets: "We was on picket the other day ... they wanted us to come over and swap them tobacco for coffee but it was against orders ... or I would have went over and got a mess of coffee." Some of the men of the Thirty-seventh did go over and swap with the yankees, usually getting newspapers or the much beloved "coffee."[18]

Conditions in and around the Moss Neck camp were rough. The regiment slept in Sibley tents—large canvas tents that looked like teepees but had a single pole that ran up the middle. "We slept on the ground, two and two, our feet toward the middle of the tent and our heads to the wall," wrote Ashe County native William H.

Private William H. Miller, Company A (courtesy of the Ashe County Historical Society).

Miller, of Company A. "Our tent was small; there was only room for ten or twelve men in it. It was supported by a big pole in the middle to which the rigging and canvas were fasten."[19]

The Thirty-seventh stayed in their Sibleys until January 15, 1863, when they moved about one mile to Camp Gregg. One reason for the move may have been the storm reported on January 15 by a chaplain attached to another regiment in Lane's brigade: "The wind is blowing a perfect gale and has been doing so for twenty-four hours. Several tents have gone over and several more will doubtless fall before morning." The men constructed winter "huts to stay in and shelter us from the weather." Eminent historian Bell Irvin Wiley left an excellent description of the process of constructing winter quarters:

The prevailing type of shelter was a small hut made of logs, chinked and daubed after the fashion of a pioneer cabin.... First the builders went into a wood or thicket with axes ... and chopped down the necessary trees. These were trimmed ... and snaked back to camp. With the logs assembled each group ... began the heavy and tedious work of notching and laying the logs. When the walls were about eight feet high, some sort of roof had to be devised ... often a tent cloth would be used.[20]

After the construction of semi-decent places to live, food was next on the minds of the soldiers. Many of their winter quarters had fireplaces with which to heat the cabins and to cook. "We were given enough food too do," wrote Private William H. Miller after the war, "mostly bean soup. Western salt pork, crackers, and meal. Occasionally we got some beef. We baked our own bread — sometimes we had flour; we drew two days rations at a time.... We had coffee for a while, but that was cut off. There was no sugar." Private Green (Company B) wanted some of his kin, if they were able to come and visit him, to bring him "a bowl for we have nothing fit to make dough in[,] that was one thing that I intended to ... fetch with me...." Green would go on to describe the rations the men received in the middle of January: "just been making me some biscuits and I doubt aunt could imitate them ... for they was part corn mill[.] as to our fair... we get flour beef pork and a little sugar and if we get anything else we have to buy it." Luxuries were still rare. Private Bennett Smith, also of Company B, asked the people at home "to send me som dried fruit ... [and a] cake of sugar if you have any chance to send me thing to eat it will bea ver[y] acceptable." Alexander County native Andrew J. Teague was a little more precise on what he wanted: "I want you to send me 2 or 3 chickings & I want you to salt them raw and send them...." He would write again in April: "i wold be glad to hav sume more dried frut dried beaf or eny thing you can send ... you may send eny thing you can at eny time at will do to eate almost any thing will be good ... you wanted to no whether i got the brandy or not i did git it and was glad to git it...." Major Morris

Private Jacob Taylor, who deserted from Company A in January 1863, and his wife (courtesy of the Ashe County Historical Society).

also wrote in April: "I recd the trunk you Sent Me. Every thing right there. Was Not One of the Eggs broken." Another member of Company B, Jordan S. Councill, also wrote home, in an undated letter, for things he wanted to improve his rations. He wrote: "I want 2 or 3 gallons of brandy and 15 or 20 pound of butter and about 2 gallons of molases and about 2 hams of meate some dried fruit and dried beares gren aples ... some sweet bread and if Paw has killed his hog and they have any saseges I want a mess or two...."[21]

In February the roads turned so bad that the commissaries were hampered bringing food to the camp. One soldier of the Thirty-seventh wrote on February 25th: "Rations have been very scarce for the last ten days, on account of the bad roads.... The men here do not apear to mind death half so much as they do missing their rations." To solve the problem, a "pole" road was constructed from the camp to the depot, which, the soldiers hoped, "will make rations a little more plenty."[22]

Once they had food, either from the commissary or from home, they had to prepare it. Private Smith wrote home on March 24: "I mess to my self I do my one cooking It would make you laf to sea me a baking pyes & to sea them after they was baked I think they eat prime[.]" William H. Miller, of Ashe County, reminisced after the war: "we each had a frying pan; each man cooked his own food, but four of us cooked and messed together." Bennett Smith wrote: "I will tel you who I mess with George Lowrance & Dav Dugger Jest us three[.]"[23]

Payday was to come every two months, on the last day of the second month. This did not always happen. The Thirty-seventh was paid first on December 31, 1861. The next payday was six months later, June 30, 1862, and the men were paid next on October 31, 1862. While not in an active campaign mode, they were paid quite regularly: December 31, 1862, February 28, 1863. Basically, the men were never quite sure when they would get paid again. "I would have sent you more money but I did not no when we would draw any more," wrote one soldier in Company E. Some of the men sent large portions of their pay home to help support their families. Private Teague wrote in April: "i will send you all the money i can i think that i can send you about twenty dollars about the first of June...."[24]

The weather seemed exceptionally bad that winter. Major Morris wrote to his family on January 22: "It has been raining heare for 3 Days & tolerably Cold." He wrote again on the 29th: "We had a heavy snow a fiew Days ago. it is 12 inches Deep at this time.... The roads heare are Knee Deep in Mud...." Private Smith wrote on February 26: "We Don't drill non nor stand gard much the weather is to bad...." Just how bad was it? Doctor Alexander wrote home on February 25: "Last Sunday has not been equaled for snow and wind since the furious 'wind and snow Sunday' of 1856: our tents and huts were all wet with it. It lay on the ground about 12 inches...." April seemed even worse to one private: "it Snode a bout 6 inch deep the 5th of this Month it is a dredful windy place hear & mudy you hav no idy how mudy it does git hear & the stickeyes mud I ever saw...." Private Teague echoed his fellow soldiers' writings: "we have hard times hear & rain and snow evry day or to we had a snow hear the 3 [April] half a leg deep...." The "half a leg deep" snow was probably the one that Sergeant Tally was referring to in his letter home on April 5: "Yesterday was very cold and to day we have a Snow 10 inches deep and still a snowing."[25]

Furloughs, or passes home for certain periods of time, were granted to many. Colonel Barber received a thirty-day furlough, as did Major Morris. "They have commenced giving furlows," wrote Private Francis on January 18. "The old soldiers will get furlows first. Some start home today out of our Regiment." Those who could not get furloughs sometimes tried to walk to the nearest town or depot. Private Bennett Smith tried to go to the depot to get a Richmond newspaper for his wife back in Watauga County. "As we got to the depot," wrote the private, "they put us under guard & tuck us to the Soldiers home & cep us all nite & we had to Start [back to camp] before day...."[26] A few used the time to secure special duties, usually located away from the boredom of camp. Thomas L. Eason of Company D was on detached service in January and February, serving as a brigade pioneer by preparing roads for the army. Roads that might be adequate for normal local traffic would have to be widened to allow the passage of army wagons and artillery caissons. John S. Farthing of Company E was detailed to the provost guard from December 20, 1862, through January 1863, probably guarding prisoners back to Richmond. Marcus D. L. Moody, of Company I, was a little luckier. He was absent on detail in Charlotte, North Carolina, from November 1863 until February 1865, probably at one of the state's clothing or equipment manufactories.

When soldiers were seriously ill the regimental surgeon sent their cases to higher authorities. Doctor Alexander wrote about one such case in the winter of 1862-63. "I sent Sam Whitley up to the Ex. Board yesterday to try for a discharge. I think I will be able to put him through ... I expect to get him off in ten days. He has consumption." Private Samuel Whitley, of Company C, was discharged on February 9, 1863, by reason of "incipient phthisis." He was only 18 years old at the time of his discharge, and had only been with the regiment since November 15, 1862.[27]

An order went out in mid–January stating that those who were absent without leave, or had overstayed their furloughs, would be given a reprieve if they returned to the regiment by March 10. The order further stated that those who failed to return by March 10 were to be court-martialed and shot for desertion. Many letters went out at this time asking family members to talk to those who had deserted, asking them to come back to the regiment. Private Smith wrote his wife on January 27: "Jiney if you hav any chance to cend Jo Shull Nin Coffey & Jonas Coffey word to com back Do So for one good the Capt told me when I roat home to let them no his intention he Sed that he would gave them time to come rite away & if not he intended to advertise them & giv a big reward then they would be punished severe...." Nathaniel Horton would make mention of the same order in a letter home dated February 20, 1863. He concluded his letter to his cousin with: "So I thought I would write to you and apprise you of the order." Major Morris brought two soldiers, Jacob Rudisill and O. P. Byrd, with him as he returned from his furlough. He had a third man, Eli Rudisill, with him, but lost the man when they boarded the train to travel north. Morris received a letter from Caleb Hallett, around March 20, asking that Colonel Barber not have him shot if he returned to camp. Orders had also been going out to the militia and home guard companies in each county to look for and arrest certain men, usually naming the men from each regiment who were absent without leave or who had overstayed their furloughs. Davis S. Isenhour (Company F) was one such soldier. Corporal Isenhour was declared absent without leave in November-December 1862. He underwent courts-martial on January 1, 1863, and was reduced back to the rank of private. He returned to the regiment sometime before February 28, 1863, but deserted again on May 30 of the same year, returning to Alexander County. The local home guard company caught Isenhour on November 19, took him out behind Paul Bowman's store in Taylorsville, Alexander County, and shot him.[28]

Those soldiers who were caught and returned to the Thirty-seventh's camp were brought before a brigade level courts-martial. These trials took place the week of February 21. "A large number of cases are to be tried," wrote Doctor Alexander, " and I fear that some of them will be shot.... Our men who have overstayed their furloughs, without a valid excuse, are being treated *rather* roughly." Alexander mentioned one soldier in particular, Private Dallas S. Maxwell. Maxwell had originally enlisted on October 22, 1861. He deserted on August 20, 1862, but was returned to duty on February 2, 1863.

The view of life in camp differed from soldier to soldier. Private Collins spoke of suffering "inexpressibly or indescribably in consequence of our being exposed as we were, to the intensely cold weather and smoke of the camp fires that prevailed ... at that place." Private Smith, who suffered from some ailment that caused his legs to swell, wrote: "I don't do anything only law a bout the fire it is a cold disagreeable place hear...." Others recalled a more pleasant time in the winter of 1862-63, a time of "snowball battles ... jokes, songs and dances in our little shanties." Private Holland of Gaston County related this scene: "there was two men [who] fell out playing cards today and walked over the guard line and took a regular fight and they were both put in the guard house." Some of the time was passed to the fiddle tunes of Color Sergeant Daniel C. Robinson (Company I), who "played dances, including 'Philadelphia girls won't you come out tonight & dance by the light of the moon.' At the all-soldier dances, soldiers who played the girls would tie a rag around one arm." Even enemy technology was sometimes seen more as an entertaining novelty, as an officer made mention in an April letter home of seeing two Federal balloons scanning the area, an odd sight for sure. One soldier in the ranks wrote in April:

> I am tird of so many masters & Sutch tite rules. I want to git So I can go when I pleas & whar I plese with out a pas. it is pore living the way we hav to liv hear no liberty a tal & hav to do jest as others say. I long to Sea the time when the officers has no cawl for their offis So they can quit exercizen authority over men that is as good as they are if not better than a heap of them.[29]

Another soldier related this story of one of his pards, Robert A. Sharpe of Company I:

> Robert Sharp ... was fine looking, active, talked well, and was a great ladiesman. He was opposed to doing camp duty, for which the colonel had him put in the guard house for a week at a time, He was not in the least abashed; but drew the sign "Sharp's Picture Gallery," and pinned it to his tent; and all day long he had applicants for pictures, which brought him considerable revenue. He did not object going into all the battles, but he would not stay in camp. At the grand review ... he was standing in the shade, dressed handsomely, with a woman on each arm bowing to his acquaintances.... He was always neat, a cleaver talker and popular wherever he went....[30]

Doctor Alexander also penned a few lines about his life in camp to his wife on April 1: "I have just finished the last of my stock of tobacco; and have just taken a chew of a new kind, it is as black as ink, and tastes like liquorish and sweet oil mixed. I want you to send me some by the first opportunity."[31]

The soldiers spent a great deal of their time in camp writing and reading letters to and from home. "This morning finds Me well as usual & trust when these Lines reach you they May find you all Well," wrote Major Morris on December 28, 1862. Their letters talked of friends and relatives who were coming home on furlough, and soldiers who were sick or who had died. They talked of the weather, of picket duty and conversations between the lines, and of the morale of the men on both sides. They often sought news of the conditions at home and gave advice on planting, harvesting, and selling crops, rearing the children, and other details of an everyday simple life that they had known before the war had interrupted. And they wrote of being homesick. "I want to Sea you & Joney the worst in the world," wrote one soldier. Another member of the Thirty-seventh penned these lines to his "Dear Wife … [when] this war is over, and I am sparred to get home, I want to see you looking as young and pretty as I saw you on the evening of the 13th of May [18]53." They closed their letters with passionate requests for more letters from home. Bennett Smith wrote: "you must rite often & tel Father to rite." Private Teague finished with: "so i will close by asking you to rite as soon as this comes to hand[.]" Major Morris concluded: "Give My Love to all the Children & your Mother allso all the black famely."[32]

Christianity was still one of the ways in which men sought solace from their homesickness. "We have Preaching Nearly every day in camp. considerable revivals attend the Meetings. Benick from Catawba is Chaplin of the 34 NC Reg. he is an able Preacher. I think the Soldiers are becoming More Interested in the Salvation of there Souls." So wrote Major Morris. If there was one topic that predominated the soldier's letters more than anything, it was Christianity and the condition of their souls. Private Teague wrote home: "i hope god will spaire me to come home agin i put all my trust and hope in him and i want you to do the same and pray for me i pray for you day and nite." One officer wrote: "Our chaplin Preached us a very good sermond which I trust will have a Good effect." Private M. L. Holland of Gaston County also relayed those feelings: "we have preaching hear by the Methodist and Camelites…. Oh that some more [men] could feel what I have felt. I think they would change their ways before it is everlastingly two late…." Major Morris further expounded in another letter: "May God prepare us for the trials that awaits us and cause us to trust in the arm of his Power, the onley Power that can Save." He wrote again in April: "The time will Soon come When all those that turn away from the Invitations of Gods Holey Sperrit Will repent but Everlastingly to late. Every year has its Seasons, So has the Grace of God With Man." Private Daniel W. Chambers wrote to the *Biblical Recorder*, a Baptist North Carolina journal:

> [S]even weeks ago a religious association for the promotion of morality and piety was formed in the Thirty-seventh Regiment, North Carolina troops, at the instance of the chaplain and with the aid of the colonel. It numbers 132 members, belonging to seven or eight denominations. Fifty-five soldiers have asked the prayers of their believing associates, and five have found relief in the Saviour's blood. "Our chaplain and colonel," he says, "are, with many good brethren, ministering spirits throughout our camp."[33]

The men of the Thirty-seventh were becoming a part of something much larger. Revivals were breaking out all across the Army of Northern Virginia. The soldiers, now isolated from their homes and loved ones and confronted by the reality of death,

Captain William T. Nicholson, Adjutant and commander of Company E (courtesy of the North Carolina Division of Archives and History).

sought the Christ of their childhoods. The revivals had started in early September of 1862 and continued on until the commencement of the Gettysburg campaign, but picked up again in the winter of 1863-64. Denominational differences were all but forgotten in what would become an ecumenical movement to supply the men with religious education. T. H. Pritchard wrote in late September of 1862, while the regiment was still stationed near Winchester: "For the past four or five days I have been preaching in Lane's North Carolina brigade, with great pleasure, by reason of interest manifested by the soldiers in the important subject of salvation. There have been as many as twenty-five and thirty forward for prayer at a time. Three were baptized last Thursday, and others have connected themselves with other denominations." Also in September, Lt. William A. Nicholson, adjutant of the regiment, would pen a few lines to the *Biblical Recorder* regarding the religious instruction in the Thirty-seventh's camp: "The tracts were read and re-read by our brave men with eagerness. Many of them to whom I had given only one, came back to know if they could not get more of the instructive messages. I am anxious to have all the men of our regiment supplied with the teachings of Jesus."[34]

March 27, 1863, was declared a day for fasting and prayer. Major Morris's letter home that day was very poignant: "Though we are Engaged in a Just cause in the defence of our country and rights We Must Not Expect Peace Without the proper Respect and Recognition of the divine Power." Chaplain Kennedy of the Twenty-eighth would leave this view of the day in his diary: "I preached this morning from Psalms 8th Cp., 3–4 verses, the largest audience I have ever addressed in camp — nearly the entire regiment was out and quite a number from neighboring Regiment [Thirty-seventh].... The men seem to appreciate the importance of a proper observance of the day.... Pretty nearly all the men too *fasted*.... I feel hopeful of the influence of the day's work in the Confederacy."[35] The verses that Kennedy selected as his text read:

> When I consider thy heavens
> The work of thy fingers
> The moon and stars,
> Which Thou hast ordained;
> What is man that thou art mindful of him?
> And the son of man, that thou visitest him? [Psalms 8 KJV]

At end of March the officers of the regiments in the brigade assembled on "a beautiful, bright, sunshiny day" for a special service, one in which the officers of the brigade presented General Lane with a new saddle, bridle, sash, and sword. Colonel Barber made the presentation speech, giving a short history of the brigade, eulogizing Colonels Lee and Campbell, and General Branch, and promising Lane to never falter in the line of duty. Lane replied to his subordinate's token of gratitude by stating that North Carolina should "be proud of such gallant sons...."[36]

8

"One of the bloodiest pages of history"
April–May 1863

By mid–April the long, dreary months of inactivity for the Thirty-seventh were coming to a close. General Joseph Hooker, mislabeled by the yankee press as "Fighting Joe Hooker," had replaced Burnside as commander of the Army of the Potomac. Hooker had arrogantly boasted in a meeting with President Lincoln that in taking Richmond, "there is no if in this case. I am going straight to Richmond if I live." Lincoln responded: "It seems to me that he [Hooker] is overconfident. The hen is the wisest of all the animal creation because she never cackles until after the egg is laid."[1]

Lieutenant Octavius Wiggins of Company E wrote: "On 29 April, 1863, the familiar boom of cannon comes wafted on the spring breezes from the direction of Fredericksburg."[2] The men of the Thirty-seventh quickly cooked rations, rolled blankets, and packed knapsacks, knowing that the time of winter doldrums ended with the new spring campaign. The Federal troops had seized a foothold on the western side of the Rappahannock River. To be nearer the main lines, Colonel Barber led the men of the Thirty-seventh out of their encampment near Moss Point. As they took up the march, one of the many spring-time rains that made travel so arduous poured forth upon the Tar Heels. They took up a position, for the night, near their old lines at Hamilton's Crossing and strengthened their entrenchments as a drubbing rain hounded them all night. The Thirty-seventh, along with the rest of Lane's brigade and A. P. Hill's division, was positioned behind Early's division, with Rodes's division on Hill's right. The entire Second Corps of the Army of Northern Virginia was ready to face Hooker. But it was not Hooker's plan to duplicate Burnside's blunders at Fredericksburg a few months before. The forces that crossed over the Rappahannock were merely a diversion. Lee was not deceived. While not sure of the number or objective of the Federals crossing far up river, he knew they were there and waited to see what course of action they took before he committed to a plan of his own.

The contest on April 30 proved trivial for the Thirty-seventh. Most of the action involved long range artillery duels between the two forces. Toward evening, the sortie came a little closer when the Federal artillery began targeting a battery located in front of the brigade. On the morning of Friday, May 1, the members of the Thirty-seventh, along with the rest of A. P. Hill's division, quietly moved out of their entrenchments before first light, around 4 A.M., and moved down along the Plank Road, toward Chancellorsville. A thick fog prevented each side from knowing what the other side was doing. McClaws's division had already moved out around midnight, to be followed by Rodes, Hill, and then Coleston. Lee was going to confront Hooker's grand flanking maneuver. Lieutenant Wiggins recalled: "all ... fresh in my memory ... the slow march to Chancellorsville, the many halts, the deafening cheer given General Lee as he passes going to the front, the order to load, the picture of Lee and Jackson seated under a tree." That afternoon, General Hill sent Lane's brigade, along with the brigades of Heth and McGowan, to reconnoiter the Orange Plank Road toward Chancellorsville. Parts of Heth's and McGowan's brigades found the enemy and skirmished with them, but darkness halted the operation. The Thirty-seventh's troops rested on their arms that evening, believing that they would be called to assault the Federal works at any time. Their bivouac was near the junction of the Orange Plank Road and the Furnace Road. Lee, Jackson, and Stuart would also meet near that junction to plan Jackson's flanking movement of the next day. This was the famous "last meeting" between Lee and Jackson.[3]

May 2 greeted the soldiers of the Thirty-seventh with a chill, but the day promised to be warmer than the day before. A. P. Hill's division was the last to move out on the now-famous flanking march of Stonewall Jackson. The Confederates had found the open right flank of the Federal army and intended to attack that exposed flank and cut the Federals off from the fords they had used to cross the river. While Jackson had said that his entire Second Corps would move out by 4 A.M., it was actually between 7 and 8 A.M. when the movement finally got underway. Jackson used some of the artillery of Hill's division to test the Federals. They were still present and responded with some artillery fire of their own, wounding some of the members of the Eighteenth. Lane did not pass by Lee's headquarters until 11 A.M. The men covered ten miles before taking a two-hour rest. The roads used by the brigade and other members of the corps were just right for the infantry. They were damp enough to prevent much dust, and only muddy in low places. The wagon trains and artillery did not make many ruts to turn the ankles of the members of the Thirty-seventh. For some of the men on the march, however, the route may have presented a different perspective. A member of Company E said that this was one of the hardest marches he had ever made. "The day was very warm, the route poor.... On we rushed jumping bushes, branches up and down hill.... Every man bends to his work, not a murmer is heard; we laugh and joke about it as one of old 'Jacks' hustlers."[4]

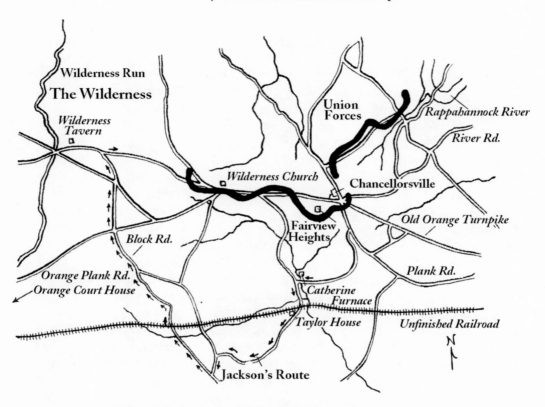

Jackson's flank march at Chancellorsville, Virginia, May 2, 1863.

The lead elements of Jackson's corps arrived on Hooker's open right flank around 4 P.M., and at 5 P.M. Jackson ordered the attack to begin. Rodes's division was the first to attack, followed by Colston's. Part of Hill's division was first deployed, but, unable to keep up, was moved back into the road and marched by the left flank. Colonel Barber and the Thirty-seventh led Hill's division, with Company E in the vanguard. Jackson was up and down the line with all the eyes of his men following him. The Thirty-seventh, being in the lead on the road, was the target for Federal artillery throughout the late afternoon battle. The men were also witness to the success of Jackson's attack. Lieutenant Lewis Battle remarked: "Our spirits were so high we could scarcely hold ourselves to the ground, for we could see as we passed along the road at least ten dead Yankees to our one." Lieutenant Wiggins, after the war, said this about the attack:

> I then witnessed the grandest sight I have ever seen ... two lines of Confederate soldiers rushing on to victory with Jackson in full view leading them. As they burst from the woods like a pack of hounds and become conscious of what was going on under their own observation, animation seemed to take possession of them. On they rushed like an avalanche.... They [Howard's Eleventh Corps] did run ... I would have done the same things and so would you and I reckon the Devil himself would have run with Jackson in his rear.

The Thirty-seventh found itself in a unique position: While being stacked on the road, the troops were under constant artillery fire. But they were also able to take advantage of the spoils of war. Wiggins continued his story:

> Fires were burning in every direction over which were pots filled with fresh beef. The Yankees were cooking supper for Jackson's men, and there is where Lane's men had the advantage of the line of battle. It was an easy thing to slip out of ranks and charge these pots and many was the old "reb" who brought his supper from the bottom of them on the point of his bayonet.[5]

Lieutenant Wesley Lewis Battle, Company D (courtesy of the North Carolina Division of Archives and History).

Noah Collins of Company D echoed Wiggins's culinary description of the regiment's advance: "…[we helped] ourselves to the scattered haversacks of provisions, occasionally passing the dead and wounded and coming in sight of the flying Union troops, and the pursuing Rebels…." Sergeant Tally (Company I) was a little more specific with his description: "They left nearly everything on the battlefield, Knapsacks, havre sacks. Cantines, Overcoats, Blankets, beef just in the act of being skined. and pickled also. Crackers—in fact Evrything that belongs to the army … guns was more plenty than Sticks … [the yankees] left their coffee pots on the fire making coffee but they never came back to get it. I think there must have been thousands of gallons of coffee making."[6]

The Thirty-seventh spent about two hours on the Plank Road, barely able to keep up with the two divisions ahead, driving the yankees through the woods in mass confusion. About dark, Jackson ordered Hill to deploy his brigades to resume the fight. The two other divisions had been so broken by the thick tangle of undergrowth that they now needed time to re-form. They had driven the Federals at least three miles.

"Press them! Cut them off from United States Ford, Hill. Press them!" were Jackson's orders. The Thirty-seventh moved up the Plank Road until hit by murderous artillery fire that forced them to the woods and as close to the ground as they could get. One member of the regiment remarked: "we sought protection on the edge of the road and buried our faces as close to the ground as possible and I expect some of us rubbed the skins off our noses trying to get under it." Another of the men "resorted to prayer … he went down low and loud—long and strong[.]" The artillery fire was coming from a battery of U.S. regulars that was posted at Fairview. They were responding to the fresh guns of William Carter's Virginia battery that had just gone into action behind Hill's columns. Pvt. George Patrick, of Company E, emphatically stated:

"Gentlemen, I want to tell you all something and I want these officers to remember it; I never intend to stay in another such place as that. You can shoot me if you want to but I'm going to leave if you carry me in another such place as that." Hill's chief of staff, Colonel William H. Palmer, arrived during the cannonade and queried Lane as to why he had not deployed his men. Lane responded that the Federal artillery was too much and that if Hill would order the Virginia battery to cease fire, Lane thought that the Federals would do the same. Palmer relayed the message and the Federal fire stopped within fifteen minutes. Lane later remarked that "all old soldiers know how difficult it is to maneuver the bravest troops in the dark, under a murderous fire, through scrubby oak and pine thickets and over the abatis of the enemy's abandoned works."[7]

Lane's brigade deployed and advanced 100 yards before coming upon the abandoned works of the Federals and the lone artillery pieces of Captain Marcellus Moorman, in command of one of the horse batteries that were for a time the leading element of the attack. It was dreadfully dark, but clear. The moon would not rise for another hour or so. Lane deployed two regiments to the right of the road and two to the left, with the Thirty-third as skirmishers to their front. The Thirty-seventh and the Seventh were deployed to the right of the Plank Road, and the Eighteenth and Twenty-eighth to the left of the road, with the left of the Thirty-seventh and the right of the Eighteenth resting on the road. The woods and wilderness that surrounded them were a hazardous place. They were full of wounded and dead Federal soldiers, along with tons of abandoned guns, knapsacks, canteens, blankets, and other elements of the North's war machine. To add to the problem, no one quite knew where the Federals were. After Lane had moved his men into position, he sent back to find Hill for a further clarification of his orders. Instead, he met Jackson, who ordered Lane to "Push right ahead...." When Lane returned to the brigade to prepare the troops for a night attack, he had a new problem: Lieutenant Colonel Levi H. Smith, One-hundred-and-twenty-eighth Pennsylvania, had come into the lines supporting a flag of truce, under the pretext of seeing if Union or Confederate soldiers were in his front. Lane wrote a few days later in his official report: "Considering this an illegitimate use of the white flag, as he expressly stated it was not his object to surrender, and not wishing to let him return, I sent Lt. O. Lane to General A. P. Hill to know what I should do."[8]

But these were not all of the Tar Heels' problems. The group of Federal soldiers under Lieutenant Colonel Smith's command was threatening to open fire upon the Tar Heels if their Colonel was not returned. Lane sent a small detachment under Lt. James Emack of the Seventh to find out how many Federals were on his right. At the same time, Union Brigadier General Joseph Knipe rode into Lane's skirmishers. The Thirty-third opened fire. The Federals responded with infantry and artillery. Then Lane's main line, the Thirty-seventh included, returned the Federals' fire. The skirmishers of the Thirty-third were caught between the two lines of lead. As this firing died down, Emack and his four-man squad returned with 198 prisoners of the One-hundred-and-twenty-eighth Pennsylvania.

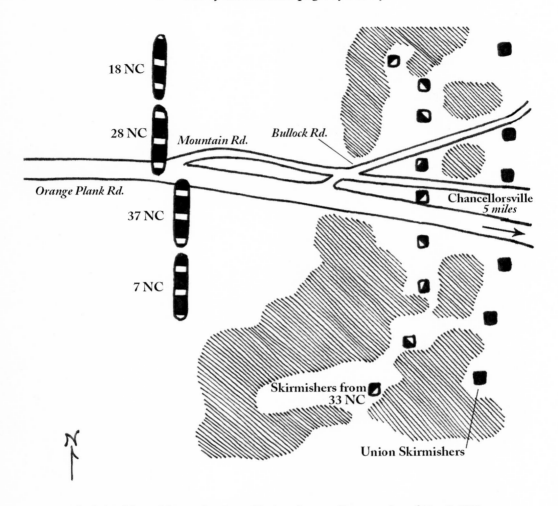

18 NC

28 NC   *Mountain Rd.*   *Bullock Rd.*

Orange Plank Rd.

37 NC

Chancellorsville
5 miles

7 NC

Skirmishers from
33 NC

Union Skirmishers

N

The brigade's position at the time of Jackson's wounding, evening of May 2, 1863.

Some time soon after the encounter (9 P.M.), General Jackson and his staff rode forward to reconnoiter the Federal position. According to a story passed down through the Lowery family, Private Thomas Lowery, who was possibly acting second sergeant for Company D of the Thirty-seventh, the company posted along the Orange Plank Road, saw General Jackson ride by, saying to the general, "I wouldn't go in there now. It's too dark, and your men may take you for the enemy and shoot you."[9] A. P. Hill and his staff were also in the woods somewhere in front of Lane's men, but not as far as the skirmishers. A few moments later, as Jackson and his staff returned to the Confederate lines, the men of the Thirty-seventh, who could just barely see the mounted figures, fired into the woods at the unknown figures, driving the parties across the Plank Road and in front of the Eighteenth, killing Jackson's engineer Keith Boswell and his signalman Cunliffe. The Eighteenth, having heard of a cavalry charge by the Federals earlier that day and seeing the carnage of dead Federal cavalry horses, were spooked into thinking that Jackson and Hill's party was another cavalry attack. As the thirty or so horsemen crashed through the thick, dead underbrush, a few shots rang out from an unknown location on the field. Then a few members of the Eighteenth fired, and someone yelled to stop firing because they were hitting their own men. Major John D. Barry of the Eighteenth questioned the order, and calling it a lie, ordered the Eighteenth to "Pour it into them...." Many members of the party not wounded by the Thirty-seventh were hit by the Eighteenth. Jackson's wounds would prove mortal.

When questioned about the incident later, not one of Lane's officers knew that the two parties were out in front of the Confederate lines. So no one in Lane's brigade was held responsible for the death and injuries to Jackson and his party.

A few moments after Jackson was brought through the lines and placed upon an ambulance, Hill was also wounded. As he came to Lane on foot, "pistol in hand," he informed him of Union cannons preparing to rake the Plank Road. Artillery fire erupted again and a shell fragment tore through both calves of the division commander, who had succeeded Jackson in the command of the Second Corps. Hill's injuries prevented him from riding, and hence from commanding the corps. Command of Hill's division passed to Henry Heth, and Corps command passed to Robert Rodes. But Rodes was only a Brigadier General, having only recently gained command of a division. Hill sent for Major General Stuart to take command of the corps.

It was now after 10 P.M. and chaos ruled. The Confederates knew that there were Federals in front of them and on their right flank. Jackson, their beloved commander, had been wounded and so had Hill, who had given fame to Lane's brigade and the "Light Division." The night attack that Jackson had pushed so hard for was postponed.

That night was a long, sleepless affair for the members of the Thirty-seventh. Both their Corps commander and their Division commander had been wounded near their lines. They had been under fire for most of the evening, with a fair amount of action on their right, as Sickles's Union Corps groped around in a night attack and made contact with members of Lane's brigade. They could also plainly hear the sound of the Federals entrenching in their front. Clearly, tomorrow's work would come at a high price.

All of Lane's brigade had been shifted to the right, or south, of the Plank Road. The order of line was now the Twenty-eighth, Eighteenth, part of the Thirty-third, Seventh, and the Thirty-seventh, with its left still resting on the road. The other part of the Thirty-third remained out as skirmishers. The Federal works that the Thirty-seventh were to attack had been crudely built, but still formed a formidable obstacle. Trees had been felled with a "thick abatis of interwiding tree tops pointing towards the advancing Confederates." The Tar Heels struck two Federal units of Ross's XII Corps, the One-hundred and twenty-third New York and the Third Maryland. The attack began around 5:30 A.M. and met with initial success. Captain Nicholson gave his men an inspirational oration before they moved out: "Keep cool men

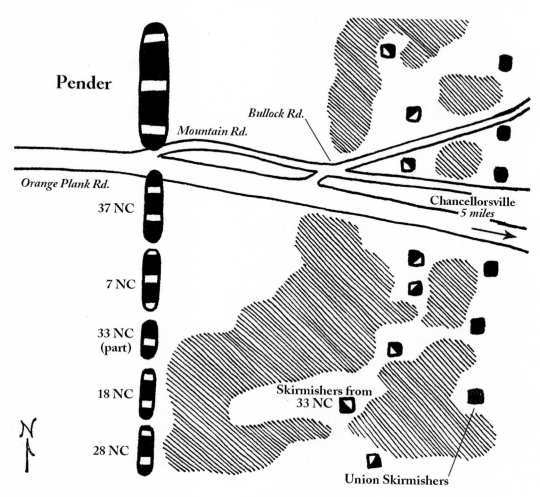

Pender

Bullock Rd.

Mountain Rd.

Orange Plank Rd.

37 NC

Chancellorsville
5 miles

7 NC

33 NC
(part)

18 NC

Skirmishers from
33 NC

28 NC

N

Union Skirmishers

The brigade's position near dawn, May 3, 1863.

and do your duty." Colonel Barber echoed his words: "Yes, men do as Captain Nicholson tells you to and let us die on this battle field or gain victory."[10]

"We were orderd into it rite and made a charge uppon the Yankees," wrote Sergeant Tally a few days after the battle. As the Thirty-seventh and her sister regiments advanced, one of the Federal skirmishers reported back to his fellow New Yorkers: "Get ready boys, for they are coming and coming strong." Lieutenant Wiggins would chronicle after the war in an address given to a chapter of the United Daughters of the Confederacy: "We moved forward as if on parade, and the bloody work commence…. Inch by inch, foot by foot we press forward; nothing is heard but the roar of cannon and the rattling of rifle. At times the lines would not be more than thirty paces apart, shooting into each others faces." Captain Bost (Company D) recalled the contest as the "hotest place that ever I was in on account of the enemy's artillery…." The Third Maryland (US), which had never been in this type of conflict,

was the first to break. As Lane's brigade charged with bayonets and went in scream-
ing "Remember Jackson!" the Marylanders went streaming to the rear. In the Thirty-
seventh's ranks, "some were killed and wounded directly after starting to charge,"
recalled one Thirty-seventh officer, " and a good many skulked out of it by pre-
tending to be wounded by the bursting of bombs near them and laging behind." But
even with the reduced numbers, "A few of the 37th [and Seventh] charged over their
breast works at one point" and were able to penetrate the Federal line. They leaped
over the Federal abatis and captured several prisoners. Sergeant Albert F. Montgomery planted the colors of the Thirty-seventh on the seized works. The Federal
cannoners who manned the guns that had fired on the Thirty-seventh the previous
evening fled their guns. The Thirty-seventh and the Seventh then formed a line at a
right angle to the rest of the Federal line and sent an enfilade fire down upon the Federals. Lane sent for the Eighteenth to support the Thirty-seventh and the Seventh,
and ordered the two regiments to lie down and keep up their fire. But they could not
hold on to their breakthrough for any prolonged duration.[11]

The Federals quickly reorganized and sent in a murderous fire upon the Confederates. "It was bad ... times," recorded Private Thorton Sexton (Company A) to his
parents. "The trees and bushes was [shot] all to peses with balls and grape shoot...."
Another member of the regiment wrote: "Both men and ammunition are nearly
exhausted. Cartridge boxes are cut from both friend and foe and strewn on the
ground by our men." The fire came from three directions and after about a half hour
was too much for the men from the old North State. "[T]he shelling becam[e] so
very spirited that our progress or advancement was greatly retarded or hindered [by]
grape and cannister shot; till all bacame a general roar, like that of the approach of
a very severe and destructive southern thunderstorm." The Twenty-seventh Indiana
fixed bayonets and charged, and the Tar Heels were forced to withdraw to their original lines of the night before. "I received a slight wound in the head directly after
starting the fight," recalled Captain Bost, "four small pieces of a bomb ... through
my hat into my scalp of my head which bled considerably ... [I had] two more shots
in my hat brim ... [and had a] few of them brush my hair which is cut short." Noah
Collins was wounded and captured by the Federals:

> I was pierced in the right thigh, by a very large musket ball; which mashing itself
> about haft flat against, and fracturing the bone, glided over and located itself just
> on the inside of it; about which time the [Thirty-seventh] fell back ... leaving me
> under the cross fire of both armies; at which place shells, grape and cannister shot
> kept the dirt limbs and chunks that they knocked off the green trees, constantly
> falling on me, till I became so intensely alarmed and ardently or keenly anxious to
> extricate myself from such a perilous or dangerous condition that I raised my head
> and looking around saw the plank road, which being but a few paces off, I crawled
> to it, in consequence of its being a lower position than that of the one I then occu-
> pied ... soon after ... two of the Union soldiers came out and capturing me, com-
> manded me to arise from thence and go to their rear ... one of them came up to my
> right side, the other to my left, and placing my arms around their necks, started with
> me to the hotel at Chancellorville; when upon coming into the Union lines, I became

so weak sick and faint that I commenced lying down to rest; when a Union Captain seeing me, commanded me to go on … I replied that I could not possibly go any further … he drew back his sword, advancing two or three paces towards me at the same time, and angrily told me I must and should so on … I replied [that] I must have assistance; when the same two soldiers … carried me to the hotel at Chacellorsville, amidst a very severe and destructive shower of Rebel cannon shot and shells, and set me down behind the hotel, to shelter me from the same…. General Hooker … was knocked down speachless in the piazza of the hotel, soon after my arrival at that place, by a shell … the Union soldiers [then] carried me to their third line of fortifications, and set me down behind them … at which place I remained, the battle still raging with unabated fury, till about twelve o'clock; when I was recaptured by the Rebels….[12]

Only a rally by the Twenty-eighth saved the line. The brief time the Thirty-seventh had spent in battle that morning would prove to be the regiment's worst fight of the war. Colonel Barber was wounded in the right arm, but continued to command. Lieutenant Colonel Ashcraft was wounded, as was Major Morris, who was wounded in the right foot. Morris would leave the hospital and rejoin the Thirty-seventh's ranks, helping to rally the regiment from horseback. First Sergeant George W. Baucom (Company D) was struck in the leg. He lay upon the ground and cried out for help to his messmates, but when no one came, he got up, and with a bloody and broken leg, hobbled back to where the company was positioned. Also wounded was Private Francis M. Blevins of Company K, who was injured in the foot. Less fortunate was Private Andrew J. Derr of Company C, who would later lose a leg to the injury he received. Total casualties for the Thirty-seventh were as follows: "One officer killed, 19 officers wounded; 35 men killed, 175 wounded; 8 missing[.]" Many of the wounded would spend days in temporary field hospitals before being transferred to Richmond.[13]

Private Francis M. Blevins, Company K, and his wife (courtesy of the Ashe County Historical Society).

Private Andrew J. Derr, Company C (courtesy of James L. McElveen).

The Thirty-seventh was done fighting for the day. In time, it was re-formed, issued ammunition, and served as a reserve for Colquitt's brigade. As they were recovering and acting as a reserve, the Thirty-seventh's troops witnessed a striking tragedy. The woods in front of them caught fire and "the dead, Confederates as well as Federals were on fire," chronicled General Lane after the war. The

helpless wounded Federals-officers & men begged to be removed from the approaching devouring flames but we could render no assistance. On reaching Colquitt, we had to wait until the woods on his left was burnt over, before we could prolong his line. There we remained until the next day in the ashes & the charred scrubby oaks, & it was hard to tell whether we [were] white or black, Federal or Confederate so far as the color of our clothes were concerned. When we were orded back, the troops in rear received us with boisterous laughter & cheer.

As the men of the Thirty-seventh retired, they were tired, hungry, dirty, and mourning the loss of many a brother. Colonel Barber, in concluding his official report, stated: "I do not hesitate to say that it was the bloodiest battle that I have ever witnessed." Major Bost would second Barber's report in a letter home: "Our brigade suffered badly." General Lane completed his postwar letter with almost thirty years of retrospect: "My brigade was in nearly every great battle fought by the Army of Northern Virginia, but in none did I ever witness so many harrowing scenes as I did at Chancellorsville."[14]

May 4 and 5 would be spent in the line of battle in front of Hooker's entrenched forces. Lee was busy fighting against Sedgewick and his attempts to destroy Early and his vastly outnumbered Confederate troops on the heights of Fredericksburg. By May 6, Lee had driven Sedgewick back across the Rappahannock and once again turned his attention toward Hooker. But Hooker also had shifted the Army of the Potomac back across the river, and Lee's skirmishers found empty Federal breastworks.

On the evening of May 7, the Thirty-seventh had returned to its winter quarters at Moss Neck. Lee was concerned that Hooker might try to re-cross the river in a different location, and he quickly moved his men back to the positions they had occupied before the battle. It was now time for the flood of letters that so often commenced after a great battle. Bennett Smith wrote to his wife Jane on the eighth: "Ther has bin a big fite up at Fredricksburg hit commenced May 1st & lasted 7 dayes I wasent in it I was cent off with the wagons." Sergeant Tally wrote to his wife on "captured paper and all cut up — but I will try to arrange it so you can understand...."

The slightly wounded also wrote home. Andrew J. Teague wrote to his wife on May 14: "I am in the hospittle at Richmond I was in the fight and got wounded below the knee...." Thomas Nixon wrote to his uncle: "The Battle of Chancellorsaville will cover one of the Bloodiest pages of history in this war I wish you could have seen the field on Sunday evening after the Battle had ceased it was an awful sight to look at...." Another member of the Thirty-seventh wrote: "Our Battle was named Chanlersville. [W]e had hard time of it."

The evening of May 10 found the Regiment formed up "for dress parade on the green clover fields near the Rappohannocks[.]" General Lee had issued General Orders No. 61, which was read by the adjutant:

> With deep grief, the commanding General announces to the army the death of Lieut. Gen. T. J. Jackson, who expired on the 10th inst., at 3.15 P.M. The daring, skill, and energy of this great and good soldier, by decree of an all-wise Providence, are now lost to us. But while we mourn his death, we feel that his spirit still lives, and will inspire the whole army with his indomitable courage and unshaken confidence in God as our hope and strength. Let his name be a watchword to his corps, who have followed him to victory on so many fields. Let his officers and soldiers emulate his invincible determination to do everything in the defence of our beloved country.

One member of the Thirty-seventh described the men standing "in their old ragged gray jackets with no handkerchief to brush away the scalding tears pouring down their bronzed and battle scar[r]ed faces, seeking some secluded spot upon the banks of the river there to shed tears that come truly from the aching heart." Thomas Nixon wrote to his uncle: "I know you have heard of the Death of Gen Jackson[.] I tell you he will be greatly missed in this Army[.] I know that I should look for him if I ever get into Another Battle[.] I knew that he could not save my life But I always felt certain of victory when I could see him About and the men put such great faith in him[.]" Charles T. Haigh, a Virginia Military Institute cadet who would later serve in Company B of the Thirty-seventh, wrote from the Institute: "The death of the lamented hero 'Stonewall' Jackson is a terrible blow to the South ... his military career fills the brightest and most momentous pages of the history of our country and the achievements of our army."[15]

After Chancellorsville, life for the Thirty-seventh lapsed into a somewhat unsettled pattern. In Bennett Smith's letter of the eighth, he wrote his wife: "I hope hit [Chancellorsville] will be the last fite I fear not I think they will recruit & try it a gane I don't think it will end by fiting it looks like they hav bin whipt often a nuf if whiping would do any good." Food was always on the minds of the members of the regiment. "As to eatibles we don't git much flour & meat is the hith we git & a great deal of that damaged so we can hardly eat it," Smith continued. In the next few days, the men would spend time on picket duty on the river, and would be paid. Smith again wrote home and talked about food:

> I recon you would like to no what we git to eat we git flour a pound a day to the man Beacon & some times Beef a quarter a pound a Day Some times we git a little

sugar & some corn field peas we git a little rice Some times I hav bin a picken Salet a long for severl dayes I pick polk & Dock & plantin & some wild mustard we cuck et & I tel you it eats splendid the worst is we cant find a nuf of it their so many a picken it keeps is so scarse everybody is picking Salet hear

Rations were not just on the mind of Private Smith. His neighbor from Ashe County, Thorton Sexton, also wrote home around the same time, saying that the ration of bacon had been increased from a quarter a pound to half a pound a day. "Jeff says his boys must have more to eat when they do such good fighting."[16]

On May 11, orders came to prepare to move at a moment's notice. Those orders were later rescinded and new orders issued: to prepare for 24-hours picket duty, which would begin on May 12.[17] The casualties list kept growing for the Thirty-seventh. Between May 3 and May 24, 17 men succumbed to wounds received in the battle or died of disease. William Walker of Company Co. F died of unknown causes on May 3; Albert P. Young of Company I died of wounds on the sixth, followed by fellow Company I members Michael L. Aderholdt on the seventh and Brown Starnes on the ninth. On May 9, Company D member Charles Evans succumbed to his wounds, and the next day John A. Lackey of Company G died of the "fever." May 15 brought the deaths of Jonathan Lee (cause unknown), and on the sixteenth, Samuel P. Paysour of Company H and William Green, both of whom died of wounds. William A. Henderson of Company B died on the nineteenth of wounds, along with Starling Vanzant of Company A.

During this time, desertion loomed large in the regiment. After the battle was over, the men were mustered and paid. Many saw this time as an opportunity to go home. On May 13, at least four, perhaps five, members of Company B left: John and William Huddler, Samuel Jones, George W. Norris, and Thomas M. Phipps. On the sixteenth, Andrew Jenkins of Company H left. On May 19, the largest group left — all from Company A: Hamilton Bare, George Black, George and Jeremiah Blackburn, Eli Calloway, James W. Carpenter, Peter Goodman, Robert McCormick, Eli and James McNeil, Jasper Miller, Ephraim Osborne, Andrew Pennington, Stephen Perry, Enoch and Silas Severt, John Simmons, and Calvin Testerman. According to Thomas L. Norwood, these men deserted over a disagreement concerning promotions within the company. In all, there were 23 desertions in the month of May. Of that 23, five would stay gone permanently. Most of the others would return by September of that year. F. M. Nixon wrote home on May 20: "32 or 33 men runaway from the 37th NC last night[,] all out of one company ... they took their arms and Ammunition. I don't know all this to be true But I suppose it is." Going home was on the minds of many. Bennett Smith wrote on the seventeenth: "There was Six runaway out of Hortons oald company a few nites ago & I think there is several more a fixing to runaway the first opportunity[.] I don't think I will go yet[,] I want to wait fore the biggest crowd & then I will go[.]"[18]

Not long after the battle, the members of the Thirty-seventh gathered to vote on their nominations for the "medals and badges of distinction as a reward for courage and good conduct on the field of battle." According to General Orders Number 93, a presidential act, the men — non-commissioned officers and enlisted men — were to gather at the first dress parade after a battle and, by a majority vote, select the soldier who had demonstrated "courage and good conduct" in the recent battle. Each company was allowed to select one man. The nominations were then forwarded to the president. "If the award [should] fall upon a deceased soldier," the order continued, "then the badge thus awarded him shall be delivered to his widow ... or ... to any relation...." Those that the Thirty-seventh nominated were:

Company A . . . . Pvt. William J. Goss
Company B . . . . Sgt. Joel E. Fairchild
Company C . . . . Sgt. Benjamin F. Brown
Company D . . . . Pvt. John L. Austin
Company E . . . . Pvt. John E. Coffee
Company F . . . . Pvt. William Kilby
Company G . . . . Cpl. Jesse A. Robinett
Company H . . . . Sgt. George W. McKee
Company I . . . . Sgt. John Tally
Company K . . . . Pvt. M. D. L. Parsons

A few months after the men had been selected, General Orders Number 131 was published, stating that the government had experienced difficulties in procuring the medals and badges. Instead, the names of the soldiers would be published on a "Roll of Honor." This roll was to be read at the first regimental dress parade after the roll was published, and published in at least one state newspaper. This was the only time on record that the Thirty-seventh gathered to nominate men for the Roll of Honor.

The last days of May the regiment spent on and off picket duty, watching the yanks in front of them and talking about their comrades who had deserted or died of disease or wounds. Bennett Smith wrote home again on the twenty-eighth from "Camp Gregg" to his "Dear Wif & Child":

> ...I was on picket when I got it [letter] about to miles from hear I had ruther be on picket than to stay in camps I hant no nuse mutch to rite at this time evry thing appears to be still & quiet at this time.... I hear that William Green A. C. Dotson & Williams from Alexander Co has died I hant heard how the rest of the wound is getting a long ... it is a bad time on them the weather is gitting so hot & another thing I don't expect they are more than haf tended two ... our boys keeps running a way their was thirty one run a way about a week a go from Capt Hartzog Co its from Ash they tuck their guns with them their was 3 run a way out of company K nite before las I would be glad they would quit it or awl run a way it makes harder times on the rest of us.[19]

Bennett Smith would not have long to wait to see if they would "quit it or awl run away." While his brothers and friends were on the edge of a little town in Pennsylvania, waiting for the dawn and the most costly battle of American history, he would die, on June 30, 1863, of "hydroxthrus and or dropsy" in a hospital in Lynchburg, Virginia.

9

"Things are faverable for a Glorious Campaign"

June–July 1863

On June 3, 1863, Lee put his Army of Northern Virginia into motion once again. The Confederate general's rationale was to raise enough havoc to cause General Grant to loosen his grip on the Southern city of Vicksburg. Grant and his Federal army were laying siege to this key Southern city on the Mississippi River. Lee also sought to frustrate the plans of the Federals in Virginia for the summer campaign by embarking on a new offensive campaign of his own. The Army of Northern Virginia had scored two resounding victories in the past five months: Fredericksburg and Chancellorsville. The morale of the Southern army in Virginia rose to an all-time high, while two crushing defeats brought the spirits of the Federal forces to a new low.[1]

In the weeks following the affair at Chancellorsville and the death of General Jackson, Lee reorganized his Army. The old Army of Northern Virginia had been composed of two corps, each numbering about 30,000 men, under the command of generals Longstreet and Jackson. The newly reorganized army consisted of three corps: Longstreet's, Ewell's, and A. P. Hill's. This new arrangement made the Army easier to control and maneuver. The old Light Division was placed under the command of William D. Pender and assigned to A. P. Hill's Third Corps.

William Dorsey Pender was born on February 6, 1834, in Edgecombe County, North Carolina. He grew up on his father's farm, spending his time as a boy attending school, working on the family farm, and "enjoying outdoor recreational activities on the flatlands" around the Tar River. Dorsey, as he preferred to be called, worked as a clerk in his brother's store in Tarboro before securing a recommendation to the United States Military Academy from his Congressman, Thomas Ruffin. Pender excelled at cavalry tactics and mathematics at West Point, and had as his classmates the likes of J.E.B. Stuart, Stephen Lee, John Pegram, Otis Howard, and Custis Lee. Pender graduated from West Point on July 1, 1854, and was assigned to the Second Artillery and stationed at Fort Myers, Florida. Later he was transferred to the First Regiment of Dragoons and stationed in New Mexico. He married Fanny Shepperd, of Good Spring, North Carolina, on March 3, 1859. Pender resigned his commission when his native state of North Carolina left the Union, and entered Confederate service as Colonel of the Third, later the Thirteenth, North Carolina Troops. Pender was promoted to Brigadier General on June 3, 1862, when he was given the brigade in A. P. Hill's division. Promoted to Major General on May 27, 1863, he was wounded four times; the last, received at Gettysburg, would prove fatal.[2]

Major General William D. Pender (courtesy of the Library of Congress).

The last days of spring found the Thirty-seventh's troops entrenched on the heights overlooking Fredericksburg. They, along with the rest of A. P. Hill's corps, were entrusted with keeping the pressure on Hooker's army and to counter any sudden Federal moves toward Richmond. A Federal offensive was indeed a likelihood. Since two of Lee's three corps were being sent north, Hooker perceived an opportunity to seize Richmond, and had sent numerous messages to Washington to that effect. Ewell had already left, and Longstreet was soon to follow. On June 5, portions of the Federal VI Corps started to re-cross the Rappahannock River on their pontoon boats at Franklin's Crossing in order to reconnoiter the Confederate position. The Thirty-seventh, along with the rest of the brigade, was rushed from its encampment near Hamilton's Crossing to counter this new Federal threat. After enduring an all-night march, the Thirty-seventh advanced against the Federals. The Sixth Vermont, of Grant's brigade of the Second Division, had formed a skirmish line in a "semi-circular position, the right and left resting on the river...." The Tar Heels advanced up the Bowling Green Road and made contact with the Vermont troops near the Bernard house, driving some of the Federal soldiers off of the road. The small skirmish slowed, until the firing completely died away. Excluding the occasional shell from the Federal side, the Thirty-seventh spent the next week and a half in a quiet camp, enduring "weather [that was] was dry here," in the words of one member of the Thirty-seventh, "but it suits us very well that has to be in the ditches."[3]

The Federal forces would slip back across their pontoons, which were then dismantled, on the evening of June 13. The Thirty-seventh, along with the rest of Pender's division, left its position on the heights overlooking Fredericksburg on Tuesday, June 16, and moved to join up with the rest of the army, passing the battlefield of Chancellorsville on the Orange Plank Road and crossing the Rapidan at Eli's Ford. The weather played an influential role in their movements. The unusually hot summer wreaked havoc on the men's endurance. Lieutenant Lewis Battle of Company D estimated that three-quarters of the men had succumbed to some form of exhaustion during the march. The severe weather even claimed the life of at least one member of the Thirty-seventh, Private Andrew Baird of Company E. In addition to the heat, the troops had to contend with sudden severe weather that further impeded their progress. Late on the seventeenth they passed through Culpeper. The weather turned from heat to rain, then to hail and sleet on the night of the eighteenth, and made traveling difficult on muddied roads.[4]

The Thirty-seventh crossed the Blue Ridge Mountains at Chester Gap. Both the improving weather and their surroundings served to improve morale. The change of scenery must have reminded many of home. Lieutenant Battle said it was "the prettiest country I ever saw." The column would reach Front Royal on the twentieth, crossing over both forks of the Shenandoah River. On June 22, General Lee ordered Hill's corps across the Potomac. They reached Shepherdstown on June 23 and began fording the Potomac on June 24. General Hill would issue a proclamation to his men: "We will move at 2 o'clock to cross the Potomac and conquer a glorious peace on their own soil!"[5]

"I never saw troops march as ours do," wrote General Pender to his wife. "They will go 15 to 20 miles a day without leaving a straggler and hoop and yell at once." It rained on the twenty-fourth, as the Tar Heels crossed the river under the watchful eyes of General Lee, and the rain continued intermittently throughout the twenty-fifth. They arrived in Hagerstown in the rain that same day. One British observer would write his reflections of Pender's men around this time: "The soldiers of this Division are a remarkably fine body of men, and looked quite seasoned and ready for any work. Their clothing is serviceable ... but there is the usual utter absence of uniformity as to colour and shape of their garments and hats; grey of all shades, and brown clothing, with felt hats predominant."

On the morning of the twenty-seventh, Hill's corps arrived at Chambersburg, turned east, and proceeded to Fayetteville, Pennsylvania, where they were ordered, after covering 157 miles in twelve days, to rest, wash their clothes, and to procure food from the locals. For the first time in several months the Confederate soldiers were, in the words of one historian, "living off the fat of the land." The lean Tar Heels had plenty of eggs, milk, beef, chicken, molasses, butter, and pork.[6] One Lieutenant of Company G wrote home:

> Yesterday and the day before our soldiers plundered far and wide — taking butter, milk, apple-butter, fruit, chickens, pigs and horses and everything they could get their hands on. The people are frightened out of their senses "take anything you want but don't hurt us" is their cry. They are afraid to protest against anything. It is the most beautiful country you ever saw, the neatest farms, large white barns, fine

houses, good fences. The whole county is covered with the finest crops of wheat, such wheat as is not seen in our country.

Yesterday, however, Genl. Lee sent an order around that all stealing, and plundering should be punished in each case with *death*. [T]hat officers should bee held accountable for the execution of his orders, that he made war upon armed men — not upon women and children. The plundering will be stopped now. I never saw people so submissive and badly scared as these people in my life. It must be conscience. They know how their soldiers have desolated Virginia and they fear that ours will retaliate....

William G. Morris, who was appointed Lieutenant Colonel of the Thirty-seventh on May 29, 1863, was trying to catch up to the regiment. He had been wounded in the foot at Chancellorsville and was returning from convalescent leave. On June 24 he wrote his family from New Market, Virginia: "I am well & this far on My way to My command. they was at Berryville yesterday on the March for Harpers ferry.... Our Cavalry are in Meryland & pinsilveny Gathering Cattle & Horses & things are faverable for a Glorious Campaign...."[7]

The Thirty-seventh rested at Fayetteville until the twenty-ninth. That morning the Thirty-seventh was inspected, along with the other regiments in Pender's division. During this time, many men took the opportunity to express their thoughts in letters and diaries that reveal both their everyday pursuits and their anxieties about the possibilities of battle. William D. Alexander, who served most of the war as a hospital steward (even though there is no record that he was ever officially appointed), began a diary on June 29. He wrote:

This is June 29, 1863. We are in Penn. near Chambersburg the troops are in fine spirits we are expecting to get ordered to move every minute. I eat a nice dinner yesterday and kissed a pretty lady.... We lay all day in suspense.

30th we marched early and rapid on the Balt & Pittsburg pike passing the remains of Stephens Foundry halted near Cashtown the enemy reported in front a fight expected tomorrow.[8]

Iowa M. Royster, who had been transferred from Company E, Ninth Regiment, North Carolina State Troops (First North Carolina Cavalry), to Company G of the Thirty-seventh NCT, wrote to his mother on June 29 from Chambersburg. "Dear Ma," he would begin:

I suppose you saw in the "Progress" newspaper a notice of my appointment to this regiment. It was quite unexpected. I had made a request to Capt. Nicholson of this reg't to recommend me to the Co. but did not expect any good result. When I read the appointment in the newspaper I was under arrest in my old company. In a day or two came a note from Col. Barbour of the 37th asking Col. Baker to send me to him as I had been appointed in his regiment. Col. Baker released me from arrest and sent me on with many expressions of goodwill, and wished for my future success....

I am the only office present in the company. The men are very clever. There is not one among them who swears or uses any profane language. There are about twenty four. When the co. started from N.C. it numbered 126. At Sharpsburg last

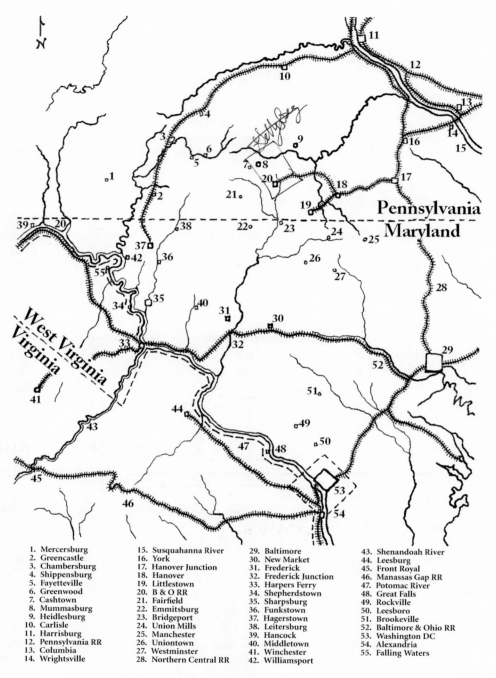

1. Mercersburg	15. Susquahanna River	29. Baltimore	43. Shenandoah River
2. Greencastle	16. York	30. New Market	44. Leesburg
3. Chambersburg	17. Hanover Junction	31. Frederick	45. Front Royal
4. Shippensburg	18. Hanover	32. Frederick Junction	46. Manassas Gap RR
5. Fayetteville	19. Littlestown	33. Harpers Ferry	47. Potomac River
6. Greenwood	20. B & O RR	34. Shepherdstown	48. Great Falls
7. Cashtown	21. Fairfield	35. Sharpsburg	49. Rockville
8. Mummasburg	22. Emmitsburg	36. Funkstown	50. Leesboro
9. Heidlesburg	23. Bridgeport	37. Hagerstown	51. Brookeville
10. Carlisle	24. Union Mills	38. Leitersburg	52. Baltimore & Ohio RR
11. Harrisburg	25. Manchester	39. Hancock	53. Washington DC
12. Pennsylvania RR	26. Uniontown	40. Middletown	54. Alexandria
13. Columbia	27. Westminster	41. Winchester	55. Falling Waters
14. Wrightsville	28. Northern Central RR	42. Williamsport	

Gettysburg, Pennsylvania, and vicinity, 1863.

September only five. The Capt. Went back a few days ago on business expecting to join the company in a few days. I fear the Yankees have got him. He is a member of the Baptist Church. When the company was first made up, the captain the three lieutenants and one private were all preachers. Every regiment in the brigade has a chaplain; I heard a sermon yesterday. In this brigade are the 18th, 7th, 33rd, and 37th and 28th reg'ts. I find a great many old acquaintances among them, and on the whole have quite a pleasant time.

Everybody told me that my feet would be blistered, but I have been marching nearly a week and have experienced no inconvenience, though several men have fallen by the road. There is no straggling. All are compelled to keep up. Those who are too week or sick ride in ambulances or wagons. Lee has fully the number of men he had at Sharpsburg. Our regiment for instance had only fifty at Sharpsburg, there are about two hundred and seventy five now. The other regiments are the same....

...I don't know what place we shall attack, most seem to think Harrisburg. For my part I want to stay here until the war is over, and take their towns and beat their armies a[n]d live on their people. Lee's men have unbounded confidence in him. The Yankees are in great perplexity — don't know what point to re-inforce — don't know whether Lee will attack Harrisburg, Pittsburg, Baltimore, or Washington. I want to take them all. It is glorious. All the fences that are burnt now are Yankee fences. They'll be willing for us to stay out of the Union hereafter. We've come back to the Union, but not as they expected....[9]

Lieutenant Iowa Michigan Royster, Company G (courtesy of the North Carolina Division of Archives and History).

Lieutenant Colonel Morris had caught up to his regiment by the end of June. On June 29 he also wrote home to his family: "I am well & trust you May all be Enjoying the Same. I reached My comd yesterday & found the Boys in Good Sperrits.... I cant say wheather We will have to fight heare [near Chambersburg] or not. Genl Ewell is Some Distance ahead of us. We came to this place Night before last...."[10] On June 30 the Thirty-seventh moved out of Funkstown at five A.M. in the rain and headed in the direction of Cashtown, crossing through the passes in South Mountain, and past the smoldering ruins of Thaddeus Stevens's ironworks. General Lee was seeking to reunite his scattered army at Cashtown. Also on the thirtieth, General Heth sent the brigade of Pettigrew to Gettysburg to search for supplies. Pettigrew's brigade ran into the Federal forces — two cavalry brigades under Brigadier General John Buford — on the outskirts of the town. Pettigrew retired before the Federal forces and made reports of his observations to both Heth and Hill, neither of whom believed the North Carolinian.

The quiet period of rest in the beautiful countryside would come to an end on the evening of June 30. The men of Pender's division were ordered to cook one day's ration and be prepared to move at 5 A.M. Most of the men nearing the field where America's greatest battle would be fought awoke to a light drizzle on July first. The sun reappeared two hours later and the humidity began to grow oppressive. Long before the Thirty-seventh became engaged in the first day's fighting, the men could

Reference this in the fiction section and mention this in the non-fiction area not just about the 37th but other regiments.

hear the early stages of the fight, as Heth's division, which they were supporting, made first contact with Federal cavalry and artillery. General Heth had advanced with his division to Gettysburg early that morning, hoping to chase out what he believed to be a few militia. Alexander wrote in his diary: "We have advanced 8 miles the ball is opened 10-o'clock … a hard battle has been fought we are victorious yet this is a calm, but the battle is not over…." The small town of Gettysburg, with its 2,400 residents, held a strategic significance: ten important roads wound through the green fields and wooded hills of southern Pennsylvania to converge on the town.[11]

The Thirty-seventh broke camp and headed out along the Chambersburg Pike about 8:00 A.M. General Heth's advance soon found the Federal cavalry in force on the west side of Gettysburg. Pender's division was deployed along the Chambersburg Pike about three miles west of town, near Marsh Creek, with Scales's and McGowan's brigades south of the road, and Lane's and Thomas's brigades to the north of the pike. After advancing half a mile, the division was ordered to halt near a small stream, where many of the men refilled their canteens. The division advanced another half a mile across the field, where they were ordered to halt behind a collection of Third corps artillery dueling with the Federals from Herr's Ridge. The regiments dropped to the ground, both to avoid the Federal artillery and out of exhaustion due to the heat and humidity. After some intense, see-saw fighting, Heth's division succeeded in driving the Federals, who had been reinforced by infantry, from McPherson's Ridge back to Seminary Ridge. Heth's men were spent, and Pender's division was called upon to continue the attack. "A line of battle was formed," wrote a South Carolina officer in the division, "with General Lane on the right, McGowan's in the center, and General Scales on the left. The left rested on the Chambersburg Pike…." At 3 P.M. Lane re-deployed his brigade, his left now resting upon the right of McGowan, to the rear of Heth's division, to the left of the Chambersburg Pike. He placed the regiments in this order: Seventh, Thirty-seventh, Twenty-eight, Eighteenth, and Thirty-third, with the right of the Seventh resting on the road.[12]

As Heth pulled back, Pender ordered Lane, along with the rest of the division, to go through Heth's division toward Buford and the shattered elements of the Federal I Corps, with each brigadier managing his brigade based on his own judgment. Lane ordered the Seventh to re-deploy on the right side of the brigade to counter the Federal cavalry. The division's action, combined with Ewell's corps's later arrival on the Federal right, would be enough to rout the Federals through town and onto Cemetery Hill, to the south of town.

Lane wrote in his official report of his brigade's participation in the afternoon battle:

> After marching nearly a mile in line of battle, we were ordered to the right of the road [Chambersburg], and formed on the extreme right of the light division. Here I ordered the Seventh Regiment to deploy as a strong line of skirmishers some distance to my right and at right angles to our line of battle, to protect our flank, which was exposed to the enemy cavalry. Pettigrew's and Archer's brigades were in the first line, immediately in our front[.] We were soon ordered forward again…. In advancing,

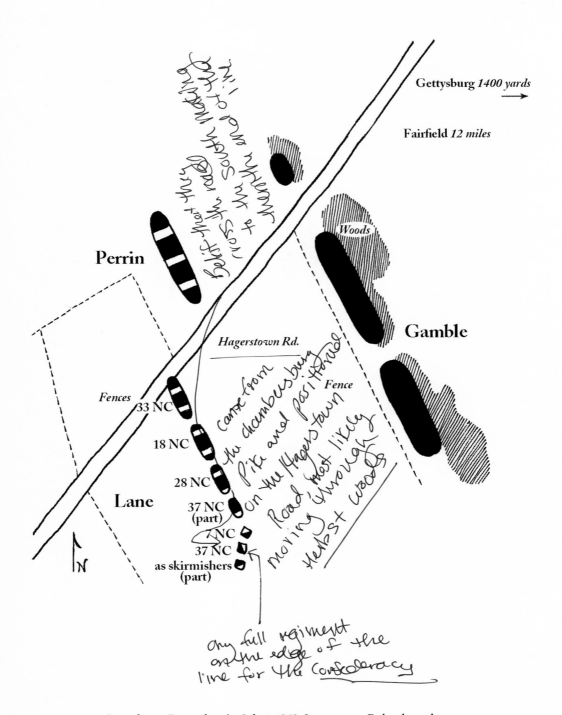

Gettysburg, Pennsylvania, July 1, 1863, Lane versus Federal cavalry.

we gained ground to the right and, on emerging from the woods in which Pettigrew's brigade had been formed, I found that my line had passed Archer's, and that my entire front was unmasked.[13]

Around 4 P.M., Lane continued his advance forward. The Eighth Illinois Cavalry moved in on his right flank, west of Willoughby Run, attempting to outflank Lane. The dismounted Illinois troops were effectively neutralized when Lane sent Captain Daniel L. Hudson, of Company G of the Thirty-seventh, with forty men, to dislodge them. Lane advanced further "when the men gave a yell, and rushed forward at a double-quick, the whole of the enemy's force beating a hasty retreat to Cemetery Hill." The Thirty-seventh then moved into a peach orchard, but was ordered to halt by General Pender.[14] The Yankee artillery opened on the Thirty-seventh and the rest of Lane's brigade. Lane ordered the brigade back behind the stone wall they had taken earlier that day, to afford the men shelter from the yankee missiles. The Thirty-seventh encamped on Seminary Ridge as hostilities subsided for the evening. The first day of battle was over for the Tar Heels.

The night was passed as comfortably as possible, with the weather clear until some early morning showers passed over. The men of the Thirty-seventh awoke to find that "those people" had been entrenching on the high ground in front of them during the night. When the Federal artillery opened fire, Lane ordered the Thirty-seventh and the Eighteenth regiments to the left of Garnett's battalion of artillery to shield them from the Union guns. Pender then ordered Lane to take possession of the sunken road in their front, and to drive the yankee skirmishers from it. The assignment was placed under the command of Major Owen N. Brown of the Thirty-seventh. Major Brown had been promoted from his position as Captain of Company C only a month previously. Lane wrote in his official report: "Brown … executed the order very handsomely, driving the enemy's skirmishers from our front."[15]

The enemy was made up of men from the One-hundred-and-thirty-sixth New York and the Seventy-third Ohio. The Confederates took the fence flanking the road, but were harassed by Federal artillery fire from Cemetery Hill. It was probably during this time frame that First Sergeant Joel E. Fairchild (Company B) was wounded. According to a family story, an incoming artillery round was rolling along the ground toward Fairchild. When he attempted to stop the round with his foot, the ball was both moving faster and was heavier than he thought, and it broke his ankle. The Federals soon mounted a counterattack and "followed the retreating rebs too far." The Confederates re-formed and pushed the Federals back again; this time the Union forces took heavy losses. The Thirty-seventh took up positions in the sunken road behind a skirmish line. William D. Alexander sketched in his diary later that day: "all was quiet until four PM when a furious cannonading commence on the right and was carried along the entire line an awful fight was kept up until 9 PM the result is not known[.]"[16]

The Thirty-seventh, along with the rest of Lane's brigade and Pender's division, was ordered to support an attack by Rodes. About this time, near sunset, Captain Thomas, of Pender's staff, informed Lane that Pender had been wounded, and Lane

[handwritten margin notes:]

Day 1

cavalry cooperated flanking morning fight

not much action for them but important nonetheless.

Enough to note a difference, however. They were the official left end of the Union line of fighting was placed in charge of the division, with the orders to advance if an opportunity presented itself. Major General Pender's wound, a shell fragment in the leg, would prove fatal, claiming his life on July 18 in Staunton after he failed to recuperate from an amputation. Rodes's night attack never fully materialized, and the Thirty-seventh spent another night in the field.[17]

Patchy fog and dark clouds greeted the men of the Thirty-seventh on the morning of July 3rd. The night had been warm, with temperatures in the seventies. The rising sun quickly burned off the fog and the day began to heat up, promising a hot and humid afternoon. The regiments of Thomas's and Scales's brigades were involved in heavy skirmishing early in the morning, "requiring at times whole regiments to be deployed to resist the enemy and drive them back." General Lee's first plan of attack for July 3 had been curtailed. Lee had wanted Longstreet to continue with his attack on the Federal left, while Ewell attacked on the Federal right. Longstreet was in the act of repositioning his troops when his orders arrived and was not in a position to renew the attack of July 2. Lee then chose to assault the center of the Federal lines with Longstreet's whole corps. Longstreet protested, saying that the use of two of his divisions, under Law (who had replaced Hood) and McLaws, would leave the right flank of the Confederate line exposed and open to a counterattack. General Lee relented, and assigned two of Hill's divisions to Longstreet for the attack: Heth's, commanded by Pettigrew, and half of Pender's, commanded by Lane.[18]

General Lee's plan had some credence. The Confederates believed in a number of factors that, if true, would act in their favor: the Union center appeared weak, based upon the flank attacks of the previous day and earlier that morning; the terrain between the Confederate lines and the Emmitsburg Road would partially safeguard the advancing Confederate troops; the artillery of the Confederates would suppress the artillery of the Federals; the Confederate infantry would be supported by their artillery; the right and left flanks of the attacking Confederate force would be secured from Federal attack; and there "was historical precedence for the tactical plan from Napoleon III's victory over the Emperor Francis Joseph of Austria near Castiglione, Italy, at the 1859 battle of Solferino."[19]

Later that morning, Lane was ordered to move to the right with two of the four brigades under his command and report to Longstreet. About noon, the Thirty-seventh, with the rest of Lane's and Scales's brigades, moved into position to the rear of Marshall's brigade of Heth's division, and behind the batteries of Wingfield, Graham, and Wyatt. The infantry was commanded to keep out of sight until orders were received to advance. General Trimble was ordered to take over the command of the small division, and Lane returned to the command of the brigade. Colonel Avery, who had been in command of the brigade during Lane's absence, returned to his regiment.

Isaac Ridgeway Trimble was born in Culpeper County, Virginia, on May 15, 1802. During his 61 years prior to the battle of Gettysburg, he had graduated from West Point, served 10 years in the regular army and 29 years as a engineer for several Eastern and Southern railroad construction projects. At the outbreak of the war,

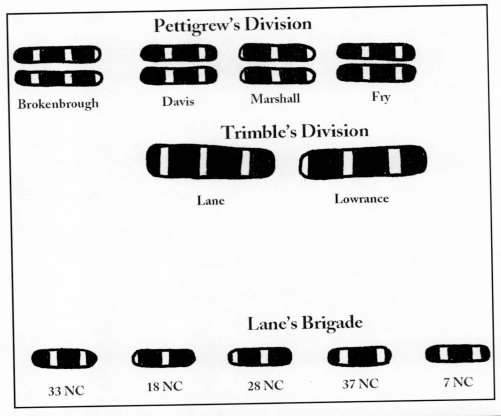

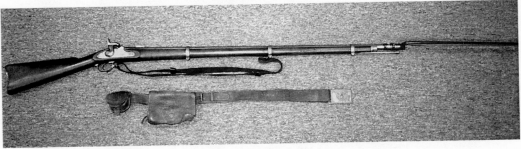

Top: The division and brigade placement, noon, July 3, 1863, Gettysburg, Pennsylvania. *Bottom:* 1861 Springfield, cartridge box, cap pouch, and belt reportedly worn by a member of the Thirty-seventh during the battle of Gettysburg (courtesy of the American Military Museum of Gastonia).

he was commissioned a colonel of engineers in the Virginia state forces. On August 9, 1861, Trimble was appointed a brigadier general and assigned a brigade in Ewell's division. He was wounded in the battle of Second Manassas and was unattached at the time of Gettysburg, having been promoted to major general on January 17, 1863. His wound on the third day cost him a leg and months in a Federal prison. He would not take active field command again.[20]

As Lane returned to his brigade, Trimble and Lee rode over to inspect the brigades of Lane and Lowrance (who had replaced the injured Scales), and Heth's division under the command of Pettigrew. Seeing many of the men with wounds and bandaged heads, Lee remarked to Trimble: "Many of these poor boys should go to the rear; they are not fit for duty." General Trimble had only about 1,533 men present in both brigades. He recorded what happened next: "On taking command of these troops, entire strangers to me, and wishing as far as I could to inspire them with confidence, I addressed them briefly, ordered that no gun should be fired until the enemy's line was broken, and that I should advance with them to the farthest point. Lieutenant Wiggins (Company B), after the war, also recalled the moment when Trimble "rode down the line and halted at different regiments and made little speeches— saying he was a stranger to us and had been sent to command us in the absence of our wounded general, and would lead us upon Cemetery Hill at 3 o'clock." General Longstreet also inspected the lines at least twice before the attack began.[21]

At 1:00 P.M., Sgt. W. T. Hardie and his Alabamians fired one of their Whitworths located on Oak Hill, a couple of miles to the north of the Federal line. Brown's section of the Third Company of the Washington Artillery fired next; these two shots commenced the artillery barrage. One-hundred-and-forty-four Confederate guns then opened upon the Federals. "One of the severest artillery duels the world has ever known," recalled one officer of Company B. The Thirty-seventh was positioned in the woods along Seminary Hill, with the shelter of the woods affording them some protection from the shells. Lieutenant Wiggins would recall that the "earth fairly shook for two hours...."[22]

The artillery "firing ceased almost as suddenly as it had commenced and infantry moved forward," recalled the Lieutenant. Lane's brigade moved out of the protection of the woods and began the arduous journey across the field at about 3 P.M. William Alexander wrote: "3 P.M. we are charging the heights." Pettigrew's division, in front of the Thirty-seventh, was composed of (from left to right) Brokenbrough's Virginia brigade, Davis's North Carolina and Mississippi brigade, Pettigrew's (under Marshall) North Carolina brigade, and Archer's (under Fry) Tennessee and Alabama brigade. In their rear were the brigades of Lane and Lowrance. Lane's brigade was composed of, from left to right, the Thirty-third, Eighteenth, Twenty-eighth, Thirty-seventh, and Seventh. "It was a grand site," continued Wiggins, "as far as the eye could see to the right and to the left two lines of Confederate soldiers with waving banners pressing on into the very jaws of death." The Thirty-seventh passed through the batteries that had been pounding the Union positions a mile away and started down the slope of Seminary Hill.[23]

Little realizing that they were about to take part in one of the most famous charges in history, the Thirty-seventh, along with the rest of Lane's brigade, soon began a complicated series of actions, taking just over an hour. What later would come to be called Pickett's Charge or the Pickett-Pettigrew-Trimble charge was, for the men of the Thirty-seventh, often a confused muddle of events that, even in retrospect, is often difficult to clearly sort out.

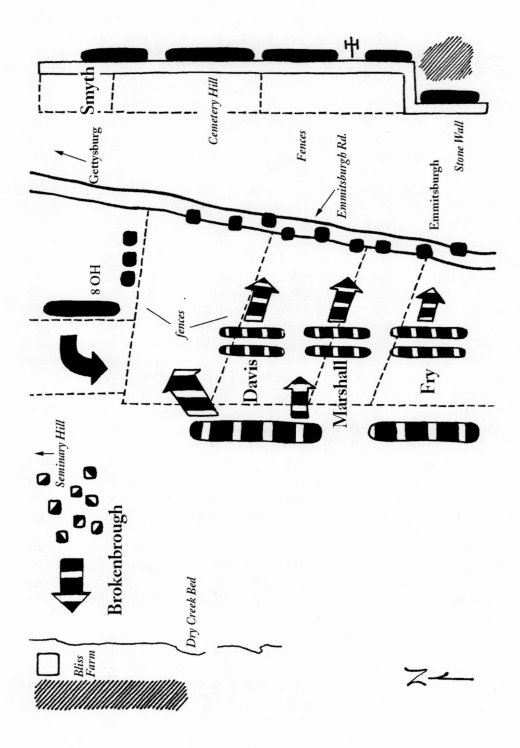

Lane's brigade was positioned 140 yards behind Marshall's North Carolinians and Davis's Mississippians, a distance that General Trimble thought "sufficient … to prevent the adverse fire raking both ranks as we marched down the slope." In front of the Thirty-seventh was one of its sister units, the Eleventh North Carolina State Troops, the "Big Bethel" regiment. Both the Thirty-seventh's former Colonel, Charles C. Lee, and its current brigade commander, James H. Lane, had served in this regiment when it was known as the First North Carolina Volunteers. While the dynamics of the Bethel Regiment had changed, Lane probably could have found some familiar faces among its thin ranks. All the regiments were under heavy, long-range Federal artillery fire from the start of their long march. The Virginians of Brokenbrough's brigade were one of the first units to falter under the artillery and musket fire of the Federals on their left, primarily the Eighth Ohio and the One-hundred and Twenty-fifth New York. The flight of these Virginians, along with other members of Pettigrew's command, would have demoralized Lane's brigade if the men of the Seventh had not leveled their bayonets and forced the panicked soldiers to move around the right flank of Lane's brigade. The Thirty-seventh continued its advance past the smoldering ruins of the Bliss farm at the double quick, "press[ing] rapidly forward and in spite of numerous obstacles, such as fences, ditches, &c." General Trimble, who was riding to the left of the Thirty-seventh, watched in amazement as Marshall's brigade entered a creek bottom that ran through the Blisses's orchard. Most of the left wing of Marshall's command, composed of the Eleventh and Twenty-sixth North Carolina Troops, did not emerge from the shelter, while the right wing, the Forty-seventh and the Fifty-second North Carolina Troops, continued to charge uphill.[24]

Meanwhile, in addition to causing confusion and disorder, the disintegration of Brockenbrough's brigade had an even more devastating effect upon Lane's brigade, as the Virginians' absence exposed the left flank of Lane's brigade to direct Federal fire. The Federals took advantage of this opening and took a position at a stone wall on the left flank of Lane. Lane moved ahead, and "without even halting, took position on the left of the troops [Pettigrew's] which were still contesting the ground with the enemy. My men never moved more handsomely." As Lane and his men reached the Emmitsburg Road, he ordered his brigade to a left oblique to bolster up that flank and counter the Federal threat to his flank. The Seventh and half of the Thirty-seventh did not follow the order for the left oblique because they were in a small depression in the landscape. Instead of following Lane's orders, they followed a conflicting order issued by General Trimble over on their right for a bayonet charge and continued straight ahead. Trimble did not realize the gravity of the flanking maneuver taking place on his left and saw an opportunity for an effective advance. Federal artillery, under Captain William A. Arnold's Battery A, First Rhode Island, and Lieutenant George Woodruff's Battery I, First U.S. Artillery, opened with canister upon what was left of Pettigrew's and Trimble's divisions, causing some con-

Opposite: The brigade in the Pickett-Pettigrew-Trimble charge, Gettysburg, Pennsylvania, July 3, 1863.

fusion and delay. As the North Carolinians finally entered the Emmitsburg Road, they were getting raked from both the front and the left. Col. Franklin Sawyer of the Eighth Ohio wrote:

> ...the front of the column was nearly up the slope ... when a suddenly terrific fire from every available gun, from the Cemetery to Round Top Mountain. The distinct, graceful lines of the rebel underwent an instantaneous transformation.
> They were at once enveloped in a dense cloud of smoke and dust. Arms, heads, blankets, guns and knapsacks were thrown and tossed in to the clear air.

As the Confederates approached Emmitsburg Road, they quickly knocked down the first fence and poured into the two-foot road bed. But the second fence proved to be better built and halted the advance. Many of the men started firing from the road. Some men simply quit, dropping to the ground and hoping to survive the furious onslaught of death and destruction; while some of these demoralized troops would later be captured, others would make their way to the rear, eventually rejoining their units. Others kept going.[25]

General Trimble, who had followed the right part of the division, looked into the smoke and called out to an aide, "Charlie, I believe those fine fellows are going into the enemy's line." About this time, as the general was riding near the fence, a bullet struck him in the left leg and wounded his horse as well. As he tried to gain control of his wounded mount, he sent a message to Lane: "General Trimble sends his compliments to General Lane, and wishes him to take charge of the division, as he has been wounded." The aide further added: "He also directs me to say that if the troops he had the honor to command today for the first time couldn't take that position, all hell can't take it." Trimble would lose his leg and spend the next 20 months in a Federal prison.[26]

Part of the Thirty-seventh veered off to the left to contend with the threatened left flank and to bolster what was left of Pettigrew's line. The other part, the right wing containing at least companies A, K, and G, along with the Seventh regiment, continued to advance to their front, crowding part of Lowrance's brigade. A chaplain of the Fourteenth Connecticut wrote, after the war, about the rebs in his front (Lowrance and part of Lane):

> Our men were ordered to withhold their fire until the Confederates were across the Emmitsburg road. As soon as the Confeds. began to climb the hither fence the men opened fire upon them. As many were armed with Sharps' rifles, the distance, about 270 yards, was an easy one for effectiveness with veterans, and indeed it was for the Springfield rifles the others used, and the result was a dreadfully bloody one.

One section of the fence along the road, measuring 14 inches by 16 feet, was perforated by 836 minié balls. As the right wing of the Thirty-seventh approached a fence at the base of Cemetery Hill, Lieutenant Thomas L. Norwood of Company A "advanced firmly and cheerfully to within thirty yards of the enemy's work, where we encountered a plank fence. Several officers, myself among the number, sprang over the fence,

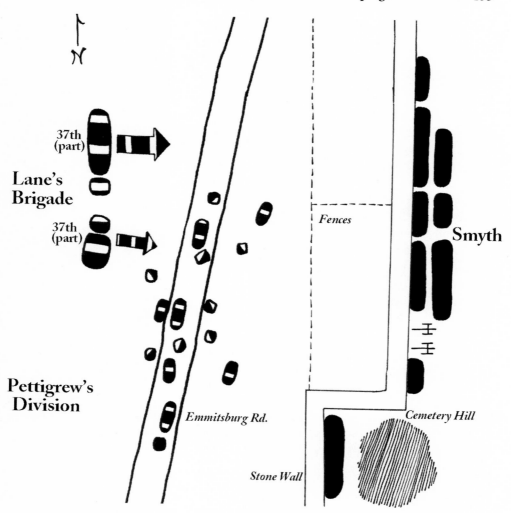

Lane's Brigade

37th (part)

37th (part)

Pettigrew's Division

Fences

Smyth

Emmitsburg Rd.

Cemetery Hill

Stone Wall

The Thirty-seventh splits, July 3, 1863.

followed by the whole of the command, so far as I know. I rushed forward thinking the day was ours, and when within twenty yards of the enemy's works was called by Lieut. Mickle who told me that our line had fallen back." Right after Mickle called out to Norwood, Norwood was struck in the chest, Second Lieutenant William N. Mickle of Company K was killed, and Second Lieutenant Iowa Royster, of Company G was struck in the chest and thigh. Norwood wrote later of Mickle's death: "He [Mickle] and I were shot at the same moment…. He uttered one shriek; was afterwards motionless and quiet, so there is no doubt he was killed." Lieutenant Norwood was dragged over the works by a Federal sergeant, and soon passed out. Pettigrew then issued orders for those who were left to retire from the field.[27]

The left wing of the Thirty-seventh that had followed Lane's order fared no better. The Eighth Ohio came in on their left flank and rear. The Thirty-seventh, along with the rest of Lane's brigade, was forced to retire from the field. And retire they did, in good order. Lane and Lowrance could not muster more than 800 in their two brigades. They retired across the field in a somewhat orderly fashion, the last organized Confederate troops upon the field. They re-formed as they were ordered, in the rear of the artillery on Seminary Ridge, to be ready for the expected Union counterattack.[28]

William Alexander wrote later on the afternoon of the third: "We are repulsed with great slaughter." The casualties for the three days had been overwhelming. Morris, who was in command of the regiment in the absence of the wounded Barber, was captured, and, according to family history, used the logs of a barn to break his sword in half, preventing its being captured by the Federals. Major Owen N. Brown, from Mecklenburg County, was wounded and would later die of his wounds at a hospital in Chambersburg, Pennsylvania. Of the twenty-four company grade officers, nine were wounded and seven were captured, including five wounded men. Second Lieutenant William W. Doherty of Company C was killed, along with William N. Mickle of Company K and Third Lieutenant John P. Elms of Company I, all along the heights of Gettysburg. Most of the Thirty-seventh's casualties from the battle of Gettysburg were received in the Pickett-Pettigrew-Trimble charge on the third. Among these was Private Robert N. Bivens, of Company D, who was wounded in the face and right leg. While separate figures for each day do not exist, we know that, excluding the officers, another 11 were killed, 95 were wounded, 14 died of wounds, 91 were captured, seven were missing in action, and four deserted. These figures do not account for the slightly wounded or the men who went down from the extreme heat. This was the second most costly action for the Thirty-seventh during the war. Third Lieutenant Wesley Lewis Battle was wounded in the left arm during the charge. The arm was amputated. On August 11, this optimistic article appeared in the *Raleigh Daily Progress*:

> A letter has been received by one of his parents from Lt. W. L. Battle of the 37th Regiment in which he says his left arm was shattered by a ball just below the shoulder and that three or four inches have been taken out. A note was kindly appended to the letter by Lt. Battle's attending surgeon, who says he is doing well and unless something unforeseen occurs he will be able to leave the hospital at Gettysburg in a few weeks. It may be a consolation to those who had friend or relation left wounded in Pennsylvania to know that these officers met with very kind treatment from the surgeons and nurses into whose hands they fell. We have reason to hope many others have fared as well.

Battle died in Gettysburg on August 22. He was not the only soldier who clung to life in a yankee hospital, only to die long after the guns of Gettysburg had fallen silent. Second Lieutenant Iowa M. Royster, of Company G, was also wounded. As he lay at the base of Cemetery Hill, a chaplain of a Maine Regiment heard him cry out, calling "Dr. come here." The minister went to Royster and found him "fearfully wounded...." The chaplain told Royster that he was not a doctor, "but a minister of Christ." Royster's reply was, "You are the doctor that I need, none other will do me any good now." Royster gave the chaplain his parents' address and asked him to write them of his death. The chaplain took Royster to one of the field hospitals, and "nursed him tenderly." There were high hopes for Royster's recovery, until on July 15 "a sudden ... hemorrhage carried him off." The chaplain would recall that Royster "died trusting in Jesus without a doubt of his acceptance." Royster's body was buried "without a coffin" in the "corner of woods on the south side of Henry Beitler's tenant house." A leather belt with "I. M. Royster" carved on it and a small notebook were interred with his body, and a headboard with his carved initials was placed on the grave. As promised, the chaplain wrote to Royster's father, giving him directions so he could find the grave.[29]

Private Robert Nathaniel Bivens, Company D (courtesy of the North Carolina Division of Archives and History).

After the battle, Gettysburg would become one vast hospital. "I have been in one more battle and received a ball in my hip," wrote Private Smith Barnes (Company G). "I am in the hospital of the enemy doing fine." There were over two-hundred buildings or sites used as hospitals by the two armies during and after the battle. Private Barnes was doubtless taken to one of these facilities, where he penned his letter home to his wife.[30]

The Thirty-seventh moved on July 4 to the rear of Thomas and Perrin's brigades, taking a position near the McMillan house and preparing breastworks and rifle pits. A Federal counterattack was still anticipated. Alexander continued in his diary: "July 4 all quiet we are caring for the wounded; no fight today[.]" That evening, Hill's corps started off first down the Fairfield Road toward the safety of Virginia's soil. Lane's brigade led the Third Corps, with the Thirty-seventh leading Lane's brigade. One officer of Company B recalled seeing both General Lee and General Hill riding in front of the Thirty-seventh the entire day. Alexander continued:

> ...at dark we took up a retreat it rained all night we moved very slow[.]
> 5th at 10 AM we halted at Fairfield to eat & rest we moved agan at 4PM firing was soon herd in the rear we wer at night in the road but did not go far.
> July 6 at dawn we are moving up south mountain 5 PM we pased Wainsborough our regt is in advance; quite a compliment to the old 37th (advance guard for Gen Lee & Hill) 7 PM some cannonading in front for 2 hours we may make a fight tomorrow. We camped in four miles of Hagerstown[.]

After enduring rain soaked roads, the Thirty-seventh stopped and bivouacked near Hagerstown on July 7, waiting for the Potomac to recede enough to grant them passage. Federal cavalry had destroyed the bridge over the river three days earlier. The only means of crossing over the river were two flatboats attached by wires. These flatboats were used to remove the wounded and to bring ammunition and other supplies to the Confederates on the other side of the river. The days were spent in rest for the Tar Heels. During the days of July 11 and 12, the men of the Thirty-seventh dug in. Lee firmly believed that Meade was going to pursue him, and he wanted to be prepared for the Federals. The works the Thirty-seventh prepared were on an expanse of hills west of town, fronted by Marsh Creek. The overall Confederate defensive line stretched nine miles, from Concocheague Creek a mile west of Hagerstown to Doensville, near the Potomac River. There was also an inner line covering the river crossings at Falling Waters and Williamsport. Several roads in the rear of the Confederate lines provided access for swift reinforcements anywhere along that line. Two Federal officers described the Confederate works: "the position was naturally strong, and was strongly intrenched; it presented no vulnerable points [and] much of it was concealed from view…. Its flanks were secure and could not be turned." The other would add that the works were "by far the strongest I have seen yet … built as if they meant to stand a month's siege. The parapet was a good six feet wide on top, and the guns, which were very thick, were all placed so as to get a perfect cross fire and to sweep their whole front." On July 12, what was left of the Light Division was combined with Heth's division, General Heth in command. Lane, who had served as division commander for Pender's division, returned to his brigade. Alexander again wrote on the twelfth: "we have made good earthworks, the men are anxious to fight 1PM the enemy are advancing sharp skirmishing is going on the night passed quiet."[31]

Lieutenant Thomas L. Norwood, of Company A, wandered back into camp around the twelfth. A few days later he wrote home of his experiences:

> Richmond, Va.
> July 16, 1863.
>
> My Dear Father:
>   By the mercy of God, I find myself again comfortably quartered in Uncle William's room. In the battle of the 3rd at Gettysburg, I received a wound in the left shoulder, the ball passing entirely through and coming out without wounding injuring bone or leader. I have the use of the arm almost unimpaired, but the wound is a very long one….
>   BUT YOU MUST HEAR ABOUT MY ADVENTURE. I was taken prisoner when I was wounded. I was very near the batteries when I was shot, and undertook to retreat, but fainted from the loss of blood and general exhaustion. So the first thing I knew the Yankees picked me up and hurried over the breastworks and carried me, as soon as I could walk, about three miles to the rear where they kept us until our army fell back from Gettysburg. They treated us kindly and did the best they could towards making us comfortable, but that was not much. There were so many of us that every thing was divided by a long division.
>   For my part, I lost everything, and lay two days and nights on the ground with

nothing on me but a pair of pants and half a shirt, and it raining all the time at that; but I stood it very well and excited the amazement and admiration of friend and foe by my indifference to the unpleasant circumstance.

After our army left the vicinity of Gettysburg they put us in the big college at that place. We got there last Tuesday a week ago. Think the prospect rather gloomy as far as parole or exchange was concerned, and seeing no guard around, I determined to make my escape; so I walk off on the next day after we arrived there on the Chamersburg Pike (the road our army came over) with a student's blouse around me about two hours by sun and went on unmolested until about nine o'clock that night, when I had nearly reached the top of the South Mountain. Here a man who came into the road from a by path hailed me and asked who I was, and where I was going. I gave him an indefinite answer but he would not be bluffed and asked if I wasn't a rebel. I told him plainly, I was. "Ah, then," said he "You have found a friend!"; I am a Southern Rights man, come, go home with me, and I will take care of you.: So off I went with him to his home right on top of the mountain at a distance of four miles from the road, going through torrent, cliffs, and everything else in the pitch darkness until finally at about twelve o'clock we reached his house. He gave me supper or rather his wife did. Next morning he gave me a suit of citizens clothes, such as the laborers there wear. He was a smaller man than I, so you can imagine the figure I cut in his clothes. Then I set out on my journey with nothing that appertained to the army.

I wandered about over rocks, dens, and coves of the earth until I reached the road our army had taken in the retreat. I followed this road until about two hours by sun in the afternoon, everybody taking me for a laborer looking for harvest, for the whole country was turning out harvesting. I frequently fell in with the Yankee soldiers and went along conversing freely and exciting no suspicion whatever. In the late afternoon I came into Waynesboro, which is twelve miles from Hagerstown on the Chamersburg road. Here I stumbled upon the whole Yankee Army!

So just as I was beginning to think my joke about played out, an old citizen hailed me and wanted to hire me to do work on towards the rebel lines in the vicinity of Hagerstown. I agreed and gave my name as "John Knauss!" "Oh, yes, he knew my folks very well!" he being well known locally secured a pass for me from the provost marshall and had it signed by the Brigadier General. With this pass we made our way through the enemy pickets with no trouble, then I gave my abolittionst friend the slip and hurried on to our lines. Our guards sent me to General Johnson, commander of the outpost, who sent me to General Ewell, and he again to General Lee. I arrived at General Lee's headquarters about midnight, having walked a distance of 40 miles. Here I slept until morning, and then went in to see the General.

General Lee received me very politely, got from me the information I had discovered about the Yankee Army which was very considerable for I had successfully reconnoitered their position and found something of their plan of operation. He complimented me upon my adventure and then insisted on my taking breakfast with him, which I accordingly did, sitting by the General in my uncouth garb and feeling at ease....

Next, I reported to Col. Barber who sent me to the hospital here at Richmond. Of corse I will be allowed to stay with Uncle William. I am in robust health and suffering very little from my wound....[32]

Back in the field, Alexander wrote again in his diary on July 13: "It is raining this morning 11 AM no fight yet 9PM we started to falling waters to cross the river after hard march through the mud we crosed the river at 12 oclock on the 14th the enemy dashed up on us at ten this morning 'we took them in out of the wet'. [O]ur men wer fed at night for the first time in three days." A pontoon bridge had been constructed at Falling Waters to help aid in the removal of Lee's men. Lane, in his official report after the campaign, wrote: "The retreat from Hagerstown the night of the 13th was even worse than from Gettysburg." The men in the Thirty-seventh were so tired that they immediately went to sleep as soon as they stopped. About a mile from the river, Heth, who was deployed as the rear guard, was attacked by Federal Cavalry. Lane ordered his "command to fix bayonets, as our guns were generally unloaded, and moved down the road after General Thomas." Heth ordered Lane to halt and re-formed the brigade as a new line of rear guard as he moved the division out. Lane deployed some skirmishers, with the Thirty-seventh being held in the main body. The Thirty-seventh retreated slowly, and they, along with the other members of the brigade, were the last group to cross the Potomac, ending the Army of Northern Virginia's second Northern campaign, and possibly the hopes of the Confederacy for independence.[33]

10

"Able to give the enemy a good fight whenever it is necessary"
August 1863–April 1864

For many members of the Thirty-seventh, the aftermath of Gettysburg brought an unwelcome experience. More than 100 men were captured and sent to Northern prisons. Some, like Lieutenant Colonel Morris, would spend almost two years in incarceration before being released. Others would never leave, dying of one of the many diseases that hovered within the interior of the prison walls. The exchange system, in which a Confederate prisoner was exchanged for a Union prisoner of the same rank, had come to a stop. And the conditions in the prisons were much worse than they had been in June 1862 when another large number of the Thirty-seventh were captured at Hanover Court House. Captured officers of the Thirty-seventh were first taken to Fort Delaware, Delaware. For those not wounded, their stay at Fort Delaware was short, and on July 18 many of the officers were moved to Johnson's Island, Ohio.

Located in Lake Erie, opposite Sandusky, Ohio, Johnson's Island was a three-hundred acre, one-mile-long and half-mile-wide barren island that almost exclusively held Confederate officers. The captured officers of the Thirty-seventh were housed in wooden barracks, with one single wood-burning stove for heat. Each officer slept on a straw tick or mattress, and was allowed three blankets. Lieutenant Colonel Morris would write his wife in August: "the health of the prisoners at this place is verry good. Our quarters are comfortable & rations verry Good. We are not kept in close confinement but have the priviledge of several acres." For those officers that did not have money, nor friends at home, a commissary issued clothing to them. "You should not bee uneasy about me as I am not suffering for anything," Morris would continue. "[A] friend supllied Me with what Clothing I want for the present. Confederate money is Worthless heare Except among ourselves but a friend from Tennessee Supplied me with Some Federal Money." The Confederate officers also had use of a sutler, from whom they could purchase items: "We can buy any thing that we want to Eat or Weare." The officers at Johnson's Island found many things to occupy their time. They had a library of over 800 books and magazines. Many engaged in playing baseball, or carving rings and trinkets from shells and wood. In the winter time, there were snowball battles. Also, there were string bands and theatrical groups that performed regularly.[1]

The enlisted men, such as Private Adam Black (Company D) or Private Henry Tredway, would not have the comforts that the officers would enjoy. After their capture, they too were taken to Fort Delaware. After a few days they were transferred to Point Lookout, Maryland. Point Lookout was situated at the confluence of the Potomac River and the Chesapeake Bay, at the southernmost tip of St. Mary's County, Maryland. It has been described by a later historian as "a low, sandy spit, with a good deal of marshy land, indented with the coves and ponds.... Due to its exposure, the Point is hot in the summer and freezing cold in the winter." The prisoners were kept in deplorable conditions: their clothing was tattered and they were dirty; they never had enough firewood for their thin, smoky tents; every three men shared a blanket; they never had enough food, and the three most common afflictions were scurvy, diarrhea, and lice. A solder in the Sixth North Carolina, Sergeant Bartlett Y. Malone, described the camp in his diary for the last few days of 1863:

> Our rations at Point Lookout was 5 crackers and a cup of coffee for Breakfast. And for dinner a small ration of meat 2 crackers three Potatoes and a cup of Soup. Supper we have non. We pay a dollar for 8 crackers or a chew of tobacco for a cracker.
> A yankee shot one of our men the other day[,] wounded him in the head[,] shot him for peepen threw the cracks of the planken[.]
> All the wood we get to burn at Point Lookout is one sholder tirn of pine brush every other day for a tent[,] 16 men to every tent.
> The 25th was Christmas day and it was clear and cool and I was boath coal and hungry all day[.] [O]nley got a peace of bread and a cup of coffee for Breakfast and a small slice of meat and a cup of Soop and five Crackers for Dinner[,] and Supper I had non.[2]

Over one hundred members of the Thirty-seventh would pass through the gates into the Confederate Prison camp at Point Lookout. Nineteen would perish. They would die of typhoid fever, of chronic diarrhea, of diphtheria, and of pneumonia, or a combination of these things.

Life in a Northern prison was too much for some members of the Thirty-seventh. Private James P. Gwaltney (Company G) took the Oath of Allegiance to the United States and joined the Federal Army. After being assigned to a Federal regiment, he was "sent to the Canadian border to guard the Indians."[3]

For those fortunate enough to survive Gettysburg and the deprivations of prison, life in the army continued. On August 9, another North Carolinian was named to replace General Pender as commander of the "Light Division." Cadmus Marcellus Wilcox was born in Wayne County, North Carolina, on May 29, 1824, the second of four children born to Reuben Wilcox, a merchant, and Sarah Garland. While Wilcox was still young, the family moved to Tipton County, Tennessee. He attended the University of Nashville and was admitted to the United States Military Academy in 1842. He graduated a member of the famed class of 1846, a class that provided several generals to the Confederate and Union armies. During the war with Mexico, Wilcox was breveted for bravery while leading a charge at Chapultepec. After the war he served on garrison duty for a time in Florida, and in 1852 became an instructor of infantry tactics at West Point. Wilcox traveled in Europe in 1858, and in 1859, after his return, published *Rifles and Rifle Practice*, a manual that would benefit the Confederates greatly in the upcoming struggle. On June 8, 1861, while stationed in New Mexico, he resigned his captaincy in the United States Army. Wilcox was soon given a colonelcy in the Ninth Alabama Infantry, and led the regiment during the first

Lieutenant General Cadmus Wilcox (courtesy of the Library of Congress).

battle of Bull Run. On October 21, 1861, he was promoted to brigadier general, and assigned a brigade of Alabamians and Mississippians in Longstreet's division. He led his men gallantly, and on August 9, 1863, he was promoted to major-general and assigned command of Pender's old division, composed of the brigades of Lane, McGowan, Scales, and Thomas.[4]

One may wonder why General Lane, the senior brigadier general in the "Light Division," was not given command. Lane had been in command of the division since Pender's wounding, and also again after Trimble had been wounded and captured on July 3. General Lee simply wrote that "Lane the senior brigade commander of the division is not recommended for promotion...." Lee also would pass over the next senior brigade commander, Thomas, finally recommending Wilcox to President Davis. Wilcox was undoubtedly helped by Congressman Landon C. Hayes; his brother, Congressman John A. Wilcox; and fourteen other representatives, along with the officers of his brigade, who had petitioned the president in February 1863 for Wilcox's promotion to major general.[5]

In the fall of 1863, General Lane organized a group "of picked marksmen and brave men" for a battalion of sharpshooters. The battalion was established by a levy on the five regiments in the brigade for three or four of the finest shots per company. Enough men were gathered to form three companies for the battalion. "Intelligence, sound judgment, accuracy of marksmanship, fidelity to the Southern cause, and unfaltering courage in the trying ordeal of battle were the *conditiones sine qua non*, or necessary qualifications to membership in this command," the commander of another battalion of sharpshooters wrote. The battalion used General Wilcox's *Rifles and Rifle Practice*, and troops were trained using the "American skirmish and French zouave drills."[6]

The first lesson was "in calculating and stepping off distances...." In this first lesson, the men were each brought up to a predetermined point, and a man, or an object the same size as a man, was placed at an unrevealed distance, starting at one hundred yards. As each soldier's name was called, he would step forward and estimate the distance to the target. The distance of the target from the line of soldiers was increased, from one to nine hundred yards, each solder learning what that distance looked like. From sighting practice, the soldiers went to target practice. A target was the size of a man out on the firing range. The targets all had a center bullseye of five inches, within a circle of 14 inches, enclosed by an outer circle of 24 inches. At 100 yards, the target was one inch thick and two by six feet in size. At 500 yards, the target was one inch thick and four by six feet. And at 900 yards, the target was one inch thick, six by six feet. A rifle rest was constructed with a bag of sand on which to rest the rifle. The preferred weapon of the sharpshooter was the British-made Enfield in .577 caliber. If the sharpshooter was lucky, he was able to receive a British-made Whitworth, in .450 caliber, with an accurate distance of 1,500 yards. One by one the names of the sharpshooters were called. They walked to the rest, placed their rifles upon the sandbag, took aim, and fired. Their hits were recorded and a record was kept of their improvements. Besides the practices of estimating distances and shooting at targets, the men drilled in the evolutions of the battalion: how to deploy, how to advance *en echelon*, or by the right or left flanks, how to fight in the woods, an open field, or in the streets of a town. Many of the brigades would form sharpshooting battalions in the coming months. The battalions would prove themselves the elite attacking force that General Lee would need in the last half of the war. Captain John G. Knox of Company A, Seventh North Carolina Troops, was the first commander of Lane's battalion of sharpshooters. Although there is no known roster of men from the Thirty-seventh who served in the sharpshooting battalion, family tradition has it that Solomon V. Cox, of Company A, served within their ranks.[7]

On July 23 the partially revived Tar Heels moved over the Blue Ridge once more, passing through Chester Gap and into the area around Culpeper Court House. A week later, on August 1, information was received that Federal cavalry had advanced on a Confederate picket post. Wilcox formed his division and set out beyond Culpeper, in the direction of the picket post. There was little conflict, and the men bivouacked that night in the field and resumed their hunt the following day. Monday, August 3, was another hot and dry day, and the brigade moved from the area around Culpepper Court House to south of the Rapidan River, near the rail line north of Orange Court House. The Tar Heels were assigned to guard Morton's Ford. General Lee had chosen the area south of the river, near his supply routes, as his defensive line. The southern banks of the Rapidan were steep, with few fords where the enemy could cross. These fords were easily patrolled by small groups of cavalry or infantry. Sometime during the first two of weeks of August, Colonel Barber wrote to the Adjutant-General of North Carolina, informing him of the Thirty-seventh's condition:

> The regiment has lost one hundred and fifty men killed, seventy who have died of wounds, three hundred and two who have died of disease, and three hundred and thirty-two who have been wounded and recovered. Total loss killed and wounded, five hundred and fifty-two; to which add three hundred and fifty-two who have died of disease, and we have a total of casualties amounting to eight hundred and fifty-four men. Fourteen commissioned officers of this regiment have been killed or mortally wounded, and ten others permanently disabled by wounds. This does not embrace the names of those officers who have been wounded but were not disabled by their wounds. There are but six officers in this regiment who have not been wounded, and a large number (both officers and men) have been wounded several times.
>
>   Notwithstanding the heavy loss of my regiment I now have present four hundred and forty-two officers and men, and am able to give the enemy a good fight whenever it is necessary.[8]

The Thirty-seventh's time was not spent in inactivity: there were daily drills, usually company drill in the morning and battalion drill in the afternoon, and inspections, along with troop reviews, for visiting dignitaries, or once for General Lee's daughters.[9]

"We heard ... to Day That North Carolina was a goeing Back in the Union," wrote Sergeant Tally on July 30. What Tally had heard was that William W. Holden, editor of the Raleigh *North Carolina Standard*, had begun to organize anti-war meetings across the state. At first, Holden had urged that peace negotiations begin between the Southern and Northern states. His stance became stronger as time passed, urging individual states to pursue peace with the Federal government. One lieutenant colonel in the Twenty-eighth would write home: "There is much excitement among the NC Troops about the peace talks at home ... meetings have been held in all Regts. & a convention held ... the 12th passed many resolutions denouncing an unconditional peace...."[10]

The meeting for the Thirty-seventh was actually held on August 10. The entire regiment gathered in the camp near Orange Court House, and upon a motion made by Colonel Barber, Chaplain Albert Stough was called to chair the meeting, with First Lieutenant Thomas J. Armstrong (Company K) and Second Sergeant Henry M. Bryan (Company F) appointed secretaries. The object of the meeting was explained by Stough, and the following soldiers were appointed to a committee to draft a resolution:

Capt. William T. Nicholson (Company E)

First Lieutenant John B. Petty (Company F)

First Lieutenant William D. Elms (Company I)

Sergeant Elijah A. Carter (Company A)

Musician John R. Carlton (Company B)

Private John W. Pettus (Company C)

Sergeant Joseph Griffin (Company D)

Sergeant Jonathan Hartley (Company E)

Sergeant Robert M. Staley (Company F)

Private Noah J. Deal (Company G)

Sergeant Robert B. Tucker (Company H)

Private Thomas G. Brown (Company I)

Sergeant William N. Ross (Company K)

While the committee met and drafted the resolution, the soldiers called upon Colonel Barber to speak, and he did so, "in a very happy manner." The committee soon returned with their resolutions, which were read and adopted unanimously. The resolution stated that:

> With profound indignation the course pursued by ... papers in our State in reference to our existing affairs, and that the sentiments enunciated by those journals are in the highest degrees treasonable ... [and that] we can recognize no other basis than the full and complete recognition of our nationality and independence, and that we hereby pledge anew "our lives, our fortunes and our sacred honor" in defense of our rights, our homes and our family altars ... [and] That if actuated by no other nor stronger motive, the blood that our State Troops shed, should have commemorated the cause in the hearts of all true sons of North Carolina.

The resolution also called for delegates to meet with other North Carolina regiments in the Army of Northern Virginia for the purpose of adopting a unified set of resolutions.[11]

A convention of North Carolina Troops in the Army of Northern Virginia was held at 11 A.M. on August 12 at Orange Court House. Among many others present were Lieutenant T. J. Armstrong (Company K) and Private S. W. McKee (Company H) of the Thirty-seventh. Colonel Bryan Grimes, of the Fourth North Carolina State Troops, was called to chair the meeting. A committee was formed, to include one representative from each brigade. Colonel John D. Barry of the Eighteenth North Carolina Troops was elected representative of Lane's brigade. The committee met while the other conventioneers were entertained by speeches from notable orators, and music provided by the regimental bands of the Fourth North Carolina State Troops and the Twentieth North Carolina Troops. The meeting reassembled and the convention adopted the resolution as a whole, ordering that their findings be published in Richmond and North Carolina newspapers. One member of the Thirty-seventh wrote directly to the *Charlotte Western Democrat* concerning the tax in kind issue, voicing his displeasure of those who were "encouraging the enemy by their conduct," and giving credence to the peace movement. The soldier wrote:

> If it ever happens that the enemy's army gets into their midst these grumblers will have cause to complain. What is the tenth of your produce compared with the poor

soldier's time and labor and sufferings? Any soldier, if his conscience would permit him to leave the lines, would be willing to give one-half of all he made to have the privilege of enjoying the comforts of home. Now, croaker, when you begin to think that the tax is rather high, just consider in your mind for a minute what your neighbor, a soldier, pays and never grumbles. If you have any soul at all you will never complain again of "high taxes."[12]

Private Andrew J. Teague (Company K) returned from the hospital in September and continued to write to his wife back in Alexander County. One of his biggest concerns was his possibility for a furlough home. "[I] hope that i will git a furlow sume day yet," he wrote. To try and combat the rising desertion rates among the soldiers of the Army of Northern Virginia, General Lee took two steps. The first was to issue General Order 26, ordering all men absent without leave back to their regiments. The order partially read: "While you proudly boast that you belong to the Army of Northern Virginia, let it not be said that you deserted your comrades in a contest in which everything you hold dear is at stake." Along with this order came a promise of amnesty if the soldiers returned by the end of August. The second phase of the plan was to start offering more furloughs to the present soldiers. "[T]hay air giving furlow in the regment now thay is two men gone home now and thay will be back in a few days and then sume body elce will git to go," continued Private Teague, "and i think if i have good luck i will git [to go home] agin sume day."[13]

General Lee's plan did not work. The offer of amnesty caused more men to desert, since they knew that they would not be punished as long as they returned by the end of the month. First Lieutenant Thomas N. Norwood, now in command of Company A after their captain's capture at Gettysburg, wrote home to his uncle about more of his adventures. After returning from a convalescence leave following his ordeal at Gettysburg, Norwood had journeyed to Ashe County in search of deserters, or, in his words, "to persuade my lost sheep to return to duty...." When he arrived in the state, Norwood found that most of the deserters from Company A had enlisted in a regiment near Saltville, Virginia. "I went and found a good many of them and applied to Col. Peter for their relase; but he refused to give them up until I should come with an order for them from the Secretary of War." Norwood procured his order, and was able to bring back fifteen members of the Company.[14]

General Lee would need to implement sterner measures for the army's deserters, measures that would bring the prescribed sentence of death to soldiers caught and then convicted of desertion. Thorton Sexton (Company A) wrote to his parents back in Ashe County: "tell him [Marion Sexton] to come back hear as quick as he can and tell him not to come under guard for if he does he will be shot and if he will come rite on he will come clear...."[15]

The Thirty-seventh would witness the execution of two members of their brigade, Allen Abosher and Esom Fugit of the Thirty-third. Both of these soldiers had been pardoned before for desertion and had been ordered to report back to their regiment, but had taken the opportunity to desert again. They were captured on August 27 and ordered to be executed on September 19. The entire Light Division would witness the procedure. The division was drawn up into a "hollow square," a formation that contained troops on three sides, with the last side open. The two condemned men, with their hands tied, along with their guards, passed in front of each regiment, to the slow beat of a drum. Abosher and Fugit then were tied to separate stakes, a few feet apart, and were blindfolded. At the command to fire, 24 men detailed as executioners fired their rifle-muskets from a distance of fifteen feet, killing both deserters instantly. Each regiment then passed in review of the bullet-riddled bodies before they were buried, impressing on the minds of the soldiers of the Light Division the consequences of desertion. Chaplain Kennedy of the Twenty-eighth called the gruesome occasion "a very revolting site."[16]

An unofficial gathering of officers and men of the brigade was held at the camp of the Thirty-seventh the day following the executions. Several men offered "temperate and patriotic" speeches to boost the morale of the men and to counter the sway of the anti-war movement back in their home regions. But the desertions and the executions continued. Seven more men were executed the next week, four for desertion and three, from the Thirty-seventh, for misbehavior in the presence of the enemy while the brigade was in line of battle at Fredericksburg, Chancellorsville, and Gettysburg. The three from the Thirty-seventh were Private James S. Greer (Company B), who had deserted first during the battle of Fredericksburg, and then again on March 21, 1863; Private Green W. Ford (Company H), who deserted sometime after February 1863; and Private Sampson Collins, who deserted sometime around the battle of Gettysburg. Private Greer had also sought to persuade two of his nephews, "over which he had unbounded influence," to desert from the Thirty-seventh. All the men were tried by a courts-martial, convicted, and ordered to be executed. Private Greer, in his testimony before the court, stated that Holden's newspaper had provided the motivation for his crime, and that of the others.[17] All seven men were executed on October 6.

The executions would continue on through the fall. Private James Holman (Company F) was convicted of desertion after fleeing from the enemy during the battle of Chancellorsville and deserting again after the battle of Gettysburg. He was captured on October 27, courts-martialed on November 4, and executed on November 14. "Poor fellow!" wrote Chaplain Kennedy of the Twenty-eighth, "his nerves were terribly unstrung; and I fear he was not prepared for his charge. Just before the guard was ready, he asked that I should request them not to shoot him in the face. His wish was respected and he died from the first voley, pierced with three balls in the heart and one in the thigh." As the winter wound to a close, two more members of the Thirty-seventh were brought before the firing squad to answer for their crimes: Jeremiah Blackburn and George Black, both of Company A. Both of these men had deserted four times each. Privates Black and Blackburn were both men who had been with the regiment since its inception. And both men were married with families. Black "was a jolly fellow and applied to be a good soldier...." He had originally been captured at Hanover Court House on May 27, 1862, and when he had been exchanged he deserted. He returned, but deserted again with the large group that left after the battle of Chancellorsville (May 3, 1863). Black was arrested before he could return home, and was imprisoned at Castle Thunder in Richmond. When the proclamation of President Davis was issued that pardoned all deserters who returned to their companies, Black was released. As soon as he was released, he deserted again and returned home to Ashe County. When General Hoke issued a proclamation pardoning all deserters in the state of North Carolina, Black returned to the army, but did not stay more than two months before he was gone again. He was soon apprehended, tried by a courts-martial, and condemned to be shot. Blackburn, who was some kin to Black, shot off his own finger during one of the battles around Richmond in the summer of 1862. When Blackburn came back to the company after his furlough due to his wound, he was detailed to light duty with a hospital. He forged a furlough "from General Lee," and attempted to get back to Ashe County, but was arrested in the process. The pass he had forged was lost, so Blackburn was not tried and was detailed back to the hospital. He once again created a pass from General Lee, this time granting himself a furlough of 1,000 days, and made it back home, but was arrested by militia officers and returned to the army. He deserted once again on March 14, with Black, and they were both arrested at the same time, with three others, after only three days away from camp. They were brought back and placed in the guard house. Black and Blackburn suffered the same penalty: death by firing squad. "God love them," William F. Campbell would write to his wife Jane. He was saddened to inform her that "[G]eorge Black and Jessie Blackburg [sic] is to be shot this day a week to come for disertion in front of this brigade."[18]

While some of the officers, like Norwood, thought that the executions were doing good work keeping the men in the army, others did not seem to care. Private Marion L. Holland (Company H) wrote home that "the men is running away in spite of what they shoot...."[19]

"The talk ... her[e] in camp is that wee are going to advance on the yankes," wrote Thorton Sexton on October 5 to his parents back in Ashe County. Sexton would not have long to wait. Active campaigning would begin once more during those early days of October. General Longstreet's corps had been transferred to the Army of Tennessee, and two Federal corps soon followed to that theater. The Army of the Potomac was in between the Rappahannock and the Rapidan rivers, between Lee's army and Richmond. General Lee sought to turn the right flank of the Federal army and to attack the Army of the Potomac as it was falling back toward Washington. Preparations would get underway on October 6, sending excess baggage to the rear, along with those who were sick in the camps. The Thirty-seventh would march out of camp before daylight on October 8, crossing the Rapidan near Cave's Ford the next day and going into bivouac ten miles beyond the river, on the road to Madison Court House. Around 5 A.M. on the morning of October 10, following a cold and frosty night, the men of Hill's corps began moving out of their encampments, and passed through Madison Court House and on to the northwest towards Criglersville. It had been raining intermittently during the past several days, and would continue as the Tar Heels moved out of Criglersville toward Woodville and

Slates Mill. General Lee ordered Hill's men to be on the road by dawn on Sunday, the eleventh. The Thirty-seventh only covered eight to ten miles over what one member of the brigade called "terribly rough roads, fields, and new road that had been cut by the pioneer corps." The Tar Heels camped for the night northwest of Griffinsburg, and that night, the wagon trains caught up with the brigade, issuing the men three days' worth of rations, which the men prepared and ate.[20]

To date, the campaign had gone much the way that General Lee had wanted it to go. General Meade, fearful of a flanking movement (much like the one that had occurred a little over a year before when General Jackson had captured and destroyed the Federal depot at Manassas), had withdrawn his Army of the Potomac from Culpeper, back up the Orange and Alexander Railroad. It appeared that the Federal army was in a frantic retreat, with the Confederate army in sharp pursuit.

Wilcox's division would not get underway until 8:00 A.M. on the twelfth. Most of the day's journey would be over farm trails and newly created roads. The weather was described as being "cool and bracing" with the road dry from all of the recent rain. The Tar Heels crossed the Hazel River at Hill's Mill where the Thorton River joined the Hazel two miles northwest of Rixeyville, and encamped for the night near Amissville, seven miles from the right flank of the Army of the Potomac. A crossing of the North Fork of the Rappahannock, also known as Hedgeman's River, was planned for the thirteenth, and they would bivouac outside of Warrenton that night.[21]

Around noon on October 14, General Hill arrived at Broad Run, north of Bristoe Station. Below his position, he spied thousands of Federal soldiers waiting to ford the swift-moving stream, while many of their comrades, who had already crossed, awaited them on the far side. It appeared that a solitary Federal corps was within the easy grasp of the lead elements of his divisions. Heth's division was at the head of the column, and Hill sent word to Heth to deploy his men in a line of battle and attack at once.

The Thirty-seventh had been up before dawn that day, marching through the town of Warrenton by the time the rays of sunlight touched the fall colors and the Northern Virginia soil. After a short pause to allow two divisions of Ewell's corps to pass by, the Thirty-seventh headed out on the Warrenton and Alexandria Turnpike. Anderson's division was in the lead, followed by Heth, with Wilcox in the rear. The column continued on through the gap in Baldwin Ridge at New Baltimore. Anderson's division traveled ahead on the Warrenton Turnpike, while Heth and Wilcox turned off the pike and moved toward Greenwich. As the columns of Confederate soldiers moved through Greenwich, they saw signs of the retreating enemy: camp fires were still smoldering and Federal equipment, discarded in the hasty withdrawal, littered the ground. Lane's brigade was still a few miles away as Heth committed two of his brigades, under the watchful eyes of General Hill, to attack the Federal crossing over Broad Run.

As two of Heth's brigades swung forward to attack elements of the Federal III Corps attempting to cross the river, the Confederates were caught on the flank by Federal troops hidden in the woods on the Confederate right. The Confederates were

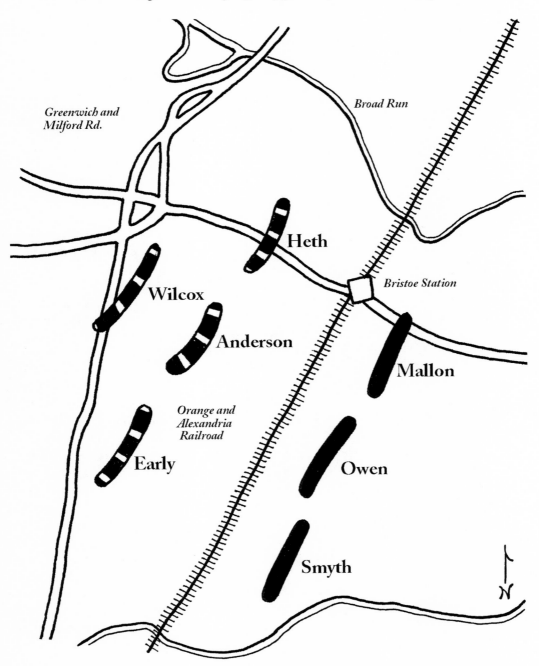

Battle of Bristoe Station, Virginia, October 14, 1863.

forced to retire after a 40 minute "skirmish," losing some 1,300 in casualties and several pieces of artillery. Cadmus Wilcox's division would not arrive on the field until 4:00 P.M., after portions of Heth's division had been pushed back. Wilcox would form his troops into a line of battle and move over the crest of a hill at the double quick, but would arrive a little too late to help Heth's men.[22] He formed his division in the rear of Anderson's division as a support. During the night, the Federal forces slipped across the river, as the rain fell on the men left wounded upon the field.

A cold front passed through the next morning, bringing more rain and cold temperatures, thoroughly drenching the men of the Thirty-seventh. The Tar Heels would have little to chronicle home about the battle. One member of Company I wrote: "we were not in the fight for the first time that our Brigade has ever missed Since I have been in the war...." The Thirty-seventh spent the day in position behind Anderson's division. Wilcox moved his division out around sunset and progressed, in the rain, on a route parallel to the railroad, toward Rappahannock Station, halting at around 11:00 P.M. after covering three or four miles. They would resume their march the next morning, October 16, continuing to follow the railroad tracks for some distance. As they reached Warrenton Junction, all of the regiments in the division received orders to destroy the tracks of the railroad to their front. "Perhaps it may be of interest to know how this was done," wrote Lieutenant Wiggins (Company E) after the war. "The rails were ripped up and pens made of cross-ties, the rails then laid on the pens which were set on fire, the irons soon become red hot in centre, when half a dozen soldiers would seize each end and run to a telegraph post, or tree, and play circus by running rapidly around it — bending the rail three of four times around the post." The regiment continued to march and destroy sections of the railroad throughout the day. That night they were caught in a blinding and violent storm, and on the next day they continued on their mission alongside the tracks.[23]

On Sunday, October 18, the brigade rested for the day, and on Monday they crossed the Rappahannock and made camp a few miles on the other side. "We are camped near Brandy Station where wood and water is plenty," Sergeant Tally (Company I) wrote home to his wife. Some thought that this last campaign during the waning fall days of 1863 would be the end of the active campaign season. "[W]e have been in camp about two weeks," Private Teague wrote home to his wife, "and taking up winter quarters here...." Lieutenant Norwood (Company A) echoed Private Teague's sentiments when he wrote: "the men all have very comfortable quarters built, huts with chimneys ... and covered with boards.... We find it more difficult to get flooring than anything else. I don't call these winter quarters, because it is not winter yet, nor do I know how long we are to stay...." But the commanding generals were not quite finished with active campaigning for the year 1863, and Norwood was soon to find out just how short a time they would have to stay at their new camp.[24]

At dusk on November 7, Federal forces seized Confederate positions at Kelly's Ford and Rappahannock Station. General Meade, under pressure from his government, started on a campaign to drive deep into the Confederate-held territory, hoping for a decisive battle against General Lee. Lee withdrew from his now undefendable position to a new line in the earthworks south of the Rapidan River. The Thirty-seventh fell back towards Culpeper Court House and entrenched. Soon General Lane received orders to move forward to the Warrenton Road and to stop a detachment of Federal cavalry. It is unclear as to whether the Thirty-seventh or the Eighteenth were the ambush force, but the Federal cavalry was forced to retreat after suffering minor casualties. The Thirty-seventh continued its retreat the next day in the cold and snow, fording the icy waters of the Rapidan. The regiments of Lane's brigade went into winter quarters in the vicinity of Liberty Mills.

The next week was spent in constant anticipation of either a Federal attack on the Confederate works, or of a Confederate offensive to drive the Federals out of the area. "We Cooked up two days Ration to day," Sergeant Tally again wrote to his wife on November 13, a few days after entering camp. "We are Expecting the enemy to Advance but it is uncertain what they will do [when] they apear." Thorton Sexton (Company A) would add, in a letter dated the same day: "we will have a bully of a fite before long...." The Confederates spent the following days strengthening their field works. General Meade's strategy was to put the Army of the Potomac into motion on November 24. He wanted to march part of his force quickly to the east, cross over the lower fords of the Rapidan River, and swing in behind Mine Run, hoping to capture a portion of Lee's army unawares.[25]

A heavy rain fell on the night of November 23, postponing the Federal advance until the twenty-sixth. On the morning of the twenty-sixth, a thick fog shrouded the valley surrounding the Rapidan River, restricting the views of both the Federal assaulting force and the Confederate pickets protecting the river. In response to the Federal army's movements, General Lee ordered the Confederates to abandon their lines along the upper Rapidan during the night and move eastward. Hill's corps, including the Thirty-seventh, was to use the Orange Plank Road. Before setting out on their march, they were issued three days' rations and ordered to prepare them. The weather was bitter cold, with icicles forming on the men's beards. The brigade left camp at 2:30 A.M., moved east twenty-three miles, and camped in a pine thicket that could render only green wood and old, dry boughs for warmth. Snow soon began to fall on the already cold Tar Heels.

Lane's cold brigade would reach the field on the twenty-eighth and commence to throw up breastworks. Portions of the Federal army soon appeared in their front, and the skirmishing became quite heavy at times. The weather alternated between blinding snow and cold rain for the next few days. Men on picket duty were required to be relieved every half-hour, due to the cold. Wilcox's division was placed in the center of Hill's line, across the Orange Plank Road, with Anderson's division to his right and Heth's division to his left. Some Federal probes found that Hill's left was weak, so on the twenty-ninth, Federal General Warren moved into the area. Hill was quick to respond, shifting his entire corps to the left of the Plank Road. His men quickly started to entrench the new area, working throughout the night. "We had no tools except one axe to each company and made spades of planks," one Confederate of Hill's corps wrote home. "These answered the purpose very well and it took us but a very short time to make a very good entrenchment, for every man worked hard." The night was again extremely cold, with reports of the thermometer dropping below zero. Water froze in the men's canteens. The morning would bring little relief, especially for the Federals, who were under orders to assault the Confederate works shortly after dawn. "Jackson's old corps had worked like beavers all night and kept themselves in a sweat 'to give the Yanks a warm reception in the morning,'" wrote one Federal soldier close enough to the Confederate lines to hear them throughout the night. Wilcox's new lines of defense now crossed over an unfinished railroad.[26]

Federal forces fell into their battle lines at 3 A.M. to await the order to charge the Confederate works. The order never came. As soon as it was daylight enough to see the strong works that the Confederates had built during the night, the Federal commander on that portion of the field called off the attack and sent word back to General Meade that he thought the Confederate lines could only be carried with a large loss to the Federal troops. This was enough to stop the whole Federal assault planned for that morning. Skirmishing would continue throughout the day. When the Federal assault failed to develop by December 1, General Lee began planning for his own flanking campaign. He ordered the divisions of Anderson and Wilcox to the right, opposite the Federal left, which was reported to be largely devoid of works.

Beginning at dawn on the next day, December 2, Hill's men were ordered to advance on the Federal position, only to discover that the Union troops had abandoned their lines during the darkness of the night and retreated across to the northern bank of the Rapidan. With the Federal forces back in their works, there was little left for the Confederates to do but to return to their winter quarters near Liberty Mills. The Confederates had been able to deny the Federals a victory, but in turn had not been able to crush the Union army.

The Thirty-seventh returned to their camp at Orange Court House near Liberty Mills and drew clothing. John Black (Company A) would write his wife on December 4: "I have just drawn a large lot of clothing — 2 shirts pr of drawers and a splendid Woolen shirt — in fact I have more clothes than I care about." Thorton Sexton (Company A) would also write home about the same time as Black, saying that he had also drawn "plenty of clothes and a splendid blanket and ... a excellent pair of shoes."[27]

With the return to their winter camp at Liberty Mills, the Thirty-seventh settled into the more mundane aspects of military life. This would be the third winter they had spent away from home for many of the Tar Heels. But many sought to make it as pleasurable as possible. Lieutenant Norwood would write to his uncle, Walter W. Lenoir, formerly a captain of Company A: "Lt. Carter and myself occupy a tent. We have a neat chimney an[d] fire place, and at night [sit] on our wooden stools enjoying a bright cheerful fire.... I often imagine you sitting in the corner with that old cap on...." Sergeant Tally (Company I) would spend part of his time making mementos for loved ones at home: "I have a ring to send you the first chance [I get]," he wrote, "a nice bone ring." Others would poke fun at visitors in camp. "One of those cries a man with a high hat on is obliged to hear [is] ... 'Hello Mister ! Has your cow gone dry?' or 'I see you wear the church for a hat,' or 'what's the price of butter Mister? I see the churn on your head!'" Added to these outbursts were many types of nighttime activities. "[T]he 37th carries around at night with deafening sounds of laughter and applause," chronicled Lieutenant Norwood.

> The boys have divers kinds of shows at night. Such as the mule: two men with a tent cloth around them in such a position that look a little like the body of a mule: then a big head and ears tail etc. the giant: a man standing erect upon another's shoulders: both wrapped in a cloth; the top man carrying a gun: which looks like a twelve foot man…. Co. A always takes the prize at such games as that. An fighting with the cobs of roasting ears.[28]

Several of the men's winter time activities involved members of the fair sex. At Christmas the writer of this letter wrote of his adventures, from the headquarters of the Thirty-seventh, but left us only his first name, "Tommie":

> No doubt you had a very pleasant time during Christmas. I should like to have been with you. And I wish I was there now to have some fun skating, Providing my gallante would not lead me into such luck as happened a few days ago on the Rapid Ann river while I was skating. One or two of Virginia['s] fair sex were present and it happened that one of the hats of the crowd blew off and went across the river. I of course immediately darted after it. [A]fter having obtained this hat on my return shake came off and I went through the ice in about twenty feet of water. Of course I fell in I let loose the hat. [B]ut soon I got out and found that the damsel had her hat. She (of course) said she was sorry—and (of course) I said it did not matter. ([B]ut it did make a considerable matter for I thought I would Freeze.) She insisted that I should take her shawl. I declined for I knew what the consequences would [be]. [S]he might never get her shawl again. [B]ut she kept insisting I should take it so to my great pleasure she folded it around me. I immediately got on my horse and started for camp. But the best part now … when she put the shawl around me [I forgot] to inquire her name and her place of residence. [S]o there I was—had some lady's large double shawl and I perfectly ignorant of anything about her.[29]

Some of the men continued to occupy themselves with thoughts of the girls at home. Calvin Childers wrote on December 10 to Miss Nancy Welch: "I have nothing interesting to rite at the present only I would be glad to see you…." He would finish with, "no more at present only remember me."[30]

Private William F. Campbell (Company A) would write home a few days later, on December 29, and paint a truer picture of the conditions around the Thirty-seventh's camp in Orange County. "We are suffering without a doubt," Campbell wrote to his "Dear and Loving Wife." "[W]e are drawing flower [rations] but mute [meat] not regular a tall[;] we hante drawn but one rashing of meat in five days until today…." Campbell would write that their ration on Christmas day had been "the more of pound of horse beefe…." He would conclude with, "one pint of flower and nothing with it aint a nuff you now for man a day. Wife if you have anything you can spare and has a chance please send me it. There is many boxes brote to the regt. But there is no chance of buying anything…."[31]

Private Jordan S. Councill wrote home on January 17, 1864, about the boxes sent from home that Private Campbell mentioned. Councill wrote that the officers of Company B & E had appointed men from the two companies to go home and get as many boxes from the soldiers' families as they could get. These boxes often contained articles of clothing and food. Councill wanted "15 or twenty pounds of butter and a bout 2 galons of molases an a bout 2 hams of meat some dried fruit and dried green beans gren aples some onions and some sweere bread," among other things.[32]

Extensive revivals continued to sweep through the army, including Lane's brigade. Nightly prayer meetings, with singing and other "devotional exercises," continued on throughout the camps. One chaplain left this picture of the winter of '63-'64: "One of the most interesting features in this revival is, that the young converts ... take hold of the work, and pray, and frequently exhort in public, any may be seen *conversing* with the *unconverted*...." Some were not that impressed with the services. "Tommie" continued in his letter home: "I went to church last Sunday ... as for the sermon I can preach as good a one myself." On February 7, 1864, General Lee issued General Order No. 24, praising the men for their "proper observance of the Sabbath," and "directing that none but duties strictly necessary shall be required to be performed...." General Lee believed, and justifiably so, that a proper relationship with Christ was just as important to the "personal health and well-being" of the soldiers as to their spiritual lives. "Soldiers!" General Robert E. Lee continued, "Let us humble ourselves before the Lord our God, asking that Christ [forgive] ... our sins, beseeching the aid of the God of our forefathers in the defense of our homes and our liberties, thanking him for his full blessings and imploring their continuance upon our cause and people."[33]

Even with the revivals sweeping through camp, there were still problems. In a letter dated January 20, 1864, Thorton Sexton wrote home to his father, who had recently visited Thorton there in camp, of a thief. Thorton writes: "Marion [Sexton] is still in the guard house. Lieutenant Carter says that Marion will com clear for Cal[vin] Testerman has owned taking the money." Testerman was also of Company A, but from whom the money was taken was not recorded. Testerman was found guilty and sent to a prison in Richmond, sentenced to 12 months of hard labor while wearing a ball and chain.[34]

The winter of 1863-64 was remarkably cold, and at times the men would suffer greatly from exposure. "The weather was so very intensely cold," wrote one private, "that in washing one's face and hands, when a persons dipped his hands into the water before he would get ready to dip again a skim of ice would freeze over the water." Another private in Company K would write: "we heiv veary could wether [here, it] snow heair now about 3 or 4 inches deep and the ether is v[ery] cold." But the soldiers were still likely to have their fun. Both Lieutenant Wiggins (Company E) and Private Collins (Company D) left detailed descriptions of snowball battles that took place on March 23 among the regiments of Lane's brigade. Collins had only recently returned from convalescent leave, for his wound on May 3, 1863, at Chancellorsville. Wiggins would call the affair the "only event of interest that occurred during the winter."[35]

On the twenty-third day of March, the snowball battles began under the command of Lieutenant Colonel R. V. Cowan, of the Thirty-third, who captured the Seventh without a fight. These two regiments then proceeded to the camp of the Eighteenth and demanded its surrender, which they agreed to without a contest. The Thirty-third, Seventh, and Eighteenth then proceeded to the camp of the Thirty-seventh and formed a line of battle about four hundred yards away. Lieutenant Colonel Cowan then sent a challenge to the Thirty-seventh and the Twenty-eighth for battle. The Twenty-eighth quickly created some artillery by "uncoupling a wagon and mounting a flour barrel on each ... of the wagons...." The call to battle was answered and the Thirty-seventh threw out skirmishers and waited for the "enemy" to appear. Soon the enemy "appeared across an open field with a strong line of skirmishers in front...." The enemy drove in the skirmishers posted by the Thirty-seventh and the Twenty-eighth, but the Seventh, Eighteenth, and Thirty-third, who "came to the attack beautifully," were driven back by one volley from the Twenty-eighth and Thirty-seventh. The Thirty-third, Seventh, and Eighteenth re-formed and "made a vigorous assault," causing first the Twenty-eighth, and then the Thirty-seventh, after they had been flanked, to retreat. A second stand was made by the Thirty-seventh and Twenty-eighth in the camp of the former. The battle now became "exasperated and very furious, and the air became very thickly mingled with snow bals, sticks and stones...." The Thirty-seventh and Twenty-eighth then retreated "to our shanties and surrendered" after "a Captain of the 28th Regiment [with] one eye seriously injured, several knocked down with stones, several [in] hand to hand fights and several severely bruised...." Lieutenant Wiggins wrote that his regiment "surrendered to a pot of rice, bacon and corn bread."[36]

Reports were mixed as to how the Thirty-seventh fared with their clothing during the winter of 1863-64. On January 30, Lieutenant Norwood (Company A) reported that about half of his men were barefoot. "I could turn out a handsome company at any time," he wrote to his Uncle, "but more [than] half of the men are entirely bare footed." One of the solutions, Norwood hoped, was the establishment of a brigade shoe shop, for "the relief [of] these suffers." Sergeant Tally (Company I) would write home a few times wanting a new pair of suspenders, and later, a pair of gloves. On January 1, Private Teague wrote home about having just drew "a pair of pants drawers and shirt and a jacket ... [and an] overcoat i gave 9 dollars for it...." But he still wanted his wife to send him a pair of gloves and some socks.[37]

The winter would again bring shortages of food. General Order Number 7, issued January 22, 1864, apologized for the "temporary reduction of rations," but praised the soldiers for their dedication. "Soldiers!" the order continued, "You tread with no unequal step the road by which your forefathers marched through, suffering privation and blood to independence."[38] But no matter how much acclamation was heaped upon them by General Lee, their haversacks were still more empty than they were full.

Lane's brigade would get a welcomed visitor on March 3. Governor Zebulon Baird Vance visited the camp on a rainy and snowy afternoon. In a letter, General Lane left his impression of Vance's visit on March 3:

His appeal to the soldiers to stand by their colors, his enumeration of the qualities of heroes out of whose blood springs nations and empires, and his showing that all things earthly as well as heavenly that are truly worth having must be purchased at the sacrifice of blood, were really grand, and brought tears to the eyes of many of the old battle-scarred veterans.

With his visit, Governor Vance sought to inspire the sagging morale of North Carolina's soldiers. Private Holland (Company H) wrote on March 13, a few days after Vance's visit, that he thought that "the soldiers is getting very tired of this war and seem whilling to except peace on any terms almost...." It was also around this time that the term of three years expired for the men of the Thirty-seventh. There was much talk about reenlisting, even though to not reenlist meant to be drafted. Most supported the measures but some did not, including Private Noah Collins (Company D), who left his thoughts in his diary:

> On the 10th instant I went out with the regiment, when an opportunity was offered it for reinlistment, on which day a majority of the 37th North Carolina Regiment reinlisted for the war by voting for certain resolutions which [w]ere drafted by Captain W. T. Nicholson of Company "E" and two private members from each company in the regiment. The two members sent out of Company "D" were K. M. Hasty and K. M. Dees; but neither I, nor a majority of company "D" reinlisted or voted for these resolutions, but boldly walked out four paces in front of a hollow square against them, amid threats of being published in the Richmond and Raleigh newspapers as revolters, deserters and base cowards.... Colonel Barber ... took a great deal of trouble upon himself in sending papers around for us to sign that our names might not be published; but the most would not sign them; the two clauses of these resolutions that I and the majority of company "D" discarded, were that we were satisfied with the present organization, which was not so, and that all skulkers and deserters be tied to the stake and shot indiscriminately, let their excuse be what it may, and that we would never lay down our arms till we had gained our independence over the North; I could not see how any person [with] reasonable sense, or regard for man, justice or obligation, to say nothing about the future, could vote for such resolutions.[39]

But the Thirty-seventh, and other elements of Lee's Army of Northern Virginia, would not get to spend the entire winter engaging in snowball battles, hearing speeches, and sitting around their fires thinking of past winter encampments. There was still a foe out there, sometimes just a few miles away, and the Tar Heels would often be called upon to be ready to move at a moment's notice to protect what they had struggled so hard for since their arrival in Virginia. On February 7, Federal cavalry attacked the Confederate cavalry patrolling beyond the Rapidan River, driving them into the main Confederate lines. McGowan and Lane's brigades were called upon to meet the enemy force, possibly to flank or get into the rear of the Federal forces. A cold rain was falling and the roads were muddy. Thorton Sexton chronicled in a letter to his parents: "We had a tolerable hard march last night...." After spending the night in the field, the brigades returned to camp without having caught the Union forces. Sergeant Tally would sum up the affair with "not much done on either side...."[40]

"It is now too dark to write," concluded Lieutenant Norwood in one of his letters to his uncle. "My fire burns brightly and the wind blows bleakly [through the] pine thicket across the hollow, but much more agreeable is its melancholy voice than the howl of the shell and shot...." It would be all too soon before Norwood and the other members of the Thirty-seventh would again hear the "howl of the shell and shot...."[41]

11

"Let us drop a tear to the memory of that noble boy who now sleeps upon that bloody battlefield"

May 1864

On May 4, 1864, at 1:00 P.M., the Thirty-seventh ventured out again from its comfortable winter quarters to face a new foe: Ulysses S. Grant. Grant had launched his forces across the Rapidan River in an effort to outflank the Army of Northern Virginia and force them out into the open where they could be brought to battle and defeated. General Lee reacted quickly to the threat and caught the Army of the Potomac in the Wilderness.

After covering some 18 miles on the Orange Plank Road, the Thirty-seventh went into camp near Vidiersville. They continued their march the following morning in a heavy, impeding fog. By noon, the boom of the cannon was heard coming from the direction the Tar Heels were heading. "Continuing our march we soon came upon the enemy's dead in great numbers on either side of the road," chronicled Lt. Wiggins after the war. The Thirty-seventh was approaching a seventy-square acre area known as the "Wilderness." The Wilderness, described by one historian, was a forest "overgrown with vines, briars, and other tangled vegetation, and it was divided by many small creeks and swampy areas."[1]

Wilcox's division, of which the Thirty-seventh was still a part, trudged along the dusty roads behind Heth's division. The regiment halted between 2 and 3 P.M. Wilcox, under the watchful eye of General Lee, formed his division in the tangled undergrowth. The advance was called, and the Thirty-seventh swept forward with the rest of the line. After traveling about 200 yards and capturing some 147, the division was halted, withdrawn, and re-deployed to assist Heth's division, which was hard pressed at the time. The Thirty-seventh was the last regiment in the rear of the division as it moved along the plank road, coming to the assistance of Heth. Lt. Wiggins wrote: "as [the Thirty-seventh] was leaving the Plank road it was reported that the enemy was approaching from the left of the road; it was detained there and did not take part in the engagement that evening, but lay still, watched, and listened...." It was now 6:30 P.M., and as they "lay ... watched, and listened..." the regiment must have thought back to a year ago when they spent another restless night in these very woods.[2]

The Thirty-seventh was relieved during the evening and rejoined Lane's brigade, which had met and driven back a portion of the Federal forces. The brigade went into a reserve position behind Scales's brigade, in two lines, facing the northwest. The Thirty-seventh was on the left of the front line. At approximately 9 P.M. the brigade pulled back a little further to a small hill, but still waited in reserve behind Scales. Early the next morning, Lane repositioned the brigade once more, this time in a fishhook-shaped line, with the Eighteenth, Thirty-seventh, and part of the Thirty-third facing the enemy to the northeast, and part of the Thirty-third, Twenty-eighth, and Seventh still facing the northwest.

Dawn came; the men were roused and began to fix a breakfast that had been scrounged from the yankee supplies littering the area where the Federal attack began. Crocker's and a part of Ward's New York, Indiana, Pennsylvania, and Maine brigade slammed into Scales's brigade. As the men from Scales's brigade streamed to the rear, they took the Thirty-seventh with them. "[T]he men were willing to fight, but had no chance," wrote Lt. Wiggins. "The Thirty-seventh was borne gradually back ... without firing a gun." Minié balls sailed through the trees like a swarm of angry bees. Alexander W. H. Price of Company D caught a round in the leg. Company C's Captain, Lawson A. Potts, was struck in the wrist. William G. Ford of Company H was wounded in the neck; John A. Edwards of Company I was struck in the left hand. David R. Alexander of Company C was killed. Sergeant Major Thomas C. Wright also went down with a wound. General Lane would make mention of Wright in his official report, calling him "a brave and noble boy...." Company A's Enoch Osborne, Jr., Josiah G. Roten, William M. Royal, and Hiram Tomlinson were not quick enough to get away and were captured by the Federals, as were 10 others of the regiment. Absalom Bare of Company A is still listed as missing in action. All of Hill's line gave way that morning.[3]

They fell back about 100 yards before meeting the lead elements of Longstreet's Corps coming onto the field. Lane then took up a position near the Orange Plank Road and began reorganizing his brigade. Soon after the brigade was re-formed, it was ordered to plug a gap in the Confederate lines. The brigade moved into the Chewing field, closed up on Ramsuer's brigade, and began to entrench, inviting the Federals to attack across the open field. That Thursday slowly faded without any attack. The Thirty-seventh's casualties for the day had been moderate: one killed, 13

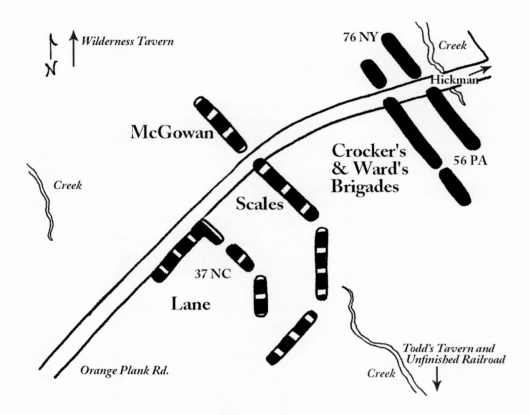

Battle of the Wilderness, evening of May 5, 1864.

wounded, 14 captured, and one missing in action. Two of the wounded, Sergeant Major Wright and David F. Harmon of Company G, would later die of their wounds.

May 7 dawned with heavy fog and smoke from the many fires filling the air. Some of the dry underbrush had caught fire during the attack of the previous day, and many of the wounded of both sides, unable to move, perished in the flames. The area surely must have resembled a hellish scene out of Dante's *Divine Comedy*. The lack of visibility screened the movements of both armies. "We were moved frequently," General Lane wrote, speaking of the activities of the brigade for the next day and a half, "and made to occupy various points on the line to the left of the plank road, at all of which the men worked with untiring energy, cutting down trees, making abattis and throwing up entrenchments." At 3:30 on the afternoon of the eighth, Lane was ordered toward Spotsylvania Court House. Lane's brigade took the lead in the division, marching until 2:00 A.M. before stopping for a few hours of rest. They took up the line of march again at 6:00 A.M. and arrived just north of the little hamlet around noon on the ninth, and once again began to cut down trees and build breastworks. The men no longer needed to be told to build breastworks: they did it whenever they stopped. The next day they shifted about a quarter of a mile to the

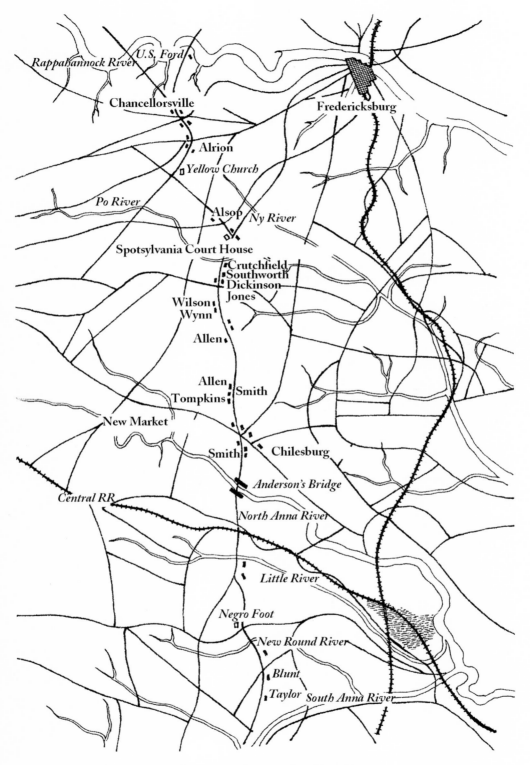

Overland Campaign overview, May 1864.

left, dressing on Johnson's brigade, Early's Division, Second Corps. The yankees in their front were Burnsides's IX Corps. The brigade was positioned from left to right: Twenty-eighth, Eighteenth, Thirty-third, Seventh, and the Thirty-seventh. As the brigade started to entrench, the rain began, not ending until the fifteenth.[4]

That evening, portions of the Federal Army, under the command of Colonel Emory Upton, broke through a section of the Confederate line to the left of Lane, dubbed "the mule shoe." Lane formed his command quickly and moved rapidly toward the breach. The Federal attack was quickly countered and the line sealed. Lane's men returned without seeing any action. Lane readjusted his lines once more. The Thirty-seventh stayed in position while the other regiments moved forward, establishing a new line. Lane wrote in his official report:

> The Twenty-eighth formed close upon Stewart in the "Double Sap" which had been thrown up by Johnston's pioneer corps, with its right resting on a boggy piece of ground. The Eighteenth entrenched itself on an elevated point on the opposite side of this boggy place, with its right resting on a swampy branch. The Seventh and Thirty-third regiments entrenched on the same line between the swampy branch and the left of the Thirty-seventh, the right of the Seventh resting on the Thirty-seventh, and the left of the Thirty-third on the branch. This new line of entrenchments, thrown up and occupied ... formed an exterior obtuse angle with the line occupied by the Thirty-seventh, and was nearly at right angles to an abandoned arm of the old works, which ran to the rear from the apex of this obtuse angle.[5]

A cold, bone-chilling rain fell throughout the night, and another vexing fog greeted the men on the morning of May 12. Shortly after daylight, the Federals rushed the Confederate works once again. Upton's attack the day before had consisted of 12 Federal regiments. This renewed attack had real strength in it — nineteen thousand men. The Federals poured over the works, some continuing straight, others peeling off to the left and right. Federal soldiers of Brooke's, Owen's, and Carroll's brigades got into the last ranks of Lane's brigade and captured 241 men of the Eighteenth and Twenty-eighth regiments. Lane pulled back the survivors of the other four regiments and formed on a crest at a right angle to the Thirty-seventh. There he ordered the men to open fire upon the Federals, with "a severe oblique fire from the Thirty-seventh and the direct fire from the rest of the brigade ... [which] drove them from the field." Lane ordered the advance, and the brigade moved off into the pine thickets and drove the bewildered yankees for two to three hundred yards before being recalled by General Wilcox. The gap in the Confederate line had been sealed, but the fighting was intense. On the front opposite Lane's brigade, the Confederate soldiers were on one side of the works, with the Federal soldiers on the other side, dealing out death at close intervals in the rain. Lane would write concerning the performance of the brigade: "In the best of spirits the brigade welcomed the furious assault, which soon followed, with prolonged cheers and death dealing vollies — the unerring rifles of the 37th and part of the 7th thinning the ranks of the enemy in front...." More accolades were given the brigade for that performance. A British newspaper correspondent would write: "Lane's North Carolina veterans stopped the tide of Federal victory as it came surging to the right." One of Lee's staff officers would also praise the Tar Heels: "They [the Federals] were checked by General Lane, who, throwing his left flank back from the trenches, confronted their advance."[6]

According to General Lane, General Lee and some other mounted officers were sitting on their horses in front of the works when Lane returned with his brigade and positioned it in some woods behind the front line. General Lee called for Lane's Sharpshooters: a battery of Federal guns was position in front of Lane and to the rear of the Federal battle line. General Lee wished "to ascertain … whether that battery was supported by a line of infantry at right angles to the enemy's line" or, as Lt. Wiggins put it, to "ascertain … how far the enemy's left extended." William D. Alexander of Company C relates what happened next:

> Captain Nicholson took five men, also carried a litter, and went out immediately in front to our outpost pickets. The captain of the pickets said he could not raise his head without being shot at—it would never do to go in front of that line. Captain Nicholson assured him that General Lee had authorized him to go out there. Leaving four of his men with the litter in the rifle pit, Captain Nicholson took one man with him to a little elevation out in front where he could see the enemy battery of which General Lee had spoken. The enemy was perfectly quiet as he walked out—did not fire a gun at him until he got to the point where he could see. He raised his glasses to take observation and the enemy turned the sharpshooters for six hundred yards each side of him on him. However, Captain Nicholson was not touched and got the information he wanted. The man he had with him had a leg broken. Captain Nicholson picked that man up on his shoulder and carried him back to our picket lines where he left the wounded man with the litter bearers…. Captain Nicholson was able to report to General Lee when he returned to the rear that the battery he had been sent to observe was not supported by infantry.[7]

A shell fragment soon killed the unnamed soldier that the captain had brought back. Lane's brigade was relieved from the front for a short time, to rest, replenish ammunition, and clean their fouled guns. Soon thereafter, McGowan's brigade moved off, and the Thirty-seventh, with the rest of the brigade, moved into the gap in the line created by McGowan's shuffle.

With the information that Captain Nicholson had provided in hand, General Lee ordered Lane to prepare to charge and take Burnside's artillery, which continued to enfilade the Confederate position. The brigade was arranged, from left to right: the Seventh, Thirty-third, Thirty-seventh, Eighteenth, and the Twenty-eighth.

At 2:00 P.M. skirmishers were thrown out, and as General Lane would write: "My men, as usual, moved forward very handsomely and, encouraged by their officers, drove the enemy's sharpshooters out of the woods." Lane's brigade moved by the right flank, then fronted, marched straight into the woods "cheerfully and quickly" in the words of an officer of the Thirty-third, then started to wheel toward the left and the guns. As they broke through the woods, the gunners turned the pieces toward the charging Confederates and opened fire. One shell fell into Company

Lieutenant Charles T. Haigh, Company B (courtesy of the Virginia Military Institute).

D, mortally wounding Captain Henry C. Grady and taking several other men out of action. The battery "opened upon us with grape and canister," chronicled Lt. Wiggins, "but it had no effect upon the Thirty-seventh." Lieutenant Charles T. Haigh, a recent Virginia Military Institute graduate who had transferred to Company B at the end of December 1863, "rushed twenty odd yards in front, with hat in one hand and sword in the other, shouting to his men to come on," recalled Lt. Wiggins. As the brigade wheeled, "poor Charley Haigh fell dead...."[8]

Other officers, inspired by the young Lieutenant, took the lead at the head of the advancing battle line. One officer of the Thirty-seventh would write: "It was the only instance [that I knew of] where a charge was led by officers. We read often of such things, but they seldom happen; they generally remain in rear of their men to keep from being shot by them." Joseph W. Green of Company B went down with a shell wound in his right side. Lorenzo D. Ward caught iron in the face, neck, left foot and knee. Third Lieutenant Barhabas A. Johnston (Company C) was killed, as was the company's First Sergeant, James H. Alexander. Company H's Amos A. Morris stumbled to the ground with a painful wound in the groin. First Lieutenant Edwin H. Russell of Company I struggled to the rear with a wound in the face. As the brigade neared the field pieces that they had been assigned to capture, four Napoleons and two rifles, the men unloosed a volley, killing or wounding almost all the members of the Nineteenth New York Battery. Lane later asserted: "we were unable to bring off ... the battery of six guns ... for the want of horses, and because there were no roads by which we could bring it off by hand...."[9]

The brigade surged ahead past the guns into another section of woods. "Then and there in those oak woods a scene with clubbed musket and bayonet took place which was too horrible to describe," wrote one officer. Lane sent back for reinforcements, Weisiger's (Mahone's) brigade, to support Lane and his attack, but Weisiger had become disoriented in the woods and soon began to fire upon the rear of Lane's men. The Thirty-seventh swelled ahead and caught the Seventeenth Michigan on its left flank and a grapple ensued. Lieutenant Colonel Swift of the Seventeenth attempted to rally his regiment. He was captured, along with the Seventeenth's color bearer and flag, by First Lieutenant James M. Grimsley of Company K of the

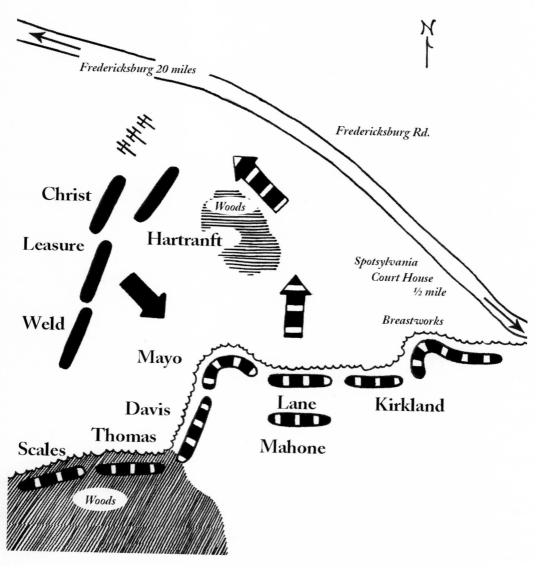

Lane's flank attack, battle of Spotsylvania Court House, Virginia, May 12, 1864.

Thirty-seventh. General Lane called Lieutenant Grimsley "a very brave man." Ensign Robert M. Staley of the Thirty-seventh went down with a wound in his right leg and passed the Tar Heels' colors to another member of the color guard. The Seventeenth Michigan collapsed into the Fifty-first Pennsylvania Volunteers. Their Color Sergeant, Patrick McKeevin, was shot and killed. Another member of the color guard raised their standard, but he too was struck down. Captain William Allebaugh of Company C of the Fifty-first raised the colors once again, but was captured by Lieutenant

Ensign Robert M. Staley, field and
staff (courtesy of the North Carolina
Division of Archives and History).

Wiggins (Company E, Thirty-seventh). Lieutenant Wiggins himself had just escaped capture
when General Lane distracted two federal soldiers
who had backed Wiggins up to a tree.[10]

The Second Michigan Infantry, who had
been detailed to support a section of Wright's battery, rushed into the melee. Lane was forced to
call a retreat due to lack of support, and the regiments moved back to the Confederate entrenchments. As Lane was returning to the lines, he
came across a Federal soldier "not more than ten
paces from [me] ... level[ing] his gun and was
in the act of firing" when Private P. A. Parker
(Company D) stepped up and fired his rifle-mus-
ket, killing the yankee. General Lane wrote of Private Parker, "[he] is a brave young man, and has
shown himself an excellent soldier in camp and
on the march, as well as in battle." Many of the
Thirty-seventh, over the din of battle, did not
hear the order to retire and were captured. Among
those was the fearless Colonel Barber, who was captured by Sergeant Daniel McFall
of the Seventeenth Michigan. Sergeant McFall would later be awarded a Congressional Medal of Honor for the deed. Command of the Thirty-seventh fell upon Major
Jackson L. Bost. Casualties were much higher than they had been a few days before
in the Wilderness. The regiment suffered 19 killed, 51 wounded (of which eight would
die), 58 captured, and one missing in action.[11]

General Lee sent for General Lane again, requesting more service from Lane's
Sharpshooters. General Lane wrote:

> ...he had witnessed the gallantry of these brave men, as well as the cheerfulness with
> which they had endured the hardships of the day, and that he had such a high appre-
> ciation of their services as to make him unwilling to order them forward again, but
> as they had been thoroughly tried and he wished to make another very important
> reconnaissance on the Fredericksburg road he would be glad if they would make it
> for him. I at once told him that however tired they might be I knew they would go
> wherever he wished them. To which he replied, "I will not send them unless they are
> willing to go." I went for Captain W. T. Nicholson, at that time commanding them,
> and introduced him to General Lee, who repeated what he had just said to me....

As Nicholson moved his men out, they took off their slouch hats and kepis, and
cheered the General. Lee returned the salute by doffing his hat. Nicholson soon
returned and reported to Lee that the Federal flank was stronger than ever. Lee did
not send the men in again.[12]

The brigade re-formed near the courthouse and returned to the works, where
they drew rations and rested for the evening in the rain, ever alert for another attack

by the Federals. The men would spend the next few days in the trenches. One third of the brigade was required to stand guard behind the works all night. Also, the men could not leave the breast works, nor remove their cartridge boxes and cap pouches at any time. The regiments were awakened every morning at 3:00 A.M., prepared to counter a surprise morning Federal attack. They spent their daylight time improving their entrenchments while constantly dodging minié balls and artillery shells. On May 14 Captain Nicholson was "wounded in the shoulder by a piece of shell." Between May 13 and May 20, the Thirty-seventh would have one soldier killed and six wounded while in the trenches and behind the breast works they had constructed.[13]

Some dispute later arose over the capture of the colors of the Seventeenth Michigan. General Mahone claimed that his brigade had captured the flag, along with a large portion of the Federal prisoners whom Lane's men had sent back during the fight. Lieutenant Grimsley, while clutching the banner behind the lines, was heard to state: "I captured this flag with my own hands and I can whip the man who says I did not." The next day the following order was read to the brigade:

> Headquarters Army of Northern Virginia
> On Battlefield
> *Major-General C. M. Wilcox, Commanding Division*
>   General: General Lee directs me to acknowledge the receipt of the flags captured by Lane's Brigade in its gallant charge yesterday, and to say that they will be forwarded to the honorable Secretary of War, with the accompanying note and the names of the brave captors.
>   I am, very respectfully, your obedient servant,
> C. S. Venable
> A. D.C.[14]

Lieutenant Colonel Speer, of the Twenty-eighth, would leave the best account of the actions of the brigade for the next seven days:

> On the night of the 16th ... [we were] relieved by ... Gen'l McGowan ... after which ... [we] moved ... to the rear of the second line near the Brick Kiln and rested for the night. The 18th was spent in this position. On the 19th [we] moved to the left ... and formed on a second line as support for Gen'l Gorden.... Here [we] fortified under heavy shelling. On the 19th we moved back to the right to await orders.... On the 21st we moved back to the right to the position on the line occupied formerly by Gen'l Gorden's Brigade.[15]

General Lee would call upon the Thirty-seventh again on the afternoon of the twenty-first. Reports had been coming to General Lee of large bodies of Federal troops moving to the east. Lee needed to know what was in front of him inside the Federal works. At 5 P.M. Lee sent the Thirty-seventh, with the rest of Lane's brigade and all of Scales's brigade, forward to reconnoiter the Federal position. The regiments "moved by the right flank along the works to a church south of the Court House, where we filed to the left, passed beyond the works, [and] formed line of battle...." The brigade then moved toward the Federal works without encountering any resistance until within 200 yards, when a body of Federal soldiers rose up and volleyed into the Confederates. The Thirty-seventh charged and captured the works. Near dark, Lane's brigade was recalled back into the Confederate lines. Once again the men of the Thirty-seventh had provided the information that General Lee had needed. Casualties for the individual regiments of Lane's brigade are not known. As a whole, the brigade suffered three killed, seventeen wounded, and eight missing.[16]

The Thirty-seventh re-formed on the road near the church. Soon, they were on the move again, headed toward Hanover Junction. They marched until 2:00 A.M., when a halt was called and the men fell out for some rest. After resting for two hours, they resumed the march at 4:30. They continued until reaching the Virginia Central Railroad and made camp at Hewlett's Station. The march resumed the next morning, crossing over the North Anna River at Butler's Bridge. The men moved along the railroad toward Anderson's Crossing, where they were allowed to rest. During this time, some of the soldiers apparently took the opportunity to liberate some livestock from local farmers. One such farmer came to General Lane demanding the return of his pilfered sheep. Although an inspection revealed no misplaced livestock, one member of the Thirty-seventh happened to wander by as he polished off a leg of lamb. He was promptly arrested and forced to march in a circle, carrying a wooden pole, upon which was suspended the farmer's property. After seeing that justice was carried out, the farmer requested that the man be released and allowed to finish his much deserved meal. After the short period of rest, the brigade moved to the railroad and formed in a line of battle, its left resting on General McGowan's right. Soon the order came to move and engage the enemy. The brigade moved by the left flank, parallel to the railroad, and formed at Noel's Station. Wilcox placed Thomas's brigade on the left, Brown's in the center, Lane's on the right, with Scales's brigade behind Thomas in reserve. The regiments of Lane's brigade were posted, from left to right: Twenty-eighth, Thirty-third, Thirty-seventh, and the Eighteenth. The Seventh had been sent to hold the ford at Quarles's Mill.[17]

General Wilcox had been misinformed about the size of the Federal force in front of him. Instead of only two or three Federal brigades, the 6,000 men of Wilcox's Division faced 15,000 Federals of Griffin's and Cutler's Division of the V Corps. The advance was called, and the Confederate brigades moved out into the woods that stretched before them. Encountering little resistance from the Federal skirmishers, they ran into the main Federal line, "posted on a commanding ridge...." At this point, Lane's and Brown's brigades drifted to the right, while Thomas's and Scales's brigades headed for the left. When the Confederate brigades of Lane and Brown emerged from the woods they were at an angle to the Union lines. The Federal Ayres's brigade swept the exposed Confederate left flanks. First Lieutenant James M. Grimsley (Company K) was wounded in the face and struggled to the rear. Peter Dellinger (Company H) was struck in the right hand. After re-forming, the brigades charged ahead again, this time straight toward the Union works. The Federals manning the works waited until the last moment before unleashing a volley that staggered the Carolinians. The Confederates re-formed, and, giving a rebel yell, opened fire upon the Federal battle lines.[18]

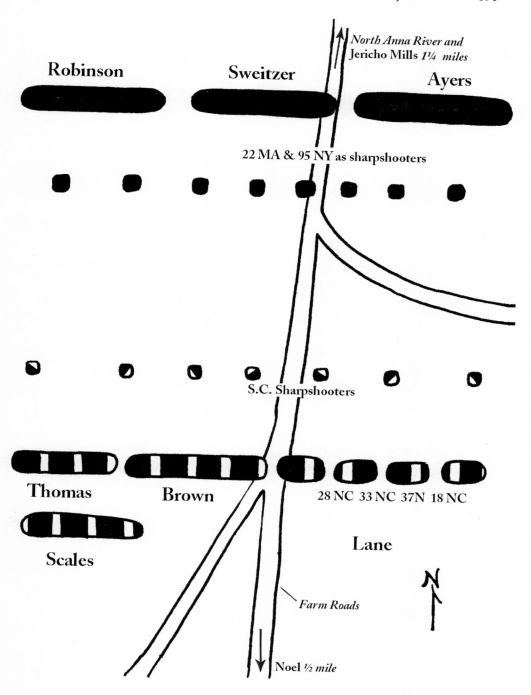

Brigade's position along the North Anna River, Virginia, May 23, 1864.

In the confusion, the brigades of Lane and Brown became separated. The Federals began to falter under the fire of the Tar Heels, but at the same time, they began to receive reinforcements. Now the Confederates began to falter under the Federal fire. Daniel Blevins (Company B) was struck in the right thigh; John W. Parker dropped, in agony, with a ball in the head, beginning his struggle with death. Company K's Eli A. Blevins was struck in the arm, side, and right lung. This, too, would be his last earthly struggle. The Federal firepower became greater than the Thirty-seventh could stand. Amid the taunts of bleating sheep from their fellow Carolinians, the Thirty-seventh's troops broke to the rear. Left with a gap in the center of his line, Lane was forced to pull back the rest of the brigade. The Thirty-seventh rallied, re-formed after gaining order, and resumed their place in the line. Wilcox ordered Lane to break Ayres's line, and the Tar Heels charged ahead once again. Ayres's line began to receive heavy reinforcements: two of Bartlett's regiments, the Forty-fourth New York and the One-hundred-and-eighteenth Pennsylvania. Bigelow's Massachusetts Battery began to fire over the heads of Ayres's men into the Confederates. Also, Lyle's brigade arrived in time to shore up Ayres's men.

Once again this was more than the Thirty-seventh could stand. Despite the attempts of the officers, like Lieutenant John M. Cochran (Company D), to steady the men, they once again broke toward the rear, leaving Lane with only three regiments, which he soon recalled. The brigade fell back to a field on the edge of the woods. The Thirty-seventh had suffered one killed, twelve wounded (of whom three would die of their wounds), and five captured. Around 11:00 P.M., Lane's brigade was relieved by Davis's brigade of Heth's division. The Thirty-seventh moved to the railroad and halted for a short time. Then they moved down the railroad to near the Anderson House, where they were allowed to rest for the remainder of the night. The morning of May 24 brought little rest to the fatigued men. The Thirty-seventh spent that morning entrenching and fortifying their position. They would stay in the general area, strengthening their positions and undergoing shelling from artillery until the afternoon of the twenty-seventh.

Colonel Barber; Captain Andrew J. Critcher (Company B), captured during this last engagement; and Captain William J. Alexander (Company A), captured at Gettysburg, would all have memorable and horrific experiences as prisoners of war. After Colonel Barber's capture, he was escorted behind the lines and moved to the Old Capital Prison in Washington, D.C. On June 15, 1864, the colonel was transferred to Fort Delaware, Delaware. Barber, along with Lieutenant Colonel William Dee Davidson of the Seventh North Carolina and 48 other high ranking officers, was selected as part of a group to be used as human shields by the Union Army outside Charleston, South Carolina. Fifty Union prisoners had been housed in the city and were subject to Federal artillery bombarding the civilian sections of Charleston. The fifty Confederate officers left Fort Delaware around July 26, guarded by a portion of the One-hundred-and-fifty-seventh Ohio. The group arrived in Charleston Harbor a few days later. After three tense weeks aboard ship, an exchange agreement was made, and the fifty Confederate officers were exchanged. Kentucky Brigadier General Basil Duke would chronicle the events:

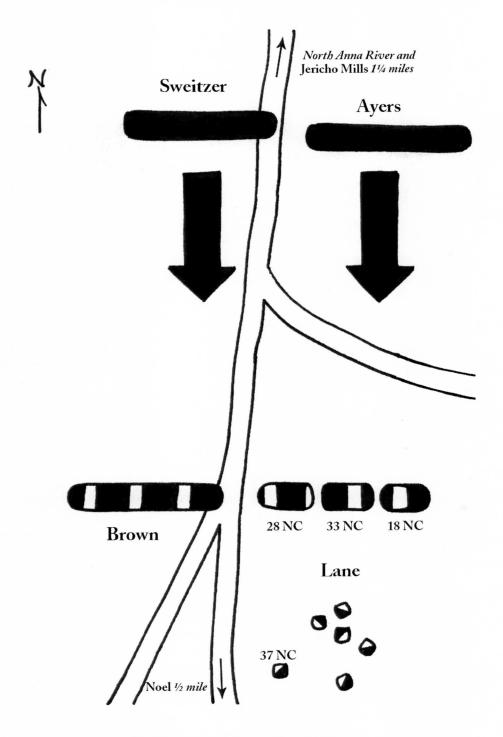

The Thirty-seventh falters, May 23, 1864.

After the customary formalities had been gone through with and the exchange completed, a banquet was given the prisoners on both sides, in which the officers conducting the exchange and some officers of the fleet participated. To the Confederates
and doubtless others so long accustomed to prison fare, this feast seemed ambrosial,
almost incredible, and was done ample justice.... It had been agreed upon that all
real firing should be suspended for the day, both by the fleet and the Confederate
batteries, but, in honor of the occasion, the big guns on both sides boomed out thun-
derous salutes when the exchange was concluded.[19]

Captains Critcher's and Alexander's affairs were remarkably different. Twenty-
eight-year-old Alexander had been captured during the charge on July 3, 1863, at Gettysburg, and he had been moved around continually since that date, first being
imprisoned at Fort Delaware. On July 18, Alexander was transferred to Johnson's
Island, Ohio. Johnson's Island was one mile long and a half mile wide and was located
at the mouth of the Sandusky Bay near Sandusky, Ohio. It was used primarily to
house Confederate officers. Captain Alexander was transferred via Baltimore to Point
Lookout, Maryland, on February 9, 1864. From there he returned to Fort Delaware
on June 23, 1864. Captain Critcher, thirty-four years old at the time, was first taken
to the Old Capital Prison in Washington, D.C., after his capture on the North Anna
River. On June 15, 1864, he was transferred to Fort Delaware. Fort Delaware could
be described as a bug- and mosquito-infested, bemired piece of ground called Pea
Patch Island, located in the middle of the Delaware River, which separates the states
of Delaware and New Jersey.

Prison life at Fort Delaware was at best a dull and predictable existence. Barracks had been constructed along the outside walls of the fort to house line officers:
field and general officers were quartered within the interior of the fort. A lamp was
kept lit 24 hours a day inside the damp barracks. The men were allowed to receive
money and packages from home, but the money was taken out and traded for sutler
checks. The men were only allowed one suit of clothes. The Confederate prisoners
received two meals a day. Breakfast, served at 8:00 A.M., usually consisted of "a cup
of water, about four ounces of the light bread, and ... five ounces of pork. Several
times the pork was omitted." Two P.M. brought dinner, "a small amount of bread
and meat, and, in addition, we received a pint of bean soup. This soup was generally burned, and always made of old beans."[20]

During the first few days of August, six-hundred Union officers from Macon,
Georgia, were moved into the residential sections of Charleston, on their way to Confederate prisons elsewhere. General Grant had ordered a cease to the prisoner exchange,
and the South was left with thousands of prisoners that it could not care for. These
six hundred Federal officers were some of the unfortunate men that were allowed to
starve and perish through the neglect of their own government. As soon as the Federal officer in command of the siege of Charleston was notified of the presence of the
Union officers, he sent for six-hundred Confederate officers for retaliatory measures,
although there is no evidence that the Union officers in Charleston were strategically
placed to be human shields. Early on Saturday, August 13, six hundred names were

Captain Andrew Jackson Critcher, Company B (courtesy of the North Carolina Division of Archives and History).

called from the prisoners at Fort Delaware. Captain J. Ogden Murray of the Eleventh Virginia Cavalry would write: "We soon fell into line, the roll call began and went on, while the prisoners stood in death-like silence awaiting the call of their names, each man showing on his face the hope of his heart; each asking God, in silent, earnest prayer, that his name would be called." This group of Confederates thought that they would soon be paroled, like the officers who had gone before. Alexander and Critcher were among the six hundred.[21]

Their journey began August 20. The officers packed what little they had managed to keep — letters, a few books, tattered blankets, and clothing. The roll was called; the soldiers marched out of the prison around 4:00 P.M. and boarded an old sidewheel steamship, the *Crescent City*. Around 5:00 P.M. the cargo freighter weighed anchor and set sail for Charleston Harbor. Bunks for the Confederates had been constructed in the hold of the ship: two rows of three-tiered bunks on either side of the vessel. Each bunk was approximately five feet ten inches square and housed four men. The conditions were unbearable. Captain Walter G. McRae of the Seventh North Carolina left this description: "Only one hatch was left open, so that the place was very close and dark. The August heat was intense even on deck. Imagine, then, the situation in this foul hold, near the steaming boilers and glowing furnaces, with six hundred sea sick men, already enfeebled by the close confinement, sweltering and gasping for water, which was doled out hot from the condensers."[22]

August 30 was a good day for Captain Critcher. While the men aboard the *Crescent City* awaited their fate, Critcher was one of forty men sent to the federal hospital in Beaufort, South Carolina. He had a case of chronic diarrhea. Captain Critcher was paroled at Charleston Harbor on December 15, 1864. He would never return to the Thirty-seventh. The dark-haired and blue-eyed captain was captured by General Stoneman's men in Boone, North Carolina, on March 28, 1865, and sent to Camp Chase, Ohio. He took the oath of allegiance and was released from that prison on June 14, 1865.

The remaining officers reached Charleston Harbor on September 1. Finally, on September 7, the six hundred men landed on Morris Island. They had spent eighteen days in the cargo hold of the freighter that had transported them there. Morris Island was described by one federal officer as "a long sand spit, facing Charleston Harbor for a part of its length and the ocean for the balance...." The prison pen was made of logs, consisting of one and one-half acres of sand. It was located between forts

Wagner and Gregg, in one of the most fired-upon sections of land. Five cartloads of iron shell fragments had been removed before the six-hundred men had arrived. The Confederate officers were marched off the vessel and placed in the charge of their guards, the Fifty-fourth Massachusetts and the Twenty-first United States Colored Troops. The prisoners marched three miles in the rain from the landing to the stockade, several needing help due to their abhorrent treatment aboard the ship. The officers were quartered in 160 A-frame tents, four men per tent.[23]

Regulations inside the palisade fort were severe. There was a "dead line" running around the inside of the stockade. Any man crossing that line would be shot. No lights were permitted after taps. The entire compound was illuminated by a large calcium light at night. Men were confined to their tents after dark, and there were no gatherings of groups over ten men. No fires, loud talking, or talking to friends across the stockade was allowed. A battery of Billinghurst-Requa machine guns guarded the stockade. A daily, regimented routine was also in order. Reveille was sounded at sunrise (6:30 A.M.), followed by a roll call and assigned camp duties: policing the grounds, raking the sand smooth, and emptying the sinks. Around 8:00 A.M., breakfast was brought in by the guards. Another roll call was held at noon, and dinner arrived at 2:00 P.M. A final roll was held at tattoo, with retreat, or lights out, at 9:00 P.M. All mail was being withheld from the Confederates. Also, many of the Confederate prisoners had been forced to relinquish any equipment marked US as "stolen property." Rations issued were considered "starvation rations": "three army crackers per day and a half a pint of soup.... It was called bean soup, but we could never discover any traces of that vegetable in the mixture." In contrast, the Federal officers held in Charleston received "Three quarters pound of fresh meat or one-half pound of salt meat, One-fifth pint rice, One-half pound of hard bread or one-half pound of meal [and] one-fifth pint of beans" per man.[24]

The day after his arrival, Captain Alexander experienced the horrors of the fort's exposed position. The "Third Great Bombardment of Charleston" began on September 8. The Confederates were exposed to the fire on all four sides: Wagner in the rear, forts Sumter and Moultrie in the front, the federal monitors on the seaside, and two other batteries, Simkins and Johnson, in a cul-de-sac near the mouth of Charleston Harbor. Some of Alexander's comrades wrote of the terrifying ordeal. Lieutenant W. A. Ford (20th Virginia Cavalry): "The shells from 'Wagner' ... pass directly over us and could be seen directly. In a short time our shells in reply are seen to fall and explode with great accuracy over Fts. Gregg and Chatfield, in our front." Captain Henry Dickinson (2nd Virginia Infantry): "Most of our shells were from mortars and looked as if they would fall directly on us, but, whilst we held our breath in anxious expectation, its parabolic course would land it in the fort." Captain John Dunkle (Twenty-fifth Virginia Infantry): "Oh, the misery of having the ear constantly filled with such doleful sounds, the misery, the horrible misery, the wretched agony of anticipating death at every moment! The battle-field was pleasure compared with this...."[25]

The Confederate prisoners would stay in this position, with these rations, for fifty days. None of them was ever wounded by the artillery shells, neither the ones fired by the Confederate batteries nor the prematurely exploding ones fired by the Union batteries. By the first of October, all of the Union prisoners housed in Charleston had been moved to Columbia, South Carolina. At last, on October 21, Captain Alexander and his comrades received orders to pack what few belongings they had. Many thought that they had been, or were going to be, exchanged. But another prison awaited them, this one at Fort Pulaski near Savannah, Georgia. Captain Alexander would spend three days without rations on board a schooner in route to the fort. After arriving at the fort, the captain and his fellow prisoners were billeted in the cold and drafty brick casements on bunks made of hard planking. But the prisoners received full rations for the first time in several weeks: "8 to 10 ... crackers ... a cup full of soup and as much meat as I want." During the cold winter, Captain Alexander would stay at Fort Pulaski, suffering from the want of clothing and blankets, as well as a reduction in rations to corn meal and pickles (supplemented by rats and cats), until March 4, 1865, when he, along with the other prisoners, was transferred back to Fort Delaware. They would arrive on March 12, many unable to walk, many on the verge of death due to their depleted condition. On May 30, 1865, Captain Alexander took the oath of allegiance to the United States and was released from prison, his horrific experiences over.[26]

12

"Only the sharp shooters and canonade"
May 1864–December 1864

By the spring of 1864, Lieutenant General Ulysses S. Grant had achieved little success in his overland campaign. The Army of the Potomac had been stalled in the Wilderness, at Spotsylvania Court House, and along the banks of the North Anna River. The ventures had cost the Federal Army 50,000 casualties, and Grant had been forced to call upon reserves being held in the Washington defenses. General Lee would have few, if any, reserves to rely upon.

General George Meade, under the instruction of General Grant, would again move his army to the southeast and closer to Richmond. This would entail another hard march on the boys from North Carolina. The Thirty-seventh left its position behind the North Anna River breastworks during the late afternoon of May 27. The heavens once more opened upon the marching soldiers, placing large sections of the Ashland road completely under water. The Tar Heels kept plodding along until 10 P.M., when the order to halt was given. The men fell into the mud for a little slumber, about a mile from Ashland. Three A.M. the next morning would find the Thirty-seventh on the road again. One officer of Lane's brigade would describe the march as moving along "very rapidly all day...." That afternoon, the Thirty-seventh reached the vicinity of Shady Grove Church, not far from where General Hill had set up his headquarters, and made camp. The Tar Heels would stay here until the afternoon of the twenty-ninth, when they would move a short distance and make camp near General Heth's division.[1]

On the morning of the thirtieth, the brigade formed a line of battle on the right of McGowan's brigade and commenced building breastworks near the railroad. The next day the brigade was ordered to Storr's farm on the Totopotamoi Creek, near

Pole Green Church, where they relieved Wofford's brigade. The Thirty-seventh was on the left of the Twenty-eighth. Intense skirmishing erupted throughout the day. The Federal forces were both testing the strength of Lee's lines and covering their army's further movement to the east. Different writers in the brigade would record the action. A member of the Thirty-third described the action as "a severe fire both of infantry and artillery...." A member of the Twenty-eighth wrote, "heavy skirmishing and ... a terrible artillery fire." Another member of the Twenty-eighth would record "a most terrific shelling and [we] did ... skirmish all day...." During the day-long action, Private John Armstrong (Company H) was wounded in the armpit; Benjamin H. Kilby (Company F) was mortally wounded; Company A's James H. Vannoy was wounded in the chest, right arm, and side; and Leonard L. Parlier (Company F) was killed. The Thirty-seventh would remain in the works for a short time, resting.[2]

The regiment took up the line of march again and arrived on the old battlefield of Gaines's Mill, also known as Cold Harbor, around 2 P.M. on June 2. The Federals had control of a position called Turkey Hill, a gentle ridge that overlooked the Confederate lines along the Chickahominy. As soon as General Breckinridge and General Hill had their men in position, Lee ordered a charge to drive the Federals off that hill. The Thirty-seventh went into position with the Twenty-eighth on its left and the rest of the brigade to the right. The advance was called after the hill had been bombarded by the artillery. The Thirty-seventh rushed forward, and the Federals scattered from the hilltop. The only casualty sustained by the Thirty-seventh was Company A's Thorton Sexton, who later died of his wounds. A more serious casualty was the brigade's commander, General Lane. While observing the Confederate offensive, he was struck in the midsection by a Federal bullet. Lane was "borne, profusely bleeding, from the field...." He was so severely wounded that he was not expected to live. He was taken by ambulance to Richmond and would not return to the brigade until late August. Command of the brigade would devolve upon Colonel John D. Barry of the Eighteenth.[3]

John Decatur Barry was the son of a graduate of the United States Naval Academy, and the grandson of General James Owen, brother to North Carolina Governor John Owen (1828–1830). John D. was born on June 21, 1839, in Wilmington, North Carolina, and he attended the University of North Carolina from 1856 to 1859. In 1861 he enlisted as a private in the "Wilmington Rifle Guards," later Company I, Eighteenth North Carolina Troops. On April 24, 1862, the Eighteenth was reorganized as a "three years" or "for the war" regiment. The young Barry was elected captain of Company I. In October the regiment reorganized again, and Barry was elected major. Barry was one of the commanders of the Eighteenth during the battle of Chancellorsville, ordering his men to fire at Jackson, Hill, and their staffs. The generals had ridden out in the dark between the lines to survey the Union positions, and Barry had received orders to shoot anything in the front. Jackson was mortally wounded during the fray. Barry was promoted to colonel after the battle, and led his men in the battles of Gettysburg, Mine Run, the Wilderness, Spotsylvania Court House, and

Cold Harbor. At the latter, General Lane was wounded and Barry assumed command of the brigade. On August 8, 1864, Barry was appointed temporary brigadier general of Lane's brigade.[4]

The Thirty-seventh would not be actively involved in the second battle of Cold Harbor the next day. Grant threw three corps against the Confederate lines and gained nothing but 7,000 killed and wounded in less than half an hour. Casualties for the Thirty-seventh would amount to three men wounded: Daniel W. Chambers (Company D), right leg; Henry S. Beam (Company H), back/left shoulder; and Second Lieutenant Adam F. Yadle (Company I). They would spend the next ten days in their suffocating and filthy entrenchments. Life in the trenches was testing, even for the battle-hardened soldiers. Colonel Speer of the Twenty-eighth wrote home to his parents on June 5: "They have got to fighting of a night. We can't sleep any…. We have fought behind breastworks. It is raining on us and quite disagreeable. The Men are getting sick very fast…." Sergeant Tally (Company I) would echo Colonel Speer's thoughts when he wrote home on June 7: "I am well enough in health but am about Broke down a marching & throwing up breast-works to gether every day since the 3rd of last May[.] [W]e have never been in camps sinc then[.] [W]e have pretty hard times in the hot sun & raining every 2 or 3 days untill we are all completely broken down."[5]

A set of orders from General Lee would circulate on June 5 among the Thirty-seventh and the other regiments in the Army of Northern Virginia. The first ordered officers to inspect and, if necessary, adjust their lines, to replenish ammunition and to issue rations, and to keep at least one-third of the men on duty at all times. The second, issued on the same day, ordered men who had been on detail to return to the ranks. The third directive "criticized many officers' willingness to allow their able-bodied men to go to the rear for trivial reasons or no reason at all." The period of inactivity was welcomed by the men. Rations had been increased, so much that some regiments and brigades gave some of their rations to the poor and needy in Richmond. On June 7, Breckinridge would move his division out and Hill would re-occupy his lines. They would hold here until their next trial came, 8 A.M. on June 13.[6]

Lee had discovered on the morning of June 13 that the trenches in front of his army were empty. Grant was again moving his army to the east. The Thirty-seventh, with the rest of the Light Division, was soon on the dusty road once again. They crossed over the Chickahominy at McClellan's Bridge, continuing across the York River Railroad to the Charles City Road. The Confederates made contact with the Federals late in the afternoon. The brigades of McGowan and Scales were placed in front, followed by Thomas and Lane in support. The fight was brief, sharpshooters driving back the Union cavalry before the main Confederate force arrived. The main Confederate body pressed ahead approximately a mile and a half before halting for the evening.

For the next three days the Thirty-seventh would be occupied by position shifts and entrenchment building, all in the proximity of Riddle's Shop, on the fields of

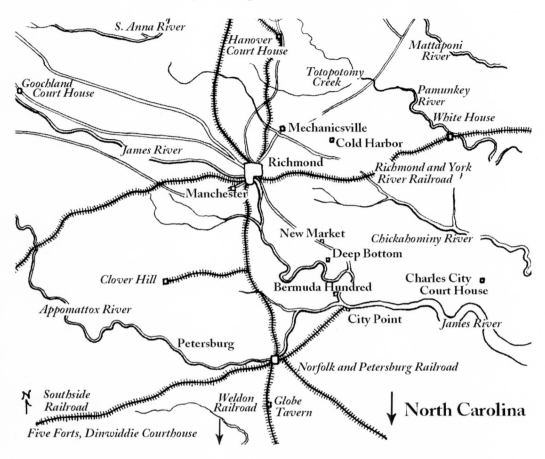

Petersburg, Virginia, and vicinity, June 1864 through April 1865.

battle of the summer of 1862. Around 4 P.M. on the seventeenth, the men of the Thirty-seventh, along with the rest of the brigade, marched to Darbytown, where they bivouacked for the night. By 3 A.M. on June 18, General Lee had decided to cross his army over the James River. Lee had been uncertain about Grant's intentions, but the General now believed that Grant was headed for Petersburg. One historian related the details of that day's 22-mile march:

> The march to Petersburg ... began without breakfast and become one of the most severe that the brigade endured throughout the war. Under the severe heat, the men choked on the thick clouds of dust raised with each step. Each man's clothes and face was soon blanketed with a powdery gray mantle. A scarcity of water led to fights at every well passed by the marching column.... The brigade stretched out for miles as soldiers fell by the way side with every mile, unable to maintain the pace demanded by the officers.

One officer of the brigade called the march "one of the hardest and most disagreeable marches [we] ever [made]."[7]

The Tar Heels of the Thirty-seventh arrived in Petersburg around 6 P.M. They passed through the city to the works south of town, took up a position on the east side of the Weldon Railroad near Battery number 37, and rested for the night. The next day the men would dress on General Mahone's division, near Battery number 34, but rest would be in short supply. On June 21, A. P. Hill was ordered to move two of his divisions to confront a Union attempt on the right flank of Lee's army. The Thirty-seventh moved out around midday. Two P.M. brought word from the Confederate cavalry pickets of the presence of a Federal force near the Weldon Railroad. Wilcox ordered two of his brigades, including Lane's, out to meet the Union forces. The brigades were deployed in a battle line, and swept forward, driving the yankees back to within a few hundred yards of the Jerusalem Plank Road.[8] That evening the Confederate regiments returned to their positions within their lines near Battery number 34.

The following morning, the Union forces returned with greater force — the II and VI Corps, augmented by 7,500 cavalrymen. General Wilcox was soon ordered to meet and drive back the enemy. He deployed his brigades in a line of battle parallel to the railroad, deployed his skirmishers, and started the advance. The advance continued until 1:00 P.M., when the Confederates were forced to halt. Around 2 P.M., General Hill arrived on the field. Hill directed the brigades of Scales and Lane, still under the command of Colonel Barry, to advance towards the north in an endeavor to locate the flank of the Federal forces. The brigade sharpshooters took up the skirmish line once more and moved forward. Lane's brigade was deployed, from left to right: the Thirty-seventh, Twenty-eighth, Eighteenth, Seventh, and Thirty-third. The Thirty-seventh was the left-most regiment in the line, and part of the regiment was refused to guard the flank of the two brigades. The Thirty-seventh would see very little of the yankees this day but would be under the effects of the Federal artillery. Colonel Speer of the Twenty-eighth, the regiment on the right of the Thirty-seventh, wrote that they were under a heavy shelling while formed in a field. The two right regiments of the brigade were engaged with the yankees for about thirty minutes, but the whole brigade was soon withdrawn by the left flank from their position in front of the VI Corps and re-deployed in support of General Mahone's division, which had routed much of the II Corps. Around 10:00 P.M. on the night of the twenty-second, the Thirty-seventh returned to its former position in the works. The next day the brigade relieved General Finnigan's Florida brigade. Casualties for the operations from June 22 till June 30 would be light. Nine men were captured, six were wounded, and one, William P. Lawing (Company I), was killed "by a bomb shell," probably on June 22.[9]

Constant danger would be the rule for the next few days. The Tar Heels were in the trenches and would be on the move, relieving this brigade here, supporting this portion of the line there. One soldier in the brigade would leave a good description of life on the line during the last weeks of June:

> The works we are now in are so close to the enemy's lines we can't stick up our heads without getting shot at. We are in the open field. No shade's over us in the boiling

sun & the hottest weather I ever did see & no rain. We have had no rain in over a month ... it is a horrible to be in this place. We are first shot down, day or night, any time. Our sharpshooters & the enemy are all the time looking for each other. As soon as a man shows his head he is plugged at & often killed or wounded. It is a perfect state of horror here.[10]

The first of July would bring another shift in locale and another dusty march. Around 8 o'clock on the evening of July 2 the Thirty-seventh, along with the rest of Lane's brigade and McGowan's brigade, struck out to the north for a defensive line near Richmond. They crossed the James River at Chaffin's Bluff on the morning of the third, and took up a position around noon below the bluff on a farm near Four Mile Creek. The weather would continue to be unfavorable. One officer wrote: "The weather is awful hot & dry — no rain since the 12th of May — everything is nearly burnt up." The brigade was situated across the river from the Federal forces. They could on occasion see the Union gunboats, lying a few miles out, and were constantly under the threat of artillery: "They throw shells over us here that weigh 180lb., 2 ft. long, 15 in. through & look like churns," an officer would chronicle. Life here was less volatile than in the trench east and south of Petersburg, even though there were occasional forays.[11]

The region around Deep Bottom, where the Union and Confederate troops faced each other, had been personally reconnoitered by Grant on June 19. Named for a narrow spot on the James River where fast-moving currents had carved a deep channel in the river, Deep Bottom was an ideal place for a defensive line. Its high bluffs on the North bank would protect the Union supply lines from Confederates from nearby Bermuda Hundred. Based on Grant's observations, a defensive line was constructed on the bluffs and a pontoon bridge spanned the river. Not long after the Union forces gained control of the area, General Lee instructed Major General Ewell to sink Federal supply boats with artillery and torpedoes, also called floating mines. Due to the intense fire that the Confederates were able to mount, General Grant, who had come under fire himself when inspecting the area, ordered the small garrison reinforced and the Confederate artillery fire stopped. The Federal forces also constructed a second pontoon bridge farther up the river. This bridge was on a more direct road to Richmond, and General Lee ordered some of the Confederate forces to drive the Union soldiers away from their bridge head.

On July 8, Federal forces stole into the Confederate picket lines and captured three members of the Thirty-seventh: Calvin C. Davis (Company B), Newton Greer (Company B), and Jesse Salyer (Company F). Daniel L. Spencer, also of Company F, was wounded in the right shoulder. It is likely that these men were interrogated by the Federals and the information they provided, including what brigade, division, or corps they belonged to, was sent on up to the Union high command. Skirmishing continued for several days between the two forces. Colonel John D. Barry was wounded in the hand and replaced by Colonel Cowan of the Thirty-third North Carolina as the brigade commander.

In late July, two Federal cavalry divisions and the II Corps, under Hancock, were sent north across the James River. The Federal forces in the trenches in front of Petersburg had been constructing a mine under the Confederate line, in hopes of exploding the mine and rushing troops into the breach to split General Lee's army. Hancock had been sent North to deny the Confederates the opportunity of reinforcing their lines to the south, and to draw away some of the Confederate defenders manning the lines where the crater was being dug. Grant wanted Hancock to cut off the Confederates north of the James River. The Federals attacked on the twenty-seventh, driving the Confederate pickets into their fortified lines. But in the hours after the initial Federal advance, Confederate reinforcements arrived, including the Thirty-seventh. The Confederate battle plan for the day was to recapture the Long Bridge Road, force Foster and Hancock back across the James River, and destroy the Federal pontoon bridges. McGowan and Lane's brigades, the former under Kershaw and the latter under Conner, were ordered to attack the right end of the Federal line. Those very Federals that they were ordered to flank had received similar orders: to flank the Confederates out of their works on the left.

The morning's activities had started around 5 A.M. for the Thirty-seventh. Orders were received and the brigade moved out by the left flank, past Heth's division, toward Fussell's Mill. After fording a creek, the brigade was deployed around 10 A.M. The Seventh was on the left, their left along a road, followed by the Eighteenth, Thirty-seventh, Twenty-eighth, and the Thirty-third on their right. McGowan's brigade was deployed to the right of the Thirty-third. There was a low, marshy section to the front of the brigade, then a cornfield. The Federals had taken a position in the field. Skirmishers were deployed, and the order to advance was given, guiding on the road. The left regiments of the brigade advanced with little difficulty, while the right side of the line became entangled due to the terrain. Captain J. S. Harris, commanding the Seventh and on the left of the line, wrote: "we moved forward passing through a dense swamp and attacked the enemy posted in a field in front of our line. We drove him across the field and a mile, when the whole line halted and kept up a fire for about 20 minutes." The Thirty-seventh would not have such luck. A week later in his official report, Major Bost, still in command of the Thirty-seventh, chronicled the regiment's actions:

> ...officials orders were given to forward with the guide on the left and executed in good faith but in a short time the line became very much crowded so that giving way to the right did not seem to give room enough when orders were given by the Brigade Commander to march by the right flank which was repeated by me but rather badly executed owing to the right of the line not moving off by the flank, when the regt on my _____ broke in front of mine and I did the same thing as soon as I could get to where it was. In a short time the Brigade Commander gave the command forward double quite which caused the regt to lap over each other and my left was considerably covered by those on my left so that at the very time Col Cowan comdg Brigade happened to be present to whom I reported and I then received my orders from him to move on to the right of the Brigade.[12]

The skirmishing had now begun, and Major Bost had his hands full. The regiment had been ordered forward, and now the order changed to march by the right flank. "[I] only succeeded in getting a portion [of the regiment] to move to the right[,] the rest having gone on with the Brigade," continued Major Bost,

> [when] some [of the Thirty-seventh] became mixed up with McGowan's brigade. With that I could make understand to move to the right of the brigade I marched by the right flank ... before I had gone far was fired into from the right & rear which confused the ... [men] ... and made them think they were flanked. At this time I was between two corn fields near the end of a ridge which is between two swamps and as soon as I could get [the men] into line and find out which way to go I proceeded to cross the swamp on my left and did not get beyond the left corn field until the left were falling back....

Bost moved the Thirty-seventh to protect the flank, forming a skirmish line along a fence in between the two fields of corn. A courier was sent to Colonel Cowan for orders. David W. Oates, adjutant for the Thirty-seventh, was wounded in the neck; Second Lieutenant George W. McKee (Company H) was wounded in the right buttock; Henry N. Rape (Company D) was struck in the left shoulder and hand. Men of the Thirty-seventh were dispersed all over the field. Orders soon arrived, and the Thirty-seventh fell back a short distance and re-formed "on a county road to my rear." Adjutant Oates, Noah J. Gilbreath (Company E), who was wounded in the right thigh and left leg, and sixteen others were captured. Julian C. Plummer (Company K) was killed. The brigade was soon flanked on the right and forced to fall back about two hundred yards to a ridge. The short, spirited fight had produced thirty casualties in the Thirty-seventh: one killed, fourteen wounded (of whom three would die), and eighteen captured (including two of the wounded). Casualties for the month of July were one killed, nineteen wounded, two wounded and captured, and twenty-four captured.[13]

Confederate forces fell back to their defensive line near Chaffin's Bluff around 12:30 P.M.. The mine the Federals had labored at so hard was exploded on the morning of July 30 and the assault that followed ended in dismal defeat for the Federals. Hancock and the II Corps were recalled back south of the James River the same day to reinforce a section of the Union line. Keeping the head down was the rule for both sides the next few weeks. Not only was there the continual pop-pop of the skirmishers, but the intolerable heat was excessive both during the day and night. Having recently returned from his excursion to Charleston, courtesy of the Federals and their human shield policy, Colonel Barber succeeded Colonel Cowan as commander of Lane's brigade, by virtue of seniority.

August 14 would bring the next clamor of activity. General Grant believed that a feint toward the Confederate capital would make Lee weaken his Petersburg defenses by sending troops north of the James to combat the Federal forces. Hancock had once again crossed over the river and was threatening Richmond. The Federals had attempted to take the Confederate line, but had been beaten back, as much by Southern heat as by Southern lead. The Thirty-seventh would see no action that day, nor the next. The battle of Fussell's Mill would be fought on August 16 in an intense heat that would reach ninety-four degrees by 3:00 P.M., overshadowing the preceding days. Federal skirmishers deployed early in the morning, and the day-long duel began. Around 1 P.M., after repeated assaults, the Western Brigade of the Federal forces broke the Confederate line held by Wright's Georgians, on Lane's right. The Confederate forces were now split in half. The retreating Georgians caused the Tar Heels in Lane's brigade to waiver, and several members of the Thirty-seventh were captured. But Colonel Barber soon had the North Carolinians re-formed on the Darbytown Road, and the brigade joined Little's brigade and McGowan's brigade to counter the attack on the left of the Union line.

Under the watchful eye of General Lee, who had arrived on the field to take charge of affairs, Barber re-formed Lane's brigade. General Lee "spoke kindly and encouragingly to Barbour's [sic] Tarheels," wrote one historian, and "expressing confidence in the North Carolina troops, and telling them they 'must not fail.'" A little before 2 P.M., the attack pressed forward. The three brigades pushed forward slowly, stopping several times to re-dress their ranks in the thick wood or on rough ground. After nearing the Federal line in a pine thicket, the brigades charged forward to within sixty yards of the Federal soldiers before being forced to halt by the terrific small arms fire being delivered by Pond's brigade and the Ninth United States Colored Troops. For fifteen minutes the two sides traded volleys just sixty yards apart. Colonel Barber was wounded in the right leg, and command of the brigade was passed to Colonel Speer of the Eighteenth. With a cheer, the Tar Heels sprang forward and captured the line of works, along with a number of prisoners.[14]

The members of the Thirty-seventh left no impression or thoughts on seeing black Union soldiers for the first time. They certainly had enough to do without noticing the ethnicity of their foes. At dusk the Federals retreated, leaving the Thirty-seventh with nineteen casualties: two killed, six wounded, and eleven captured. There would be no fighting for the members of the Thirty-seventh on the next day. At 4 P.M. a truce was called for the exchange of the dead between the two forces. The Confederates had already removed the wounded from both sides.

On August 18, Brigadier General James Conner was relieved of commanding McGowan's brigade, and, by Special Order Number 196, was temporarily placed in command of Lane's brigade. Conner had been born in Charleston, South Carolina, on September 1, 1829. He attended the South Carolina College and graduated in 1849, entering the legal profession after graduation. In 1856 he was a United States attorney. Conner enlisted in the Hampton Legion, and was appointed a captain. He was present at the battle of First Manassas, and after the battle of Seven Pines he was appointed Colonel of the Twenty-second North Carolina. Wounded in the leg at the battle of Gaines's Mill, he was promoted to brigadier general on June 1, 1864. Conner had been in command of McGowan's South Carolina Brigade during the previous battle.[15]

There was very little action the next day, August 18. At 5:00 P.M. an assault was made on the Union lines, but it only succeeded in capturing the Federal picket line. During the night of August 18, in the middle of a storm (the first that occurred in weeks), Major Bost led the Thirty-seventh back over the James River to the Petersburg works. The storm-drenched Tar Heels arrived near Battery 45 on the Dinwiddie Plank Road late in the day on August 19. On the same day that the Thirty-seventh arrived from north of the James, a Federal force composed of Warren's V Corps captured a portion of the Weldon Railroad near Globe Tavern. The Weldon and Petersburg Railroad linked Petersburg and the Confederate capital of Richmond with Wilmington, North Carolina. Thousands of supplies and munitions of war ran the blockade at Wilmington and were transported either west, further into North Carolina, or north to the Army of Northern Virginia. The Thirty-seventh would have a few days' rest while other portions of the Confederate army battled elements of the Army of the Potomac.[16]

Rain had changed the terrain from a dry and dusty one to mud. Around 10 A.M. on the morning of August 24, orders were received to be in readiness to move at a moment's warning. Those orders came at about 3 o'clock that same afternoon. Robert E. Lee, acting on the advice of his cavalry commander, Wade Hampton, was sending a large force to drive the Federals from the Weldon Railroad area. The Thirty-seventh, in order to avoid the Federals around Globe Tavern, took an indirect march to their staging area. They headed southwest out of the Petersburg entrenchments on the Boydton Plank Road toward the Dinwiddie Court House. After reaching the intersection of Duncan Road, they moved south toward Armstrong's Mill. The Tar Heels crossed Hatcher's Run at Armstrong's Mill and bivouacked for the night three miles beyond the mill, near Holly Point Church and the intersection of the Vaughan and Monk's Neck Roads, three miles from the Federals at Reams's Station.

Orders were to be ready to march at 4 A.M. The regiments started at 8 A.M., moving two miles before halting for a few hours. The march resumed once again, but stopped once more around noon. Because of the presence of Federal cavalry patrols, General Hill, in command of the expedition, deployed Wilcox's command, including Lane's brigade, a mile before reaching the Federal lines. When the threat had passed, "the command was faced about and moved back down on the road leading to Reams Station...." Around 3 P.M. the brigade deployed once more, this time in support of Scales's brigade in a wooded stand of pines on the left side of the Depot Road. The Seventh was on the left, followed by the Twenty-eighth, Thirty-seventh, Thirty-third, and the Eighteenth. General Wilcox deployed his three battalions of sharpshooters (McGowan, Scales, and Lane), and ordered Scales's and Lane's brigades to keep under the shelter of the woods. Scales's sharpshooters led the advance, followed by McGowan's, and lastly, the sharpshooters of Lane. As the sharpshooters advanced, the Federals quickly overlapped the Confederate line. Scales's sharpshooters wheeled to the right and came up on McGowan's right. Lane's sharpshooters wheeled to the left and came up on McGowan's left. The row of sharpshooters advanced cautiously through the pines, driving the Union skirmishers from the woods. The Confederates found the entrenched Federal picket line in a cornfield beyond the woods. With a loud cry, the Confederates advanced, forcing the Federal pickets to flee toward their main lines.[17]

The main Union line at Reams's Station was U-shaped. Hancock, whom the

Thirty-seventh had been fighting on the North side of the James River, had positioned his Corps in a precarious position, where incoming rounds that did not strike the Federal soldiers in the front had a chance of striking other Federals in the back. The Confederate attack commenced in earnest when Wilcox ordered Scales and Anderson forward. The Federal fire proved too much for these brigades, and they fell back to the protection of the woods. General Heth arrived on the field with reinforcements, and the Confederates charged ahead again. This time, Lane's brigade, with Cooke's brigade of Wilcox's division, moved toward the Federal entrenchments. Elements of the two brigades moved forward around 5 P.M. through the pines, toward the railroad embankment. The Federal lines were on the other side, at a distance of about 40 yards. A thunderstorm began at about the same time as the assault did. The Federal skirmishers were driven back to their works by the main Confederate body. A few moments after Lane and Cooke had made contact with the Federals, another Confederate brigade, under General MacRae, crashed into the Federal works and gained a foothold inside. The Thirty-seventh, positioned in the center of Lane's brigade, made the next breakthrough. Hysteria-stricken Federal soldiers streamed to the rear. The color bearer of the Thirty-seventh rushed ahead into the Federal entrenchments. The Federal officers attempted to get their men to counterattack, but their efforts were in vain, as the Union soldiers started surrendering or heading for the rear. But the fire concentrating on the Thirty-seventh was intense. "In gaining this point," Major Bost would write, "the Regt was exposed to a heavy fire of grape shot and bulletts." Portions of Lane's brigade started falling back, while other portions, including most of the Thirty-seventh, intermixed with elements of Cooke's brigade, pressed ahead, "capturing prisoners, caisons, horses...." Much of the fighting was done hand-to-hand.[18]

"The Rail Road cut was continuous until dusk in consequence of the enemy being near, and attempting to recapture the works," Major Bost added to his report. "The engagement lasted some three hours." The Thirty-seventh would sustain fifteen casualties. (Bost's official report of the action claims twenty-nine, which may include some slightly wounded.) One man, Enoch Phillips (Company K), was killed; one, William H. Cable (Company E) was listed as missing in action; Kenneth M. Hasty (Company D) was captured; and twelve were wounded, of which one, Jonas C. Fronebarger (Company H), later died of his wound to the left lung.[19]

Private Thomas M. Hanna (Company H) was one of the soldiers slightly wounded during the battle. He would pen this account of his ordeal to his wife a few days after the battle:

> Dear wife: ...God has spared my life through another bloody battle.... The day I commence it we were marched all night and fought the yankees at Ream Station ... we had to march 20 miles to get around them in the hottest weather I ever felt. We had a desperate fight, made the attack and drove them from their breat works.... We also lost pretty heavily.... I myself slightly wounded in the right breast. The ball struck my pocket Bible, and went half way through it. [It] kill[ed] a man dead just in front of me and the doctor said it would have killed me if it had not struck my

pocket Bible. I told them I was killed when I was hit, it hurt me desperately, and I thought I was shot in the heart. I went to the rear and stayed there two or three hours and went back again. But the Book saved my life…. I have the bullet. It stopped in the Book. It went through my coat….

A Gaston County pastor would relate many years after the war that the bullet had made "a track through [the Bible] from Genesis to John…" and that the minié had come to rest on the "14th chapter of John … 'Peace I leave with you, my peace I give unto you.'" Hanna would continue in his letter to his wife after the battle: "I don't know what I will do for a Bible, mine is ruined, torn and bursted all to pieces."[20] Hanna struggled back to the front through the storm to join his comrades.

Rain continued to fall until a little after midnight. Orders went out to bring in the wounded and bury the dead. Union losses would amount to 2,700, including 2,150 men who were marched off to confinement in Confederate prisons. The Confederates also captured nine cannons, 3,100 small arms, and 32 horses. Praise for the actions of the Thirty-seventh and the other men of Lane's brigade, and Cooke's and MacRae's brigades, came a few days later from General Lee in a dispatch to Governor Vance:

> I have been frequently called upon to mention the services of North Carolina soldiers in this army, but their gallantry and conduct were never more deserving the admiration than in the engagement at Reames's Station on the 25th instant.
>
> The brigades of Generals Cook, MacRae, and Lane, the last under the temporary command of General Conner, advanced through a thick abatis of felled trees under a heavy fire of musketry and artillery, and carried the enemy's works with a steady courage, that elicited the warm commendations of their corps and division commanders and the admiration of the army.

A few days later, President Jefferson Davis was in Charlotte, North Carolina, addressing a group of people. In his remarks, he praised the North Carolinians: "her sons were foremost in the first battle of the war, Great Bethel, and they were foremost in the last fight near Petersburg, Reames's Station."[21]

That night, after the battle was over and after the wounded were cared for and the dead buried upon the field, the Thirty-seventh made its way back to the entrenchments in Petersburg, near Battery number 45. On August 29 General Lane returned from his convalescence and resumed command of his brigade. On August 30 Colonel Barber returned and resumed command of the Thirty-seventh. Once again there would not be much rest for the members of the Thirty-seventh. On September 7 they were involved in a small fight near the Davis house, but apparently no casualties occurred. About this time, Major Wooten, in command of Lane's sharpshooter battalion (which included several members of the Thirty-seventh), began a series of raids entitled "Wooten's seine-haulings." In these raids the sharpshooters would steal forward in between the lines in the middle of the night and capture the Federal pickets, bringing back prisoners with information and much needed munitions of war. "[H]e [Wooten] was very successful, and never lost a man." These audacious raids would continue on throughout the winter. Adjutant William H. McLaurin of the Eighteenth described Major Wooten's methods:

His method was to reconnoiter, during the day, the lines to be gone through that night and at such hour as would suit his purpose would approach "in twos" with his selected men, sufficiently near to make a dash at them. At a signal the column would go through the line with as little noise as possible, halt, face out, and each rank swing around right and left, taking the skirmish line in the rear, capturing men with the minimum of danger to his command. His success was phenomenal, and he received the commendation of Generals Lee and Hill in congratulatory orders.[22]

In a letter home on September 11, 1864, Captain Norwood related that "the situation on the right is unchanged, except that our brigade moved 300 yds, 30 ft. and 3 in. exactly, to the right the other day." While skirmishes and battles raged all around them, the men in the Thirty-seventh seemed somewhat oblivious to the raging tide. Norwood would continue in his letter:

> Though I mentioned in a letter to one of the family ... what I would need in the way of winter clothing, I will let you know exactly what I have and then you can judge for yourself what I will need.
> Coats— My homespun is perfectly new, the campaign having caught me in my "other" coat, which having weathered the storm for upwards of four months is now fading into nothingness.
> Pants. One new pair of the Confederate gray; my blues having long since suffered complete shipwreck.
> Shirts. Two flannel, the other pr. Worn out.
> Socks. One pr. thin cotton.
> Such is my wardrobe ... I shall hereafter be able to supply myself I think as to coats and pants. There seems to be a pretty good supply on hand most of the time.[23]

On September 16 the sharpshooters of Lane's and McGowan's brigades were sent out again. This time the orders were to drive in the Federal sharpshooters and "Discover the attitude and temper of their main line in front of the light division." Lane's sharpshooters took up a position on the right of the Weldon railroad, and McGowan's sharpshooters deployed on the left. General Wilcox himself supervised the action. The advance was called and the men stepped off into a cornfield. Soon the Federals discovered the sharpshooters and opened fire. The sharpshooters responded by raising a yell and charging through their picket line. The Federal pickets retreated into their own main lines, and the sharpshooters dueled with the main body of Federals for a short time before being recalled into their own lines, bringing a number of prisoners with them. It was later discovered that the action had been a demonstration against the Federal army, hoping to draw attention away from a raid being conducted by General Hampton on the Federal beef supply. The raid was a success, and Hampton returned with 2,500 head of cattle.[24]

Union forces moved north again, over the James River, and attacked the Confederate lines on September 29. They succeeded in capturing a portion of the Confederate line, including Fort Harrison. The Tar Heels would spend the balance of that September day under marching orders. On the morning of the thirtieth, orders came for the Thirty-seventh, with the rest of the brigade, to re-deploy north of the James River. After crossing the Appomattox, they were ordered back, to counter a new threat. Federal forces had captured Fort Archer and a portion of the Confederate lines south of Petersburg, defended only by dismounted cavalry. Private Collins called all the marching "[being] put on the Zig Zag ... first ordered to the left ... then to the right...."[25]

It was almost 5 P.M. when the Thirty-seventh arrived and took up positions. Lane's brigade was formed to the right of the Harman road, leading to the Jones House, described as an "elegant residence" by one member of the Thirty-seventh. Major Wooten deployed his sharpshooters, and "the obstinate or stubborn and bloody battle of Jones' Farm, Dinwiddie County, Virginia, commenced." The sharpshooters moved forward at the double quick, capturing many prisoners. One general was heard to remark that the charge of the sharpshooters "was the handsomest thing of the kind he had seen during the war." Orders soon came, and the Thirty-seventh advanced about 100 yards into an open field and went prone. It was here that Colonel Barber received his sixth and final wound, a stray bullet in the right hip, while conferring with Lieutenant Wiggins (Company E). Colonel Barber was carried beyond the lines and died of his wounds on October 3. His body was removed to the St. James Episcopal Church Cemetery in Wilkesboro, North Carolina. On August 15, 1866, Robert E. Lee would write to Colonel Barber's son, Edward, this moving letter:

Master Edward A. Barbour [*sic*]

The grief which I experienced at your father's death, is greatly relieved on learning that you possess a large share of his mental vigour; and bid fair at a future day to fill the place he held in the love and estimation of his fellow citizens. That you may the more certainly do this permit me to urge upon you to study in your youth the holy precepts of the Bible, to practice virtue in preference to all things; and to avoid falsehood and deception of every kind, which will be sure to debase the mind and to lead every vice and misery.

In contemplating the virtues and achievements of the good and great men of whom history presents so many examples, keep constantly in mind the conduct of your father, and endeavor to equal him in goodness, tho you may fall short his greatness. Wishing you every happiness and success in life, I am very truly your friend

R. E. Lee
Lexington, Va.

Gravestone of Colonel William M. Barber, St Paul's Episcopal Church, Wilkesboro, North Carolina.

Major Bost once again resumed command of the Thirty-seventh, a position he would retain until the end of the war.[26]

Lane's brigade was deployed as follows (from left to right): the Eighteenth, Seventh, Twenty-eighth, Thirty-seventh, and Thirty-third. The sharpshooters' advance was checked by the main Union force, and they were forced to fall back about 150 yards. Major Bost moved the Thirty-seventh to the right of a ravine, and as soon as the regiment was in position, he called for the Thirty-seventh to advance. While advancing, he changed direction to the left and directed his men to fire at the left oblique. Thomas Davis (Company B) was killed. Joseph S. Selvy (Company H) was struck in the chin. The Thirty-seventh had outdistanced all of the other regiments of Lane's brigade, causing it to suffer from small arms fire from the front and the flanks. Company K's James B. Johnson was struck and killed. Redmond Price (Company E) was wounded in the knee. Private Collins wrote: "the 37th North Carolina Regiment out-charged the other Rebel troops on its right and left, in so much as to drive the Union line into the form of a 'V'; which exposed it to a terrific cross-fire of the Union line...." It took a few moments for the rest of the Tar Heels to catch up. "The direction," related Major Bost, "was then changed to the right along a certain road[,] driving the enemy before us until we reached the crest of a corn field, and another house." It was now near dusk, and the Thirty-seventh was again intermingled with other commands. "Night put an end to the flagitious or grossly wicked and bloody days work," concluded Private Collins. As dark settled on the battlefield, the brigade moved back a few yards to the edge of the woods, "through the mud and rain," for some much needed rest. Casualties for the day were three killed, eight wounded (of which two would die, including Colonel Barber), and one captured.[27]

"The battle-field was a rich one," General Lane wrote, "and my brigade bears me out in the assertion, as they have a great many sugar-loaf hats, blue overcoats, oil-cloths, shelter-tents.... All of the [Federal] dead that had on passable clothes were stripped." It may have well been a member of the Thirty-seventh that Lane was referring to when he wrote: "There was a disposition on the part of some to pillage.... I commenced upbraiding one of them ... while his comrades were fighting, and ordered him forward, he replied that he only wanted a blanket to sleep on these cold nights, and I could but be amused as he went running to the front with a fine Yankee blanket under his arm." Major Bost would write that the Thirty-seventh was not engaged on October 1, losing only one man killed and two wounded. Private Noah Collins would see things differently:

> The next morning ... I was detailed on skirmish, and being thrown forward in sight of the Union troops, we were halted at a fence by a large cornfield, where we remained, fortifying with the fence rails, till our line of battle came up ... we were again thrown forward, with orders to charge the Union troops out of their temporary or advance line ... which we did by the assistance of a battery which was located a little to our right, in a position to enfilade the Union ... line of works.... I did not get to fire but one round ... at the Union troops, which was a squad of about twenty retreating Union soldiers, soon after which I rejoined my company ... we all marched down and took possession of the vacated Union temporary of advance works.

The Thirty-seventh, with the rest of the brigade, continued to hold these works, in the rain, until dark, when they fell back to their position of the night before, near the Jones house. General Lane would write in his official report: "The whole brigade behaved nobly in these two engagements, and again proved themselves worthy of the high esteem of our Commanding General."[28]

There would be little rest for the battle-weary and worn Thirty-seventh. On the night of October 2, all of Company B and part of Company D were detailed to reinforce the Fourth North Carolina Cavalry. The rest of the regiment took up the march to meet a Union raiding party, but returned with no losses. The detailed companies of the Thirty-seventh relieved the pickets of Wright's brigade on the night of the third, and were relieved themselves by pickets from Scales's brigade on the fourth. The main body of the Thirty-seventh would dig in around the Jones Farm. Alexander wrote in his diary on October 3: "scarcely a gun has been fired." A member of Company D that had been out on picket duty would find his regiment "tollerably well fortified at the Jones' Farm battle field."[29]

"We learned this morning that Col Barbour died last night at 8 o. clock (a stunning loss to the 37th)," Alexander recorded on the morning of October 4. Captain Norwood would echo Alexander's feelings: "Tis sad to think of the Col's young wife now left desolate of heart." Not all were mournful over the loss of their beloved colonel. Private Collins, who had harbored ill will towards the Colonel for some time, would write: "I had the pleasure of seeing Colnel William M. Barbour ... fall mortally wounded ... to rise no more." Life continued for the Tar Heels of the Thirty-seventh. General Lane penned a few words about a visit of a minister: "Last Sunday [October 9] I had an Episcopal minister with me, who comes from North Carolina not only to preach, but to visit the North Carolina hospitals, and give clothing to the sick and wounded from the 'Old North State.'"[30]

Their short respite would end at 2 A.M. the next morning. "[W]e were all aroused from our sweet slumbers, and shivering with cold, were soon marching for Petersburg," General Lane would write. The Thirty-seventh took up a position in the second line of works near Reeve's salient just before daylight. They would hold this line under an artillery barrage until night. One private in Company D related his experiences when the "Union troops mortor-shelled us sharply":

> I heard a mortor shell coming, making a curious noise through the air, perpendicularly of straight above us. When upon looking up and discovering it, I dashed as close to the wall ... as I could get ... about which time the mortor shell struck in the edge of the magazine and sank so deep in the ground that when it exploded or bursted not a single piece of it flew out ... not long ... a mortor shell exploded about the height of a man's head, about six feat in the rear of Company "B" of the 37th ... which fortunately injured no person.

That night the Thirty-seventh, with the rest of the brigade, moved to the area around Battery number 45. The men were issued new clothing, a boost to anyone's morale, though the Thirty-seventh's morale seemed to be high during this time. Over the course of the next few days the men would start to construct their winter quarters near the Jones house. "We have been busy fixing up our tent with log walls—hospital tents are being fixed up," the Thirty-seventh's hospital steward would write.[31]

The next few days were quiet. On October 20, Colonel Barber's body started back to North Carolina. Everything would remain tranquil until 8 A.M. on the morning of the twenty-seventh, when Lane's brigade received marching orders. The brigade would head about a mile to the southwest, where MacRae's brigade was engaged with portions of the Federal army. The Thirty-seventh would not see action that day, being held in reserve. Nor would they see action the next day. The Federals fell back before the main Confederate body could be brought to bear upon their lines, but the Confederates were able to recover needed supplies. Captain Norwood chronicled: "There was literally no end to the plunder of all description that we brought off after the action." The Thirty-seventh returned to their camp that evening.[32]

Construction now began in earnest on their winter quarters, or "shanties," as some called them. General Lane pitched his tent right there with the men, not using any of the nearby houses as headquarters. He would leave this description of his humble abode:

> Lieutenant Meade and myself are living in two nicely-pitched tents, which are joined together and open into each other. The back tent is used as a sleeping apartment, and the front one, which has a nice brick chimney to it, is our sitting room. When we get the floors and doors completed we will be very comfortably fixed. Our chamber is furnished with a plank floor, a bedstead and blankets, two trunks and a clothes pole (suspended from the ridge pole), which serves as an excellent wardrobe. In the front of my tent [can] be seen an old camp-table, a few chairs, an old bent tin candlestick, an inkstand and pens, tobacco and pipes, and sometimes a great deal of smoke.

Things were also somewhat comfortable for others in the Thirty-seventh. Alexander would confide in his diary on October 30: "I rec[ieved] a bundle from home of clothes and a bottle of Ellen boy [sic] brandy[;] it was the first that I had seen[,] it is a delicious drink…. We had a gay time at my expence."[33]

November 1 brought an inspection. "Brig. hospt. Camp was complimented as being the nicest in the corps," Alexander related with pride. November 2 would bring the much dreaded foul weather of winter—sleet and rain. Orders were received on November 8 for the Thirty-seventh to prepare to march, but the day passed off quietly. This November day was also the United States election day. Many had hoped that the almost constant fighting and loss of Union soldiers from May until the present would persuade the Northern people to elect another president, one to replace the current administration and possibly sue for peace with the Southern Confederacy. Their hopes were soon dashed.[34]

The subsequent weeks would remain frigid and the men placid. Federal deserters continued to come into the lines. "Desertions from the enemy are of nightly occurrence," General Lane would write on December 3. The Thirty-seventh was not idle during this time, although even the skirmishers had stopped their firing. Construction was always, weather permitting, being done on some portion of the line:

one position being strengthened, another position being totally rebuilt. Some soldiers were constructing a dam to flood a portion of the field, and effectively used water to prevent a Federal attack.[35]

The solitude was brought to a temporary halt on December 9. The Federal cavalry was conducting a raid, and Lane's brigade was sent out to try and catch the Union troopers. Orders went out on the eighth for everyone to be in light marching order. The Thirty-seventh took to the road in snow around 9 P.M. that evening, and would continue until 6 P.M. the evening of the next day, before making camp for the night about two miles from the bridge over the Nottoway river. As soon as the halt was called, the Thirty-seventh's soldiers busied themselves pitching their shelter tents, a protection from the "ground-covering and timber-breaking sleet" that was falling. Reveille was called the next morning, and the men were soon moving through the mire, rain, and icy precipitation. They bivouacked for the night two miles beyond Jarratt's Station. The next day they returned in the direction that they had come, because the Federal forces retired before Lane's brigade could arrive. The Tar Heels made camp that night near the bridge over Nottoway, and the next night, a mile from the Dinwiddie Court House. Alexander penned in his diary: "this is a lovely moonlight night; 8 P.M. we have eaten supper and are all sitting around a good fire.... [We had] some singing and many big [lies] told[;] last night we retired at a late hour...." The next day, December 13, they returned to their camps, "very nearly completely broken down, in consequence of the unfavorableness of the weather, marching so far over the snow and ice and suffering so indescribly from cold." Many a poor soldier would sleep soundly that evening.[36]

Major Wooten and his command of sharpshooters received orders on December 18 to provide two or three yankees for interrogation at headquarters. The major assembled his men, and that night advanced to within one hundred yards of the skirmish line. At a given signal, the sharpshooters fired several volleys and, with the old yell, charged the Federal skirmishers. The yankees had little opportunity to fire back before they were overwhelmed and forced to flee back to their main line. The sharpshooters returned with eleven Federal prisoners. General Lane praised his young officer: "He is certainly one of the most successful, most gallant, most unassuming and most modest officers that I have ever seen. He is worth a million of the stay-at-home somebodies."[37]

A grand ball was held in the city of Petersburg for the officers of Hill's corps on the night of December 23. The attendees from the Thirty-seventh are not known. The following Sunday was Christmas. "Many boxes have been sent from N.C. to the army—the boys are having a nice time," related a member of the Thirty-seventh. The boxes sent from the state were a welcomed relief. "Tell the kind donors, with thanks, that the boxes reached us in very good time, as the soldiers have been living on short rations for the past few days.... My brigade has some kind friends at home, and Christmas boxes have been pouring in," the general would write. Rations, especially meat, had been in extremely short supply. In one instance in the month of December, the soldiers went three days without receiving beef or pork. But North

Carolina, above all other states, was working the hardest to supply her soldiers in the field. In the same letter, General Lane would continue: "The State is also trying to get vegetables to her soldiers. Governor Vance ... says he is willing to send his "tar-heels" a great many things to help along." Every once in a great while the commissary was able to issue "The London Times"—beef cooked and canned in London, and brought over through the blockade. "[I]t makes an excellent hash and is superior to any other meat-ration that is issued." Many members of the Thirty-seventh attended church services that Sunday morning. "[T]he church was handsomely dressed," scribbled one soldier of the Thirty-seventh, "the music was excellent, I have never heard better." The services probably reminded many of the loved ones at home.[38]

13

"The support of a completely fallen cause"
January–April 1865

The beginning of 1865 would find the Thirty-seventh a mere skeleton of its former self. Colonel Lee had died on the field of battle in 1862. Colonel Barber had died of wounds in a hospital in Petersburg in October of 1864. The regiment was on its third lieutenant colonel and its fourth major. The current lieutenant colonel, William G. Morris, was still confined in a Yankee prison camp on Johnson's Island, Ohio. The current major, Jackson L. Bost, a thirty-two-year-old doctor from Union County and former captain of Company D, would command the regiment through the ending days of the war. All told, the regiment could only muster, at the most, 320 men, some of whom were not fit for duty and were in one of the many hospitals in the Petersburg and Richmond area. The command structure of the Thirty-seventh in January 1865 reveals many vacancies:

Colonel . . . . vacant
Lieutenant Colonel . . . . William G. Morris (prisoner of war)
Major . . . . Jackson L. Bost

Company A
Captain . . . . William J. Alexander (prisoner of war)
1st Lieutenant . . . . Thomas L. Norwood
2nd Lieutenant . . . . vacant
3rd Lieutenant . . . . vacant

Company B
Captain . . . . Andrew J. Critcher (prisoner of war)
1st Lieutenant . . . . vacant

2nd Lieutenant . . . . Nathaniel Horton (prisoner of war)

3rd Lieutenant . . . . Thomas M. Wiggins

Company C

Captain . . . . John D. Brown

1st Lieutenant . . . . vacant

2nd Lieutenant . . . . Abraham P. Torrence (absent, wounded)

3rd Lieutenant . . . . vacant

Company D

Captain . . . . John M. Cochrane

1st Lieutenant . . . . vacant

2nd Lieutenant . . . . Albert T. March (appointed February 10, 1865)

3rd Lieutenant . . . . Joseph E. Griffin

Company E

Captain . . . . William T. Nicholson

1st Lieutenant . . . . Johiel S. Eggers (would resign January 13, 1865)

2nd Lieutenant . . . . Octavius A. Wiggins

3rd Lieutenant . . . . vacant

Company F

Captain . . . . John B. Perry

1st Lieutenant . . . . Felix Tankersley

2nd Lieutenant . . . . John T. Forrester (prisoner of war)

3rd Lieutenant . . . . William S. McGee

Company G

Captain . . . . Daniel L. Hudson

1st Lieutenant . . . . James B. Pool (prisoner of war)

2nd Lieutenant . . . . vacant

3rd Lieutenant . . . . William W. Glenn

Company H

Captain . . . . vacant

1st Lieutenant . . . . John J. Ormand

2nd Lieutenant . . . . George W. McKee (absent, wounded)

3rd Lieutenant . . . . vacant

Company I

Captain . . . . William D. Elms

1st Lieutenant . . . . vacant

2nd Lieutenant . . . . Adam F. Yandle

3rd Lieutenant . . . . Dallas M. Rigler

Company K

Captain . . . . Thomas J. Armstrong

1st Lieutenant . . . . James M. Grimsley

2nd Lieutenant . . . . William N. Ross
3rd Lieutenant. . . . . vacant

The dearth of officers would hardly be noticed in the understrength companies as the war hobbled to a close.

Lieutenant John T. Forrester, Company F (courtesy of the North Carolina Division of Archives and History).

The weather was still cold and bitter during the first few days of January. But the snow and frigid air did not hamper the two armies' constant forays. On the night of January 6, Union skirmishers probed the position held by Scales's brigade. The skirmishers of the Thirty-seventh countered, flanking the Union skirmishers, capturing 14 prisoners, and killing and wounding several others. The same thing occurred again two nights later, when Union skirmishers again rushed the skirmishers and pickets in the same locale. Again the Thirty-seventh responded, this time capturing 25 Federal soldiers. The Confederate works in front of Petersburg were 37 miles long, stretching from the Darbytown Road to Hatcher's Run. As a rule, on this section of the line the Confederate pickets were posted some 600 yards in front of the main line, protected by a line of rifle pits. The Union pickets were 300 yards to their front. Six hundred yards behind the picket line were the main Confederate trenches, formidable earthworks built out of Virginia soil and logs. The Tar Heels constructed their winter quarters, log huts, and bombproofs right behind the lines. The pickets and sharpshooters on both sides made life miserable. Any show of a part of one's body above the works almost always brought a bullet or two.[1]

Besides keeping the head down, there was little to do inside the trenches. The pickets rotated on and off every day, with the men serving on the picket line one out of every three or four days. Another duty was the constant construction and strengthening of the works. Private Collins was a part of such a detail during the last days of 1864 and the first two weeks of 1865:

> I was detailed with nine other members of Company "D" of the 37th ... as regular fatigue of the line on the 20th day of December 1864 ... during which time we suffered a great deal in consequence of the extreme unfavorableness of the weather, in constructing and strengthening our Rebel lines, Southwest of and near Petersburg, many days of which it snowed, ice and water was full knee-deep in the moats and ditches in which we had to labor.... I was relieved on the 15th day of January 1865.[2]

For the men not on duty there was company drill in the morning and battalion or brigade drill in the afternoons, and every evening before supper, dress parade. Added to this were the frequent inspections of the lines by General Lee or General Hill and other members of their staffs.

Sickness would still plague the Thirty-seventh. Private James A. Myers, of Davidson County, was a late enlistee of the regiment. He had joined in October 1864, after his eighteenth birthday, leaving his young bride at home. Myers soon became sick with "typhoid pneumonia" and was sent to the hospital in Petersburg, where his brother wrote to his wife, saying "that if [he] didn't get some attention [he] would not be here long...." According to a story recorded many years after the war, Myers's wife, Susie, with their six-month-old daughter, acquired a railroad pass and made her way to Petersburg, and found Myers lying outside a hospital in the snow. "She said she raked the snow off many faces before she finally recognized mine," Myers recalled. "She found me lying on a bed of pine needles in the snow, with my one thin blanket to keep me warm ... she saw that I was, indeed, very sick and that something would have to be done for me in a hurry." Susie soon found a local family that was willing to take Myers, who was "more dead than alive," into their home and nurse him back to health. On February 8, 1865, the partially recovered Myers was granted a 30-day furlough, and the young family started back to Davidson County.[3]

Desertions among the companies of the Thirty-seventh began to increase. Often, men would simply walk off the picket line and into the Federal lines. John Q. Adams (Company D) went over on the night of December 29. Coleman Williams (Company B) would follow him on December 30. Frequently, family or friends in the same company or from the same area or township back in North Carolina would make the decision to desert together. James A. Swanner, his brother William G., David C. Thomas, and Alexander B. Watts, all of Company D, would cross over into the Union lines on January 19. In all, 38 men would desert and go home, or voluntarily go over to the Federals during the first two months of 1865. Their reasons to leave the army, when some of them had been with the Thirty-seventh since the latter months of 1861, were varied. Many were hungry or cold. Pvt. John N. Adams of Company E stated after the war that he "At last ... got so hungry that the site of a well fed yankee troop was too much. Taking a flag of truce, [I] crossed to the other side...."[4] Others were disillusioned at the prospect of four more years of war given the reelection of Abraham Lincoln, or were concerned, with just cause, with the protection of their families at home: activity in the western North Carolina mountains by Tennessee Unionists and non-partisan bushwhackers had increased since the departure of Confederate forces in eastern Tennessee in late 1863. Another threat was General Sherman and his Federal armies that were approaching from South Carolina.

Marching orders came on February 5. General Grant had sent part of his army to try and cut off the flow of supplies coming up the Boydton Plank Road southwest of Petersburg. The Thirty-seventh would only move about 250 yards from their current position, stretching their already thin lines to cover for the men that General Lee had withdrawn to counter this latest offensive. On the morning of the sixth, the Thirty-seventh would be allowed to return to quarters. On the seventh, they again would head 250 yards to the right, to garrison the works. Private Collins would write of the weather on the seventh: "a very intensely cold day, on which it rapidly sleeted all day." Alexander would echo his fellow member of the Thirty-seventh: "The ground is covered in sleet, which is still falling." The cold and sleet made fighting conditions dreadful; men too wounded to crawl to the rear often froze to death before help could be rendered. The Confederate forces succeeded in driving the Federals back, with losses, but the Federals succeeded in extending their lines another three miles, forcing the Confederates to do the same.[5]

Beginning in mid–February and continuing into the month of March, the prisoner exchange system began to work once again. Thirty-six members of the Thirty-seventh, including Lieutenant Colonel Morris, were exchanged and paroled during a six-week time period. None of these men returned to the army. They all went home and awaited the end of the hostilities.

Things would remain quiet for a few more days. Orders to prepare to march were again received on February 22, but the regiment did not move. Those orders came again on March 12, and the brigade moved to General Mahone's division's portion of the lines. "The weather has been quite wet," chronicled Alexander, "making the roads very muddy, it is thought that the campaign will soon open." The Thirty-seventh would stay in this position until the twenty-fourth, when they moved once again through "the mud full knee deep in the moats or ditches which were cut for the purpose of sheltering advancing or receding or retreating troops" to relieve Grimes's brigade. Due to the conditions, the brigade did not reach its assigned place at the appointed time, and was moved to another position in the rear, in support of the Confederate assault on Fort Stedman. The attack, led by General Gordon, commanding Stonewall Jackson's old Second Corps, was initially successful, capturing many Union soldiers. But once daylight broke, the Confederates were overwhelmed, and they were forced to withdraw back to their own lines.[6]

The last weeks of the month of March brought about many new cases of desertion. Isaac Ham, James J. Testerman, and John A. Henderson (Company A), and David L. Beam (Company H) all left on March 3. They were followed on March 6 by Milton C. Mullis, and Calvin C., Hurley G., and James C. Price (Company D). On March 8, William C. Land (Company C) deserted, followed by John W. Kilby (Company F), Ambrose Liles and Jasper M. Miller (Company A) on the twenty-second. March 23 would bring the desertion of Miles R. Eacher, Jason and Samuel Stegall, and Emberry and James H. Walters, all of Company D. Lee's army was evaporating before his eyes. Part of the incentive for deserting was a decree from General Grant offering amnesty to deserting Confederates, promising "subsistence and free transportation to their homes, if ... [they] are within the lines of Federal occupation" and money if these deserters brought their "arms, horses, mules, or other property" with them. Private Noah Collins, who had been with the army since the beginning, deserted on the night of March 30:

> I went on picket duty again ... on the night of the 30th of March 1865, in quite a
> pensive, or thoughtful, and sad, or sorrowful mood ... being sorely pressed down

in mind, with regard to my savage treatment of my officers; who for no possible offense that I ever committed had been base principle enough to deny me a single furlough of indulgence during the whole war ... and the failure on the part of our Rebel officials, any conciliatory, or peace making measures, with the Northern head officials ... when nearly every person possessed of sound reason, both North and South well knew that this great Southern Rebellion was virtually crushed at that time; and that it was no better than wilful murder on the part of our Rebel officials, to continue the ... bloody war any longer; I consequently resolved to hazzard my life and health no longer for the support of a completely fallen cause....

Collins's actions, even though he went alone, were probably much like all those who had gone before him:

I voluntarily went out on vidette on the [10] o'clock relief that night, about thirty-yards in front of our skirmish line and taking a post near a large persimon tree, sat down on the south ... side ... and ... await [for] the going down of the moon ... [this] was one of the most pensive, or sad and thoughtful hours I ever experienced... I was extremely and impatient for the moon to go down.... I commenced hurry the moon in such ejaculatory phrases as "Hurry Moon Hurry, Oh Moon hurry, may the Lord hurry the moon down"... I heard the 10 o'clock relief alarm start down the line from the right, "Ten O'Clock, Ten O'Clock, Ten O'Clock," and knowing the relief would be there in a very few minutes, as it had but about thirty yards to come, and thinking that might be the last chance that might ever present itself to me, I got down on my hands and knees, thinking I might crawl off, as about half the moon was yet visable over the top of the hill ... proving to be very slow, I arose to my feet for the purpose of forever abandoning ... the fallen rebel cause, walked hurriedly and very cautiously over into the Union ... crossing a ravine ... and from thence an old road through an open field to a piece of woods ... thence through the wood, carefully examining every large tree that I passed by, for Union videttes; crossing a small creel ... till I came within about forty yards of the a union vedette post.... I looked up and seeing five or six dark figures in the distance, hollowed out "Don't shoot, I am coming over." "Are you?" said they, "Well come on; Come this way. Come this way," exclaimed about a half a dozen voices....

No matter how many felt like Noah Collins, there were still two weeks of war left. The Confederate authorities soon countered with two General Orders concerning desertion: General Order Number 8 stated that there was an "evil habit ... with some in the army of proposing to their comrades in jest to desert and go home ... the penalty for advising or persuading a soldier to desert is death: and those indulging in such jest will find it difficult on a trial to rebut the presumption of guilt arising from their words." A second order soon came out, offering a pardon to deserters "and men improperly absent [who] shall return to the commands to which they belong within the shortest possible time, not exceeding twenty days from the publication of this order...." Those who did not return to the army "Shall suffer as the courts may impose, and no application for clemency will be entertained." It appears that no member of the Thirty-seventh took up the offer of "clemency" from President Jefferson Davis.[7]

Around noon on the twenty-fifth, the Thirty-seventh was on the road again, back to the area of Mahone's division's winter quarters. Earlier that day the Federals had attempted to capture a large portion of the Confederate picket line in front of Petersburg. Their first attempt had not been successful. The Thirty-seventh soon arrived near their old quarters bordering the old Jones Farm battlefield. Not long after the men had finished their dinners, the Federals stormed the picket line again. The Union soldiers formed about 350 yards in front of the main Confederate line, in an open field. The Confederate and Federal skirmishers began to duel, and the Confederate batteries, firing over the heads of the Thirty-seventh, "open[ed] gap after gap through their ranks ... we began to inquire amongst ourselves whether they, the Union troops were men, or that they could be, that they would stand such a destructive fire from our Rebel Artillery fire so long...." The Federals were soon forced to retire to the protection of a small woods between the Confederate and Union lines. Reinforced, the Federals advanced once more, this time overwhelming the Confederate pickets and capturing their entrenched picket line. The Confederate pickets and skirmishers gave ground grudgingly, but were forced to flee. When the Federal troops had advanced to within 40 yards of the main Confederate line, the Thirty-seventh, along with the other members of the brigade, gave the Federals a volley, halting their advances. The Federal soldiers fell back a short distance and started building an advanced picket line, not far from the main Confederate line.[8]

Sunday, March 26, was a quiet day for the Thirty-seventh. The following day the sharpshooters from the brigades of McGowan, Scales, Thomas, and Lane would advance and retake portions of the ground that had been lost on the twenty-fifth. McIlwaine's Hill was a strategic point in front of the main Confederate line which had been held by the Southerners for the duration of the siege. It now lay in the hands of the Federal army, and if Union artillery was positioned on the hill, then its fire could infiltrate the Confederate lines. The four battalions of sharpshooters, approximately 400 soldiers, assembled early on the morning of the twenty-seventh. They were deployed with Lane's sharpshooters on the right, McGowan on their left, and Scales and Thomas in support in the rear. The battalions began to move forward at 5:00 A.M., under orders not to fire until the opposing force opened fire. One South Carolinian wrote: "The stillness of death settled down upon the dark valley which intervened between the lines, as this little band of devoted Confederates sallied forth with undaunted courage to encounter a foe five times their number, in a strong position well fortified[.]"[9]

After moving through the pre-dawn fog and crossing a waterless tributary of the Rohoic Creek, the Confederates approached to within 30 to 50 yards of the Federal line before encountering any of the Union pickets. One picket cried out a demand, and the Confederates answered with a yell and rushed ahead, capturing numerous soldiers. As the Confederate battalions reached the crest of the small hill, the sharpshooters of Lane's brigade changed front to the right, with McGowan's changing front to the left. The two battalions in reserve then moved up into position in the center of the line. With the hill secure, other elements of Wilcox's division, including the Thirty-seventh, moved forward to support the sharpshooters and to guard against a

Federal counterattack. They suffered four wounded during their advance. By noon, a flag of truce had been sent out and the two opposing forces worked to gather the wounded and bury the dead of the day's action, as well as those of the skirmishes that took place on the twenty-fifth.[10]

Alexander chronicled in his diary on Tuesday, March 28: "All quiet This is a beautiful day — warm and pleasant." March 29 would bring more action, an interruption to the "all quiet" of the day before. Grant had sent General Sheridan, with two Federal corps, to attack the Confederate right in an attempt to turn Lee's flank and cut off the Confederate supply lines. Lee countered by sending his cavalry (under Fitz Lee), Pickett's division, McGowan's brigade, and other Confederate troops in an attempt to destroy the Union forces. With McGowan pulling out of the Petersburg entrenchments, General Wilcox's other brigades, including Lane's, were forced to once again lengthen their already thin, over-extended lines to cover the gaps. The Confederate soldiers were now spaced, according to General Wilcox, an average of ten feet apart. Rain began to fall again on the night of the twenty-ninth, and would continue on until mid-morning of the thirty-first. Lane's brigade, still containing the Thirty-seventh, was positioned between Thomas's brigade on the left and Erson's brigade on the right. Lane's right flank rested on a ravine that contained one of the lesser tributaries of Arthur's Swamp. The Thirty-third was on the left, followed by the Eighteenth, and then the Thirty-seventh, next to the ravine, with the Twenty-eighth on the other side of the ravine. On the evening of April 1, the Union artillery once again opened upon the Confederate fortifications, blasting the Confederates for three hours. General Wilcox called the barrage "an almost incessant cannonade, solid shot and shell whizzing through the air and bursting in every direction, at times equal in brilliancy to a vivid meteoric display." General Grant had found the weakness that had eluded the Union forces for so long, and that weakness was Arthur's Swamp.[11]

The small tributary that bordered on Lane's flank was approximately 60 feet wide, but "broadened into a flat marsh as it approached the Union picket lines." The ravine had started the winter full of timber, but the timber had been cut by the Confederates to heat their crude cabins as the cold season had progressed. Now all that was left was a field of stumps. One historian would write of the area: "Because of the swampy nature of this ground, the once-thick tree cover, and the emplacement of artillery on either side of the drainage, the Confederates had not deemed it necessary to extend their entrenchments across the miniature valley." This was an unguarded avenue into the Confederate works.[12]

At 4:40 A.M. on the dark morning of a day that promised to be clear and mild, a Federal artillery piece fired from the Union-held Fort Fisher. Grant's Federal troops, nearly 60,000 in number, stepped off in the early morning darkness toward the Confederate lines, defended by, at most, 25,000 men. At 5:15 the Confederate lines that had withstood so many assaults were broken. "At dawn this morning the enemy broke through in Lane's front, and carried the entire line," one member of the Thirty-seventh would chronicle in his diary. As the men of the Thirty-seventh peered out into the pre-dawn blackness, shapes began to appear. With a yell, the Union soldiers

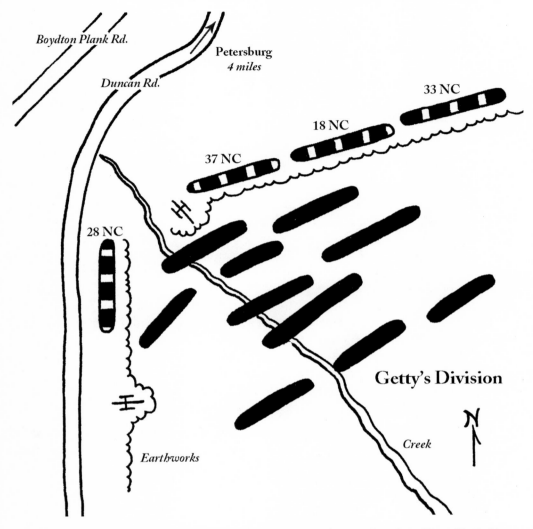

Boydton Plank Rd.

Petersburg
4 miles

Duncan Rd.

33 NC

18 NC

37 NC

28 NC

Getty's Division

N

Creek

Earthworks

Breakthrough on April 2, 1865, south of Petersburg, Virginia (current location of Pamplin Park).

charged the line. The Vermont brigade was in the lead, but were largely entangled in the ravine. The Thirty-seventh Massachusetts Volunteers, of Wheaton's Division, rushed the Confederate line held by the Thirty-seventh. The first Massachusetts soldier to enter the Tar Heels' section of line was Captain J. C. Robinson, who was soon wounded. Other Federals soon came pouring into the works. The fight was brief, but sharp. First Lieutenant Octavius A. Wiggins (Company E) "received a scalp wound, the muzzle of the gun being in such close proximity to his head as to blow powder into his face, nearly destroying his eyes and knocking him senseless upon the ground." Captains William T. Nicholson (Company E), John B. Petty (Company F), and Daniel L. Hudson (Company G) were all killed in the melee. The Thirty-seventh's only field officer, Major Bost, would chronicle: "I was driven from the works, the line on the right and left of me in the regt. Was broken and the enemy were filing down in the rear of our works toward Petersburg. I had to fall back directly to the rear and formed a skirmish line as best I could to keep the enemy from advancing too fast in our rear, and to give our wagons time to get out[.]"[13]

Several members of the Thirty-seventh Massachusetts, including Corporal Richard Welch of Company E, rushed up to the Thirty-seventh's color-bearer and knocked him down, taking the flag the Thirty-seventh had borne since December 1862. Welch, an Irish-born yankee soldier, would be awarded the Congressional Medal of Honor for his actions. Lieutenant William A. Waterman, Corporal Luther M. Tanner, and Private Michael Kelly, of the Thirty-seventh Massachusetts, were also involved in the fray around the flag of the Tar Heels. Waterman was wounded in the wrist, and Tanner and Kelly were killed. Another member of the Thirty-seventh North Carolina Troops, who had tried to shoot the commanding officer of the Massachusetts regiment as he came over the top of the parapet, was bayoneted by Corporal Patrick Kelly before Kelly was killed. All told, the Thirty-seventh North Carolina Troops would lose six men killed, seven wounded (of which one died), and 168 captured (including four of the wounded).

Lieutenant Wiggins, after his capture, was taken to the rear as a prisoner. He found several friends in the Thirty-seventh behind the lines, including Private Rufus G. Culler of Company F, and they commenced to pick out the tiny grains of powder that had embedded themselves in the lieutenant's face. The Thirty-seventh prisoners were marched back to City Point, and from there taken by boat to Washington, D.C. From there the Confederate officers were loaded on a train and started to the prison on Johnson's Island. Lieutenant Wiggins would write of his journey:

> ...in the dead of the night, the writer jumped from the window of the car while it was running at the rate of forty miles an hour. Why he did not break his neck, the Lord only knows, but he was not even hurt, except a few scratches on the forehead where it plowed in the sand. Fortunately for him, he had on a suit of clothes made of an old gray shawl, such as the students at Chapel Hill wore before the war, cutting off the brass buttons from the coat and vest and substituting wooden pegs, he was in perfect disguise and passed as a laborer, working a day or so at one place, then moving farther south, until he reached Baltimore, thence by steamer to Richmond, but too late to do any more fighting[,] for General Lee had surrendered.[14]

After the breakthrough, the remnants of the Thirty-seventh would make a couple of stands against the Federals, but were forced to retreat back toward Battery Gregg and the inner Petersburg lines.

Ambrose P. Hill, the Thirty-seventh's corps commander, had been up before daylight and had ridden to General Lee's headquarters. A member of Lee's staff, Colonel Charles Venable, soon brought word of the collapse of a part of the Confederate line, the part under the command of Hill where the Thirty-seventh was stationed. Hill, with a couple of members of his staff, rushed toward the right to assess the damage and to try to stabilize things. As they rode through the early morning light, shots rang out nearby, possibly fire by members of the Thirty-seventh, and the mounted officers came across two Federal infantrymen. The two aides, courier William H. Jenkins and Sergeant George W. Tucker, quickly darted in front of the General with drawn revolvers and demanded the surrender of the Federal infantrymen. They dropped their rifles, and Hill sent them to the rear with Jenkins. Hill and Tucker continued on toward the Confederate right. Federals were lurking everywhere in the woods. Tucker tried to keep in

Private Rufus G. Culler, Company F, and his wife (courtesy of Rufus W. Culler).

front of the general. In their front, they saw two Federals run behind a large tree for cover. Both Federals aimed their rifles in the direction of the two Confederates. Tucker demanded their surrender: Hill rode up beside Tucker, with his pistol drawn, and echoed Tucker's ultimatum. Both of the Federals, members of the One-hundred-and-thirty-eighth Pennsylvania, fired. One shot missed Tucker. The other struck Hill, cutting off his left thumb and striking him in the heart, making a large exit wound. The impact spun the general around, and Hill's lifeless corpse fell to the ground. Tucker grabbed Hill's horse and rode swiftly back to Lee's headquarters. By 9:30 A.M. that morning, Alexander jotted in his diary: "Hill reported killed...."[15]

Along the lines, the desperate struggle for the life of the Confederacy would continue without General Hill. Portions of the Thirty-seventh rallied on the Church Road, but were soon forced back to the Boydton Plank Road. Other members of the Thirty-seventh moved into Fort Gregg, an unfinished earthen fort, with walls that were eight feet thick, the top protected by a palisade of logs. The fort contained six artillery embrasures, only three of which would have guns in them during the upcoming contest. The majority of the men huddled inside of the fort were members of Lane's brigade. There were a few others—artillerists, and a few men from Harris' Mississippi Brigade. Private Angelum A. Garrison (Company C) would recall: "General Lane 'gathered' his men (sixteen in all), one of whom was Lieutenant Riglar, [and] turned us over to him.... We were all of the 37th North Carolina Regiment." Lieutenant George H. Snow of the Thirty-third, in command of the men of Lane's brigade inside the fort, would write: "at least three-forths were of your [Lane's] brigade. I think I had between seventy-five and eighty men all told...." General Wilcox rode up to the fort and admonished the soldiers inside: "Men, the salvation of Lee's Army is in your keeping; you must realize the responsibility, and your duty; don't surrender this fort; if you hold the enemy in check for two hours, Longstreet, who is making a forced march, will be here, and the danger to the army in the trenches will be averted." The Confederate and Union artillery soon began to play, the Federals "directing a brisk and well-directed fire upon Gregg...."[16]

The Federal infantry soon came into sight. One Mississippian later wrote: "Ah, what a contrast, what a soul-sickening spectacle to behold. 25,000 men, flushed with recent victory, to be hurled against 250 ... half starved heroes, whose hearts of steel qualled not even at such fearful odds." These were men of Foster's divisions. With two brigades of Turner's division in support, all of the XIV Corps, under the command of John Gibbon, commenced the attack. "About ten o'clock the enemy commenced charging with four or five lines," Lieutenant Rigler would write a few years after the war.

> We did not fire until they were within forty yards, and then gave them one volley; they wavered, and the first line gave way; the second came forward, and came within thirty yards of the fort. We yelled and fired—they stood a few seconds and then broke. The third retreated also, but the forth and fifth came to the ditch around the fort. While this fighting was in the front, one line came in the rear and almost got inside of the fort through the door. About twenty men charged them, drove them back. About eleven o'clock they scaled the walls of the fort, and for several minutes we had a hand to hand fight. We used the bayonet, and killed almost all of them that came on the top.

Things from the private's point of view were just as heated inside the fort. Private Garrison chronicled: "A man of Company D, of our regiment, volunteered to shoot while three of us loaded, and we did the best that was possible. I had eighty rounds of new cartridges; and when I surrendered, my cartridge box was nearly empty. This soldier of Company D took good aim, and I think he must have killed or wounded scores of the enemy."[17]

Twenty-year-old Lieutenant Rigler would conclude his story of the defense of the fort:

> About half-past eleven they attempted to scale the walls again. We met them with the bayonets, and for several minutes it was the most desperate struggle I ever witnessed; but it did not last long. Soon they were all killed or knocked back, and then a deafening shout arouse from our boys. Near twelve, they tried to force they way through the door in the rear of the fort, and succeeded in getting almost in, but we meet them with the bayonet and drove them back. By this time the ammunition was almost out, and our men threw bats and rocks at them in the ditch. No ammunition would we get, and after a short struggle, they took the fort, and some few did fire on us after they got possession, but their officers tried to stop them.

General Wilcox would add this, viewing things from outside the fort while in the Confederate lines: "As they [Federals] appeared at this point [Gregg], they were either shot or thrust off with the bayonet. Again and again this was done. At length numbers prevailed, and the parapet of the little work was thickly covered with men, six flags being seen on it at the same time; and from this dense mass a close, and of necessity destructive fire, was poured down upon the devoted band within."[18]

Casualties resulting from the battle of Fort Gregg are unknown for the Thirty-seventh. It is known that Lieutenant Rigler and Private Garrison were captured. After their capture, they were marched to the observation tower near Fort Fisher, and then forwarded to City Point and then to Point Lookout, Maryland. General Gibbons would inform General Wilcox on the day of the surrender that they had found 67 Confederates dead inside the fort. The attack had cost the XIV Corps close to 800 casualties. The sacrifice by the members of the Thirty-seventh and the other regiments in Lane's brigade (along with a few from Harris's brigade and a handful of artillerymen) had saved the Army of Northern Virginia, at least for the time being. Longstreet had gotten his men into a position in the inner line of works that protected the town of Petersburg.[19]

The remaining members of the Thirty-seventh fell back into the inner line of Petersburg's defenses and prepared to evacuate the city. Alexander, who was stationed at the hospital during the morning's assault, received his orders to move to the 2 P.M. trains, as "minié balls were falling in our camp...." His train did not leave until sunset, headed for Chesterfield Court House. A few of the wounded had been transferred the day before to hospitals in Farmville and Lynchburg. Many of the sick and wounded in the hospitals around Richmond were left to be captured by the Federals as they advanced upon the city.[20]

Orders came to withdraw from the lines at midnight. The remnants of Hill's corps were to cross over the Battersea Cotton Factory pontoon bridge to the north side of the Appomattox River, and then to march west along the River Road. Barrels of tar had been lit to provide light during the dark night, and the fragrance of tobacco that had been burning in the warehouses in Petersburg for hours filled the cold night air and stung at the eyes of the weary Tar Heels. The magazines of the Confederate forts and batteries exploded with earth-jarring concussions as they were destroyed. Added to this were countless women and children, weeping, "lamenting the fate which they knew daylight would bring." Many members of the Thirty-seventh were captured within the town of Petersburg. They had either been sick or too tired to continue on. At least 12 members of the regiment were captured the next day in the hospitals of Richmond. The exhausted, worn, and hungry men of the Thirty-seventh continued to move throughout a night of gloom and uncertainty, continuing on the following spring day, bivouacking at Amelia Court House on the night of April 4. When they reached Amelia, the 350,000 rations that General Lee had ordered brought to Richmond to feed his men had not arrived, due to confusion in the War Department. Wagons were sent out into the country to forage for food. They came back almost empty. The countryside had already been scoured for supplies during the past year and had little to offer the Confederates.[21]

The rain and chilly wind continued on the night of the fourth and into the morning of the fifth, making the muddy roads still more impassable. Around noon, the Tar Heels resumed their march, halting that evening some four or five miles from

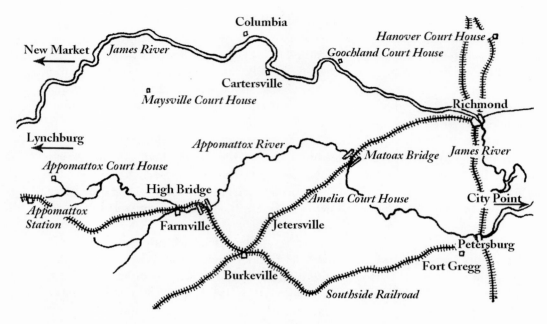

Appomattox, Virgina, and vicinity, April 1865.

Amelia Court House, near the railroad. "A line of battle was formed," General Wilcox wrote, "and slight skirmishing [occurred] between our and the enemy's cavalry." The Confederate column would begin moving again that night, after dark, toward Burkeville. The night was brisk and overcast.[22]

On the afternoon of April 6, the Thirty-seventh would be called upon once more to meet the enemy. Longstreet deployed his troops in a line of battle covering the roads to Rice's Station and at right angles to the South Side Railroad. Field's division was placed across the Burkeville Road, with Mahone's division in support. Wilcox's division, with Lane's brigade and the Thirty-seventh, was on the right, with Heth's division in support. Orders were issued for the men to entrench. At 8 P.M. that evening the Confederates were pulled from their works and began another night march. Field's division was in the lead, followed by Heth, and then Wilcox in the rear. As they marched along, "the troops (Heth and Wilcox) halted for wagons to pass, the bridge had been injured by the breaking of a plank, the approach to it was over a muddy flat, covered with water in some parts.... Lights were made and men stationed to warn the teamsters when and how to drive." Some of the soldiers had begun to slip away. Between April 2 and April 9, twenty-eight men would disappear into the surrounding countryside, only to turn up at home a few days later.[23]

They continued to march until 9 A.M. on the seventh, when they reached Farmville. The famished soldiers piled out to receive rations: "bread ... meat ... [and] dried French soup packaged in tinfoil...." The remaining members of the Thirty-seventh would have little time to enjoy their small meal. They were soon called upon to form again in a line of battle, this time extending the Confederate flank and providing support in the battle around Cumberland Church. Lane's sharpshooters, still under the command of Major Wooten, were engaged by the Federals, and the Thirty-seventh lost two men: Lorenzo D. Triplett (Company B), wounded in the left foot and captured, and Jonas Clemmer (Company H), also captured.[24]

During the evening they would once again march through the night, with Longstreet's men moving by way of the Piedmont Coal Mines Road (Old Lynchburg Wagon Road), and the rest of the Confederates following the Maysville or Bucking-ham Court House Plank Road. When the two corps reached the crossing of these two roads, Lee moved Gordon's Corps, which had been in the rear, to the front, and Longstreet's men fell in behind them. The Thirty-seventh would leave eight of its members at Farmville to be captured by the Union forces. They were either too sick or too tired to continue.

On April 8 the Army of Northern Virginia was officially consolidated and placed under two field commanders: John B. Gordon and James Longstreet. The Thirty-seventh was still in Lane's brigade, Wilcox's division, but the men were now in Long-street's corps, under the same commander that they had been under three years earlier after the Seven Days campaign. Many soldiers awoke on the morning of the eighth with frost covering them, and rain continued off and on all day and into that night. Private Alexander, still with the medical wagon, wrote in his diary: "we have heard no firing today so far it is the first quiet day ... that we have had...."[25]

April 9 would greet the men with a chill in the air and a heavy fog. The fog later burned off to a blue cloudless sky that had a smell of spring in the air. Just before dawn, orders were received by General Lane to order his men to fall in and march toward Appomattox Court House. Gordon had begun to battle the Federals early that morning, hoping to cut through the Federal forces so Lee could join up with General Johnston and the remnants of the Army of Tennessee in North Carolina. The brigade would halt two miles east of the courthouse. At 10 A.M., orders came for the members of the brigade to take up the march once again, toward the sounds of the battle. But before they could arrive, they were diverted to the south to counter a Federal movement in that direction. They had commenced the change in direction when orders were received to halt and stack arms. One member of the regiment, Featherson W. Armstrong (Company H), recalled after the war that Robert E. Lee had passed so close to him "that I could of touched his coat" and he overheard the general say that "A soldiers life isn't worth that," referring to the battle currently tak-ing place. "The army has been surrendered," Private Alexander would scribble in his diary on April 9, "Our arms have all been stacked — in the evening the terms were made known — all to be paroled — private property to be respected — we will all be sent home."[26]

Generals Lee and Grant were in the process of meeting to discuss the surrender of the Army of Northern Virginia, even as the Thirty-seventh marched toward the sound of the battle. Terms had been reached as the generals met in the parlor of the William McLean House. Those terms were:

Rolls of all the officers and men to be made in duplicate — one copy to be given to an officer designated by me, the other to be retained by such officers as you may designate; the officers to give their individual paroles not to take up arms against the Government of the United States until properly exchanged, and each company or regimental commander sign a like parole for the men of their commands. The arms, artillery and public property to be parked and stacked and turned over to the officer appointed by me to receive them. This will not embrace the side-arms of the officers, nor their private horses or baggage. This done, each officer and man will be allowed to return to their homes, not to be disturbed by the United States authority so long as they observe their paroles and the laws in force where they may reside.[27]

General Lee accepted General Grant's terms laid out in the document and surrendered his army.

"The life of the C. S. 'is gone,'" Private Alexander would write. Rations were issued to the Confederate troops by their captors on April 9. The only thing remaining to the men for the Thirty-seventh would be the stacking of their arms. On April 10, General Lee would issue his final General Order to the Army of Northern Virginia:

GENERAL ORDER NO. 9
Headquarters, Army of Northern Virginia
April 10, 1865

After four years of arduous service, marked by unsurpassed courage and fortitude, the Army of Northern Virginia has been compelled to yield to overwhelming numbers and resources.

I need not tell the brave survivors of so many hard fought battles, who have remained steadfast to the last, that I have consented to this result from no distrust of them.

But feeling that valor and devotion could accomplish nothing that would compensate for the loss that must have attended the continuance, I determined to avoid the useless sacrifice of those whose past service have endeared them to their countrymen.

By the term of the agreement officers and men can return to their homes and remain until exchanged. You will take with you the satisfaction that proceeds from the consciousness of duty faithfully performed, and I earnestly pray that a Merciful God will extend to you His blessing and protection.

With an increasing admiration of your constancy and devotion to your country, and a grateful remembrance of your kind and generous consideration for myself, I bid you all an affectionate farewell.

R. E. Lee
Genl.[28]

On that morning the generals agreed to issue paroles to the Confederate troops. A printing press was secured and the process was finished the next day. Private Alexander would provide a glimpse into the Army of Northern Virginia on the same day:

Apl 10th -65 We are all prisoners but you would not know it were it not told us, as the enemy are kept at their lines and our men not mix with them....

Apl 11th We are still in sus-
pence not knowing when we will
get off the cavalry & artillery are
being paroled We have not drawn
any bread rations since our surrender — the weather still damp —

Apl 12th -65 4 P.M. we have
received our parole papers and
have started —

The Thirty-seventh would surrender
115 men on April 12. They would
march up, in between two Federal brigades, stop, front, stack their rifled-
muskets, and furl their colors. The
paroles that each man received read:
"All officers and men of the Confederate service paroled at Appomattox
Court House who to reach their homes
are compelled to pass through the lines
of the Union armies, will be allowed
to do so, and to pass free on all Government transports and military railroads."[29]

The former members of the
Thirty-seventh would start on their
way home that evening. Alexander
would chronicle their trip:

Private Andrew Spears, Company I, who surrendered at Appomattox Court House on April 9,
1865.

(April 12) [we] traveled very
rapidly through the rain &
mud — I slept in a haystack....

(April 13) We started early to
Carmichael C. H. got their at 1
P.M. I got some beans and they
are being cooked — we have
drawn but two rations of bread
in ten days but we have plenty of
meat — we ... slept in a fence corner — we have a nice supper of
beef & bread, and a good nights
sleep on a bed of leaves

(April 14) We started at sunrise feeling fresh 55 miles to Danville ... we have had
a plenty to eat

(April 15) We found it raining this morning — marched into town ... and rested
untill 2 P.M. [and] eat something — the road was desperately muddy — but we
marched within 8 miles of Danville — and halted before sunset — to rest and eat —
and to push on to Danville

> (April 16) We arrived at D[anville] at sunrise and got a train to the half way sta-
> tion and there we were ordered off and the train sent back — we walked to the river
> ten miles — the R.R. bridge was burned, and trains come unto the other side — the
> train left....
>
> (April 17) We spent the night near the river ... the conductor refused to carry us
> untill he was compelled — I got to Greensboro at 10 A.M. and dined with a. Cald-
> well and spent the night with George Donell — the first good sleep that I have had.
>
> (April 18) I went to town and drew two suits of cloth — a truce is pending between
> Johnson & Sherman....
>
> (April 19) Returned to town and heard that Abe Lincoln and several [others] have
> been killed — an armistice of ten days have been agreed upon....
>
> (April 20) We started early ... and walked to High Point (five miles) spent a pleas-
> ant day with some cousins — the train came down from Salisbury, to secure a seat,
> we got on and went back to the river the cars were very much crowded, also loaded
> with ammunition — it was quite dangerous ride — arrived at Salisbury at 11 P.M. and
> walked out on the road expecting to meet a train but were disappoint.
>
> (April 21) We started early and walked to "China Grove" meeting no train we
> hurried on to Cousin Bettie Rankins — a long hard march 20 miles from Salisbury —
> we have nothing to eat for 24 hours ... expect to get home this evening — I arrived
> at home at dark — I found all well.[30]

The adventure home was not without mishap. While traveling down the rails,
some of the members of the Thirty-seventh "were in and on top of the box cars, when
the burden to one was breaking in the top and threatening serious disaster," related
one veteran after the war's end. Other members of the regiment braced the roof and
finally got the train to stop.

> The conductor and engineer went back to the broken car and ordered the men to
> get down, but they guyed and ridiculed the railroaders. The Federal officer in charge,
> who was riding in a passenger car, was appealed to, and he ordered the men to get
> down, but with like result. The hardy Confederates were defiant to the last. It was
> reckless of them to take such peril on their own account, but they were accustomed
> to peril, and there seemed to be a fascination in it to them. When their own com-
> mander ... realized the situation, he said, "Come down, boys!" That was enough. In
> quicker time than it could be written they got off the broken car.[31]

For many, the trip home was probably like that of James Addison Myers. After
being granted a sick furlough in the waning days of the war, Myers, his wife Susie,
and their infant daughter made their way to the train station. Trains were running
somewhat irregularly and the adventure was toilsome for the weak soldiers. "Every
car of any train was loaded," chronicled Myers after the war,

> and people were hanging on the cars from the outside. We waited ... thinking ... we
> would be able to get enough space ... to get us home. We were so very tired! I made
> up my mind I was going to get on the next train to get us home. I don't know where
> my strength came from.... I pushed with every once of strength in my entire body
> to get into one of those box cars. I took Susie by the hand, we ducked our heads and
> pushed with all our might until we forced our way into the middle of a box car. They
> warned us that nobody else could get into that car, but I was tired of waiting, sick
> and homesick.... [the] old box car [had] been used to haul cattle. There were no
> seats of any kind and we had to sit on the floor.... War is a terrible thing.[32]

14

"Grand, grim, titantic warrors of a cause"
April 1865–Present

"April 20, [1865 ... we] spent a pleasant day with some cousins," wrote former hospital steward William D. Alexander. Thus began the rest of the lives of the remaining members of the Thirty-seventh North Carolina Troops. But when they returned, what was the condition of the land they had left?[1]

Since Burnside's invasion in early 1862, which constituted the Thirty-seventh's baptism of fire, the coastal plain area of eastern North Carolina had been under Federal control longer than any other region. Many of the pro–Southern families of the area had fled farther inland to escape rule under the dreaded yankees, leaving their fields to lie fallow, and their homes and possessions unprotected. The piedmont area of the state had provided much of the war matériel for North Carolina. It was their crops that fed the Army of Northern Virginia, and their cotton and wool that were woven into jeanscloth to clothe the Confederate soldiers. But General George Stoneman's raiders moved into portions of the piedmont, along with elements of General Sherman's Federal army during the latter days of the war. Much military and personal property was destroyed.

The western areas of the state had escaped the larger campaigns of war until the very end, when Stoneman moved through the counties of Watauga and Wilkes and down into the piedmont, skirmishing with Confederate home guards and burning houses, factories, and other buildings. But the war in the western mountains had raged on a small scale throughout the entire four years. Union sympathizers had crept into the state from Tennessee and had stolen horses, food, and other provisions; and Confederate militia and home guard units tracked them back into Tennessee and regained their property. To further complicate matters, many inter-kinship group

235

Lieutenant Isaac Wilson, Company E (courtesy of Clinton Getzinger).

struggles took place. Such struggles were not just relegated to the mountains, but, due to the close ties of families in that area, they seemed to be more common. The violence that erupted in these conflicts can be seen in the case of Lieutenant Isaac Wilson of Company A.

Isaac Wilson was born December 16, 1822, in Ashe County. Apparently, his first cousin had married Andy Potter, of whom her parents had strongly disapproved. They objected so much that the young couple moved to Missouri for some time. When the war came, Isaac Wilson enlisted in the "Watauga Minute Men" on September 18, 1861. He was elected third lieutenant on the same day, and soon thereafter, the regiment transferred to one of the camps of instruction established near Raleigh. Army life must not have been to the liking of the twenty-eight-year-old lieutenant, for on December 13, 1861, Wilson resigned from the newly formed Thirty-seventh. He continued to serve the Confederate cause as a recruiting officer in Ashe County. The home guard units in Ashe and Watauga counties worked hard to round up deserters and conscription evaders. On one of their missions they were sent to arrest some of the Potters and members of another family named Arnold. Shots were exchanged and Jack Potter was killed. Three members of the company of the home guard were Wilsons, but Isaac Wilson was not among their number. When word reached Andy Potter that the Wilsons had killed Jack, he began plotting his revenge. Isaac Wilson was out plowing his fields one morning, not long after sunrise, when two shots rang out from the woods, striking Wilson in the back. Family members found Wilson, carried him back to the house, and "placed [him] on a cot [or coat] which had been moved to the middle of the room. [H]e was still alive but not able to speak." Isaac Wilson soon died of his wounds, another life lost for the Confederate cause. The date was June 17, 1864. The retaliations between the families continued on after the war.[2]

Turbulence was general throughout the state after the official end of the war. Governor Vance had been arrested on May 13 in Statesville and sent to a military prison in Washington, D.C. On May 29, President Andrew Johnson appointed William W. Holden provisional governor of the state and issued an Amnesty Proclamation, pardoning all who would swear their allegiance to the United States. Holden was widely disliked all across the state, namely for the wartime peace movement that he had joined and promoted. Holden called for an election on September 21 for the purpose of electing delegates to a convention to be held in Raleigh. At that meeting the act of secession was repealed, slavery was abolished, and a date in November was set for the election of a new governor and representatives to the General Assembly. Jonathan Worth was elected governor; the Thirteenth Amendment was ratified; and "Union men" were elected as the state's representatives to Congress.[3]

However, all was not well. When Congress met in December 1865, the representatives from the Southern states were not seated, based upon the grounds that only the congress, and not the president, could determine a state's readmission to the Union. A radical group, close to the new president, believed that, "the time has not come for holding any relations with her [Virginia] but that of the conqueror to the conquered." That sentiment was true for all of the Southern states. In March 1867 the Congress passed the Reconstruction act, which reinstituted Government control over the states; placed an appointed United States general in control of each state; charged the commander with maintaining peace and with the protection of rights and property, using force if necessary; made existing state governments provisional and subject to modification or abolishment by the powers of the military commander; and required each state to follow a program to qualify it and its representatives for readmission to Congress. North Carolina and South Carolina constituted the Second Military District and were placed first under the command of General Daniel E. Sickles, and then later, General Edward R. S. Canby. Governor Worth was allowed to remain as governor, but with limited powers.[4]

Between January 14 and March 17, 1868, a Constitutional Convention met in Raleigh to produce a new state constitution. This constitution simulated the constitutions of Northern states in that it abolished slavery; repudiated the debt created by the war; created a bill of rights that forbade the suspension of the writ of *habeas corpus*; upheld the freedom of the press; abolished property and religious qualifications for voting; fixed the voting age at twenty-one; and provided for a public school system with a state-wide superintendent of public instruction. One month after the close of the convention, North Carolinians ratified their new constitution, and elected state and county officers (as well as representatives to the lower house of Congress). The Federal Congress accepted the state's new constitution, and North Carolina's representatives were allowed to take their seats in the House. The war had finally come to a close for many members of the Thirty-seventh.

However, while the war was legally over, it continued to rage in the minds and bodies of many men who had served in the Thirty-seventh. Not all of those returning from the front lines to their native state returned whole. Many would suffer from what doctors would eventually term Post Traumatic Stress Disorder, sometimes called "soldier's heart" during the war. Unfortunately for these soldiers, their actions led to "imputations of malingering, allegations of cowardice or charges of desertion." In later conflicts, such soldiers might have been diagnosed with combat trauma, but during their war they were often executed for cowardice. It was much more than just the personal horrors of combat that brought about the disorder. "In addition to directly experiencing an event," wrote one modern doctor, "threatening death, serious injury, or loss of physical integrity, an individual may witness or be confronted with such events."[5]

Many other veterans suffered from more obvious scars. Leander R. Gryder (Company G) was wounded during the battle of Chancellorsville and carried a yankee minié ball in his leg for the rest of his life, walking with a limp. According to his family, he stumbled over a log one day, breaking the leg. Blood poisoning set in and he died shortly thereafter. John C. Black, Jr. (Company C), who was captured on April 3, 1865, near Petersburg, suffered a hernia while in prison at Hart's Island, New York. This would lead to bladder and kidney problems for the rest of his life. Added to this, he suffered an ear infection that resulted in a loss of hearing. Even though his wound was not recorded in his compiled service record, Corporal William P. Perteete's (Company F) leg wound never healed and, according to family, had to be dressed every day of his life. After being wounded in both legs during the battle of New Bern in March 1862, Company A's Andrew Jackson Stuart shot and killed a yankee, but during his recuperation he contracted an unknown illness that led to blindness and his discharge on December 6, 1862. Despite these hardships, he continued with life — fathering fourteen children, twelve of whom would live past infancy — and died in 1907.[6]

James P. Griffin (Company D), who moved to Weakly County, Tennessee, after the war, carried his wound for many years. Griffin was wounded on August 29, 1862, during the battle of Second Manassas, "in the leg between the knee and ankle." After moving to Tennessee in 1877 and working as a farmer, "he had the wounded leg taken off ... on April 10, 1894 ... after a period of nearly thirty-two years, having suffered very much at times.... Before having his leg amputated he made for himself a wooden leg.... He is now well, cheerful, and happy, and sends greetings to old comrades who remember him." North Carolina provided some relief for her soldiers who had lost limbs due to combat injuries. Thirty-three of the members of the Thirty-seventh applied for aid and received prosthetics.[7]

Other families were denied even the return of a maimed loved one. Private James M. Tugman's (Company B) story illustrates the grief and sadness for many. Tugman, the oldest of four children, had marched away with the men of Company B in the early days of the war. He soon contracted typhoid fever and was sent to a hospital in Richmond. From there he drafted a letter home, saying that he was unwell and had lost the use of his legs. "Dear Father," his letter read, "I want you to come after me the doctor says he will discharge me if you will come after me.... I want you to come as quick as you can for I can't live here...." As the postwar story goes, James's mother read and re-read the letter as James father made his way to Abington, Virginia, to take a train to Richmond. "I will have Jim walking again soon," thought his mother, Nancy. James's father arrived in Richmond and found his sick son in one of the hospital wards. He spent some time with James, sometimes called Jim by his family, and had left to procure a wagon to take James back to the train station. When his father returned, James was dead. They acquired a coffin, dressed James in his uniform, wrapped him in his "heavy army blanket," and placed him in the coffin. He was taken to the train station and started back home to Ashe County. James's mother, who did not know that her son had died, made a comfortable bed for him and cooked plenty of food. She had gone out on the porch of their home when she soon heard a wagon coming up the mountain…. The wagon seemed to be coming very slowly and Jim's mother was sure someone was bringing Jim and his father home in a wagon. Just then she saw a neighbor man and his wife coming out from the road toward the house. As they came closer, Nancy sensed something was wrong… Nancy walked out to meet the neighbors and the man started speaking, telling her that Cajer had stopped at their house and asked them to go and tell Nancy that he was bringing Jim home and that Jim was dead…. Nancy didn't say a word, but started walking swiftly toward the big gate. She thought the saddest sound she had ever heard was the noise the wagon made coming up the mountain bringing her boy home…. Behind the wagon Cajer was walking with his head down and with one hand holding to the wagon bed. On the wagon was a rough box-like casket… she stepped around the wagon to walk home beside him. When they got to the house, the casket was lifted from the wagon and placed on the porch…. The neighbors all gathered at the home the next morning. A grave was dug for Jim on the top of the hill back of the house…. At least two songs were sung while Jim's casket was lowered into the grave and dirt shoveled on it, "Life's Railway to Heaven" and Nancy's favorite, "Snow White Angel Band."[8]

Tragic homecomings were also in order for the families of the Thirty-seventh's two colonels. The regiment's first colonel, Charles C. Lee, had been killed on June 30, 1862, during the battle of Frayser's Farm. Lee's remains were taken back to Charlotte and interred in Elmwood Cemetery. Lee's wife, Anna Tripp, and his four children, Anna C., Eula, Chillers, and Florence, continued to live in the Charlotte area. Tripp married a man named Moyle, and applied for a widow's pension in 1911. The Lees and Moyles are all buried together near the Confederate section of Elmwood Cemetery.[9]

The Thirty-seventh's only other colonel, William M. Barber, had tried to resign on two different occasions during the war. The first time was on July 30, 1862. He again tendered his resignation on September 24, 1864, not long after he was wounded. Either his resignation was not accepted or had not been approved before he was wounded a second time. He died of those wounds on October 3, 1864, at the General Hospital in Petersburg. Colonel Barber's remains were interred at the St. Paul's Episcopal Churchyard in Wilkesboro, North Carolina. After the war, Barber's widow, Ada Alexander, sold the Colonel's laws books and moved, with their three children, Edward A., Annie Powell (born during the war), and Mary Ellis, to Van Buren, Arkansas, where she worked as a tutor.[10]

Other former members of the Thirty-seventh survived combat only to meet tragic ends after the close of the war. First Lieutenant Richard G. Goodman (Company A) was killed in 1867 at a dance in Jefferson. After the war, Private Jacob Finley Tolliver (Company K) had moved to Elliot County, Kentucky, with his wife, Orleana Watts. On August 10, 1901, Tolliver and his six sons were murdered, victims of the infamous Martin-Tolliver feud. Joseph B. Burleyson, a private in Company C, survived the war and Union prison camps only to lose his life in a cotton gin accident after the war. His arm became entwined in the contraption, and Burleyson bled to death in his own living room after he loosened the tourniquet that the doctor had placed on him.[11]

Top left: Ada Alexander Barber, wife of Colonel William M. Barber. *Top right:* Annie Powell Barber, born c. 1862, daughter of Colonel William M. Barber. *Bottom left:* Edward Barber, born c. 1860, son of Colonel William M. Barber. *Bottom right:* Mary Ellis Barber, born c. 1864, daughter of Colonel William M. Barber (courtesy of Betsy Barber Hawkins).

But there were also happy moments for the many veterans of the Thirty-seventh. James A. Myers, whose wife had traveled to Petersburg to bring him home, prospered after the war, having eight more children (in addition to the one born during the war) and building a very prosperous farm. In one season, it was reported, he grew and harvested one hundred and twenty-five bushels of corn from one acre of land. Rufus Govan Culler (Company F) was released from Point Lookout, Maryland, on June 24, 1865, and, according to family history, it took him over a year to walk home, due to his injuries and poor health. His wife, Salena, and her mother were sitting on the front porch of their home "when they noticed a man slowly making his way up the road to the house ... they finally recognized [the man] as Govan and Selana ran out to great him with many hugs and kisses."[12]

Many former soldiers were able to adjust to civilian life despite grievous injuries. Joseph Lemmond Orr (Company I), who had lost an arm due to his wounding at Chancellorsville, returned to Charlotte after the war and was selected as a member of the local police force. "Notwithstanding the fact that he had only one arm[,] Mr. Orr made a most excellent officer, arresting all offenders without regard to class or condition." So wrote a local paper. "He was always fair and fearless." Orr was promoted to the rank of sergeant, and later, assistant chief of the Mecklenburg Police force.

Former Captain W.W. Lenoir returned home to Caldwell County after he was wounded during the battle of Ox Hill, September 1, 1862, and subsequently ordered a wooden leg from a firm in Philadelphia. The leg, Walter said in a letter, was "as good as they make 'em, but ... a wretched substitute for the one that I left in Virginia." After the war concluded, Walter farmed on a piece of property entitled "Crab Orchard," in Haywood County. He sold this piece of property in 1874 and relocated to the Shull's Mill area of Watauga County, where he worked at improving his land by clearing it, building fences, and planting grass for his cattle and sheep to graze upon. In 1882 Lenoir won a seat to the North Carolina House of Representatives, where he served one term. In June of 1887, Walter sold his Watauga County holdings, some 7,890 acres, which included Grandfather Mountain.[13]

A member of Company F, William Riley Price, sharecropped on Lenoir's land after the war. Price, according to family history, had helped save Lenoir's life after the captain had been wounded at Ox Hill. Lenoir let Price, Price's wife, Barbara Ann Cline, and their nine children live in a cabin that General William Lenoir, Captain Lenoir's grandfather, had built when he moved to the area not long after the end of the American Revolution. Price died in 1879 and is supposedly buried in a hollow with another Confederate soldier there in the Yadkin Valley.[14]

Not everyone who returned to North Carolina after the war remained within the Old North State. Some of the men would move just across the state line into Tennessee. Alexander B. Watts (Company D) moved to Madison County; James H. Teaster (Company E) moved to Carter County; and Albert F. Montgomery (Company I) moved to Weakly County. Some would seek new lives on the western frontier. William J. Goss (Company A) had been captured at Falling Waters, Virginia, on July 14, 1863. He was sent to Point Lookout, Maryland, where on February 2, 1864, he took the Oath of Allegiance and joined the Federal Army. Given the choice of fighting fellow Southerners or fighting Indians, he chose the latter and was assigned to Company I, First Regiment United States Volunteer Infantry. After his term of service was up, he went back to Ashe County, collected his belongings, and moved back out west, first to Pueblo, and then to Fruita, Colorado.[15]

Captain Thomas J. Armstrong (Company K) also headed west. Born on August 30, 1834, in Rockford, North Carolina, Armstrong was a civil engineer prior to the war, surveying roads for the Western North Carolina Railway. After the war concluded, he took his wife, Laura Clark of Iredell County, and moved first to Arago, Nebraska, and then in 1871, to Highland, Kansas, where he was employed as a bookkeeper in the insurance industry. He passed away on August 15, 1908, and is buried with his wife in Highland, Kansas.[16]

Watauga County's Jonathan H. Hartley (Company E) had three brothers also in the war: two Confederates, who died during the war, and one Union soldier. In 1868 Hartley left the mountains and headed west with his wife, first to Benton, Kansas, and then in 1895 to Mt. Vernon, Missouri, where he died. Another member of Company E's family also headed west. Nathaniel C. Shull had married Elmrya Green prior to the war and had fathered four children: Mary S., William C., Cencia E., and Phebe. Shull enlisted on September 18, 1861, and served until December 13, 1862, when he was killed by a "shot in breast" during the battle of Fredericksburg. After the war, according to family stories, Shull's widow loaded the children up in a wagon and set off for Missouri. Unfortunately, the horse died along the way, and the family had to abandon the wagon and walk the rest of the way, carrying whatever of their possessions that they could manage.[17]

The Swanner brothers of Company D would not head west after the war, but north, to Baltimore. By 1865, both brothers, James A. and William G., had seen enough of the war. On January 19 they both went on picket duty and deserted to the Union lines sometime during the night. They were transferred to Titusville, Pennsylvania, a week after their capture, where they took the Oath of Allegiance and were released on an unknown date. William G. never returned to North Carolina. He made his way to Rockbridge County, Virginia, where he married Margaret Sanders in 1868. His wife's sister and her husband had moved to Baltimore in 1869, and William and Margaret soon followed. William's brother James did return to the Tar Heel state, where he married in 1866. In 1885 James, his wife, and their 10 children loaded up into a wagon and headed to join William in Baltimore. As the family story goes, "Margaret Swanner was standing on the porch of their home in Baltimore County when a wagon pulled into the yard. Margaret yelled for William to get the rifle because there was a band of gypsies in a wagon in the yard. It was the very dusty, dirty James Swanner family." James died on November 18, 1891, and William on February 7, 1912. Both brothers are buried in the Oakdale Cemetery in Baltimore, Maryland.[18]

Postwar life sometimes brought a change of profession as well as a change of location. The first surgeon of the Thirty-seventh, Dr. James Hickerson, was born May 14, 1832, in Wilkes County. James attended the Jefferson Medical College in Philadelphia, Pennsylvania, where he received his medical education. He enlisted in Company F at the start of the war, and was promoted to regimental surgeon on November 20, 1861, when the Thirty-seventh was officially mustered into service. He resigned on December 28, 1862, due to "indigestion and general debility." After the war, Dr. Hickerson settled in Valley Spring, Arkansas, where he practiced his profession and married Anna Eliza Weaver. In 1879 Dr. Hickerson gave up his practice and moved with Anna back to Wilkes County, where he purchased "Round About," the family home, from his father. He settled into the life of a farmer and was quite successful for a number of years. His son, Felix Hickerson, wrote many years later:

My father's hobby as a farmer was raising watermelons. As many as 30 covered wagons came from the mountains of Virginia across the Blue Ridge during a season to carry back a load of his melons. A layer of wheat straw was carefully packed around each melon to prevent bruises on the bumpy road back home…. His corn and wheat crops on the Yadkin [River] bottoms were very fine. One year 1700 bushels of wheat were harvested….

Doctor Hickerson died on April 6, 1918, and is buried in the Ronda Cemetery in Wilkes County.[19]

Some men not only survived after the war, but prospered and contributed to their communities. Robert Luckey Steele was a man involved in many of the important aspects of his community. He was born to James and Martha Steele on Tuesday, May 31, 1808, in what is today Alexander County. He married and settled to farm, raise his growing family, and pastor many local churches. In 1836 Reverend Steele was appointed Justice of the Peace for Wilkes County, and in 1844 he served as a member of the House of Commons. In 1847 he was elected Superintendent of Schools for Alexander County, a post he held until the outbreak of the war. When the war did come, Reverend Steele and other Alexander County pastors, John G. Bryan, James Reed, and Daniel Austin, all formed the "Alexander Soldiers." Steele resigned on November 18, 1862, due to his advanced age and his inability to "stand hard marches," and possibly due to the fact that his son Benjamin had been conscripted into the Thirty-seventh in August. After returning home, he continued to work with local churches, pastoring the Sulphur Springs Baptist Church from 1868 until 1873, and opening a literary school in the area in 1868. Also in 1868 he served as moderator of the Annual Session of the United Baptist Association. He continued to work and minister until his death in 1883.[20]

A few members of the Thirty-seventh would seek to better their war-torn communities by serving in political offices. Lieutenant Colonel William G. Morris would serve in the state legislature from 1876 until 1877. Captain John D. Brown (Company C) was a mayor of Davidson, North Carolina. John L. Jetton, also of Company C, was another who led his district in postwar political affairs. Jetton was born on August 12, 1827, in Mecklenburg County, the son of Alexander Brevard Jetton and Elizabeth Nantz (Nance). He, along with Colonel Barber, studied under the tutelage of Peter S. Ney before the war, and graduated from Davidson College in 1851. After his wartime service as a Lieutenant in the Thirty-seventh, Jetton served from 1873 to 1875, and from 1891 to 1893 in the North Carolina House of Representatives. He died in 1907 after suffering a second stroke.[21]

John Doderidge Brown, Captain of Company C and later, mayor of Davidson, North Carolina (courtesy of Maudie Keniston-Bullman).

James T. Lowery, the soldier from Company D who supposedly warned Jackson during the battle of Chancellorsville, moved to the Wingate area of Union County. He built the third house ever built in the community and was elected the first mayor of the new town. Lowery and his wife, Julia Fincher, of Anson County, had eight children. Lowery died February 18, 1901, on what is now the property of Wingate College. He was out plowing one day, and a traveling salesman saw him get down off his horse and lie down in the field. When the salesman reached him, Lowery was dead. He and Julia are buried in the Mt. Olive Church Cemetery, Anson County, North Carolina.[22]

Nereus Mendenhall Thayer was another member of the Thirty-seventh who rose to the call of service in postwar politics in North Carolina. Thayer was born November 17, 1845, in Ophir, North Carolina. He was a student prior to enlisting at the age of seventeen on August 15, 1864. He served during the final year of conflict, including the battles of Reams's Station, Jones Farm, and the siege of Petersburg. Thayer surrendered on April 9, 1865, with the other remaining members of the Thirty-seventh, and returned home. Between 1867 and 1920 he variously listed his occupation as operating a tanning yard, a shoe shop, a casket shop, a harness shop, and a grist mill on the Uwharrie River. He served as Postmaster of Eldorado from 1880 to 1893. In 1903 Thayer was a state senator for Montgomery County in the General Assembly, and in 1913 was a School Board Committeeman for the Eldorado School. From 1916 until 1918 he was Chairman and Commissioner for Montgomery County. Thayer was married twice, first to Letha (Aletha) Coggin (December 15, 1857–June 13, 1889) and second to Mary Ada Mittie Kirk (April 14, 1871–March 1, 1939). He was a member of the Macedonia Methodist Episcopal Church and died July 1, 1934.[23]

After the war, many men sought to start life anew with marriage. Captain Thomas J. Armstrong (Company K) married Miss Laura Clark of Iredell County in 1864. "I am happy that God has so signally helped me," the Captain wrote to his sister in August 1865. "He has not only protected me through many dangers but has helped me with one of the best wives in the world. She is now looking at me while I am writing." Lieutenant Colonel John B. Ashcraft married Miss Sallie Lavinia Marsh in Union County on October 25, 1865. Ashcraft settled down after the war to practice veterinary surgery and to sell "various remedies for diseased stock," including Ashcraft's Colic Mixture, Ashcraft's Acme Ointment, Ashcraft's Eureka Liniment, and Ashcraft's Condition Powders, just to name a few. Thomas Franklin Holcomb (Company F) eventually fathered twenty-five children from two marriages. Commissary Sergeant Charles Theodore Stowe was the father of thirteen children, five of whom succumbed to scarlet fever. George Washington Lawrence (Company E) sired fourteen children by his two wives, Elizabeth Norris and Hiley Stout.[24]

Some members of the regiment would seek to better their communities through religious service. The Reverend Alfred L. Stough, after resigning from the Thirty-seventh, returned to working with churches in the piedmont section of North Carolina. He served as pastor to churches in Cleveland and Lenoir counties, including the First Baptist Church of Shelby, before returning to Mecklenburg County in the late 1890s. Several members of the community met in 1894 to organize a Missionary

Baptist Church in Pineville, Mecklenburg County. The church was later named the Stough Memorial Baptist Church, in honor of Reverend Stough.[25]

Sion H. Harrington, Jr. (Company G), and his wife, Sara Watts, were charter members of the Taylorsville Baptist Church in Alexander County. His brother, John Harrington (Company G), and his wife, Catherine, were members of the Salem Evangelical Lutheran Church, also in Alexander County. Daniel C. Robinson (Company I) was a charter member of Matthews Presbyterian Church in Mecklenburg County. On the same day the church was chartered, he was elected a deacon, and later served as an Elder.[26]

Unfortunately, some members of the old Thirty-seventh harbored some bitterness after the war. One officer wrote in 1865: "I wrote a letter at the surrender of General Lee and gave it to a Yankee to mail and he proved like all other Yankees not to be a man of his word." Bitterness would even lead some men to join secret societies, such as the Ku Klux Klan. According to one family researcher, Dallas M. Rigler joined the Klan in Charlotte "for reasons of secular self-aggrandizement. During the war, he received a wound which emasculated him."[27] Fortunately, it appears that such incidents were few, and members of the Thirty-seventh were far more likely to pursue more positive outlets for their postwar energies.

Many members of the Thirty-seventh would venture into rebuilding the wartorn South. During the first half of 1867, Charlotte showed remarkable growth, when twelve new stores and seventy-five other buildings were constructed. Robert Marcus Oates was one of those responsible for helping with Charlotte's growth, and is credited with setting "into motion a series of forces which made Charlotte a leading center of textile manufacturing in the United States." Oates, from Cleveland County, served first as a lieutenant in Company I before his appointment to assistant quartermaster and his transfer to the field and staff. On June 1, 1863, he was transferred to the staff of Major General William Dorsey Pender, and placed in charge of Pender's division's commissary train. Oates rose to the rank of colonel and "was reputed to be one of the best quartermasters in the Confederate Army." After the war, Oates, along with three of his nephews, including David W. Oates, also of the Thirty-seventh, started the Charlotte Cotton Mill in 1880. The mill was the only one of its kind in Charlotte for almost ten years, employing sixty workers, mostly women. Robert M. Oates also served as president of the First National Bank and various terms as County Commissioner and City Alderman. He would die in 1897, but the business would be carried on by his nephews. One writer described Colonel Oates as:

> One person who was literally what he appeared to be. He was candid and outspoken, saying always what he thought, and meaning what he said. If he liked you, you knew it. He was strong in his convictions, conservative in his ideas, and these two characteristics together with his mental ability and correctness of life made him a tower of strength to the community.[28]

The war had scarcely been over for a year when the backbone of the South, the women, started to gather in grass-roots efforts to interpret the meaning and implications of the South's defeat and conquest. One of the first of these organizations was the Ladies Memorial Association of Wake County, led by the widow of General Branch, Mrs. Nancy Haywood Blount Branch. The association's goal was to seek out the graves of Confederate soldiers in and around Raleigh, and move them to a common burial ground, one that had been purchased just for these honored dead.[29]

Since the 1830s, the cemeteries in America's urban landscape had moved from simple, family burial places to "resorts" or "asylums." The genteel had "favored their use for meditative promenades ... [and other] edifying leisure times ... before the creation of public parks, these green, pastoral places also functioned as 'pleasure grounds' for the general public." This usage of cemeteries as a 'pleasure ground' would be heightened after the war, with the creation of Confederate Memorial Day.[30]

It is generally believed that Confederate Memorial Day, celebrated on different days in the spring throughout the South, was a reworking of a Catholic custom brought over from Germany. On All Saints Day, people would gather at the local churches and decorate the graves of the deceased. In May 1866, when the Ladies Memorial Association, composed of both women and men, was formed, their goal was to "protect and care for the graves of our Confederate soldiers." At their June 1866 meeting, several members reported on the conditions of the graves of several hundred Confederate soldiers buried in the Rock Quarry Cemetery, adjacent to the Pettigrew Hospital in Raleigh. The hospital, at the conclusion of the war, had been commandeered by Federal soldiers, and the cemetery "lay neglected, with the inscriptions on the headboards defaced and nearly effaced." Union soldiers had also been interred in the cemetery. The committee recommended the establishment of a new cemetery. Grounds were located, land donated, and funds were being raised to clear the land. Plans proceeded in an orderly fashion, until February 20, 1867, when the Ladies Memorial Association was notified that the Confederate dead would need to be moved out of the Rock Quarry Cemetery immediately, to make room for the Union soldiers being re-interred from other areas. The bones of those Confederates not removed would be dumped in the streets.[31]

By the end of March, all of the Confederates had been re-interred at the new cemetery, a Confederate section within the Oakwood cemetery, and plans were made for a "decoration" day. May 10, the date of the death of Thomas "Stonewall" Jackson, was chosen. On May 10, 1867, the ladies quietly met at the capitol at 3:30 P.M. and made their way to the cemetery "for the purpose of decoration and other observances." In the years following that day in 1867, the Ladies Memorial Association raised the funds necessary to place a memorial in the cemetery, and to replace the wooden head boards with granite markers.[32]

Raleigh was not the only North Carolina town where a Ladies Memorial Association was formed. Charlotte also had such an organization, which, in 1889, erected a monument to their Confederate soldiers in Elmwood Cemetery. Many other groups would follow.

Erecting monuments was not the only work of these Ladies Memorial Associations. In 1884 many began to talk of raising funds to help the "unfortunate victims

Confederate Monument, Monroe, Union County, North Carolina.

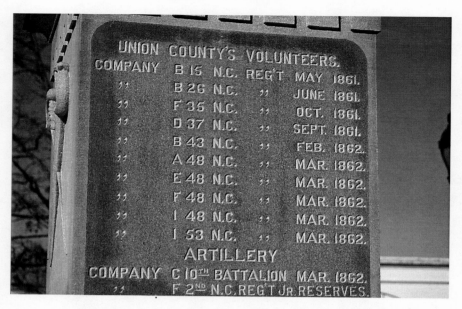

Side view of Confederate Monument, Monroe, Union County, North Carolina.

of the Lost Cause." One of the leaders behind this movement was former governor and then United States Senator Zebulon B. Vance. The movement took on new life in the 1890s, when the Wake County Ladies Memorial Association, along with the Confederate Veteran Association of North Carolina, raised enough money to lease an eight-room house in downtown Raleigh. Several members of the Thirty-seventh would live out their days at the old soldiers home, located on the site of the war-time Pettigrew Hospital. Solomon V. Cox (Company A) was one of those soldiers.[33] Eli McNeil, also of Company A, died in 1924 at the Confederate Soldiers home in Higginsville, Missouri. He is buried in the Confederate Cemetery there. McNeil's service record describes him as a deserter. However, he had been wounded at Petersburg and sent home to recover. He was then unable to return to his heavily engaged unit before the war ended. Apparently, this blot on his record did not disqualify him from living out his days in the soldiers home.[34]

Besides the Home for Confederate Veterans in Raleigh, the state also sought to grant financial assistance to her veterans. In 1867 the state began granting pensions to Confederate veterans who were blinded or who had lost a limb during their tenure to the state. Twenty years later, on December 23, 1887, the North Carolina General Assembly authorized pensions to Confederate veterans who were unable to earn a living or who had income of less than $250 a year. An applicant had to go before a county official, usually a justice of the peace, and a doctor, before he could receive his allowance. In 1895 the eligibility was expanded to include all veterans or their widows over the age of 60 who had an income of less than $100 a year. The state would continue to broaden the scope of its benefits to veterans and their wives as time progressed. In 1900 disabled veterans were able to receive $150 per year. In 1919 all veterans,

Confederate Monument, including a cannon used at Gettysburg by the Confederates, Taylorsville, Alexander County, North Carolina.

Monument to Confederate Dead, Elmwood Cemetery, Charlotte, North Carolina.

as well as widows over the age of 60 who had married veterans before 1890, were eligible. In 1923 pensions were approved for black Confederate soldiers who had served at least six months. The age of eligibility for widows was dropped to fifty-five in 1920, to fifty in 1921, and to forty-five in 1930. North Carolina continued to pay Confederate widow pensions until the last applicant died in 1990.

Members of the Thirty-seventh who moved to other states were also eligible to receive pensions. A good example of the process of applying for a pension can be found

Right: Private Solomon V. Cox, Company K (courtesy of the Ashe County Historical Society). *Bottom:* Private Simon Timothy Cline, Company F, and wife, Clarrissa (Price) Cline (courtesy of David L. Cline).

Private Jacob Orrant, Company F, and his wife Mary (courtesy of Margaret Arrant).

in the case of Jacob A. Orrant (also spelled Arrant). Private Orrant resided in Watauga County in 1862 when he enlisted, at the age of eighteen, at Camp Holmes near Raleigh. He was "Burnt badly by accident" on December 12, 1862, just a day prior to the battle at Fredericksburg. Orrant returned to duty in January or February 1863, and was wounded in both thighs at Fussell's Mill on August 16, 1864. He returned to duty again in November or December 1864, and was captured in the trenches at Petersburg on April 2, 1865. He was released from Point Lookout, Maryland, after taking the Oath of Allegiance, on June 22, 1865. At the turn of the century, Orrant and his wife, Mary Ann Norwood, were living in Monroe County, Tennessee. On July 14, 1911, Orrant applied for a Tennessee Confederate veteran's pension. The application posed many questions: where did he presently live, where was he born, what regiment did he serve with and who were his company officers. Another question concerned the battles he was engaged in, and "what disabilities did [he] receive, if any?" Orrant replied that he was in several engagements, including Gettysburg, Manassas, and Wilderness, and that in one of the battles, "I was shot through both hips and am now suffering with running sores on my legs caused by said wounds." Other questions asked if he was discharged on account of his wounds, if he had ever been in prison, the size of his family, what business he was engaged in (he would respond to this question with, "Nothing. Not able to do anything"), and how long he had been a resident of the state. The application was then signed by a witness and a county trustee. Orrant's application was approved. On November 22, 1919, Jacob Orrant died, leaving his widow, Mary. She submitted an application for a Tennessee Widow's Indigent Pension on February 21, 1920. Mary would also have to answer several questions, such as how long she had resided in the state, how many children she had, how long Jacob had been in the army, and whether she had remarried. Also, a questionnaire for the witness had to be submitted. After clarification regarding how long she had been a resident in the state, Mary's application was accepted. She died on July 12, 1923, and both Mary and Jacob are buried in Maple Springs, Monroe County, Tennessee.[34]

In October 1881, North Carolina's Society of Ex-Confederate Soldiers and Sailors was one of the first statewide Confederate Veteran organizations. A few years later, in Virginia, the Robert E. Lee Camp #1 was formed. Several other independent camps formed across Virginia, and in 1887, the Grand Camp of Confederate Veterans of Virginia was created. This organization spread to Tennessee and Georgia, and later Louisiana. In February 1889, the Virginia and Tennessee groups, along with the Benevolent and Historical Association, Veteran Confederate States Cavalry, met in New Orleans and endorsed a plan for a comprehensive organization. This was the beginning of the United Confederate Veterans. Major General John B. Gordon, of Georgia, became the first commander.

In January 1893, a monthly magazine was begun by Sumner Archibald Cunningham, entitled *Confederate Veteran*. The *Confederate Veteran* would become the official publication of the United Confederate Veterans. Articles found within the pages of the *Confederate Veteran* were largely penned by the veterans themselves. Colonel H. A. Brown wrote an article on Colonel Barber. Angelum A. Garrison (Company C) published a piece in the magazine about seeing General Lee at Petersburg on April 2, 1865.

Prior to the organization of the United Confederate Veterans, many local communities started holding local reunions. The "old soldiers of Union County" held a meeting on August 2, 1879, at the courthouse in Monroe "for the purpose of making arrangements and appointing the time for a general re-union...." A committee was appointed for each of the companies that had come out of the counties. For Company D of the Thirty-seventh, the committee was composed of Lieutenant Colonel John B. Ashcraft, lieutenants Vachel T. Chears and Joseph E. Griffin, and privates Ananias R. Broom, Charles L. Helms and Hurley G. Price. The veterans met again in Union County at the Court House on August 20, 1890. After finishing the "business" of the meeting, the veterans "adjourned to 'Stewart Grove' where a table had been spread...." The Charlotte *Democrat* went on to report, "At least one thousand persons partook of the feast," after which a "Permanent Relief Association for the benefit of indigent soldiers, their widows and orphans" was organized. The members of the association unanimously adopted a resolution, saying that

> Whereas, The success of the barbecue this day enjoyed by us, has been assisted by the zeal, energy and kindness of certain young ladies connected with the contribution committees, and whose names have been reported to us; now therefore be it,
> Resolved, That in these young ladies we recognize the true and perfect type of the genuine "Southern Girl," and as worthy daughters of those matrons whose heroism, in the dark days of the South, is an honor to all womanhood.

The old Union County veterans then dissolved their meeting until the next year.[35]

Blowing Rock, on the border of Watauga and Caldwell counties, was the site for

A gathering of Union County Civil War Veterans.

one of the first reunions in the mountain counties. In August 1890, the veterans met at the resort town, even though the reunion planners had tried to cancel the affair due to the rainy weather. The old veterans came despite the rain, and the speakers included the Reverend Doctor Rumple, of Salisbury, and Captain (and later Reverend) G. W. Sanderlin, State Auditor. Sanderlin was a fellow brigade member, having served in the Thirty-third. On Thursday, August 3, 1893, there was a reunion of members of Company C, Thirty-seventh North Carolina Troops; Company K, Fifty-sixth North Carolina Troops; and the Black Boys of Cabarrus County in the Hopewell community of Mecklenburg County. Doctor John B. Alexander, former surgeon of the Thirty-seventh, was scheduled to speak, after which dinner was served.[36]

The United Confederate Veterans soon began organizing national reunions. The local United Confederate Veteran camps would elect different members to attend the reunions as their representatives. William D. Norris (Company B) was a delegate to the 1905 National Confederate Soldiers' Reunion in Louisville, Kentucky. These reunions were held all across the South, such as the reunion in Birmingham, Alabama, in 1894, at which there were an estimated 20,000 veterans. The pinnacle of the reunions was in 1917, when Woodrow Wilson attended the parade that was held in Washington, D.C.

Local reunions also continued to take place, and the local Confederate Veteran organizations largely merged into the United Confederate Veterans. By 1901 there were 72 camps in North Carolina, including the Nimrod Triplett Camp (#1273) in Boone; the Mecklenburg Camp (#382) in Charlotte; the William Gamble Camp (#1184) in Gastonia; and the Walkup Camp (#781) in Monroe.

Confederate Veterans' parade, Blowing Rock, Watauga County, North Carolina, August 1917.

The typical local reunion looked much like the one in Watauga County in August 1917. The Nimrod Triplett Camp met at Henson's Chapel in Amantha, Watauga County, for the twenty-sixth annual reunion on Thursday, August 9, and Friday, August 10. A prelude of fife and drum music summoned the crowd; Captain Elijah J. Norris of the Fifty-eighth North Carolina Troops called the meeting to order, and the Reverend J. F. Eller led the gathering in a devotional service. Professor D. J. Horton then delivered the address of welcome. Horton would make references to the old veterans, calling them the "noblest of any class in any age of the world's history" and calling them as "brave as Hannibal's troops who fought for Carthage — as brave as the Trojans who were masses of courage." After his remarks, various committees were appointed, and Colonel F. A. Olds of Raleigh spoke, followed by Captain John Fuller of Mountain City, Tennessee, speaking on the current war with Germany. Following Captain Fuller, the old soldiers talked of their experiences, and the roll was taken of the old Confederates attending. Present from the Thirty-seventh were William T. Blair (Company E); James B. Blair (Company E); Thomas A. Cable (Company E); Henry H. Farthing (Company E); Robert H. Farthing (Company E); Edmond M. Greer (Company B); Pinkny Gryder (Company G); Thomas Love (Company E); William D. Norris (Company B); William L. Norwood (Company E); Joseph C. Shull (Company E); and George Younce (Company E). The meeting was then adjourned for the afternoon. On Thursday night, camp fires were lit, and the old soldiers had "foot races" and "stories of the 'Sixties.'"

On Friday, there was once again a prelude of drum and fife music, and a devotional service, this time lead by the Reverend J. L. L. Sherwood. Then Miss Anna Smith, the granddaughter of Abner Smith of Company E, who was killed, gave a "splendid address." The title of her oration was the "Soldier of N.C." She spoke about the "bravery and devotion that North Carolina's soldiers had displayed during the war" and that no other army in history had "ever fought as they did; they battled against overwhelming odds and their many victories were only achieved by death-defying courage and devotion to duty." Miss Smith continued:

> Although every Southern State furnished thousands of brave men who fought and died in defense of the cause which they believed so right ... North Carolina will always feel that she deserves to rank first among them all; both for the number of men contributed to defend the Confederacy and for the bravery displayed by those men on the field of battle....
>
> The Civil War cost us thousands of our bravest men and left desolate homes and weeping women and children in every part of our state.... Watauga, though a small county in population at that time, furnished a large number of soldiers for the Confederacy. Many lost their lives, either in battle, by disease or from other causes. The first soldier from Watauga county to give his life for the South was Abner Smith of Silverstein. When the first call to arms was sounded and the land of his forefathers was threatened with invasion, he cast his lot with the South and with many other men from Watauga was mustered into the 37th Regiment of N.C. Infantry.
>
> The 37th Regiment was sent to the eastern part of this state and took part in the battle of Newbern. After this battle the Confederate forces fell back to Kinston and here, March 4, 1862, Abner Smith was killed by the accidental discharge of a gun in the hands of a careless comrade. Although not killed in battle, Abner Smith gave his life for the Southern cause.

After Miss Smith concluded her remarks, several of the old soldiers in the crowd gave short speeches, and the Reverend J. L. L. Sherwood concluded the event with a short sermon "commending the old soldiers for their deeds of valor during the Civil War and painting several of the necessary requisites for a good soldier of Christ." The local newspaper pronounced the event "The greatest time ever!" These reunions, both local and national, continued until the Confederate veterans were too old to attend, or were dead.[37]

There are two organizations which still survive as offshoots of the United Confederate Veterans: the United Daughters of the Confederacy and the Sons of Confederate Veterans. The United Daughters of the Confederacy trace their origins back to the war-time enterprises of ladies all across the South. These "patriotic" women organized hospital associations, knitting circles, and sewing organizations that helped the Southern war effort. After the war concluded, cemetery, memorial, monument, auxiliaries to Confederate veteran camps, and Confederate home associations were all formed. The United Daughters of the Confederacy were formally organized on September 10, 1894, in Nashville, Tennessee. By 1912, the Daughters had 800 chapters and 45,000 members.[38]

One of the things that the United Daughters of the Confederacy did was to present medals to "veterans, soldiers or sailors, or they being dead, upon their widow or eldest lineal descendant." These medals were entitled the "Southern Cross of Honor," and were made of bronze. The medals were adopted in 1899, and the design was a "cross with a battle flag on the face, surrounded by a wreath of laurel, with the inscription 'Southern Cross of Honor'; on the reverse, the motto of the Confederate States *Deo Vindice* (God our Vindicator) 1861–1865, with the inscription 'From the U. D.C. to the U. C. V.'" All that a veteran had to do was fill out the appropriate forms and submit them through his local camps. By 1901, the United Daughters of the Confederacy in Charlotte alone had presented 209 of the medals.[39] The United Daughters of the Confederacy continue to meet today in camps all across the world.

The Sons of Confederate Veterans was the other organization created from the United Confederate Veterans. In July 1896, with forty delegates representing twenty-four "sons" camps, a constitution was adopted, and the "United Sons of Confederate Veterans" was created. There were three North Carolina camps represented in that group of twenty-four. The goal of the Sons of Confederate Veterans is to preserve "the history and legacy of these heroes, so future generations can understand the motives that animated the Southern Cause." The Sons of Confederate Veterans continues today, with an international membership of 31,000, including many descendants of members of the Thirty-seventh.[40]

One of the highlights for both the United Daughters of the Confederacy and the Sons of Confederate Veterans is the reinternment of Confederate soldiers to their native soil of North Carolina. These events began right after the conclusion of the war, evident through the work of Mrs. Branch, but they did not stop there. On May 10, 1883, Colonel A. M. Waddell, while addressing a gathering in the Elmwood Cemetery in Charlotte to commemorate North Carolina's Confederate Memorial Day, called for the citizens of the state to petition the governor and other state officials to bring home the bodies of North Carolinians that were "buried in an out-of-the-way corner in Arlington Cemetery ... [and have them] interred within the borders of the State to which they belonged." Waddell went on to state that "they are buried in a corner of the cemetery, grown up in weeds and grass, and on each head board is the single word 'Rebel.'"[41]

Colonel Waddell's pleas for a proper burial for North Carolina soldiers would not fall on deaf ears. In 1883 one-hundred and seven of the Old North State's sons were disinterred from the soil around Arlington. Their remains were placed in four large caskets, loaded aboard a steamer and transported from Alexandria to Norfolk. Then the caskets were transferred to railcars and moved to Raleigh. In Raleigh the remains would lie in state in the rotunda of the capital overnight. Then, on the morning of October 17, 1883, with much pomp and circumstance, the remains were taken to Oakwood Cemetery and reinterred in the Confederate section. A monument is there today, with all of the names of these soldiers inscribed upon it. Two members of the Thirty-seventh who were part of the group reinterred were Marion C. Abernathy (Company H) and Joshua D. Frazier (Company F). Private Abernathy was captured May 6, 1864, during the battle of the Wilderness. He was confined in Washington, D.C., where on June 9, 1864, he died of chronic diarrhea. Private Frazier was wounded

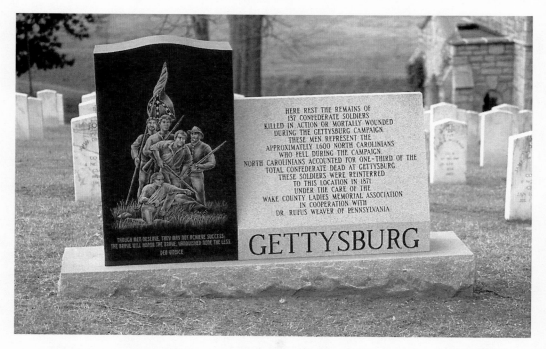

Memorial to the North Carolina Confederate Dead, Oakwood Cemetery, Raleigh, North Carolina.

in the left foot and right thigh and captured a few days after Abernathy, on May 12, at the battle of Spotsylvania Court House. He was hospitalized in Washington, D.C., where he died on July 7, also of chronic diarrhea.[42]

But not all of the members of the Thirty-seventh who died in the Federal capital would find final resting places in their native soil. Private Alexander L. Bullison (Company A) was wounded and captured December 13, 1862, at Fredericksburg. He succumbed to his wounds on January 10, 1863, in a hospital in Washington. Private Thomas R. Carlton (Company B) died in Washington of typhoid fever on July 14, 1862. He had been captured June 30 at Frayser's Farm. Neither of these soldiers was ever returned to North Carolina; the location of their graves remains a mystery. Like so many soldiers, they lie in graves that have been lost to history.[43]

The soldiers killed at Gettysburg were not among the forgotten. After the battle was over, the remains of the Confederates were buried in shallow trenches, or thrown into ditches and gullies. From 1870 until 1873, Dr. Rufus Weaver of Gettysburg worked as an agent for various Ladies Memorial Associations across the South. He and his associates disinterred 3,320 sets of remains of Confederate soldiers, boxed them up and shipped them to different states. Soldiers that could be identified were shipped to their native state capitals. Private Jacob McGrady (Company K) was one of those soldiers. The twenty-nine-year-old McGrady was wounded and captured on July 3, during Pickett's Charge. After the battle he was taken to a hospital located on the property of Peter Conover, off the Baltimore Pike. McGrady died of his wounds on July 14, 1863, and was interred on Conover's Farm. His remains were some of the ones disinterred, and he now lies in the Oakwood Cemetery in Raleigh, North Carolina. A total of 137 remains identified as North Carolinians were reinterred in Raleigh. Other remains identified simply as Confederate were shipped to Richmond, Virginia, and interred in the Hollywood Cemetery. In June 1872, Richmond officials and at least 1,000 veterans held a procession to Hollowood Cemetery, where the first 708 of 2,935 boxes were laid to rest.

Lieutenant Iowa Royster, who had died at Gettysburg and had his belt and notebook interred with him, was also found and returned to North Carolina. In 1870 a notice was published, requesting that all the Confederate soldiers buried on private property be removed so the land could be put back into cultivation. Royster's father wrote to a local physician, sending a copy of the letter that Mr. Adams had written. Iowa Royster's remains were found, along with the lettered belt, and sent back to Raleigh. He was first interred in the soldiers' section of Oakwood, with remarks being made by Professor Phillips of the University of North Carolina. Later, Royster was reinterred in a family plot there in Oakwood. A newspaper clipping, published a few days after his death, had this to say about the young lieutenant:

Gravestone of Lieutenant Iowa M. Royster, Company G. Oakwood Cemetery, Raleigh, North Carolina.

Lieut. Royster, was from his boyhood distinguished for high honor, and a purity of heart and conduct almost womanly. Heaven has not taken home from the hecatombs slain in this merciless war, a gentler and more christianized spirit. He had the talents of a very high order; a mind deeply imbued with science and literature; spotless integrity, which shrunk at the approach of pollution; a lofty scorn for everything mean and contemptible; and a heart that knew no fear in the discharge of duty. To crown all he was a true christian hero.[44]

The remains of the soldiers were not the only relics returned to the South. In time, many of the battle-flags would also be returned. After the Thirty-seventh's flag was captured in the trenches south of Petersburg on April 2, 1865, it was forwarded to the Adjutant General with details of its capture. By the end of 1865 there were over 500 flags in the Adjutant General's office in Washington. Each flag was assigned a number as it came in. The Thirty-seventh's flag was number 384. In 1867 the flags were moved to the office of the Superintendent of the War Department. In 1875 some of the flags were moved to the Ordnance Museum, and in 1882 the flags were moved to the basement of the State, War, and Navy Building. The Adjutant General, in 1887, suggested that the flags, as a gesture of good will, be returned. President Grover Cleveland agreed, but many politicians and Northern veterans were opposed to the idea, and the flags continued to mold and decay. In 1905 Congress passed legislation returning flags to the states whose troops had fought under them. Since the Thirty-seventh's flag was not labeled "Thirty-seventh," it was not included in the group returned to North Carolina. But, in 1906, Congress voted to return the remaining 252 flags without provenance to the Confederate Museum in Richmond. Through research, the flag of the Thirty-seventh was correctly identified and, since its return, has seen more active service. For years the Thirty-seventh's flag, on its original staff, hung above the statue of General Lee in the Lee Chapel in Lexington, Virginia. Eventually a replica was made to replace the flag on the original staff. The flag is still owned today by the Museum of the Confederacy, but is on loan to Pamplin Park, in Petersburg, Virginia, and is displayed just yards from the location where it was captured on April 2, 1865.[45] The original flagstaff continues to display the replica flag in honor to the beloved General Lee.

While the flag has endured, the men of the Thirty-seventh passed with the years. The old soldiers started to "cross over the river and rest in the shade" in great numbers toward the turn of the twentieth century. Eleven died in each of the years 1918 to 1924, twelve each in 1900, 1907, 1909, 1915, and 1917. The largest group passed on in 1921, when sixteen Thirty-seventh veterans died.

Albert P. Wilson, first sergeant of Company E, lived to be 103 years old and died in 1928, in Boone. He was "the oldest citizen of the region," and his funeral was held "in the oldest church west of the Blue Ridge [Three Forks Baptist Church]." Wilson was both deaf and blind, and "afflicted with the palsy," but "retained the activity of a clear mind until his death." During the latter years of his life, a big celebration was held on each of his birthdays, and the old soldiers in attendance would tell the stories of their trials during the war. During the celebration of his 102nd birthday, one "hundred or more guests gathered around the dinner table, piled high with only such food as can be prepared in country homes. Albert Wilson and his old buddies of the Civil War told of the heroic exploits of Company E, 37th North Carolina Infantry...."[46]

It appears that the last of the gallant Thirty-seventh faded away in 1938, when her last two soldiers passed on. Private Socrates Justice was born April 10, 1845, enlisted at Camp Vance on October 10, 1863, and was assigned to Company G of the Thirty-seventh. He was present for the surrender at Appomattox Court House on April 9, 1865. Justice moved west after the end of the war, first to Springfield, Missouri, then to Center Point, Arkansas, and finally to Valliant, Oklahoma, where he operated a mercantile store. Socrates Justice died on February 19, 1938, at the age of 93, in Hugo, Oklahoma, and is buried in the Valliant Cemetery there.[47]

The last soldier was Private John M. Hoover, born August 30, 1846, in Mecklenburg County. He served first with Company B, Second North Carolina Junior Reserves

Gravestone of Private John M. Hoover, Company C, last surviving member of the Thirty-seventh, Paw Creek Presbyterian Church, Mecklenburg County, North Carolina.

until coming of age, when he transferred to Company C, Thirty-seventh Regiment of North Carolina Troops, on or about October 10, 1864. He was wounded in the last days of the war and sent to a hospital in Richmond, Virginia, where he was captured on April 3, 1865. He was taken to Newport News, Virginia, where he arrived on April 24, 1865, and was released there on June 30, after taking the Oath of Allegiance. He died on June 25, 1938, and is buried in the cemetery at the Paw Creek Presbyterian Church in Mecklenburg County.

"The thunder of cannon on foreign shore cannot disturb the sleep of Colonel William Morris," wrote the *Gaston Gazette* on January 31, 1941. The Gaston Chapter of the United Daughters of the Confederacy was seeking to mark "the graves of all the Civil War veterans" of Gaston County. They honored Lieutenant Colonel Morris, a "stalwart son of the Old South," on February 1, 1941, with a military stone at the cemetery were he was buried, the old Philadelphia Lutheran cemetery in Gaston County.[48]

The struggle to mark the graves of members of the Thirty-seventh and other Confederate soldiers continues today. In 1996 the Hoke Chapter of the United Daughters of the Confederacy went before the Salisbury City Council, seeking permission to mark the 175 graves of Confederates buried in the Old Lutheran Cemetery. Permission was granted, and on June 2, 1996, the markers were erected. Among the 175 who died in a Salisbury hospital during the war were Calvin Hicks (Company B), who died on May 28, 1864, of "hydrothorax," and Junius A. Milholland (Company B), who died June 6, 1863, of wounds received during the battle of Chancellorsville, Virginia.[49]

Lieutenant Barnabas Alexander, of Company C, was killed at the battle of Spotsylvania Court House. He has a cenotaph in the churchyard of Gilead church in Mecklenburg County. His epitaph is a fitting conclusion to the story of the Thirty-seventh. It reads:

> He died as a soldier prefers, if he must fall, in the front of battle, with his face to the foe, gallantly fighting for his country's right. His body lies on the field of battle, ensanguined by his blood. Though the cause for which he fought and fell is lost, his memory is cherished in the hearts of those who loved him living, as a Martyr for Southern honor and liberty.[50]

Appendix A: Roster

Non-commissioned officers and enlisted men appear in alphabetical order. All others appear in chronological order with the first-listed as the first to hold the position followed by his replacements. Birth and death dates and burial locations are included. Unless otherwise noted, all burials are in North Carolina. For detailed service records for each soldier, see Manari and Jordan, *North Carolina Troops*.

KEY TO ABBREVIATIONS

1LT	First Lieutenant	GA	Georgia
2LT	Second Lieutenant	Jun. Res.	Junior Reserves
3LT	Third Lieutenant	Maj.	Major
1Sgt.	First Sergeant	Mus.	Musician
A.O.W.	Article of War	NC	North Carolina
As. Surg.	Assistant Surgeon	NCST	North Carolina State Troops
Cap.	Captured	NCT	North Carolina Troops
Capt.	Captain	NC Vol.	North Carolina Volunteers
Co.	County	Pvt.	Private
Comp.	Company	SC Inf.	South Carolina Infantry
Cpl.	Corporal	Sgt.	Sergeant
F&S	Field and Staff	TN	Tennessee

FIELD AND STAFF

Colonels

Lee, Charles Cochrane; 2 Feb. 1834–30 June
1862; Elmwood Cemetery, Mecklenburg Co.
Barber, William Morris; 24 Jan. 1834–3 Oct.
1864; St. Paul Episcopal Church Cemetery,
Wilkes Co.

Lieutenant Colonels

Hickerson, Charles Napoleon; 1829–1915;
Ronda Cemetery, Wilkes Co.
Ashcraft, John Benjamin; 15 Jul. 1834–7 Feb. 1901;
Bethel Baptist Church Cemetery, Union Co.
Morris, William Groves; 20 Nov. 1825–29 Nov.
1918; Old Philadelphia Church Cemetery,
Gaston Co.

Majors

Bryan, John Gilson; c.1807–1902; Silver Shoals
Baptist Church Cemetery, Banks Co., GA
Rankin, William Rufus; 7 Mar. 1823–17 Nov.
1883; Goshen Prebyterian Church Cemetery,
Gaston Co.
Brown, Owen Neil; 1837–24 Jul. 1863; Gettys-
burg, PA
Bost, Jackson Lafayette; 31 Jan. 1832–27 Oct.
1909; Olive Branch Baptist Church Ceme-
tery, Union Co.

Surgeons

Hickerson, James; 14 May 1832–6 Apr. 1918;
Ronda Cemetery, Wilkes Co.
Alexander, John Brevard; 27 May 1834–29 Jun.
1911; Elmwood Cemetery, Mecklenburg Co.
Trescott, George E.
Moffett, George B.; 20 Oct. 1820–21 Aug. 1887;
Cook/Riverview Cemetery, Wood Co., WV

Adjutants

Nicholson, William Thorne; 1840–2 Apr. 1865;
Petersburg, VA
Oates, David William; 1844–1911; Elmwood
Cemetery, Mecklenburg Co.

Assistant Quartermasters

Oates, Robert Marcus; 13 Jan. 1829–27 Dec.
1897; Elmwood Cemetery, Mecklenburg Co.

Pegram, Miles Pickney; 27 Nov. 1834–16 Dec.
1915; Elmwood Cemetery, Mecklenburg Co.

Assistant Commissaries of Substance

Stowe, Hebert DeLambert; 22 Sept. 1831–8 Feb.
1907; Steele Creek Presbyterian Church Cemetery, Gaston Co.
Pegram, Miles P. (See above)

Assistant Surgeons

Tracy, James Wright; 1819–1896
Graham, Daniel McLean; 1833–1898; Cumberland Co.

Chaplain

Stough, Alfred L.; c.1827–

Ensign

Staley, Robert M.; 11 Mar. 1844–20 May 1911;
Old Presbyterian Church Cemetery, Wilkes
Co.

Sergeant Majors

Elms, John Irvin; c.1843–
Torrance, John Albert; 18 Nov. 1835–25 Oct.
1916; Long Creek Presbyterian Church Ceme-
tery, Gaston Co.
Glenn, William Wallace; c.1837–4 Nov. 1878;
Bethel Presbyterian Church Cemetery, Clover,
York Co., SC
Wright, Thomas C.; –26 May 1864
Austin, Joseph H.; c.1844–

Quartermaster Sergeant

Alexander, John O.; c.1832–1912; Providence
Presbyterian Church Cemetery, Mecklenburg Co.

Commissary Sergeants

Triplett, Pickens Lewis; c.1840–25 Jul. 1862;
Richmond, VA

Gaston, Larkin B.; 16 Nov. 1813–11 Aug. 1881; Goshen Presbyterian Church Cemetery, North Belmont, Gaston Co.

Stowe, Charles Theodore; 29 Jan. 1833–18 Sep. 1907; Goshen Presbyterian Church Cemetery, North Belmont, Gaston Co.

Ordnance Sergeant

Abernathy, James W. C.; c.1840–

Hospital Steward

Sparrow, Thomas W.; 1814–1890; Davidson College Cemetery, Mecklenburg Co.

Chief Musician

Carlton, John R.; c.1835–after 1880; Kentucky

COMPANY A

Captains

Hartzog, John; 27 Feb. 1812–18 Jun. 1863; Calloway Cemetery, Ashe Co.[1]

Lenoir, Walter Waightstill; 13 Mar. 1823–26 Jul. 1900; Fort Defiance Cemetery, Caldwell Co.

Alexander, William J.; c.1837–

Lieutenants

Carter, Elijah Allen; 3LT; c.1837–13 May 1864; Confederate Cemetery, Spotsylvania C. H., VA

Goodman, James Gordon; 1LT; 1 Aug. 1836–15 Jan. 1913; Bethel Baptist Church Cemetery, Ashe Co.

Goodman, Richard G.; 2LT; c.1843–1867[2]

Goodman, William Harrison; 1LT; 19 May 1835–8 Jan. 1881; Goodman-James Cemetery, Ashe Co.

Greer, Catlett Aquilla; 2LT; 21 Mar. 1844–17 Feb. 1887; Elisha Anderson Cemetery. Ashe Co.[3]

Hartzog, Isham C.; 1LT; c.1826–June 27, 1862; Battlefield of Gaines's Mill, VA

Norwood, Thomas Lenoir; 1LT; 9 Oct. 1845–28 Jul. 1888; Lenoir Cemetery, Loudon Co., TN

Stuart, William Anderson; 1LT; 11 Sep. 1835–8 Dec. 1910; Carter-Stuart Cemetery, Ashe Co.

Whitaker, Willis; 2LT

Non-Commissioned Officers and Enlisted Men

Adams, Abraham; Pvt.; c.1836–17 Apr. 1928; Miller-Roten Cemetery, Ashe Co.

Adams, Charles W.; Pvt.; c.1842–

Anderson, Floyd R.; Pvt.; c.1833–after 1880; Pennington-Anderson Cemetery, Ashe Co.

Ashley, Tivis; Pvt.; c.1842–[4]

Baker, James M.; Pvt.; c.1845–

Bare, Absalom; Pvt.; c.1844–; Missing in action, May 6, 1864, Wilderness, VA

Bare, Fallow; Pvt.; c.1842–

Bare, Hamilton; Pvt.; 19 Apr. 1839–5 Nov. 1920; Farrington-Koonts Cemetery, Ashe Co.

Barker, Abraham; Pvt.; c.1844–Mar. 1863

Bentley, Nathan

Black, Andrew; Pvt.; c.1844–11 Aug. 1862

Black, George; Pvt.; c.1835–14 Apr. 1864; Executed in Virginia.

Black, John M.; 1Sgt.; 24 Apr. 1833–6 Apr. 1907; Greenwood Methodist Church Cemetery, Ashe Co.

Black, Joseph; Pvt.; c.1838–16 Apr. 1862

Blackburn, George W.; Pvt.; c.1844–

Blackburn, Jeremiah; Pvt.; c.1838–14 Apr. 1864; Executed in Virginia

Blevins, William Harrison; Pvt.; 27 Dec. 1840–19 Nov. 1925; Davis Cemetery, Smyth Co., VA

Bryant, George H.; Pvt.; c.1842–29 Aug.1862; Virginia

Bullison, Alexander L.; Pvt.; c.1833–10 Jan. 1863; Washington, D.C.

Burgess, Andrew; Pvt.; c.1840–31 Oct. 1864; Hollywood Cemetery, Richmond, VA

Calloway, Eli; Pvt.; c.1844–

Capehart, Francis M.; Pvt.; c.1837–

Carpenter, James W.; Pvt.; c.1840–

Carter, Clarence M.; Pvt.; 6 Dec. 1842–20 Jan. 1876; Ashe Co.

Carter, Columbus R.; Pvt.; c.1841–1 Oct. 1862; Oakwood Military Cemetery, Richmond, VA

Childers, Calvin; Cpl.; c.1843–12 May 1864; Jackson-Testerman Cemetery, Ashe Co.

Childers, James Franklin; Pvt.; 1819–

Childers, John; Pvt.; 10 Nov. 1845–10 Jan. 1933; Jackson-Testerman Cemetery, Ashe Co.

Church, Jackson; Pvt.; c.1831–

Coldiron, Benjamin C.; Pvt.; c.1843–6 Jun. 1862[5]

Comach, Robert; Pvt.

Cooke, Harrison Garland; Pvt.; 14 Jun. 1846–12 May 1926; Mt. View Cemetery, Chilhowie, VA

Cox, Leander A.; Pvt.; c.1843–8 Jul. 1862; Cypress Hill National Cemetery, Brooklyn, NY

Cox, Payton; Pvt.; 11 Nov. 1837–8 Jun. 1917; Annie Cox Cemetery, Russell Co., VA

Cox, William, Jr.; Pvt.; c.1841–16 Jul. 1862; Hollywood Cemetery, Richmond, VA

Cox, William, Sr.; Pvt.; c.1824–6 Aug. 1862; Blandford Cemetery, Petersburg, VA

Craven, George; Pvt.; c.1842–12 Jun. 1862

Davidson, J. R.; Pvt.

Davis, William M.; Pvt.; 15 Jul. 1840–10 Dec. 1909; William Davis Cemetery, Ashe Co.

Davis, William J.; Pvt.; c.1840–

DeBoard, Elijah C.; Pvt.; 10 Jan. 1840–Aug. 1862

Eldrich, David; Pvt.; c.1822–9 Jul. 1862; Cypress Hill National Cemetery, Brooklyn, NY

Eldrich, Jacob; Pvt.; c.1844–

Eldrich, John; Pvt.; c.1840–27 May 1862

Farrington, Mathias; Pvt.; c.1839–

Faw, Elijah Frank; Pvt.; c.1830–12 Dec. 1898; Tom Calloway Family Cemetery, Ashe Co.

Fisher, John P.; Pvt.; c.1835–5 Apr. 1863; Oakwood Military Cemetery, Richmond, VA

Garvey, Thomas; Pvt.; c.1826–

Garvy, Aaron L.; Pvt.; c.1842–19 Jun 1863; Oakwood Military Cemetery, Richmond, VA

Gentry, Andrew, Jr.; Pvt.; 12 Feb. 1832–13 Dec. 1862

Gentry, Andrew C.; Pvt.; c.1841–; Yorktown National Cemetery, Yorktown, VA

Gentry, Levi R.; Pvt.; c.1844–20 May 1863; Oakwood Military Cemetery, Richmond, VA

Gentry, Robert T.; Pvt.; c.1838–27 Jun. 1862; Hampton National Cemetery, Hampton, VA

Goodman, Calvin Peter; Pvt.; c.1829–

Goodman, Peter Calvin; Pvt.; 25 Aug. 1842–3 Feb. 1914; Goodman-Walters Cemetery, Ashe Co.

Goss, William J.; Pvt.; 4 Jan. 1846–27 Jun. 1922; Elmwood Cemetery, Fruita, Mesa Co., CO[6]

Green, Jesse W.; Pvt.

Griffin, Levi G.; Pvt.; c.1843–

Griffin, William Harrison; Pvt.; –3 May 1863

Ham, Isaac; Pvt.; 1820–1908; Isaac Ham Cemetery, Ashe Co.

Ham, Jackson; Pvt.; c.1840–[7]

Ham, Levi; Pvt.; c.1819–

Ham, Thomas; Pvt.; 20 Jan. 1839–29 Apr. 1893; Thomas Ham Family Cemetery, Ashe Co.

Ham, William M.; Pvt.; c.1844–after 1863; Sexton Family Cemetery, Ashe Co.

Hawthorne, Alexander B.; Sgt.; c.1837–13 Apr. 1862; Willow Dale Cemetery, Goldsboro, Wayne Co.

Henderson, John A.; Pvt.; c.1840–

Hendricks, Henry H.; Pvt.; c.1821–10 Sep. 1862; Sharon Cemetery, Middlesburg, VA

Hines, John Henry; Sgt.; c.1839–23 Dec. 1862; Oakwood Military Cemetery, Richmond, VA

Holdaway, Rufus M.; Sgt.; 8 Feb. 1831–22 Dec. 1903; Blue Ridge Baptist Church Cemetery, Ashe Co.

Holloway, James; Pvt.; –25 Aug. 1864; Confederate Cemetery, Point Lookout, MD

Houck, George; Pvt.; c.1843–Apr. 1862

Houck, Lowry; Pvt.; c.1843–; Cox-Danner Cemetery, Ashe Co.

Houck, Solomon S.; Pvt.; 1817–5 Oct. 1879; Briston Community Cemetery, Ashe Co.

Huffman, Joel; Pvt.; c.1825–

Hurley, Andrew; Pvt.; c.1827–3 Oct. 1911; James A. Hurley Cemetery, Ashe Co.

Hurley, Solomon M.; Pvt.

Hurley, William H.; Pvt.; c.1841–8 Jun. 1862

Johnisee, George; Pvt.; c.1843–Aug. 1862

Johnisee, Samuel C.; Pvt.; c.1843–6 Aug. 1862

Johnson, John; Pvt.; c.1842–12 Jan. 1863; Oakwood Military Cemetery, Richmond, VA

Johnson, Sandy A.; Pvt.; c.1843–27 Jun. 1862

Jones, William Reid; Pvt.; 18 Apr. 1845–1 Jan. 1915; Old Phipps Cemetery, Ashe Co.

Jones, Wilson; Pvt.; c. 1836–13 Jun. 1863; Maplewood Cemetery, Gordonsville, VA

Key, William N.; Pvt.; c.1844–

Lane, Robert M.; Sgt.; 18 Jan. 1842–21 Apr. 1916; Old South Fork Cemetery, Allegheny Co.

Leagan, James H.; Pvt.; –Mar. 1863

Light, Matthias M.; Pvt.

Liles, Ambrose; Pvt.; c.1842–

Marlow, Edmond; Pvt.; c.1840–3 Jul. 1863

Mash, George; Pvt.; 17 Jan. 1836–29 Nov. 1862; Old Soldiers Cemetery, Mount Jackson, VA

Mash, James; Pvt.; 4 Mar. 1828–c.1895; Mash-Severt Cemetery, Ashe Co.

Mash, John; Pvt.; c.1840–

Mash, Thomas; Pvt.; c.1843–

Matherly, Thomas J.; Pvt.; c.1837–3 Apr. 1863; Old City Cemetery, Lynchburg, VA

May, George Washington; Pvt.; 10 Jan. 1841–1881; May-Roland Cemetery, Ashe Co.

May, Marshall Saunders; Pvt.; 25 Aug. 1839–18 Dec. 1920; Jackson Teasterman Cemetery, Ashe Co.

May, Silas Mercer; Pvt.; c.1844–20 Dec. 1862; Old City Cemetery, Lynchburg, VA

McCormick, Robert B.; Pvt.; c.1842–

McGuire, William W.; Pvt.; 13 May 1842–Jan. 1862; Milas McGuire Cemetery, Ashe Co.

McNeil, Eli Henderson; Cpl.; –1924; Confederate Cemetery, Higginsville, MO

McNeil, James A.; Sgt.; 12 Feb. 1842–[8]

Miller, Ambrose; Pvt.; c.1845–30 Jan. 1864

Miller, Bartlett; Pvt.

Miller, Jacob; Pvt.; c.1837–1 Mar. 1863[9]

Miller, Jasper M.; Pvt.; c.1845–

Miller, John H.; Pvt.; 15 Mar. 1841–10 May 1927; David Miller Cemetery, Ashe Co.

Miller, Lewis Williams; Pvt.

Miller, Lowery; Pvt.; c.1842–12 Dec. 1862; Richmond, VA

Miller, Richard; Pvt.; c.1838–4 Dec. 1861

Miller, Shadrach; Pvt.; c.1841–13 Dec. 1862

Miller, William Harrison; Pvt.; 19 Nov. 1832–25 Feb. 1935; Senter Primitive Baptist Church Cemetery, Ashe Co.

Miller, William P.; Pvt.

Mullis, Madison; Pvt.; c.1839–13 Dec. 1862; Poe Family Cemetery, Ashe Co.

Mullis, Martin V.; Pvt.; c.1842–5 Jun. 1862[10]

Norman, Benjamin Franklin; ---; 11 Mar. 1841–28 May 1913; Union Rice Cemetery, Boone Co., KY

Osborne, Enoch, Jr.; Pvt.; 15 Dec. 1844–9 Dec. 1931; Pines Primitive Baptist Church Cemetery, Ashe Co.

Osborne, Enoch Sr.; Pvt.; c.1835–7 Nov. 1862; Hollywood Cemetery, Richmond, VA

Osborne, Ephraim; Pvt.; 8 Oct. 1840–17 Oct. 1932; Burt Hill, Ashe Co.

Owens, Benjamin; Pvt.; c.1840–14 Nov. 1861

Owens, Elijah; Pvt.; 19 May 1838–7 May 1909; Elijah Owens Cemetery, Ashe Co.[11]

Owens, Zachariah; Pvt.; c.1828–12 Feb. 1864

Parish, Robert S.; Pvt.

Parsons, George P.; 1Sgt.; c.1843–

Patrick, William; Pvt.; c.1813–

Pendergrass, Alexander; Pvt.; –12 May 1864; Confederate Cemetery, Spotsylvania C. H., VA

Pennington, Andrew; Pvt.; c.1840–

Perry, Basil; Pvt.; c.1843–

Perry, Hiram; Pvt.; c.1836–1 Jan. 1864; Ashe Co.

Perry, Jonathan; Pvt.; c.1840–2 Sep. 1862; Oakwood Military Cemetery, Richmond, VA

Perry, Richard Matthew; Sgt.; 1836–12 May 1864

Perry, Stephen; Pvt.; c.1837–

Perry, William; Pvt.; c.1832–21 Oct. 1862; Stonewall Cemetery, Winchester, VA

Price, John William; Pvt.; c.1843–

Roark, Ephraim; Pvt.; c.1843–24 Mar. 1864[12]

Roark, William

Rose, Alexander; Pvt.; c.1844–

Rotan, David; Pvt.; c.1830–13 Dec. 1862; Oakwood Military Cemetery, Richmond, VA

Roten, Josiah G.; Pvt.; c.1843–; Benjamin Brown Cemetery, Ashe Co.

Roten, William M.; Pvt.; c.1840–

Royal, William M.; Pvt.; c.1834–19 Mar. 1865; Woodlawn Cemetery, Elmira, NY

Severt, Enoch; Pvt.; 1 May 1844–6 Nov. 1917; John Severt Cemetery, Ashe Co.

Severt, John; Pvt.; 10 May 1841–4 Apr. 1924; John Severt Cemetery, Ashe Co.

Severt, Silas; Pvt.; 2 Feb. 1825–22 Aug. 1918; Severt Family Cemetery, Ashe Co.

Severt, Wiley; Pvt.; c.1841–2 Mar. 1863

Sexton, Joseph Enoch; Pvt.; c.1834–15 Jan. 1865; Woodlawn Cemetery, Elmira, NY

Sexton, Marion; Pvt.; c.1840–; Ashe Co.

Sexton, Reuben; Pvt.; 1829–6 May 1885; Family Cemetery, Helton Creek, Ashe Co.

Sexton, Thornton; Pvt.; c.1842–5 Jun. 1864

Shannon, James Newton; Pvt.

Sheets, Wesley; Pvt.; c.1837–3 May 1863

Shepherd, John; Pvt.; c.1843–21 Jul. 1862

Sherwood, Isaac F.; 1Sgt.; c.1839–4 Jul. 1862

Simmons, John; Pvt.; c.1835–

Stamper, Joshua; Pvt.; c.1826–

Stringer, Missouri B.; Pvt.; 18 Aug. 1838–11 Jan. 1924; Micagar O. Lewis Cemetery, Ashe Co.

Strunks, Absalom; Pvt.; c.1827–4 Jun. 1863; Hollywood Cemetery, Richmond, VA

Stuart, Andrew Jackson; Pvt.; c.1839–1907

Stuart, Elijah; Pvt.; 30 Apr. 1843–16 Sep. 1862

Swaine, Abel W.; Pvt.; c.1840–after Jun. 1862

Taylor, Calvin; Pvt.; 7 Nov. 1830–11 Sept. 1892

Taylor, George P.; Pvt.; c.1844–

Taylor, Harrison; Pvt.; 5 Jun. 1841–1 Mar. 1863

Taylor, Jacob; Pvt.; 8 Oct. 1835–9 Jul. 1924; Taylor Family Cemetery, Ashe Co.

Taylor, John; Cpl.; 2 Sept. 1833–3 May 1863

Taylor, Marshall; Pvt.; 29 Nov. 1845–29 Aug. 1864; Woodlawn Cemetery, Elmira, NY

Teague, George W.; Cpl.; c.1843–8 Jun. 1862; Hollywood Cemetery, Richmond, VA

Testerman, Calvin; Pvt.; c.1844–

Testerman, James J.; Cpl.; c.1838–1870

Testerman, Johnson; Pvt.; c.1840–1 Jul. 1862; Danville, VA

Tomlinson, Hiram; Pvt.; c. 1833–

Trivett, Thomas; Pvt.; c. 1830–24 Jun. 1864

Vannoy, James Humphery.; Sgt.; 8 May 1837–3 May 1916; James H. Vannoy Cemetery, Ashe Co.

Vanzant, Starling; Pvt.; c.1839–May 1863; Oakwood Military Cemetery, Richmond, VA[13]

Walker, William A.; Pvt.; c.1835–
Walters, Benjamin Franklin; Pvt.; c.1843–
Walters, John O.; Pvt.; c.1826–Dec. 1862[14]
Ward, John; Pvt.; c.1839–May 1862[15]
Ward, Lorenzo Dow; Pvt.; c.1831–10 May 1865; Woodlawn Cemetery, Elmira, NY
Weaver, John Ketterson; Pvt.; c.1842–1862[16]
Weaver, William H.; Pvt.; c.1844–29 Aug. 1862; Andrew Weaver Cemetery, Allegheny Co.
Welch, Porter; Pvt.; c.1834–27 Jun. 1862; Oakwood Military Cemetery, Richmond, VA

Williford, Nelson W.; Pvt.
Woods, Henry Absalom; Pvt.; c.1837–2 Jul. 1862; Richmond, VA
Wyatt, John; Pvt.; c.1831–10 Nov. 1862; University of Virginia Confederate Cemetery, Charlottesville, VA
Yates, James C.; Pvt.; c.1841–11 Jul. 1862; Hollywood Cemetery, Richmond, VA[17]
Yaunce, John W. H.; Pvt.; c.1844–May 1862
Young, John B.; Sgt.; c.1829–Apr. 1862

COMPANY B

Captains

Horton, Jonathan; 26 Feb. 1806–29 Nov. 1895; Horton Family Cemetery Watauga Co.
Cook, Jordan; 5 Oct. 1836–10 Jan. 1900; Jordan Cook Cemetery, Watauga Co.
Critcher, Andrew Jackson; Sept. 1834–7 Jul. 1909; Greer Cemetery Watauga Co.

Lieutenants

Brown, John M.; 3LT; 26 May 1835–15 Mar. 1909; Middle Fork Cemetery, Watauga Co.
Carlton, Calvin C.; 2LT; c.1826–; Caldwell Co.
Cook, Thomas D.; 2LT; 25 Mar. 1827–7 May 1897; Cook Cemetery Watauga Co.
Green, David J.; 2LT; c.1825–
Green, William M.; 2LT; c.1835–29 Aug. 1862; Second Manassas
Haigh, Charles T.; 1LT; Mar. 1845–12 May 1864; Spotsylvania Court House, VA
Horton, Nathaniel; 2LT; 22 Oct. 1829–25 Oct. 1898; Horton Cemetery, Watauga Co.
Somerville, James B.; 3LT
Todd, Joseph Beckwith; 1LT; 2 Sept. 1822–11 Dec. 1903; Old Boone City Cemetery Watauga Co.
Wiggins, Thomas Medicus; 3LT[18]

Non-Commissioned Officers and Enlisted Men

Asher, Fielden E.; Pvt.; c.1842–
Ball, John B.; Pvt.; 1835–1866; "Out West"
Barlow, Abram; Pvt.; c.1836–
Bebber, John G.; Pvt.; c.1835–3 July 1863; Gettysburg, PA

Beckham, William J.; Pvt.; Nov. 1841–
Benfield, Jackson VanBuren; Pvt.; 1834–6 Jul. 1862; Hollywood Cemetery, Richmond, VA
Benfield, Joseph L.; Pvt.; 27 May 1834–17 Aug. 1893; Benfield Cemetery, Avery Co.
Bennet, Benjamin N.; Pvt.; c.1828–1 Dec. 1862; Stonewall Cemetery, Winchester, VA
Bishop, Larkin C.; Cpl.; c.1842–15 Jul. 1862; Richmond, VA
Bishop, Lindsey M.; Pvt.; c.1843–27 Jun. 1862; Gaines's Mill, VA
Bishop, Samuel J.; Pvt.; 18 Sep. 1839–27 Jan. 1933; Fairview Cemetery, Watauga Co.
Blevins, Daniel; Pvt.; c.1836–
Boyd, Andrew E.; Pvt.; c.1836–8 Jul. 1862; Hollywood Cemetery, Richmond, VA
Brown, Jesse; Pvt.; c.1838–15 Jul. 1862; Oakwood Military Cemetery, Richmond, VA
Brown, Martin R.; Pvt.; c.1829–27 May 1862; University of Virginia, Charlottesville, VA
Broyhill, Stephen; Pvt.; c.1842–
Bryant, William; Pvt.; c.1839–9 Aug. 1862; Cedar Mountain, VA
Burgess, James; Pvt.; c.1844–12 May 1864; Spotsylvania Court House, VA
Burke, Charles H.; Pvt.; c.1838–1902; Daniel's Creek, Johnson Co., KY
Calhoun, Felix A.; Pvt.; c.1832–6 Oct. 1863; "at home"
Campbell, David W.; Pvt.; c.1845–
Campbell, Hilton H.; Pvt.; c.1836–17 Jul. 1864; Hollywood Cemetery, Richmond, VA
Campbell, William F.; Pvt.; c.1829–
Carlton, Cornelius M.; Pvt.; c.1844–6 Jul. 1863; Gettysburg, PA
Carlton, John R. (See Field and Staff)
Carlton, Lindsey H.; Sgt.; 1 Jun. 1838–13 May 1910; Fix Ridge Cemetery, Juliette, Idaho

Carlton, Thomas R.; Pvt.; c.1842–14 Jul. 1862; Washington, D.C.

Carroll, James; Pvt.; c.1842–

Carroll, Lewis William; ---; c.1839–[19]

Carroll, William; Pvt.; c.1840–[20]

Church, Jordan C.; Pvt.; c.1834–

Church, William R.; Pvt.; c.1842–

Clanton, Francis; Pvt.; –24 May 1865; Woodlawn Cemetery, Elmira, NY

Cook, David A.; Pvt.; 31 May 1832–14 Jun. 1909; Cook Cemetery, Watauga Co.

Cook, Henry; Pvt.; c.1842–13 Dec. 1862; Fredericksburg, VA

Cook, Jonathan; Pvt.; c.1841–2 Mar. 1864

Cossens, Franklin; Pvt.; c.1833–29 Aug. 1862; Manassas, VA

Councill, Jordan D.; Pvt.; c.1839–30 Nov. 1862; Winchester Cemetery, Winchester, VA

Councill, Jordan S.; Pvt.; c.1842–17 Nov. 1864; Woodlawn Cemetery, Elmira, NY

Cozzens, William Henry; Pvt.; c.1840–

Curtis, John C.; Pvt.; c.1838–6 Mar. 1863

Danner, William R.; Pvt.; c.1832–

Davis, Bartlett; Pvt.; c.1840–; Mt. Olive Baptist Church Cemetery, Alexander Co.

Davis, Calvin C.; Pvt.; 14 Dec. 1842–20 Jan. 1916; C.C. Davis Cemetery, Ashe Co.

Davis, Charles H.; Pvt.; c.1838–

Davis, Solomon; Pvt.; c.1838–21 Jan. 1863; Stonewall Cemetery, Winchester, VA

Davis, Thomas; Pvt.; c.1838–30 Sep. 1864; Jones Farm, VA

Day, William D.; Pvt.; c.1840–

DeBoard, Levi H.; Pvt.; 1 Oct. 1827–6 Nov. 1896; Chilichothe, Ross Co., OH

DeBoard, Thomas J.; Pvt.; 9 Sep. 1843–20 Jun. 1863; Old City Cemetery, Lynchburg, VA

Dula, Thomas; Pvt.; c.1832–1 Aug. 1862; Caldwell Co.

Estep, Allen; Pvt.; c.1825–

Estes, Amos; Pvt.; c.1843–

Fairchild, Joel Edden; 1Sgt.; 26 Jan. 1835–31 Jul. 1909; Oklahoma Cemetery, Tecumseh, OK

Faircloth, Ethelbert Andrew; Pvt.; Dec. 1824–1915; Fee Ridge Community Cemetery, Grayson Co., VA

Francis, Robert; Cpl.; c.1841–1908

Garland, Alfred L.; Pvt.; c.1842–13 May 1864

Gentry, Robert L.; Pvt.; c.1832–4 Dec. 1862; Hampton National Cemetery, Richmond, VA

Gortney, Francis G.; Pvt.; c.1836–2 Jul. 1864; Hollywood Cemetery, Richmond, VA[21]

Gragg, William Smith; Pvt.; c.1845–2 May 1863; Knoxville, TN

Green, David J.; Pvt.; c.1841–10 Aug. 1862; "Divisional Hospital"

Green, Joseph W.; Sgt.; c.1838–

Green, Levi; Pvt.; –26 Mar. 1933; Franklin/Oaks Cemetery, Avery Co.

Green, Smith; Pvt.; c.1836–

Green, Solomon; Pvt.; c.1844–12 May 1864

Green, William; Pvt.; c.1839–26 Jan. 1863

Greer, Edmond Marshall; Pvt.; 4 Mar. 1841–16 Jan. 1927; Benjamin Greer Cemetery, Watauga Co.

Greer, James S.; Pvt.; c.1834–1863; executed in Virginia.[22]

Greer, Newton; Pvt.; 28 Jul. 1841–26 Feb. 1934; Rymer Cemetery, Watauga Co.

Greer, Vinson; Pvt.; c.1840–27 Jun. 1862; Gaines's Mill, VA.[23]

Greer, William M.; Pvt.; c.1836–

Hagaman, Hamilton D.; Sgt.; c.1836–3 Jun. 1864

Hartley, Alexander; Pvt.; c.1834–7 Nov. 1863; Confederate Cemetery, Point Lookout, MD

Hartley, Azor; Pvt.; 4 Aug. 1839–22 May 1913; Hartley Family Cemetery, Watauga Co.

Hartley, Finley E.; Pvt.; c.1842–

Hartley, Harrison; Pvt.; 24 Jun. 1844–1925; Norway Cemetery, Coos Co., OR

Hartley, John Carlton; Sgt.; c.1838–27 Mar. 1863

Hayes, James Madison; Pvt.; c.1825–11 Apr. 1865; Fort Delaware National Cemetery, Finn's Point, DE

Hayes, John A.; Sgt.; c.1836–30 Sep. 1864; Hollywood Cemetery, Richmond, VA

Hayes, Thomas; Pvt.; c.1840–29 Aug. 1862; Manassas, VA

Hayes, Wyatt; Pvt.; 4 Oct. 1844–22 Dec. 1930; Fairchild Cemetery, Watauga Co.

Hays, William; Pvt.; c.1838–c.1900; Oregon

Heath, William R.; Pvt.; 1 Dec 1832–12 Nov. 1914; Dixon Cemetery, Ashe Co.

Hendrix, Tarlton; Pvt.; c.1843–17 Jul. 1862; Oakwood Military, Richmond, VA

Hicks, Calvin; Pvt.; –28 May 1864; Old Lutheran Cemetery, Iredell Co.

Hicks, John; Pvt.

Hilderth, David A.; Pvt.

Hodges, Demarcus; Pvt.; c.1846–

Hodges, Edmund; Pvt.; c.1831–

Hodges, Hilery J.; Pvt.; c.1843–

Hodges, Larkin; Pvt.; 16 Nov. 1841–13 Oct. 1933; Maney Cemetery, Weaverville, Buncombe Co.

Hodges, Thomas M.; Pvt.; c.1837–27 Jun. 1862; Gaines's Mill, VA

Hodges, William; Pvt.; c.1833–

Hodges, William, Jr.; Pvt.; c.1838–

Hodges, William H.; Pvt.

Holder, Sidney K.; Pvt.; c.1842–26 Jul. 1862; Hollywood Cemetery, Richmond, VA

Holdman, John; Pvt.; c.1831–

Howell, Calvin; Pvt.; c.1839–

Hudler, David; Pvt.; 1838–c.1920

Hudler, John W.; Pvt.; 26 Mar. 1832–23 Dec. 1921; Liberty Hill Baptist Church Cemetery, Ashe Co.

Hudler, Robert; Pvt.; c.1837–19 Mar. 1863; "at home"

Hudler, William; Pvt.; c.1830–

Hughes, James W.; Cpl.; c.1837–

James, John A.; Pvt. Hollywood Cemetery, Richmond, VA

James, Jordan S.; Pvt.; c.1817–15 Dec. 1862; Oakwood Military Cemetery, Richmond, VA

Jones, Edmond R.; Pvt.; 9 May 1828–1 Nov. 1886; Meat Camp Baptist Church Cemetery, Watauga Co.

Jones, Henderson J.; Pvt.; c.1824–13 Dec. 1862; University of Virginia Confederate Cemetery, Charlottesville, VA

Jones, Joseph Hampton; Pvt.; 25 Jul. 1844–

Jones, Samuel; Pvt.; c.1832–

Jordan, William D.; Pvt.; c.1844–4 Dec. 1862; Lynchburg, VA

Keller, Edmund; Cpl.; c.1832–7 Oct. 1864; Hollywood Cemetery, Richmond, VA

Land, William T.; Cpl.

Littleton, Robert H.; Pvt.; c.1831–

Long, Isaiah; Pvt.; Aug. 1831–1900; Ashe Co.

Lookabill, David; Pvt.; c.1813–22 Dec. 1862; Hollywood Cemetery, Richmond, VA

Lowe, James M.; Pvt.; c.1842–7 Feb. 1864; Confederate Cemetery, Point Lookout, MD

Lowe, William Tilford; Pvt.; 18 Apr. 1836–10 May 1905; Mt. Olive Baptist Church Cemetery, Alexander Co.

Massey, William; Pvt.; c.1844–

Meggs, James R.; Pvt.

Milholland, Junius A.; Pvt.; c.1844–1863; Old Lutheran Cemetery, Iredell Co.[24]

Miller, Alfred; Pvt.; c.1834–3 Jul. 1863; Missing, Gettysburg, PA

Miller, Calvin C.; Pvt.; c.1830–

Miller, George Washington; Pvt.; 30 Aug. 1843–1906; Oklahoma

Miller, Jesse Mark; Pvt.; c.1840–27 Jan. 1892; Hope Cemetery, Cooke Co., TX

Mitchell, Alexander S.; Pvt.; c.1840–31 Aug. 1864; Oakwood Military Cemetery, Richmond, VA

Moore, George Dumas; Pvt.; c.1835–

Morris, George T.; Pvt.; c.1843–7 Oct. 1862; Danville, VA

Musgraves, John C.; Pvt.; c.1836–4 Dec. 1862

Myers, James Addison; Pvt.; 30 Aug. 1845–23 Apr. 1928; Reeds Baptist Church Cemetery, Davidson Co.

Nelson, David; Pvt.; c.1844–29 Aug. 1862; Manassas, VA

Nelson, William R.; Pvt.; c.1842–23 Dec. 1863; Point Lookout, MD

Norris, George Washington; Pvt.; 15 Aug. 1831–7 Feb. 1926; Fairview Church Cemetery, Watauga Co.

Norris, John M.; Pvt.; c.1842–

Norris, John Riley; Pvt.; 22 Oct. 1828–3 Nov. 1889; Norris Cemetery, Watauga Co.

Norris, William D.; Pvt.; 12 Apr. 1841–11 Apr. 1924; Sands Cemetery, Watauga Co.

Norris, William S.; Pvt.; c.1839–3 May 1863; Chancellorsville, VA

Osborne, John S.; Pvt.; c.1840–

Oxendine, Larkin; Pvt.; c.1835–13 Mar. 1921; Peters Cemetery, Carter Co., TN

Page, Joseph J.; Pvt.

Payne, Franklin; Pvt.; c.1841–

Penley, Luther L.; Pvt.; c.1845–20 Jul. 1862; Brook Church Cemetery, VA

Phipps, Thomas M.; Pvt.; 16 Sep. 1827–16 Oct. 1901; Phipps Cemetery, Ashe Co.

Pipes, Thomas M.; Pvt.; c.1819–22 Apr. 1862; Lenoir Co.

Pitts, John; Pvt.; c.1843–12 Mar. 1864

Pitts, William; Pvt.; c.1844–13 Dec. 1862; Fredericksburg, VA

Potter, Levi; Pvt.; c.1846–26 Jan. 1863; Jacksborough, TN

Privett, Sampson C.; Pvt.; –1 Jan. 1865; Woodlawn Cemetery, Elmira, NY

Randle, William M.; Pvt.; c.1839–

Richardson, Robert; Pvt.; c.1844–after Aug. 1863

Robbins, Thomas; Cpl.; c.1841–31 May 1864

Robbins, William R.; Pvt.; c.1839–13 Dec. 1862; Fredericksburg, VA

Shoaf, Jesse; Pvt.; c.1825–29 Mar. 1936; Concord United Methodist Church Cemetery, Davie Co.

Simmons, John; Pvt.; c.1828–15 Jul. 1862; Emanuel Episcopal Church Cemetery, Richmond, VA

Smith, John E.; Pvt.; c.1844–5 Aug. 1862; Hollywood Cemetery, Richmond, VA

Stafford, Anderson Franklin; Pvt.; c.1833–

Stafford, John; Pvt.

Stafford, John C.; Pvt.

Stitt, Wellborn; Pvt.; c.1843–17 Jan. 1863

Storie, Amos; Pvt.; c.1830–; possibly killed at Spotsylvania

Storie, Jesse P.; Sgt.; Dec. 1833–1 Aug. 1863; Old City Cemetery, Lynchburg, VA

Storie, Rufus; Pvt.; c.1828–

Thayer, Nereus Mendenhall; Pvt.; 17 Nov.

1845–1 Jul. 1934; Macedonia United Methodist Church Cemetery, Montgomery Co.

Triplet, Larkin Hodges; Pvt.; 29 Jun. 1848–5 Nov. 1916; Lewis Fork Cemetery, Wilkes Co.

Triplett, Calvin; Pvt.; c.1844–27 Jun. 1862; Gaines's Mill, VA

Triplett, Franklin M.; Pvt.; c.1836–c.1908

Triplett, George Washington; Pvt.; Nov. 1835–26 Feb. 1920; Bend, OR

Triplett, James Wellington; Pvt.; c.1836–9 Dec. 1861

Triplett, Lorenzo Dow; Pvt.; 23 May 1838–4 Sep. 1930; Whitnel Methodist Church Cemetery, Caldwell Co.

Triplitt, Darby; Pvt.; 8 Aug. 1844–28 Mar. 1929; Triplett Cemetery, Watauga Co.

Tucker, John R.; Pvt.

Tucker, John W.; Pvt.; 25 Dec. 1844–1 Mar. 1921

Tugman, James M.; Pvt.; 19 Jan. 1843–8 Aug. 1862; Richmond, VA

Tugman, Mecager; Pvt.; c.1817–

Turner, Francis Marion; Pvt.; c.1842–18 Feb. 1863

Turnmire, David L.; Pvt.; c.1826–14 Sep. 1864; Woodlawn Cemetery, Elmira, NY

Turnmire, Peter Wilburn; Pvt.; Dec. 1833–13 Apr. 1917; Caldwell Co.

Williams, Coleman; Pvt.

Company C

Captains

Potts, James Monroe; 11 Dec. 1839–21 Sep. 1869; Iredell Co.

Brown, Owen N. (See Field and Staff)

Potts, Lawson A.; 14 Aug. 1841–3 May 1886; Bethel Presbyterian Church Cemetery, Micklenburg Co.

Brown, John Doderidge; c.1840–1915; Davidson College Cemetery, Mecklenburg Co.

Lieutenants

Beatty, George; 2LT; –29 Aug. 1862; Manassas, VA

Doherty, William W.; 2LT; –3 Jul. 1863; Gettysburg, PA

Gillespie, Joseph R.; 2LT; c.1829–18 Apr. 1877; Bethel Presbyterian Church Cemetery, Mecklenburg Co.

Jetton, John L.; 2LT; 12 Aug. 1827–30 Jan. 1906; Davidson College Cemetery, Mecklenburg Co.

Johnston, Barhabas A.; 3LT; c.1838–12 May 1864; Spotsylvania Court House, VA

Johnston, James S.; 2LT; 9 Mar. 1840–30 Mar. 1867; Gilead Presbyterian Church Cemetery, Mecklenburg Co.

Kerns, Thomas J.; 1LT; c.1831–

Osborne, William B.; 3LT; c.1828–

Pettus, John W.; 3LT

Sample, John W.; 2LT

Torrence, Abraham Perry; 2LT; 6 Aug. 1833–7 Jun. 1918; Bethel Presbyterian Church Cemetery, Mecklenburg Co.

Wilson, Thomas A.; 1LT; c.1827–

Non-Commissioned Officers and Enlisted Men

Alcorn, Thomas P.; Pvt.; c.1838–24 Mar. 1863; Camp Gregg, VA

Alexander, David Rankin; Sgt.; c.1834–3 May 1864; Virginia

Alexander, James H.; 1Sgt.; c.1836–12 May 1864; Spotsylvania Court House, VA

Alexander, John Brevard (See Field and Staff)

Alexander, Thomas Lafayette; Pvt.; c.1832–

Alexander, Thomas Roberson; Pvt.; 18 May 1840–13 Jul. 1914

Alexander, William D.; Pvt.; c.1840–

Armour, Thomas S.; Pvt.; 15 May 1838–14 Dec. 1901; Pleasant Ridge M. Church Cemetery, Bolton, TN

Armstrong, Mathew; Pvt.; 17 Oct. 1823–4 Nov. 1885; Lowell, GA

Barnett, W. R.; Pvt.; c.1828–9 Dec. 1862; University of Virginia Confederate Cemetery, Charlottesville, VA

Barnette, James F.; Pvt.; –26 Jul. 1864; Hollywood Cemetery, Richmond, VA

Barnette, John D.; Pvt.; c.1831–

Barnette, John W.; Pvt.; c.1838–

Beard, James Francis Marion; Cpl.; c.1842–1 Oct. 1917; Gilead ARP Cemetery, Mecklenburg Co.

Beard, John C.; Sgt.; c.1835–

Beard, John M.; Pvt.; c.1842–30 Jun. 1862; Frayser's Farm, VA

Bell, J. B.; Pvt.

Bell, John A.; Cpl.; c.1837–8 Jul. 1862; Brook Church Cemetery, VA[25]

Bell, John D.; Pvt.

Black, Allison W.; Pvt.; c.1836–

Black, Andrew J. L.; Pvt.; c.1840–22 Oct. 1862; Sharon Cemetery, Middlesburg, VA

Black, John Calvin; Pvt.; c.1838–; Mt. Lebanon Baptist Church Cemetery, Covington, TN

Black, John C., Jr.; Pvt.; 3 Sep. 1846–3 Jan. 1925; Tipton Co., TN

Black, Samuel; Pvt.; c.1828–

Blakely, John B.; Pvt.; c.1834–30 Jun. 1862; Hollywood Cemetery, Richmond, VA

Blakely, W. F. M.; Pvt.; c.1842–12 Jul. 1862

Blythe, James W.; Pvt.; 25 Oct. 1839–30 Nov. 1914; Oakwood Cemetery, Wake Co.

Blythe, John Nantz; Pvt.; 20 Nov. 1830–30 Sep. 1896; Hopewell Presbyterian Cemetery, Mecklenburg Co.

Boyles, James A.; Pvt.; 3 Oct. 1836–30 Aug. 1904; Bethel Presbyterian Cemetery, Mecklenburg Co.

Brady, Rufus A.; Pvt.; c.1844–

Britt, John; Pvt.; c.1837–

Brown, Benjamin F.; 1Sgt.; c.1842–

Brown, Henry W.; Pvt.; c.1840–after 27 Jun. 1862

Brown, Jonas; Pvt.; c.1832–24 May 1863

Burleyson, Joseph Benjamin; Pvt.; 12 Mar. 1842–18 Sep. 1900; Rocky Rover Presbyterian Church Cemetery, Cabarrus Co.

Caldwell, William W.; Pvt.; c.1838–21 Oct. 1864; Loudon Park National Cemetery, Baltimore, MD

Carpenter, Jacob A.; Pvt.; 12 Sep. 1837–after 16 May 1864

Carpenter, John C.; Pvt.; c.1842–; Old Town Cemetery, Tarboro, Edgecombe Co.

Carrigan, William F.; Pvt.; 17 Dec. 1816–13 Feb. 1907; Coddle Creek A. P. R. Cemetery, Iredell Co.

Cathey, James W.; Pvt.

Christenburg, Samuel B.; Pvt.; c.1837–

Cochran, James C.; Pvt.; c.1830–8 Oct. 1862; Winchester, VA[26]

Cox, J. Thomas; Pvt.; c.1836–27 Nov. 1862; Staunton, VA

Deaton, James R.; Pvt.; c.1841–; Mount Zion Methodist Church Cemetery, Mecklenburg Co.

Deaton, John; Pvt.; c.1844–; Mount Zion Methodist Church Cemetery, Mecklenburg Co.

Dellinger, Marcus Conner; Cpl.; 11 Nov. 1835–30 Nov. 1926; Portalis, Roosevelt Co., NM

Derr, Andrew J.; Pvt.; 1831–1902

Dewease, William Alfred; Pvt.; 27 May 1824–27 Nov. 1873; Ramah Presbyterian Church Cemetery, Mecklenburg Co.

Deweese, John Walter; Pvt.; 1844–1876; Ramah

Presbyterian Church Cemetery, Mecklenburg Co.

Ewing, Samuel R.; Pvt.

Fesperman, John C.; Pvt.; c.1840–1 Jul. 1862; Danville, VA

Fidler, David H.; Cpl.; c.1823–17 Jul. 1862; Oakwood Military Cemetery, Richmond, VA

Gardner, David; Pvt.; c.1838–3 May 1863; Chancellorsville, VA

Gardner, Hezekian T.; Pvt.; c.1842–28 May 1862; Old City Cemetery, Lynchburg, VA

Gardner, Samuel S.; Pvt.; 20 Feb. 1837–21 Sep. 1921; Hepbzibah Presbyterian Church Cemetery, Gaston Co.

Garrison, Angelum A.; Pvt.; 4 Oct. 1846–1918; Mecklenburg Co.

Gibbs, Jackson Matthew; Pvt.; 3 Jan. 1841–6 Jun. 1878; McKendree United Methodist Church Cemetery, Iredell Co.

Gibbs, John Alexander; Cpl.; 28 Aug. 1830–9 Aug. 1862; Cedar Mountain, VA

Gibson, James J.; Pvt.; c.1837–3 Jul. 1862; Hollywood Cemetery, Richmond, VA

Gibson, Thomas Alexander; Pvt.; 1842–1907; Gilead Presbyterian Church Cemetery, Mecklenburg Co.

Goodrum, John W.; Pvt.; c.1842–; Mt. Zion United Methodist Church Cemetery, Mecklenburg Co.

Goodrum, Joseph Z.; Pvt.; c.1844–

Graham, Adelbert J.; Pvt.; 20 Feb. 1843–5 Oct. 1864

Graham, Daniel C.; Pvt.; 20 Feb. 1843–5 Oct. 1864

Grier, John S.; Pvt.; c.1825–3 May 1863; Chancellorsville, VA

Hagons, H. M.; Pvt.; c.1824–15 Dec. 1862; Fredericksburg, VA

Hamilton, J. R.; Pvt.; c.1837–13 Dec. 1862; Fredericksburg, VA

Harrison, William Henry; Sgt.; c.1843–; Huntersville Presbyterian Church Cemetery, Mecklenburg Co.

Hastings, William C.; Pvt.; c.1842–

Henderson, Hugh E.; Pvt.; c.1839–

Henderson, William A.; Pvt.; 16 Sep. 1844–19 May 1863; Oakwood Military Cemetery, Richmond, VA[27]

Henderson, William F.; Pvt.; c.1838–15 Oct. 1862; University of Virginia Confederate Cemetery, Charlottesville, VA

Hendricks, James Martin; Pvt.; c.1838–12 Jun. 1865; Confederate Cemetery, Point Lookout, MD

Hendrix, William P.; Pvt.; c.1841–17 Oct. 1862; Winchester, VA

Holbrooks, Richard Simpson; Pvt.; c.1841–

Holt, Jackson; Pvt.; 1820–1896; Collins Family/ Peter Overby Cemetery, Stokes Co.

Hoover, John M.; Pvt.; 30 Aug. 1846–25 Jun. 1938; Paw Creek Presbyterian Church Cemetery, Mecklenburg Co.

Houston, H. Lafayette; Pvt.; c.1832–23 May 1863; Hollywood Cemetery, Richmond, VA

Houston, John M.; Pvt.; c.1834–

Howie, Andrew J.; Pvt.; c.1830–Aug. 1864; Mecklenburg Co.

Hucks, Samuel L.; Pvt.; c.1841–; Mt. Zion United Methodist Church Cemetery, Mecklenburg Co.

Hunter, Andrew J.; Pvt.; c.1845–

Hunter, Henry C.; Pvt.; c.1837–8 Mar. 1865; Confederate Cemetery, Point Lookout, MD

Hunter, Hugh Mc.; Pvt.; c.1832–

Hunter, James F.; Pvt.; c.1841–23, Jul. 1863; Philadelphia National Cemetery, Philadelphia, PA

Icehower, John W. W.; Pvt.; c.1844–

Jamison, John R.; Pvt.; c.1834–

Johnston, M. F.; Pvt.; c.1832–7 Jul. 1863

Kelly, Alexander A.; Pvt.; c.1838–1922; Center Presbyterian Cemetery, Iredell Co.

Kerns, Joseph A.; Pvt.; c.1836–27 Apr. 1862; Lenoir Co.

Kerns, Thomas J.; Pvt.[28]

Knox, John R.; Sgt.; 18 Mar. 1830–4 Jan. 1863; Presbyterian Church Cemetery, Mecklenburg. Co.

Knox, Samuel Willis; Pvt.; 8 Jun. 1821–3 Dec. 1897; Huntersville Presbyterian Church Cemetery, Mecklenburg Co.

Leach, Levi; Pvt.; c.1836–23 Feb. 1863; Fredericksburg Confederate Cemetery, Fredericksburg, VA

Lentz, Rufus S.; Sgt.; c.1839–

Little, John S.; Pvt.; c.1844–

Luckey, T. S.; Pvt.; c.1844–12 Jun. 1862; Hollywood Cemetery, Richmond, VA

Martin, Samuel D.; Pvt.; c.1836–

McAlister, Cephas; Pvt.; c.1839–19 Apr. 1864

McAulay, Hugh E.; Pvt.; c.1840–23 May 1862; Old City Cemetery, Lynchburg, VA

McAuley, Daniel N.; Pvt.; –22 Feb. 1865

McAuly, Ephraim Alexander; Pvt.; 1826–1909; Gilead A. P. R. Church Cemetery, Mecklenburg Co.

McCoy, Albert; Pvt.; 1 Sep. 1843–10 Apr. 1925; St. Mark's Church Cemetery, Mecklenburg Co.

McCoy, Columbus Washington Pvt.; c.1833– 1922; St. Mark's Church Cemetery, Mecklenburg Co.

McCoy, John F.; Pvt.; c.1830–3 Jul. 1863; Gettysburg, PA[29]

McFadden, John F.; Pvt.; c.1844–

Miller, Robert C.; Pvt.; c.1835–

Monteith, R. A.; Pvt.; c.1835–27 Jun. 1862; Gaines's Mill, VA

Moore, J. T.

Moore, Robert D.; Pvt.; c.1844–8 Mar. 1863; Richmond, VA

Morrison, Norman; Pvt.

Morrison, William L.; Pvt.

Nantz, Clement R.; Pvt.; c.1829–25 Jul. 1862; Old City Cemetery, Lynchburg, VA

Nantz, David J.; Pvt.; c.1830–

Onton, William Richard; Pvt. (See Company F)

Page, J. F.; Pvt.; c.1833–29 Nov. 1862; Old Soldiers Cemetery, Mount Jackson, VA

Parks, Isaac F.; Pvt.; c.1828–

Pettus, John W.; Pvt.[30]

Pippins, Milus B.; Pvt.; c.1830–4 Aug. 1864; Point Lookout, MD

Potts, Sidney X.; ---; 24 Apr. 1844–17 Jan. 1925; Bethel Presbyterian Church Cemetery, Mecklenburg, Co.

Puckett, E. McCamy; Pvt.; c.1837–

Reid, John L.; Pvt.; c.1844–3 Aug. 1862

Rhyne, John Jones; Pvt.; 18 Nov. 1827–Dec. 1862; Richmond, VA

Rodgers, James M. L.; Pvt.; c.1827–17 Sep. 1884; Bethel Presbyterian Church Cemetery, Mecklenburg, Co.

Rodgers, John R.; c.1822–8 Mar. 1863; Old City Cemetery, Lynchburg, VA

Sample, Elam A.; Pvt.; c.1844–

Sample, Isaac W.; Sgt.; c.1844–3 May 1863; Chancellorsville, VA

Sample, William Leroy; Sgt.; c.1841–1 Sep. 1862; Ox Hill, VA

Sellers, Eli; Pvt.; 5 Oct. 1819–31 Mar. 1902; Concord United Methodist Church Cemetery, Cherryville, Gaston Co.

Shaver, Monroe; Pvt.; c.1836–

Shaw, Andrew; Pvt.; c.1814–

Sloan, Walter S. Pharr; Pvt.; 5 Oct. 1846–26 Dec. 1929; Davidson College Cemetery, Mecklenburg Co.

Sloane, Thomas A.; Pvt.; 1829–1878; Ramah Presbyterian Church Cemetery, Mecklenburg Co.

Sloane, Thomas C.; Pvt.; 1840–1917; Ramah Presbyterian Church Cemetery, Mecklenburg Co.

Solomon, David A.; Pvt.; c.1837–22 Dec. 1862; Oakwood Military Cemetery, Richmond, VA

Sparrow, Thomas W.; Pvt.; c.1814–(See Field and Staff)

Stearns, Ambrose Lee; Pvt.; c.1838–2 Aug. 1862

Stearns, William Russell; Pvt.; c.1833–1913; Mt. Zion United Methodist Church Cemetery, Mecklenburg Co.

Stewart, Samuel Jackson; Pvt.; c.1840–

Strickland, Quincy

Stroupe, Cephus; Pvt.; c.1833–

Stroupe, Maxwell; Pvt.; c.1833–3 May 1863; Chancellorsville, VA

Taylor, W. A.; Pvt.; c.1831–24 Oct. 1862; Hollywood Cemetery, Richmond, VA

Todd, J. A.; Pvt.; c.1841–May 1863; Chancellorsville, VA

Torrance, John A.; c.1840–(See Field and Staff)

Torrence, Hugh L. W.; Pvt.; c.1837–10 Sep. 1863; Fort Delaware National Cemetery, Finn's Point, DE

Torrence, James Harvey; Pvt.; Mount Zion Methodist Church Cemetery, Mecklenburg Co.

Torrence, William Land; Cpl.; 1843–1865; Mt. Mourne, Iredell Co.

Turnmire, Larkin G.; Pvt.

Varner, John L.; Pvt.; c.1836–14 Mar. 1862; Craven Co.

Wagstaff, James R.; Pvt.; c.1839–

Wagstaff, John F.; Pvt.

Walker, Joseph C.; Pvt.; c.1832–

Wallace, Charles S.; Pvt.; c.1843–25 Jun. 1862; Hollywood Cemetery, Richmond, VA

Warsham, Alexander; Pvt.; c.1834–8 Jul. 1862; Richmond, VA

Weddington, Joseph Young; Pvt.; 3 Oct. 1843–

18 Dec. 1932; Elmwood Cemetery, Mecklenburg Co.

White, Joel H.; Pvt.; 1 Jul. 1840–19 Feb. 1908; Mt. Zion United Methodist Church Cemetery, Mecklenburg Co.

Whitely, Samuel; Pvt.; c.1845–

Wiley, John; Pvt.; c.1842–30 Jun. 1862; Frayser's Farm, VA

Williams, C. R.; Pvt.; c.1841–1 Jul. 1862; Blandford Cemetery, Petersburg, VA

Williams, Franklin C.; Pvt.; c.1837–23 Jun. 1862; Oakwood Military Cemetery, Richmond, VA

Wilson, Gilberth M.; Sgt.; c.1841–18 Jun. 1862; Richmond, VA[31]

Wilson, Thomas C.; Pvt.; c.1844–30 Jun. 1862; Richmond, VA[32]

Wood, John M.; Pvt.; –25 Aug. 1864; Reams's Station, VA.

Worsham, Francis Marion; Pvt.; 18 Dec. 1832–1 Jun. 1911; Beth Presbyterian Church Cemetery, Cornelius, Mecklenburg Co.

Worsham, Rufus Richard; Pvt.; 21 Oct. 1835–20 Jul. 1918; Mt. Zion Presbyterian Church Cemetery, Mecklenburg Co.

Worsham, Thomas Lafayette; Cpl.; c.1830–3 Jul. 1863; Gettysburg, PA

Worsham, William; Pvt.; c.1829–7 Jun. 1862; Hollywood Cemetery, Richmond, VA[33]

COMPANY D

Captains

Ashcraft, John B. (See Field and Staff)

Bost, Jackson L. (See Field and Staff)

Grady, Henry C.; c.1844–12 May 1864; Spotsylvania Court House, VA

Cochrane, John McKinley

Lieutenants

Battle, Wesley Lewis; 3LT; –22 Aug. 1863; Gettysburg, PA

Bost, Aaron Junis; 1LT; 7 Apr. 1802–9 Aug. 1871

Chears, Vachel T.; 1LT; c.1837–

Davis, George W.; 2LT; c.1839–20 Jul. 1862; Fredericksburg, VA

Gaddy, William Alexander; 3LT; 29 Nov. 1839–21 Jun. 1931; Unity Chapel Presbyterian Church Cemetery, Polkton, Anson Co.

Griffin, Joseph E.; 3LT; 28 May 1839–12 Jul. 1898; Wingate/Old Meadow Branch Cemetery, Union Co.

Marsh, Albert T.; 2LT; 1 Aug. 1830–

Walters, Daniel L.; 1LT; c.1838–17 Nov. 1862; Confederate Cemetery, Winchester, VA

Non-Commissioned Officers and Enlisted Men

Adams, John Q.; Pvt.; c.1837–

Austin, James Knox P.; Pvt.; 9 Jan. 1845–9 Nov. 1931; Union Co.

Austin, John J.; 7 Aug. 1820–30 Jan. 1884

Austin, John L.; c.1839–19 Nov. 1863; Confederate Cemetery, Point Lookout, MD

Austin, Jonathan L.; Pvt.; 25 Apr. 1835–13 Jan. 1886

Austin, Joseph H.; Sgt. (See Field and Staff)

Austin, Milton A.; Pvt.; c.1843–3 Apr. 1863; "in camp" near Richmond, VA

Austin, Milton S.; Pvt.; c.1839–2 Apr. 1865; Federal field hospital, VA

Baker, Charles E.; Pvt.; c.1842–

Ballard, William; Pvt.; c.1840–22 Feb. 1863; Camp Gregg, VA

Barco, William T.

Baucom, Ellis G.; Pvt.; 4 Dec. 1840–17 Dec. 1876; Baucom Family Cemetery, Union Co.

Baucom, George Wilson; 1Sgt.; 27 Jul. 1837–16 Jun. 1921; Primitive Baptist Church Cemetery, Jerusalem, Union Co.

Baucom, James C.; Pvt.; c.1839–

Baucom, James R.; Pvt.

Bennett, Henry; Pvt.; c.1841–9 Apr. 1864; Confederate Cemetery, Point Lookout, MD

Bivens, Robert Nathaniel; Pvt.; 2 Mar. 1831–7 Apr. 1899; Williams Cemetery, Union Co.

Black, Adam; Pvt.; c.1839–11 Aug. 1864; Confederate Cemetery, Point Lookout, MD

Bradley, Saunders; Pvt.; –1 Dec. 1862

Broom, Ananias R.; Pvt.; c.1841–

Brown, John C.; Pvt.; c.1841–20 Dec. 1861

Carelock, Samuel T.; Cpl.; c.1844–

Carson, W. G.

Caudle, Archibald Benjamin; Pvt.; 24 Jul. 1845–19 Nov. 1908; Eastview Cemetery, Wadesboro, Anson Co.

Chambers, Daniel W.; Pvt.; c.1832–

Cockerham, Jack

Collins, Calvin; Pvt.; c.1839–16 Jul. 1862; Richmond, VA

Collins, Lawson G.; Pvt.; c.1842–

Collins, Noah; Pvt.; c.1835–

Collins, Sampson; Pvt.; c.1841–26 Sep. 1863; executed

Crowell, John W.; Pvt.; 9 Apr. 1819–18 Aug. 1864; Fussell's Mill, VA

Cuthbertson, Thomas Lee; Cpl.; 7 Jul. 1839–7 Jan. 1884; Old Union Cemetery, Union Co.

Dees, Kenneth Mert; Cpl.; 20 Mar. 1835–2 Mar. 1897

Dees, William R.; Pvt.; c.1841–18 Aug. 1862; Blandford Cemetery, Petersburg, VA

Dickens, William

Duncan, Andrew Jackson; Pvt.; 15 Jan. 1833–25 Nov. 1862; Staunton, VA

Eacher, Hiram Peter; Pvt.; c.1835–

Eacher, Jonas P.; Pvt.; c.1842–3 May 1863; Chancellorsville, VA

Eacher, Miles R.; Pvt.; c.1845–

Earing, Abram; Pvt.; –6 Jul. 1862; "died at sea"

Eason, John Wilson; Sgt.; 20 Apr. 1839–27 Aug. 1919; Pleasant Grove Church/Campground Cemetery, Union Co.

Eason, Thomas Lee; Pvt.; 22 Feb. 1835–8 Oct. 1913; Old Haney Family Cemetery, Union Co.

Edwards, David J.

Edwards, Mathew Green; Pvt.; 1 May 1834–2 Jun. 1874; Edwards Graveyard No. 2, Anson Co.

Evans, Charles; Pvt.; c.1841–9 May 1863; Oakwood Military Cemetery, Richmond, VA

Fincher, Henry H.; Pvt.; 10 Feb. 1828–23 Dec. 1869; Monroe, Union Co.

Gaddy, David T.; Pvt.; c.1841–2 Jul. 1863; Gettysburg, PA

Gaddy, Elijah Gaston; Pvt.; 4 Oct. 1843–22 Jul. 1922; Olive Branch Baptist Church Cemetery, Union Co.

Gaddy, James Neville; Pvt.; 27 Dec. 1837–

Gaddy, John M.; Pvt.

Gaddy, Wilson P.; Pvt.; c.1833–

Gardner, Ransom J.; Pvt.; c.1829–13 Dec. 1862; Fredericksburg, VA

German, John D.; Pvt.; c.1841–; Missing, Gettysburg, PA

Green, Henry T.; Pvt.; c.1842–23 Jul. 1862; Oakwood Military Cemetery, Richmond, VA

Green, Thomas J.; Pvt.; c.1828–19 Nov. 1863; Hollywood Cemetery, Richmond, VA[34]

Griffin, Ellis P.; Sgt.; c.1836–3 Jul. 1863; Gettysburg, PA

Griffin, Hampton B.; Pvt.; c.1840–

Griffin, James Pleasant; Pvt.; Jan. 1842–28 Feb. 1915; Travis Chapel Cemetery, Weakly Co., TN

Griffin, James T.; Pvt.; c.1842–; Missing, Gettysburg, PA

Griffin, Joseph H.; Pvt.; c.1844–29 Aug. 1862; Manassas, VA

Griffin, Phillip C.; Pvt.; c.1843–

Griffin, Stanly J.; Pvt.; c.1844–3 May 1863; Chancellorsville, VA

Griffin, T. E.

Griffin, William A.; Pvt.; 6 Jun. 1839–21 Jul. 1863; Hollywood Cemetery, Richmond, VA[35]

Griffin, William T.; Pvt.; c.1843–

Gurley, Tilman; Pvt.; c.1829–10 Nov. 1862; Richmond, VA[36]

Hall, John W.; Pvt.; c.1834–1 Nov. 1862

Hancock, James P.; Pvt.; c.1842–20 Jul. 1862; Richmond, VA

Harington, Edmund P.; Pvt.; c.1845–

Hasty, Andrew J.; Pvt.; 6 Apr. 1836–27 May 1862; Hanover Court House, VA

Hasty, Jesse Caswell; Pvt.; Sep. 1832–

Hasty, Kenneth M.; Pvt.; 30 Aug. 1834–26 Sep. 1901; Old White Oak Cemetery, Union Co.

Hasty, William Jasper; Pvt.; c.1843–

Helms, Adam Clark; Pvt.; 25 Aug. 1845–11 Mar. 1898; Hillrest Baptist Church Cemetery, Unionville, Union Co.

Helms, Charles Leander; Pvt.; 14 Apr. 1838–13 Sep. 1916; Helms Cemetery, Union Co.

Helms, Gilbert Moore; Pvt.; c.1841–27 Mar. 1863; Camp Gregg, VA

Helms, Nathaniel; Pvt.; c.1830–29 Dec. 1862; Oakwood Cemetery, Richmond, VA

Helms, Solomon A.; Pvt.; c.1834–; Trulland Holmes Cemetery, Union Co.

Helms, William A.; Pvt.; c.1835–

Hendricks, William Thomas; Pvt.; 1843–1867; McFarland, SC

Hill, William; Pvt.; c.1824–6 Jan. 1863; "at home"

Hodges, Daniel

Hollaway, Emmet

Holsclaw, Elisha; ---; –15 Jun. 1898; Avery Co.

Honeycutt, Andrew; Pvt.; c.1838–30 Aug. 1862; Manassas, VA

Horne, Thomas J.; Sgt.; c.1842–23 May 1864; Jericho Mills, VA

Horne, William F.; Cpl.; c.1844–

Huffstetler, John P.; Pvt.; 12 Nov. 1843–; Old Smynra Cemetery, Bessemer City, Gaston Co.

Humphrey, William

Hyatt, James M.; Pvt.; c.1839–10 Aug. 1862; Richmond, VA

Keziah, Allen; Pvt.; c.1840–30 Aug. 1862; Manassas, VA

Keziah, Pinkey; Pvt.; c.1844–27 Aug. 1862; Oakwood Military Cemetery, Richmond, VA

Kirby, James

Kiser, Joseph; Pvt.; c.1835–3 May 1863; Chancellorsville, VA

Kiser, Philip; Pvt.; c.1837–11 Dec. 1862; Chancellorsville, VA

Kizer, William L.; Pvt.; c.1825–12 Jul. 1862; Fort Columbus, NY

Laney, Rowland A.; Pvt.; c.1839–10 Oct. 1863; Laney Cemetery, Union Co.

Liles, David T.; Pvt.; c.1834–

Liles, Dennis A.; Pvt.; c.1837–4 Jun. 1865; Confederate Cemetery, Point Lookout, MD

Liles, Emerson Hampton; Sgt.; 29 Aug. 1839–30 Jun. 1862; Old City Cemetery, Lynchburg, VA

Liles, Jesse W.; Pvt.; 2 Feb. 1844–3 Jul. 1862; Petersburg, VA

Little, Ellis P.; Pvt.; c.1837–23 Jul. 1863; Soldier's Section, Hollywood Cemetery, Richmond, VA

Little, Patrick; Pvt.; c.1839–

Little, William A.; Pvt.

Livingston, John E.; Pvt.; c.1827–28 Jun. 1862; Cypress Hill Cemetery, Brooklyn, NY

Lowery, James Thomas; Sgt.; 10 May 1843–18 Feb. 1901; Mt. Olive Church Cemetery, Anson Co.

Manus, B. A.; Pvt.; c.1845–

Manus, Nathan E.; Pvt.; c.1838–5 Aug. 1862; Petersburg, VA

Marsh, Joseph W.; Pvt.; c.1839–8 Jul. 1862; Richmond, VA

Marsh, Solomon F.; Pvt.; c.1837–; Missing, Gettysburg, PA

Marsh, William T.; Pvt.

Mauney, Christopher; Pvt.; c.1824–26 Jul. 1864; Oakwood Military Cemetery, Richmond, VA

Mauney, Manassas; Pvt.; 1840–

Medlin, Garrison; Pvt.; c.1841–29 Dec. 1864; Point Lookout, MD

Melton, Thomas; Pvt.; c.1819–10 Nov. 1862; Hollywood Cemetery, Richmond, VA

Mitchum, Burton Milton; Pvt.; c.1841–29 Aug. 1862; Manassas, VA

Moore, Sid D.

Mullis, John P.; Pvt.

Mullis, Milton Culpepper; Pvt.; 30 Sep. 1847–30 Sep. 1917; Shiloh Truelight Church Cemetery, Mecklenburg Co.

Nance, James C.; Pvt.; c.1843–27 Dec. 1862; Richmond, VA

Nash, Abner; Pvt.; c.1832–23 May 1863; Richmond, VA

Neal, David; Pvt.; c.1840–; Long Creek Presbyterian Church Cemetery, Gaston Co.

Neal, Green Berry; Pvt.; c.1838–27 Aug. 1863; Philadelphia National Cemetery, Philadelphia, PA

Neil, John H.; Pvt.; c.1840–

Neil, John H.; Pvt.; 23 Jun. 1831–7 Dec. 1863; Richmond, VA[37]

Newsom, Edmond T.; Pvt.; c.1841–2 Sep. 1862; Lynchburg, VA

Outon, Wiley; Pvt.; c.1844–12 May 1862; Maplewood Cemetery, Gordonsville, VA

Parker, David H.; Pvt.; c.1841–6 May 1862

Parker, Elijah J.; Pvt.; c.1841–; Smynra Cemetery, Union Co.

Parker, Franklin D.; Pvt.; c.1841–10 Aug. 1862; Oakwood Military Cemetery, Richmond, VA

Parker, Gary N.; Pvt.; c.1842–24 May 1862; University of Virginia Confederate Cemetery, Charlottesville, VA

Parker, James E.; Pvt.; c.1845–8 Jun. 1864; Confederate Cemetery, Spotsylvania Court House, VA

Parker, John W.; Pvt.; c.1836–9 Jun. 1864; Hollywood Cemetery, Richmond, VA

Parker, Levi G.; Pvt.; c.1843–

Parker, Peter A.; Pvt.; c.1843–

Parker, William T.; Pvt.; c.1837–12 Jul. 1863; Hollywood Cemetery, Richmond, VA

Parker, Zachariah; Pvt.; c.1844–6 Aug. 1863; Staunton, VA

Parks, Thomas Martin

Perry, James F.; Pvt.; c.1843–9 Aug. 1862; Cedar Mountain, VA

Phillips, Evan; Pvt.; c.1845–14 Jul. 1864; Hollywood Cemetery, Richmond, VA

Pierce, Jesse D.; Pvt.; c.1838–Nov. 1861; "at home"

Pierce, Jesse H.; Pvt.; c.1844–

Presler, Elijah; Pvt.; c.1828–15 Dec. 1864

Price, Andrew Wade Hampton; Pvt.; c.1840–9 Aug. 1915; Hopewell Churchyard, Union Co.

Price, Calvin Calaway; Pvt.; 6 Aug. 1839–7 Apr. 1921; Union Co.

Price, Hurley G.; Pvt.; 9 Sep. 1845–7 Jul. 1924; Cabarrus Co.

Price, James Cull; Pvt.

Price, Thomas A.; Pvt.; 2 Apr. 1842–

Pyron, Milus A.; Sgt.; 10 Oct. 1838–4 Jan. 1895; Union Baptist Church Cemetery, Old Union, AR

Rape, Henry N.; Pvt.; 25 Sep. 1836–8 Nov. 1904

Rape, Samuel M.; Pvt.; c.1842–4 Jul. 1862; Cypress Hill Cemetery, Brooklyn, NY

Rodgers, Thomas A.; Pvt.; c.1839–21 Jan. 1863; Richmond, VA

Rowland, John F.; Pvt.; c.1842–12 Aug. 1862; Richmond, VA

Rudisill, Jonus E.; Pvt.

Rushing, Felix G.; Pvt.; c.1840–3 Jul. 1862; Fort Columbus, NY

Rushing, George M.; Cpl.; c.1836–1 Jul. 1862; Malvern Hill, VA

Sellers, Abraham; Pvt.; 12 Oct. 1824–29 Sep. 1864; Hollywood Cemetery, Richmond, VA[38]

Sellers, George Lee; Pvt.; c.1827–22 Jul. 1864; Drewery's Bluff, VA

Sellers, William Monroe; Pvt.; c.1823–

Simpson, Marcus B.; Pvt.; c.1840–; Wingate/Old Meadows Branch Cemetery, Union Co.

Smith, Abraham; Pvt.; 24 Aug. 1837–16 Jun. 1862; Hollywood Cemetery, Richmond, VA

Smith, John E.; Pvt.; c.1824–

Smith, William P.; Pvt.; c.1839–19 Mar. 1863; Staunton, VA

Snider, David A.; Pvt.; c.1844–

Snider, Moses Stradler; Pvt.; 28 Apr. 1839–1 May 1888; Faulks Church Cemetery, Union Co.

Stack, Jackson; Sgt.; c.1831–10 Jun. 1862; Hollywood Cemetery, Richmond, VA

Staton, Malachi; Sgt.; c.1835–16 Aug. 1863; Cypress Hill Cemetery, Brooklyn, NY

Steel, Thomas H.; Pvt.; c.1844–7 Sep. 1937; Gray Cemetery, Carroll Co., MS

Stegall, Alexander; Pvt.; 6 Jan. 1840–30 Sep. 1920; El Dorado, Union Co., AR

Stegall, Jason; Pvt.; c.1840–

Stegall, John N.; Pvt.; c.1830–30 Aug. 1862; Manassas, VA

Stegall, Samuel; Pvt.; 3 Jan. 1845–8 Feb. 1926; Marshall Cemetery, Union Co.

Stegall, William Cicero; Pvt.; c.1832–21 Dec. 1862; Oakwood Military Cemetery, Richmond, VA

Swanner, James Alfred; Pvt.; Aug. 1840–18 Nov. 1911; Oakdale Cemetery, Baltimore, MD

Swanner, William G.; Pvt.; Dec. 1846–7 Feb. 1912; Oakdale Cemetery, Baltimore, MD

Syms, Richard; Pvt.; c.1843–

Tadlock, Alexander; Sgt.; c.1839–

Tadlock, James T.; Pvt.

Terrell, Josiah J.; Pvt.

Thomas, David C.; Pvt.; c.1844–

Thomas, Nathan G.; Pvt.

Thomas, William; Pvt.; c.1839–10 Sep. 1862; Blandford Cemetery, Petersburg, VA

Treadaway, John; Pvt.; c.1834–25 Aug. 1862; Petersburg, VA

Trull, Hampton H.; Pvt.; c.1843–30 Jun. 1864; Hollywood Cemetery, Richmond, VA

Trull, Thomas S.; Cpl.; Oct. 1840–

Trull, William H.; Pvt.; 9 Dec. 1833–13 Jun. 1898; Old Meadows Branch Cemetery, Union Co.

Tucker, George T.; Pvt.; c.1843–

Tucker, Jesse M.; Pvt.; c.1843–24 Aug. 1862; Blandford Cemetery, Petersburg, VA

Usry, Hampton; Pvt.; c.1845–

Usry, Thomas; Pvt.; c.1826–

Walden, Asa; Pvt.; c.1841–28 Nov. 1862; Oakwood Military Cemetery, Richmond, VA

Walker, Leonidas J.; Pvt.; c.1842–6 Jul. 1862; Fort Columbus, NY

Walters, Emberry; Pvt.; 10 Nov. 1843–16 Mar. 1885; Gaston Co.

Walters, George W.; Sgt.; c.1842–

Walters, James H.; Pvt.; 1845–1918; Willow Valley Cemetery, Iredell Co.

Walters, Joshua K.; Pvt.; c.1843–21 Jan. 1863; Richmond, VA

Walters, Leonard R.; Pvt.; c.1842–1 Sep. 1863; Oakwood Military Cemetery, Richmond, VA

Walters, Moses W.; Pvt.

Watts, Alexander B.; Pvt.

Watts, Thomas N.; Pvt.; c.1838–

Webb, James T.; Pvt.; c.1832–29 Sep. 1862

Williams, Bryant; Pvt.; c.1828–

Wilson, John T.; Pvt.; –1 Nov. 1862

COMPANY E

Captains

Farthing, William Young; 29 Jun. 1812–28 Nov.
1862; Winchester, VA

Nicholson, William T.; –2 Apr. 1865; Five Forks,
VA

Lieutenants

Bingham, Harvey M.; 3LT; 13 Feb. 1839–17 Mar.
1895; Oakwood Cemetery, Iredell Co.

Eggers, Johiel Smith; 1LT; 10 Oct. 1834–15 Apr.
1898; Eggers Cemetery, Watauga Co.

Farthing, Paul; 1LT; 17 Apr. 1821–11 Apr. 1865;
Camp Chase, OH

Hartley, Jonathan H.; 3LT; 13 Mar. 1841–19 Jul.
1925; Mt. Vernon, MO

Moore, Martin Van Buren; "Lt."; 12 Apr. 1837–1
Sep. 1900; Belleview Cemetery, Caldwell Co.

Nicholson, Edward A. T.; 2LT; –c.1864

Shull, William Finley; 1LT; 18 Sep. 1837–18 Jan.
1912; Brown Cemetery, Mill Creek, Johnson
Co., TN

Wiggins, Octavius Augustus; 2LT; 8 Apr. 1844–
1904; Madison, MS

Wilson, Isaac; 3LT; c.1833–17 Jun. 1864

Non-Commissioned Officers and Enlisted Men

Adams, James Winslow; Pvt.; 20 Dec. 1833–1
Mar. 1879

Adams, John N.; Pvt.

Adams, John Norman; Pvt.; 21 Jul. 1830–

Adams, Nelson; Pvt.; c.1830–28 Feb. 1863; "in
camp"

Adams, Squire, Jr.; Pvt.; 2 Mar. 1833–12 Dec.
1862; Maplewood Cemetery, Gordonsville,
VA

Adams, Wellington; Sgt.; c.1829–

Alexander, Thomas A.; Pvt.; c.1831–11 Aug.
1864; Woodlawn Cemetery, Elmira, NY

Bailey, Richmond; Pvt.; 1826–1896; Gilboa
United Methodist Church Cemetery, Marsh-
ville, Union Co.

Baird, Andrew; Pvt.; c.1842–; "died on the march
to Gettysburg"

Baird, John A.; Pvt.; c.1843–1863; Missing, Gettysburg, PA

Baird, Jonathan; Pvt.; c.1844–3 May 1863;
Chancellorsville, VA

Baker, Henry M.; Pvt.; c.1841–15 Dec. 1863;
Orange Court House, VA

Baker, Henry Simpson H.; Pvt.; c.1839–1 Aug.
1863; Philadelphia National Cemetery, Philadelphia, PA

Beckham, Lemon J.; Pvt.; c.1843–

Blair, James Benton; Pvt.; 20 Jan. 1845–

Blair, William Thomas; Pvt.; 24 Jan. 1843–6 Mar.
1923; Boone City Cemetery, Watauga Co.

Blankenship, James T.; Pvt.; c.1833–13 Jan.
1863; Old City Cemetery, Lynchburg, VA

Bowman, Logan; Pvt.

Brewer, David E.; Pvt.

Brewer, James; Pvt.; c.1820–

Brewer, Phillip M.; Pvt.; 14 Apr. 1843–21 Sep.
1921; Fork Mountain Cemetery, Avery Co.

Brickell, Joseph W.; Pvt.; c.1846–

Cable, Alexander L.; Pvt.; c.1842–23 Nov. 1908;
Tyrola Community Cemetery, Pontotoc, OK

Cable, Anderson; Pvt.

Cable, George Washington; Pvt.; c.1840–1921;
Dugger Cemetery, Johnston Co., TN

Cable, Thomas Anderson; Pvt.; 22 Jun. 1846–31
Jan. 1919; Cable Cemetery, Watauga Co.

Cable, William H.; Pvt.; c.1840–1864; Missing,
Reams's Station, VA

Calloway, William Henderson; Pvt.; 27 Sep.
1845–3 May 1916; Foscoe Community Cemetery, Watauga Co.

Clark, Francis M.; Pvt.; c.1834–27 Jun. 1862;
Gaines's Mill, VA

Clark, Samuel C.; Pvt.; c.1843–

Coffey, Cornelius Jones; Pvt.; c.1840–10 Feb.
1917; White Springs Cemetery, Watauga Co.

Coffey, James C.; Pvt.; c.1840–

Coffey, John E.; Pvt.; c.1841–3 May 1863; Chancellorsville, VA

Coffey, Joseph D.; Pvt.; c.1839–

Coffey, Thomas N.; Pvt.; c.1839–3 May 1863;
Chancellorsville, VA

Coon, Maxwell A.; Pvt.; c.1840–

Craig, William A.; Pvt.; –27 Oct. 1862; Staunton, VA

Crain, James A.; Pvt.

Crain, Wesley A.; Pvt.

Croom, Nathan Richard; Pvt.; 13 Mar. 1844–10
May 1920; Moore Creek Gap Church Cemetery, Pender Co.

Croom, William R.

Danner, Frederick; Pvt.; c.1814–1888; Danner
Cemetery, Watauga Co.

Danner, Peter F.; Pvt.; c.1845–

Dotson, Abner C.; Cpl.; c.1843–14 May 1863; Hollywood Cemetery, Richmond, VA.

Dugger, David Crocket; Pvt.; 13 Apr. 1838–26 May 1920; Howell Cemetery, Watauga Co.

Eggers, Brizilla; Sgt.; 10 Jun. 1825–

Eggers, Richard E.; Pvt.; 1 Feb. 1834–

Epps, Henry R.; Pvt.

Farmer, Lawson A.; 1Sgt.; c.1843–5 Feb. 1863; "in camp"

Farthing, Henry Harrison; Pvt.; 7 Oct. 1841–28 Aug. 1922; Farthing Cemetery, Watauga Co.

Farthing, James Martin; Sgt.; 25 Jul. 1835–13 Dec. 1862; Fredericksburg, VA

Farthing, John Sherman; Pvt.; 7 Aug. 1841–4 Aug. 1916; Mill Creek, TN

Farthing, John Young; Pvt.; 17 May 1840–7 Aug. 1920; Farthing Cemetery, Watauga Co.

Farthing, Linley Whitfield; Pvt.; 18 Aug. 1838–11 Feb. 1917; L. W. Farthing Cemetery, Watauga Co.

Farthing, Robert Hallyburton; Pvt.; 22 Jan. 1842–31 Oct. 1929; Watauga Co.

Farthing, Thomas Jefferson; 1Sgt.; 13 Aug. 1838–23 May 1862; Old City Cemetery Lynchburg, VA

Flannery, Joseph D.; Pvt.; 10 May 1834–16 Sep. 1924; John Adams Cemetery, Watauga Co.

Ford, Ephraim Wellington; Pvt.; c.1843–31 May 1862; Old City Cemetery, Lynchburg, VA

Foster, T. L.; Pvt.

Foster, William L.; Pvt.; c.1843–

Foushee, Valmore DeRosenberg; Pvt.; c.1828–3 May 1863; Chancellorsville, VA

Fox, Moses; Pvt.

Fox, William; Pvt.; c.1830–1 Jan 1863; Richmond, VA

Glenn, Henry H.; Pvt.; c.1817–30 Aug. 1862; Richmond, VA

Goodwin, Michael; Pvt.; c.1806–Nov. 1862; Rockingham Co., VA

Green, Alfred; Pvt.; c.1844–1898; Jont. Brown Cemetery, Watauga Co.

Green, Brazilla Carol; Pvt.; c.1843–18 Jul. 1863; "at home"

Green, Burzilla; Pvt.; c.1838–17 Jun. 1863

Green, John; Sgt.; c.1839–27 Jun. 1862; Gaines's Mill, VA

Green, Silas; Pvt.; c.1841–3 May 1863; Chancellorsville, VA

Green, William; Sgt.; c.1840–16 May 1863; Richmond, VA

Gurley, Jacob; Pvt.

Harden, William; Pvt.; c.1827–

Harmon, Cicero Decatur; Pvt.; 27 Jul. 1841–16 Jul. 1913; Harmon Cemetery, Watauga Co.

Hartley, Bartlett; Pvt.; 19 Dec. 1841–29 May 1865; Woodlawn Cemetery, Elmira, NY

Hartley, William; Pvt.; 21 Oct. 1831–3 May 1863; Chancellorsville, VA

Helms, Jacob; Pvt.

Henderson, Joel; Pvt.

Henson, James; Pvt.; 25 Feb. 1825–3 Apr. 1894; Henson's Chapel United Methodist Church Cemetery, Watauga Co.

Hicks, David; Pvt.; c.1832–

Hicks, William Thomas

Hilliard, Bartlett Young; Pvt.; Aug. 1832–7 Jan 1914; Watauga Co.

Hilliard, George W.; Pvt.; c.1838–27 Oct. 1862; Watauga Co.

Hilliard, Harrison H.; Pvt.; c.1842–

Hilliard, James R.; Pvt.; c.1834–

Hodges, Burton; Pvt.; c.1840–1 Sep. 1862; Huguenot Springs, VA

Hollars, William B.; Pvt.

Horrell, George W.; Pvt.; 1 Apr. 1831–17 Jul. 1915; New Hanover Co.

Howington, Joseph H.; Cpl.; c.1827–after 1900; Russell Co., VA

Howington, William M.; Pvt.

Johnson, Riley; Pvt.; c.1842–14 Dec. 1861; "in camp"

Johnson, William Riley; Pvt.; c.1847–

Knight, Levi H.; Pvt.; c.1836–

Lamb, Michael; Pvt.

Lawrance, George Washington Cpl.; 24 Apr. 1842–22 Apr. 1900; Union Cemetery, Watauga Co.

Love, James Anderson; Pvt.; 24 Sep. 1823–16 Mar. 1904; Love Cemetery, Watauga Co.

Love, Thomas Jefferson; Pvt.; 17 Apr. 1845–2 Mar. 1933; Adams Community Cemetery, Watauga Co.

Lunceford, Noah; Pvt.; c.1836–30 May 1862; Old City Cemetery, Lynchburg, VA

Lunsford, Joseph H.; Pvt.; c.1832–27 Dec. 1862; Guinea Station, VA

Lusk, John C.; Pvt.; c.1845–

Martin, George; Pvt.; c.1831–25 Jun. 1863; Old City Cemetery, Lynchburg, VA

McLain, James F.; Pvt.; c.1838–; Linney Grove Baptist Church Cemetery, Alexander Co.

McLain, John F.; Pvt.; c.1828–

Miller, Joseph W. S.; Pvt.; –after Oct. 1862; Stonewall Cemetery, Winchester, VA

Mitchell, Alexander F.; Pvt.; c.1831–21 Feb. 1863; Richmond, VA

Mitchell, John W.; Pvt.; c.1838–

Moody, Golson D.; Pvt.; 3 Apr. 1833–15 Sep. 1862; Swift Cemetery, Watauga Co.

Moody, Hedges; Pvt.; c.1843–

Morrison, Amos; Pvt.; c.1838–

Munday, George; Pvt.; c.1841–5 Jul. 1863; Gettysburg, PA

Munday, Heldon; Pvt.; c.1821–

Munday, James W.; Pvt.; c.1842–13 May 1864; Spotsylvania Court House, VA

Munday, Moses Erwin; Pvt.; 23 Apr. 1844–27 Nov. 1865; Antioch Baptist Church Cemetery, Alexander Co.

Munday, William F.; Pvt.; 1835–1914; Antioch Baptist Church Cemetery, Alexander Co.

Muse, Willis; Pvt.

Norwood, William L.; Pvt.; 4 Feb. 1841–17 Jun. 1928; Dutch Creek Cemetery, Watauga Co.

Orrant, Jacob A.; Pvt.; 10 Oct. 1839–22 Nov. 1919; Maple Springs, Monroe Co., TN

Orrant, Lewis; Pvt.; c.1844–

Patrick, George W.; Pvt.; c.1840–; Asheville, NC

Patterson, Julius H.; Pvt.; –17 Dec. 1862; Stonewall Cemetery, Winchester, VA

Phillips, Jordan Bower; 1Sgt.; 18 May 1841–21 Jan. 1923

Pilkinton, Henry A.; Pvt.; c.1844–12 Dec. 1861; "in camp"

Presnell, Elisha L.; Pvt.; c.1843–; Swift Cemetery, Watauga Co.

Price, Calvin; Pvt.; c.1838–24 Aug. 1862; Richmond, VA

Price, John; Pvt.; c.1833–13 May 1862; University of Virginia Confederate Cemetery, Charlottesville, VA

Price, Redmond; Pvt.; c.1808–

Price, Thomas; Pvt.

Pritchard, J. Anderson; Pvt.; c.1841–7 Mar. 1863; "in camp"

Reece, Hugh; Pvt.; 17 Aug. 1806–31 May 1885; Beech Community Cemetery, Watauga Co.

Ricks, George M. C.; Pvt.; c.1839–7 Apr. 1865; Richmond, VA

Rogers, Columbus M.; Pvt.

Rooney, Michael; Pvt.; c.1817–

Satterthwaite, George W.; Pvt.

Setzer, Harvey

Shell, William J.; Pvt.; c.1834–

Shoemaker, Theophilus; Pvt.; c.1840–

Shook, John Alexander; Pvt.; 22 Jun. 1846–15 Oct. 1930; Balm Cemetery, Avery Co.

Shull, Joseph Carroll; Pvt.; 21 Apr. 1842–18 Mar. 1921; Shull's Mill Cemetery, Watauga Co.

Shull, Nathaniel Canada; Pvt.; c.1825–13 Dec. 1862; Fredericksburg, VA

Shull, Philip Patterson; Pvt.; 20 Jul. 1842–1930; Nodaway Co., MO

Shull, Simon Philip; Sgt.; 8 Jul. 1840–17 Jun. 1923; Shull Cemetery, Watauga Co.

Slade, Henry; Sgt.

Smith, Abner; Pvt.; 22 Oct. 1826–24 Mar. 1862; Cove Creek Baptist Church Cemetery, Watauga Co.

Smith, Bennett; Pvt.; 29 Jan. 1835–30 Jun. 1863; Lynchburg, VA

Smith, Henry; Pvt.; 3 Mar. 1846–22 Apr. 1862; Lenoir Co.

South, Britton; Pvt.; c.1837–17 Dec. 1862; Richmond, VA

South, Eli; Pvt.; 4 Dec. 1834–4 Jul. 1919; Thomas Family Cemetery, Watauga Co.

Stevens, Lazarus; Pvt.; 31 May 1836–16 Jul. 1921; Stephens Family Cemetery, Ashe Co.

Stevens, Thomas; Pvt.; 1 Dec. 1844–1 Jan. 1916[39]

Storie, Jonathan; Pvt.; c.1831–9 Mar. 1863; Richmond, VA

Strickland, William; Pvt.; c.1843–

Swift, Dudley; Pvt.; c.1837–31 Mar. 1863; Fredericksburg Confederate Cemetery, Fredericksburg, VA

Swift, Samuel; Mus.; c.1831–31 Jul. 1864; Iredell Co.

Swift, Sherman; Pvt.; c.1839–

Swift, Young; Cpl.; c.1834–

Teague, Andrew Jackson; Pvt.; c.1829–25 Apr. 1865; Elmira, NY[40]

Teague, Daniel; Pvt.; 30 Dec. 1843–27 Mar. 1882; Antioch Baptist Church Cemetery, Alexander Co.

Teague, Moses; Pvt.; 18 Jul. 1823–8 May 1886; Macedonia Baptist Church Cemetery, Alexander Co.

Teaster, James Harrison; Pvt.; 1 Aug. 1842–16 Mar. 1928; Shell Creek, TN

Teaster, Samuel; Pvt.; c.1843–12 Dec. 1861; "in camp"

Thompson, John C.; Pvt.; c.1843–10 Oct. 1862; Stonewall Cemetery, Winchester, VA

Thompson, Milton F.; Pvt.; c.1828–12 Dec. 1862; Stonewall Cemetery, Winchester, VA

Townsend, George; Pvt.; c.1832–3 Jun. 1862; Cypress Hill National Cemetery, Brooklyn, NY

Townsend, John C.; Pvt.; c.1843–

Trivett, John E.; Cpl.; c.1833–15 Jan. 1863; Old City Cemetery, Lynchburg, VA

Ward, John; Pvt.; c.1831–6 Jul. 1862

Webster, James H.; Pvt.; c.1837–

Williams, Alfred; Pvt.; c.1830–13 May 1863; Hollywood Cemetery, Richmond, VA

Williams, Thomas R.; Pvt.; c.1825–6 Aug. 1862; Petersburg, VA

Wilson, Albert Pinkey; 1Sgt.; 14 Apr. 1862–4 Feb. 1928; Ray-Hollers Cemetery, Watauga Co.

Wilson, Hiram, Jr.; Pvt.; c.1835–after 1862
Wilson, Marion Francis; Pvt.; 14 Feb. 1828–30 Mar. 1902; Upper Beaver Dams Baptist Church Cemetery, Watauga Co.

Wilson, William Carroll; Pvt.; c.1838–6 Sep. 1862
Younce, George; Pvt.; 19 Mar. 1830–
Younce, Jacob Lewis; Pvt.; 5 Apr. 1844–26 Sep. 1921; Macon Co.

COMPANY F

Captains

Barber, William M. (See Field and Staff)
Hickerson, Charles N. (See Field and Staff)
Clary, Daniel L.; c.1836–20 Nov. 1862; Stonewall Cemetery, Winchester, VA
Beard, William W.; c.1844–
Petty, John B.; c.1843–2 Apr. 1865; Petersburg, VA

Lieutenants

Forrester, John T.; 2LT; c.1840–
Gilbreath, George R.; 2LT; c.1834–31 May 1862; Richmond, VA
Hickerson, James; 1LT; c.1834–
McGee, William S.; 3LT; c.1827–
Redding, William A.; 2LT; c.1838–19 Dec. 1862; Maplewood Cemetery, Gordonsville, VA
Shepherd, Samuel N.; 1LT; c.1828–
Smith, John K.; 2LT; c.1839–7 Sep. 1862; Martin Family Cemetery, Wilkes Co.
Tankersley, Felix; 1LT; 4 Jan. 1843–2 Apr. 1865; Petersburg, VA

Non-Commissioned Officers and Enlisted Men

Anderson, A. M.; Pvt.; c.1834–
Anderson, Harrison; Pvt.; c.1843–6 Oct. 1862; Hollywood Cemetery, Richmond, VA
Anderson, Isaac; Pvt.; c.1831–
Anderson, Samuel; Pvt.; c.1832–14 Aug. 1862; Richmond, VA
Anderson, Wesley; Pvt.; c.1837–27 May 1862; Hanover Court House, VA
Barbour, Franklin J.; Pvt.
Barlow, John B.; Pvt.; c.1841–23 Dec. 1862; Hollywood Cemetery, Richmond, VA
Barlow, Larkin C.; Pvt.; c.1839–27 May 1862; Hanover Court House, VA
Bell, Archibald L.; Pvt.; c.1824–13 Dec. 1862; Fredericksburg, VA
Bell, Joseph S.; Pvt.

Benfield, Andrew; Pvt.; c.1827–20 May 1863; Guinea Station, VA
Benfield, Jonathan A.; Pvt.; c.1831–17 Apr. 1863; Alexander Co.
Bowman, Daniel L.; Pvt.; c.1840–
Bowman, J. W.; Pvt.; c.1836–12 Jun. 1863; University of Virginia Confederate Cemetery, Charlottesville, VA
Bowman, John; Pvt.; c.1843–c.1910; Adams Cemetery, Clackamas Co., OR
Bowman, Joshua W.; Pvt.; c.1832–2 Apr. 1865; Petersburg, VA
Bowman, Marcus M.; Pvt.; c.1843–
Bradley, George McD.; Pvt.; c.1844–13 Jul. 1862
Brown, John W.; Pvt.
Bryan, Henry M.; Sgt.; c.1836–12 May 1864; Spotsylvania Court House, VA
Bumgarner, Eli H.; Pvt.; c.1842–
Bumgarner, Joseph A.; Pvt.; c.1840–
Carlton, Henry; Pvt.; c.1842–30 May 1862
Carwell, James L.; Pvt.; c.1844–30 May 1862
Caudle, Jonathan
Clary, Benjamin F.; Cpl.; 8 Dec. 1841–7 Jul. 1922; Collin, TX
Cline, Elijah; Pvt.; c.1838–23 Nov. 1862; Old City Cemetery, Lynchburg, VA
Cline, Elijah H.; Pvt.; c.1829–
Cline, Simon Timothy; Pvt.; 24 Mar. 1832–24 Jan. 1912; Friendship Lutheran Church Cemetery, Alexander Co.
Coleman, Robert; Pvt.; c.1825–1862[41]
Combs, William; Pvt.
Cook, Pettis
Corley, D. P.; Pvt.
Crouse, Andrew; Pvt.; 18 Sep. 1844–25 Nov. 1919; Duncombe Cemetery, Duncombe, IA
Crouse, Henry; Pvt.; 30 Apr. 1841–6 Mar. 1912; Duncombe Cemetery, Duncombe, IA
Crouse, Shubael Bureham; Pvt.; 14 Jun. 1842–17 Oct. 1923; Malvern Cemetery, Malvern, IA
Culler, Rufus Govan; Pvt.; c.1841–1920; Old Presbyterian Church Cemetery, Wilkes Co.
Daganhart, George; Pvt.; c.1835–10–11 Jan. 1863; Hollywood Cemetery, Richmond, VA
Davidson, William R. D.; Pvt.; 26–27 Oct. 1864; Elmira, NY

Davis, Alfred; Pvt.

Davis, Nesbet C.; Pvt.; c.1837–

Davis, Samuel P.; Pvt.; c.1842–4 Sep. 1862; Wilkes Co.

Davison, Bennet L.; Pvt.; –8 Jun. 1864; Hollywood Cemetery, Richmond, VA

Deal, George W.; Pvt.; c.1829–4 Apr. 1864; Orange Court House, VA

Deal, W. A.; Pvt.; c.1834–Sep. 1863; "at home"

Dula, Bennett; Pvt.; c.1840–4 Jul. 1862; Danville, VA

Dula, Linsey; Pvt.; c.1840–8 Aug. 1862; Richmond, VA

Dula, Lowery; Pvt.; c.1842–1935; Shepherd-Ferguson Cemetery, Wilkes Co.

Duncan, Isaac C.; Cpl.; c.1843–25 Jun. 1864; City Point, Petersburg, VA

Earp, Wilson H.; Sgt.; 1 Feb. 1843–21 Dec. 1897; Prospect Church Cemetery, Iredell Co.

Edwards, David A.; Pvt.; c.1840–1 Aug. 1862; Richmond, VA

Edwards, Joseph T.; Pvt.; c.1843–

Eller, John; Pvt.; c.1842–30 May 1862; University of Virginia Confederate Cemetery, Charlottesville, VA

Ferguson, Samuel S.; 1Sgt.; c.1841–

Fletcher, Enoch H.; Pvt.; 1845–1913

Fox, Alexander; Pvt.; c.1839–13 Sep. 1863; Ft. Delaware National Cemetery, Finn's Point, DE

Fox, Daniel J.; Pvt.; c.1832–8 Nov. 1862; Berryville, VA

Fox, David A.; Pvt.; c.1835–

Fox, Wallace; Pvt.; c.1842–3 May 1863; Chancellorsville, VA

Frazier, Joshua D.; Pvt.; 1847–7 Jul. 1864; Oakwood Cemetery, Raleigh, Wake Co.[42]

Garland, Pryor; Pvt.

Garner, John A.; Pvt.; c.1836–

Garner, William; Pvt.; c.1806–

Gaultney, Edward S.; Pvt.; c.1839–after 1864

Gentry, Austin; Pvt.; 2 Aug. 1827–11 Nov. 1896

Gibbs, Robert J.; Pvt.; c.1834–

Gilbreath, Noah J.; Cpl.; c.1844–c.15 Aug. 1864; City Point, VA

Goodnight, James M.; Pvt.; c.1837–30 Nov. 1862; Stonewall Cemetery, Winchester, VA

Grimes, Brunnel R.; Pvt.; c.1843–

Hanner, Simpson A.; Pvt.; c.1842–

Harris, E. D.

Harris, J. H.

Hartin, Rufus J.; Pvt.; c.1839–5 Aug. 1862; Richmond, VA

Hawkins, James S.

Hawkins, Samuel S.; Pvt.; c.1826–

Hefner, William R.; Pvt.; c.1843–

Helms, Thomas D.; Pvt.; 16 Apr. 1820–20 Apr. 1900; Hillrest Baptist Church Cemetery, Unionville, Union Co.

Hendricks, Joseph F.; Sgt.; c.1838–27 Jun. 1862; Gaines's Mill, VA

Hickerson, John C.; Pvt.

Hickerson, Robert Gwyn; Pvt.; c.1836–1922

Higgens, W. L.

Hinchey, Richard M.; Pvt.; c.1843–27 May 1862; Hanover Court House, VA

Holcomb, Thomas Franklin; ---; 26 Apr. 1846–26 Feb. 1924; Brooks Cross Roads, Yadkin Co.

Holman, James; Pvt.; c.1823–1 Jan. 1864; executed

Howel, John Obediah; Pvt.; 14 Jun. 1844–20 Mar. 1894

Howell, Ancey B.; Pvt.; c.1839–

Howell, George Washington; Pvt.; 23 Mar. 1844–23 Nov. 1917; Howell Cemetery, Wilkes Co.

Isenhower, Daniel L.; Pvt.; c.1838–

Isenhower, David S.; Pvt.; c.1836–19 Nov. 1863; Friendship Church Cemetery, Alexander Co.

Isenhower, James L.; Pvt.; –6 Jan. 1863; Hollywood Cemetery, Richmond, VA

Jewell, C. W.; Pvt.

Jimmerson, Samuel W.; Pvt.

Joins, James H.; Pvt.; c.1844–28 Nov. 1862; Winchester, VA

Keever, Jacob Artamis; Pvt.; 1828–1918; Oak Grove Cemetery, Wolf Bayou, AR

Keever, Jacob Clark; Pvt.

Kilby, Benjamin H.; Pvt.; c.1840–2 or 3 Jun. 1864; Richmond, VA

Kilby, John W.; Cpl.; 27 Mar. 1843–9 Mar. 1886; Wilkes Co.

Kilby, William; Pvt.; c.1827–3 May 1865; Woodlawn Cemetery, Elmira, NY

Killen, John A.; ---; 17 Apr. 1846–Jan. 1915; Saddle Mt. Baptist Church Cemetery, Allegheny Co.

Lackey, William H.; Pvt.; 23 Mar. 1836–16 Apr. 1912; Pisgah Methodist Church Cemetery, Allegheny Co.

Little, Joseph K.; Pvt.

Livingston, John Orell; Pvt.; c.1844–

Luffman, William; Pvt.; –29 Nov. 1864; Woodlawn Cemetery, Elmira, NY

Luther, Jesse Elihu; Pvt.; 10 Sep. 1843–

Luther, Walter J.; Pvt.; c.1840–10 Jul. 1862; Emanuel Episcopal. Church Cemetery, Richmond, VA

Lyons, Allen; Pvt.; 20 Nov. 1820–2 Jul. 1864; Point Lookout, MD

Lyons, James; Pvt.; 13 Oct. 1827–18 Nov. 1883; Surry Co.

Lyons, William; Pvt.; 1843–1913; Oakwood Cemetery, Raleigh, Wake Co.

Mastin, Felix; Pvt.; –3 Jul. 1864; Wilkes Co.

Mastin, William J.; Cpl.; c.1839–

McClelland, Joseph; Pvt.; –7 Aug. 1864; Alexander Co.

McDaniel, William Harrison; Sgt.; c.1840–

Menius, James Matthew; Pvt.

Milam, J. W.; Pvt.; c.1843–

Milam, James S.; Pvt.; c.1838–

Minton, Lovelace; Pvt.; c.1818–

Onton, William Richard; Pvt. (See Company C)

Owens, Daniel L.; Pvt.; c.1841–after 1862; Yorktown National Cemetery, VA

Parker, Alexander; Pvt.; c.1834–3 May 1873; Liberty Baptist Church Cemetery, Wilkes Co.

Parks, William Franklin; Pvt.; 20 Oct. 1837–17 May 1921; Zion Baptist Church Cemetery, Yadkin Co.

Parks, Willis; Pvt.; 12 Mar. 1839–19 Jun. 1905; Macedonia Baptist Church Cemetery, Wilkes Co.

Parlier, Leonard Lafayette; Pvt.; c.1844–1 Jun. 1864; Bethesda Church Cemetery, VA

Parsons, James C.; Pvt.; c.1842–15 Jun. 1862

Parsons, John; Pvt.; c.1835–

Parsons, John W.; Pvt.; –30 Sep. 1864; Jones Farm, VA

Pearson, George L.; Pvt.; c.1835–

Pendry, W. R.

Perteete, William P.; Cpl.; 14 Feb. 1840–18 Apr. 1921; Old Broadtree Cemetery, Nevarro Co., TX

Pillows, T. J.; Pvt.

Pollard, James Lee; Pvt.; 1839–; Steffleg Cemetery, Smythe Co., VA

Pollard, Thomas; Pvt.; 1844–

Pratt, Little J.; Pvt.; c.1840–20 Sep. 1862[43]

Price, William Riley; Pvt.; c.1827–

Rabin, Charles; Pvt.

Rex, George W.; Pvt.

Rhyne, John; Pvt.; –23 Dec. 1864; Petersburg, VA

Rice, Wilson; Pvt.; c.1836–

Roberson, Alexander; Pvt.; –14 Sep. 1864; Woodlawn Cemetery, Elmira, NY

Roberts, Eli A.; Pvt.; c.1838–

Roberts, Langly H.; Pvt.; c.1840–

Roberts, Rufus F.; Pvt.; c.1835–

Rogers, James M. L.; Pvt. (See Company C)

Rouse, J. W.; ---; 15 Apr. 1847–

Rowe, J. L.; Pvt.; c.1840–19 Dec. 1862; Camp Gregg, VA[44]

Rowe, John W.; Pvt.; c.1838–

Sale, Francis M.; Pvt.; c.1837–

Sale, George W.; Pvt.; 14 Mar. 1839–14 Jun.

1930; Brier Creek Baptist Church Cemetery, Wilkes Co.

Salyer, Daniel; Pvt.

Salyer, Jesse; Pvt.

Shew, Constine; Pvt.; c.1829–18 Sep. 1864; Woodlawn Cemetery, Elmira, NY

Shew, Killis; Pvt.; c.1844–20–24 Jul. 1862; Richmond, VA

Shew, William Payton; Pvt.; c.1841–

Shumate, Esley; Pvt.; c.1843–

Shumate, Samuel; Pvt.; 1 May 1839–15 Jun. 1910; Shumate Family Cemetery, Wilkes Co.

Simpson, Evin A.; Pvt.

Smith, Jacob

Smith, Lewis H.; Pvt.; c.1829–17 Dec. 1863; Richmond, VA

Snow, R.

Spencer, Daniel L.; Pvt.; c.1838–8 Jun. 1864; Hollywood Cemetery, Richmond, VA

Spencer, Joseph R.; Pvt.; c.1839–

Spencer, Terrell

Staley, Robert M.; 1Sgt. (See Field and Staff)

Stapleton, William S.; Pvt.

Stokes, James C.

Summerland, Benjamin Franklin; Pvt.; c.1832–

Summerlin, James M.; Pvt.

Thomas, Joel; Pvt.; 16 Jul. 1836–16 Dec. 1929; Oakdale Cemetery, Surry Co.

Travis, Peter

Treadaway, Moses; Pvt.; 12 May 1812–7 Nov. 1890; Cherokee, Swain Co.

Triplett, Pickens Lewis; Pvt.; c.1840–25 Jul. 1862; Richmond, VA

Triplett, William T.; Pvt.; c.1837–21 Sep. 1862; Weldon, VA

Turner, George; Pvt.

Turner, Marcus B.; Pvt.; c.1837–13 Dec. 1862; Fredericksburg, VA

Vannoy, Thomas J.; Sgt.; c.1842–

Walker, William; Pvt.; c.1839–3 May 1863

Wall, Thomas H.

Wallace, Elbert; Pvt.; 4 Jul. 1847–10 Mar. 1914

Wallace, John G.; Pvt.; c.1831–

Wallace, Joseph G.; Pvt.

Wallace, Matthew; Pvt.; c.1844–

Wallace, Noah H.; Pvt.; c.1843–

Walsh, Phillip; Sgt.; 11 Feb. 1837–16 Jun. 1911; Mt. Pleasant Baptist Church Cemetery, Wilkes Co.

Walsh, Thomas F.; Pvt.

Wetherspoon, Lucius L.; Pvt.; c.1844–

Wilcoxen, David; Pvt.; c.1843–14 Jun. 1862; University of Virginia Confederate Cemetery, Charlottesville, VA

Wiles, Hiram; Pvt.; 30 Apr. 1834–10 Sep. 1914; Liberty Grove Baptist Church Cemetery Wilkes Co.

Wiles, William; Pvt.; c.1839–27 May 1862; Hanover Court House, VA

Willis, Jacob C.; Pvt.; 17 Dec. 1821–28 Sep. 1883; Kauesh Methodist Church Cemetery, Cleveland Co.

Wyatt, Jesse W.; Pvt.; c.1839–18 Jul. 1864; Hollywood Cemetery, Richmond, VA

Wyatt, John Carlton; Pvt.; 4 May 1842–25 April 1931; Reddies River Church Cemetery, Wilkes Co.

Young, John F.

COMPANY G

Captains

Bryan, John G.; c.1830–(See Field and Staff)

Reed, James; c.1820–

Steele, Robert Luckey; 31 May 1808–19 Sep. 1883; Three Forks Baptist Church Cemetery, Alexander Co.

Hudson, Daniel L.; c.1837–2 Apr. 1865; Petersburg, VA

Lieutenants

Austin, Daniel; 2LT; c.1820–

Brown, Joel H.; 1LT; c.1835–

Brown, John Levi; 3LT; –17 May 1863

Cochrane, George Washington; 2LT; 4 Sep. 1840–15 Mar. 1908; Eastview Cemetery, Catawba Co.

Glenn, William Wallace; 3LT (See Field and Staff)

Pool, James B.; 1LT; c.1841–

Royster, Iowa Michigan; 2LT; c.1840–15 Jul. 1863; Oakwood Cemetery, Raleigh, Wake Co.[45]

Non-Commissioned Officers and Enlisted Men

Allen, John P.; Pvt.

Allen, Marcus A.; Pvt.

Austin, David A.; Pvt.; c.1836–8 Mar. 1865; Point Lookout, MD

Austin, Jehua N.; Pvt.; c.1838–27 May 1862; Hanover Court House, VA

Austin, John L.; Pvt.; c.1837–22 May 1863; Oakwood Military Cemetery, Richmond, VA

Austin, Merret; Pvt.; c.1822–

Austin, Samuel; Pvt.; c.1834–13 Jul. 1862; Richmond, VA

Austin, William; Pvt.; c.1841–

Baker, Daniel M.; Pvt.

Baker, John; Mus.; c.1831–2 Jul. 1862; Emanuel Presbyterian Church Cemetery, Richmond, VA

Barnes, Brinsley; Pvt.; c.1844–27 May 1862; Hanover Court House, VA

Barnes, Elijah; Pvt.; 23 Nov. 1848–29 Dec. 1921; Three Forks Baptist Church Cemetery, Alexander Co.

Barnes, George; Sgt.; c.1828–3 Jul. 1863; Gettysburg, PA

Barnes, George W.; Pvt.; c.1840–27 Mar. 1863; Confederate Cemetery, Huguenot Springs, VA

Barnes, Peter Q.; Pvt.; 26 Jul. 1843–28 Jan. 1925; Munday-Teague Cemetery, Alexander Co.

Barnes, Smith F.; Cpl.; c.1831–20 Jul. 1863; Soldiers Section, Hollywood Cemetery, Richmond, VA

Barnes, Tobias; Sgt.; 1 Mar. 1844–15 Dec. 1929; New Salem Presbyterian Church Cemetery, Alexander Co.

Bentley, Joel Johnson; Pvt.; 24 Sep. 1820–26 Apr. 1906; Walnut Grove Baptist Church Cemetery, Wilkes Co.

Bentley, John J.; Pvt.; 25 Dec. 1844–1936; Walnut Grove Baptist Church Cemetery, Wilkes Co.

Blackwelder, Philip Augustus; Pvt.; c.1839–8 Jun. 1911; Salem Cemetery, Alexander Co.

Bowles, Alfred G.; Pvt.; 3 Oct. 1840–13 Apr. 1926; Pleasant Hill Baptist Church Cemetery, Alexander Co.

Bowles, Bentley A.; Pvt.; c.1841–17 Jun. 1862; University of Virginia Confederate Cemetery, Charlottesville, VA

Bowman, David; Pvt.

Bowman, Miles; Pvt.; c.1837–

Brookshire, Benjamin Hamilton; Pvt.; 5 May 1828–5 Jul. 1866; Three Forks Baptist Church Cemetery, Alexander Co.

Brookshire, William; Pvt.; c.1834–1 Oct. 1863; Stonewall Cemetery, Winchester, VA[46]

Brown, Archer; Pvt.; c.1844–30 Sep. 1864; Jones Farm, VA

Brown, Franklin Manley; Pvt.; 1824–2 Sep. 1864; Hollywood Cemetery, Richmond, VA

Brown, Lawson; Pvt.; c.1844–

Brown, Noah A.; Pvt.; c.1846–

Bumgardner, Andrew G.; Pvt.; c.1832–23 Jun. 1862; Hollywood Cemetery, Richmond, VA

Bumgardner, David L.; Pvt.; –30 Jun. 1862; Gaines's Mill, VA

Bumgardner, John Miller; Pvt.; 9 Sep. 1821–11 Feb. 1887; Bumgardner Cemetery, Alexander Co.

Bumgardner, Tobias; Pvt.; c.1834–24 Jul. 1862; Old City Cemetery, Lynchburg, VA

Campbell, Alexander; Pvt.; c.1839–

Campbell, Harrison; Pvt.

Campbell, James; Pvt.; c.1805–

Campbell, Squire B.; Pvt.; c.1821–

Chapman, Archy B.; Pvt.; 25 Dec. 1841–12 Feb. 1931; Three Forks Baptist Church Cemetery, Alexander Co.

Chapman, Clinton Boone; Pvt.; c.1844–17 May 1907; Three Forks Baptist Church Cemetery, Alexander Co.

Chapman, Edwin F.; Pvt.; –14 Oct. 1864; Richmond, VA

Chapman, Elisha; Pvt.; c.1840–29 May 1862; University of Virginia Confederate Cemetery, Charlottesville, VA

Chapman, Emmit F.; Pvt.; 16 Aug. 1830–7 Oct. 1911; Three Forks Baptist Church Cemetery, Alexander Co.

Chapman, James Wiley; Sgt.; 30 Jun. 1841–18 Sep. 1916; Little River Baptist Church Cemetery, Alexander Co.

Chapman, Larkin J.; Pvt.; c.1823–8 May 1865; Greenlawn Cemetery, Newport News, VA

Chapman, Richard C.; Pvt.; 29 Dec. 1811–30 Sep. 1893; Three Forks Baptist Church Cemetery, Alexander Co.

Chapman, Thomas H.; Pvt.; c.1826–

Chapman, William Franklin; Cpl.; 30 Jun. 1838–23 Feb. 1922; Macedonia Baptist Church Cemetery, Alexander Co.

Childers, Noah A.; ---; 22 Aug. 1844–14 Mar. 1910; Macedonia Baptist Church Cemetery, Alexander Co.

Cochrane, Francis M.; 1Sgt; 4 Sep. 1840–3 May 1863; Chancellorsville, VA

Crouch, John L.; 1Sgt.; c.1838–21 Jul. 1862

Crouch, Joseph; Pvt.; c.1828–

Crouch, Lawson; Pvt.; c.1841–10 Jun. 1863; Hollywood Cemetery, Richmond, VA

Daniel, Doctor A.; Pvt.; c.1841–

Daniel, William; Pvt.; c.1838–; Salem Evan Lutheran Church Cemetery, Alexander Co.

Davis, Jehu W.; Cpl.; c.1840–29 Aug. 1862

Davis, John B.; Pvt.

Davis, Solomon; Pvt.; c.1838–; (See Company B)

Davis, Thomas W.; Pvt.; c.1834–

Deal, David L.; Sgt.; c.1834–10 Apr. 1865; Woodlawn Cemetery, Elmira, NY

Deal, Noah; Pvt.; c.1827–1 Sep. 1862

Deal, Noah J.; Sgt.; c.1831–

Dickson, Stephen

Dison, William; Pvt.; c.1830–

Dison, William F.; Pvt.; c.1846–

Drum, David; Pvt.; c.1833–15 Aug. 1862; Hollywood Cemetery, Richmond, VA

Echard, Henry Franklin; Pvt.; 20 May 1829–1 Jul. 1902; Three Forks Baptist Church Cemetery, Alexander Co.

Echerd, Peter E.; Sgt.; 22 Jan. 1835–26 Jun. 1899; Antioch Baptist Church Cemetery, Alexander Co.

Faulkner, Miles A.; Pvt.; c.1823–9 Aug. 1864; "at home"

Flowers, Adam A.; Pvt.; c.1829–17 Jul. 1880; Pisgah Cemetery, Catawba Co.

Fortner, Edwin; Pvt.; c.1834–30 Jun. 1862; Frayser's Farm, VA

Fortner, John G.; Pvt.; c.1832–17 Nov. 1863; Confederate Cemetery, Point Lookout, MD[47]

Fox, Ambrose Calvin; Pvt.; 9 Dec. 1845–29 Mar. 1921; Oakwood Cemetery, Raleigh, Wake Co.

Fox, Elcany; Pvt.

Fox, Hugh; Pvt.

Fox, Jordan C. A.; Pvt.; –15 Jun. 1864; "near Petersburg"

Fox, Moses G.; Pvt.; c.1835–27 May 1862; Hanover Court House, VA

Fox, Wesley; Pvt.; –30 Jan. 1865; Woodlawn Cemetery, Elmira, NY

Fox, William, Jr.; Pvt.; c.1841–11 Dec. 1862; Old City Cemetery, Lynchburg, VA

Fox, William, Sr.; Pvt.; c.1834–27 May 1862; Hanover Court House, VA

George, N. L.

German, John; Pvt.; c.1836–25 Aug. 1862; Richmond, VA

Greay, George F.; Pvt.

Gryder, Adam Adolphus; Sgt.; c.1845–12 May 1864; Spotsylvania Court House, VA

Gryder, Pinkny L.; Pvt.; 11 Jun.1831–29 Nov. 1918; Adam Green Cemetery, Watauga Co.

Gryder, Leander Rufus; Pvt.; 7 Feb. 1825–15 Dec. 1882; Bethel Baptist Church Cemetery, Alexander Co.

Gryder, Wiley W.; Pvt.; c.1828–14 Jun. 1863; Hollywood Cemetery, Richmond, VA

Gwaltney, James Perry; Pvt.; 18 Feb. 1840–7 Apr. 1932; Linney Grove Baptist Church Cemetery, Alexander Co.

Harmon, David F.; 1Sgt.; c.1834–8 May 1864; Orange Court House, VA

Harmon, Marcus; Pvt.

Harrington, John; Pvt.; 7 Feb. 1822–7 Apr. 1932;

Salem Evan Lutheran Church Cemetery, Alexander Co.

Harrington, Sion H.; Pvt.; 22 Mar. 1820–26 Mar. 1891; Three Forks Baptist Church Cemetery, Alexander Co.

Hase, J. F.; Pvt.; c.1843–1 Oct. 1862

Hatton, Manley; Pvt.; c.1824–12 Sep. 1862

Hefner, George W.; Cpl.; c.1836–

Hendren, J.; Pvt.; –30 Jul. 1864; Richmond, VA

Hendrics, Josiah; Pvt.; –30 Jul. 1864; near Chaffin's Bluff, VA

Hickman, M. E.; Pvt.; c.1844–17 Aug. 1864; Richmond, VA

Holder, Maybry

Hollar, Martin; Pvt.; c.1827–

Hudson, Thomas A.; Cpl.; Salem Evans Lutheran Church Cemetery, Alexander Co.

Humphries, William; Pvt.

Johnson, John Covington

Johnston, Samuel; Pvt.; c.1841–

Jones, Samuel G.; Pvt.

Justice, Noah; –––; c.1818

Justice, Socrates; Pvt.; 10 Apr. 1845–19 Feb. 1938; Valiant Cemetery, Hugo, OK

Keller, Anthony C.; Pvt.; c.1833–1 Dec. 1862

Kerley, Hiram; Pvt.; c.1833–27 May 1862; Hanover Court House, VA

Lackey, John A.; Pvt.; c.1832–10 May 1863; Hanover Junction, VA

Lackey, Robert F.; Pvt.; 14 Sep. 1841–22 Mar. 1912; Sulpher Springs Baptist Church Cemetery, Alexander Co.

Lewis, Andrew Jackson; Pvt.; c.1840–8 Oct. 1863; "at home"

Little, David Boone; Pvt.; 30 Aug. 1837–24 Sep. 1904

Loudermilk, Jacob; Pvt.; c.1837–Oct. 1910; Calloway Cemetery, Avery Co.

Loudermilk, Thomas J.; Pvt.; c.1845–12 May 1864; Spotsylvania Court House, VA[48]

Lowe, James M.; Pvt.; c.1842–; (See Company B)

Lowe, William T.; Pvt.; c.1835–; (See Company B)

Lowrance, James P.; Pvt.; 21 Oct. 1839–; Taylorsville City Cemetery, Alexander Co.

Mathiser, John; Pvt.

McAlpin, Malcolm A.; Pvt.

McAlpin, Malee; Pvt.; c.1845–

McAlpin, William F.; Pvt.; c.1843–22 Jan. 1863; Richmond, VA

McCracken, William Davidson; Pvt.; 25 Aug. 1830–1 Jan. 1863

McDaniel, Alexander C.; Pvt.; c.1835–27 Jun. 1862; Gaines's Mill, VA

McRee, Robert David; Pvt.; 2 Mar. 1846–22

Feb. 1931; St. James Lutheran Church Cemetery, Catawba Co.

Meadows, David A.; Pvt.; c.1835–13 Dec. 1862; Fredericksburg, VA

Miller, Joseph W. S.; Pvt.; c.1841–; (See Company E)

Miller, Solomon; Pvt.; c.1839–6 Apr. 1863; Camp Gregg, VA

Mitchell, John J.; Pvt.; c.1821–5 Feb. 1863; Richmond, VA

Mitchell, William E.; Pvt.; c.1843–15 Jul. 1862

Murphy, Eli; Pvt.

Patterson, Julius H.; Pvt.; c.1841–; (See Company E)

Payne, Robert B.; Pvt.; c.1826–22 Dec. 1862; Old City Cemetery, Lynchburg, VA

Pearce, Wesley T.; Pvt.; c.1840–11 Aug. 1863; Gordonsville, VA

Pennell, Jesse A.; Pvt.; c.1833–

Phillips, Archer A.; Pvt.; c.1842–15 Aug. 1862

Pimon, Jesse; Pvt.; c.1835–

Pool, Christopher C.; Cpl.; 26 Apr. 1845–14 Oct. 1900; Antioch Baptist Church Cemetery, Alexander Co.

Pool, George W.; Pvt.; Feb. 1829–14 May 1909; Macedonia Baptist Church Cemetery, Alexander Co.

Pool, James F.; Cpl.; c.1837–4 Jun. 1863; Richmond, VA

Pope, Pinkey W.; Pvt.; c.1834–21 Sep. 1862; Oakwood Military Cemetery, Richmond, VA

Pope, Samuel; Pvt.; c.1835–

Presnell, Aaron L.; Pvt.; c.1844–11 Jul. 1862

Presnell, Harrison C.; Pvt.; c.1822–13 Dec. 1862; Fredericksburg, VA

Price, Elkanah; Pvt.; c.1839–

Queen, Radford B.; Pvt.; c.1840–; Bethel Baptist Church Cemetery, Alexander Co.

Rayfield, F. M.

Rector, Elihu W.; Pvt.; c.1830–

Rector, Willis A.; –––; 1816–1901; Wilkes Co.

Reed, Andrew J.; Pvt.; c.1842–

Reed, Elijah; Pvt.; c.1823–2 Oct. 1864

Reed, George R.; Pvt.; c.1833–10 Sep. 1862; Staunton, VA

Reed, Henry M.; Cpl.; c.1840–29 Aug. 1862; Manassas, VA

Reed, James S.; Pvt.; c.1836–13 Oct. 1864; Richmond, VA[49]

Reed, Joel; Pvt.; c.1809–

Reed, John A.; Pvt.; c.1834–30 Aug. 1862

Reed, Larkin N.; Pvt.; c.1837–6 Oct. 1862

Reed, Thomas W.; Pvt.; c.1838–May 3, 1863; Chancellorsville, VA

Robnett, Abner E.; Pvt.; c.1840–7 Dec. 1862; Gordonsville, VA[50]

Robnett, Elisha Leander; Pvt.; –4 Aug. 1894; Three Forks Baptist Church Cemetery, Alexander Co.

Robnett, James W.; Pvt.; c.1841–27 May 1862; Hanover Court House, VA

Robnett, Jesse A.; Sgt.; c.1842–22 Jul. 1863; Gettysburg, PA

Robnett, Jesse F.; Sgt.; c.1832–24 Jul. 1862; Hollywood Cemetery, Richmond, VA

Robnett, Joel B.; Pvt.; c.1840–27 May 1862; Hanover Court House, VA

Robnett, John C.; Pvt.; c.1844–27 May 1862; Hanover Court House, VA

Robnett, Lawson C.; 1Sgt.; c.1843–9 Aug. 1863; Cypress Hill Cemetery, Brooklyn, NY

Robnett, William A., Jr.; Mus.; c.1837–7 Jun. 1863; Oakwood Military Cemetery, Richmond, VA

Robnett, William Anson, Sr.; Cpl.; c.1835–24 Jun. 1862; Hollywood Cemetery, Richmond, VA

Robnett, William Payton; Pvt.; c.1844–27 May 1862; Hanover Court House, VA

Robnett, William W.; Pvt.; c.1841–12 May 1864; Spotsylvania Court House, VA

Rogers, Jesse Turner; Pvt.; 22 Dec. 1820–12 May 1864; Spotsylvania Court House, VA

Rufty, E.; Pvt.

Rufty, James H.; Pvt.; c.1830–

Russell, John J.; Pvt.; 3 Apr. 1832–24 Jul. 1925; Boomer, Wilkes Co.

Sherrell, Alfred S.; Pvt.; c.1837–24 Aug. 1862; Hollywood Cemetery, Richmond, VA

Sifford, William Alexander; Pvt.; 13 Jan. 1826–20 Nov. 1877

Smith, Henry; Pvt.; –2 Jun. 1865; Baltimore, MD

Smith, Leander F.; Pvt.; c.1837–3 May 1863; Chancellorsville, VA

Smith, Robert Burton; Pvt.; 8 Sep. 1839–8 Feb. 1934; Antioch Baptist Church Cemetery, Alexander Co.

Smith, T. A.; Pvt.; c.1844–25 Nov. 1862

Smith, Thomas W.; Pvt.; c.1831–30 Dec. 1862; Stonewall Cemetery, Winchester, VA

Smith, William J.; Pvt.; c.1830–8 Oct. 1864; "at home"

Snow, James; Pvt.; c.1822–

Steele, Benjamin F.; Pvt.; 24 Mar. 1839–3 May 1885; Mt. Nebo Baptist Church Cemetery, Alexander Co.

Stevenson, Joseph C.; Pvt.; –27 Aug. 1864; Woodlawn Cemetery, Elmira, NY

Stine, Jonas L.; Pvt.; 29 Jan. 1837–3 May 1885; Antioch Baptist Church Cemetery, Alexander Co.

Summers, James M.; Pvt.; c.1844–

Summers, Lewis W.; Pvt.; c.1843–17 Apr. 1863; Oakwood Military Cemetery, Richmond, VA

Tant, James Wesley; Pvt.; c.1838–25 Nov. 1861; High Point, Guilford Co.

Teague, George Granderson

Teague, John A.; Pvt.; 17 Nov. 1830–18 Jun. 1892; Macedonia Baptist Church Cemetery, Alexander Co.

Teague, Vandever; 1Sgt.; c.1816–

Teague, Vandiver S.; Pvt.; c.1819–

Thomas, Burton; Pvt.; c.1842–12 May 1864; Spotsylvania Court House, VA

Tritt, Elkannah (Elcany); Pvt.; c.1836–

Tritt, George W.; Sgt.; c.1838–20 Jan. 1864; "in camp"

Tritt, Henry F.; Pvt.; c.1827–

Tritt, William L.; Cpl.

Turner, Edward; Pvt.; c.1796–

Tyre, Joseph; Pvt.

Walker, Benjamin; Pvt.; c.1812–

Walker, Jeremiah; Pvt.; c.1840–

Walker, L. C.

Walker, Michael S.; Pvt.; c.1838–10 Jun. 1862

Walker, William C.; Cpl.; c.1844–2 Jun. 1862

Warren, James R.; Pvt.; c.1839–2 Feb. 1863; Hanover Junction, VA

Watts, Andrew C.; ---; 11 Apr. 1824–2 Dec. 1895; Three Forks Baptist Church Cemetery, Alexander Co.

Watts, James F.; Pvt.; c.1844–14 Jun. 1863; Hollywood Cemetery, Richmond, VA

Watts, John; Pvt.; c.1816–30 Jun. 1862; Fort Delaware, DE

Watts, Levy L.; Pvt.; c.1837–17 Jun. 1863; "at home"

Watts, Manley L.; Pvt.; c.1839–; Taylorsville City Cemetery, Alexander Co.

Watts, Thomas C.; Pvt.; 1 Feb. 1838–28 May 1902; Macedonia Baptist Church Cemetery, Alexander Co.

Watts, William; Pvt.; 15 Feb. 1844–14 Aug. 1921; Three Forks Baptist Church Cemetery, Alexander Co.

Webster, Merriman; Pvt.; 1819–1879; Alexander Co.

White, Henry; Pvt.; c.1826–

Wike, Andrew Jackson; Pvt.; c.1837–13 Aug. 1862; Gordonsville, VA

Wike, Franklin Hinkle; Pvt.; 26 Feb. 1833–13 Jan. 1917; Salem Evan Lutheran Church Cemetery, Alexander Co.

Wike, Pinkey C.; Pvt.; 3 May 1831–24 Mar. 1882; Oak Grove Baptist Church Cemetery, Watauga Co.

Winkler, James; Pvt.; c.1844–; Confederate Section, Spotsylvania Court House, VA

Winkler, Thomas; Pvt.; c.1842

COMPANY H

Captains

Rankin, William Rufus; c.1823–; (See Field and Staff)

Morris, William Groves; c.1826–; (See Field and Staff)

Fite, Henry Cathy; 16 Nov. 1819–9 Jan. 1896; Mabank, Kautman Co., TX

Ragin, William C.; –16 Aug. 1864; Fussell's Mill, VA

Lieutenants

Alexander, William J.; 3LT; c.1837–

Glenn, William Wallace; 2LT; c.1837–

Hanks, George W.; 1LT; c.1831–

McKee, George W.; 2LT; c.1843–

Moore, John Cathy; 1LT; 3 Jan. 1829–5 Apr. 1890; Gaston Co.

Ormand, John Jackson; 3LT; c.1829–10 Feb. 1889; Long Creek Presbyterian Church Cemetery, Gaston Co.

Roberts, John H.; 1LT; c.1820–

Non-Commissioned Officers and Enlisted Men

Abernathy, Christian M.; Pvt.; 23 Dec. 1827–29 Mar. 1881; C. M. Abernathy Family Cemetery, Gaston Co.

Abernathy, James W. C.; Cpl.; c.1841–; (See Field and Staff)

Abernathy, Marion C.; Pvt.; c.1834–9 Jun. 1864; Oakwood Cemetery, Raleigh, Wake Co.[51]

Abernathy, Munroe; Pvt.; c.1835–

Abernathy, William R. D.; Pvt.; c.1834–18 Jun. 1862; Cypress Hill National Cemetery, Brooklyn, NY

Alexander, James L.; Sgt.; –13 Dec. 1862; Fredericksburg, VA

Allison, Hugh Laban; Pvt.; c.1835–1 Aug. 1862; Richmond, VA

Armstrong, Featherston W.; Pvt.; c.1841–1913

Armstrong, James W.; Pvt.

Armstrong, John; Pvt.; c.1818–

Armstrong, John L.; Pvt.

Armstrong, John M.; Pvt.; c.1843–

Armstrong, John R.; Pvt.; c.1843–27 May 1862; Hanover Court House, VA

Armstrong, Logan; Pvt.; c.1838–18 Dec. 1861

Armstrong, Whiten J.; Pvt.

Arowood, Benjamin Franklin; Pvt.; 18 Dec. 1829–2 Apr. 1863; Old City Cemetery, Lynchburg, VA[52]

Beam, David L.; Pvt.

Beam, George M.; Pvt.; –7 Sep. 1862

Beam, Henry Simpson; Pvt.; 9 Nov. 1838–31 Jan. 1913; St. Mark's Lutheran Church Cemetery, Gaston Co.

Beaty, John Allison; Pvt.; c.1841–6 Jul. 1863

Bell, George; Cpl.; c.1835–12 May 1864; Spotsylvania Court House, VA

Black, Benaja; Pvt.; 28 Oct. 1827–19 Dec. 1917

Black, Joseph; Pvt.

Black, Matthew; Pvt.; 7 Jul. 1845–8 Jan. 1915

Black, Thomas; Pvt.; 15 Feb. 1834–14 Aug. 1898

Blackwood, Joseph; Pvt.; –3 Mar. 1865; Woodlawn Cemetery, Elmira, NY

Brimer, George; Pvt.; c.1834–15 Aug. 1862; Oakwood Military Cemetery, Richmond, VA

Brimer, James P.; Pvt.; c.1841–

Brown, David L.; Pvt.; –12 May 1864; Missing, Spotsylvania Court House, VA

Brown, James Logan; Pvt.; c.1812–

Brown, Oliver; Pvt.; Feb. 1837–27 May 1862; Hanover Court House, VA

Byrd, Oliver Pryor; Pvt.; c.1837–

Canady, Laban; Pvt.; c.1838–

Canely, Samuel; Pvt.

Cannon, James A.; Pvt.

Cansler, Martin Luther; ---; 14 May 1836–10 Nov. 1919; Christ Church Cemetery, Gaston Co.

Clemmer, Andrew; Pvt.

Clemmer, Cephas M.; Pvt.; c.1841–29 Jun. 1862; Oakwood Military Cemetery, Richmond, VA

Clemmer, John M. L.; Pvt.; c.1836–

Clemmer, Jonas; Pvt.

Clemmer, Larkin D.; Pvt.; 1845–1909; Clemmer Cemetery, Gaston Co.

Clemmer, Lemuel L.; Pvt.; c.1837–

Clemmer, Lewis J.; Pvt.; c.1822–

Clemmer, Perry E.; Pvt.; –16 Jun. 1862

Clemmer, Rufus M.; Pvt.; –1 Sep. 1862; Richmond, VA

Cloninger, Emanuel; Pvt.; 22 Oct. 1840–1 Dec. 1924; Cloninger Cemetery, Gaston Co.

Cody, William; Pvt.; c.1835–

Cook, J. C.; Pvt.

Cook, John; Pvt.; c.1843–

Costner, Caleb; Pvt.; 1836–3 May 1863; Chancellorsville, VA

Costner, David M.; Pvt.; c.1842–1 Jan. 1863

Costner, Jacob Melchi; Pvt.; 29 Mar. 1829–15 Sep. 1862; University of Virginia, Charlottesville, VA

Costner, Jacob V.; Pvt.; c.1833–1880/99; Gaston Co.

Costner, John; Pvt.; c.1840–25 Nov. 1862; Old Soldiers Cemetery, Mount Jackson, VA

Cox, John; Cpl.; c.1835–14 Jan. 1862; Raleigh, Wake Co.

Craig, J. Porter; Pvt.; –1–3 Jul. 1863; Gettysburg, PA

Craig, John Starr; Pvt.

Craige, R. A.; Pvt.; c.1843–28 Dec. 1861

Cronister, William; Pvt.; c.1843–

Dameron, John N.; Pvt.; c.1840–12 Jan. 1862; Raleigh, NC

Dellinger, Nathan; Pvt.; 12 Jun. 1828–3 May 1863; Chancellorsville, VA

Dellinger, Peter; Pvt.; c.1830–; Charlottesville, VA

Dickerson, John; Pvt.; c.1840–

Dickson, John; Pvt.; c.1833–

Dickson, John Thomas; Pvt.; 20 Apr. 1825–27 Jun. 1890; Onley Presbyterian Church Cemetery, Gaston Co.

Dickson, William F. A.; Pvt.; 21 Mar. 1835–27 Sep. 1872; Onley Presbyterian Church Cemetery, Gaston Co.

Digh, John Pickney; Pvt.; 8 Apr. 1845–11 Feb. 1919; Mt. Lebannon Baptist Church Cemetery, Rutherdford Co.

Dunn, David R.; Pvt.; c.1833–28 Jul. 1863; Hollywood Cemetery, Richmond, VA

Elmore, Henry R.; Sgt.; 28 Feb. 1844–19 Jan. 1924

Elmore, Jesse; Pvt.

Ewing, Hugh F.; Pvt.; c.1841–

Featherston, William E.; Pvt.; –12 Jul. 1864; Hollywood Cemetery, Richmond, VA

Fergusson, Thomas W.; Pvt.

Fite, James H.; Cpl.; c.1843–29 Aug. 1862; Manassas, VA

Ford, Green W.; Pvt.; c.1843–6 Oct. 1863; executed

Ford, Robert T.; Pvt.; c.1840–4 Sep. 1862; Oakwood Military Cemetery, Richmond, VA

Ford, Thomas L. P.; 1Sgt.; –12 May 1864; Spotsylvania Court House, VA

Ford, William G.; Sgt.; c.1843–

Foster, Robert; Pvt.; c.1842–12 Dec. 1861

Friday, Ephraim; Pvt.; c.1839–18 Aug. 1862; Richmond, VA

Fronebager, Jonas C.; Sgt.; c.1837–29 Nov. 1864; Clemmer Cemetery, Gaston Co.

Furgurson, George N.; Pvt.; c.1843–14 Jul. 1862; Fort Columbus, NY

Furgurson, Robert; Pvt.; c.1842–27 May 1862; "in the hands of the enemy"

Furgusson, Andrew; Pvt.; –14 Feb. 1863; Old City Cemetery, Lynchburg, VA

Gaston, Larkin B.; Pvt. (See Field and Staff)

Glenn, James Polk; 1Sgt.; c.1843–

Glenn, William Wallace; Pvt. (See Field and Staff)[53]

Good, William C.; Cpl.; c.1843–

Gullick, George W.; Pvt.; c.1841–6 Jun. 1862; Hollywood Cemetery, Richmond, VA

Gullick, Green J.; Pvt.

Hallett, Caleb; Pvt.

Hand, James H.; Pvt.; c.1821–12 Jul. 1862; "below Richmond"

Hanna, Samuel Blackwood; Pvt; 1 Jun. 1830–1 Sep. 1913

Hanna, Thomas MacKnight; Pvt; 25 Sep. 1828–10 Mar. 1900

Harmon, Henry Holmes; Pvt.; 1837–1918; Oakwood Cemetery, Raleigh, Wake Co.

Hawkins, A.; Pvt.; –21 Nov. 1862; Winchester, VA

Henry, Robert N.; Pvt.

Hoffman, Frederick L.; Pvt.

Holbrook, Ralph C.

Holland, Marion Ligget; Pvt.; c.1823–23 Jun. 1893; Christ Lutheran Church Cemetery, Stanley Co.[54]

Hovis, Jacob D.; Pvt.

Hovis, Levi; Pvt.

Howell, Oliver Perry; Pvt.

Ireland, Roberson F.

Jenkins, Andrew Berry; Pvt.; c.1833–10 Aug. 1864; Confederate Cemetery, Point Lookout, MD

Jenkins, David; Pvt.

Kendrick, John F.; Pvt.

Kendrick, Thomas L.; Sgt.

Lewis, James J.; Pvt.; c.1824–

Linebarger, Feph C.; Pvt.; –13 Dec. 1862; Fredericksburg, VA

Linebarger, John D.; Pvt.; 1829–1869

Linebarger, Jonas Laban; Pvt.; 1 Dec. 1820–6 May 1898; Linebarger Cemetery, Gaston Co.

Long, Pleasant G.; Pvt.; –30 Sep. 1862; Old City Cemetery, Lynchburg, VA

Lynch, John W.; Pvt.; c.1816–

Mauney, Wiley; Pvt.; c.1838–

Mauney, William; Pvt.; c.1832–

McAlister, George W.; Pvt.; –23 Jul. 1863; Old Soldiers Cemetery, Mount Jackson, VA

McCullough, J. F.; Pvt.; –5 Apr. 1863; Oakwood Military Cemetery, Richmond, VA

McGinnas, George L.; Pvt.; c.1828–27 May 1862; Hanover Court House, VA

McGinnas, Robert M.; Pvt.

McKee, James L.; Pvt.; –2 Jun. 1862; Hollywood Cemetery, Richmond, VA

McKee, Logan L.; Pvt.; c.1844–

McLane, John; Pvt.

Mellon, George Worth; Pvt.; 28 Oct. 1820–20 Nov. 1895; Bethel Presbyterian Church Cemetery, Clover, SC

Moore, John H.; Pvt.

Morris, Amos Alexander; Pvt.; c.1844–

Morrison, David; Pvt.; –prior to 28 Mar. 1863

Morrison, Levi; Pvt.

Neal, James; Pvt.; c.1828–

Paysour, Eli F.; Pvt.; c.1843–6 Apr. 1914; Beauvoir Confederate Soldiers Cemetery, MS

Paysour, Ephraim W.; Pvt.; –3 May 1863; Chancellorsville, VA

Paysour, Philip H.; Pvt.; c.1837–

Paysour, Samuel P.; Pvt.; –15 May 1863

Peterson, Ireneus A.; Pvt.; c.1844–May 1862

Pursley, Samuel M.; Pvt.; c.1825–

Ragan, Jasper; Pvt.; –Dec. 1862; Lynchburg, VA

Ragan, Robert F.; Cpl.; c.1843–24 Jul. 1863; Richmond, VA

Ramsey, William H.; Pvt.

Rankin, Alexander Nathaniel; Pvt.; 1824–24 Jul. 1862; Lincoln Co.

Rankin, Cephas Lafayette; Cpl.; c.1839–1 Sep. 1862

Ratchford, John Addison; Pvt.; 15 Aug. 1829–27 Sep. 1897

Ratchford, John F.; Pvt.

Reynolds, Caleb; Pvt.; c.1827–

Reynolds, Nathan A.; Pvt.; c.1843–

Rhyne, Alfred; Pvt.; c.1840–1 Sep. 1862; Ox Hill, VA

Rhyne, Henry Malachi; Pvt.; 27 Jul. 1838–1 Jun. 1907; Linville, Burke Co.

Rhyne, Henry R.; Pvt.; c.1834–

Rhyne, Peyton S.; Pvt.; Dec. 1837–13 Feb. 1906; Oakwood Cemetery, Gaston Co.

Roberts, Thomas M.; Pvt.

Robertson, James R.; Pvt.

Rudisell, Eli Jonas; Pvt.; 11 Apr. 1829–25 Nov. 1897

Rutledge, Ruburtus Gamwell; Pvt.; c.1843–

Selvy, Joseph S.; Pvt.

Smith, David J.; Pvt.; 14 Nov. 1843–22 Jun. 1935; Paw Creek Presbyterian Church Cemetery, Mecklenburg Co.

Smith, John B.; Pvt.; –22 May 1863; Oakwood Military Cemetery, Richmond, VA

Smith, Marcus; Pvt.; c.1843–

Smith, Robert L.; Pvt.

Stowe, James A.; Pvt.; c.1835–27 May 1862; Hanover Court House, VA

Stroup, Columbus C.; Pvt.

Stroup, William M.; Pvt.; –31 May 1864; Hollywood Cemetery, Richmond, VA

Summy, Andrew; Pvt.; c.1825–27 May 1862; Hanover Court House, VA

Thomasson, George L.; Sgt.; c.1835–16 Aug. 1863; Philadelphia National Cemetery, Philadelphia, PA

Thomasson, J. A.

Thomasson, J. Beverly; Pvt.; c.1841–

Thomasson, John A.; Pvt.; 18 Jul. 1838–

Thompson, John D.; Pvt.; c.1840–7 Aug. 1862; Old City Cemetery, Lynchburg, VA

Tucker, Robert B.; Sgt.; c.1823–

Warren, George R.; Pvt.

Watson, Pinkney W.; Pvt.; c.1840–27 May 1862; Hanover Court House, VA

Weathers, Martin R.; Pvt.; –Apr. 1862; "in Virginia"[55]

West, David F.; Pvt.; c.1841–

Whitesides, Caleb; Pvt.; c.1843–30 Jun. 1862; Frayser's Farm, VA

Whitesides, James J.; Pvt.

Whitesides, John Lanthan; Pvt.; Old Presbyterian Cemetery, Dallas, Gaston Co.

Wilson, Thomas A.; Sgt.; c.1840–3 May 1863; Chancellorsville, VA

Wingate, Daniel; Pvt.; c.1834–15 Mar. 1863; "at home"

Withers, John L.; Pvt.; 15 Sep. 1834–18 May 1877

Withers, Miles; Cpl.; 8 Mar. 1839–29 Jul. 1902

Wright, Harvey A.; Pvt.; c.1841–3 Jul. 1863; Gettysburg, PA

Young, Joseph; Pvt.; –22 Jun. 1863; Hollywood Cemetery, Richmond, VA

COMPANY I

Captains

Harrison, John K.; c.1815–
Hart, Moses N.; c.1822–
Elms, John Irvin; 19 Apr. 1844–16 Jun. 1912; Elmwood Cemetery, Mecklenburg Co.
Elms, William D.
Stitt, William M.; c.1836–

Lieutenants

Crowell, Elias M.; 3LT; c.1840–
Elms, John P.; 3LT; –3 Jul. 1863; Gettysburg, PA
McCoy, James G.; 2LT; c.1838–
Oates, Robert M.; 1LT; c.1829–
Price, Julius G.; 2LT; c.1832–; Steele Creek Presbyterian Church Cemetery, Mecklenburg Co.
Rigler, Dallas Mifflin; 3LT; 1 Nov. 1844–before 1900
Russell, Edwin H.; 1LT
Samonds, Thomas Kirkpatrick; 1LT; c.1828–
Wilson, John J.; 3LT; c.1826–
Yandle, Adam F.; 3LT; c.1834–

Non-Commissioned Officers and Enlisted Men

Adams, Lowrie; Pvt.; c.1827–
Aderholdt, Michael L.; Pvt.; c.1829–6 May 1863; Fredericksburg Confederate Cemetery, Fredericksburg, VA
Alexander, Adolphus W.; Pvt.; c.1842–1863
Alexander, James A.; Pvt.; c.1843–
Alexander, John O.; Pvt.; c.1832–(See Field and Staff)
Alexander, Thomas Neely; Pvt.; 13 Dec. 1844–12 Jan. 1940; Pleasant Hill Presbyterian Cemetery, Mecklenburg Co.
Allen, James H.; Pvt.; c.1827–
Auton, John W.; Pvt.; c.1825–3 May 1863; Chancellorsville, VA
Ballard, William H.; Pvt.; c.1840–26 Mar. 1863; Old City Cemetery, Lynchburg, VA
Barnhill, John W.; Pvt.; c.1841–
Beam, John Tighlman; Pvt.; 18 Dec. 1836–18 Oct. 1905
Black, Joseph P.; Pvt.; c.1818–10 Jun. 1862; Gaines's Mill, VA
Black, Samuel J.; Pvt.; c.1835–1899; Sardis Presbyterian Church Cemetery, Mecklenburg Co.

Blanchard, James G.; Pvt.; –3 May 1863; Chancellorsville, VA
Blankenship, Thomas E.; Pvt.; c.1837–23 Sep. 1862; Cypress Hill Cemetery, Brooklyn, NY
Blume, Michael; Pvt.
Blume, William T.; Pvt.
Blythe, Samuel W.; Pvt.; c.1839–20 Sep. 1864; Woodlawn Cemetery, Elmira, NY
Boatwright, Samuel W.; Pvt.
Bridges, William A.; Pvt.; c.1822–15 Feb. 1863; Richmond, VA
Brines, James W.; Pvt.; Rocky River Presbyterian Church Cemetery, Cabarrus Co.
Brown, James K. P.; Pvt.; c.1844–
Brown, Thomas G.; 1Sgt.; c.1841–
Bruce, James; Pvt.; c.1823–25 Dec. 1861; High Point, Guilford Co.
Burns, Samuel A.; Pvt.; c.1830–
Carpenter, Levi B.; Pvt.; c.1830–1 Mar. 1865; Woodlawn Cemetery, Elmira, NY[56]
Carpenter, Marcus; Pvt.; 20 Oct. 1845–15 Nov. 1918
Cathey, Green Benjamin; Pvt.; c.1839–14 Sep. 1864; Hollywood Cemetery, Richmond, VA[57]
Clark, James; Pvt.; c.1814–3 May 1863; Chancellorsville, VA
Clark, James W.; Pvt.; c.1844–
Clark, John; Pvt.
Clark, John F., Jr.; Pvt.
Clark, John F., Sr.; Pvt.; c.1828–
Clontz, Abraham C.; Pvt.; c.1832–27 May 1862; Hanover Court House, VA
Coffee, Benjamin M.; Pvt.
Crocker, William J.; Pvt.; c.1832–3 Nov. 1864; Confederate Cemetery, Point Lookout, MD
Cross, William D.; Pvt.; c.1827–
Devine, William Thomas; Pvt.; 12 Feb. 1830–12 May 1908; New Prospect Baptist Church Cemetery, Cleveland Co.
Drury, Andrew J.; Pvt.; c.1838–
Dulin, Thomas Stuart; Pvt.; c.1822–
Edwards, John Anderson; Cpl.; c.1835–
Elliott, Sidney Harralson; Pvt.; 1820–1909; Zoar Baptist Church Cemetery, Cleveland Co.
Featherston, R.; Pvt.
Featherston, W. E.; Pvt.; –14 Jul. 1864; Richmond, VA
Flanagan, Benjamin M.; Pvt.; c.1817–
Flow, James C.; Sgt.; 9 Mar. 1821–31 Dec. 1876; Philadelphia Presbyterian Church Cemetery, Mecklenburg Co.
Freeman, George

Freeman, Jacob J.; Pvt.; c.1846–7 Mar. 1863; Richmond, VA

Freeman, McAmy; Pvt.; c.1834–

Fronabarger, John; Pvt.; c.1829–3 May 1863; Chancellorsville, VA

Gates, Marcus William; Pvt.; 1816–18 May 1907; Pisgah Methodist Church Cemetery, Lincoln Co.

Gordon, James P.; Pvt.; c.1816–

Gordon, James R.; Pvt.; c.1839–

Griffith, Thomas; Pvt.

Gurley, William D.; Pvt.; c.1843–27 Apr. 1863; Richmond, VA

Hall, Joseph L.; Pvt.; c.1838–

Haney, Elijah H.; Pvt.; –16 Dec. 1864; Richmond, VA

Hargett, Andrew J.; Sgt.; 1838–1895; Monroe City Cemetery, Union Co.

Harris, Newell J.; Pvt.

Hawkins, J. A.

Hayes, Elijah Lee; Pvt.; c.1837–

Headley, William L.; Pvt.; c.1840–26 Dec. 1862; Maplewood Cemetery, Gordonsville, VA[58]

Henderson, John Wood; Pvt.; c.1829–17 Apr. 1917; Paw Creek Presbyterian Church Cemetery, Mecklenburg Co.

Henry, Berry Grove; Pvt.; c.1842–

Henry, Terrell B.; Pvt.; c.1839–

Herron, George

Higginson, John; Pvt.; c.1836–

Hill, Thomas M.; Pvt.

Hipp, James Franklin; Pvt.; 11 Feb. 1830–31 Jan. 1924; Paw Creek Presbyterian Church Cemetery, Mecklenburg Co.

Hipp, Larkin A.; Pvt.; 20 Oct. 1832–19 May 1896; Paw Creek, Presbyterian Church Cemetery, Mecklenburg Co.

Hood, Henry C.; Pvt.; –19 Oct. 1862; Stonewall Cemetery, Winchester, VA[59]

Hovis, Andrew J.; Pvt.; c.1837–13 Dec. 1862; Fredericksburg, VA

Hunsucker, James A.; Pvt.

Hunsucker, John W.; Pvt.; c.1844–

Hunsucker, William J.; Pvt.; c.1841–

Hunter, Charles L.; Cpl.

Icehower, Hugh Franklin; Pvt.; c.1838–7 May 1862; Louisa Court House, VA

Johnston, Alfred Nathaniel; Pvt.; 9 Mar. 1842–5 Mar. 1908; Robinson Presbyterian Church Cemetery, Mecklenburg Co.

King, George W.; Pvt.; 13 Apr. 1836–30 Jan. 1890; Trinity Methodist Church Cemetery, Mecklenburg Co.

King, William J. A.; Pvt.; 15 Jan. 1840–8 Nov. 1867; Trinity Methodist Church Cemetery, Mecklenburg Co.

Kirkley, Thomas; Pvt.; c.1839–27 Oct. 1864; Hollywood Cemetery, Richmond, VA[60]

Kissiah, George W.; Pvt.; c.1839–

Kissiah, Thomas Alleson; Pvt.; c.1839–

Kissiah, William Macam; Pvt.; c.1836–

Kistler, George H.; Pvt.; c.1841–

Kizer, David W.; Pvt.; c.1833–

Kizer, Solomon; Pvt.; c.1843–

Kizer, Thomas P.; Pvt.; c.1829–

Lawing, David F.; Pvt.; c.1834–

Lawing, George A.; Pvt.

Lawing, William Pickney; Pvt.; 1 Oct. 1834–29 Sep. 1864; Petersburg, VA

Lemonds, Jay; Pvt.

Looker, John C.; Pvt.; c.1813–

Lowrie, Samuel J.; Pvt.; c.1828–

Manning, James; Pvt.; c.1836–

Manning, John W.; Pvt.; c.1831–

Mason, Robert Gideon; Pvt.; c.1821–

Masters, Franklin A.; Pvt.; c.1843–16 Feb. 1863; Lynchburg, VA

Maxwell, Dallas S.; Pvt.; c.1843–

McCall, James C.; Pvt.; c.1842–

McCall, Sylvester; Pvt.

McCord, David L.; Pvt.; 10 May 1829–27 Dec. 1908; Paw Creek Presbyterian Church Cemetery, Mecklenburg Co.

McCoy, Marshall A.; Pvt.; c.1846–

McCoy, William L.; Pvt.; c.1841–14 Sep. 1862; Sharon Cemetery, Middlesburg, VA

McGee, Isaac; Pvt.; c.1837–12 Dec. 1864; Woodlawn Cemetery, Elmira, NY

McGinn, James M.; Pvt.; 11 Mar. 1828–24 Apr. 1902; Harrison Methodist Church Cemetery, Mecklenburg Co.

McKeele, Major; Pvt.

Montgomery, Albert F.; Sgt.; 12 Jan. 1840–17 Dec. 1928; New Hope Church Cemetery, Carroll Co., TN

Montgomery, James M.; Pvt.; c.1818–

Moody, Marcus D. L.; Pvt.; 1826–1869

Mooney, Caleb; Pvt.; c.1829–

Mullis, Coleman; Pvt.; c.1817–17 Jul. 1864; Chaffin's Bluff, VA

Nicholson, John B.

Orr, Cunningham Miller; Pvt.; Nov. 1843–1907

Orr, James L. Virginius, Sr.; Cpl.; Sep. 1833–1907; Greenville, SC

Orr, John Garrison Alexander; Cpl.; 4 Sep. 1830–15 Oct. 1904; Sugar Creek Presbyterian Church Cemetery, Mecklenburg Co.

Orr, Joseph Lemmond; Pvt.; 13 Mar. 1835–16 Apr. 1906; Elmwood Cemetery, Mecklenburg Co.

Orr, Silas Gilbright, Jr.; Pvt.; Jan. 1847–1927

Patterson, Eli; Pvt.; c.1829–7 Jul. 1862

Patterson, John H.; Pvt.; 1819–22 Sep. 1893; Raleigh National Cemetery, Wake Co.

Paysour, Caleb; Pvt.; c.1836–

Phelan, Pat O.; Pvt.

Phillips, Jesse; Pvt.

Phillips, Junius A.; Pvt.; c.1838–7 Jul. 1862; Richmond, VA

Raffield, Franklin A.; Pvt.; c.1835–

Reid, George F.; Pvt.; c.1834–5 Nov. 1862; Winchester, VA

Reid, John C.; Sgt.; c.1827–

Robinson, Daniel Columbus; Sgt.; 13 Aug. 1826–4 Sep. 1906; Philadelphia Presbyterian Church Cemetery, Mecklenburg Co.

Robinson, James A.; Pvt.; c.1838–18 Jun. 1862; Onley Presbyterian Church Cemetery, Gaston Co.

Rudisill, Jacob; Pvt.; 28 Nov. 1836–1925

Rumage, Lindsay; Pvt.; c.1837–11 Mar. 1863

Russell, Sterling H.; Pvt.; c.1839–28 Jun. 1862; Hampton National Cemetery, Hampton, VA

Sanderford, James O.; Pvt.

Sharp, Thomas A.; Pvt.; c.1823–

Sharpe, Robert A. Landis; Pvt.; 21 Oct. 1836–5 May 1896; Paw Creek Presbyterian Church Cemetery, Mecklenburg Co.

Shaw, Duncan C.; Pvt.; c.1836–9 May 1896; Paw Creek Presbyterian Church Cemetery, Mecklenburg Co.

Shoe, Jacob; Pvt.; c.1841–

Simpson, Cyrus L.; Pvt.; c.1846–1862/63[61]

Simpson, Ira P.; Pvt.; c.1839–

Smaw, John O.; Pvt.

Smith, Franklin; Pvt.; c.1837–

Smith, Lawson S.; Pvt.

Spears, Andrew Jackson; Pvt.; 1830–1920; West's Chapel, Union Co.

Spears, Jeptha J.; Pvt.; c.1831–27 May 1862; Hanover Court House, VA

Starnes, Brown; Pvt.; c.1841–7 May 1863

Starnes, Dulin; Pvt.; c.1836–after Oct. 1862; executed

Starnes, Jacob M.; Pvt.; c.1838–29 Jun. 1863; Hollywood Cemetery, Richmond, VA[62]

Stegall, Griffin; ---; 7 Feb. 1836–5 Mar. 1907; Pleasant Grove Primitive Baptist Church Cemetery, Union Co.

Stewart, Archie A.; Pvt.; c.1828–

Stewart, Patrick J.; Pvt.; c.1836–21 Nov. 1862; Richmond, VA

Stinson, David W.; Pvt.; c.1837–10 Jun. 1862

Stowe, Charles Theodore; Com. Sgt. (See Field and Staff)

Taggart, James S.; Pvt.; c.1842–3 Jul. 1863; Gettysburg, PA

Tally, John; 1Sgt.; c.1816–12 May 1864; Spotsylvania Court House, VA

Tally, Michael; Pvt.; c.1836–30 Jul. 1864; Hollywood Cemetery, Richmond, VA

Taylor, Charles W.; Pvt.; c.1837–; Elmwood Cemetery, Mecklenburg Co.

Taylor, Elias A.; Mus.

Taylor, Jesse S.; Pvt.; c.1834–

Todd, Robert Jamison; Pvt.; 18 Sep. 1834–12 Oct. 1906; Paw Creek Presbyterian Church Cemetery, Mecklenburg Co.

Turner, Stephen R.; Cpl.; c.1838–

Turner, William; Pvt.; c.1841–7 Jan. 1862; "at home"

Walker, Robert; Pvt.; c.1845–after Oct. 1863

Wallace, Albert; Pvt.; 29 Jan. 1817–6 Oct. 1882; Philadelphia Presbyterian Church Cemetery, Mecklenburg Co.

Whitely, George M. D.; Pvt.

Whitely, John H.; Pvt.

Williamson, George W.; Pvt.; 24 Apr. 1842–1 Dec. 1921; Paw Creek Presbyterian Church Cemetery, Mecklenburg Co.

Windley, Asa Oden; Pvt.; 12 Nov. 1832–12 May 1896; Beaufort Co.

Wolf, Elam B.; Pvt.; c.1829–27 May 1862; Hanover Court House, VA

Woodall, William C.; Pvt.; c.1838–4 Dec. 1863; Point Lookout, MD

Young, Albert P.; Pvt.; c.1844–5 May 1863

COMPANY K

Captains

Ross, John; 1819–

Fetter, William M.; c.1841–

Armstrong, Thomas Jay; 30 Sep. 1834–15 Sep. 1908; Highland, KS

Lieutenants

Davidson, William Lee; 2LT; 9 Nov. 1842–8 Nov. 1902; Lone Star Cemetery, Rains Co., TX

Grimsley, James Monroe; 1LT; 6 Jul. 1833–1 Apr. 1915; Jones-Cox-Greer Cemetery, Ashe Co.

Grimsley, Lowery; 1LT; Dec. 1811–c.1900; Sedgewick Co., KS

Halsey, William; 1LT; 20 Nov. 1837–12 Jun. 1913; William Hasley Cemetery, Allegheny Co.

Mickle, William N.; 2LT; –3 Jul. 1863; Gettysburg, PA

Owens, John J.; 2LT

Ragan, Charlton H.; 2LT; –3 May 1863; Chancellorsville, VA

Ross, William N.; 2LT; c.1844–5 May 1865; Fort Monroe, VA

Wiggins, Thomas Medicus; 3LT; 11 Aug. 1842–16 Oct. 1928; Elmwood Cemetery, Oxford, Granville Co.

Williams, John; 3LT; 14 May 1820–17 Jun. 1903; Old South Fork Cemetery, Allegheny Co.

Williams, Melvin C.; 2LT; c.1841–

Non-Commissioned Officers and Enlisted Men

Adams, Martin; Pvt.; c.1842–23 Jun. 1862; Richmond, VA

Aker, Johnston B.; Pvt.; 12 Oct. 1845–29 Jul. 1935; Rose Hill Cemetery, Ardmore, OK

Anderson, Amos; Pvt.; c.1843–8 Dec. 1862; University of Virginia Confederate Cemetery, Charlottesville, VA

Anderson, Enoch; Pvt.

Arvens, J. J.; Pvt.

Beamon, Marion; Pvt.

Bingham, Jeptha K.; Pvt.; c.1836–27 May 1862; Hanover Court House, VA

Black, Lawrence K.; Pvt.

Blevins, Alfred C.; Pvt.; 8 Aug. 1832–16 Mar. 1884; Pleasant Home B. C. Cemetery, Allegheny Co.

Blevins, Alvis; Pvt.; 18 Mar. 1828–22 Sep. 1905; Buchanan Co., VA

Blevins, Eli A.; Sgt.; c.1834–6 Jun. 1864; Hollywood Cemetery, Richmond, VA

Blevins, Elijah; Pvt.; 5 Aug. 1827–31 Dec. 1862; Guinea Station, VA[63]

Blevins, Ephraim; Pvt.; 27 Dec. 1842–7 Dec. 1919; Azen Cemetery, Konnarock, Smyth Co., VA

Blevins, Francis Marion; Pvt.; Nov. 1845–12 Dec. 1933; Azen Cemetery, Smyth Co., VA

Blevins, Granville H.; Pvt.; c.1841–17 Nov. 1862; Stonewall Cemetery, Winchester, VA

Blevins, Hugh; Pvt.; 9 Oct. 1834–3 May 1863; Chancellorsville, VA

Blevins, Isham; Pvt.; 16 Apr. 1830–3 Jul. 1863; Gettysburg, PA

Blevins, Meredith; Pvt.; c.1838–16 Apr. 1863

Blevins, Robert; Pvt.; 18 Sep. 1830–15 Feb. 1909; Scott Blevins Cemetery, Ashe Co.

Blevins, Wells; Pvt.; 4 Sep. 1841–1900; Healing Springs Baptist Church Cemetery, Ashe Co.

Blevins, Wesley; Pvt.; 22 Apr. 1837–1900; Senter Primitive Baptist Church Cemetery, Ashe Co.

Boran, Clark T.; Pvt.; c.1837–15 Nov. 1862; Winchester, VA

Brown, Eli; Pvt.; c.1841–

Brown, Jackson B.; Pvt.; c.1830–9 Apr. 1863; Fredericksburg Confederate Cemetery, Fredericksburg, VA[64]

Brown, John; Pvt.; c.1836–9 Jun. 1862; Richmond, VA

Bumgarner, A. L. D.; ---; 23 Jan. 1833–31 Oct. 1879; Three Forks Baptist Church Cemetery, Alexander Co.

Burny, Yancey; Pvt.

Caldwell, John M.; Pvt.; c.1834–27 Nov. 1922; Lawrence Co., KY

Caldwell, Morris; Pvt.; c.1844–1878; Floyd Co., KY

Caldwell, William Haynes; Pvt.; 21 Dec. 1840–5 Mar. 1918; Los Angeles, CA

Cameron, William; Pvt.

Caudill, Calvin C.; Pvt.; c.1840–; Grayson Co., VA

Caudill, Mark R.; Pvt.; 25 Mar. 1848–27 Mar. 1923; Helton Baptist Church Cemetery, Ashe Co.

Caudill, William R.; Pvt.; 26 Jul. 1824–

Chandler, Elijah; Pvt.; c.1823–

Cox, Cicero M.; Pvt.

Cox, Martin C.; Pvt.; c.1841–

Cox, Solomon V.; Pvt.; 18 Sep. 1840–2 Nov. 1913; Senter Primitive Baptist Church Cemetery, Ashe Co.

Davis, John; Pvt.; 24 Mar. 1846–8 May 1936; John Davis Cemetery, Ashe Co.

Davis, John W.; Pvt.; c.1820–; Ashe Co.

DeBoard, Benjamin, Jr.; Pvt.; 6 Feb. 1823–24 Mar. 1897; DeBoard Family Cemetery, Ashe Co.

Douglas, Daniel H.; Pvt.; c.1824–24 Aug. 1864; Confederate Cemetery, Point Lookout, MD

Douglas, George Y.; Pvt.; c.1843–29 Jul. 1862; Fort Columbus, NY

Douglas, John O. J.; Pvt.; c.1821–30 Nov. 1862; Old Soldiers Cemetery, Mount Jackson, VA

Duncan, George W.; Pvt.; c.1840–

Duncan, Jesse; Pvt.; c.1843–

Ellis, Nathan; Pvt.; c.1840–3 May 1863; Chancellorsville, VA

Evans, Abram; Pvt.; c.1820–27 May 1862; Hanover Court House, VA[65]

Evans, David K.; Pvt.; c.1833–23 Jun. 1862; Oakwood Military Cemetery, Richmond, VA

Evans, John W.; Pvt.; c.1837–13 Apr. 1864; Richmond, VA

Griffith, Harvey; Pvt.; c.1825–16 Jun. 1862; Hollywood Cemetery, Richmond, VA[66]

Grubb, John; Pvt.; c.1831–1922; Mt. Zion United Methodist Church Cemetery, Allegheny Co.

Halsey, Granville; Pvt.; c.1844–14 Aug. 1863; Richmond, VA

Halsey, Ira M.; Sgt.; 17 Oct. 1842–6 Oct. 1890; John Milton Cemetery, Allegheny Co.

Halsey, John; Pvt.; 14 Feb. 1840–4 Jan. 1871; John Milton Cemetery, Allegheny Co.

Hart, Madison; Pvt.; 31 May 1836–1915; Oregon

Hensley, James O.; Pvt.; c.1842–3 Jul. 1863; Gettysburg, PA

Hill, Alexander; Pvt.; c.1842–31 Oct. 1862; Winchester, VA[67]

Hill, Horton; Pvt.; –14 Jun. 1862; Richmond, VA

Hill, Meredith; Pvt.; –19 Nov. 1862; Winchester, VA

Jenkins, Henry; Pvt.; c.1842–

Jester, R. F.

Johnson, Hartwell B.; Pvt.

Johnston, James B.; 1Sgt.; c.1835–1 Oct. 1864; Jones Farm, VA

Jones, Isaac; Pvt.

Jones, Isham H.; Pvt.; c.1841–

Jones, James C.; Cpl.; c.1841–

Jones, Levi Fielding; Pvt.; 2 Aug. 1844–22 Jul. 1886; Allegheny Co.

Jones, William D.; Pvt.; c.1825–; Allen Jones Family Cemetery, Allegheny Co.

Jones, William R.; Pvt.; c.1838–21 Oct. 1862; Phipps Family Cemetery, Ashe Co.

Landreth, Samuel; Pvt.; 15 May 1830–21 Feb. 1919; Cox-Landreth-Perkins Cemetery, Ashe Co.

Laxton, Morris; Pvt.; c.1843–5 Aug. 1862; Richmond, VA

Lee, Jonathan; Pvt.; c.1837–15 May 1863; Guinea Station, VA

Lewis, William R.; Pvt.; –27 Dec. 1862; Oakwood Military Cemetery, Richmond, VA

Long, Felix; Pvt.; c.1843–27 May 1862; Hanover Court House, VA

Marlin, Josephus S.; Pvt.; c.1843–26 Feb. 1865; Woodlawn Cemetery, Elmira, NY

Marlin, Thomas; Pvt.; c.1835–

Marshall, John G.; Pvt.; c.1843–3 May 1863; Chancellorsville, VA

McAllister, Joseph; Pvt.

McGrady, Jacob; Pvt.; c.1834–14 Jul. 1863; Oakwood Cemetery, Raleigh, Wake Co.[68]

McGrady, John M. C.; Pvt.; c.1839–17 Nov. 1862

Mendenhall, Obadiah S. R.; Pvt.; c.1843–

Miles, John; Pvt.; c.1843–15 Nov. 1862; Winchester, VA

Miller, John Sam; Sgt.; 29 Mar. 1835–10 Jan. 1924; Miller Cemetery, Allegheny Co.

Miller, William R.; Pvt.; c.1843–27 May 1862; Hanover Court House, VA

Money, Lewis; Pvt.; c.1817–23 Oct. 1862; Confederate Cemetery, Huguenot Springs, VA

Mulkey, James; Pvt.; c.1833–

Osborne, Jonathan; Pvt.; 24 Oct. 1836–31 Mar. 1919[69]

Ousmint, Henry L.; Pvt.

Owens, John J.; Pvt.

Parker, John A.; Pvt.

Parson, J. M.; ---; –Apr. 1916; Avery Co.

Parsons, Alexander D.; Pvt.; 3 Jun. 1839–30 Jan. 1863; Richmond, VA[70]

Parsons, Craig S.; Pvt.; –28 Apr. 1864; Old City Cemetery, Lynchburg, VA

Parsons, Franklin B.; Pvt.; c.1837–

Parsons, Marcus D. L.; Pvt.; c.1843–23 Jul. 1863; Hollywood Cemetery, Richmond, VA

Parsons, William M.; Pvt.; c.1847–

Perish, Pleasant; Pvt.; c.1843–

Perry, William; Pvt.; c.1837–20 Oct. 1862; Maplewood Cemetery, Gordonsville, VA

Philips, Ransom; Pvt.; 10 Jul. 1837–12 Aug. 1912; Gideon Ham Cemetery, Ashe Co.

Phillips, Jackson

Phillips, Zachariah; Pvt.; c.1843–

Phipps, David; Pvt.; c.1834–3 Sep. 1864; Woodlawn Cemetery, Elmira, NY

Phipps, Enoch; Pvt.; c.1832–25 Aug. 1864; Reams's Station, VA

Plummer, Jesse B.; Pvt.; c.1829–

Plummer, Julian C.; Cpl.; c.1846–28 Jul. 1864; Gravel Hill, VA

Price, John, Jr.; Pvt.; c.1831–

Privitt, Isaac M; Pvt.; c.1841–13 Dec. 1862; Fredericksburg, VA

Pugh, John L.; Pvt.; 7 Jul. 1827–26 Jan. 1910; Dancy Cemetery, Allegheny Co.

Pugh, Lee Wesley; Pvt.; c.1845–5 Oct. 1910; Scott Blevins Cemetery, Ashe Co.

Reynolds, Martin; Pvt.

Rhinehart, John W.; Pvt..; –20 Apr. 1865; Point Lookout, VA

Richardson, Alvin; Pvt.; c.1834–

Richardson, James; Pvt.; c.1831–

Richardson, John; Pvt.; c.1841–14 Mar. 1862; New Bern, Craven Co.

Richardson, John R.; Pvt.; c.1843–19 Aug. 1862; Old City Cemetery, Lynchburg, VA

Richardson, William; Pvt.; 15 Mar. 1839–13 Aug. 1884; Richardson Cemetery, Ashe Co.

Richardson, William Anderson; Pvt.; 3 Aug. 1827–12 May 1893; Ashe Co.

Roop, Jacob C.; Pvt.; c.1834–

Ross, L. W.

Royal, John O.; Pvt.; c.1837–

Rutherford, Andrew; Pvt.; –2 Sep. 1863; Hollywood Cemetery, Richmond, VA

Saunders, Alfred M.; Pvt.; c.1842–14 Jun. 1863; Maplewood Cemetery, Gordonsville, VA

Saunders, William; Pvt.; 1 Apr. 1833–9 May 1893; Senter Primitive Baptist Church Cemetery, Ashe Co.

Smith, Harrison; Pvt.; c.1839–15 Nov. 1862; Stonewall Cemetery, Winchester, VA[71]

Smithdeal, William; Pvt.; 2 Nov. 1827–

South, Samuel C.; Pvt.; 15 Feb. 1831–3 May 1863; Chancellorsville, VA

Speaks, Isaiah; Pvt.; 20 Apr. 1830–26 Jan. 1903; Jacob Walters Cemetery, Ashe Co.

Spears, Jesse; Pvt.

Spears, William Nelson; Pvt.

Spencer, Goodman   .

Stamper, Joseph Samuel; Pvt.; 17 Nov. 1843–10 Nov. 1928; Mt. Zion Primitive Baptist Church Cemetery, Allegheny Co.

Stamper, Madison; Pvt.; c.1838–1920; Hash Family Cemetery, Grayson Co., VA

Stamper, Nathaniel; Pvt.; c.1831–

Stamper, William H.; Pvt.; c.1843–13 Oct. 1862; Richmond, VA

Steadham, William; Pvt.; c.1837–19 Jan. 1865; Woodlawn Cemetery, Elmira, NY

Sturgill, James; Pvt.; c.1936–19 Mar. 1865; Elmira, NY

Sturgill, Jehu; Pvt.; 19 Sep. 1841–19 Jun. 1862; South Fork Old Cemetery, Allegheny Co.[72]

Sturgill, Joseph K.; Pvt.; c.1837–27 Oct. 1864; Hollywood Cemetery, Richmond, VA

Sturgill, Levi B.; Pvt.; c.1836–; Elliott Co., KY

Sturgill, William E.; Cpl.; 1 Nov. 1843–

Sumbers, W. M.; Pvt.

Tilley, James M.; Pvt.; c.1833–

Tilley, John Calvin; Pvt.; 17 Jan. 1839–20 Sep. 1906; Gunter/Tilley Cemetery, Wyoming Co., WV

Tilley, Joseph; Pvt.; c.1836–

Tilly, James; Pvt.; c.1830–

Toliver, Drury Senter; Pvt.; 1841–26 Dec. 1926; Johnson Co., KY

Toliver, Jacob Finley; Pvt.; 2 Feb. 1830–19 Aug. 1901; Elliott Co., KY

Tredway, Henry; Pvt.; c.1843–

Tredway, John; Pvt.; c.1814–

Vanzant, Leander; Pvt.; c.1831–12 Mar. 1863

Waddell, Huston; Sgt.; 26 Jan. 1838–20 Nov. 1881; Burgess-Walden Cemetery, Allegheny Co.

Waddle, Alson; Pvt.; 14 Mar. 1832–31 Jan. 1923; Cranberry Community Cemetery, Ashe Co.

Walters, Bower; Pvt.; c.1833–

Weaver, Andrew J.; Pvt.; 20 Mar. 1843–2 May 1932; Andrew Weaver Cemetery, Allegheny Co.

Weaver, William H.; Pvt.; 11 Feb. 1841–2 Jun. 1863; Old City Cemetery, Lynchburg, VA

Webb, Hugh W.; Pvt.

Webb, Jason C.; Pvt.; c.1847–

West, James L.

Western, William; Pvt.

White, John

Willey, Allen; Pvt.; c.1844–3 May 1863; Chancellorsville, VA

Williams, Felix J.; Pvt.; c.1844–3 May 1863; Chancellorsville, VA

Williams, Jesse P.; Sgt.; c.1842–22 Dec. 1863; "on his way home"

Williams, Killis F.; Pvt.; c.1844–19 Aug. 1863; Davis Island, NY

Williams, Melvin C.; Pvt.

Williams, William; Pvt.

Wood, Zebedee C.; Pvt.; c.1838–

Wyatt, James H.; Pvt.; –Oct. 1864; "at home"

Wyatt, Robert M.; Pvt.; c.1841–

Wyatt, William W.; Cpl.; c.1843–17 Apr. 1863

Miscellaneous

Records attest that the following soldiers served with the Thirty-seventh, but the companies in which they served were not recorded.

Black, Joseph M.; Pvt.

Hampton, William

Lewis, W. M.; Pvt.

McNair, John N.

Roswell, B.; Pvt.

Rue, P.

Thomas, H. L.; Pvt

Appendix B: Transferred to the Thirty-seventh North Carolina Troops

These men were members of other regiments before they enlisted in or transferred to the Thirty-seventh North Carolina Troops.

Name	Rank	Previous Regiment	Date of Transfer	Company in Thirty-seventh
Armstrong, Thomas J.	Capt.	Co. A, 4th NCST	15 Aug. 1862	K
Barnette, James F.	Pvt.	Co. A, 11th NCT (1st NC Vol.)	1 Jan. 1864	C
Battle, Wesley L.	3LT	Co. I, 43rd NCT	15 Jan. 1863	D
Beatty, George H.	2LT	Co. K, 18th NCT (8th NC Vol.)	1 Aug. 1862	C
Bell, John D.	Pvt.	Co. E, 2nd NC Jun. Res.	11 Oct. 1864	C
Bell, Joseph S.	Pvt.	Co. G, 16th GA. Inf.	1 Oct. 1863	F[1]
Black, John C., Jr.	Pvt.	Co. E, 2nd NC Jun. Res.	11 Oct. 1864	C
Blanchard, James G.	Pvt.	Co. K, 42nd NCT	11 Mar. 1862	I[2]
Bost, Aaron J.	1LT	Co. A, 20th NCT (10th NC Vol.)	16 Nov. 1862	D
Brown, John D.	Capt.	Co. I, 63rd NCT (5th NC Cav.)	16 May 1863	C
Brown, John L.	3LT	Co. D, 12th SC Inf.	2 Jan. 1863	G
Brown, John W.	Pvt.	Co. K, 26th TN Inf.	6 Oct. 1863	F
Cable, Anderson	Pvt.	Co. G, 18th NCT	Sep.-Oct. 1864	E
Carlton, Cornelius M.	Pvt.	Co. I, 58th NCT	28 Feb. 1863	B
Cochrane, John M.	Capt.	Co. B, 53rd NCT	27 Oct. 1863	D
Combs, William	Pvt.	Co. K, 26th TN Inf.	13 Oct. 1863	F[3]

Name	Rank	Previous Regiment	Date of Transfer	Company in Thirty-seventh
Corley, D. P.	Pvt.	GA.	1 Oct. 1863	F
Crain, Wesley A.	Pvt.	Co. H, 1st NC Jun. Res.		E
Crowell, Elias M.	3LT	Co. B, 1st NC Inf.		I
Davis, John W.	Pvt.	Co. G, 18th NCT (8th NC Vol.)	Sep.–Oct. 1864	K
Davis, Thomas	Pvt.	Co. D, 9th NCST (1st NC Cav.)	21 Jul. 1864	B
Davidson, William	Pvt.	Co. K, 26th TN. Inf.	1 Oct. 1863	F[4]
Doherty, William W.	2LT	Co. F, 9th NCST (1st NC Cav.)	1 Jun. 1863	C
Elliott, S H.	Pvt.	Co. C, 1st NC Inf.		I
Elms, William D.	Capt.	F&S, 45th NCT	1 Aug. 1862	I
Elms, John P.	3LT	Co. A, 11th NCT (1st NC Vol.)	1 Jun. 1863	I
Fetter, William M.	Capt.	Co. D, 1st NC Inf.		K
Frazier, Joshua D.	Pvt.	26th TN Inf.	1 Oct. 1863	F[5]
Garland, Pryor	Pvt.	Co. K, 26th TN Inf.	1 Oct. 1863	F[6]
Garrison, Angelum A.	Pvt.	Co. B, 2nd NC Jun. Res.	10 Oct. 1864	C
Gillespie, Joseph R.	2LT	Co. B, 19th NCST (2nd NC Cav.)	21 Feb. 1862	C
Graham, Adelbert J.	Pvt.	Co. D, 9th NCT (1st NC Cav.)	21 Jul. 1864	C[7]
Graham, Daniel M.	As. Surg.	Co. A, 63rd NCT (5th NC Cav.)	11 Jun. 1863	F&S
Greer, Catlett A.	2LT	Co. A, 22nd NCT (12th NCV)	17 Feb. 1865	A
Haney, Elijah H.	Pvt.	Co. F, 2nd NC Jun. Res.	20 Sep. 1864	I
Harris, Newell J.	Pvt.		1 May 1864	I
Hickerson, John C.	Pvt.	Co. B, 1st NCST	4 Dec. 1861	F
Hoover, John M.	Pvt.	Co. B, 2nd NC Jun. Res.	10 Oct. 1864	C
Horton, Nathaniel	2LT	Co. A, 9th NCST (1st NC Cav.)	1 Dec. 1862	B
Hunsucker, James A.	Pvt.	Co. D, 42nd NCT	28 Jan. 1864	I
Jewell, C. W.	Pvt.		1 Oct. 1863	F
Kirkley, Thomas	Pvt.	Co. F, 2nd NC Jun. Res.	20 Sep. 1864	I
Lee, Charles C.	Col.	F&S, 1st NC Vol.	20 Nov. 1861	F&S
Lenoir, Walter W.	Capt.	Co. H, 58th NCT	18 Jul. 1862	A
Lowrie, Samuel J.	Pvt.	Co. C, 10th NCT (1st NC Art.)		I
Marsh, Albert T.	2LT	Co. I, 53rd NCT	10 Feb. 1865	D
Mickle, William N.	2LT	Co. I, 41st NCT	3 May 1863	K
Moore, Martin V.	"LT"	Co. D, 9th NCT (1st NC Cav.)	20 Nov. 1861	E[8]
Morrison, William L.	Pvt.	Co. E, 2nd NC Jun. Res.	11 Oct. 1864	C
Mullis, John P.	Pvt.	Co. I, 53rd NCT	19 Jan. 1864	D
Nicholson, Edward	2LT	F&S, 19th NCT (2nd NC Cav.)	1 Dec. 1862	E

Name	Rank	Previous Regiment	Date of Transfer	Company in Thirty-seventh
Nicholson, John B.	Pvt.	Co. G, 34th NCT	1 Jan. 1862	I
Parks, Willis	Pvt.	Co. B, 1st NCST	15 Apr. 1862	F
Perry, Richard M.	Pvt.	"58th NCT"	13 Jan. 1863	A[9]
Pettus, John W.	3LT	Co. K, 1st NC Vol.	20 Nov. 1861	C[10]
Phelan, Pat O.	Pvt.	Co. D, 16th NCT (6th NC Vol.)		I[11]
Pillows, T. J.	Pvt.	"Edward's Battalion."	6 Oct. 1863	F
Potts, Lawson A.	Capt.	Co. C, 1st NC Vol.	28 Feb. 1862	C
Ragan, Charlton H.	2LT	Co. A, 25th SC Inf.	9 Mar. 1863	K
Ragin, William C.	Capt.	Co. L, 1st SC Inf.	1 Oct. 1862	H
Rogers, Columbus M.	Pvt.	Co. F, 2nd NC Jun. Res.	2 Sep. 1864	E
Royster, Iowa M.	2LT	Co. E, 9th NSCT (1st NC Cav.)	5 Jun. 1863	G
Russell, Edwin H.	1LT	Co. C, 12th NCT (2nd NC Vol.)	10 Mar. 1864	I
Sample, John W.	2LT	Co. C, 1st NC Inf.		C
Salyer, Daniel	Pvt.	Co. C, 5th KY Mnt. Inf.	6 Oct. 1863	F
Slade, Henry	Sgt.	Co. A, 10th NCT (1st NC Art.)	24 Jan. 1865	E
Sloan, Walter S. Pharr	Pvt.	Co. B, 2nd NC Jun. Res.	10 Oct. 1864	C
Somerville, James B.	3LT	Co. F, 12th NCT (2nd NC Vol.)	17 Mar. 1864	B
Spears, William N.	Pvt.	Co. E, 2nd NC Jun. Res.	11 Oct. 1864	K
Stapleton, William S.	Pvt.	Co. C, 5th KY Mnt. Inf.	6 Oct. 1863	F
Starnes, Dulin	Pvt.	Co. F, 35th NCT	22 Oct. 1861	I[12]
Stowe, Charles T.	Sgt.	Co. M, 16th NCT (6th NC Vol.)	Jun. 1862	I
Tankersley, Felix	1LT	Co. G, 5th Al. Inf.	20 Jan. 1863	F
Todd, Joseph B.	1LT	Co. D, 9th NCST (1st NC Cav.)	15 Mar. 1862	B
Thomas, Nathan G.	Pvt.	Co. F, 2nd NC Jun. Res.	10 Oct. 1864	D
Turner, George	Pvt.	"26th TN Inf."	1 Oct. 1863	F[13]
Turnmire, Larkin G.	Pvt.	Co. D, 9th NCST (1st NC Cav.)	21 Jul. 1864	C
Walsh, Thomas F.	Pvt.	Co. F, 13th NCT (3rd NC Vol.)	1 Jan. 1865	F
Watts, Alexander B.	Pvt.	Co. F, 2nd NC Jun. Res.	6 Jul. 1864	D
Whitaker, Willis A.	2LT	Co. A, 1st TX Inf.	9 Mar. 1863	A
Wiggins, Octavius A.	2LT	Co. G, 41st NCT (3rd NC Cav.)	12 Jan. 1863	E
Wood, John M.	Pvt.	Co. D, 9th NCST (1st NC Cav.)	21 Jul. 1864	C

Appendix C: Transferred from the Thirty-seventh North Carolina Troops

These men were members of the Thirty-seventh who transferred to other regiments in Confederate service.

Name	Rank	Transferred to	Date of Transfer	Company in Thirty-seventh
Ashley, Tivis	Pvt.	Co. A, 26th NCT	1 May 1862	A
Blevins, William H.	Pvt.	Co. L, 58th NCT	14 Feb. 1865	A
Carrigan, William F.	Pvt.	Co. F, 4th NC Sen. Res.		C[1]
Church, Jordan	Pvt.	Co. M, 58th NCT		B
Cloninger, Emanuel	Pvt.	C. S. Navy	10 Apr. 1864	H
Cook, Jordan	Capt.	Co. B, 11th Batt. NC Home Guard		B
Crowell, Ellias M.	3LT	Co. H, 11th NCT		I
Cuthbertson, Thomas L.	Pvt.	Co. I, 53rd NCT	19 Jan. 1864	D
Davis, Alfred	Pvt.	Co. F, 13th NCT	1 Jan. 1865	F
Elms, John I.	Capt.	Co. K, 56th NCT		I
Estes, Amos	Pvt.	Co. D, 9th NCST (1st NC Cav.)		B
Farthing, Paul	1LT	Co. A, 11th Batt. NC Home Guard		E
Fetter, William M.	Capt.	Co. I, 18th NCT (8th NC Vol.)		K
Gaddy, William A.	3LT	Co. C, 10th Batt., NC Heavy Art.		D
Goodman, James J.	1LT	Co. D, 5th Batt. NC Cav.		A

Name	Rank	Transferred to	Date of Transfer	Company in Thirty-seventh
Goodman, Richard G.	2LT	Co. A, 9th NCST (1st NC Cav.)		A
Gragg, William S.	Pvt.	Co. I, 58th NCT		B
Grimsley, Lowery	1LT	Co. I, 61st NCT		K
Hartley, Finley F.	Pvt.	Co. D, 9th NCST (1st NC Cav.)		B
Hartley, Harrison	Pvt.	Co. D, 9th NCST (1st NC Cav.)		B
Henry, Berry G.	Pvt.	Co. H, 11th NCT		I
Henry, Terrell B.	Pvt.	Co. H, 11th NCT		I
Hilliard, Bartlet Y.	Pvt.	Co. I, 58th NCT		E
Hunter, Charles L.	Cpl.	Co. F, 63rd NCT (5th NC Cav.)		I
Jones, Edmond R.	Pvt.	Co. M, 58th NCT	28 Feb. 1863	B
Jones, William R.	Pvt.	Co. C, 2nd VA Inf. (Local Def.)		A
Mash, Thomas	Pvt.	Co. H, 38th NCT		A
Moore, Martin V.	"LT"	F&S, 7th Batt. NC Cav.		E
Norris, John R.	Pvt.	Co. M, 58th NCT	26 Sep. 1862	B
Oates, Robert M.	Capt.	Pender's division	1 Jun. 1863	F&S
Osborne, William B.	3LT	Co. K, 56th NCT		C
Pettus, John W.	Pvt.	Co. A, 11th NCT	Jan.-Feb. 1864	C[2]
Potter, Levi D.	Pvt.	Co. D, 58th NCT		B
Price, John W.	Pvt.	Co. A, 9th NCST (1st NC Cav.)	13 Mar. 1862	A
Pursely, Samuel M.	Pvt.	Co. C, 38th NCT		H
Rankin, William R.	Maj.	Co. B, 28th NCT		F&S
Rector, Elihu W.	Pvt.	Co. D, 18th NCT (8th NC Vol.)	Nov. 1863	G
Rutledge, Ruburtus G.	Pvt.	Co. B, 28th NCT		H
Samonds, Thomas K.	1LT	Co. E, 59th NCT (4th NC Cav.)		I
Snow, James	Pvt.	Co. F, 4th NCST	28 Mar. 1864	G
Steel, Thomas H.	Pvt.	Co. B, 43rd NCT		D
Teague, Vandever	1Sgt.	Co. H, 55th NCT	5 Apr. 1862	G
Toliver, Drury S.	Pvt.	Co. I, 21st VA Cav.		K
Torrance, John A.	Sgt. Maj.	Co. D, 7th NCST	28 Apr. 1863	F&S
Tracy, James W.	Surg.	F&S, 14th NCT	1 Jul. 1862	F&S
Tritt, Henry F.	Pvt.	Co. A, 19th NCT (2nd NC Cav.)		G
Usry, Hampton	Pvt.	Co. K, 45th NCT		D

Appendix D: Invalid Corps

These members of the Thirty-seventh were wounded and unable to take active duty, but were well enough to do light duty as guards or hospital attendants. They were transferred to the Invalid Corps.

Name	Rank	Reason Transferred	Date of Transfer	Company in Thirty-seventh
Armstrong, John	Pvt.	disability from wounds	28 Dec. 1864	H
Brown, Eli	Pvt.	Not Recorded	17 Nov. 1864	K
Derr, Andrew J.	Pvt.	Not Recorded	4 Aug. 1864	C
Cable, George W.	Pvt.	Not Recorded	28 Sep. 1864	E
Clemmer, John M. L.	Pvt.	Not Recorded	31 May 1864	H
Cochrane, George W.	2LT	disability from wounds	17 Dec. 1864	G
Coffey, Cornelius J.	Pvt.	disability from wounds	17 Nov. 1864	E
Dula, Lowery	Pvt.	disability	6 Jul. 1864	F
Fox, David A.	Pvt.	"necrosis"	7 Oct. 1864	F
Griffin, James P.	Pvt.	Not Recorded	5 Oct. 1864	D
Hasley, John	Pvt.	Not Recorded	19 Oct. 1864	K
Hipp, Larkin A.	Pvt.	disability from wounds	13 Apr. 1864	I
Hucks, Samuel L.	Pvt.	disability	18 Apr. 1864	C[1]
Kizer, David W.	Pvt.	Not Recorded	10 Aug. 1864	I
Manning, John W.	Pvt.	disability	18 Apr. 1864	I
Morris, Amos A.	Pvt.	Not Recorded	29 Nov. 1864	H
Nantz, David J.	Pvt.	disability	19 May 1864	C
Orr, Joseph L.	Pvt.	Not Recorded	17 Aug. 1864	I
Potts, Lawson A.	Capt.	Not Recorded	17 Dec. 1864	C
Shull, Joseph C.	Pvt.	disability from wounds	11 Jan. 1865	E
Somerville, James B.	3LT	disability	24 Jan. 1865	B
Staley, Robert M.	1LT	disability	23 Mar. 1865	F&S

Name	Rank	Reason Transferred	Date of Transfer	Company in Thirty-seventh
Steele, Benjamin F.	Pvt.	Not Recorded	9 Nov. 1864	G
Tadlock, James T.	Pvt.	Not Recorded	28 Dec. 1864	D
Tilley, James	Pvt.	disability	26 Oct. 1864	K
Townsend, John C.	Pvt.	Not Recorded	14 Jan. 1865	E
Walker, Joseph C.	Pvt.	Not Recorded	9 Nov. 1864	C
Walters, George W.	Sgt.	Not Recorded	21 Dec. 1864	D
Whitaker, Willis	2LT	Not Recorded	6 Jan. 1865	A
Wood, Zebedee C.	Pvt.	disability	25 Jul. 1864	K
Worsham, Rufus R.	Pvt.	Not Recorded	18 Apr. 1864	C

Appendix E: Transfers to the United States Army

These members of the Thirty-seventh, generally prisoners-of-war, enlisted in various regiments of the United States Army.

Name	Rank	Regiment in the U.S. Army	Enlistment Date	Company in Thirty-seventh
Baker, James M.	Pvt.	Co. E, 1st U.S. Vol. Inf.	18 Feb. 1864	A
Campbell, David W.	Pvt.	Co. F, 1st U.S. Vol. Inf.	25 Feb. 1864	B
Comach, Robert	Pvt.	U.S. Army	27 May 1864	A
Davis, Nesbet C.	Pvt.	Co. I, 1st U.S. Vol. Inf.	22 Jun. 1864	F
Davis, William	Pvt.	Co. B, 1st U.S. Vol. Inf.	2 Feb. 1864	A
Duncan, Jesse	Pvt.	Co. D, 3rd MD Cav.	5 Sep. 1863	K
Farthing, John S.	Pvt.	Co. G, 1st U.S. Vol. Inf.	26 Feb. 1864	E
Goss, William J.	Pvt.	Co. I, 1st U.S. Vol. Inf.	2 Feb. 1864	A
Hanner, Simpson A.	Pvt.	U.S. Army	25 Jan. 1864	F
Kizer, Solomon	Pvt.	U.S. Army	15 Oct. 1864	I
Miller, Robert C.	Pvt.	Co. E, 1st U.S. Vol. Inf.	15 Feb. 1864	C
Parsons, Franklin B.	Pvt.	U.S. Army	29 Jan. 1864	K
Simpson, Ira P.	Pvt.	1st U.S. Vol. Inf.	22 Jan. 1864	I
Strickland, William	Pvt.	Co. F, 1st U.S. Vol. Inf.	26 Feb. 1864	E
Tomlinson, Hiram	Pvt.	Co. I, 1st U.S. Vol. Inf.	27 May 1864	A
Tritt, Elcany	Pvt.	Co. G, 3rd MD Cav.	22 Sep. 1863	G
West, David F.	Pvt.	Co. B, 4th U.S. Vol. Inf.	9 Feb. 1865	H

Appendix F: Courts-Martial

These members of the Thirty-seventh appeared before courts-martial at various times during the war.

Name	Rank	Co.	Date of Trial	Charge	Sentence
Alexander, Thomas A.	Pvt.	E	13 Jan. 1864	Not Recorded	Confinement
Armstrong, Whiten J.	Pvt.	H	6 Jan. 1865	Absent Without Leave	Hard Labor
Beam, David L.	Pvt.	H	28 Jan. 1864	Desertion	Hard Labor
Beam, Henry S.	Pvt.	H	14 Aug. 1863	Desertion; Misbehavior before the enemy	Death, remitted
Bell, Archibald L.	Pvt.	F	8 Nov. 1862	Absent Without Leave	Company punishment
Benfield, Joseph L.	Cpl.	B	2 Nov. 1864	Desertion	Hard Labor
Black, George	Pvt.	A	23 Mar. 1864	Desertion	Death by firing squad
Black, Joseph	Pvt.	H	28 Jan. 1864	Desertion	Hard Labor
Blackburn, Jeremiah	Pvt.	A	23 Mar. 1864	Desertion	Death by firing squad
Blair, James B.	Pvt.	E	23 Jan. 1865	Leaving post without permission	Hard Labor
Blevins, Alvis	Pvt.	K	22 Sep. 1864	Desertion	Confinement on bread/water
Blythe, Samuel W.	Pvt.	I	7 Mar. 1863	Desertion	Company Punishment
Bost, Jackson L.	Maj.	F&S	5 Jan. 1865	Disobedience of orders	Company Punishment
Bowman, Marcus M.	Pvt.	F	1 Feb. 1864	Desertion	Hard Labor

Name	Rank	Co.	Date of Trial	Charge	Sentence
Brimer, James P.	Pvt.	H	1 Nov. 1864	Misbehavior before the enemy	Hard Labor
Brow, David L.	Pvt.	H	1 Feb. 1864	Not Recorded	Hard Labor
Cable, Anderson L.	Pvt.	E	16 Dec. 1863	Not Recorded	Acquitted
Canady, Laban	Pvt.	H	20 Feb. 1864	Not Recorded	Confinement
Carroll, James	Pvt.	B	18 Dec. 1863	Thief	Hard Labor
Caudill, William R.	Pvt.	K	9 Oct. 1862	Absent Without Leave	Company Punishment
Chambers, Daniel W.	Pvt.	D	24 Mar. 1864	Not Recorded	Acquitted
Chapman, James W.	Sgt.	G	19 Nov. 1864	Absent Without Leave	Acquitted
Church, Jackson	Pvt.	A	4 May 1864	Desertion	Death, inconclusive
Clark, Franklin	Pvt.	I	25 Mar. 1863	Desertion, Violation of A. O. W. #44	Company Punishment
Coffey, J.	Pvt.	E	16 Dec. 1863	Not Recorded	Acquitted
Collins, Sampson	Pvt.	D	1 Sep. 1863	Misbehavior before the enemy	Death by firing squad
Coon, Maxwell	Pvt.	E	22 Dec. 1863	Not Recorded	Acquitted
Councill, Jordan S.	Pvt.	B	26 Nov. 1863	Absent Without Leave	Company Punishment
Daniel, Doctor A.	Pvt.	G	24 Apr. 1862	Not Recorded	Hard Labor
Daniel, William	Pvt.	B	26 Nov. 1863	Not Recorded	Acquitted
Davis, Bartlett	Pvt.	B	26 Nov. 1863	Absent Without Leave	Company Punishment
Deal, George W.	Pvt.	F	18 Dec. 1863	Not Recorded	Fined and/or pay stopped
Farthing, John S.	Pvt.	E	24 Mar. 1863	Violation of A. O. W. #46	Reprimand
Fergusson, Thomas W.	Pvt.	H	20 Feb. 1864	Not Recorded	Confinement
Fite, Henry C.	3LT	H	21 Apr. 1862	Not Recorded	Acquitted
Ford, Green W.	Pvt.	H	11 Oct. 1862	Violation of A. O. W. #21	Fined and/or pay stopped
Ford, Green W.	Pvt.	H	1 Sep. 1863	Misbehavior before the enemy	Death by firing squad
Foster, William L.	Sgt.	E	16 Sep. 1863	Disobedience of orders; Disrespect	Confinement
Greer, James S.	Pvt.	B	3 Sep. 1863	Desertion; Misbehavior before the enemy	Death by firing squad
Greer, William M.	Pvt.	B	4 Apr. 1864	Desertion	Hard Labor
Griffin, Phillip C.	Pvt.	D	23 Feb. 1863	Violation of A. O. W. #20, 52	Death, remitted
Harmon, Henry H.	Pvt.	H.	25 Apr. 1862	Desertion	Confinement on bread/water
Harmon, Henry H.	Pvt.	H	10 Nov. 1863	Desertion; Misbehavior before the enemy	Acquitted

Name	Rank	Co.	Date of Trial	Charge	Sentence
Hicks, David	Pvt.	E	24 Mar. 1864	Desertion	Hard Labor
Holloway, James	Pvt.	A	23 Mar. 1864	Not Recorded	Hard Labor
Holman, James	Pvt.	F	30 Oct. 1863	Desertion; Misbehavior; Inciting deserter	Death by firing squad
Howell, Oliver P.	Pvt.	H	6 Apr. 1863	Violation of A. O. W. #6, 9, 45	Confinement
Howington, Joseph	Pvt.	E	17 Feb. 1864	Desertion	Hard Labor
Icehower, Hugh F.	Pvt.	I	25 Apr. 1862	Not Recorded	Confinement on bread/water
Jenkins, Andrew B.	Pvt.	H	4 Nov. 1863	Desertion	Confinement on bread/water
Kilby, Benjamin H.	Pvt.	F	30 Oct. 1863	Desertion	Company Punishment
Lackey, John A.	Pvt.	G	31 Mar. 1863	Violation of A. O. W. #20, 43	Company Punishment
Love, James	Pvt.	E	22 Dec. 1863	Absent Without Leave	Fined and/or pay stopped
Maxwell, David S.	Pvt.	I	26 Feb. 1863	Absent Without Leave	Remitted
McCall, James C.	Pvt.	I	23 Apr. 1862	Not Recorded	Confinement on bread/water
McRicks, George	Pvt.	E	24 Mar. 1864	Not Recorded	Company Punishment
Miller, John	Pvt.	A	6 Nov. 1862	Absent Without Leave	Company Punishment
Miller, John	Pvt.	A	24 Mar. 1864	Not Recorded	Acquitted
Miller, Lewis W.	Pvt.	A	24 Mar. 1864	Not Recorded	Hard Labor
Moore, John C.	1LT	H	14 Sep. 1864	Not Recorded	Reprimand
Morrison, Amos	Pvt.	E	16 Dec. 1863	Not Recorded	Acquitted
Neal, James	Pvt.	H	4 Nov. 1863	Desertion	Confinement on bread/water
Norwood, William L.	Pvt.	E	16 Dec. 1863	Not Recorded	Acquitted
Orrant, Jacob A.	Pvt.	E	16 Dec. 1863	Not Recorded	Acquitted
Orrant, Lewis	Pvt.	E	27 May 1863	Desertion	Death, not carried out
Osborne, Ephraim	Pvt.	A	22 Dec. 1863	Desertion	Death, remitted
Patrick, Churchill W.	Sgt.	E	13 Jan. 1864	Not Recorded	Acquitted
Payne, Franklin	Pvt.	B	25 Apr. 1862	Not Recorded	Confinement on bread/water
Pendergrass, Alexander	Pvt.	A	23 Mar. 1864	Not Recorded	Hard Labor
Petty, John B.	Capt.	F	24 Mar. 1864	Not Recorded	Suspended from rank
Potts, James M.	Capt.	C	15 Apr. 1862	Not Recorded	Acquitted
Price, Redmond	Pvt.	E	16 Dec. 1863	Not Recorded	Acquitted
Price, Redmond	Pvt.	E	29 Sep. 1864	Absent Without Leave	Fined and/or pay stopped

Name	Rank	Co.	Date of Trial	Charge	Sentence
Queen, Radford	Pvt.	G	24 Apr. 1862	Not Recorded	Confined on bread/water
Reynolds, Caleb	Pvt.	H	28 Jan. 1864	Desertion	Hard Labor
Roberts, Thomas M.	Pvt.	H	4 Nov. 1862	Not Recorded	Fined and/or pay stopped
Robnett, William W.	Pvt.	G	4 Nov. 1863	Desertion	Confinement on bread/water
Rudisell, Eli	Pvt.	H	28 Jan. 1864	Desertion	Hard Labor
Rufty, James	Pvt.	G	2 Sep. 1863	Tampering with sentinel	Acquitted
Rutherford, Andrew	Pvt.	K	27 May 1863	Not Recorded	Death, not carried out
Sexton, Marion	Pvt.	A	26 Jan. 1864	Desertion	Hard Labor
Shoe, Jacob	Pvt.	I	5 Jan. 1863	Desertion	Confinement on bread/water
Shull, Simon P.	Sgt.	E	16 Dec. 1863	Not Recorded	Acquitted
Shumate, Samuel	Pvt.	F	9 Feb. 1865	Desertion	Death, remitted
Simpson, Ira P.	Pvt.	I	23 Mar. 1863	Desertion; Violation of A. O. W. #22	Hard Labor
Smith, John E.	Pvt.	D	9 Sep. 1863	Absent Without Leave	Confinement
South, Eli	Pvt.	E	22 Dec. 1863	Absent Without Leave	Fined and/or pay stopped
Taylor, Calvin	Pvt.	A	29 Mar. 1864	Not Recorded	Confinement
Taylor, Charles W.	Pvt.	I	23 Mar. 1863	Absent Without Leave	Company Punishment
Taylor, Charles W.	Pvt.	I	31 Oct. 1863	Desertion	Confinement on bread/water
Teague, John A.	Pvt.	G	26 Nov. 1863	Desertion	Death, not carried out
Testerman, Calvin	Pvt.	A	26 Jan. 1864	Desertion	Hard Labor
Thomas, Burton	Pvt.	G	8 Nov. 1862	Violation of Article #52	Fined and/or pay stopped
Walker, Jeremiah	Pvt.	G	2 Sep. 1863	Disrespect to his superior officer	Confinement
Wallace, John G.	Pvt.	F	1 Feb. 1864	Desertion	Hard Labor
Wallace, Matthew	Pvt.	F	21 Feb. 1863	Desertion	Company Punishment
Warren, James R.	Pvt.	G	8 Nov. 1862	Violation of A. O. W. #52	Company Punishment
West, David F.	Pvt.	H	28 Jan. 1864	Desertion	Hard Labor
White, Henry	Pvt.	G	4 Nov. 1864	Desertion	Confinement on bread/water
Williams, Alfred	Pvt.	E	25 Mar. 1863	Desertion; Violation of A. O. W. #44	Company Punishment

Appendix G:
Appomattox Parolees

These men surrendered on April 9, 1865. An asterisk (*) denotes members of the Thirty-seventh that were present when the regiment was mustered into service on November 20, 1861. This list was compiled from *North Carolina Troops*, by Manari and Jordan, and *Appomattox Paroles*, by Nine and Wilson.

FIELD AND STAFF

Major Jackson L. Bost
Surgeon George E. Trescott
Assistant Surgeon Daniel M. Graham
Sergeant Major Joseph H. Austin

Quartermaster Sergeant John O. Alexander
Commissary Sergeant Charles T. Stowe
Ordnance Sergeant James W. C. Abernathy

COMPANY A

First Lieutenant Thomas L. Norwood
Black, John M., 1Sgt.
Childers, John, Pvt.
Light, Matthias M., Pvt.
Miller, Bartlett, Pvt.

Miller, Lewis W., Pvt.
Osborne, Ephraim, Pvt.
Rusher, A. W., Sgt.[1]
Severt, Enoch, Pvt.

COMPANY B

Jones, Joseph H., Pvt.
Stafford, John C., Pvt.

Thayer, Nerlos M., Pvt.
Triplett, Pickens L., Pvt.[2]

COMPANY C

Alexander, Thomas L., Pvt.
Beard, James F. M., Cpl.
Deaton, John Z., Pvt.
Harrison, William H., Sgt.
Kelly, Alexander A., Pvt.

Knox, Samuel W., Pvt.
Lents, Rufus R., Sgt.
Sample, Elam A., Pvt.
White, Joel H., Pvt.

COMPANY D

Captain John M. Cochrane
Second Lieutenant Albert T. Marsh
*Third Lieutenant Joseph E. Griffin
*Baucom, George W., 1Sgt.
* Bivens, Robert N., Pvt.
Caudle, Archibald B., Pvt.
*Eason, Thomas L., Pvt.
*Fincher, Henry H., Pvt.
Gaddy, Elijah G., Pvt.[3]

Gaddy, James N., Pvt.[4]
*Griffin, Phillip C., Pvt.
Griffin, William T., Pvt.
Helms, Adam C., Pvt.
Helms, Charles L.,
*Little, Patrick, Pvt.
*Lowery, James T., Sgt.
*Stegall, Alexander, Pvt.

COMPANY E

Adams, Wellington, Sgt.
*Coffey, James C., Pvt.[5]
Croom, Nathan R., Pvt.
Foster, T. L.[6]
*Harmon, Cicero D., Pvt.

Harrington, John[7]
*Howington, Joseph H., Cpl.[8]
Morrison, Amos, Pvt.
Munday, William F., Pvt.
Slade, Henry, Sgt.

COMPANY F

Brown, John W., Pvt.[9]
*Crouse, Shubael B., Pvt.[10]
Edwards, Joseph T., Pvt.
*Ferguson, Samuel S., 1Sgt.
Hefner, William R., Pvt.
Hendricks, James F.[11]

Keever, Jacob C., Pvt.[12]
Mastin, William J., Pvt.
*Parks, William F., Pvt.
Parks, Willis, Pvt.[13]
Rex, George W., Pvt.[14]
Willis, Jacob C., Pvt.

COMPANY G

Bently, John J., Pvt.
*Chapman, James W., 1Sgt.[15]
Fox, Hugh, Pvt.

Justice, Socrates, Pvt.
McRee, Robert D., Pvt.
Smith, Robert B., Pvt.

COMPANY H

Black, Matthew, Pvt.
Black, Thomas, Pvt.
Byrd, Oliver P., Pvt.[16]
Craig, John S., Pvt.
Digh, John P., Pvt.[17]
Hallett, Caleb, Pvt.
Hoffman, Frederick L., Pvt.

Kendrick, John F., Pvt.[18]
*Linebarger, Jonas L., Pvt.
*McKee, Logan L., Pvt.
Morrison, Levi., Pvt.[19]
*Paysour, Eli F., Pvt.
Selvy, Joseph S., Pvt.
Thomasson, J. Beverly, Pvt.

COMPANY I

* Second Lieutenant Adam F. Yandle
Alexander, James A., Pvt.
*Barnhill, John W., Pvt.
Clark, John F., Jr., Pvt.[20]
*Flow, James C., Sgt.
Hill, Thomas M., Pvt.
*Kissiah, George W., Pvt.
*Kistler, George H., Pvt.

Lawing, George A., Pvt.
McCall, James C., Pvt.
*Patterson, John H., Pvt.
*Robinson, Daniel C., Sgt.
Smith, Franklin, Pvt.
*Spears, Andrew J., Pvt.
Todd, Robert J., Pvt.

COMPANY K

Captain Thomas J. Armstrong
Third Lieutenant Thomas M. Wiggins
Arvens, J. J., Pvt.[21]
Blevins, Alfred C., Pvt.
Jenkins, Henry, Pvt.

Owens, John J., Pvt.[22]
Parker, John A., Pvt.
Saunder, William, Pvt.
Sumbers, W. M., Pvt.
Webb, Hugh W., Pvt.

Notes

Chapter 1

1. For more information on the beginnings of North Carolina, please see Wheeler, John Hill, *Historical Sketches of North Carolina from 1584 to 1851*, 2 vols. (Baltimore, Maryland: Regional Publishing Company, 1864). For more information on antebellum North Carolina and the secession movement within the state, please see Harris, William C., *William Woods Holden: Firebrand of North Carolina Politics* (Baton Rouge: Louisiana State University Press, 1987); Jeffery, Thomas E., *State Parties and National Politics, North Carolina 1815–1861* (Athens: University of Georgia Press, 1989); Johnson, Guion Griffis, *Ante-bellum North Carolina: A Social History* (Chapel Hill: University of North Carolina Press, 1937); and Sitterson, Joseph Carlyle, *The Secession Movement in North Carolina* (Chapel Hill: University of North Carolina Press, 1939).

2. Cope, Robert F., and Manly Wade Wellman, *The County of Gaston, Two Centuries of a North Carolina Region* (Gastonia: Gaston County Historical Society, 1961), pp. 66–78.

3. Blythe, LeGette, and Charles Raven Brockhamnn, *Hornet's Nest: The Story of Charlotte and Mecklenburg County* (Charlotte: McNally of Charlotte for the Public Library of Charlotte and Mecklenburg County, 1961), p. 398; Gianneschi, Matthew Everett, "A Man from Mecklenburg: 1st Sergeant John Tally and the 'Hornet's Nest Riflemen,' North Carolina 37th Regiment, Company I" (Master's thesis, University of Denver, 1998), p. 14.

4. Walden, H. Nelson, "History of Union County, North Carolina: A Thesis" (Master's thesis: Appalachian State Teacher's College, 1963).

5. Inscoe, John C., and Gordon McKinney, *The Heart of Confederate Appalachia: Western North Carolina in the Civil War* (Chapel Hill: University of North Carolina Press, 2000), pp. 8, 12–13; also see Arthur, John Preston, *Western North Carolina: A History from 1730 to 1913* (1914 reprint, Johnson City, TN: The Overmountain Press, 1996); Crawford, Martin, "Mountain Farmers and the Market Economy: Ashe County during the 1850s" (*North Carolina Historical Review*, Vol. 72, Oct. 1994), pp. 430–50; and Inscoe, John C., "Mountain Masters as Confederate Opportunists: The Profitability of Slavery in Western North Carolina, 1861–1865" (*Slavery and Abolition*, Vol. 16, Num. 1, Apr. 1995), pp. 85–100.

6. Crouch, John, *Historical Sketches of Wilkes County* (no publication information, c.1902); Inscoe and McKinney, *Heart of Confederate Appalachia*.

7. Charlotte *Bulletin*, quoted in the Raleigh *Register*, Sep. 7, 1859; Ibid., Oct. 12, 1859; North Carolina *Standard*, Aug. 6, 1859.

8. Raleigh *Register*, Oct. 26, 1859; Wilmington *Journal*, Oct. 28, 1859; Raleigh *Register*, Nov. 2, 1859; Vance, Zebulon B., quoted in Inscoe and McKinney, *The Heart of Confederate Appalachia*, p. 35; Sitterson, *The Secession Movement in North Carolina*, pp. 149–150; Harris, *William Woods Holden*, pp. 82–3.

9. *Asheville News*, Jan. 29, 1857; Jan. 9, 1860.

10. For more information on John Bell, please see Parks, Joseph Howard, *John Bell of Tennessee*. For more information on John C. Breckinridge, please see Davis, William C., *Breckinridge: Statesman Soldier, Symbol*. For more information on Stephen Douglas, please see Johannse, Robert W., *Stephen A. Douglas*; Inscoe and McKinney, *The*

Heart of Confederate Appalachia, p. 40; Sitterson, *The Secession Movement in North Carolina,* p. 175.

11. Wilmington *Journal,* Oct. 25, 1860; Sitterson, *The Secession Movement in North Carolina,* p. 172; Inscoe and McKinney, *The Heart of Confederate Appalachia,* p. 41; Crawford, Martin, *Ashe County's Civil War* (Charlottesville, VA: University Press of Virginia, 2001), pp. 67–68; Raleigh *Register,* Nov. 6, 1860.

12. Raleigh *North Carolina Standard,* Feb. 5, 1861; Crawford, *Ashe County's Civil War,* p. 72.

13. Barrett, John G., *The Civil War in North Carolina* (Chapel Hill: University of North Carolina Press, 1963), pp. 9–10, 15.

14. Manari, Louis H., and Weymouth T. Jordan, eds., *North Carolina Troops, 1861–1865: A Roster* (14 volumes to date, Raleigh: North Carolina Department of Archives and History, Vol. 9, 1961–), pp. 462–604.

15. *Ibid.;* Hardy, Michael C., *Watauga County's Confederate and Union Civil War Soldiers: A Biography* (unpublished manuscript, in possession of the author).

16. Manari and Jordan, *North Carolina Troops,* pp. 462–604.

17. Heath, Raymond A., Jr., "The North Carolina Militia on the Eve of the Civil War" (Master's thesis: University of North Carolina, 1974), pp. 9–12.

18. Moore, Bartholomew F., and Asa Biggs, *Revised Code of North Carolina* (Boston: Little, Brown, and Company, 1855), pp. 396–399.

19. Manari and Jordan, *North Carolina Troops,* pp. 462–604; Robinson, Daniel C., unpublished family notes.

20. Record Group 109: War Department Collection of Confederate Records, Orders, and Circulars issued by the Army of the Potomac and the Army and Department of Northern Virginia, C. S. A., 1861–1865; Hardy, *Watauga County's Confederate and Union Civil War Soldiers.*

21. "Bounty Payrolls: Alexander, Ashe, Union, Watauga, and Wilkes Counties, Dec. 21, 1861," Civil War Collection, Military Collection, Archives, Division of Archives and History, Raleigh.

22. Hardy, *Watauga County's Confederate and Union Civil War Soldiers.*

23. Austin family, email to author, Mar. 5, 1999.

24. Gianneschi, "A Man from Mecklenburg," p. 24.

25. Manari and Jordan, *North Carolina Troops,* p. 471.

26. *Ibid.,* pp. 485–86.

27. *Ibid.,* pp. 591–92.

28. *Ibid.,* pp. 497–98.

29. *Ibid.,* pp. 509–10.

30. *Ibid.,* pp. 523–24.

31. *Ibid.,* pp. 537–38.

32. *Ibid.,* pp. 566–67.

33. *Ibid.,* pp. 551–52.

34. *Ibid.,* pp. 578–79.

35. Crawford, *Ashe County's Civil War,* p. 78; Puett, Minnie S., *History of Gaston County* (Charlotte: Laney-Smith, Inc., 1939, 1998); *Watauga Democrat,* Feb. 3, 1898; Whitener, Daniel J., *History of Watauga County* (no publication information, c.1949), p. 43.

36. Kautz, August V., *Customs of Service for Non-Commissioned Officers and Soldiers* (Philadelphia: J. B. Lippincott & Co., 1864, reprint), pp. 116–123, 102.

37. Collins, Noah, Papers, 1861–1865. (North Carolina Department of Cultural Resources, Division of Archives and History, Raleigh, N.C.), p. 5; Bruton, Teresa, email to the author, Sep. 22, 2001; Iobst, Richard W., "North Carolina Mobilizes: Nine Crucial Months, Dec. 1860-Aug. 1861" (Ph.D. dissertation, University of North Carolina, Chapel Hill, 1968), p. 206.

38. Western *Democrat,* quoted in Gianneschi, "A Man from Mecklenburg," p. 34; Chapel Church *Records Abstract, 1859–1904* (Ashe County Public Library, Genealogy Room).

39. Robinson, Daniel C., unpublished family notes.

Chapter 2

1. Harsh, Joseph L., *Confederate Tide Rising: Robert E. Lee and the Making of Southern Strategy, 1861–1862* (Kent, Ohio: Kent State University Press, 1998), pp. 32–35.

2. Collins, Noah, p. 5; Tugman, James H., Letters, 1861–1863 (William E. Eury Appalachian Collection, Appalachian State University, Boone, NC), to Friend, Nov. 10, 1861; Sterns, A. L., Letters, 1861–1862 (Manuscript Department, Duke University Library, Durham, N.C.), to Wife, Dec. 1, 1861.

3. Morris, William G., Letters, 1861: 1865: 1877: 1894: 1941: 1957 (Southern Historical Collection, University of North Carolina, Chapel Hill), to Wife, Oct. 31, 1861.

4. Iobst, "North Carolina Mobilizes," p. 248.

5. Harsh, *Confederate Tide Rising,* p. 177.

6. Collins, Noah, p. 8; Tugman, James H., to Wife, no date; Alexander, John B., Papers (University of North Carolina at Charlotte Library), to Wife, Nov. 14, 1861; Alexander, John B., to Wife, Nov. 19, 1861; Alexander, John B., to Wife, Nov. 26, 1861.

7. Morris, William G., to Wife, Nov. 12, 1861; Mast, Greg, *State Troops and Volunteers: A Photographic Record of North Carolina's Civil War Soldiers, Volume 1* (Raleigh: North Carolina Department of Cultural Resources, Division of Archives

and History, 1995), see note 19 on page 24; Iobst, "North Carolina Mobilizes," p. 38.

8. Morris, William G., to Wife, Nov. 12, 1861; Mast, *State Troops and Volunteers*, p. 24.

9. Morris, William G., to Wife, Nov. 12, 1861: "we have Preaching Every Night in Camp or at High Point which is ½ Mile from Camp very often 3 Sermons Going on at the same time."; Iobst, "North Carolina Mobilizes," p. 276.

10. Morris, William G., to Wife, Nov. 12, 1861; Green, Barzilla C., and Silas Green, Letters (Private Collection), to Aunt and Uncle, Dec. 29, 1861; Tugman, James H., to Brother, Dec. 27, 1861; Field, Ron, *Brassey's History of Uniforms: American Civil War, Confederate Army* (London: Brassey's, 1996), pp. 98–9; Civil War Collection, Military Collection, Archives, Division of Archives and History, Raleigh, Box 43, Folder 15; *Ibid.*, Box 43, Folder 16.

11. Iobst, "North Carolina Mobilizes," p. 38.

12. Stevens, William, *Dictionary of North Carolina Biography* (Chapel Hill: University of North Carolina Press, Vol. 4, 1979, 6 Vols.), p. 43.

13. Collins, Noah, p. 6.

14. Madaus, Howard M., email to author, Feb. 8, 2000.

15. Morris, William G., to Wife, Nov. 12, 1861; Green, Silas, to Aunt and Uncle, Dec. 29, 1861; Tugman, James H., to Father and Mother, undated; this listing was compiled from a search in Manari and Jordan, *North Carolina Troops*, Vol. 9, pp. 462–604.

16. *Ibid.*

17. Morris, William G., to Wife, Nov. 12, 1861.

18. Civil War Collection, Military Collection, Archives, Division of Archives and History, Raleigh, Box 43, Folder 16.

19. Lord, Francis A., *Civil War Collector's Encyclopedia, Vol. 1* (Secaucus, N.J.: Castle Books, 1977), pp. 168–171.

20. Alexander, John B., to Wife, Jan. 1, 1862.

21. Tugman, James H., to Father and Mother, undated; Alexander, John B., to Wife, Apr. 7, 1862.

22. Morris, William G., to Wife, Jan. 7, 1862.

23. *Ibid.*

24. *Ibid.*; Green, Silas, to Aunt and Uncle, Jan. 5, 1862.

25. *Regulations for the Army of the Confederate States, 1863* (Richmond, VA: J. W. Randolph, 1863), pp. 176–177.

26. Morris, William G., to Wife, Jan. 7, 1862: "We have a heavy sleet at this time heare"; Alexander, John B., to Wife, Jan. 7, 1862; Morris, William G., to Wife, Jan. 7, 1862.

Chapter 3

1. Morris, William G., to Wife, Jan. 10, 1862; Alexander, John B., to Wife, Jan. 15, 1862; Robin-son, Blackwell P., *The North Carolina Guide* (Chapel Hill: University of North Carolina Press, 1955), p. 219.

2. Brawley, James Shober, "The Public and Military Career of Lawrence O'Bryan Branch" (Master's thesis: University of North Carolina at Chapel Hill, 1951), pp. 54, 58.

3. *Ibid.*, pp. 116–118.

4. *Ibid.*, p. 131.

5. *Ibid.*, p. 134; Raleigh *Standard*, Nov. 23, 1861.

6. Lee, Charles C., to James H. Lane, quoted in McDaid, William K., "Four years of Arduous Service: The History of the Branch-Lane Brigade in the Civil War" (Ph.D. dissertation, Michigan State University, 1987), p. 30.

7. Collins, Noah, pp. 6–8.

8. Morris, William G., to Wife, Jan. 18, 1862; Alexander, John B., to Wife, Jan. 15, 1862; *The War of the Rebellion: A Compilation of the Official Records of the Union and Confederate Armies*, 128 vols. (Washington, D.C., 1880–1901), vol. 51, part 1, p. 450; Sauers, Richard A., *A Succession of Honorable Victories: The Burnside Expedition in North Carolina.* (Dayton, Ohio: Morningside House, Inc., 1996), p. 247.

9. Barrett, John G., *The Civil War in North Carolina* (Chapel Hill: University of North Carolina Press, 1963), p. 26; Bilby, Joseph G., *Civil War Firearms* (Pennsylvania: Combined Books, 1996), p. 16.

10. Compiled Service Records of Confederate Soldiers Who Served in Organizations from North Carolina, Record Group 109.

11. Morris, William G., to Wife, Jan. 18, 1862; Council, Jordan S., to Mother, Feb. 4, 1862 (Mary A. Council Papers, Manuscript Department, Duke University Library); Carrigan, William, to Father and Mother, Feb. 26, 1862 (Hayer, Larry, email to the author, Oct. 7, 2001); Smith, Bennett, to Wife, Feb. 24, 1862 (private collection).

12. Collins, Noah, p. 8; Green, Silas, to Uncle, Feb. 18, 1862; Collins, Noah, p. 9; Alexander, John B., to Wife, Jan. 15, 1862.

13. Morris, William G., to Wife, Feb. 8, 1862.

14. *Ibid.*

15. *Ibid.*, Jan. 27, 1862; *Ibid.*, Feb. 8, 1862.

16. Smith, Bennett, to Wife, Feb. 24, 1862; Morris, William G., to Wife, Feb. 15, 1862; Council, Jordan S., to Mother, Feb. 4, 1862; Smith, Bennett, to Wife, Feb. 24, 1862; Morris, William G., to Wife, Feb. 15, 1862.

17. Carrigan, William, to Father and Mother, Feb. 26, 1862; Carrigan, William, to Daughter, Feb. 26, 1862.

18. *Official Records*, Vol. 9, pp. 241–42.

19. The state of North Carolina gave two designations to artillery and cavalry regiments: the first was the order in which they were mustered into state service; they were also numbered according to branch of service. For example, the

Tenth North Carolina Troops was more commonly known as the First North Carolina Artillery.

20. Sauers, *A Succession of Honorable Victories*, p. 116.

21. Morris, William G., to Wife, Feb. 15, 1862.

22. Smith, Bennett, to Wife, Feb. 24, 1862; Alexander, John B., to Wife, Jan. 25, 1862; *Ibid.*, Jan. 19, 1862; Morris, William G., to Wife, Feb. 23, 1862; Alexander, John G., to Wife, Jan. 19, 1862.

23. *Ibid.*, Apr. 7, 1862; Stough, Alfred, to *Biblical Recorder*, Mar. 5, 1862.

24. Smith, Bennett, to Wife, Mar. 6, 1862; Stough, Alfred, to *Biblical Recorder*, Mar. 5, 1862; Morris, William G., to Wife, Feb. 26, 1862.

25. Smith, Bennett, to Wife, Mar. 6, 1862; Morris, William G., to Wife, Feb. 26, 1862.

26. Lee, Charles C., to E. S. Shoolbred, Jan. 22, 1862, quoted in McDaid, "Four Years of Arduous Service."

27. Lee, Charles C., to James H. Lane, Mar. 3, 1862 (James H. Lane Papers, Auburn University); Marcotte, Frank B., *Private Osborne, Massachusetts 23rd Volunteers: Burnside Expedition, Roanoke Island, Second Front Against Richmond* (Jefferson, NC: McFarland, 1999), p. 63.

28. *Official Records*, Vol. 9, p. 242; Sauers, *A Succession of Honorable Victories*, pp. 236–37; *Official Records*, Vol. 9, p. 243; Alexander, John B., to Wife, Mar. 12, 1862.

29. Collins, Noah, p. 10.

30. *Official Records*, Vol. 9, pp. 264–65.

31. Johnson, Robert Underwood, and Clarence Clough Buel, eds., *Battles and Leaders of the Civil War*, 4 vols. (New York: Thomas Yoseloff, 1956), 2:648.

32. Sauers, *A Succession of Honorable Victories*, p. 261.

33. Dugger, David C., to *Watauga Democrat*, Jun. 18, 1891.

34. Collins, Noah, p. 11; *Official Records*, Vol. 9, p. 265; Smith, Bennett, to Wife, Mar. 15, 1862; Sauers, *A Succession of Honorable Victories*, p. 266; Collins, Noah, p. 12; Smith, Bennett, to Wife, Apr. 13, 1862.

35. Alexander, John B., to Wife, Mar. 14, 1862.

36. Collins, Noah, p. 12; Sauers, *A Succession of Honorable Victories*, p. 274; Collins, Noah, p. 12; Smith, Bennett, to Wife, Mar. 15, 1862; Collins, Noah, p. 13; Dugger, David C., to *Watauga Democrat*, Jun. 18, 1891.

37. *Raleigh Register*, Mar. 22, 1862; Smith, Bennett, to Brother, Apr. 13, 1862.

38. *Official Records*, Vol. 9, p. 266; Sauers, *A Succession of Honorable Victories*, p. 298; Collins, Noah, p. 14.

39. Collins, Noah, p. 14; *Raleigh Register*, Mar. 15, 1862; *Official Records*, Vol. 9, p. 266; Smith, Bennett, to Brother, Apr. 13, 1862; Morris, William G., to Wife, Mar. 16, 1862.

40. Barrett, John G., *The Civil War in North Carolina*, p. 126.

41. Morris, William G., to Wife, Feb. 23, 1862; Manari and Jordan, *North Carolina Troops*, p. 501; Alexander, John B., to Wife, Apr. 27, 1862.

42. Manari and Jordan, *North Carolina Troops*, pp. 498, 538.

43. *Raleigh Register*, Apr. 23, 1862.

44. Collins, Noah, p. 15; *Charlotte Daily Bulletin*, Mar. 25, 1862; *Western Democrat*, Apr. 8, 1862; *North Carolina Whig*, Nov. 5, 1861.

45. Morris, William G., to Wife, Apr. 16, 1862; Alexander, John B., to Wife, Apr. 7, 1862; Chamber, Daniel W., to *Biblical Recorder*, Apr. 16, 1862.

46. Smith, Bennett, to Wife, Mar. 30, 1862; *Ibid.*, Apr. 13, 1862; *Ibid.*, Mar. 30, 1862; Green, Silas, to Uncle, Mar. 23, 1862.

47. Alexander, John B., to Wife, Mar. 29, 1862.

48. Thirty-seventh North Carolina Regiment, Letter Book (Manuscript Department, Duke University Library, Durham, North Carolina).

49. Manari and Jordan, *North Carolina Troops*, p. 592; *Ibid.*, p. 498; Alexander, John B., to Wife, Mar. 29, 1862.

50. Bunch, Jack A., *Military Justice in the Confederate Armies* (Shippensburg, PA: White Mane Books, 2000), p. 4.

51. *Ibid.*, pp. 2–3.

52. *Ibid.*, pp. 16–24.

53. Thirty-seventh North Carolina Regiment, Letter Book.

54. Green, Silas, to Uncle, Apr. 11, 1862.

55. Smith, Bennett, to Wife, Apr. 6, 1862; Manari and Jordan, *North Carolina Troops*, p. 462.

56. Bost, Jackson L., to Rev. E. S. Davis, Apr. 26, 1862 (Manuscript Department, Duke University Library, Durham, N.C.).

Chapter 4

1. Harsh, *Confederate Tide Rising*, p. 36.

2. Lee, Robert E., to Theophilus Holmes, May 13, 1862, quoted in Harsh, *Confederate Tide Rising*, p. 218, see note 95; Ripley's brigade from South Carolina was the other brigade transferred to General Johnston's army.

3. Alexander, John B., to Wife, May 7, 1862; Phillips, Kenneth Edwards, "James Henry Lane and the War for Southern Independence" (Master's Thesis: Auburn University, 1982), p. 44; *Biblical Recorder*, May 14, 1862; Smith, Bennett, to Wife, May 8, 1862.

4. Smith, Bennett, to Wife, May 8, 1862; *Biblical Recorder*, May 14, 1862.

5. Morris, William G., to Wife, May 4, 1862; *Biblical Recorder*, May 14, 1862; Hewett, Janet B., Noah Andre Trudeau, and Bruce A. Suderow, eds., *Supplement to the Official Records of the Union and*

Confederate Armies (Wilmington, NC: Broadfoot, 1994), 2:365.

6. Brawley, "The Public Life and Military Career of Lawrence O'Bryan Branch," p. 159.

7. Alexander, John B., to Wife, May 14, 1862; Morris, William G., to Wife, May 22, 1862; Tally, John, to Wife, May 20, 1862 (Private Collection); Brawley, "The Public Life and Military Career of Lawence O'Bryan Branch," p. 163; Alexander, John B., to Wife, May 19, 1862.

8. Collins, Noah, p. 17; Alexander, John B., to Wife, May 23, 1862.

9. Morris, William G., to Wife, May 30, 1862; *Biblical Recorder*, Jun. 11, 1862.

10. Morris, William G., to Wife, May 27, 1862; Hewett, *Supplement to the Official Records*, 2:366; Morris, William G., to Wife, May 27, 1862.

11. *Official Records*, Vol. 11, Pt. 1, pp. 702; McLaurin, William H., "Eighteenth Regiment," in Clark, Walter, ed., *Histories of the Several Regiments and Battalions from North Carolina in the Great War, 1861 to 1865* (Raleigh: E. M. Uzzell, 1901), 2:22.

12. Morris, William G., to Wife, May 27, 1862; *Official Records*, Vol. 11, Pt. 1, p. 709.

13. Morris, William G., to Wife, May 27, 1862.

14. Hart, Moses, to *Weekly Catawba Journal*, Jun. 10, 1862.

15. Manari and Jordan, *North Carolina Troops*, p. 556.

16. Morris, William G., to Wife, May 27, 1862.

17. Lane, James H., "History of Lane's North Carolina Brigade," *Southern Historical Society Journal*, Vol. 7 (1879), pp. 513–522; Collins, Noah, p. 18.

18. Morris, William G., to Wife, May 27, 1862; Chambers, Daniel W., to *Biblical Recorder*, Jun. 11, 1862.

19. Wiggins, Octavius A., "Thirty-seventh Regiment," in Clark, Walter, ed., *Histories of the Several Regiments and Battalions from North Carolina in the Great War, 1861 to 1865*, 3:24.

20. Clark, 3:24; Richmond *Examiner*, quoted in *Weekly Catawba Journal*, Jun. 19, 1862.

21. *Raleigh Register*, Jun. 17, 1862.

22. Hewett, *Supplement to the Official Records*, 2:369.

Chapter 5

1. Robertson, James I., *General A. P. Hill: The Story of a Confederate Warrior* (New York: Random House, 1987), p. 5.

2. *Ibid.*, pp. 34, 22.

3. Archer, James Jay (1817–1864), prewar lawyer and Mexican war officer, he was colonel of the Fifth Texas Infantry until Oct. 2, 1861, when he was promoted to brigadier general. He was wounded and captured at Gettysburg, and died of pneumonia in Richmond, Virginia, on Oct. 24, 1864. He is interred at Hollywood Cemetery, Richmond, Virginia. William Dorsey Pender (1834–1863) was a prewar officer in the United States Army. He resigned and was a captain of artillery in the Confederate Army, then colonel of first the Third North Carolina State Troops (Thirteenth North Carolina Troops), then the Sixth North Carolina Troops. He was promoted May 27, 1862, to brigadier general (temporary) and later served as the Thirty-seventh's divisional commander. He was mortally wounded on Jul. 2, 1863, at Gettysburg, and died on Jul. 18, 1863. He is buried in the Calvary Churchyard, Tarboro, North Carolina. Maxcy Gregg (1814–1862) was an amateur astronomer, ornithologist, botanist, language teacher, lawyer, and Mexican War veteran prior to the war. He served as colonel, 1st South Carolina Infantry, before being promoted to brigadier general in Dec. 1861. He was mortally wounded on Dec. 13, 1862, at Fredericksburg, Virginia, and died on Dec. 15. He is buried in the Elmwood Cemetery, Columbia, South Carolina. Charles William Field (1828–1892), a prewar officer in the United States Army, resigned on May 30, 1861, and rose through the ranks from captain to colonel in the Virginia Provisional Army. He was commissioned a brigadier general on Mar. 9, 1862, and major general on Feb. 12, 1864. After the war he served in the Egyptian Army, and as doorkeeper of the United States House of Representatives. He died in Washington, D.C., on Apr. 9, 1892, and is interred at Loudon Park National Cemetery, Baltimore, Maryland. Joseph Reid Anderson (1813–1892) was also a prewar army officer, and later an engineer for both the Valley Turnpike Co. and the Tredegar Iron Works in Richmond, Virginia. He was commissioned major in May 1861, and promoted to brigadier general Sep. 3, 1861. He resigned Jul. 19, 1862, and served as chief executive, Tredegar Iron Works. He died at Isle of Shoals, New Hampshire, Sep. 7, 1892, and is interred at Hollywood Cemetery in Richmond, Virginia. For more information, see Warner, *Generals in Gray*.

4. Alexander, John B., to Wife, Jun. 2, 1862; Miller, John, to Brother, Jun. 17, 1862 (private collection); Tally, John, to Wife, Jun. 22, 1862; Alexander, John B., to Wife, Jun. 5, 1862.

5. *Ibid.*

6. *Ibid.*, Jun. 15, 1862, Jun. 20, 1862.

7. Harsh, *Confederate Tide Rising*, pp. 56–58.

8. *Ibid.*, p. 65.

9. Robertson, *A. P. Hill*, p. 68.

10. Morris, William G., to Wife, Jul. 6, 1862.

11. Collins, Noah, p. 21; Phillips, *James Henry Lane*, p. 63; Alexander, John B., *Reminiscences of the Past Sixty Years* (Charlotte: privately printed, 1908), p. 72.

12. Collins, Noah, p. 21; Alexander, *Reminiscences*, p. 72.

13. Collins, Noah, p. 22.

14. Collins, Noah, p. 23; Alexander, John B., to Wife, Jul. 4, 1862.

15. Collins, Noah, p. 24.

16. Collins, Noah, p. 25; Morris, William G., to Wife, Jul. 6, 1862; Collins, Noah, p. 25.

17. Brawley, "The Public Life and Military Career of Lawrence O'Bryan Branch," p. 179.

18. Johnson, *Battles and Leaders*, 2:400; Sears, Stephen W., "The Battle of Glendale" (*North & South*, Vol. 5, Num. 1, Dec. 2001), pp. 13–17.

19. Sears, Stephen W., *To the Gates of Richmond* (New York: Ticknor & Fields, 1992), p. 301; Morris, William G., to Wife, Jul 6, 1862.

20. Manari and Jordan, *North Carolina Troops*, p. 468; Alexander, *Reminiscences*, p. 73; Morris, William G., to Wife, Jul. 6, 1862; Lane, "History of Lane's North Carolina Brigade," Vol. 8 (1880), p. 4; *North Carolina Standard*, Jul. 9, 1862; *Western Democrat*, Jul. 8, 1862; *North Carolina Whig*, Jul. 8, 1862.

21. Wegner, Ansley Herring, "Phantom Pain: Civil War Amputation and North Carolina's Maimed Veterans" (*North Carolina Historical Review*, Vol. 75, Num. 3, Jul. 1998), p. 269.

22. Cunningham, H. H., *Doctors in Gray: The Confederate Medical Service* (Baton Rouge: Louisiana State University Press, 1958, 1993), pp. 75, 116.

23. Collins, Noah, pp. 17–19.

24. Cunningham, *Doctors in Gray*, pp. 47–52.

25. Alexander, John B., to Wife, Jul. 6, 1862.

26. Alexander, *Reminiscences*, p. 73.

Chapter 6

1. Cunningham, *Doctors in Gray*, p. 195.

2. Manari and Jordan, *North Carolina Troops*, p. 475; LeGrand, Louis, M.D., *The Military Handbook and Soldier's Manual* (New York: Beadle and Company Publishers, 1861), pp. 90–92.

3. Miller, John V., to Brother, Jul. 17, 1862; Morris, William G., to Wife, Jul. 21, 1862; Green, Brazilla, to Uncle, Jul. 26, 1862; Alexander, John B., to Wife, Jul. 24, 1862.

4. Alexander, John B., to Wife, Aug. 6, 1862.

5. *Ibid.*, Oct. 5, 1862.

6. Hickerson, Thomas F., *Echoes of Happy Valley* (Chapel Hill: privately printed, 1962), p. 83.

7. Morris, William G., to Wife, Aug. 8, 1862.

8. Hickerson, *Echoes of Happy Valley*, pp. 83–4.

9. Alexander, John B., to Wife, Aug. 18, 1862; Krick, Robert K., *Stonewall Jackson at Cedar Mountain* (Chapel Hill: University of North Carolina Press, 1990), p. 204; Hickerson, *Echoes of Happy Valley*, p. 84; Collins, Noah, p. 27; Hickerson, *Echoes of Happy Valley*, p. 84.

10. Wiggins, "Thirty-seventh Regiment," p. 655; Hickerson, *Echoes of Happy Valley*, p. 84.

11. Collins, Noah, p. 28.

12. Krick, *Stonewall Jackson at Cedar Mountain*, pp. 344–5.

13. Collins, Noah, p. 29.

14. Green, Brazilla C., to Uncle, Aug. 19, 1862.

15. Robertson, *A. P. Hill*, p. 114.

16. Alexander, *Reminiscences*, pp. 78–9.

17. *Ibid.*, p. 79.

18. Robertson, *A. P. Hill*, p. 117.

19. Hickerson, *Echoes of Happy Valley*, p. 85.

20. Brawley, "The Public Life and Military Career of Lawrence O'Bryan Branch," p. 193; Hickerson, *Echoes of Happy Valley*, p. 85; Wiggins, "Thirty-seventh Regiment," p. 656.

21. Hickerson, *Echoes of Happy Valley*, p. 85; Alexander, *Reminiscences*, p. 79.

22. McDaid, "Four Years of Arduous Service," p. 108.

23. Robertson, *A. P. Hill*, p. 125; Hennessy, John J., *Return to Bull Run: The Campaign and Battle of Second Manassas* (New York: Simon & Schuster, 1993), p. 438.

24. Harsh, Joseph L., *Taken at the Flood: Robert E. Lee and Confederate Strategy in the Maryland Campaign of 1862* (Kent, Ohio: Kent State University Press, 1999), p. 169.

25. Hickerson, *Echoes of Happy Valley*, p. 85; Morris, William G., to Wife, Sep. 2, 1862; Lane, "History of Lane's North Carolina Brigade," Vol. 8 (1880), p. 154; Hickerson, *Echoes of Happy Valley*, p. 85.

26. *Ibid.*, p. 86.

27. *Ibid.*, pp. 86–88.

28. Brawley, "The Public Life and Military Career of Lawrence O'Bryan Branch," p. 196.

29. Morris, William G., to Wife, Sep. 2, 1862.

30. Harsh, *Taken at the Flood*, pp. 72, 88.

31. Morris, William G., to Wife, Sep. 7, 1862.

32. Harsh, *Taken at the Flood*, p. 175.

33. *Ibid.*, pp. 182–83.

34. Lane, "History of Lane's North Carolina Brigade," Vol. 8, p. 193.

35. Morris, William G., to Wife, Sep. 23, 1862; Robertson, *A. P. Hill*, 139; Harsh, *Taken at the Flood*, p. 321; Morris, William G., to Wife, Sep. 24, 1862.

36. *Official Records*, Vol. 10, Part 1, pp. 452–53; *Ibid.*, pp. 454–55.

37. *Ibid.*, p. 467; Morris, William G., to Wife, Sep. 23, 1862.

38. Wiggins, "Thirty-seventh Regiment," p. 656; Robertson, *A. P. Hill*, p. 147.

39. *Confederate Veteran*, Vol. 12, p. 234; *Raleigh Register*, Oct. 1, 1862; Lane, James H. (Papers, Auburn University), Petition, Officers of Lane's Brigade (ca. 1862)—Memorial for Brigadier General L. O'Brien Branch.

40. Wiggins, "Thirty-seventh Regiment," p. 657; Lane "History of Lane's North Carolina Brigade," Vol. 8, p. 195; Morris, William G., to Wife, Sep. 23, 1862; Alexander, *Reminiscences*, p. 27.

41. Robertson, *A. P. Hill*, p. 151.

Chapter 7

1. Manari and Jordan, *North Carolina Troops*, pp. 475, 489.

2. Green, Brazilla C., to Aunt and Uncle, Sep. 19, 1862; Morris, William G., to Wife, Sep. 23, 1862; *Ibid.*, Sep. 24, 1862; *Ibid.*, Sep. 28, 1862; *Ibid.*, Oct. 4, 1862.

3. Manari and Jordan, *North Carolina Troops*, p. 468.

4. Thirty-seventh Letter Book, p. 7; Teague, Andrew J., to Wife, Oct. 25, 1862, *Kinfolk*, Vol. 15, Issue 1, 1997 (Alexander County Historical Society), p. 16; Morris, William G., to Wife, Oct. 5, 1862; Tally, John, to Wife, Oct. 11, 1862.

5. Tally, John, to Wife, Oct. 11, 1862; Thirty-seventh Letter Book, p. 17; Compiled Service Record, Paul Hartzog.

6. Alexander, John B., to Wife, Oct. 11, 1862; Morris, William G., to Wife, Oct. 10, 1862.

7. Thirty-seventh Letter Book, p. 18.

8. Phillips, "James Henry Lane," p. 102.

9. *Ibid.*, p. 37.

10. *Ibid.*

11. Complied Service Record, William Y. Farthing; Manari and Jordan, *North Carolina Troops*, p. 529.

12. Morris, William G., to Wife, Nov. 19, 1862.

13. Robertson, *A. P. Hill*, p. 158; Shull, Finley P., to Cousin, Dec. 21, 1862 (Mary Councill papers).

14. Morris, William G., to Wife, Dec. 18, 1862.

15. *Ibid.*; Lane, James H., "History of Lane's North Carolina Brigade," Vol. 8, p. 399; Collins, Noah, p. 34; Morris, William G., to Wife, Dec. 18, 1862; Barber, William M., draft of official report, Thirty-seventh Letter Book.

16. Morris, William G., to Wife, Dec. 28, 1862.

17. *Ibid.*, Jan. 22, 1863.

18. Green, Brazilla C., to Uncle, Jan. 12, 1863.

19. Miller, William Harrison, "William Harrison Miller, Confederate States Army 'Memories of the War Between the States,'" *The Heritage of Ashe County*, Vol. 2, p. 28.

20. Kennedy, Francis Milton, *Diary*, 1863–1864 (Southern Historical Collection, University of North Carolina, Chapel Hill, N.C.), p. 2; Collins, Noah, p. 35; Wiley, Bell Irvin, *The Life of Johnny Reb* (Baton Rouge: Louisiana State University Press, 1943), p. 60.

21. Miller, William H., "Memories of the War"

p. 23; Brazilla C. Green, to Aunt and Uncle, Jan. 12, 1863; Smith, Bennett, to Wife, May 17, 1863; Teague, Andrew J., to Wife, Apr. 7, 1863; Morris, William G., to Wife, Apr. 15, 1863; Council, Jordan S., to Wife, undated.

22. Alexander, John B., to Wife, Feb. 25, 1863.

23. Smith, Bennett, to Wife, Mar. 24, 1863; Harrison, William H., "Memories of the War," p. 23; Smith, Bennett, to Wife, Mar. 24, 1863.

24. Teague, Andrew J., to Wife, Feb. 12, 1863; *Ibid.*, Apr. 7, 1863.

25. Morris, William G., to Wife, Jan. 22, 1863; *Ibid.*, Jan. 29, 1863; Smith, Bennett, to Wife, Feb. 28, 1863; Alexander, John B., to Wife, Feb. 25, 1863; Smith, Bennett, to Wife, Apr. 16, 1863; Teague, Andrew J., to Wife, Apr. 7, 1863; Tally, John, to Wife, Apr. 5, 1863.

26. Francis, Robert, to Cousin, Jan. 18, 1863 (private collection); Smith, Bennett, to Wife, Jan. 27, 1863.

27. Alexander, John B., to Wife, Feb. 12, 1863; Manari and Jordan, *North Carolina Troops*, p. 508.

28. Smith, Bennett, to Wife, Jan. 27, 1863; Horton, Nathan, to Mother, Feb. 20, 1863 (Mary Council Papers); Manari and Jordan, *North Carolina Troops*, p. 544; Davis, Keith, email to author, Sep. 18, 2001.

29. Alexander, John B., to Wife, Feb. 21, 1863; Manari and Jordan, *North Carolina Troops*, p. 587; Collins, Noah, p. 35; Smith, Bennett, to Wife, Apr. 7, 1863; Wiggins, Octavius A., "Address to the United Daughters of the Confederacy" (North Carolina Department of Cultural Resources, Division of Archives and History, Raleigh, N.C.), p. 1; Holland, Marion L., to Mother and Father, undated (Gaston County Historical Society); Robinson, Daniel C., postwar interview (private collection); Smith, Bennett, to Wife, Apr. 16, 1863.

30. Manari and Jordan, *North Carolina Troops*, p. 589.

31. Alexander, John B., to Wife, Apr. 1, 1863.

32. Morris, William G., to Wife, Dec. 28, 1862; Smith, Bennett, to Wife, Feb. 26, 1863; Alexander, John B., to Wife, Feb. 12, 1863; Smith, Bennett, to Wife, Mar. 24, 1863; Teague, Andrew J., to Wife, Apr. 7, 1863; Morris, William G., to Wife, Dec. 28, 1862.

33. *Ibid.*, Apr. 15, 1863; Teague, Andrew J., to Wife, Apr. 7, 1863; Morris, William G., to Wife, Mar. 27, 1863; Holland, Marion L., to Mother and Father, no date; Morris, William G., to Wife, Mar. 27, 1863; *Ibid.*, Apr. 15, 1863; Chamber, Daniel L., to *Biblical Recorder*, quoted in Jones, J. William, *Christ in the Camp* (Harrisonburg, VA: Sprinkle Publications, 1887, 1986), p. 39.

34. Jones, J. William, *Christ in the Camp*, p. 332; Nicholson, William A., to *Biblical Recorder*, Sep. 10, 1862.

35. Morris, William G., to Wife, Mar. 27, 1863; Kennedy, Francis M., *Diary*, p. 10.

36. McDaid, William, "Four Years of Arduous Service," p. 167.

Chapter 8

1. Sears, Stephen W., *Chancellorsville* (New York: Houghton Mifflin Company, 1996), p. 116.

2. Wiggins, Octavius, "Thirty-seventh Regiment," p. 658.

3. Kennedy, Francis M., Diary, Apr. 30, 1863; Robertson, James I., *A. P. Hill*, p. 181; Furgurson, Ernest B., *Chancellorsville 1863: The Souls of the Brave* (New York: Alfred A. Knopf, 1992), p. 120; Wiggins, Octavius, "Address to the United Daughters of the Confederacy," p. 2.

4. Robertson, James I., *A. P. Hill*, p. 182; Wiggins, Octavius, "Address to the United Daughters of the Confederacy," p. 2.

5. Battle, Lewis, to Mother and Father, May 13, 1863; Wiggins, Octavtius, "Address to the United Daughters of the Confederacy," p. 3.

6. Collins, Noah, p. 36; Tally, John, to Wife, May 10, 1863.

7. Furgurson, *Chancellorsville 1863*, p. 195; Wiggins, "Address to the United Daughters of the Confederacy," p. 4; *Ibid.*, p. 5; Lane, James H., to Augustus C. Hamlin, 1892, p. 4 (James H. Lane Collection, Auburn University).

8. Lane, James H., "History of Lane's North Carolina Brigade," Vol. 8, p. 489.

9. Lowery, Ray, email to the author, Jun. 12, 2001.

10. Furgurson, *Chancellorsville 1863*, p. 223; Nicholson and Barber, quoted in McDaid, "Four Years of Arduous Service," p. 283.

11. Tally, John, to Wife, May 10, 1863; Sears, *Chancellorsville*, p. 321; Wiggins, "Address to the United Daughters of the Confederacy," p. 7; Bost, Jackson L., to Rev. E. L. Davis, May 11, 1863; Tally, John, to Wife, May 10, 1863.

12. Sexton, Thorton, to Mother and Father, May 9, 1863 (Manuscript Department, Duke University Library); Wiggins, "Address to the United Daughters of the Confederacy," p. 7; Collins, p. 37; Bost, Jackson L., to Rev. E. L. Davis, May 11, 1863; Collins, pp. 37–8.

13. Manari and Jordan, *North Carolina Troops*, pp. 468–9; Lane, "History of Lane's North Carolina Brigade," Vol. 8, p. 492; Baucom, John H., email to the author, Apr. 26, 2000; Wiggins, "Thirty-seventh Regiment," p. 600.

14. *Ibid.*, 660; Lane, James H., to Augustus C. Hamlin, 1892; Bost, Jackson L., to Rev. E. L. Davis, May 11, 1863; Lane, James H., to Augustus C. Hamlin, 1892.

15. Smith, Bennett, to Wife, May 8, 1863; Tally, John, to Wife, May 10, 1863; Teague, Andrew J., to Wife, May 14, 1863; Nixon, Thomas, to Uncle, May 20, 1863 (Manuscript Department, Duke University Library); Tally, John, to Wife, May 10, 1863; Wiggins, "Address to the United Daughters of the Confederacy," p. 8; Furgurson, *Chancellorsville 1863*, p. 342; Wiggins, "Address to the United Daughters of the Confederacy," p. 8; Nixon, Thomas, to Uncle, May 20, 1863; Haigh, Charles T., *Diary* (Virginia Military Institute Archives, Lexington, VA), May 11, 1863.

16. Smith, Bennett, to Wife, May 8, 1863; *Ibid.*, May 17, 1863; Sexton, Thornton, to Father and Mother, May 16, 1863.

17. Bost, Jackson L., to Rev. E. L. Davis, May 11, 1863.

18. Norwood, Thomas L., to Uncle, Jun. 16, 1863; Nixon, Thomas, to Uncle, May 20, 1863; Smith, Bennett, to Wife, May 17, 1863.

19. Smith, Bennett, to Wife, May 28, 1863.

Chapter 9

1. Coddington, Edward B., *The Gettysburg Campaign: A Study in Command* (New York: Scribner's, 1968, Morningside Reprint, 1979).

2. Hassler, William Woods, *One of Lee's Best Men: The Civil War Letters of General William Dorsey Pender* (Chapel Hill: University of North Carolina Press, 1965, 1999) pp. 3–6; Warner, *Generals in Gray*, p. 233.

3. Trudeau, Noah Andre, "False Start at Franklin's Crossing," *American's Civil War* (Vol. 14, Num. 3, Jul. 2001), pp. 32–37, 86–88; Tally, John, to Wife, Jun. 11, 1863.

4. Coddington, *The Gettysburg Campaign*, p. 76.

5. Lewis W. Battle, quoted in McDaid, "Four Years of Arduous Service," p. 202; Coddington, *The Gettysburg Campaign*, p. 113; Robinson, *A. P. Hill*, p. 201.

6. Hassler, *One of Lee's Best Men*, p. 254; Phillips, "James Henry Lane," p. 143; Robertson, *A. P. Hill*, p. 203; Coddington, *The Gettysburg Campaign*, p. 259.

7. Royster, Iowa, to Mother, Jun. 29, 1863 (Southern Historical Collection, Chapel Hill); Morris, William G., to Wife, Jun. 22, 1863.

8. Pfanz, Harry W., *Gettysburg: The First Day* (Chapel Hill: University of North Carolina Press, 2001), p. 24; Alexander, William D., *Diary*, Jun. 29–30, 1863 (Southern Historical Collection, Chapel Hill).

9. Royster, Iowa, to Mother, Jun. 29, 1863.

10. Morris, William G., to Wife, Jun. 29, 1863.

11. Elmore, Thomas L., "A Meteorological and Astronomical Chronology of the Gettysburg Campaign," *Gettysburg Magazine* (Vol. 13, Jul. 1995), pp. 7–19; Alexander, William D., *Diary*, Jul. 1, 1863.

12. Pfanz, *Gettysburg: The First Day*, p. 300; Miller, J. Michael, "Perrin's Brigade on Jul. 1, 1863," *Gettysburg Magazine* (Vol. 13, pp. 22–32), p. 24; McDaid, "Four Years of Arduous Service," p. 207; Brown, Varina D., *A Colonel at Gettysburg and Spotsylvania Court House* (Columbia: The State Company, 1931), p. 41; Miller, "Perrin's Brigade," p. 24.

13. *Official Records*, Vol. 27, part 2, p. 665.

14. Phillips, "James Henry Lane," p. 150.

15. *Official Records*, Vol. 27, part 2, p. 664.

16. *Official Records*, Vol. 27, part 2, p. 665; Alexander, William D., *Diary*, Jul. 2, 1863; Pfanz, Harry W., *Gettysburg: Culp's Hill and Cemetery Hill* (Chapel Hill: University of North Carolina Press, 1993), p. 148.

17. Tucker, Glenn, *High Tide at Gettysburg* (New York: Bobbs-Merrill Company, Inc., 1958), p. 296; Warner, *Generals in Gray*, pp. 233–34; *Official Records*, Vol. 27, part 2, p. 666.

18. Wert, Jeffry D., *Gettysburg: Day Three* (New York, Simon and Schuster, 2001), p. 34; Elmore, "A Meteorological and Astronomical Chronology of the Gettysburg Campaign," p. 14; Phillips, "James Henry Lane," p. 152.

19. Cooksey, Paul Clark, "The Plan for Pickett's Charge," *Gettysburg Magazine* (Vol. 22, 2000, p. 66–79), p. 67.

20. Warner, *Generals in Gray*, p. 310.

21. Stewart, George R., *Pickett's Charge: A Microhistory of the Final Attack at Gettysburg, July 3, 1863* (Greenwich, CN: Fawcett Publications, 1959), p. 106; Priest, John Michael, "Lee's Gallant 600?" *North & South* (Vol. 1, No. 6, 1998: 42–56), p. 45; Taylor, Michael W., "North Carolina in the Pickett-Pettigrew-Trimble Charge at Gettysburg," *Gettysburg Magazine* (Vol. 8, Jan. 1993: 67–93), p. 76; Priest, John Michael, *Into the Fight: Pickett's Charge at Gettysburg* (Shippensburg, PA: White Maine Company Publishing, 1998), pp. 51–53, 92; Wiggins, "Thirty-seventh Regiment," p. 661; Wert, *Gettysburg: Day Three*, p. 129.

22. Wiggins, "Thirty-seventh Regiment," p. 661.

23. *Ibid.*, Alexander, William D., *Diary*, Jul 3, 1863; Wiggins, "Thirty-seventh Regiment," p. 661.

24. Taylor, "North Carolina in the Pickett-Pettigrew-Trimble Charge at Gettysburg," p. 76; most of Brokenbrough's troops probably passed to the left of Lane's brigade. The troops that the Seventh had to force around to their right were other elements of Pettigrew's command, probably from Davis's and Marshall's brigades.

25. *Ibid.*, pp. 73–78; Stewart, *Pickett's Charge*, p. 175; Campbell, Eric A., "'Remember Harper's Ferry!' The Degradation, Humiliation, and Redemption of Col. George L. Willard's Brigade, Part 2," *Gettysburg Magazine* (Vol. 8, 1993), p. 105; Taylor, Michael W., "The Unmerited Censure of Two Maryland Staff Officers, Maj. Osmun Latrobe and First Lt. W. Stuart Symington," *Gettysburg Magazine* (Vol. 8, 1993), see note on page 78.

26. Stewart, *Pickett's Charge*, p. 212; Priest, *Into the Fight*, p. 156; Warner, *Generals in Gray*, p. 311.

27. Taylor, "The Unmerited Censure," see note p. 78; Priest, *Into the Fight*, p. 135, 157; Taylor, "North Carolina in the Pickett-Pettigrew-Trimble Charge," pp. 77–8.

28. Tucker, *High Tide at Gettysburg*, p. 371.

29. *Raleigh Daily Progress*, Aug. 11, 1863; Alexander, William D., *Diary*, Jul. 3, 1863; Puett, Minnie S., *History of Gaston County* (Charlotte: Laney-Smith, Inc., 1939, 1998), p. 208; *Official Records*, Vol. 27, part 2, p. 667.

30. Barnes, Smith, to Wife, Jul. 12, 1863, in Allen, Sara C., *The Heritage of Alexander County* (Winston-Salem, N.C.: Hunter Publishing Corporation, 1986).

31. Alexander, William D., *Diary*, Jul. 4, 1863; Wiggins, "Thirty-seventh Regiment," p. 661; Alexander, William D., *Diary*, Jul. 12, 1863: Wert, *Gettysburg, Day Three*, pp. 171, 187.

32. Norwood, Thomas L., to Father, Jul. 16, 1863.

33. Alexander, William D., *Diary*, Jul. 13, 1863; McDaid, "Four Years of Arduous Service," p. 224; *Official Records*, Vol. 27, part 2, p. 667.

Chapter 10

1. Morris, William G., to Wife, Aug. 27, 1863; Downer, Edward T., "Johnson's Island," *Civil War History* (Vol. 8, Num. 2, 1962), pp. 202–217.

2. Beitzell, Edwin W., *Point Lookout Prison Camp for Confederates* (Leonardtown, MD: St. Mary's County Historical Society, 1983), pp. 1, 56.

3. Pittard, Pen Lile, and W. C. Watts, *Alexander County's Confederates* (No publication information, c.1960), p. 65.

4. Warner, *Generals in Gray*, pp. 337–8; Patterson, Gerard A., "Wilcox the Paradox," *Civil War Times Illustrated* (Vol. 39, Num. 6, Dec. 2000), pp 56–62.

5. Phillips, "James Henry Lane," pp. 167–68, 202.

6. Dunlop, W. S., *Lee's Sharpshooters; or, the Forefront of Battle* (reprint Dayton: Morningside, 2000), pp. 18–19.

7. Lane, "History of Lane's Brigade," Vol. 9, p. 226; Dunlop, *Lee's Sharpshooters*, pp. 19–22; Shepherd, Ruth Weaver, *The Heritage of Ashe County* (Winston-Salem, N.C.: Hunter Publishing Corporation, 1984).

8. Dozier, Graham Town, "The Eighteenth North Carolina Infantry Regiment, C.S.A." (Master's thesis: Virginia Polytechnic Institute, 1992), p. 111; Weston, J. A., "Thirty-Third Regiment," Clark, Walter, ed., *Histories of the Several Regiments*

and Battalions from North Carolina in the Great War, 1861 to 1865 (Raleigh: E. M. Uzzell, 1901), p. 568; Henderson, William D., *The Road to Bristoe Station* (Lynchburg: H. E. Howard Inc., 1987), p. 26; Phillips, "James Henry Lane," p. 168; Wiggins, "Thirty-seventh Regiment," p. 662.

9. Caldwell, J. F. J., *The History of a Brigade of South Carolinian* (Philadelphia: King and Baird, 1866), p. 156; Robertson, *A. P. Hill*, p. 231.

10. Tally, John W., to Wife, Jul. 30, 1863; Speer, Allen P., *Voices from Cemetery Hill: The Civil War Diary, Reports, and Letters of Colonel William Henry Asbury Speer (1861–1864)* (Johnson City, TN: The Overmountain Press, 1997), p. 110.

11. *Raleigh Register*, Aug. 12, 1863.

12. *Western Democrat*, Sep. 15, 1863.

13. Teague, Andrew J., to Wife, Sep. 4, 1863; McDaid, "Four Years of Arduous Service," p. 233; Teague, Andrew J., to Wife, Sep. 4, 1863.

14. Norwood, Thomas L., to Uncle, Sep. 25, 1863.

15. Sexton, Thorton, to Wife, Nov. 13, 1863.

16. McDaid, "Four Years of Arduous Service," p. 235.

17. *Ibid.*, p. 235–6.

18. Kennedy, *Diary*, Nov. 14, 1863; Norwood, Thomas L., to Uncle, May 4, 1864; Campbell, William F., to Wife, Apr. 6, 1864 (*Letters, 1863–1864*, private collection).

19. Holland, Marion L., to Mother and Father, Mar. 13, 1864 (*Letters, 1863–64*, Gaston County Historical Society).

20. Sexton, Thorton, to Mother and Father, Oct. 5, 1863; Henderson, *The Road to Bristoe Station*, pp. 60, 72, 74, 84, 103–4.

21. Caldwell, *History of a Brigade of South Carolinians*, p. 159.

22. Henderson, *The Road to Bristoe Station*; Phillips, "James Henry Lane," p. 171.

23. Tally, John W., to Wife, Oct. 27, 1863; Wiggins, "Thirty-seventh Regiment," p. 663; Caldwell, *History of a Brigade of South Carolinians*, pp. 161–62.

24. Tally, John W., to Wife, Oct. 27, 1863; Alexander, *Diary*, Nov. 4, 1863; Norwood, Thomas L., to Uncle, Oct. 31, 1863.

25. Tally, John W., to Wife, Nov. 13, 1863; Sexton, Thorton, to Mother and Father, Nov. 13, 1863.

26. Graham, Martin F., and George F. Skoch, *Mine Rune: A Campaign of Lost Opportunities, October 21, 1863-May 1, 1864* (Lynchburg, VA: H. E. Howard, 1987), pp. 71, 74.

27. Black, John, to Wife, Dec. 4, 1863 (in Thorton Sexton letters); Sexton, Thorton, to Father and Mother, undated.

28. Norwood, Thomas L., to Uncle, Oct. 31, 1863; Tally, John W., to Wife, Jan. 4, 1864; Norwood, Thomas L., to Uncle, Oct. 31, 1863; *Ibid.*, Sep. 25, 1863.

29. Tommie to "Mamie," Jan. 20, [1864] (Giles

family papers, Southern Historical Collection, University of North Carolina). It is unclear whom this letter is from. It was written from "Headquarters, 37th."

30. Childers, Calvin, to Nancy Welch, Dec. 10, 1863 (Thorton Sexton letters).

31. Campbell, William F., to Father and Mother, Dec. 29, 1864.

32. Councill, Jordan S., to Wife, Jan. 17, 1864.

33. Jones, *Christ in the Camp*, p. 352; Tommie to "Mamie," Jan. 20, 1864; Thirty-seventh Letter Book, vol. 2, p. 28.

34. Sexton, Thorton, to Father, Jan. 20, 1864; *Ibid.*, Feb. 8, 1864.

35. Collins, Noah, p. 47; Teague, Andrew J., to Wife, Jan. 9, 1864; Wiggins, "Thirty-seventh Regiment," p. 664.

36. Collins, Noah, p. 48–49; Wiggins, "Thirty-seventh Regiment," p. 664.

37. Norwood, Thomas L., to Uncle, Jan. 30, 1864; Tally, John W., to Wife, Dec. 15, 1863; *Ibid.*, Jan. 4, 1864; Teague, Andrew J., to Wife, Jan. 1, 1864.

38. Thirty-seventh Letter Book, Vol. 2, p. 22.

39. Phillips, "James Henry Lane," p. 174; Holland, Marion L., to Wife, Mar. 13, 1864; Collins, Noah, p. 47.

40. Sexton, Thorton, to Mother and Father, Feb. 8, 1864; Tally, John W., to Wife, Feb. 9, 1864.

41. Norwood, Thomas L., to Uncle, Oct. 31, 1863.

Chapter 11

1. Wiggins, "Thirty-seventh Regiment," p. 665; Power, J. Tracy, *Lee's Miserables: Life in the Army of Northern Virginia from the Wilderness to Appomattox* (Chapel Hill: University of North Carolina Press, 1998), p. 18.

2. Wiggins, "Thirty-seventh Regiment," p. 665.

3. *Ibid.*, Lane, "History of Lane's North Carolina Brigade," Vol. 9, p. 127.

4. *Ibid.*, p. 128.

5. *Ibid.*, vol. 9, p. 146.

6. *Ibid.*, vol. 9, pp. 146–7.

7. Wiggins, "Thirty-seventh Regiment," p. 666; Lane, "History of Lane's North Carolina Brigade," Vol. 9, p. 146; Weston, "Thirty-third Regiment," p. 571; Alexander, William D., undated letter.

8. Lane, "History of Lane's North Carolina Brigade," Vol. 9, p. 148; Weston, "Thirty-third Regiment," p. 572; Wiggins, "Thirty-seventh Regiment," p. 667.

9. *Ibid.*, Lane, "History of Lane's North Carolina Brigade," p. 149.

10. Wiggins, "Thirty-seventh Regiment," p. 667; Lane, "History of Lane's North Carolina Brigade," p. 151; Parker, Thomas H., *History of the 51st Regiment of P. V. and V. V.: From Its Organization at Camp Curtin, Harrisburg, Pa., in 1861, to Its Being Mustered Out of the United States Service at Alexandria, Va., July 27th, 1865* (Salem, Mass: Higginson Book Co., 1869, 2000), pp. 547–550; *Official Records*, Vol. 36, Part 1, pp. 947–950.

11. Lane, "History of Lane's North Carolina Brigade," p. 150. Because the battles of the Wilderness and Spotsylvania Court House are so close in date and place, the dates of casualties are sometimes unclear in the Compiled Service Records.

12. Lane, "History of Lane's North Carolina Brigade," p. 150.

13. Wiggins, "Thirty-seventh Regiment," p. 668.

14. Lieutenant Grimsley, quoted in Rhea, Gordon C., *The Battles for Spotsylvania Court House and the Road to Yellow Tavern, May 7–12, 1864* (Baton Rouge: Louisiana State University Press, 1994), p. 301; Wiggins, "Thirty-seventh Regiment," p. 668.

15. Speer, *Voices from Cemetery Hill*, pp. 133–34.

16. *Ibid.*, p. 134.

17. Miller, J. Michael, *"Even to Hell Itself": The North Anna Campaign* (Lynchburg, VA: H. E. Howard, Inc., 1989), p. 51.

18. Lane, "History of Lane's North Carolina Brigade," p. 247.

19. Joslyn, Mauriel, *Captives Immortal: The Story of 600 Confederate Officers and the United States Prisoner of War Policy* (Shippensburg, PA: White Mane Publishing Company, Inc. 1996), p. 22.

20. *Ibid.*, p. 48.

21. *Ibid.*, p. 58.

22. *Ibid.*, p. 65.

23. *Ibid.*, p. 85.

24. *Ibid.*, pp. 89, 99, 100.

25. *Ibid.*, pp. 94–97.

26. *Ibid.*, p. 142.

Chapter 12

1. Speer, *Voices from Cemetery Hill*, p. 135.

2. Weston, "Thirty-third Regiment," p. 574; Lane, James H., "Twenty-eighth Regiment," Clark, Walter, ed., *Histories of the Several Regiments and Battalions from North Carolina in the Great War, 1861 to 1865* (Raleigh: E. M. Uzzell, 1901), p. 480; Speer, *Voices from Cemetery Hill*, p. 135.

3. Phillips, "James Henry Lane," p. 192.

4. Branch, Paul, "John Decatur Barry," *North Carolina Biographical Dictionary*, vol. 1, pp. 104–5.

5. Speer, *Voices from Cemetery Hill*, p. 136; Tally, John W., to Wife, Jun. 7, 1864.

6. Power, *Lee's Miserables*, p. 70.

7. McDaid, "Four Years of Arduous Service," p. 292; Speer, *Voices from Cemetery Hill*, p. 139.

8. Trudeau, Noah Andre, *The Last Citadel: Petersburg, Virginia, June 1864–April 1865* (Baton Rouge: Louisiana State University Press, 1991), p. 68.

9. Speer, *Voices from Cemetery Hill*, p. 138; McDaid, "Four Years of Arduous Service," p. 294; Manari and Jordan, *North Carolina Troops*, pp. 585–586.

10. Speer, *Voices from Cemetery Hill*, p. 142.

11. *Ibid.*, p. 144.

12. Harris, J. G., to James H. Lane, Aug. 25, 1864 (Lane papers, Auburn University); Bost, Jackson L., to James H. Lane, Aug. 29, 1864.

13. *Ibid.*

14. Suderow, Bryce, "Glory Denied: First Deep Bottom," *North & South* (Vol. 3, Num. 7, Sept. 2000, 17-32), p. 29.

15. *Official Records*, Vol. 42, Pt. 2, p. 1185; Warner, *Generals in Gray*, p. 61.

16. Suderow, "Glory Denied," p. 30.

17. Lane, "History of Lane's North Carolina Brigade," Vol. 9, p. 243.

18. Bost, Jackson L., to James H. Lane, Aug. 29, 1864.

19. *Ibid.*

20. Hanna, Thomas M., to wife, undated letter (Collins, J. M., email to the author, Sep. 27, 2001).

21. Lane, "History of Lane's North Carolina Brigade," Vol. 9, p. 246.

22. *Ibid.*, p. 354; McLaurin, "Eighteenth Regiment," p. 59.

23. Norwood, Thomas L., to Uncle, Sep. 11, 1864.

24. Dunlop, *Lee's Sharpshooters*, p. 206.

25. Collins, Noah, p. 62

26. *Ibid.*, pp. 62–63; Lane, "History of Lane's North Carolina Brigade," Vol. 9, pg. 355: Lee, Robert E., to Edward A. Barbour (Barber), Aug. 15, 1866 (private collection).

27. Collins, Noah, p. 63; Bost, Jackson L., to James H. Lane, Oct. 6, 1864; Collins, Noah, p. 63; Lane, "History of Lane's North Carolina Brigade," Vol. 9, p. 413.

28. Lane, "History of Lane's North Carolina Brigade," Vol. 9, p. 413; pp. 414–415; Collins, Noah, pp. 63–64; Lane, "History of Lane's North Carolina Brigade," Vol. 9, p. 356.

29. Alexander, William D., *Diary*, Oct. 3, 1864; Collins, Noah, p. 64.

30. Alexander, William D., *Diary*, Oct. 4, 1864; Norwood, Thomas L., to Uncle, Oct. 22, 1864; Collins, Noah, p. 63; Lane, "History of Lane's North Carolina Brigade," Vol. 9, p. 414.

31. Lane, "History of Lane's North Carolina Brigade," Vol. 9, p. 414; Collins, Noah, p. 65; Alexander, William D., *Diary*, Oct. 9, 1864.

32. Norwood, Thomas L., to Uncle, Oct. 22, 1864.

33. Lane, James H., "Glimpses of Army Life in 1864," *Southern Historical Society Papers* (Vol. 18, pp. 406–422), p. 419; Alexander, William D., *Diary*, Oct. 30, 1864.

34. Alexander, *Diary*, Oct. 30, 1864.

35. Lane, "Glimpses of Army Life in 1864," Vol. 19, p. 416.

36. Collins, Noah, p. 67; Alexander, William D., *Diary*, Dec. 12–13, 1864; Collins, Noah, p. 68.

37. Lane, "Glimpses of Army Life in 1864," Vol. 19, pp. 418–19.

38. Alexander, William D., *Diary*, Dec. 23, 1864; Lane, "Glimpses of Army Life in 1864," pp. 419–420; Alexander, William D., *Diary*, Dec. 25, 1864.

Chapter 13

1. Dunlap, *Lee's Sharpshooters*, p. 240.

2. Collins, Noah, p. 68.

3. Eaves, Etta Snyder, *James Addison Myers — My Grandfather* (unpublished manuscript, 1926).

4. Pittard, Pen Lile, and W. C. Watts, *Alexander County's Confederates* (no publication information, c.1960), p. 65.

5. Collins, Noah, p. 70; Alexander, William D., *Diary*, Feb. 7, 1865.

6. *Ibid.*, Mar. 12, 1865; Collins, Noah, p. 71.

7. Greene, A. Wilson, *Breaking the Backbone of the Rebellion: The Final Battles of the Petersburg Campaign*, (Mason City, Iowa: Savas Publishing Company, 2000), p. 119; Collins, Noah, pp. 75–76; Greene, *Breaking the Backbone of the Rebellion*, p. 125.

8. Collins, Noah, pp. 72–73.

9. Greene, *Breaking the Backbone of the Rebellion*, pp. 201–2.

10. *Ibid.*, pp. 201–205.

11. Alexander, William D., *Diary*, Mar. 28, 1865; Greene, *Breaking the Backbone of the Rebellion*, pp. 219, 233, 271, 298.

12. *Ibid.*, p. 261.

13. Alexander, William D., *Diary*, Apr. 2, 1865; Wiggins, "Thirty-seventh Regiment," p. 671; Greene, *Breaking the Backbone of the Rebellion*, pp. 298–9.

14. Wiggins, "Thirty-seventh Regiment," p. 671.

15. Greene, *Breaking the Backbone of the Rebellion*, p. 370; Alexander, William D., *Diary*, Apr. 2, 1865; Robertson, *A. P. Hill*, pp. 314–318.

16. Greene, *Breaking the Backbone of the Rebellion*, p. 382; Garrison, Angelum, "Saw General Lee at Petersburg" (*Confederate Veteran*, Volume 16), p. 514; Snow, George H., to James H. Lane in "Defence of Fort Gregg," *Southern Historical Society Papers* (Vol. 3, pp. 19–28), p. 23; Greene, *Breaking the Backbone of the Rebellion*, pp. 386–7; Wilcox, Cadmus M., "Defence of Batteries Gregg and Whitworth and the Evacuation of Petersburg" (*Southern Historical Society Papers*, 4 [1878]: 19–33), p. 28.

17. Greene, *Breaking the Backbone of the Rebellion*, p. 393; Rigler, D. M., to James H. Lane, Jun.. 17, 1867, quoted in "Defence of Fort Gregg," p. 27; Garrison, "Saw General Lee at Petersburg," p. 514.

18. Rigler, D. M., to James H. Lane, Jun. 17, 1865; Wilcox, Cadmus M., "Defence of Batteries Gregg," p. 29.

19. Greene, *Breaking the Backbone of the Rebellion*, p. 406.

20. Alexander, William D., *Diary*, Apr. 2, 1865.

21. Trudeau, *The Last Citadel: Petersburg, Virginia, June 1864 — April 1865*, p. 401.

22. Wilcox, Camdus, quoted in Chapman, Craig S., *More Terrible Than Victory: North Carolina's Bloody Bethel Regiment, 1861–1865* (Washington: Brassey's, 1998) p. 301.

23. Calkins, Chris M., *Thirty-Six Hours Before Appomattox: The Battles of Sayler's Creek, High Bridge, Farmville and Cumberland Church* (Farmville, VA: Farmville Publishing, 1980), p. 43; Wilcox, Cadmus, quoted in Chapman, *More Terrible Than Victory*, p. 305.

24. Calkins, *Thirty-Six Hours Before Appomattox*, p. 47.

25. Alexander, William D., *Diary*, Apr. 9, 1865.

26. Abernathy, David, email to the author, Mar. 26, 2001; Alexander, William D., *Diary*, Apr. 9, 1865.

27. Nine, William G., and Ronald G. Wilson, *The Appomattox Paroles: April 9–15, 1865* (Lynchburg: H. E. Howard, Inc., 1989), p. 1.

28. Alexander, William D., *Diary*, Apr. 9, 1865; Nine and Wilson, *The Appomattox Paroles*, p. 4.

29. Alexander, William D., *Diary*, Apr. 10–12, 1865; Nine and Wilson, *The Appomattox Paroles*, p. 5.

30. Alexander, William D., *Diary*, Apr. 12–21, 1865.

31. Undated and untitled article, *Confederate Veteran*, Vol. 1, Num. 9, p. 273.

32. Eaves, *James Addison Myers — My Grandfather*, pp. 7–8.

Chapter 14

1. Alexander, William D., *Diary*, Apr. 20, 1865.

2. Wilson, William, family history written Jan. 7, 1941. Copy in author's possession.

3. Blackman, Ora, *Western North Carolina: Its Mountains and Its People to 1880* (Boone, N.C.: Appalachian Consortium Press, 1977), pp. 360–362.

4. Bowers, Claude G., *The Tragic Era: The Revolution After Lincoln* (Cambridge, Mass: The Riverside Press, 1929), p. 7; Morrill, James R., "North Carolina and the Administration of Brevet Major General Sickles," *North Carolina Historical Review* (Vol. 42, Num. 3, Jul. 1965: 291-305), p. 292.

5. Weir, Erica, "Veterans and Post-Traumatic Stress Disorder," *Canadian Medical Association Journal* (Vol. 163, Num. 9, Oct. 2000), p. 2; Talbot, John, "Combat Trauma in the American Civil War," *History Today* (Vol. 46, Num. 3, Mar. 1996: 47–54), p. 47; Tucker, Phebe, and Richard Trautman, "Understanding and Treating PTSD: Past, Present, and Future," *Bulletin of the Menninger Clinic* (Vol. 64, Num. 3, Summer 2000: 37–52), p. 2.

6. Gryder, Ray G. II, email to the author, Nov. 19, 1999; Horton, Era, email to the author, Dec. 3, 2000; Davis, Boyce W., email to the author, Sep. 27, 2001; Crawford, *Ashe County's Civil War*, p. 151.

7. "His Leg Amputated After Thirty-two Years," *Confederate Veteran* (Vol. 2), p. 203; Hollowell, Clarence, email to the author, Oct. 7, 1999.

8. Shepherd, Ruth Weaver, *The Heritage of Ashe County, Vols. 1 & 2* (Winston-Salem, N.C.: Hunter Publishing Corporation, 1984–), pp. 357–8.

9. "Charles Cochrane Lee," *North Carolina Biographical Dictionary* (Vol. 4), p. 43.

10. Barber, William Morris, *Compiled Service Record*; Interview with Betsy Barber Hawkins.

11. Parmerton, Velma L., email to the author, Sep. 22, 2001.

12. Culler, Robert W., email to the author, Apr. 24, 2000.

13. *Charlotte Daily Observer*, Apr. 17, 1906; York, Maurice C., *The Many Faces of Fort Defiance: A Report Submitted to Fort Defiance, Inc.* (Chapel Hill, 1979), pp. 159, 174–76.

14. Price, Roy, email to the author, Dec. 20, 2001.

15. Graham, Zeta, email to the author, Oct. 10, 2000.

16. *Highland Vidette*, undated article, copy in possession of author.

17. Hardy, *Biographical Roster*.

18. Jouse, Nancy, email to the author, Jun. 15, 2001.

19. Hickerson, *Happy Valley*, p. 162; Stuart, John C., Jr., *Our Family*, unpublished manuscript, copy in collection of author.

20. Renn, Lydia S., *The Reverend Robert Luckey Steele* (Wake Forest, NC: privately printed, 1976).

21. Puett, *History of Gaston County*, p. 208;

Bullman, Maudie-Keniston, email to the author, Aug. 26, 2000; Jetton, Kay F., email to the author, Jun. 21, 2001.

22. Lowery, Ray, email to the author, Jun. 12, 2001.

23. Thayer, D., email to the author, Apr. 10, 2001.

24. Armstrong, Thomas J., *Letter, August 26, 1865*, private collection; Kendrick, Virginia A. S., *The Heritage of Union County, North Carolina: 1842–1992* (Monroe, NC: Carolinas Genealogy Society, 1993), p. 93; Brown, William E., email to the author, Mar. 21, 2001; Stowe, Kay, email to the author, Jul. 17, 2001; Wingfield, Rebecca, email to the author, Mar. 29, 2000.

25. Gains, Julie H., email to the author, Jul. 4, 2001.

26. Young, Jo, email to the author, Aug. 16, 2001; Hartis, Timothy N., letter to the author, Jun. 3, 1999.

27. Armstrong, *Letter, August 26, 1865*; Coyne, Timothy C., email to the author, Aug. 19, 2001.

28. Reynolds, D. R., ed., *Charlotte Remembers*, (Charlotte Pub. Co., 1972), p. 13; Manari and Jordan, *North Carolina Troops*, p. 469; Dowd, Jerome, *Sketches of Prominent Living North Carolinians* (Raleigh: Edwards and Broughton, 1888), pp. 283–4.

29. Bisher, Catherine W., "A Strong Force of Ladies: Women, Politics, and Confederate Memorial Associations in Nineteenth-Century Raleigh," *North Carolina Historical Review* (Vol. 77, Num. 4, Oct. 2000: 455–491), pp. 455–7.

30. Linden-Ward, Blanche, "Strange but Genteel Pleasure Grounds: Tourist and Leisure Uses of Nineteenth-Century Rural Cemeteries," in Meyer, Richard E., ed., *Cemeteries and Gravemarkers: Voices of American Culture* (Logan, Utah: Utah State University Press, 1992), p. 293.

31. Bisher, "A Strong Force of Ladies," pp. 456, 459.

32. *Ibid.*, p. 467.

33. Rosenburg, R. B., *Living Monuments: Confederate Soldiers Homes in the New South* (Chapel Hill: University of North Carolina Press, 1993), p. 36; Hermon, Greg, email to the author, Mar. 16, 2002.

34. Manari and Jordan, *North Carolina Troops*, p. 533; Orrant, Jacob, Tennessee Confederate Pension Application.

35. *Monroe Enquirer*, Aug. 9, 1879; *Charlotte Democrat*, Sep. 12, 1890.

36. *Watauga Democrat*, Aug. 28, 1890; *Charlotte Observer*, Aug. 2, 1893.

37. *Watauga Democrat*, Sep. 6, 1917; *Ibid.*, Aug. 16, 1917.

38. Lawton, Ruth Jennings, et al., *The History of the United Daughters of the Confederacy, 1894–1955* (Raleigh: Edwards & Broughton Company, 1956), pp. 1–4.

39. *Ibid.*, pp. 145–7; *Confederate Veteran* (Jul. 1901, Vol. 9, Num. 7), p. 456.

40. *Confederate Veteran* (Vol. 3, 1996), pp. 12, 20–21; Deason, Edwin L., "Report from the Commander-in-Chief," *Confederate Veteran* (Vol. 6, 2001), pp. 2–3.

41. *Charlotte Chronicle*, May 11, 1883.

42. Dixon, Steve, email to the author, Jan. 10, 2002; Manari and Jordan, *North Carolina Troops*, pp. 567, 542.

43. *Ibid.*, pp. 473, 488.

44. Undated newspaper clipping, Royster Family Collection, Southern Historical Society.

45. Rollins, Richard, ed., *The Returned Battle Flags* (Redondo Beach, CA: Rank and File Publications, 1995), pp. iii, 32; Rose, Rebecca Ansell, *Colours of the Gray* (Richmond: Carter Printing Company, 2000), pp. 23, 37.

46. *Watauga Democrat*, partially dated newspaper clippings, 1927, 1928.

47. Martin, Debbie, email to the author, Feb. 1, 2002.

48. *Gastonia Gazette*, Jan. 31, 1941.

49. "Confederate Soldiers Receiving Markers," *Kinfolk*, Feb. 1997.

50. Davidson, Chalmers Gaston, *The Plantation World Around Davidson: The Story of North Mecklenburg "Before the War"* (Davidson, NC: Mecklenburg Historical Association, 1969), p. 22.

Appendix A

1. Military records state that Captain Hartzog died at home on Jun. 18, 1863. Family records state that he died of a gunshot wound to the stomach on Jun. 8, 1864.

2. Lieutenant Goodman was murdered at a dance in Jefferson, North Carolina, in 1867. No place of burial could be ascertained.

3. Military records spell this name as Collet A. Greer. Family records state his name as Catlett Aquilla Greer.

4. Private Ashley may have died prior to Mar. 1, 1864.

5. Records state that Private Coldiron died on Jun. 6 or 11, 1862. Manari and Jordan, *North Carolina Troops*, p. 474.

6. Military records state that Private Goss was 16 years old when he enlisted in 1861. Family records state that he was born on Jan. 4, 1840. Another source states that his birth date was Jan. 4, 1846.

7. Private Ham was declared missing at Gettysburg, PA, on Jul. 3, 1863. Manari and Jordan, *North Carolina Troops*, p. 476.

8. Sergeant McNeil was reported missing in action at or near Gravel Hill, Virginia, and never returned home. *Ibid.*, p. 479.

9. The Ashe County cemetery records have a listing for a Jacob Miller, a member of Company A, Thirty-seventh North Carolina Troops, who was born on 30 Jul. 1847, died on 31 Jan. 1923, and is buried at the John S. Miller Cemetery, Allegheny County. Hamilton, Russell, *Ashe County, N.C. Cemetery Records*, 2 Vols. (West Jefferson, NC: Creative Printers, 1999), Vol. 1, p. 474.

10. Private Mullis died between Jun. 5 and 9, 1862, of tetanus. Manari and Jordan, *North Carolina Troops*, p. 480.

11. Private Owens was reported missing in action on Nov. 10, 1863. He survived the war and applied for a pension in 1901 in Wilkes County under the name of Eligha Owens.

12. Ephraim Roark died of disease in Nashville while serving in Company G, Thirteenth Tennessee Cavalry (Union).

13. Private Vanzant was wounded between May 1 and 4, 1863, during the battle of Chancellorsville, Virginia, and died in Richmond, Virginia, of his wounds on May 19 or 20, 1863. *Ibid.*, p. 484.

14. Private Walters died between Dec. 22 and 24, 1861, of disease.

15. Private Ward died after May 27, 1862, of wounds received at Hanover Court House, Virginia.

16. Family history states that Private Weaver was taken prisoner and confined at Point Delaware, Delaware, where he died in 1864.

17. Private Yates died on Jul. 11 or 26, 1862, of disease. Manari and Jordan, *North Carolina Troops*, p. 484.

18. Wiggins served in Company K, but was reported as acting commander of Company B from Sep. 1864 to Feb. 1865.

19. Jordan's *North Carolina Troop Roster* lists an L. W. Carroll who applied for a pension, saying that he served in Company B. Jordan also lists a William Carroll in Company B. The author believes that these are the same person and that his name was Lewis William Carroll.

20. See note 19.

21. According to notes by Jeffery Weaver, this soldier's name was Franklin Green Gaultney. He died from wounds on Jul. 2, 1864, and is buried in Petersburg, VA.

22. Private Greer was executed for desertion sometime after Aug. 8, 1864.

23. Vinson Greer has a cenotaph at the McGuire Cemetery, Watauga County, North Carolina.

24. Private Milholland died of wounds after being transferred to a hospital in Salisbury, North Carolina.

25. Private Bell has a cenotaph at the Gilead ARP Cemetery, Mecklenburg County, North Carolina.

26. Records also state that Private Cochran died on Nov. 20, 1862.

27. Private Henderson has a cenotaph at the

Hopewell Presbyterian Church Cemetery, Mecklenburg County, North Carolina.

28. Thomas J. Kerns served as a lieutenant in Company C, but resigned on May 15, 1863, and reenlisted as a private in the same company.

29. Private McCoy might be buried in the Hopewell Presbyterian Church Cemetery, or this marker may be a cenotaph. McCoy was reported missing at Gettysburg, Pennsylvania, on Jul. 3, 1863. Manari and Jordan, *North Carolina Troops*, p. 505.

30. John W. Pettus served as a Lieutenant in Company C, but resigned on May 8, 1863, and reenlisted as a private.

31. Sergeant Wilson has a cenotaph at the Hopewell Presbyterian Church, Mecklenburg County, North Carolina.

32. Private Wilson has a cenotaph at the Hopewell Presbyterian Church Cemetery, Mecklenburg County, North Carolina.

33. Death dates for Private Worsham are Jun. 7, Jun. 12, or Jul. 7, 1862.

34. Private Green might be buried in the Watson Baptist Church Cemetery, Union County, North Carolina.

35. Private Griffin has a cenotaph in the Griffin Cemetery, Gaston County, North Carolina.

36. Records indicate that Private Tilman died on either Nov. 10, 1862, in Richmond, Virginia, or on Mar. 11, 1863, in Camp Gregg, Virginia.

37. Private Neil may be buried in the Long Creek Presbyterian Church Cemetery, Gaston County, North Carolina.

38. Cenotaph at Concord United Methodist Church, Gaston County, North Carolina.

39. Private Stevens is possibly buried in the Hopewell U. M. C. Cemetery, Watauga County, North Carolina

40. Private Teague has a cenotaph at the Munday-Teague Cemetery, Alexander County, North Carolina.

41. Private Coleman died between Jun. 30 and Jul. 5, 1862, of wounds received at Gaines's Mill, Virginia.

42. Private Frazier was originally interred in the Arlington National Cemetery, Washington, D.C., but was removed to the Oakwood Cemetery in Raleigh, North Carolina.

43. Private Pratt's date of death is recorded as either Sep. 20 or Sep. 30, 1862.

44. The date of death for Private Rowe is recorded as either Dec. 19, 1862, or Jan. 19, 1863.

45. Royster was first interred at Gettysburg, but was later reinterred in the Confederate section in the Oakwood Cemetery in Raleigh, North Carolina. Later, his remains were reinterred again in his family section in the same cemetery.

46. Records state that William Brookshire died on Oct. 1, 1863, in either Winchester, Virginia, or Taylorsville, North Carolina.

47. Has a cenotaph at the Bumgarner Cemetery, Alexander County, NC.

48. Private Loudermilk has a marker in the Calloway Cemetery, Jonas Ridge, Avery County, North Carolina.

49. Private Reed has a marker at the Liberty United Methodist Cemetery, Alexander County, North Carolina.

50. According to a family researcher, there are at least three ways to spell Robinett: Robinett, Robnett, and Robinette. All of the Robinetts that served in Company G were first cousins, and included three sets of brothers. Robinett, Bill, email to the author, Mar. 1, 2002.

51. Private Abernathy was originally interred in the Arlington National Cemetery, but was removed to the Oakwood Cemetery.

52. Private Arowood has a cenotaph in the Long Creek Presbyterian Church Cemetery, Gaston County, North Carolina.

53. William Wallace Glenn first served as first sergeant of Company H, was elected second lieutenant on Mar. 27, 1862, resigned due to "chronic dysentery" on Jul. 14, 1862, and reenlisted as a private with Company H in Mar.-Apr. 1863. Later in 1863, he was promoted to sergeant-major and transferred to the field and staff. In Sep. 1863, Glenn was promoted to third lieutenant and transferred to Company G. He was captured on Apr. 2, 1865, near Petersburg, Virginia, and imprisoned, being released after taking the oath on Jun. 18, 1865.

54. Military records state that Private Holland died Aug. 20, 1864, and is buried in the Confederate Cemetery at Point Lookout, Maryland. Family records state that he died on Jun. 23, 1893, and is buried in the Christ Lutheran Church Cemetery in Stanley County, North Carolina.

55. Private Weathers supposedly died "in Virginia" in Apr. 1862 of an unknown illness. The circumstances of his being in Virginia are also not known. The Thirty-seventh was not transferred to Virginia until May 1862. Manari and Jordan, *North Carolina Troops*, p. 577.

56. Death dates for Private Carpenter are Mar. 1, 1865, or May 9, 1865.

57. Private Cathey may be buried in the Paw Creek Church Cemetery, Mecklenburg County, North Carolina.

58. The family believes that Private Headley is buried at Steele Creek Presbyterian Church in Mecklenburg County, North Carolina.

59. Grave marker states name as H. C. Hovil.

60. Date of death on Private Kirkley's grave marker is May 14, 1865.

61. Private Simpson was absent in the hospital in Nov.-Dec. 1862, and died, according to company records, in Jan. or Feb. 1863.

62. Listed as J. M. Staidon in Hollywood Cemetery.

63. Death dates for Private Blevins are Dec. 31, 1862, or Jan. 8, 1863. He might be buried in the Mt. Pleasant Baptist Church Cemetery, Ashe County, North Carolina.

64. Death dates for Private Brown are Apr. 9 or Apr. 13, 1863.

65. Private Evans may be buried in the Crabb Tree Primitive Baptist Church Cemetery, Allegheny County, North Carolina.

66. Listed as R. Griffith in Hollywood Cemetery.

67. Death dates for Private Hill are Oct. 31 or Nov. 30, 1862.

68. Private McGrady was originally interred on the Peter Conover Farm in Gettysburg, Pennsylvania, but was removed to the Oakwood Cemetery, Raleigh, North Carolina.

69. John J. Osborne served as a second lieutenant of Company K before being dropped on Aug. 12, 1862. He continued to serve in the same company as a private.

70. Private Parsons has a marker in the Solomon Parsons Cemetery, Allegheny County, North Carolina.

71. Grave marker states that Private Smith died on Oct. 20, 1862. Military records state that he died on Nov. 15, 1862.

72. Private Sturgill died Jun. 19, Jun. 28, or Jul. 29, 1862.

Appendix B

1. The records of the Thirty-seventh indicate that Private Bell served as a private in Company G, 16th Regiment Georgia Infantry. However, "it appears that the soldier who served in the 16th Regiment of Georgia Infantry was killed at Malvern Hill, Virginia, Jul. 1, 1862." Manari and Jordan, *North Carolina Troops*, p. 539.

2. Private Blanchard enlisted in the Thirty-seventh while still a member of the Forty-second North Carolina Troops. *Ibid.*, p. 580.

3. Private Combs enlisted in the Thirty-seventh while being listed as a deserter from the Twenty-sixth Regiment Tennessee Infantry. *Ibid.*, p. 540.

4. Private Davidson also enlisted in the Thirty-seventh while being listed as a deserter from the Twenty-sixth Regiment Tennessee Infantry. *Ibid.*, p. 541.

5. The records of the Thirty-seventh indicate that Private Frazier served in the Twenty-sixth Tennessee Infantry. But the records of the Twenty-sixth do not support this. *Ibid.*, p. 542.

6. Private Garland enlisted in the Thirty-seventh while being absent without leave from the Twenty-sixth Regiment Tennessee Infantry. *Ibid.*, p. 542.

7. Private Graham transferred to the Thirty-seventh on Jul. 21, 1864, but never reported for duty. *Ibid.*, p. 503.

8. "Lieutenant" Moore served as a private in Company D, Ninth North Carolina State Troops before being discharged on Nov. 20, 1861. He had been elected a lieutenant in Company E, Thirty-seventh North Carolina Troops. He declined the appointment and later served as assistant quartermaster in the Seventh Battalion North Carolina Cavalry. *Ibid.*, p. 524.

9. The records of the Thirty-seventh state that Private Perry served in the Fifty-eighth North Carolina Troops before being transferred to the Thirty-seventh, but the records of the Fifty-eighth do not support this. *Ibid.*, p. 481.

10. After serving in Company K, First North Carolina Volunteers, Pettus enlisted in Company C, Thirty-seventh North Carolina Troops. On May 8, 1863, Pettus resigned and reenlisted in Company C as a private. No reason could be found for his resignation. In Jan.-Feb. 1864, he transferred to Company A, Eleventh North Carolina Troops. *Ibid.*, pp. 498, 506.

11. Private Phelan's name only appears on an "undated company record which indicates [that] his name was 'erased by the order of the Adj[utna]t Gen[era]l.'" *Ibid.*, p. 588.

12. Dulin Starnes was originally enlisted as a private in Company F, Thirty-fifth North Carolina Troops. He enlisted in Company I, Thirty-seventh North Carolina Troops on Oct. 22, 1861, while listed as a deserter from the Thirty-fifth. He deserted from the Thirty-seventh on Jul. 5, 1862, and on Oct. 21, 1862, enlisted in Company D, Fifty-second North Carolina Troops, while being listed as a deserter from the Thirty-seventh. Starnes was courts-martialed and executed for desertion on an unknown date and at an unknown place. *Ibid.*, p. 589.

13. The records of the Thirty-seventh state that Private Turner had served in the Twenty-sixth Regiment of Tennessee Infantry prior to enlisting in Company F of the Thirty-seventh, but the records of the Twenty-sixth do not support this. *Ibid.*, p. 549.

Appendix C

1. In Apr. 1862, Private Carrigan did not reenlist when the regiment was reorganized. He was 44 years of age and not required to do so under Confederate law. Carrigan may have later served in Company F, Fourth Regiment, North Carolina Senior Reserves as a private. Manari and Jordan, *North Carolina Troops*, p. 501.

2. See note 10, Appendix B.

Appendix D

1. There are two dates given for Private Hucks's transfer to the Invalid Corps: Apr. 18, 1864, and Sep. 13, 1864. Manari and Jordan, *North Carolina Troops*, p. 504.

Appendix G

1. Nine and Wilson, *Appomattox Paroles*, p. 191. Rusher is listed as second sergeant, Invalid Battalion, Company A, Thirty-seventh North Carolina Troops. No soldier by this name appears in Company A in Manari and Jordan, *North Carolina Troops*.

2. *Ibid.*, p. 213. Triplett does not appear in Manari and Jordan, *North Carolina Troops*.

3. Manari and Jordan, *North Carolina Troops*, p. 513. Private Gaddy does not appear in Nine and Wilson, *Appomattox Paroles*.

4. Nine and Wilson, *Appomattox Paroles*, p. 104. There is both a James M. Gaddy and a James N. Gaddy in *Appomattox Paroles*. There is no James M. Gaddy in Manari and Jordan, *North Carolina Troops*.

5. Nine and Wilson, *Appomattox Paroles*, p. 77; Manari and Jordan, *North Carolina Troops*, p. 526. According to Nine and Wilson, John E. Coffee [*sic*], received his parole on Apr. 9, 1865. But Manari and Jordan state that John E. Coffey was killed at Chancellorsville, Virginia, on May 3, 1863.

6. Nine and Wilson, *Appomattox Paroles*, 101; Manari and Jordan, *North Carolina Troops*, p. 529. According to Manari and Jordan, Private Foster returned to the company in Jan. or Feb. 1865 after his convalescence, and has no further record. He appears in Nine and Wilson as receiving his parole on Apr. 9, 1865.

7. Nine and Wilson, *Appomattox Paroles*, p. 116; Manari and Jordan, *North Carolina Troops*, pp. 557-8. Corporal John Harrington is listed in Nine and Wilson as being a member a Company E. But, according to Manari and Jordan, there was no John Harrington in Company E. There was a Private John Harrington in Company G, but he was discharged on Jan. 7, 1864, due to the amputation of his left leg as a result of wounds received at Fredericksburg, Virginia, on Dec. 13, 1863.

8. *Ibid.*, p. 531. Corporal Howington does not appear in Nine and Wilson, *Appomattox Paroles*.

9. Nine and Wilson, *Appomattox Paroles*, p. 65; Manari and Jordan, *North Carolina Troops*, pp. 539-40. Listed as hospital guard in Richmond, Jan. 30, 1865. Also listed as a member of Invalid Battalion.

10. Nine and Wilson, *Appomattox Paroles*, p. 83. Also appears as S. B. Crews.

11. *Ibid.*, p. 121. No soldier by this name appears in Manari and Jordan, *North Carolina Troops*.

12. Manari and Jordan, *North Carolina Troops*, p. 544. Does not appear in Nine and Wilson, *Appomattox Paroles*.

13. Manari and Jordan, *North Carolina Troops*, p. 546. Does not appear in Nine and Wilson, *Appomattox Paroles*.

14. *Ibid.*, p. 547. Private Rex surrendered on Apr. 9, 1865, but did not take the Oath of Allegiance until Jun. 7, 1865, in Salisbury, North Carolina.

15. Nine and Wilson, *Appomattox Paroles*, p. 72. Listed as G. W. Chapman.

16. *Ibid.*, p. 69. Also listed as J. P. Byrd.

17. *Ibid.*, p. 94. Appears as John P. Dye.

18. Manari and Jordan, *North Carolina Troops*, p. 573. Does not appear in Nine and Wilson, *Appomattox Paroles*.

19. Manari and Jordan, *North Carolina Troops*,, p. 575; Nine and Wilson, *Appomattox Paroles*, p.166. Manari and Jordan list Morrison as being captured on Apr. 2, 1865, in Petersburg, Virginia, and taking the Oath of Allegiance at Point Lookout, Maryland, on Jun. 29, 1865. Nine and Wilson list a Levi Morrison (Company H) receiving his parole on Apr. 9, 1865.

20. Nine and Wilson, *Appomattox Paroles*, p. 75; Manari and Jordan, *North Carolina Troops*, p. 582. Nine and Wilson list Clark as receiving his parole on Apr. 9, 1865. Manari and Jordan state that he was captured on Apr. 3, 1865, and took the Oath of Allegiance on Jun. 24, 1865, at Point Lookout, Maryland.

21. Manari and Jordan, *North Carolina Troops*, p. 593. Not listed in Nine and Wilson, *Appomattox Paroles*.

22. Nine and Wilson, *Appomattox Paroles*, p.172; Manari and Jordan, *North Carolina Troops*, p. 598-9. Nine and Wilson list Private Owens as receiving his parole on Apr. 9, 1865. Manari and Jordan list "no further records" after Jan.-Feb. 1865.

Bibliography

Manuscripts

Alexander, John B. Papers, University of North Carolina at Charlotte Library, Charlotte, NC.

Alexander, William D. *Diary, 1863–1865*. Southern Historical Collection, University of North Carolina, Chapel Hill, NC.

Armstrong, Thomas J. *Letter, August 26, 1865*. Private Collection.

Battle Family Papers. Southern Historical Collection, University of North Carolina, Chapel Hill, NC.

Bost, Jackson L. *Papers, 1849–1905*. Manuscript Department, Duke University Library, Durham, NC.

Campbell, William F. *Letters, 1863–1864*. Private Collection.

Chapel Church, *Records Abstract, 1859–1904*. Ashe County Public Library, Genealogy Room, West Jefferson, NC.

Civil War Collection, Military Collection, Archives, Division of Archives and History, Raleigh, NC.

Collins, Noah. *Papers, 1861–1865*. North Carolina Department of Cultural Resources, Division of Archives and History, Raleigh, NC.

Cook, Jordan. *Letter, January 10, 1889*. Private Collection.

Council, Jordan S. *Letters, 1861–1865*. Mary A. Council Papers, Manuscript Department, Duke University Library, Durham, NC.

Eaves, Etta Snyder. *James Addison Myers — My Grandfather*. Unpublished Manuscript, 1926.

Green, Barzilla C. *Letters 1861–1863*. Private Collection.

Haigh, Charles T. *Diary*. Virginia Military Institute Archives, Lexington, VA.

Hardy, Michael C. *Watauga County's Confederate and Union Soldiers: A Biography*. Unpublished Manuscript.

Hawkins, Elizabeth Barber. *The Barbers of Wilkesboro*. Unpublished Manuscript.

Holland, Marion L. *Letters, 1863–64*. Gaston County Historical Society.

Kennedy, Francis Milton, Chaplain. *Diary, 1863–1864*. Southern Historical Collection, University of North Carolina, Chapel Hill, NC.

Lane, James Henry. *Papers, 1854–1907*. Auburn University Archives and Manuscripts Department, Auburn, AL.

Miller, John V. *Letter, June 17, 1862*. Private Collection.

Morris, William G. *Letters, 1861; 1865; 1877; 1894; 1941; 1957*. Southern Historical Collection, University of North Carolina, Chapel Hill, NC.

Nixon, Thomas. *Papers, 1803–1884*. Manuscript Department, Duke University Library, Durham, NC.

Norwood, Thomas L. *Letters, 1863–1865*. Lenior Family Papers, Southern Historical Collection, University of North Carolina, Chapel Hill, NC.

Robinson, Daniel C. Unpublished Family Notes, copy in author's possession.

Royster, Iowa M. *Papers, 1840–1979*. Royster Family Papers, Southern Historical Collection, University of North Carolina, Chapel Hill, NC.

Sexton, Thorton. *Letters, 1862–1864*. Manuscript Department, Duke University.
Smith, Bennet. *Letters, 1861–1863*. Private Collection.
Sternes, A. L. *Letters, 1861–1862*. Manuscript Department, Duke University Library, Durham, NC.
Stuart, John C., Jr. *Our Family*. Unpublished Manuscript, copy in author's possession.
Tally, John. *Letters, 1862–1864*, Private Collection.
Thirty-seventh North Carolina Regiment, Letter Book. Manuscript Department, Duke University Library, Durham, NC.
(Tommie) 37th NCT. *Papers, 1727–1886; 1906*. Giles Family Papers, Southern Historical Collection, University of North Carolina, Chapel Hill, NC.
Tugman, James H. *Letters, 1861–1863*. William E. Eury Appalachian Collection, Appalachian State University, Boone, NC.
Wiggins, Octavius. *Address to United Daughters of the Confederacy*. North Carolina Department of Cultural Resources, Division of Archives and History, Raleigh, NC.
Wilson, William. Family history written Jan. 7, 1941. Copy in author's possession.

National Archives Microfilm

Compiled Service Records of Confederate Soldiers Who Served in Organizations from the State of North Carolina.
Record Group 109: War Department Collection of Confederate Records Orders and Circulars issued by the Army of the Potomac and the Army and Department of Northern Virginia, C.S.A., 1861–1865.

Published Works

Absher, W. O., ed. *The Heritage of Wilkes County, Vols. 1 & 2*. Winston-Salem, NC: Hunter Publishing Corporation, 1982.
Alexander, John B. *The History of Mecklenburg County: From 1740 to 1900*. Charlotte, NC: Observer Print House, 1902.
_____. *Reminiscences of the Past Sixty Years*. Charlotte: privately printed, 1908.
Alleghany County Heritage. Winston-Salem, NC: Hunter Publishing Corporation, 1983.
Allen, Sara C. *The Heritage of Alexander County*. Winston-Salem, NC: Hunter Publishing Corporation, 1986.
Arthur, John P. *A History of Watauga County with Sketches of Prominent Families*. Johnson City, TN: The Overmountain Press, 1915, 1992.
_____. *Western North Carolina: A History from 1730 to 1919*. Johnson City, TN: The Overmountain Press, 1914, 1996.
Barrett, John G. *The Civil War in North Carolina*. Chapel Hill: The University of North Carolina Press, 1963.
Bearss, Ed, and Chris Calkins. *The Battle of Five Forks*. Lynchburg: H. E. Howard, 1985.
Beitzell, Edwin W. *Point Lookout Prison Camp for Confederates*. Leonardtown, MD: St. Mary's County Historical Society, 1983.
Bennett, W. W. *The Great Revival in the Southern Armies*. Harrisonburg, VA: Sprinkle Publications, 1876, 1989.
Bilby, Joseph G. *Civil War Firearms*. Pennsylvania: Combined Books, 1996.
Birdsong, James C. *Brief Sketches of the North Carolina State Troops in the War Between the States*. Raleigh: J. Daniels, state printer, 1894.
Bisher, Catherine W. "A Strong Force of Ladies: Women, Politics, and Confederate Memorial Associations in Nineteenth-Century Raleigh." *North Carolina Historical Review*, Vol. 77, Num. 4, October 2000: 455–491.
Blackman, Ora. *Western North Carolina: Its Mountains and Its People to 1880*. Boone, NC: Appalachian Consortium Press, 1977.
Bowers, Claude G. *The Tragic Era: The Revolution After Lincoln*. Cambridge, Mass: The Riverside Press, 1929.
Brown, H. A. "Col. W. M. Barbour." *Confederate Veteran* (1899): p. 30.
Brown, Varina D. *A Colonel at Gettysburg and Spotsylvania Court House*. Columbia: The State Company, 1931.

Bunch, Jack A. *Military Justice in the Confederate States Armies*. Shippensburg, PA: White Mane Books, 2000.

Caldwell, J. F. J. *The History of a Brigade of South Carolinians*. Philadelphia: King & Baird, 1866.

Calkins, Chris M. *Thirty-six Hours Before Appomattox: The Battles of Sayler's Creek, High Bridge, Farmville and Cumberland Church*. Farmville, VA: Farmville Publishing, 1980.

Campbell, Eric A. "'Remember Harper's Ferry!' The Degradation, Humiliation, and Redemption of Col. George L. Willard's Brigade, Part 2." *Gettysburg Magazine*, 8, (1993): 95–110.

Chapman, Craig S. *More Terrible Than Victory: North Carolina's Bloody Bethel Regiment, 1861–1865*. Washington: Brassey's, 1998.

Clark, Walter, ed. *Histories of the Several Regiments and Battalions from North Carolina in the Great War, 1861 to 1865*. Raleigh: E. M. Uzzell, 1901.

Coco, Gregory A. *A Vast Sea of Misery: A History and Guide to the Union and Confederate Field Hospitals at Gettysburg, July 1–November 20, 1863*. Gettysburg: Thomas Publications, 1988.

_____. *Wasted Valor: The Confederate Dead at Gettysburg*. Gettysburg: Thomas Publications, 1990.

Coddington, Edward B. *The Gettysburg Campaign: A Study in Command*. New York: Scribner's, 1968, Morningside Reprint, 1979.

"Confederate Soldiers Receiving Markers." *Kinfolk*. Alexander County Ancestry Association (February 1997): 1–4.

Cook, Gerald Wilson. *The Last Tarheel Militia, 1861–1865*. Winston-Salem: privately printed, 1987.

Cope, Robert F., and Manly Wade Wellman. *The County of Gaston: Two Centuries of a North Carolina Region*. Gastonia: Gaston County Historical Society, 1961.

Cox, William R. *A Sketch of General James H. Lane, C. V.* No publisher listed, 1908.

Crawford, Martin. *Ashe County's Civil War: Community and Society in the Appalachian South*. Charlottesville: University Press of Virginia, 2001.

_____. "Mountain Farmers and the Market Economy: Ashe County during the 1850s." *North Carolina Historical Review*, 72 (October 1994): 430–50.

Crouch, John. *Historical Sketches of Wilkes County*. No publisher listed, c.1902.

Cullen, Joseph P. *The Peninsula Campaign of 1862*. Harrisburg: Stackpole Books, 1973.

Cunningham, H. H. *Doctors in Gray: The Confederate Medical Service*. Baton Rouge: Louisiana State University Press, 1958, 1986.

Cyclopedia of Eminent and Representative Men of the Carolinas of the Nineteenth Century. Madison, WI: Brant & Fuller, 1892.

Davidson, Chalmers Gaston. *The Plantation World Around Davidson: The Story of North Mecklenburg "Before the War."* Davidson, NC: Mecklenburg Historical Association, 1969.

Davis, Burke. *To Appomattox: Nine April Days, 1865*. New York: Holt, Rinehart and Winston, Inc., 1959.

Davis, Stephen. "Empty Eyes, Marble Hands: The Confederate Monument and the South." *Journal of Popular Culture*, 16:1 (1982): 2–21.

Deaton, Edwin L. "Reports from the Commander-in-Chief." *Confederate Veteran* 6 (2001): 2–3.

"Defence of Fort Gregg." *Southern Historical Society Papers*, III (1885): 19–28.

Dowd, Jerome. *Sketches of Prominent Living North Carolinians*. Raleigh: Edwards and Broughton, 1888.

Dowdey, Clifford. *The Seven Days: The Emergence of Lee*. Lincoln: University of Nebraska Press, 1964, 1992.

Downer, Edward T. "Johnson's Island." *Civil War History* 8: 2 (June 1962): 202–217.

Dunlop, W. S. *Lee's Sharpshooters; or, the Forefront of Battle*. Dayton: Morningside (reprint), 2000.

Elmore, Thomas L. "A Meteorological and Astronomical Chronology of the Gettysburg Campaign." *Gettysburg Magazine* 13 (July 1995): 7–19.

Faust, Drew Gilpin. "Christian Soldiers: The Meaning of Revivalism in the Confederate Army." *The Journal of Southern History* 53:1 (February 1987): 63–90.

Field, Ron. *Brassey's History of Uniforms: American Civil War, Confederate Army*. London: Brassey's, 1996.

Furgurson, Ernest B. *Chancellorsville 1863: The Souls of the Brave*. New York: Knopf, 1992.

_____. *Not War but Murder: Cold Harbor 1864*. New York: Knopf, 2000.

Gallagher, Gary W., ed. *The Third Day at Gettysburg*. Chapel Hill: University of North Carolina Press, 1994.

Garrison, A. A. "Saw General Lee at Petersburg." *Confederate Veteran* 16 (1908): 514.

Graham, Martin F., and George F. Skoch. *Mine Rune: A Campaign of Lost Opportunities, October 21, 1863–May 1, 1864*. Lynchburg, VA: H. E. Howard, 1987.

Greene, A. Wilson. *Breaking the Backbone of the Rebellion: The Final Battles of the Petersburg Campaign*. Mason City, Iowa: Savas Publishing Company, 2000.

Harris, William C. *William Woods Holden: Firebrand of North Carolina Politics*. Baton Rouge: Louisiana State University Press, 1987.

Harsh, Joseph L. *Confederate Tide Rising: Robert E. Lee and the Making of Southern Strategy, 1861–1862*. Kent, Ohio: Kent State University Press, 1998.

_____. *Sounding the Shallows: A Confederate Companion for the Maryland Campaign of 1862*. Kent, Ohio: Kent State University Press, 2000.

_____. *Taken at the Flood: Robert E. Lee and Confederate Strategy in the Maryland Campaign of 1862*. Kent, Ohio: Kent State University Press, 1999.

Hassler, William Woods. *A. P. Hill: Lee's Forgotten General*. Chapel Hill: University of North Carolina Press, 1957.

_____. *One of Lee's Best Men: The Civil War Letters of General William Dorsey Pender*. Chapel Hill: University of North Carolina Press, 1965, 1999.

Hayes, Johnson J. *The Land of Wilkes*. Wilkesboro, NC: Wilkes County Historical Society, 1962.

Henderson, William D. *The Road to Bristoe Station*. Lynchburg: H. E. Howard Inc., 1987.

Hennessy, John J. *Return to Bull Run: The Campaign and Battle of Second Manassas*. New York: Simon & Schuster, 1993.

The Heritage of Ashe County, North Carolina. Winston-Salem: Hunter Publishing Company, 1984.

The Heritage of Watauga County, North Carolina. Winston-Salem: Hunter Publishing Company, 1984.

Hewett, Janet B., Noah Andre Trudeau, and Bryce A. Suderow, eds. *Supplement to the Official Records of the Union and Confederate Armies*. Wilmington, NC: Broadfoot, 1994.

Hickerson, Thomas F. *Echoes of Happy Valley*. Chapel Hill: Privately printed, 1962.

"His Leg Amputated After Thirty-two Years." *Confederate Veteran* 2 (1894): 203.

Horn, John. *The Destruction of the Weldon Railroad: Deep Bottom, Globe Tavern, and Reams Station*. Lynchburg, VA: H. E. Howard, Inc., 1991.

Huffman, William H. *Charlotte Cotton Mills*. A report for the Charlotte-Mecklenburg Historic Landmarks Commission, Jun. 6, 1984.

Imhof, John D. *Gettysburg Day Two: A Study in Maps*. Baltimore: Butternut and Blue, 1999.

Inscoe, John C. *Mountain Masters, Slavery, and the Sectional Crisis in Western North Carolina*. Knoxville: The University of Tennessee Press, 1989.

_____. "Mountain Masters as Confederate Opportunists: The Profitability of Slavery in Western North Carolina, 1861–1865." *Slavery and Abolition* 16:1 (April 1995): 85–100.

_____, and Gordon McKinney. *The Heart of Confederate Appalachia: Western North Carolina in the Civil War*. Chapel Hill: The University of North Carolina Press, 2000.

Jeffrey, Thomas E. *State Parties and National Politics, North Carolina, 1815–1861*. Athens: The University of Georgia Press, 1989.

Johnson, Frontis W., ed. *Zebulon B. Vance Letters 1843–1862*. Raleigh: State Department of Archives and History, 1963.

Johnson, Robert U., and Clarence C. Buel, eds. *Battles and Leaders of the Civil War*, 4 vols. New York: Thomas Yoseloff, 1956.

Jones, J. William. *Christ in the Camp*. Harrisonburg, VA: Sprinkle Publications, 1887, 1986.

Joslyn, Mauriel. *The Biographical Roster of the Immortal 600*. Shippensburg, PA: White Mane Publishing Company, Inc., 1992.

_____. *Captives Immortal: The Story of 600 Confederate Officers and the United States Prisoner of War Policy*. Shippensburg, PA: White Mane Publishing Company, Inc., 1996.

Kaczor, Lucille Blankenship. *Alexander County Cemeteries, Vols. 1–6*. Hiddenite, NC, 1987.

Katcher, Philip. *The Army of Robert E. Lee*. London: Arms and Armour Press, 1994.

Kautz, August V. *Customs of Service for Non-commissioned Officers and Soldiers*. Philadelphia: J. B. Lippincott & Co. (reprint), 1864.

Kendrick, Virginia A. S. *The Heritage of Union County, North Carolina: 1842–1992*. Monroe, NC: Carolinas Genealogy Society, 1993.

Kolb, Richard K. "Thin Gray Line: Confederate Veterans in the New South." *VWF Magazine* June 1997: 22–32.

Krick, Robert K. *Lee's Colonels*. Dayton, Ohio: Morningside Bookshop, 1979.

_____. *Stonewall Jackson at Cedar Mountain*. Chapel Hill: University of North Carolina Press, 1990.

Landreth, Lou Reid. *Alleghany County Cemeteries Through 1986*. Sparta, NC: New River Graphics, 1988.

Lane, James. "Glimpses of Army Life in 1864." *Southern Historical Society Papers*, 25 (1897): 309–14.

_____. "History of Lane's North Carolina Brigade." *Southern Historical Society Papers*, VII (1879): 513–522; VIII (1880): 1–8, 67–76, 97–104, 145–154, 193–202, 241–248, 396–403, 489–496; IX (1881): 29–35, 71–73, 124–129, 143–156, 241–246, 353–361, 489–496; X (1882): 57–59, 206–213, 241–248.

Lawton, Ruth Jennings, et al. *The History of the United Daughters of the Confederacy, 1894–1955*. Raleigh: Edwards & Broughton Company, 1956.

LeGrand, Louis, M. D. *The Military Handbook and Soldier's Manual.* New York: Beadle and Company Publishers, 1861.

Lord, Francis A. *Civil War Collector's Encyclopedia, Vol. 1.* Secaucus, NJ: Castle Books, 1977.

Manari, Louis H., and Weymouth T. Jordan, eds. *North Carolina Troops, 1861–1865: A Roster,* 10 Vols. Raleigh: North Carolina Department of Archives and History, 1961.

Marcotte, Frank B., ed. *Private Osborne, Massachusetts 23rd Volunteers: Burnside Expedition, Roanoke Island, Second Front Against Richmond.* Jefferson, NC: McFarland, 1999.

Mast, Gregg. *State Troops and Volunteers: A Photographic Record of North Carolina's Civil War Soldiers Volume 1.* Raleigh: North Carolina Department of Cultural Resources, Division of Archives and History, 1995.

Matter, William D. *If It Takes All Summer.* Chapel Hill: University of North Carolina Press, 1988.

McKinney, Gordon B. "Zebulon Vance and His Reconstruction of the Civil War in North Carolina." *North Carolina Historical Review* 75:1 (January 1998): 67–85.

Meyer, Richard E., ed. *Cemeteries and Gravemarkers: Voices of American Culture.* Logan, Utah: Utah State University Press, 1992.

Miller, J. Michael. *"Even to Hell Itself": The North Anna Campaign.* Lynchburg, VA: H. E. Howard, Inc., 1989.

_____. "Perrin's Brigade on July 1, 1863." *Gettysburg Magazine* 13 (July 1995): 22–32.

Moore, Bartholomew F., and Asa Biggs. *Revised Code of North Carolina.* Boston: Little, Brown, and Company, 1855.

Morrill, James R. "North Carolina and the Administration of Brevet Major General Sickles." *North Carolina Historical Review* 42:3 (July 1965): 291–305.

Nine, William G., and Ronald G. Wilson *The Appomattox Paroles: April 9–15, 1865.* Lynchburg: H. E. Howard, Inc., 1989.

"North Carolina Reunion Proceedings." *Confederate Veteran,* June 1898, Volume 6, Number 6, p. 246.

O'Reilly, Frank A. *"Stonewall" Jackson at Fredericksburg: The Battle of Prospect Hill, December 13, 1862.* Lynchburg: H. E. Howard Inc., 1993.

Parker, Thomas H. *History of the 51st Regiment of P. V. and V. V.: From Its Organization at Camp Curtin, Harrisburg, Pa., in 1861, to Its Being Mustered Out of the United States Service at Alexandria, Va., July 27th, 1865.* Salem, Mass: Higginson Book Co., 1869, 2000.

Patterson. Gerard A. *From Blue to Gray: The Life of Confederate General Cadmus M. Wilcox.* Mechanicsburg, PA: Stackpole Books, 2001.

_____. "Wilcox the Paradox." *Civil War Times Illustrated* 39:6 (December 2000): 56–62.

Pearce, T. H., ed. *Diary of Captain Henry A. Chambers.* Wednal, NC: Broadfoot's Bookmark, 1983.

Pfanz, Harry W. *Gettysburg: Culp's Hill and Cemetery Hill.* Chapel Hill: University of North Carolina Press, 1993.

_____. *Gettysburg: The First Day.* Chapel Hill: University of North Carolina Press, 2001.

Pittard, Pen Lile, and W. C. Watts. *Alexander County's Confederates.* No publisher listed, c.1960.

Power, J. Tracy. *Lee's Miserables: Life in the Army of Northern Virginia from the Wilderness to Appomattox.* Chapel Hill: University of North Carolina Press, 1998.

Priest, John Michael. *Antietam: The Soldiers' Battle.* New York: Oxford University Press, 1988.

_____. *Into the Fight: Pickett's Charge at Gettysburg.* Shippensburg, PA: White Mane Company Publishing, 1998.

_____. "Lee's Gallant 600?" *North & South* 1:6 (1998): 42–56.

_____. *Nowhere to Run: The Wilderness, May 4th & 5th, 1864.* Shippensburg, PA: White Mane Publishing Company, 1995.

_____. *Victory Without Triumph: The Wilderness, May 6th & 7th, 1864.* Shippensburg, PA: White Mane Publishing Company, 1996.

Puett, Minnie S. *History of Gaston County.* Charlotte: Laney-Smith, Inc., 1939, 1998.

Reese, Timothy J. *Sykes' Regular Infantry Division, 1861–1864.* Jefferson, NC: McFarland, 1990.

Regulations for the Army of the Confederate States, 1863. Richmond, VA: J. W. Randolph, 1863.

Renn, Lydia S. *The Reverend Robert Luckey Steele.* Wake Forest, NC: (Private) 1976.

Reynolds, D. R., ed. *Charlotte Remembers.* Charlotte Pub. Co., 1972.

Rhea, Gordon C. *The Battle of the Wilderness, May 5–6, 1864.* Baton Rouge: Louisiana State University Press, 1997.

_____. *The Battles for Spotsylvania Court House and the Road to Yellow Tavern, May 7–12, 1864.* Baton Rouge: Louisiana State University Press, 1994.

_____. *To the North Anna River.* Baton Rouge: Louisiana State University Press, 2000.

Robertson, James I. *General A. P. Hill: The Story of a Confederate Warrior.* New York: Random House, 1987.

Robinson, Blackwell P., ed. *The North Carolina Guide*. Chapel Hill: University of North Carolina Press, 1955.

Rollins, Richard, ed. *The Returned Battle Flags*. Redondo Beach, CA: Rank and File Publications, 1995.

Rose, Rebecca Ansell. *Colours of the Gray*. Richmond: Carter Printing Company, 2000.

Rosenburg, R. B. *Living Monuments: Confederate Soldiers Homes in the New South*. Chapel Hill: University of North Carolina Press, 1993.

Sabastian, Samuel E., ed. *Cemetery Records, Wilkes County Area*. No publisher listed.

Sauers, Richard A. *"A Succession of Honorable Victories": The Burnside Expedition in North Carolina*. Dayton, Ohio: Morningside House, Inc., 1996.

Schenck, Martin. *Up Came Hill*. Harrisburg: The Stackpole Company, 1958.

"SCV Army and Division Histories." *Confederate Veteran* 3 (1996): 11–26.

Sears, Stephen W. "The Battle of Glendale." *North & South* 5:1 (Dec. 2001): 13–24.

_____. *Chancellorsville*. Boston: Houghton Mifflin Company, 1996.

_____. *Landscape Turned Red: The Battle of Antietam*. New York: Ticknor & Fields, 1983.

_____. *To the Gates of Richmond: The Peninsula Campaign*. New York: Ticknor & Fields, 1992.

Sexton, Margaret Branch. "Crosses of Honor at Charlotte." *Confederate Veteran* 9:7 (July 1901): 305.

Sitterson, Joseph Carlyle. *The Secession Movement in North Carolina*. Chapel Hill: The University of North Carolina Press, 1939.

Smoot, J. Edward. *Marshall Ney: Before and After Execution*. Charlotte: Queen City Printing Company, 1929.

Southwick, Leslie H. *Presidential Also-Rans and Running Mates, 1788–1996*. Jefferson, NC: McFarland, 1998.

Speer, Allen P. *Voices from Cemetery Hill: The Civil War Diary, Reports, and Letters of Colonel William Henry Asbury Speer (1861–1864)*. Johnson City, TN: The Overmountain Press, 1997.

Stevens, William, ed. *Dictionary of North Carolina Biography*. Chapel Hill: University of North Carolina Press, 1979.

Stewart, George R. *Pickett's Charge: A Microhistory of the Final Attack at Gettysburg, July 3, 1863*. Greenwich, CN: Fawcett Publications, 1959.

Sudarow, Bryce. "Glory Denied: First Deep Bottom." *North & South*, 3:7 (September 2000): 17–32.

_____. "Only a Miracle Can Save Us: Second Battle of Deep Bottom, Virginia, August 14–20, 1864." *North & South* 4:2 (January 2001): 12–32.

Sutherland, Daniel E. *Fredericksburg and Chancellorsville: The Dare Mark Campaign*. Lincoln: University of Nebraska Press, 1998.

Talbot, John. "Combat Trauma in the American Civil War." *History Today* 46:3 (March 1996): 47–54.

Taylor, Michael W. "North Carolina in the Pickett-Pettigrew-Trimble Charge at Gettysburg." *Gettysburg Magazine* 8 (January 1993): 67–93.

_____. "The Unmerited Censure of Two Maryland Staff Officers, Maj. Osmun Latrobe and First Lt. W. Stuart Symington." *Gettysburg Magazine* 8 (1993): 75–88.

Tompkins, Daniel Augustus. *History of Mecklenburg County and the City of Charlotte: From 1740 to 1903*. Charlotte, NC: Observer Print House, 1903.

Trudeau, Noah Andre. "False Start at Franklin's Crossings." *America's Civil War* 14:3 (July 2001): 32–37, 86–88.

_____. *The Last Citadel: Petersburg, Virginia, June 1864–April 1865*. Baton Rouge: Louisiana State University Press, 1991.

Tucker, Glenn. *High Tide at Gettysburg*. New York: Bobbs-Merrill Company, Inc., 1958.

Tucker, Phebe, and Richard Trautman. "Understanding and Treating PTSD: Past, Present, and Future." *Bulletin of the Menninger Clinic* 64:3 (Summer 2000): 37–52.

Van Noppen, Ina W., and John J. Van Noppen. *Western North Carolina Since the Civil War*. Boone, NC: Appalachian Consortium Press, 1973.

The War of the Rebellion: A Compilation of the Official Records of the Union and Confederate Armies, 128 vols. Washington, D.C., 1880–1901.

Warner, Ezra J. *Generals in Gray*. Baton Rouge: Louisiana State University Press, 1959, 1991.

Wegner, Ansley Herring. "Phantom Pain: Civil War Amputation and North Carolina's Maimed Veterans." *North Carolina Historical Review* 75:3 (July 1998): 277–296.

Weir, Erica. "Veterans and Post-Traumatic Stress Disorder." *Canadian Medical Association Journal* 163:9 (October 2000): 1187.

Wemsyel, James W. *Petersburg: Out of the Trenches*. Shippensburg, PA: Burd Street Press, 1998.

Wert, Jeffry D. *Gettysburg: Day Three*. New York, Simon and Schuster, 2001.

Wilcox, Cadmus M. "Defence of Batteries Gregg and Whitworth and the Evacuation of Petersburg." *Southern Historical Society Papers* 4 (1878): 19–33.

Wiley, Bell Irvin. *The Life of Johnny Reb*. Baton Rouge: Louisiana State University Press, 1943.
York, Maurice C. *The Many Faces of Fort Defiance: A Report Submitted to Fort Defiance, Inc.* Chapel Hill, 1979.

Newspapers

Asheville News
Biblical Recorder
Carter's Weekly
Charlotte Chronicle
Charlotte Daily Bulletin
Charlotte Observer
Gastonia Gazette
Highland Vidette (Kansas)
Monroe Enquirer
Monroe Journal

North Carolina Standard
North Carolina Whig
Raleigh Weekly Register
Watauga Democrat
Western Democrat
Wilkesboro Chronicle
Wilmington Journal

Theses and Dissertations

Brawley, James Shober. "The Public and Military Career of Lawrence O'Bryan Branch." Master's Thesis: University of North Carolina at Chapel Hill, 1951.
Dozier, Graham Town. "The Eighteenth North Carolina Infantry Regiment, C.S.A." Master's Thesis: Virginia Polytechnic Institute, 1992.
Gianneschi, Matthew Everett. "A Man from Mecklenburg: 1st Sergeant John Tally and the 'Hornet's Nest Riflemen,' North Carolina 37th Regiment, Company I." Master's Thesis: University of Denver, 1998.
Heath, Raymond A., Jr. "The North Carolina Militia on the Eve of the Civil War." Master's Thesis: University of North Carolina, Chapel Hill: 1974.
Iobst, Richard W. "North Carolina Mobilizes: Nine Crucial Months, December 1860–August 1861." Ph.D dissertation, University of North Carolina, Chapel Hill: 1968.
McDaid, William K. "Four Years of Arduous Service: The History of the Branch-Lane Brigade in the Civil War." Ph.D. dissertation, Michigan State University, 1987.
Phillips, Kenneth Edward. "James Henry Lane and the War for Southern Independence." Master's thesis: Auburn University, 1982.
Walden, H. Nelson. "History of Union County, North Carolina: A Thesis." Master's thesis: Appalachian State Teacher's College, 1963.

Letter/Email Sources

Abernathy, David. Email to the author. 26 Mar. 2001.
Ballard, Ruth Ann. Email to the author. 24 Jul. 2000.
Baucom, John H. Email to the author. 26 Apr. 2000.
Brown, William E. Email to the author. 21 Mar. 2001.
Bruton, Teresa. Email to the author. 22 Sep. 2001.
Bullman, Maudie-Keniston. Email to the author. 26 Aug. 2000.
Collins, J. M. Email to the author. 27 Sep. 2001.
Colson, Mary Frances. Email to the author. 26 Oct. 2001.
Coyne, Timothy C. Email to the author. 19 Aug. 2001.
Culler, Robert W. Email to the author. 24 Apr. 2000.
Davis, Boyce W. Email to the author. 27 Sep. 2001.
Davis, Keith. Email to author. 18 Sep. 2001.
DeBoard, Hurshel. Email to the author. 5 Apr. 2001.
Dixon, Steve. Email to the author. 10 Jan. 2002.

Fairchild, Paul. Email to the author. 13 Feb. 2002.
Gains, Julie H. Email to the author. 4 Jul. 2001.
Graham, Zeta. Email to the author. 10 Oct. 2000.
Gryder, Ray G., II. Email to the author. 19 Nov. 1999.
Hartis, Timothy N. Letter to the author. 3 Jun. 1999.
Hayer, Larry. Email to the author. 7 Oct. 2001.
Hollowell, Clarence. Email to author. 7 Oct. 1999.
Horton, Era. Email to the author. 3 Dec. 2000.
Jetton, Kay F. Email to the author. 21 Jun. 2001.
Jouse, Nancy. Email to the author. 15 Jun. 2001.
Lowery, Ray. Email to the author. 12 Jun. 2001.
Madaus, Howard M. Email to the author. 8 Feb. 2000.
_____. Email to the author. 8 Feb. 2000.
Martin, Debbie. Email to the Author. 1 Feb. 2002.
Millwood, Jerry. Email to the author. 22 Sep. 2001.
Parmerton, Velma L. Email to the author. 22 Sep. 2001.
Price, Roy. Email to the author. 20 Dec. 2001.
Robinett, Bill. Email to the author. 1 Mar. 2002.
Stowe, Kay. Email to the author. 17 Jul. 2001.
Thayer, D. Email to the author. 10 Apr. 2001.
Von Minden, Cate. Email to the author. 16 Apr. 2001.
Wingfield, Rebecca. Email to the author. 29 Mar. 2000.
Young, Jo. Email to the author. 16 Aug. 2001.

Index

Numbers in *italics* refer to photographs.